PENGUIN REFERENCE BOOKS

R40

ASIA HANDBOOK

Guy Wint was born in London in 1910 and educated at
Dulwich College, Oriel College, Oxford, and Berlin University. His first contact with Asian affairs was in 1932 when
he went to China as one of the secretarial assistants of the
League of Nations Technical Mission, which was sent to take
part in the strengthening and modernizing of China after the
Manchurian crisis. From China he went to India and spent
some years there with a grant from the Leverhulme Foundation studying the working of the Indian constitution. As a
result he wrote, with Sir George Schuster, *India and Democracy*, which was published early in the war. He spent most
of the war years in government service in India, Singapore,
America and China, and in the month when India became
independent he published *The British in Asia*, a kind of elegy
upon the Empire which was being dissolved. He became a
journalist in 1947 and was for ten years a leader writer for
the *Manchester Guardian* and wrote for the *Observer* on
Asian affairs. He is the author of two Penguin Specials:
Spotlight on Asia (1955) and *Middle East Crisis* (1957; with
Peter Calvocoressi), and his other publications include
Common Sense About China (1960), *China's Communist
Crusade* (1965), and a book about the stroke which he
suffered in 1960, *The Third Killer* (1965). He died in early
1969.

ASIA
HANDBOOK

SPECIALLY REVISED
AND ABRIDGED FOR
THIS EDITION

Editor: Guy Wint

PENGUIN BOOKS

Penguin Books Ltd, Harmondsworth, Middlesex, England
Penguin Books Inc., 7110 Ambassador Road, Baltimore, Maryland 21207, U.S.A.
Penguin Books Australia Ltd, Ringwood, Victoria, Australia

—

Asia: A Handbook first published by Anthony Blond 1966
Revised edition published in Penguin Books 1969

—

Copyright © Anthony Blond Ltd, 1966

—

Made and printed in Great Britain by
Hazell Watson & Viney Ltd
Aylesbury, Bucks
Set in Monotype Times Roman

CONTENTS

CONTENTS

PART TWO: GENERAL
Religion

Political Affairs

Minorities and Disputed Areas

Asia and the World

CONTENTS

MAPS

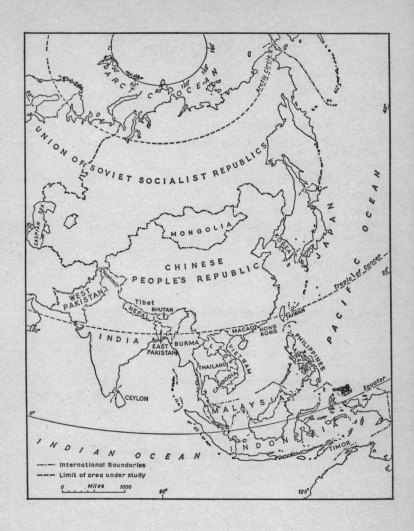

ARCTIC OCEAN

Arctic Circle

UNION OF SOVIET SOCIALIST REPUBLICS

CASPIAN SEA

MONGOLIA

CHINESE
PEOPLE'S REPUBLIC

KOREA

JAPAN

PACIFIC OCEAN

Tropic of Cancer

Kashmir

WEST
PAKISTAN

Tibet
NEPAL   BHUTAN

TAIWAN

MACAO   HONG
KONG

INDIA

EAST
PAKISTAN   BURMA

VIETNAM

PHILIPPINES

THAILAND

CAMBODIA

CEYLON

MALAYSIA

Equator

INDIAN   OCEAN

INDONESIA

TIMOR

—·—·— International Boundaries
— — — Limit of area under study

0   Miles   1000

FOREWORD

THIS book is concerned with a huge area containing over half the world's population. In the last half century much of it has undergone great political and social change, and the remainder seems destined for upheaval no less drastic, whether by revolution or by more orderly processes. The continent, which had been for the greater part subjected by the West, has been emancipated politically.

In a continent thus torn by *Sturm und Drang* three areas naturally distinguish themselves. First there is China, so huge a part of Asia, which has become Communist. Its revolution is perhaps the most weighty event of this age. China's vicissitudes, its ambition and its fate will decide much of the future of Asia and of the rest of the world.

Japan is outstanding because, though its history has been tempestuous, it has so far escaped violent revolution and a complete break with its old society. Even its defeat in the last war was absorbed. But radical change has fast been taking place. Japan has had such a peculiar history since the Meiji Restoration that it faces problems of an order different from that of other countries in Asia. First in the field as a great power, alone among Asian countries it can claim that it is fully developed. The psychology, outlook and problems of its people are different from those of the rest of Asia.

In most of the other countries of Asia the picture is of the end of colonialism. A row of nations have been reborn, and enter on a restless new life. These new nations show all the signs of growth – over-confidence and lack of confidence, assertiveness and anxiety, adventurousness and conservatism. In each case politics is controlled by nationalism, that simple, rather primitive but all-moving principle that has been incomparably the most pressing force of our time.

All these new states exist in the shadow of their colonial past. They have become free with extraordinary rapidity. Not unnaturally their cultural life has not yet caught up with the political facts, and much of Asia is still weighed down by the Westernization it has gone through in the past three centuries. Part of the Western legacy is of great value, and will not lightly be dissipated. In particular, the British achievement in India still dominates the life of that country and is likely to continue to do so, as the Roman Empire hung over Europe long after it was dissolved.

Much of this book is about relations between the new Asian states and the rest of the world. One fact stands out: Europe, which used to exercise such precedence in world affairs, has been abruptly dwarfed. Today the countries of Asia have asserted themselves and redressed the balance, so that the old inequality is being rapidly removed. Obsequiousness has disappeared, to be replaced by the determination that, in the next century, the east wind, if it does not prevail over the west, will at least blow with equal vigour.

Only in one way has the new Asia so far failed to contribute its share to world civilization. This is in ideas. Asia has borrowed, adapted, synthesized; it has not initiated. For this non-creativity there is undoubtedly an explanation, and it may lie in the fact that so much of the civilization of modern Asia is hybrid, and that the national soul of each of the various countries suffered a deep wound from the thrusting of new philosophies and ways of life upon them.

The patterns of behaviour, the ultimate ends for which men struggle, are to a great extent hidden from people's eyes. In Asia, as in the rest of the world, this is an age of confusion and obscurity. The most that can be done in a book of this kind is to illuminate the present situation against which the trends of the age will gradually become plain.

While writing this introduction I have been reading the superb memoirs of Chateaubriand. At the following passage I stopped. Chateaubriand speaks of the Europe of his day, but does it not equally fit the Asia of ours?

'Is it possible for a political system to subsist, in which some individuals have so many millions a year, while other individuals are dying of hunger, when religion is no longer there with its other-worldly hopes to explain the sacrifice? There are children whom their mothers feed at their withered breasts for want of a mouthful of bread to give their dying babies; there are families whose members are reduced to huddling together at night for want of blankets to warm them.

'As education reaches down to the lower classes, the latter gradually discover the secret canker which gnaws away at the irreligious social order. The excessive disproportion of conditions and fortunes was endurable as long as it remained concealed; but as soon as this disproportion was generally perceived, the old order received its death blow. Try to convince the poor man, once he has learned to read and ceased to believe, once he has become as well informed as yourself, try to convince him that he must submit to every sort of privation, while his neighbour possesses a thousand times what he needs: in the last resort you would have to kill him.'*

* *The Memoirs of Chateaubriand*, ed. and trans. Betty Radice and Robert Baldick, Hamish Hamilton, 1961.

The final sentence sounds ominous for the future of Asia. But at least one great cause of killing and convulsion, over-population, may be halted. The devastating torrent of babies, for which until recently no check was possible, seems suddenly likely to be brought under control. The effectiveness and cheapness of new devices of birth control may prove tremendously important.

At present only a minority of the people of Asia takes a part in politics. What will happen when the continent really wakes? In the coming century Asia is to undergo, too, the revolution of the disappearance of distance as it adopts the various devices that speed up communication. The Asiatic continent will be equipped with atomic power, and the countless miracles of material progress will be available to its needs.

The countries of Asia teem with history; it is a very old continent. Though Asia is renascent, in almost none of its countries is there a sense of starting out on a new career. All are more or less sophisticated; in this Asia differs from Africa. That is why in this present book so much space is allotted to history, along with the data of the present and surmises about the future. Nobody who wishes to study the future of the continent dare turn his back upon the past.

This book omits the region that has come to be called the Middle East. Political geography has become rather disconnected from the geography taught at school. The Middle East is now a unit which has detached itself from Asia and exists as a kind of sixth continent between Asia and Europe, with fairly well defined boundaries. This book therefore deals with Asia east of the Arab lands. It is true that Pakistan and Afghanistan seem to exist in both the Middle East and in Asia; but by and large the division chosen is sharp and definite.

A great variety of facts is set out in this book – in the form of country-by-country surveys, essays on political, social, economic, cultural and religious aspects of Asia, maps, and extracts from treaties and agreements since the last war. Contributors have been deliberately left free to describe the picture as they see it; no attempt has been made to induce a unity of view. It is hoped both that information has been presented in a businesslike manner and that what has been lost in uniformity has been gained in variety and vividness. The guiding principle in editing has been to produce an 'encyclopaedia' that can be read. Asia's problems are exciting, and this book attempts to mirror them.

It has taken longer than expected to get this book through the press, and meanwhile events have occurred remorselessly. Any reference book is bound to be a little out of date as soon as it appears. As this foreword is being written, events are happening in Vietnam, in Kashmir and on the frontiers between India and Pakistan, in Indonesia, Malaysia and China, any one of which could change the whole future of Asia. But the book cannot be held up until the outlook is clear; the most that can be offered is that it may be brought up to date and re-issued from time to time. In the meantime events have by and large been covered up to the end of 1968.

Death has removed two of the principal contributors. K. M. Panikkar, scholar, artist and statesman, is a universal loss, whose disappearance has struck away one on whose counsel the final shape of this revised edition would have relied. Derrick Sington brought to the social problems of South-East Asia a devotion which was edifying.

In committing this book to the press the editor is conscious of the huge amount of work that has gone into it and that is not reflected in the authorship of the contributions. To name everyone who has helped would mean a long list.

To George Patterson I owe a special debt. Himself the author of stimulating books about Asia, he has been responsible for the inclusion of much that is of human interest among the records of fact. I should like to express my deep gratitude to Dr Werner Klatt for his conscientious and scholarly labours in dealing with economics, and to Miss E. M. J. Campbell of Birkbeck College and Mr G. R. Versey of University College, University of London, who devoted much time and patience to the preparation of the maps. Also I owe much to the imagination and courtesy of the initial publisher of this book, Anthony Blond, and his house editor, Anthony Wood.

Oxford   GUY WINT

Publisher's Note

We have, very sadly, to record the death of Guy Wint while this book was in the later stages of production. None-the-less, as a result of much hard work on his part, his intention that the book should be, in general, up to date to the end of 1968 has been fulfilled.

PART ONE

THE COUNTRIES

South Asia

INDIA

The Political History

Percival Spear

GEOGRAPHY

ON the map of Asia, India hangs like an inverted spire or stalactite cutting into the Arabian sea. It hangs from a slanting wedge which is the Ganges valley and the Punjab, which in turn is attached to the Himalayan range, called by the early English the Great Snowy Range. From these fastnesses, where the great Hindu gods are said to dwell, India stretches out over 1,174,000 square miles, an area thirteen times as large as Great Britain but five twelfths that of the United States. It would go into Africa nearly ten times. This region forms a compact geographical area, a sub-continent of its own, which is now divided politically into the states of India, Pakistan and Nepal with the island of Ceylon as a pendant at its tip. This area contains all varieties of climate, from the Arctic of the higher mountains to the lush tropical of Bengal and the south-west corner. Physically as well as culturally, it is a microcosm of the world as a whole.

SHAPE

The shape of the country and the nature of its entrances and exits have determined much of its history and the make-up of the people today; it is therefore worth examining more closely. The mountains of the north, leading to the barren plateau of Tibet, have proved an effective barrier to intercourse with China. Physically, they have acted as a great catchment area for the annual monsoon rains. They produce the water which fertilizes the great plains of the north and provides irrigation for rainless tracts. The forests of the mountainsides are the symbols of the prosperity of the plains. To the north-east the hills are lower and more broken, but their rain-sodden and fever-haunted nature have made them as effective a barrier to human relations as their greater neighbours to the north. Until the Second World War no road or railway had been built between eastern India and Burma. The retreat from Burma in 1942 had to be conducted through forest-entangled and fever-stricken passes; even today the normal route is by sea from Calcutta to Rangoon.

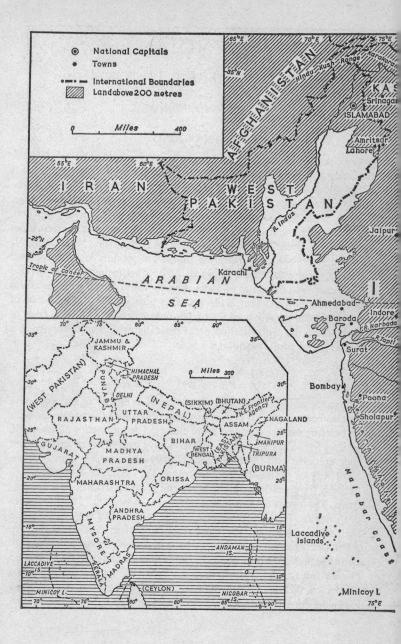

To the north-west the story is different. Here the mountains are as high as those bordering Burma, but they are bare and barren, and they are broken by well-defined passes. Moreover, the passes do not lead merely to another river valley as in Burma, itself encased in further mountains, but to the Iranian plateau which stretches to the great seats of civilization in the Middle East and to the wastes of Central Asia where nomads wandered and periodically swarmed. Here was India's window on the world, the door of access by which the stranger entered.

THE NORTHERN CORRIDOR

The traveller debouching from the north-west passes found himself in the Indus valley running roughly north and south. To travel down it was to enter a blind alley, for waterless lands crossed the route and the sea lay at its end. Progress eastward was barred by the deserts of Rajasthan, more effective, until modern times, than the highest range of mountains. But in the north an easy route led south-eastward into the northern Indian plain. The Punjab is still in the Indus basin and from the Sutlej to the Jumna valleys the transition is imperceptible. This plain, like a great diagonal cylinder on the map, stretches to the Bay of Bengal. It is so flat that there is no tunnel on the railway between Calcutta and Lahore; the land rises only 600 feet between Calcutta and Delhi. It is so fertile that fine crops will grow wherever there is a sufficiency of rain and two a year wherever there is a good monsoon.

This corridor skirts Rajasthan in its western portion. Rajasthan is a large arid region, running to complete desert in the west, which divides Sind and the Indus valley from the rest of India. It has been an historic citadel of Hinduism against Islamic invaders and is noted for its Rajput prowess, its conservative ways, its romantic castles and marble palaces set in azure lakes. From the practical point of view it is hot, infertile, poor and backward.

On the line of the Jumna where Delhi and Agra stand the corridor branches out to the plains and hills of central India. This is the route taken by all invaders of the south and this junction of routes is the factor which has given the two cities their strategic importance. On this strip of land seven decisive Indian battles have been fought. The river Narbada is the natural boundary of Hindustan and central India. Central India itself is a vast area of mingled hill and plain, forest and river. Its eastern half, stretching to Bihar and Orissa, has proved an almost complete barrier in the past. Its central portion has fertile areas; it is easy enough to allow the passage of armies and difficult enough to hinder their reinforcement. Hence the historic fact that it was far easier to conquer south India than to retain it.

THE SOUTH

Central India leads on to the Deccan plateau rising steeply from the west and sloping gradually to the east. It is a picturesque and stony region, a land of vistas rather than of wealth; with the rain of the western monsoon held by the western *ghats*. On each side of the Deccan run coastal plains with typical tropical climates. That on the west is narrow and rain-drenched, running down to the elephant-rearing forests of Malabar. Only at Cochin in the extreme south does it open out to the plain of Travancore, brilliant with palm trees and historically prosperous from their products and pepper growing. To the east the plain is wider and no less fertile until it turns due south along the Coromandel coast. Madras is set in a cotton-growing country, the land of the Tamils, which has been famous since pre-Christian times for its textiles and its wealth. With the fertile region of Gujarat on the angle of the western coast where it turns westward in the Gulf of Cambay our survey is completed. Gujarat is hot and fertile and famous for its cotton and indigo.

THE MONSOON

India is a land of periodic rains or monsoons. The south-east monsoon sweeps up the Ganges valley until (in normal years) it meets the south-west monsoon which, breaking in Ceylon early in May, reaches the hills beyond Delhi about the middle of June. The north-west has winter rains which are scanty, unpredictable but invaluable. The vagaries of these monsoons still determine the happiness of the majority of Indians. Too much rain means floods and destruction; too little, famine and death. In the northern lands of frequent droughts 'fine weather' means rainy weather.

The most fertile regions of India have traditionally been the richest; hence the concentration of political power in the north and its periodic dominations of the south. But with the advent of industrialism these conditions have changed. The sites of manufacture may now be said to be the seats of power. Two such concentrations are Bombay with Sholapur to the south, and Ahmedabad in Gujarat, where the cotton of the Deccan is made into cloth for the Indian market and exported to the Middle East, Africa and South-East Asia. Another is the iron- and coalfield of South Bihar, where the Parsi Tata built the first great Indian steel plant. Development has been assisted by transport, of which the railway system is a legacy of the British period. Generally speaking this ran eastwards and westwards, to connect the ports of Calcutta, Bombay and Madras with the interior centres of production. But north-south lines were added giving India a network which enabled her in the Second World War both to sustain a great army on her eastern frontier and to distribute food from north to south in the absence of sea transport and food imports.

India has a wealth of agricultural products, both temperate and tropical; she has all the main industrial components in quantity, except oil; and she has a transport system which enables her to make use of them. These things, joined to the skill of her people, should give her a bright future.

HISTORY

India is an amalgam of peoples and civilizations which together produced a social and cultural body which is unique in some of its characteristics and unsurpassed for its resilience and powers of absorption. The first peoples of whom we know anything concrete are the Dravidians who perhaps replaced forest-dwelling Australoid groups, of whom traces are still to be found in the south. From about the mid-third to the mid-second millenium B.C. a civilization flourished in the Indus valley, the Punjab and Gujarat, related to though not identical with the Sumerian culture of Mesopotamia. This civilization vanished without a trace until rediscovered by archaeologists in 1923, but we now know that it had an important influence upon the make-up of what was later called Hinduism. We can only surmise that the Dravidians were responsible for this culture, because human remains are few and have not yet been fully analysed. But we do know that in the late first millennium B.C. these people, in their Tamil section, produced another civilization in the south. Though later overlaid by influences from the north, Tamil culture has been an important factor in the make-up of south Indian Hinduism.

The Indus valley dwellers were probably overthrown and certainly replaced in north-west India about the middle of the second millennium B.C. by Aryan-speaking pastoral tribes entering by the north-western passes. They were tall and blond, lovers of sport, gambling and good living, worshippers of the sun and powers of nature, poets and philosophers. Their tongue developed into the classical language of Sanskrit, related to the Aryan family which includes Greek and Latin, the Teutonic and Slav languages. Their hymns of the Rig-Veda constitute some of the oldest literature in the world and begin the development of its longest lived systems of philosophy. These gifted people gradually spread over north India, assimilating more from the conquered aboriginals than they cared to admit, and developing kingdoms and philosophies with equal celerity. About 1000 B.C. occurred some conflict which caught posterity's imagination and provided the occasion for the composition of the great epic the *Mahabharata*. This, with its twin the *Ramayana*, still lies close to the heart of Indian life today.

CASTE, RELIGIONS AND EMPIRES

The first millennium B.C. saw the social development of the caste system, the momentous development of world religions and the political development of great empires. The Aryans brought with them the usual classes of king, chiefs and freemen, and they also had priests. Over the centuries and for causes which may include race and colour feeling and the conqueror–conquered relationship, but which are still largely obscure, these groups became stratified into four orders of priest, warrior, merchant and farmer, with 'outcastes' for menial tasks beyond. These orders in their turn became hereditary and subdivided until today there are some two thousand groups, each with their own social status, duties, privileges and disabilities, their rules of marriage, contact and diet. Caste is officially abolished today and is not easily to be seen in the cities, but it remains a ruling social force in rural India, that reservoir of Indian continuity.

As Hindu religion developed in the hands of the priests or Brahmins, it led to schism and creative action. Two world religions derive from this time: Jainism, an important influence within India to this day with its non-violent doctrine (an influence on Mahatma Gandhi, too), and Buddhism. Gautama the Buddha or Enlightened One was born about 560 B.C. and died about 480 B.C. His cult died out of India after flourishing for more than a thousand years, but it profoundly influenced Hinduism in the process and is still active in Ceylon, Burma, South-East Asia and Japan.

With the first of the great empires India enters upon recorded history. Alexander the Great, with his invasion of 326–5 B.C., gave the impulse. The Mauryan Empire which followed for a century and a half was the first attempt to unify India politically and gave the first Indian world political figure in the person of Asoka. He repented of conquest, preached non-violence, and engraved moralizing edicts on pillars and rocks. A second empire flourished under the Guptas in the 4th and 5th centuries A.D. when ancient Indian culture reached its full stature. It was then, with the possible exception of China, the most advanced civilization in the world with its corpus of Sanskrit literature, its great systems of philosophy (the Vedanta), its scientific and mathematical knowledge (zero and the decimal point were invented in India).

Before this time the Indian stock and culture were enriched by a number of invaders, from the Greek adventurers from what is now modern Turkestan to the mysterious Kushans, who have left mounds all over north India, and under whom Buddhism assumed a new form and winged its way across Central Asia to China. After the Guptas came fresh barbarian hordes who first fatally injured Indian Buddhism and then coalesced with the inhabitants to form the north Indian pattern recognizable today. From Brahminical compromise and barbarian might arose the Rajput clans as we know them, who were to form the life-blood of militant Hinduism in the centuries to come.

THE MUSLIMS

In A.D. 712 India was invaded by Arab adherents of the new Muslim religion, who conquered Sind. Three centuries later Turkish Muslims raided deep into India, and overran the Punjab, establishing a reputation for temple destruction and intolerance. But nearly two more centuries passed before a fresh wave of Turks burst over north India and established the first Muslim Empire at Delhi. Henceforth was established a rhythm of conquest and recovery, of attraction and repulsion which lasted for more than seven hundred years and was only ended with partition. It was 755 years before the Hindus regained Delhi after the Muslim conquest. Islam gave India many of the arts and graces of life, many fine buildings (including the Taj Mahal) and exquisite paintings, and an impetus to monotheism. It captured one quarter of its people. The Delhi Empire was overthrown by the world-conqueror Taimur in 1298. It was followed by the Mogul Empire in the 16th century, founded by the inimitable Babur and cemented by India's second secular world figure, the Emperor Akbar. The Mogul Empire provided a Persian cultural mantle for the Indian governing classes. Apart from this, with its Persianized bureaucracy, it was a working model of orderly administration upon which others could build.

INDIA AND THE WEST

The Mogul power broke up in the 18th century; the year of its death as an empire is 1761. Its would-be successors were the freedom-loving and tenacious Marathas of western India. But their triumph was fore-stalled by a world movement into whose orbit India was now moving. This was the expansion of the West with its scientific revolution now leading into the first industrial revolution with its accompaniments of new economic and military power. The first agents of the West were the Portuguese whose attempts to introduce the Europe of the Catholic renaissance foundered upon the rocks of intolerance and cruelty, in-sufficient power and Spanish conquest. Their successors were European commercial agents, Dutch, English and French mainly. These men counted their rupees and jockeyed for privileges; they had no idea that they were presently to be used as levers of a cultural destiny. Political confusion in India prompted the European companies to seek their own defence; commercial rivalry led them into war and the use of Indian allies. The new superiority of Western arms soon gave them a corner in king-making. Once the British had eliminated French power in the south they marched speedily to the dominion of all India to the river Sutlej in 1818. This success was made possible not only by military superiority but because of the distracted state of India at the time. There was no will to resist an empire; in fact a disposition to accept one.

BRITAIN AND THE NEW INDIA

The British Empire in India resembled its Mogul predecessor in many ways; it provided a dignified and static framework beneath which traditional society might revive and trade proceed. But in the 1830s a radical change occurred, which marks the birth of the India we know today. Radical and moral reforming zeal in England determined on introducing Western culture into India, believing that Indians would accept it once they were aware of it, and confident in its mission what-ever the effect on political dominion. So English became the official language and Western ideas and techniques were poured into the country through educational, official and commercial channels. Traditional India made a last convulsive effort to throw off the Western incubus in the so-called Mutiny of 1857. Thereafter there was a tacit acceptance of the Western challenge. The gifts of the West must be accepted, but the heirlooms of the past must not be abandoned. The two must be arranged in a harmonious pattern in the halls of Indian society.

One sign of this process was the educational 'explosion' which occurred about the middle of the second half of the 19th century. Then Indian individuals and groups began to set up Western-style colleges and schools themselves, thereafter providing a demand behind which government achievement lagged. A second feature was the rise of Indian machine industry, pre-eminently of cotton. A third feature was the nationalist movement, openly imported from the West, but early blending itself with local and indigenous currents of feeling. The Indian National Congress was founded in 1885. Twenty years later it was able to withstand the government's administrative partition of Bengal in a hurricane campaign which aroused mass emotion. But it was still an essentially middle-class body, divided into 'moderate' and 'extremist' wings. Then began another rhythm of concessions by the Government to rising national sentiment and demands for more rapid advance. The first sign was the Morley-Minto reforms of 1909, a first symbol the removal of the capital from Calcutta to Delhi in 1911.

THE NATIONALIST MOVEMENT

The First World War was a turning point in development. It stimulated Indian consciousness of and demand for political rights; it restricted British power and modified Britain's attitude; it provided in general discontent a fertile soil for the growth of political turmoil. The political fruit was the Montford constitution which gave India the beginnings of parliamentary government under the device of dyarchy. It also saw the steady estrangement of Hindus and Muslims into hostile camps as they saw the sceptre drawing nearer and mused as to who should grasp it first. The Congress had showed its power, but it was still a middle-class body which could not be described as an alternative government. The man who turned the Congress into a mass national organization and its executive into a potential government was Mahatma Gandhi. After a career in South Africa where he crossed swords with General Smuts, Gandhi returned to India in 1915 full of nationalist fervour, zeal for social reform, and ideas of 'non-violence' culled from Hindu, Jain and Christian sources. His opportunity came in the post-war unrest of 1919. He used the indignation aroused by European sympathy with the savage Government action at Amritsar in 1919 along with Muslim anger at the treatment of Turkey to launch a non-co-operation movement. It shook the Government but did not over-throw it and on its collapse Gandhi retired to social reform activity. The episode was none the less the writing on the wall for the British *raj*. Gandhi led a second and much better organized movement in 1930–31. Again it was defeated. But in 1937 when provincial autonomy was introduced, the Congress found itself in control of seven out of eleven provinces. A promising experiment ended with the Second World War which led on directly to independence. The Congress refused to co-operate except on terms of political advance. The Cripps offer of 1942 would have made Congress the virtual ruler of post-war India. Its rejection left the way clear for the Muslims, now led by the consummate and embittered tactician Jinnah, and fearful of the effects of Hindu domination. Jinnah declared for Pakistan, or a separate Muslim state, in 1940, but it was not until 1946 that he won the support of Muslims as a whole. Henceforth he bargained from strength and through a series of conferences, riots and massacres forced his way to partition and independence. Then in the two years after the war the Congress were faced with a double front of their former opponents, the British, now anxious to hand over, and their former compatriots, the Muslims, now insisting on separation. The division of India was the result of successive Congress errors but in perspective we may see that it had one important advantage. A united India on any terms conceivable in 1945 would have been so weak at the centre and so hampered with mutual suspicion that the great development of Nehru's India would have been impossible.

MAHATMA GANDHI

Gandhi's political mission was to turn a middle-class national movement into a mass national sentiment. In a real sense he was the creator of the Indian nation as distinct from a body of nationalists amongst the people. That he was able to do this was largely the result of the other side of his complex character and the way he combined his politics with his religion and his ethics. Starting out as an English-trained lawyer he served his community in South Africa for many years as a lawyer and champion. Here he acquired his distaste for Western civilization, his belief in reconciliation and non-violence, of 'soul-force' as he later expressed it, and here he practised his dietetic experiments. To this he added a fervent nationalism which meant that India should be free. On returning to India he identified himself with the peasant masses. It was this thought which caused him to wear, not the saffron robe of the ascetic, but the loincloth of the peasant. The people responded by making him a saint or 'great soul'. He never converted all India to non-violence, but his belief in and practice of it gave him a moral ascendancy which made his position unique and unassailable. To the peasant he was a saint who guaranteed that the nationalist movement would not overturn their cherished Hindu way of life; to the middle classes he was a gifted politician whose eccentricities (like fasting and insisting on hand spinning as a qualification of Congress membership) were condoned because he had the double knack of dealing with the British and arousing the masses. For them independence and parity with the West were worth a spinning-wheel. This analysis is confirmed by the fact that today Gandhi is still a Mahatma or great soul for the masses while he is forgotten or disregarded by the classes.

INDEPENDENCE

As the twenties and thirties were Gandhi's India, the years of independence have been Nehru's India. The new Government, inaugurated with enthusiasm on 15 August 1947 after the whirlwind Viceroyalty of Lord Mountbatten, was at once beset with difficulties. The first arose from the massacres in the Punjab which accompanied partition. These were mutual between Sikhs, Hindus and Muslims and may have cost up to half a million lives. These in turn set in motion the great migrations, which led some six million people on either side to cross the border in the next few months seeking new homes. The tide of exasperated refugees reached Delhi at the end of August. New massacres broke out and for a time threatened the existence of the Government itself. When quelled they left behind a great body of refugees to be absorbed, a large body of uprooted Muslims awaiting transport in improvised camps, and general bitterness. Not until Gandhi intervened to insist, at the cost of a threatened fast to death, on the evacuation of the Delhi mosques and security for Muslims, was confidence restored. This intervention outraged certain militant Hindus and cost Gandhi his life on 30 January 1948. The sacrifice was not in vain for it produced such a revulsion against militant Hindu groups that they have been politically insignificant ever since.

Hard on the heels of the Punjab massacres came the Pathan incursion into the Muslim majority State of Kashmir with the Hindu ruler's consequent accession to India. For a time there were hostilities between the two Dominions until a truce was arranged in April 1948. In this matter India has insisted on the ruler's right of accession, and though she offered a plebiscite in the early days of the dispute has rejected every proposal by successive United Nations missions for implementing the suggestion. The first Kashmiri leader, Sheikh Abdullah, was in prison without trial for nine years with one short break. Kashmir has now been given a constitution by its own constituent assembly which has proclaimed its union with India. But Pakistan remains unreconciled and the issue remains a running sore in the relations of the two countries. India occupies Hindu and Sikh Jammu, the coveted vale of Kashmir with Ladakh and Little Tibet to the north-east, while Pakistan has a fringe round the southern border and the regions in the north-west.

THE INDIAN STATES

The next question was the future of the Indian States, some 562 in number, of which Hyderabad, the largest, had a population of seventeen millions. The British had withdrawn their claims to paramountcy and advised all rulers to join one or other new State. In fact all of them did so except Kashmir, Hyderabad in the south and Junagarh, a small State on the Kathiawar coast. India justified the occupation of Junagarh on the ground of the popular will and of Hyderabad in 1948 as a 'police action', an action, indeed, to which the folly of its ruler, the Nizam, contributed. But the problem of integration of these often backward territories remained. This was carried through with mingled rigour and skill by Sardar Patel. The completeness of his success should not hide the greatness of the achievement. In less skilful hands this problem might have wrecked the new State.

THE CONSTITUTION

The new Government next proceeded to draft a constitution. This came into force in January 1950 and has proved so far a successful instrument of government. With a president in the place of a constitutional sovereign the constitution is of the parliamentary type, with two houses of legislature, a prime minister and a cabinet responsible to the lower house. The structure of state, or Indian Union, is federal, the constituent units now being broadly arranged on a linguistic pattern. The states thus have a life of their own, but enough authority is concentrated at the centre to enable the federal authority to dominate the country. There is universal suffrage with an electorate of 200 millions, the largest in the world. Within this constitution political life was dominated until the elections of 1967 by the National Congress compared to which other parties appeared as splinter groups. The most active of these is the Communist, but it can hardly yet be said that India has evolved a party system, let alone a two-party one. As a corollary to the constitution came the question of relationship to the British Commonwealth. Indian patriotism was satisfied by the declaration of an independent Republic and the desire not to cut adrift by continued membership with recognition of the Queen as the Head of the Commonwealth.

NEHRU'S INDIA

Since that time the years that have passed have been those of Nehru's India. At first the Government was in effect a duumvirate of Nehru and the west Indian political boss Patel. Patel died at the end of 1950 and after 1951 Nehru's supremacy remained unchallenged until his death. He led Congress to victory at three general elections and Congress knew that it could not do without him. Nehru used this ascendancy to attempt the modernization of his country. In 1950 a Planning Commission was set up from which have stemmed three successive Five-Year Plans of development. The economy has been divided into public and private sectors, agricultural and industrial fields. Broadly speaking, established industries remained in the private sector while public utilities, new projects like the three steel plants, irrigation and power plants are in the public one. The first plan, aided by the Colombo plan, emphasized agricultural production which was increased by about 25 per cent. Along with this went power plants and irrigation schemes. The second plan was much more ambitious, involving the raising of two billion pounds outside the country, and of the national income by 5 per cent per annum. The third plan, still larger, encountered difficulties. This was Nehru's bid to solve the problem of Indian poverty, to make India economically self-sufficient and the industrial centre of South Asia.

Along with industrial activity has gone development in other directions. Education has been pushed forward. The number of universities is now over sixty though primary education has lagged behind. In the field of social reform a series of Hindu Code bills have modified the traditional code of Manu to give women more equal property and personal rights with men. The English language has been retained as an alternative official language to Hindi, and till now remains so. In commerce the decimal system has been adopted for the currency.

During his premiership Jawaharlal Nehru exercised almost complete control over the conduct of foreign affairs. His first care was Kashmir, whose prince acceded to India at the height of a Pathan invasion in October 1947. At first he suggested a plebiscite to decide the future of the state but later rejected several United Nations proposals for organizing one. After Pakistan's acceptance of American aid in 1954, followed by her accession to SEATO and CENTO, his attitude hardened. He allowed the Kashmir premier, Sheikh Abdullah, to be imprisoned; in 1957 he accepted the Kashmir Assembly's declaration of union and considered the matter closed. Unfortunately his temperamental allergy to soldiers and dictators dashed any new approaches after General Ayub Khan had seized power in 1958.

In the world at large Nehru's ideas revolved around the ideas of anti-colonialism, Asianism, international co-operation and non-alignment. The first of these principles led him to support independence movements in Malaya, Indonesia and South-East Asia, and to back the Egyptians and other Arabs in the Middle East. It reached its zenith at the Bandung Conference in 1955 where India and China appeared as the joint sponsors of the ex-colonial states. It lost some of its glamour when the vigour of his denunciation of the Anglo-French action at Suez in 1956 was not matched in his rather muffled complaints of Soviet action in Hungary at the same time. It provided the plea for the unilateral occupation of Portuguese Goa in 1961.

Anti-colonialism was linked with Asianism and its extension, Afro-Asianism. Asianism was based on a belief in a common distinctive element in Asian as distinct from western culture, and Afro-Asianism on a common interest linking all underdeveloped powers. Based on faulty premises, the cult withered as the breach with China widened. More fruitful in achievement was the principle of international co-operation. India was a mediating influence in the Korean war and provided valuable services under the United Nations in such places as the Congo, Cyprus and the Israeli-Egyptian border. Most striking of all, and most successful, was Nehru's policy of non-alignment with its corollary of a third or uncommitted force. The more powers, in his view, who could keep clear of the Americo-Russian confrontation, the less risk would there be of a ruinous atomic war. This policy served India well, though it was somewhat undermined by SEATO and CENTO. The coming of the hydrogen bomb in 1956, which made atomic war less and less likely, and the widening breach with China, gradually reduced its relevance.

Nehru's last years were darkened by the dispute with China. The early years of cordiality when the *Panch Shila* or five principles of co-existence were enunciated, ended with the Chinese takeover of Tibet and the flight of the Dalai Lama in 1959. Disputes arose about the 'McMahon line' on the North-East Frontier and the desolate Aksi Chin to the north-west (claimed by India) across which the Chinese had driven a road to Sinkiang. An attempted campaign in late 1962 proved a fiasco; India was propelled by necessity towards the United States and Nehru died before he could devise any new policy.

Lal Bahadur Shastri, Nehru's Gandhi-esque successor, was only in office for eighteen months before his death. His time was overshadowed by the Pakistani infiltration into Kashmir which led to open war in late August 1965. Shastri died just as the Tashkent Conference had restored the *status quo*. His succcessor, Mrs Indira Gandhi, Nehru's daughter, now faces a complicated situation with India dependent upon and sensitive to American support.

The last few years have seen a sharpening of India's internal problems. The most fundamental is that of the population explosion which has carried Indian numbers from about 325 millions in 1947 to nearly 500 millions at the time of writing. Under the weight of this increase the growth of the national *per capita* income as a result of Nehru's development plans slowed down during the Third Five-Year Plan and then ceased altogether. The plan's target of self-sufficiency in food was not achieved; instead India has been importing 12 million tons of grain a year and is said now to need 15 million tons a year. A failure of the monsoon threatens famine and the country finds itself on a knife-edge between scarcity and bare subsistence. These conditions have in turn brought about an exchange crisis which was met by drastic devaluation (one third) in 1966. These developments found their political expression in the general elections of 1967 when the Congress Party was returned to power at the Centre with a much reduced majority and lost control altogether of a number of provinces.

Since the general election the central Congress Government, after a rather shaky start, has gradually grown in strength. The partnership of Mrs Gandhi as Prime Minister and Mr Morarji Desai as Finance Minister has proved fruitful and stable. So far from providing the starting point for fresh dissensions it seems to have enabled both to grow in stature. Congress fortunes have been assisted by the remarkable instability of many non-Congress ministries, whose prestige has been undermined by the discredit attaching to frequent changes of allegiance on the part of their followers in the Assemblies. President's rule has been proclaimed in Bengal, Bihar, the Punjab and Hariana, and in the last named the Congress has returned to power after a mid-term election.

The two chief components of the anti-Congress coalitions have been the Hindu nationalists organized as the Jan Sangha, and the Communists. The Jan Sangha are embarrassed by the RSS, extreme or militant nationalists who have clashed with the Sikhs in the Punjab. The Communists, already divided into pro-Russian and pro-Chinese wings, have now produced a revolutionary non-democratic section as well. Communists and Jan Sanghists are not easy bedfellows, for the latter lean to capitalism, though not as far as the conservative Swatantra party. The DMK holds its ground in Madras, as adamant on Hindi as ever, but no longer talking of secession. It therefore seems that, in the absence of a major economic crisis or external threat, the present government is likely to continue for some time, and even gain in strength.

BIBLIOGRAPHY

A. L. Basham. *The Wonder that was India.* (Sidgwick & Jackson, London, 1956.)

F. Bernier (ed. A. Constable and V. A. Smith). *Travels in the Moghul Empire.* (Oxford University Press, 2nd edn, 1934.)

M. Brecher. *Nehru.* (Oxford University Press, 1959.)

G. T. Garratt (Ed.). *The Legacy of India.* (Oxford University Press, 1934.)

B. G. Gokhale. *The Making of the Indian Nation.* (Asia Publishing House, 1959.)

Sir P. J. Griffiths. *Modern India.* (Ernest Benn, 1957.)

J. L. Nehru. *Autobiography.* (John Lane the Bodley Head, 1936.)

K. M. Panikkar. *A Survey of Indian History.* (Asia Publishing House, 4th edn, 1964.)

H. S. L. Polak, H. N. Brailsford and Lord Pethick-Lawrence. *Mahatma Gandhi.* (Odhams, 1949.)

H. G. Rawlinson, *India, a Short Cultural History.* (Cresset Press, 1943.)

P. Sittaramaya. *History of the National Congress,* 2 vols. (Allahabad, 1946.)

D. E. Smith, *India as a Secular State.* (Princeton University Press, Princeton and London, 1963.)

Percival Spear. *India, A Modern History.* (University of Michigan Press, Ann Arbor, 1961.) (Ed.). *The Oxford History of India.* (Oxford University Press, 3rd edn, 1958.)

R. Thapar and Percival Spear, *History of India,* 2 vols. (Penguin Books, 1965–6.)

INDIA
The Land and the People

Taya Zinkin

THE impression India makes upon the visitor is at first one of incredible poverty, a poverty so compelling that it brings tears to the eyes of those who see slums, rickety pot-bellied children and skeletal cattle for the first time. The first reaction of such people is to wonder why India has not gone Communist.

The pressure of population is tangible everywhere, in the crammed city streets, in the crowded village lanes, in the myriad of stamp-sized fields. In Calcutta sad-eyed cattle graze the pavement while hundreds of thousands of people live on that very same pavement. Everywhere the newcomer is oppressed by the combination of poverty and overcrowding. Yet to the Indians themselves the picture does not appear quite so bad.

Indians may be poor, they may lack *Lebensraum*, but much of their misery is made bearable by the extraordinarily strong warmth of belonging which characterizes the Indian way of life and is rooted in the very caste system India's well-wishers want to destroy. This warmth of belonging which is very real is not apparent to the naked eye, it has to be experienced to be understood; it is to this warmth of belonging that India owes that social and political stability which so surprises the visitor from the affluent society.

After poverty and overcrowding the visitor begins to notice the extraordinary diversity of India, a diversity as apparent to the unobservant eye as the poverty. Everybody looks different and dresses differently. Complexions range from white to black coffee; noses from Biblical spurs to Mongolian pugs; some people are very tall, others very short. Dress, like a botanical classification, reveals the exact identity of the bearer, his or her religion, caste, region and occupation. The variety is endless. Thus an urban Sikh from Patiala rolls his beard inward, not to be confused with an urban Sikh from the Punjab who rolls his beard outward, while rural Sikhs wear their beards loose. Catholic untouchable women from Kerala wear their earrings through the top of their ears, their caste sisters through the lobe. In India there are as many turbans as there are makes of cars in the West and I once counted twenty different ways of draping the sari; and many men wear hats, caps, bonnets, toppers of all shapes instead of turbans just as many women wear pyjamas, lungis, skirts or sarongs. Some people wear next to nothing, others are overdressed, some women display their breasts, others their legs, but all of them, unless they be widows, wear some sort of jewellery, be it nose rings or toe rings, glass or gold.

The unity which exists underneath the apparent diversity is as real as the warmth of belonging, and like the warmth of belonging it eludes the visitor, though he will notice that everybody has black hair and dark eyes, that everybody eats with his fingers and that many people wear unstitched clothes. Yet, in India, everybody feels Indian, because Hinduism, like Christianity in Europe, has provided a continent with an underlying attitude and a civilization which is quite different from that of Africa or China. Everybody in India, even the Muslims and the Jews, has been deeply affected by the Hindu way of looking at life. This is because of the extraordinary all-embracing pervasiveness of Hinduism, which transforms everything it touches. Thus caste, the key institution of Hinduism, has affected all religious institutions in India; even the Jews have their untouchables who cannot enter high caste synagogues and there are Catholic churches in Kerala with special benches at the back for their untouchable parishioners.

The unity which runs through a society divided by latitude, longitude, language, race, habits, cannot be described in a few words. One has to go to India to feel it, and to feel too the contrast between rich and poor, town and country, modernity and the Middle Ages, between what Mr Nehru liked to call the cowdung age and the atomic age. In this contrast lies the core of Indian politics.

POLITICS

India is overwhelmingly in the cowdung age; its leaders are determined to bring it into the atomic age, and to do so democratically. Under the British there could be no such attempt, democratic or otherwise, because it would have cut too deeply across the fabric of tradition. Indeed, Gandhi was propelled into politics by the realization that only a government of the people by their own people could attempt to reform Indian society; Gandhi was above all a social reformer dedicated to making Indians equal, be they untouchables or women; Pandit Jawaharlal Nehru, his political heir, being a Socialist, was further fired by the desire to give equality economic content. In India, since independence, the urge to equality and modernity has dominated politics. The task of modernization and equalization was not easy in a country as poor, as overcrowded and as backward as India; it was further complicated by a series of man-made cataclysms which overtook India at the time of birth. Had those cataclysms not been dealt with successfully, independent India might have been still-born.

The emergencies which faced the Government of India at independence were so enormous that for the first few years they used up most of the Government's energies. As a result of the partition of India and Pakistan there was immense dislocation in the country. This dislocation was further aggravated by the vivisection of the Punjab and Bengal and the ensuing riots with their human hecatomb and the flooding of refugees across the border by the millions. Millions of Hindu refugees from Pakistan had to be rehabilitated, a new capital had to be built for the Indian Punjab, the assets of undivided India had to be partitioned and Indian troops had to be sent to Kashmir to rescue the Maharajah from invasion, firstly by tribes from Pakistan, later by the Pakistan Army. In addition 562 independent Princely States, covering two fifths of India and 90 million people, had to be integrated into the framework of the Indian Union. All this was done. Except for a few hundred thousand refugees from East Pakistan and for the Kashmir question, everything has been settled, leaving the Government free to introduce equality, people's democratic participation and economic progress. Of these economic progress is dealt with elsewhere.

From 1950 onwards the Government of India has been steadily engaged in a programme of development, of education, of democratization, and of bringing about social and human equality.

DEMOCRACY

First a Constitution had to be framed. This Constitution, which made it possible for India to be a Republic within the Commonwealth, had to embody the federal structure of the State, guarantee fundamental rights, protect minorities, select the official language and make it impossible for the Government to be arbitrary while at the same time leaving it strong enough to rule in cases of emergency. No wonder therefore that the Indian Constitution is the longest in the world with its eight schedules and its 400 articles. Its provisions are largely taken from the American and the British Constitutions. Typical of the spirit of the new India are the fundamental rights which guarantee equality before the law, equality of opportunity regardless of sex, caste or creed and the abolition of untouchability.

38

The Constitution provided for universal adult suffrage. Since the Constitution was adopted in 1950 there have been four general elections – 1951–2, 1957, 1962 and 1967. Each time some 60 per cent, 100 million people, have voted. In the first three the Congress won three quarters of the seats at the Centre, two thirds of the seats in the States and nearly half the votes. In the first three the Congress did badly in a couple of States – Rajasthan and Pepsu in 1952; Kerala and Orissa in 1957; Madhya Pradesh and Rajasthan in 1962. The Communists came poor seconds with 180-odd seats in the States and under 30 seats at the Centre and under 10 per cent of the vote. In 1957 the Communists won the election in Kerala by one seat, but after twenty-eight months of misrule they were unseated by the President of India and defeated in an election by the Democratic Front; in the inconclusive 1965 election, however, they won more seats than any other single party. In the fourth general election Congress still got 40 per cent of the total votes but fared badly in terms of seats. At the Centre it won by 51 seats only and it found itself in a minority in 9 of the States (Madras, Kerala, West Bengal, Bihar, Madhya Pradesh, Uttar Pradesh, Orissa, Haryana and the Punjab). The Congress defeat was due largely to two very bad monsoons with their train of inflation and economic stagnation and to the electoral alignments between opposition parties and the ever growing number of dissident Congressmen. Kerala has a mainly Communist government and Madras is run by the Southern ex-separatist DMK; in the seven other States shaky coalitions were put together, some of which collapsed within months.

The stability of Indian politics comes largely from the structure of Indian society. India is basically a society of microscopic owners with a vested interest in the *status quo*. When it has been made clear to them that the *status quo* cannot endure, they vote in favour of gradual change; evolution replaces revolution, and this evolution, in India, is the product of consent. The voters have to agree before a major reform can become law; and the leaders never fail to consult them, just as when the electorate has made its wishes clear, the leaders do not fail to abide by the wishes of the people. It is this revolution by consent which is called Nehruism because Mr Nehru always insisted on taking the people into his confidence and always responded to their expressed desires, even when they were not in agreement with his own. Thus he dropped the compulsory joint co-operative farming programme dear to his heart the moment he realized it would lose the Congress Party votes, and he gave way to the popular demand for Linguistic States despite his own fear that a division of India on linguistic lines would accentuate fissiparous tendencies and end in the balkanization of the motherland. Indeed, now that India has been divided into linguistic States, the Government of India is doing its best to avoid exacerbating regionalism's potential threat to unity. Careful thought is constantly given so that no State should feel left out, whether it is over development or the appointment of central ministers. However, one major threat to Indian unity still remains because of the chauvinistic insistence of many northern Indians that Hindi – their mother tongue – should become the national language. The South does not speak Hindi and wants English to have a place equal to Hindi's as the Government of India has already promised that it will.

To make democracy more real, to give power to the villagers, the Congress Party has been developing the village councils, vesting increasing powers in them and grouping them into pyramids with an increasing say in local self-government. These elected village councils, the Panchayats, a feature of ancient India, had lost their *raison d'être* once the Pax Britannica had made the villager feel that the Government was his 'Ma, Bap' – Mother and Father – responsible for his welfare. The Government of India has been making every possible effort to foster local leadership and to break the old apathy of expecting the Government to do everything. Besides reviving the Panchayat system it has created Community Projects – India's counterpart of American Agricultural Extension – which have the twofold function of bringing new techniques to the villages and of eliciting local leadership.

The Community Projects have only begun to stir the villages out of their old apathy; there has been considerable response to agricultural improvements but little induction of spontaneous leadership. Nevertheless, the effect of the Community Projects on the administration itself has been revolutionary; for the first time administrators have had to solicit the co-operation of the villagers instead of ordering it. Indeed, the most striking change I have seen in India in the last generation has been the change of position of the administrator from a demi-god to a common mortal, sure sign that democracy is taking roots.

The administrator has not been the only one to step down from his authoritarian pedestal; the politician has had to step down also. During the days of struggle against the British, martyrdom in gaol, sacrifice, and agitation earned the Congress leaders halos. Nothing tarnishes a halo faster than office when the people learn from experience that the leaders are there to implement national policies, not to lay down the law. The politicians have, like the administrators, had to learn that they are there to serve the people, not to order them about, and that if they fail to convince them it is they, the politicians, who have to give up their schemes.

EQUALITY

There has been nothing this democracy has been keener on than equality, economic equality as well as social equality.

Economic equality is being introduced, gradually, through land reforms and a crippling system of taxation; nearly one tenth of the income even of the poorest goes in taxation, and the very rich are taxed so heavily that they have to spend some of their capital every year in order to pay all their taxes.

Beside taxation, land reforms are lopping off the tall poppies. Over 200 acts have been passed or are in the process of being passed. When they have all been put into effect, nobody will be able to hold more than a quite small quantity of land, thirty unirrigated acres in most States. The land reforms have been slow; because of State autonomy each State has had to pass its own legislation; at times the acts have been challenged in the courts; sometimes they have had to be modified, and the Constitution has once had to be amended. The delays have, however, reduced friction because people had enough warning of the ceilings to dispose of their land either by selling it to their sitting tenant or by distributing it amongst their kin. At the end of it all, land reforms will produce equality in two ways.

First of all, the income that will be left from the land once the ceiling is enforced will rarely exceed £300 per annum; moreover the land reforms are breaking the hold of the merchant and the money lender on the peasant. In addition, land reforms have an effect on the caste structure in the countryside. The very big landlords tended to belong to the top castes or to be Muslims; ceilings have meant that the land has gone from them to the middle castes which are in fact the cultivating castes and are numerically the majority everywhere in India, although the particular caste varies from place to place. Thus land reforms have in a sense given further economic strength to those to whom adult franchise was already giving political power. Moreover, wherever new lands have been reclaimed by the Government the untouchables have been given preference for settlement.

THE UNTOUCHABLES

The Congress was pledged to make all Indians equals, so the untouchables whom Gandhi named 'Harijans', the children of God, came very high on the Government's list. The practice of untouchability was made a criminal offence under the Constitution. There are some 60 million untouchables in India. They are born outside the caste system and contact with them was considered so polluting that they were debarred access to any place where they might touch others or their food or water, caste temples, wells and hotels for instance. They have now been given access by law to all public places; any obstruction of them is a criminal offence. The Government of India has done as much to abolish untouchability as the American Government to make its Negroes equals. But this still does not mean that untouchables have become full citizens everywhere in India.

The untouchables get special electoral weightage through reserved untouchable seats; they get preference for Government jobs, Government lands, and for admission to schools and colleges. Each Government has at least one untouchable senior Minister; one Congress President has been Mr Sanjivaya, an untouchable who had also been Chief Minister of Andhra. Grants, loans, scholarships, housing schemes have all been mobilized in the fight against untouchability; £40 million were earmarked during the Third Plan Period for untouchable uplift. However, legislation, even backed by money, is not enough. Untouchables can become full citizens only when they have the will and the means to insist on their legal due. So long as he is not economically emancipated, an untouchable would be foolish to enter one of the caste temples of his village. It would only annoy his caste patrons and deprive him of his job. Nobody minds when untouchables go into the big caste temples of the cities, eat in urban restaurants or live in the better part of the suburbs; but in the village where everybody knows everybody's grandfather and where tradition is paramount, every attempt to enforce the law leads to tension. Education, urbanization and industrialization are the shears with which to cut through the prejudice of millennia.

The untouchables were not alone in their need of assistance; under Hindu law women did not exist; they were minors always under the guardianship of their men; first of their father, then of their husband, and, if he died, of their sons. Women were highly respected in India, but they did not run their own affairs. The greatest feminists who have ever lived, Gandhi and Nehru, set out to change the status of the Hindu woman. Gandhi brought women into politics; he was so successful that they now quite often take the lead when it comes to courting arrest, whether it is to get rid of the Communists, or to get Bombay city incorporated into Maharashtra. Nehru piloted the reform of Hindu Law first through a general election and then through Parliament. He thus redeemed Gandhi's pledge that 'Hindu women should not suffer any disability not suffered by man'. Monogamy has been enforced, divorce is now permissible for much the same reasons as in Britain, daughters now inherit from their father, widows from their husband, mothers from their sons. Widows have been given the guardianship of their children and can claim a share of the paternal house if they do not want to remain with their in-laws. Nehru insisted that 15 per cent of the Congress candidates for elections must be women, and in every ministry there is at least one woman minister. Indeed India's third Prime Minister is Mrs Indira Gandhi. Women get full opportunity in Government posts except for a few obvious ones like the Defence Services, and during the last decade the number of women in all walks of life who have gone out to work has been very large.

There has also been a very sharp increase in female education; in the old India women were normally illiterate, but in 1960 there were no less than 200,000 girls at college. Indeed education has become a status symbol for girls; a literate daughter requires a smaller dowry than an illiterate one; this has been pushing up the age of marriage and in the case of college graduates it has been displacing arranged marriages or prepared marriages. Traditionally Indian marriages are arranged by the parents according to caste, horoscope and custom. The children have, theoretically, always enjoyed the right of veto; but since they did not meet their mate until the betrothal they had little reason or opportunity to exercise this veto; after all they knew that their parents had their interests at heart and were the best judges. But now, with education and its resultant increase in the age of marriage, children have become more discriminating. Amongst the educated, the parents now have to prepare the marriage instead of merely arranging it; that is, they must find out what their children expect out of marriage and arrange for the couple to meet before finalizing the wedding. But the old style of arranged marriage with no real say for the children is still very frequent in the villages. Love marriages, of course, are virtually unknown outside a few big cities.

In the past change was often made difficult by the existence of the joint family, which tied the younger generation to the speed at which grandmother was willing to move. Today the joint family is rapidly breaking up. Now that girls are so much more often educated and that marriages occur in the teens rather than in childhood, daughters-in-law press for their own house more often; nor are earning members of the family quite as willing as they used to be to share with the idle and the jobless. Above all, the joint family is disappearing amongst the peasantry. Those whom the increase in population has reduced to a fragment of land want to keep the pittance they earn as labourers to themselves. Those who have large farms have been frightened by the legislation imposing ceilings on landholdings into breaking their farms up amongst the different members of the family. Even in business, the joint family is being worn away by high taxation; Indian taxes are always severe, and they are especially severe on non-agricultural joint families.

If people are to be equal, they have to be educated. Only one Indian out of four is literate; illiteracy goes up with age as there used to be fewer schools in the past, and many semi-literates have become illiterate for lack of practice.

The Government of India has embarked upon an education programme which it is hoped will see nearly all the children in the age group 6–11 at school by the end of 1971. The problem is not to persuade the parents to send their children to school but to find enough money, buildings, teachers and trainers of teachers. The size of the problem is forbidding: there are in India 558,000 villages and the total population will be around 600 million by 1980.

The Government of India has allocated nearly £120 million for family planning in the Fourth Five-Year Plan. The difficulty will be to spend that amount so long as a safe, cheap oral contraceptive is not available, but clinics are spreading rapidly, and there have been hundreds of thousands of sterilizations, though it is rare for such sterilization to occur before the family has four or five living children.

Since independence the number of people who can read has doubled, to nearly 30 per cent. The number of children in school has more than trebled, to 72 million; four out of five children in the 6–11 age group now go to school. There were one million children at secondary school in 1951, three million in 1961 and over four million by 1966. Every third child goes on from secondary school to college and there is a steady shift at the university from arts to science. India has over 1,000 colleges and their number goes up every year, but the standard of education has suffered severely since 1947 from a lowering of the standard of admission and from a decline of the standard of school English; English is still the language of instruction in most colleges, although Hindi is the official language and English is only an associate language under the constitution. The regional language, not Hindi – except where it is the regional language – has been displacing English at school. The attempts that have been made to replace English in the colleges raise grave problems: there are not the textbooks in the regional languages, and the disappearance of English would tie university teachers and students to their own linguistic region.

But still not enough has been done. India's need for technicians is endless. Only £360 million was allotted to educational expansion in the Third Plan, and the emphasis is still too often on cram books and memorizing.

CASTE AND POLITICS

Caste is the dominant feature of Indian life, the feature which makes Indian civilization different from any other. While everybody has heard of untouchables, not many people realize that untouchability is only an extension of caste and that there are as many watertight compartments within the caste system as there are cells in a bee-hive. In theory there are only four main castes and the outcastes. In practice there are innumerable Brahmin sub-castes, as many untouchable sub-castes and a myriad of sub-castes in between, which all tend in their exclusiveness to behave as if they were castes, instead of sub-castes.

A caste has been defined as a group of people who can eat, sit and marry with each other without considering themselves polluted. Under the Indian social system almost everybody is polluted by almost everybody else so that sub-castes tend to be very small. For instance, a Maharashtrian potter who uses a big wheel to turn his pots will not eat with or marry into the family of a Maharashtrian potter who uses a small wheel to turn his pots; each potter thinks himself better than the other and neither has any desire to pollute himself by fraternizing. The caste system, like all hierarchy, has to be based upon a clear-cut recognition of hierarchical gradations. The Indian caste system is sufficiently prolific for so many gradations to have emerged that everybody can find comfort in the thought that there is someone lower than himself; in any case so long as distance is kept, there is little cause for conflict; nobody else cares whether the potter with the big wheel or the potter with the little wheel ranks higher, since nobody else is planning to marry into their family.

In the past what mattered was to be a big fish in a small pond; therefore sub-castes multiplied with tropical exuberance, making it possible for almost everybody to be a leader of sorts. Adult franchise has dealt a mortal blow to sub-caste. Once a leader has to represent an electorate of 75,000 people for the local Assembly, and three quarters of a million for Parliament, he has to appeal to the largest possible number. Caste has become polarized into a sandwich. Everywhere at the bottom there is the layer of untouchable bread, everywhere at the top there is the thin layer of Brahmin bread, and in the middle there is the filling which is made up by the dominant cultivator and artisan castes of the area which vary from region to region but everywhere represent perhaps two thirds of the electorate and hold political power.

As political power has shifted from the Brahmins to the major cultivating and artisan castes, the Brahmins have tended to move to the key positions of economic and technological power. Thanks to their tradition of education they provide the administrators, the engineers, the economists, the managers without whom India cannot progress from the cowdung to the atomic age; thus everybody, except the landless labourers and the untouchables who are a numerical minority everywhere, has been provided with enough power and participation in his destiny and that of his country to make Nehruism, revolution by consent, attractive and India stable.

BIBLIOGRAPHY

Paul R. Brass. *Factional Politics in an Indian State*. (University of California Press, Berkeley, 1965.)

G. M. Carstairs. *The Twice Born*. (Hogarth Press, 1957.)

L. del Vasto. *Gandhi to Vinoba*. (Rider, London, 1956.)

S. C. Dube. *Indian Village*. (Routledge & Kegan Paul, 1955.)

M. K. Gandhi. *An Autobiography*. (Phoenix, London, 1949.)

J. H. Hutton. *Caste in India*. (Oxford University Press, 1961.)

D. N. Majumdar. *Caste and Communication in an Indian Village*. (Asia Publishing House, 1958.)

McKim Marriott (Ed.). *Village India*. A collection of essays. (Chicago University Press, 1958.)

A. C. Mayer. *Caste and Kinship in Central India*. (Routledge & Kegan Paul, 1960.)

A. C. Mayer and others. *Pilot Project India*. (University of California Press, Berkeley, 1958.)

T. Mende. *Conversations with Nehru*. (Secker & Warburg, 1956.)

B. B. Misra. *The Indian Middle Class*. (Oxford University Press, 1961.)

P. Moon. *Divide and Quit*. (Chatto & Windus, 1961.)

W. H. Morris-Jones. *The Government and Politics of India*. (Hutchinson, 1964.)

V. M. Sirsikar. *Political Behaviour in India*. (University of Poona, 1965.)

N. V. Sovani and V. M. Dandekar (Eds.). *Changing India*. A collection of essays. (Asia Publishing House, 1961.)

H. Tinker. *Experiment with Freedom*. (Oxford University Press, 1967.)

Maurice and Taya Zinkin. *Britain and India: Requiem for Empire*. (Chatto & Windus, 1964.)

Taya Zinkin. *Caste Today*. (Oxford University Press, 1965.) *India Changes!* (Chatto & Windus, 1958.) *Reporting India*. (Chatto & Windus, 1962.) *India*. (Thames & Hudson, 1965.) *Challenges in India*. (Chatto & Windus, 1966.)

THE INDIAN BORDER

George N. Patterson

INDIA has approximately 2,000 miles of northern border with what is described as the 'Tibet region of China'. But over 1,000 miles of this territory is outside the effective control of India. India has no jurisdiction over Nepal and Bhutan – except for her assurances that any act of aggression against these countries would be taken as aggression against India. Since 1947 Pakistan has been in occupation of 'Azad Kashmir'. And since October 1962 the Chinese have forcibly seized some of this border territory.

LADAKH

Ladakh has never had a properly defined boundary. In or about the year A.D. 900, during one of the many revolutions in Tibet's history, a Tibetan known as Ni-ma-mgon emigrated to western Tibet, married a local chieftain's daughter and brought the area under his control, including Ladakh, or 'Maryul' as it was known at that time. This territory, with some exceptions at different times, for several centuries remained under the jurisdiction of his descendants, the 'Kings of Ladakh'.

In 1664–5 Ladakh accepted the sovereignty of the Mogul Emperor of India, Aurangzeb. In 1680, after being invaded by Kalmuks sent by the Regent of Tibet, the Ladakhis appealed to the Mogul Governor of Kashmir for help, and in this way defeated the Tibetan army. A treaty was signed which was the last formal definition of the Ladakh-Tibet frontier 'at the time of the Ladakhi Kings'.

When Kashmir, under the Dogra, Maharajah Gulab Singh, feudatory of Maharajah Ranjit Singh, attacked Ladakh in 1834 in an attempt to include it within his own boundaries, the Ladakhis appealed to the Tibetan Government for assistance. A Tibetan army, including Chinese troops, was sent to their aid. After varying success in different areas, the Dogras out-manoeuvred the Tibetans by flooding their main camp and a peace treaty in 1842 was signed broadly recognizing 'the frontiers it had during the times of the Ladakhi Kings'.

Following the First Sikh War between Britain and the Sikhs another treaty was signed, the Treaty of Lahore, in which 'the hill countries . . .

47

including the provinces of Kashmir and Hazara' were annexed to British India. Later, in 1846, in the Treaty of Lahore, Britain sold to Gulab Singh, while remaining paramount, 'all the hilly and mountainous country with its dependences situated to the eastward of the river Indus and westward of the River Ravi, including Chumba and excluding Lahul'. Article 2 of this treaty laid down that the eastern frontier of Kashmir – the frontier between Ladakh and Tibet – was to be defined by the Commissioners appointed by Britain and Maharajah Gulab Singh.

The following is part of the statement drawn up by the Commissioners:

As regards the Ladakh-Tibet boundary, the Commissioners owing to Immamudin's rebellion in Kashmir were unable to reach the Tibet border. One of the Commissioners, however, wrote a memorandum in which he pointed out that the line was, as he thought, already sufficiently defined by nature, and recognized by custom, with the exception of the two extremities. On the appointment of the Second Commission (1847) steps were taken to secure the co-operation of the Chinese and Kashmir officials, *but the Chinese delegate never appeared and the demarcation of the frontier had to be abandoned* and the northern as well as the eastern boundary of the Kashmir state is still undefined. (Italics – G.P.)

On the basis of these treaties the Indian Government claim that the whole of the Aksai Chin plateau, the Chang-chungmo valley and the Pangong, Rupshu and Hanle areas belong to India. However, Chinese maps show their boundary in this area much further to the west, and include about 4,000 square miles – the greater part of the Aksai Chin, parts of the Chang-chungmo valley, and the Pangong, Spanggur Tso and Chang-lo areas in Tibet.

The Chinese authorities contend:

1. That the then Peking Government did not participate in this treaty and that, therefore, their successors were not bound by it.

2. That the frontiers were never delimited, and that in any case they did not include the big bulge, which was part of Sinkiang and not of Tibet.

It must be stated against this, however, that the Chinese authorities in Sinkiang had set up a border pillar at a point 64 miles south of Suket, that is to say *well to the north of the territory now under dispute*, and a map published by Peking University in 1925, showing the Chinese Empire at its widest extent under the Manchu Dynasty, *excluded the Aksai Chin from China's frontiers*.

Before the dispute with China Ladakh was classified geographically as being 45,762 square miles in area with a population of 183,476. But since 1954 China has been quietly occupying 14,000 square miles of this barren north-eastern bulge of Kashmir, with India since 1960 desperately building roads and multiplying military outposts to stop the Chinese advance. According to the Indian Note of 12 July 1962, the Indian Government protests that seven of the Chinese military outposts are 'outside the Chinese claim line as shown in their 1956 map'. The Chinese boundary in this sector, according to the 1956 map, is a concave line from the Karakoram Pass to the Konka Pass, skirting the origins of the Chip Chap and Galwan rivers. But in the 1960 map the boundary has advanced to include a much wider area. South of the Konka Pass the Chinese claims have also advanced from 1956 to 1960 to include Khurnak Fort and part of the Pangong Lake. Without going into confusing details of which country's outposts are where – often they are behind each other – it is obvious that the Chinese are now well beyond their 1956 line on the entire Ladakh front.

Between Ladakh and Nepal there is also disputed territory but while this might be used as a bargaining counter in any overall settlement there is no wide area of controversy, although the territory is militarily important.

SIKKIM

In Sikkim, a small 1800-square-mile protectorate of India with a population of 165,000, there are almost 100,000 Nepalis subject to political influence from Nepal; the remainder of the population is divided between Lepchas, Bhutias and Tibetans. The ruling family is of Tibetan extraction in its origin some two centuries ago, and by inter-marriage since, and the late Maharajah was a younger brother installed by Britain in 1914. India has taken over the British agreement recognizing Sikkim as a 'protectorate' but added some points of her own. When in 1949 the political parties emerged and looked like removing the unpopular Maharajah, India stepped in at the Maharajah's request with troops to 'restore law and order', and also added a Dewan, or Chief Minister, to 'advise' the Maharajah. Sikkim receives considerable economic aid from India, and Indian technicians and engineers are assisting in the development of the country. The present Maharajah is restless under Indian pressures and would like more independence for his country.

BHUTAN

Bhutan is larger than Sikkim and its original inhabitants are of Tibetan extraction with only a slight admixture from North Assam. But in the past century there has been a great influx of Nepalis, and while the Bhutanese try to minimize the numbers and admit to 25 per cent, the local Nepali organization claims 64 per cent; the true figure is probably somewhere between. The Maharajah is young, but the victim of a serious ailment, and is opposed by relatives and other factions. The Government is composed of 130 district head-men and meets once a year – or oftener in emergency.

Bhutan's relations with India are different from Sikkim's in that Bhutan has full control over her internal affairs and an understanding regarding India handling her external affairs. There has in fact been no officially announced agreement about their dispute over the term in the Indo-Bhutanese Treaty, 'guided by the advice of the Indian Government', which was under discussion when the Prime Minister Jigme Dorji was assassinated in 1964. India claims that this gives her the right of control of Bhutan's external affairs, while Bhutan maintains that India can proffer advice but it is not incumbent on Bhutan to accept it. Bhutan has only a minuscule militia scattered thinly across 18,000 square miles of mountains to protect a population of 700,000 heavily infiltrated by Tibetan refugees with Chinese agents among them. It has a network of roads in the south under Indian supervision built with aid given by India. China has repudiated India's claims to special relationships with Sikkim and Bhutan, and has made alternative offers to both countries – such as diplomatic representation and considerable economic aid. China's invasion of Indian territory in October 1962 put a new complexion on these offers, as did the assassination of the Prime Minister. There are three major political rifts in the country which could create a crisis in the near future.

THE NORTH-EAST FRONTIER AGENCY

The North-East Frontier Agency, between Bhutan and Burma, is also claimed by China, which occupied some of it in 1960 and later invaded the whole territory, although finally vacating it with an ominous warning to India. Despite intense military preparations since 1962 this is the most vulnerable part of India's border.

The segregation of the NEFA as a separate tribal area was really begun by the implementation of the 'Inner Line Regulations' in 1873.

At the same time the geographical conformation of the territory, with its savage mountains and impenetrable forests, contributed to the separate development of distinctive tribal groupings. South of the Inner Line the territory comprising the six districts of Goalpara – Kameng, Darrang, Nowgong, Lackimpur and Sibsagar – was raised to the status of a province, known as Assam.

Throughout the period of British administration little was done in the NEFA other than sending in punitive expeditions to restrain the marauding tribes. A weak China and a weak Burma presented no external threats to the North-East. It was through the two routes from Tibet, Tawang and Rima, or Walong, that the Tibetans had come to first trade then inhabit the northern areas of the territory. It was through the Pangsu Pass in the eastern section that the earlier Ahom conquerors had come; then the later northern Burmese tribes and, finally, the Burmese army. It was through this same pass that the Indian army passed to defeat the Japanese. It is chiefly from this area that the Nagas have conducted their decade-long revolt against Indian forces. The movement of tribes over the centuries has left this area with a predominant Tibeto-Burmese people of Mongolian origin, and only a slight sprinkling of Assam admixture.

Historically, the NEFA is wide open to the claims of any of the neighbouring countries, depending on the particular basis of the claim advanced. Ethnically and economically, until the twentieth century, its associations were mostly with the north. According to one historian, in the 5th century a local Rajah sent an embassy to the Chinese court. A Muslim invasion was unsuccessful, but a more powerful invasion by the Ahoms of North Burma in the 14th century succeeded in conquering a large area, extending right up to the border of Tibet. The Ahom rulers remained in power in Assam until replaced by the British in 1839. But even the Ahoms were only able to control their territory with the help of Naga warriors.

With the coming of the British, and the rapid expansion of the tea industry in North Assam, new opportunities for trade in the south were opened up to the NEFA tribes. But, also, new confusions were introduced as independent arrangements regarding the buying and selling of land were entered into between the various tribes and European tea-planters. To safeguard the rich tea interests it became necessary to extend British administration in the area, and this was done sporadically, without a central policy, and reluctantly. District Commissioners and Political Officers on the plains of Assam interfered as little as possible with the hill people, except when there was a serious outbreak of fighting or when specifically asked to do so by the tribal councils.

When China's forceful and ambitious Frontier Commissioner, General Chao-Erh-feng, entered Tibet in 1905 with a Chinese Army bent on subjugating the country, and then turned southwards to claim 'China's' territory in NEFA, in 1910, the British Government awoke to the possible dangers threatening Assam and India in this move. With Chao Erh-feng's death in 1911, and the subsequent Tibetan defeat of the Chinese, the threat was diminished, but in 1913 the British Government convened a meeting to discuss the status of Tibet and stabilize the situation. This conference was attended by the plenipotentiaries of Britain, Tibet and China, and known as the Simla Convention. At first China objected to a Tibetan representative having equal status with the Chinese representative, but later agreed to attend. However, the terms finally proved unacceptable to China, especially those relating to the proposed boundaries between Tibet and China, and between Tibet and the NEFA. The chief Chinese objections to signing the Simla Convention, according to Ivan Chen, the Chinese plenipotentiary, were:

1. Tibet should be recognized as a region of China.

2. All the places west of the Salween shall be placed within the limits of the autonomy of Tibet but any question which may arise there of political territorial or international nature, shall be discussed between China and Great Britain.

3. The imposing of a time limit on the Tibetan and Chinese representatives by Sir Henry MacMahon in which they had to give a definite answer.

When China refused to sign, Britain and Tibet went ahead and signed the Convention. They also signed a declaration by which they agreed to regard the third party, China, as excluded from the benefits which would have accrued to her had she signed the Convention.

SINO-INDIAN BORDER DISPUTE

The border dispute between China and India is being conducted on three levels: (1) from Kashmir to Burma, and including the border states; (2) the MacMahon Line, as just described, from Bhutan to Burma; and (3) the limited NEFA districts of Tawang, or Chedong, and Longju. The Chinese policy is to try to win (1) and (2) by emphasizing (3), for if she can succeed in this then her case on the first two will be difficult to refute. For this reason we shall now concentrate on (3) in some detail to show the basis of China's claims – but this should not be taken as supporting either of them.

In 1914, as a result of the Simla Convention between Britain and Tibet, the India-Tibetan frontier was delimited from the eastern boundary of Bhutan to the Isurazi Pass on the Irawaddy–Salween water parting. This became known as the 'MacMahon Line'. Sir Henry MacMahon, who was the British representative, recommended that while great care should be taken to avoid friction with the Tibetan Government (who had objected to the proposed alterations in the Tawang area), and the vested interests of the Tawang Monastery, an experienced British official should proceed to the western part of the Line to settle its future administration. Tawang, the area of the heaviest fighting between China and India, is in what is now known as the 'Kameng Frontier Tract' of the North-East Frontier Agency, which was created by Britain in 1912; before then it was vaguely termed 'Western Section of the North-East Frontier'. The importance of this is stressed in the following excerpt from a report of the Chief Secretary of Assam to the Political Officer, Balipara Frontier Tract, dated 17 September 1936:

It amounts to this, that while the Chinese already claim a large stretch of territory East of Tawang as part of the Sikang Province of China, the Tibetan Government, over whom the Chinese Government claim suzerainty, are collecting revenue and exercising jurisdiction in the Tawang area many miles south of the international frontier. The Government of India consider that some effective steps should be taken to challenge activities which may be extended to a claim on behalf of China to Tawang itself, or even Bhutan and Sikkim. ... *The continued exercise of jurisdiction by Tibet in Tawang, and the area south of Tawang, might enable China ... to claim prescriptive rights over part of the territory recognized as within India by the 1914 Convention.* ... (Italics – G.P.)

In the autumn of 1936 the British Political Officer in Sikkim, Sir Basil Gould, had an interview with the Tibetan Government in Lhasa at which Tawang was discussed. The Tibetan Government's attitude was that: (1) up to 1914 Tawang had been undoubtedly Tibetan; (2) they regarded the adjustment of the Tibeto-Indian border as part and parcel of the general adjustment and determination of boundaries contemplated in the 1914 Convention; if they could, with British help, secure a definite Sino-Tibetan boundary they would, of course, be glad to observe the Indo-Tibetan border as defined in 1914; (3) they had been encouraged in thinking that the British Government of India sympathized with this way of regarding the matter owing to the fact that at no time since the Convention and Declaration of 1914 had the Indian

Government taken steps to question Tibetan, or to assert British, authority in the Tawang area.

In 1938, a small expedition under a Captain Lightfoot was sent to Tawang, and in his report to the Government of India, dated 7 September 1938, he warned that unless regular tours were undertaken, and some effective measures to establish administration were introduced, British authority over the area would be lost. The Central Government in reply said that a second tour could not be allowed as it 'might result in the Government of India having to undertake permanent occupation in order to fulfil their obligations. . . .' It was decided subsequently, in July 1939, that the question of future policy should be decided after the expiry of one year. The Second World War intervened, and in 1947 India became independent, but the last British Political Officer there in 1947 has told the present writer that there was no alteration in the position when he was there and that it was still necessary to obtain permission from the Tibetan authorities in Tawang to travel in that area, that Indian authority extended only to the Se-la Sub-Agency, south of Tawang, and that token tribute was paid to Tibet in recognition of this.

When India became independent in 1947 the Indian Government was almost immediately presented with a problem involving the NEFA and other border territories. The Tibetan Government, choosing the time when the Kuomintang in China was in decline, and a new Indian policy imminent, sent a telegram to the Indian Government on 16 October 1947 demanding recognition of her claims to the former territories:

. . . such as Zayul and Walong and in the direction of Pemako, Lonag, Lapa, Mon, Bhutan, Sikkim, Darjeeling and others on this side of the river Ganges and Lowo, Ladakh, etc., up to the boundary of Yarkhim.

The Indian Government sent a reply (published in White Paper No. 2) as follows:

The Government of India would be glad to have an assurance that it is the intention of the Tibetan Government to continue relations on the existing basis until new Agreements are reached on matters which either party would wish to take up. This is the procedure adopted by all other countries with which India has inherited Treaty relations from His Majesty's Government.

In 1950 the Chinese Army invaded Tibet and India recognized her right to do so under China's pre-1914 Simla Convention claims of 'suzerainty' over Tibet.

Between the earlier period of China's invasion of Tibet in 1905, and the later invasion in 1950, only fitful interest in the NEFA had been taken, as has been noted. Prior to 1914 the NEFA was divided into two sections, the Western and Eastern, each under the nominal charge of a distant Political Officer. In 1912 these sections were named as Balipara and Sadiya respectively. In 1912 units of the Assam Rifles began penetrating some of the valleys in Lohit and Siang, but Subansiri and Tawang were left as administrative voids – although several letters were sent by the Assam Governor and Secretaries to the Central Government warning that this lack of administration was in danger of letting the territory go to China by default. In 1942 another Frontier Tract was created out of the Sadiya Tract and named Tirap Frontier Tract; and in 1946 the Balipara Frontier Tract was divided into the Se-La Sub-Agency and Subansiri Area. In 1949 the remaining parts of the Sadiya Frontier Tract were divided into the two divisions of Abor Hills and Mishmi Hills. In 1949, the Subansiri Divisional Headquarters was established and Tawang was brought under Indian administration for the first time in February 1951. In 1951, also, Naga Hills was formed into a separate district and in 1953 it was named the Tuensang Frontier District. Finally, in 1954, the Divisions were given the names of Kameng (2,000 sq. miles), Subansiri (7,950 sq. miles), Siang (8,392 sq. miles), Lohit (5,800 sq. miles), and Tirap (2,657 sq. miles) and brought under a specially created administrative unit of some 31,438 sq. miles under the Foreign Ministry, with the Governor of Assam acting as the agent of the President of India.

The greatest, and most immediate, threat to India lies in the recent Chinese invasion of the NEFA, in October 1962, and her claims to this territory – according to the Chinese Government, 'illegally' occupied by Indian administrators and troops. In the 'Report of the Officials of the Government of India and the Chinese People's Republic on Boundary Questions' published in February 1961, the Chinese officials deliberately excluded Sikkim and Bhutan and equivocated on the NEFA. In an exchange of diplomatic Notes the Chinese Government made clear its claims:

The traditional, customary Sino-Indian boundary east of Bhutan follows in the main the southern foot of the Himalayas, and Chinese maps published throughout the years have all shown the location of this line. The unilateral claim about the boundary in this sector put forward by the Indian Government in its memorandum has never been accepted by the Chinese Government. In view of the fact that the Sino-Indian boundary has never been formally delimited ... and that moreover ... what is in dispute is not the question of the location of individual parts on the boundary but involves the question of larger tracts of territory, the Chinese Government has always hoped to have friendly discussions . . . so as to seek a reasonable settlement of the boundary question . . . [*But*] *the unshakeable fact remains that it is only the boundary line running along the southern foot of the Himalayas . . . which is the true, traditional, customary line of the boundary between China and India in the eastern section.* . . . (Italics – G.P.)

This was categorically refuted by India.

To sum up the basis of the dispute: (1) Until the 20th century the territory belonged to no sovereign power; (2) Britain established her claim in the early 20th century, particularly through the 1914 Simla Convention, but did not take 'effective steps' to bring large parts of it within her administration, which would have been sufficient to give her right to the territory under international law; (3) from 1947 to 1950 the Government of India began to bring the territory under her administrative control, but seriously jeopardized her claims to the territory, by (a) recognizing China's claim to a suzerainty over, and armed conquest of, Tibet in 1950, which suzerainty could be extended to include those other areas; and (b) recognizing Tibet as 'a region of China' in 1954 (which negated her own claims that she would have inherited under the 1914 Simla Convention, because these were agreed between Britain and a sovereign treaty-making Tibet).

There are two distinct schools of thought among objective scholars studying this difficult problem. One is that India lost nothing by claiming the MacMahon Line while repudiating Tibet's right as an independent nation to negotiate the Convention which produced the boundary; the argument being that Tibet was in a position to negotiate such a treaty *at the time*, but that circumstances in 1950, 1954, and 1962 were such that China was the dominant power and so in a position to dictate her own interpretations.

The other school argues that the Tibetan Government was the effective administration controlling Tibet and some parts of NEFA from 1914 to 1950, that both Britain and the later Governments recognized this in their official dealings with Tibet, and that India's claims to the MacMahon Line can only be on the basis of recognizing Tibet as an independent sovereign state.

Whatever may be the final outcome India's position has been strengthened by the late Mr Nehru's offer to take the matter to the International Court for a decision and by accepting the Afro-Asian moderated interpretation of China's cease-fire 'offer' contained in the

'Colombo proposals'. But in the light of NEFA's history, and China's own categorical claims, it is highly unlikely that the Chinese Government will agree to India's counter-proposal.

A recent proposal of China is for a 'Confederation of Himalayan States' – to include Nepal, Sikkim, Bhutan, NEFA and Nagaland. This proposal, like previous ones, is unacceptable to India. No solution to the Sino-Indian border dispute seems in sight.

BIBLIOGRAPHY

S. K. Blugai. *Anglo-Assamese Relations*. (Gurhati, Assam, 1949.)

W. J. Buchanan. *Notes on Tours in Darjeeling and Sikkim*. (Darjeeling, 1961.)

Ivan Chen. *China-Tibet-U.K.* Account of the Simla Conference, 1913–14. (Peking, 1940.)

Sir Edward Gait. *A History of Assam*. (Thacker, Spink & Co., Calcutta, 2nd edn, 1926.)

Alistair Lamb. *The China-India Border: The Origins of the Disputed Boundaries*. (Chatham House Essays, Oxford University Press, 1946.)

W. Leifer. *Himalaya: Mountains of Destiny*. (Galley Press, London, 1962.)

Sir Robert Reid. *The Frontier Areas Bordering on Assam*. (Shillong, 1942.)

Vincent A. Smith. *The Early History of India*. (Clarendon Press, Oxford, 4th edn, 1924.) *The Oxford Student's History of India*. (Oxford University Press, 15th edn, revised by H. G. Rawlinson, 1951.)

NEPAL

George N. Patterson

NEPAL is an independent kingdom, situated on the southern slopes of the Himalayas, and thus occupying a key position between the Republic of India and Communist China. It is bounded on the north by Tibet, on the east by Sikkim and West Bengal, and on the south and west by the two Indian Provinces of Bihar and Uttar Pradesh. The country is about 500 miles long by 100 miles wide and falls away from the near-30,000 feet Himalayan peaks in three distinct terraces to the plains of India. Between Nepal and the plains of India there is no natural frontier or barrier of any kind.

In this strategic area of mountains, valleys and jungles live 9 million Nepalis, the most martial being the Limbus, Rais, Magars and Gurungs, better known outside Nepal as 'Gurkhas'. Most of the 9 million inhabitants are scattered in remote valleys throughout the country, with little or no contact between them. The Katmandu Valley, which contains the capital of that name, is the largest 'valley' in Nepal, covering an area of 242 square miles at a height of 4,500 feet, and has the largest concentrated population of 415,000. Most Nepalese are Hindus. Many aristocratic families have matrimonial connexions with Indian princes. The Gurkhas constitute one of the most important sections of the Indian Army and are being recruited in increasingly large numbers in the mountain divisions raised to combat the Chinese threat from the north.

The modern history of Nepal has been shaped by three important periods. First, the conquest of the Katmandu Valley by Prithvi Narayan Shah in the 1760s that led to the unification of Nepal under one rule. The Shah dynasty continues to rule in Nepal until the present day. Secondly, the usurpation of power by Jung Bahadur in 1846, which resulted in the hegemony of the Rana family for 104 years without a break. Even today some Ranas are a significant factor in the kingdom's social and economic life. Finally, the sequence of events from 1950 onwards.

Nepal leapt from feudalism into the 20th century in 1951. That was the year when its unique agnate system of rule by a Prime Minister of the Rana dynasty was replaced by a form of constitutional monarchy with democracy. But Nepal was nowhere near prepared for modern democratic methods, for in addition to the lack of administrative machinery and means of transport and communications there was no national consciousness but only primitive tribal loyalties. The old order had been disrupted too suddenly for the speedy creation of a country-wide social, economic and political base which might have supported democratic institutions. There was no bridge between the disgruntled aristocrats used to absolute power and the idealistic Congress Party with theories and little experience. To complicate the situation further, many Nepalis are extremely sensitive to India's interest in Nepal's affairs; they question the loyalties of the Congress leaders whose associations have all been with India and who owe their positions to India's intervention on their behalf in 1951.

In 1952 a militant nationalist, Dr K. I. Singh, led a revolt against the Government, but fled to Tibet and China. Following this there was a period of maladministration, corruption and nepotism which culminated, under the threat of a national demonstration, in the King dissolving the Royal Council of State and vesting all Royal prerogatives in the then Crown Prince, now King, Mahendra.

King Mahendra began his reign in 1955 by denouncing the previous four years of democracy as 'shameful', and tried to govern by 'direct rule', but was forced by the political parties to hold elections in 1959. The Congress Party emerged clear winners with a majority of 74 seats in a House of 109. But the King, who had said at his coronation that there would never be 'two sovereigns in Nepal', quickly tired of the continued bickering, corruption and maladministration and on 15 December 1960, he announced that once again he had taken over direct rule and had imprisoned the political leaders.

The earlier attitude of superiority and contempt of the martial Nepalis for the plain-dwelling Indians had been temporarily modified by the help India had given to the Nepali Congress leaders in overthrowing the Rana regime. But this quickly disappeared. To assert their independence of India the Nepalese leaders turned to China and in 1956 a Sino-Nepalese Treaty was signed, and China gave to Nepal considerable economic aid. This friendly beginning was continued by both sides, and after agreeing to a Sino-Nepalese boundary settlement favourable to Nepal the Nepalese Government agreed to China building a strategic road from Lhasa, in Tibet, to Katmandu, thereby offsetting Indian advantages. In addition, China is now contributing over 20 crores of rupees (£15½ million) in aid of various kinds. India has also increased its aid to Nepal.

In the first two years after the King took over, according to the report of the King's hand-picked 'Intellectuals' Conference' held in June 1962, there was little change. Dr K. I. Singh, who led the abortive revolt in 1952 and returned in 1956 to be Prime Minister, declared that if the King did not change his policies he would lead another revolt against him. His chief fear was that the King's vacillating direction of Nepalese affairs was opening the way for a return of the exiled Nepali Congress Party under threat of arms and committed to a pro-Indian policy, which in turn would bring in the Chinese from the north to 'help' pro-Chinese elements – and so make Nepal into another Korea.

China's attitude towards Nepal was summed up in Mao Tse-tung's ominous words a few years ago: 'In defeating China in war the imperialists have taken away *many Chinese dependent states and parts of her territories* . . . England seized Burma, Bhutan, *Nepal* . . .' [Italics – G.P.]. It is this fear of China's long-term intentions in Nepal, together with the deterioration in Indo-Nepal relations, which led in March 1963 to a visit to Nepal by the then Indian Home Minister, Mr Lal Bahadur Shastri. China's invasion of Indian territory in October 1962 virtually altered Nepal's attitude toward its southern neighbour, dissipating much of the anti-Indian feeling that had been allowed to develop in the country and bringing about a realization that if Nepal is to remain independent it should develop closer ties with India.

THE ECONOMIC SITUATION

Over 90 per cent of the population is engaged in subsistence farming. Whilst the country is normally self-sufficient in foodstuffs, in good years the Terai region in the south provides a grain surplus for export to India. In years when the rains fail, on the other hand, and in case of widespread flooding rice or wheat has to be imported. In the Sherpa regions the introduction of the potato has helped to supplement grain production and farm income.

Farming is carried out mostly by smallholders under the traditional Zamindari (intermediary) system and on rent-free Birta land. A Land Reform Commission has been set up to control rents and interest rates in agriculture and to prohibit evictions except where rents have not been paid or land has been left idle.

Nepal's foreign trade – imports of approximately 300 million rupees and exports of approximately 150 million rupees – is primarily, if not exclusively, with India. In the past Indian rupees used to circulate freely, side by side with Nepalese rupees, but in 1964 the Government took steps to restrict the circulation of Indian currency. The official rate of exchange is 160 NRs to 100 IRs. Government revenue and expenditure runs at an annual rate of 300 million rupees.

Nepal's industry is in its infancy. Hydro-electric projects are given a certain priority in long-term planning, designed to improve communications, intensify farming and create the basis of an indigenous industry. However, the consumption of energy (1962: 4 kilogrammes of coal equivalent per head of population) is still the lowest on record for countries listed by the Statistical Office of the United Nations. Among the limited range of goods produced are sugar, jute bags, matches and cigarettes.

No official information is available on Nepal's national income, but it is believed to be no higher than US $50 (£18) per head of population. The current development plan, running from 1962–5, aims at raising the level of economic performance and the standard of living. Of the 670 million rupees (£32 million) set aside for development during the Three-Year Plan, 560 million are expected to become available in the form of foreign aid and foreign loans. The three sectors which are given priority are industry and mining (150 million), transport, communications and public works (145 million), and agriculture, irrigation and village development (110 million). Two fifths of the grants-in-aid which are used in support of the development plan are provided by the United States (Rs. 210 million); India has offered two thirds as much (140 million) and Russia and China two fifths (80 million) and one fifth (40 million) respectively. Britain offered Nepal in 1960 a programme of aid to the value of £1 million, spread over five years and including diesel generating, hydro-electric and road building equipment. In 1952 Nepal became a member of the Consultative Committee of the Colombo Plan, under which technical and training assistance has been given.

BIBLIOGRAPHY

Karl Eskelund. *The Forgotten Valley*. (Alvin Redman, London, 1959.)
Girilal Jain. *India Meets China in Nepal*. (Asia Publishing House, 1960.)
David Snellgrove. *Himalayan Pilgrimage*. (Bruno Cassirer, Oxford, 1961.)
Francis Tuker. *Gorkha: The Story of the Gurkhas of Nepal*. (Constable, 1957.)

AFGHANISTAN

William Hale

GEOGRAPHY AND POPULATION

WITH an area of some 250,000 square miles, Afghanistan is entirely landlocked. It is bounded to the west by Iran, to the south and east by West Pakistan, and to the north by the Turkmen, Uzbek and Tajik Soviet Republics. The Hindu Kush range, whose peaks rise to 25,000 feet and which splays out from the Pamirs in the north-east into central Afghanistan, dominates the physical map of the country and divides the plains of the Oxus basin to the north from the complex of river systems draining the south and east. Afghanistan's principal cities lie around the periphery of the central massif where rivers, swollen by the spring snow melt, form the basis of intensive irrigated agriculture around scattered centres. Of these the most important are Kabul (the capital), Jalalabad, Ghazni, Kandahar, Herat and Mazar-i-Sharif. Until recently the rugged and often waterless country which separates these centres of habitation has been a formidable barrier to communication between them, and has made transport between Kabul and the important agricultural areas of the north especially difficult.

The deserts of Khurasan separate Afghanistan from Iran, but important passes along her eastern frontier with Pakistan (of which the Khyber, between Jalalabad and Peshawar, is undoubtedly the most famous) have for centuries assured regular communications with the Indus basin. Routes between Herat and the Merv oasis via Kushk, and at Termez and Qizil Qala across the Oxus, connect the north and west with what is now Soviet Central Asia.

It is her climate which divides Afghanistan most distinctly from the Indian sub-continent. Only the lower part of the Kabul river valley around Jalalabad, together with isolated valleys to the south, are affected by the monsoon system. For the rest, Afghanistan enjoys a dry continental climate, with widely ranging seasonal extremes and an annual rainfall of about 10 inches, of which the bulk falls during the winter. The result is a seasonal pattern and range of vegetation fundamentally similar to that of the continent of Europe.

The Afghan government has yet to conduct a national census universally recognized as accurate. Latest sources speak of a total population of 16 millions, but unofficial estimates would reduce this figure to

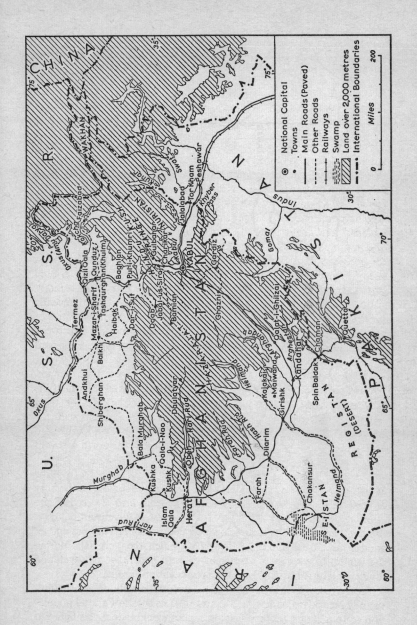

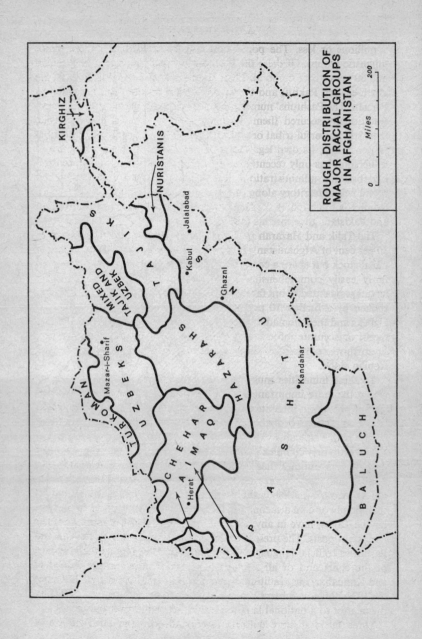

ROUGH DISTRIBUTION OF
MAJOR RACIAL GROUPS
IN AFGHANISTAN

KIRGHIZ

NURISTANIS

TAJIK

MIXED
TAJIK AND
UZBEK

UZBEKS

TURKOMAN

Mazar-i-Sharif

HAZARAS

CHEHAR
AIMAQ

Herat

PASHTUN

BALUCH

Kabul

Jalalabad

Ghazni

Kandahar

0   200
Miles

9 millions or less. The population may be divided into three major linguistic groups. Of these the Pashtuns probably represent between 50 and 60 per cent of the total. Their language has two major dialects, the north-eastern Pakhtu and the south-western Pashtu, and is related to Persian. The Pashtuns' numerical superiority and military prowess have traditionally secured them the major role in Afghan politics, while their still powerful tribal organization, with its emphasis on joint tribal responsibility, its own legal customs and its autonomous structure of leadership, has only recently retreated before the advance of a centralized national administration. The fact that Pashtuns also inhabit a broad belt of territory along the Pakistani side of Afghanistan's eastern frontier is the basis of the 'Pashtunistan' dispute between the Afghan and Pakistani governments (see p. 73).

The Tajik and Hazarah peoples, who together represent some 20 to 30 per cent of Afghanistan's population, are of fundamentally different racial stock but share a common language in Dari, a dialect of Persian fairly easily comprehensible to Persian-speaking foreigners. Turkic languages, related to but far from identical with that used in Turkey, are spoken by a further 10 per cent of the population – notably by the Uzbeks and their nomadic Turkoman neighbours. There is virtually no recent or accurate information on the Chehar Aimaq ('Four Tribes') of north-western Afghanistan, who are probably of mixed Turkic and Iranian stock.

To these minorities must be added a host of still smaller ones, of whom the more important are the Nuristanis, the presumed descendants of pre-Aryan inhabitants of Afghanistan, and the Baluch nomads, whose migrations probably take them across Afghanistan's southern border with Pakistan.

The extremely complex pattern of racial distribution, of which Map 4 presents the outlines, has a less debilitating effect on Afghanistan's politics than is sometimes supposed. Race consciousness (in Afghanistan as in other middle eastern countries) is less important in politics than family or clan attachments. Minority nationalities, and in particular the Tajiks, have in any case been represented in Cabinet and other important posts. The present Constitution recognizes both Persian and Pashtu as 'official languages of Afghanistan'. Persian, as the language of the court and of all Afghanistan's major cities except Jalalabad and Kandahar, has traditionally enjoyed the greater prestige, but since the 1930s the government has made efforts to extend the use of Pashtu, the nearest to a national language which Afghanistan possesses.

Three fairly distinct cultural layers influence the political life of modern Afghanistan. The first, the ancient tribal culture, plays an important though probably declining role in the life of the peoples of eastern and north-west Afghanistan. The second, the corpus of Islamic theological, legal and social forms, reached Afghanistan during a brief period of Arab domination during the eighth century A.D., and gradually established itself in the area in the course of the next two to three hundred years. It has resulted in the adoption of orthodox Sunni Islam by the vast majority of Afghans (though the Hazarahs follow the Shi'ite heterodoxy, as do some of the Tajiks). The third, the ideology of reform nationalism adopted by the contemporary leadership of almost all middle-eastern states, is the product of the twentieth century and affects the thinking of the small urban and educated element of Afghanistan's population.

MODERN HISTORY AND POLITICS

From the beginning of the 11th century A.D., when Sultan Mahmud of Ghazni descended into northern India, until the establishment of the Mogul empire in the 16th century, Afghan tribesmen played a major role in Indian history as the backbone of invading armies. Yet the empires they helped to found were for the most part Indo-centric and generally left their homeland in unimportant obscurity – or at best the bone of contention between the Persian and Mogul empires, as during the 16th and 17th centuries.

It was not until the middle of the 18th century that a more lasting and specifically Afghan kingdom was established. In 1747 Ahmad Shah, a former follower of the Persian conqueror Nadir Shah, was elected chief of the Abdali Pashtuns of Kandahar (subsequently known as the Duranis). By the time of his death in 1772 he had carved out a kingdom which included most of what is now Afghanistan, the Punjab and Kashmir. The reign of Ahmad's son Timur Shah (1772–93) saw little change in the territorial extent of the Durani empire, but the government of his son Shah Zeman was threatened by the rising power of the Sikhs in the Punjab, and by rivalries within the Durani tribe between the Sadozais, the royal clan, and the more numerous Barakzais. Zeman's reign was ended in 1799 when his half-brother Mahmud seized the throne with Barakzai support, only to lose it four years later to Zeman Shah's brother, Shah Shujah. Mahmud returned to power in 1809, but his defeat in 1818 by the Barakzai leader, Dost Muhammad, opened a period of prolonged civil war which ended in 1837 when Dost Muhammad proclaimed himself 'Amir of the Faithful' in Kabul.

Dost Muhammad's empire was but a fraction of that of Ahmad

Shah. The Punjab and Peshawar were now occupied by the Sikhs, while to the west Mahmud and his son Kamran preserved Herat as an autonomous Sadozai kingdom. Even the independence of what remained was interrupted in 1839 when the British authorities in India, frightened by the possibility of Russian intervention in Afghanistan, invaded the country to place Shah Shujah on the Afghan throne. A revolt in Kabul, and the murder there of the British envoy Sir William Macnaghten and his assistant Alexander Burnes, compelled the British to withdraw to Jalalabad at the end of 1841. In the course of the retreat the Kabul force was destroyed in the Khurd Kabul Pass, and when the British returned to Kabul in August 1842, it was only to undertake a punitive destruction of the city and to leave Afghanistan in Dost Muhammad's hands until his death in 1863.

Many of the features of the episode of 1839–42 were repeated in 1878–80. The Russian advance across central Asia had brought the empire to the boundaries of Afghanistan by 1875. When Dost Muhammad's son and successor, the Amir Shir Ali, began a correspondence with the Governor-General of Russian Turkistan, the British offered him an alliance with themselves whose terms the Amir felt unable to accept. A British army entered Afghanistan in November 1878, Shir Ali died the following February, and his son Yaqub was forced to accept a British Resident at his court and British control of his foreign relations. The British then withdrew to the south, but were obliged to re-enter the capital in September 1879 after the murder of their Resident, Sir Louis Cavagnari. They were however left with the task of finding a satisfactory political settlement in Afghanistan and in July 1880 the mounting cost of the occupation forced the new Liberal government in England to decide on withdrawal. Abdur Rahman, Shir Ali's nephew and former rival, was simultaneously recognized as Amir. The dangers of attempting the permanent occupation of Afghanistan were underlined shortly afterwards when a British force was defeated at Maiwand, some fifty miles north-west of Kandahar, at the hands of Yaqub's cousin, Ayub Khan.

In the agreements which he concluded with the British in 1880 Abdur Rahman accepted British direction of his foreign relations in return for a promise of British help if his kingdom was attacked by Russia. Earlier British demands for the stationing of a British Resident in Kabul were dropped and the Indian government undertook to pay the Amir an annual subsidy of 1·8 million rupees. The connexion with Britain subsequently served to arrange the demarcation of the Russo–Afghan frontier between the Hari Rud and the Oxus in 1885–8 and along the upper Oxus in 1895. Afghanistan's boundaries with British India were fixed by an agreement between the Amir and Sir Mortimer Durand, the Indian government's Foreign Secretary, which was negotiated in 1893. The establishment of fixed frontiers was itself a new departure in central Asian politics, and Abdur Rahman followed up the change by constructing a paid army and an administrational bureaucracy, and by subduing the tribes whose autonomy had contributed to the dynastic strife which had plagued Afghanistan's earlier history. When Abdur Rahman died in 1901 Afghanistan had acquired at least some of the characteristics of a modern state.

The British had accepted the agreements of 1880 because they feared a Russian march on north-west India and regarded a semi-independent Afghanistan as the best means of keeping Russia at arm's length. The fact that Russia had only agreed to the boundary alignment of 1885 after a conflict over the possession of the Panjdeh oasis helped to substantiate the assumptions on which British policy rested. For his part Abdur Rahman had been willing to sacrifice the opportunity of independent relations with Russia for the sake of a settlement with the British and as an insurance against Russian attack. Changing conditions during the reign of Abdur Rahman's son and successor Habibullah forced both sides to reconsider their earlier attitudes. The needs of European great power politics led the British to conclude the Anglo–Russian entente of 1907, which delineated Russian influence in Persia and excluded it from Afghanistan. The agreement with Russia automatically reduced the value of the alliance with the Amir. British interests during the First World War were in any case directed against a new enemy and induced the government of India to accept in 1915 a tentative recognition of Russian rights in northern Afghanistan which undermined the basis of their previous policy. Habibullah had resented the 1907 *entente* and when a German mission visited Kabul in 1915–16 he accepted promises of military help from the central powers, though on conditions which were not fulfilled by Germany. In 1919 he formally requested through the British that he should be at the Versailles conference and implicitly asked for recognition of full independence. Though they failed to reveal the fact to the Amir, the British were disinclined to reject his proposals outright.

The promised transition to a new and peacefully negotiated Anglo–Afghan settlement was abruptly interrupted by Habibullah's murder in February 1919. After a brief struggle with his uncle Nasrullah, Habibullah's son Amanullah secured the throne. The new Amir renewed his father's request for consultations with the British, and in the face of an inconclusive reply from the Viceroy he opened war on British India in May 1919. This, the third Anglo–Afghan war, was ended within a month with a limited British victory but no general advance into Afghanistan. An armistice signed at Rawalpindi in August 1919 conceded formal recognition of Afghanistan's independence, but left the final settlement of Anglo–Afghan relations to a fuller and later peace treaty. This treaty was not concluded until November 1921, and in formalizing the provisions of the Rawalpindi armistice, by confirming Afghanistan's full independence, it failed to reveal the proposals for the restitution of the Anglo–Afghan alliance against Russia which had been made by both the British and Afghan representatives. A Russo–Afghan treaty of February 1921 was equally evidence that Bolshevik Russia was prepared to treat Afghanistan as a foreign power like any other and that the Soviets had effectively abandoned their earlier plans for exploiting Afghanistan as a base for revolutionary activities in India. The principle of Russo–Afghan co-existence was confirmed by subsequent treaties in 1926 and 1931.

Whether they recognized it or not, the British and Russians had temporarily de-fused Afghanistan as an arena of great power conflict in 1921, leaving Afghanistan's rulers free to concentrate on internal reform and modernization. This was a task to which Amanullah, guided by his Turkish educated father-in-law, Mahmud Tarzi, applied himself with enthusiasm. The establishment of schools on the western pattern and attempts at industrial development were followed in 1928 by a full-scale programme of reform, embracing the foundation of a National Assembly and the introduction of compulsory female education and western dress. Amanullah's attempts to emulate the programme of Mustafa Kemal in Turkey unfortunately outran his financial resources and the desires of many of his subjects. A rebellion among the Shinwaris, east of Jalalabad, spread to Kohistan, the mountainous area north of Kabul, and in January 1929 Amanullah was forced to flee his capital for Kandahar, and thence for Europe.

The rebel leader, Bachah-i-Saqao, technically ruled as Amir Habibullah for the next nine months, but his rebellion lacked any concerted political direction and effectively reduced Afghanistan to anarchy. When Nadir Khan, a member of the royal house whose siege of the Indian fort of Thal was the major Afghan achievement in the war of 1919, entered Kabul with a force of tribesmen from the south-east in October 1929, there was a gratified reaction both in Afghanistan and abroad.

Nadir's reign as King Nadir Shah was cut short in 1933 by his murder by a supporter of Amanullah, but sufficed to see the restitution of the central government's power and the resumption of educational and economic reforms. Nadir's son, now King Zahir Shah, was only nineteen years old when his father died, but Nadir's brothers Muhammad Hashim Khan, Shah Wali Khan and Shah Mahmud ensured the continuity of firm government and steered Afghanistan through the difficult period of her neutrality during the Second World War. Some relaxation of the royal family's virtual monopoly of political power was permitted in 1950–51 by Shah Mahmud, who succeeded Muhammad Hashim as Prime Minister in 1946. The experiment proved short-lived, and the appointment to the premiership in 1953 of Muhammad Daoud (Shah Mahmud's nephew) opened a period of rapid economic development and a more active foreign policy – but no abrogation of the royal family's powers.

This situation was radically altered in March 1963 when Muhammad Daoud resigned with the explanation that increased popular participation in the government was now called for. Daoud's successor as Prime Minister was Dr Muhammad Yusuf, a commoner and a former Professor of Physics at Kabul University. A seven-member constitutional commission set to work to produce a draft Constitution, which was subsequently considered by a larger advisory committee. In September 1964 the amended draft was submitted to the 173 members of a Loya Jirgah – an assembly of provincial notables summoned on an *ad hoc* basis at other critical moments over the last fifty years.

Afghanistan's new Constitution, which was formally adopted by the Loya Jirgah on 9 September 1964, separates the legislative, judicial and executive powers of the government and excludes the royal family from membership of the Cabinet, Parliament and political parties. Legislative powers are vested in a House of the People (Wolesi Jirgah), whose 215 members are elected by universal franchise for four-year terms, and a House of the Elders (Meshrano Jirgah) of 87 members, one third of whom are appointed by the King 'from amongst well-informed and experienced persons'. The remaining two thirds of the Meshrano Jirgah seats are allotted on the basis of two per province, one member being selected by a Provincial Council and the other by universal franchise. An election law of March 1965 stipulates that women should be allowed to run as candidates and to vote, and lays down other provisions for the fair conduct of elections. Under the Constitution, the Wolesi Jirgah can eject a government by a two-thirds vote of non-confidence. Both houses have the right to initiate legislation or reject that initiated by the government.

The government's determination to put the principles embodied in the Constitution into practice was put to the test when Parliament assembled for the first time in October 1965. The foregoing elections had been carried out in orderly fashion, though with little evidence of popular interest or understanding; it was estimated that only 15 to 20 per cent of the electorate exercised its right to the franchise. Riots by university and high-school students broke out in Kabul on 24 October, however, and Parliament was unable to meet. Troops called out on the 25th killed three (or, by unofficial account, twelve) of the rioters, the Houses then assembled and Dr Yusuf received a vote of confidence, only to announce his resignation four days later 'on grounds of health' (29 October). His successor, Muhammad Maiwandwal, is a former Afghan Ambassador in Washington and for fifteen years edited the Kabul daily, *Anis*. Maiwandwal's term of office was ended without further overt disturbance on 12 October 1967, when ill health forced his resignation. (The Prime Minister had in fact been in hospital in September, and left immediately afterwards for treatment in the United States.) An interim government under Abdullah Yaftali was in office until 14 November 1967, when a new Cabinet under Nur Ahmad Itimadi was sworn in.

Afghanistan's leaders – and notably King Zahir Shah himself – are evidently determined to continue the experiment in democracy so bravely begun in 1963, but they cannot be unaware of the problems it faces. Chief among them is the fact that while many of the deputies can be classified as progressives or conservatives, an organized party system has yet to make its appearance. More serious than differences within Parliament is that between Parliament and the Cabinet as a whole. Ministers are typically members of Afghanistan's small intellectual elite and their educational and political sophistication contrasts with the homespun characteristics of most of the deputies, who are in turn anxious to test their power in the new parliamentary *milieu*.

ADMINISTRATIONAL AND JUDICIAL SYSTEMS

The preparation of the new Constitution was accompanied by a reorganization of the provincial administrational structure, which was introduced in March 1964. The country was then divided into 29 provinces, which were then subdivided into districts of the first, second and third degrees. The Governor of each province is an employee of the Ministry of the Interior, and is assisted by representatives of other Ministries – such as Finance, Education, Health and Public Works – as well as a police commandant. He is advised by a Provincial Council, elected by universal ballot. The Constitution mentions the 'extension of the councils to the village level' as an eventual aim.

The 1964 Constitution provides also for the foundation of a separate judicial establishment, as a departure from earlier forms under which the provincial Governor generally wielded effective judicial authority. Primary courts are being established in each district, staffed by professional judges. On appeal cases go to a court in the provincial capital, which may also act as a court of first instance in cases involving public servants or public security. Higher appeal courts are to be established in seven provincial towns, and a Supreme Court of Afghanistan took office in October 1967.

Afghanistan's judicial machinery is in process of rapid overhaul; reform of the legal system itself is obviously a far weightier task. Until the volume of legislation passed by Parliament increases, Afghan courts will often be forced to follow the direction of the Constitution that

whenever no provision exists under the Constitution or the laws for a case under consideration the courts shall, by following the basic principles of the Hanafi Jurisprudence of the Shariat of Islam, within the limits of this Constitution, render a decision that in their opinion secures justice in the best possible way.

FOREIGN POLICY AND FOREIGN AID

Afghanistan is one of Asia's most long-standing proponents of a non-aligned foreign policy, and has secured friendly relations with both Eastern and Western blocs without undertaking alliance commitments to either. American and Soviet rivalry for her favours has taken the form of competitive economic and military assistance. A modest programme of technical aid begun by the United States in 1952 was countered by the USSR in 1956 with a loan of $100 million. Between 1949 and 1964 Afghanistan received a total of $420 million in loans from the Soviet Union (plus an unannounced quantity of Russian military equipment), matched by $53·4 million from the United States, $60 million from West Germany and $12 million from Czechoslovakia. She additionally gained about $220 million in outright grants ($131 million from the US, $68·5 million from the USSR and $20·3 million from other sources). The servicing of the large foreign debt she has thus accumulated has become an important item in her balance of payments.

As a neighbour of China, Afghanistan has equally developed friendly relations with Peking but has remained uninvolved in the Sino–Russian conflict. A Treaty of Friendship and Mutual Non-Aggression in 1960 was followed by an agreement for the demarcation of the border with China at the tip of the north-eastern Wakhan corridor. This demarcation was carried out in 1964. In March 1965 an Agreement on Technical and Economic Collaboration marked the start of a small-scale programme of Chinese economic assistance.

Afghanistan's most serious foreign policy problem derives from her espousal of the cause of the Pashtuns inhabiting what is now north-west Pakistan. The Afghan case rests on the fact that the Pashtuns of the former North-West Frontier Province of India were given no chance to opt for independence in the referenda held preparatory to the formation of Pakistan in 1947, that 45 per cent of the electorate boycotted the polls in the settled districts, and that in the indirectly administered tribal area along the Afghan frontier only the tribal leaders were consulted. Afghan demands for a free plebiscite in the Pashtun areas of Pakistan have been consistently rejected by the Pakistanis on the grounds that the present Afghan–Pakistan frontier has international recognition, and that the fate of the eastern Pashtuns is not a matter of international concern. Intensification of the Afghan claims during the 1950s, coupled with isolated clashes between Pakistani troops and irregulars from both sides of the frontier, culminated in the closure of the border in 1961 and the mutual withdrawal of diplomatic representatives. Relations were not normalized until after Daoud's retirement in March 1963. Diplomatic and commercial links were resumed the following August, and recent Afghan ministerial statements, while not attempting to deny the existence of the 'Pashtunistan problem', have emphasized that Afghanistan seeks its settlement by peaceful means.

ECONOMIC SITUATION

Like those of most Asian countries, Afghanistan's economy is overwhelmingly agricultural; an estimated 86 per cent of the national income derives from agriculture and forestry, 6·7 per cent from industry and trade and 7·3 per cent from other activities. While it is impossible to compute accurately the *per capita* income, casual observations would suggest that living standards are slightly higher than in India, and that the typically Indian problems of mass urban destitution and periodic famine are generally absent in Afghanistan. Subsistence farming is gradually giving way to the production of cash crops, of which cotton, sugar beet and cane, oil seeds and fruit are the most important.

Industrial development is under way and plants for the manufacture of cotton and wool textiles (1966–7 production about one million metres), sugar (7,500 metric tons) and cement (177,000 metric tons) are now in operation, though as yet insufficient to meet even internal demands. Electricity production (222 million kwh in 1966–7, mainly hydro-electric) and that of coal (152,000 metric tons) have both increased rapidly over recent years, but are both capable of further expansion. Coal deposits are estimated at 70 million metric tons, and reserves of hematite (250 million tons), magnesite and chromite have also been located. Natural gas deposits exist near Shiberghan, west of Mazar-i-Sharif, and are currently being exploited with Soviet help. Of an annual production of 2,000 million cubic metres, 1·5 million are to be exported through a pipeline to the Soviet Union, and the remainder used for fertilizer and power plants at Mazar.

This development has been achieved within the context of two Five-Year Plans between the years 1958 and 1967. The first provided for a development expenditure of 10,300 million Afghanis (at the rate of 32·35 Afghanis to the dollar), while the second budgeted for an outlay of 31,300 million Afghanis. Of the latter, 25,900 million Afghanis was actually invested, and at the changed rate of 45 Afghanis to the dollar. The third plan, commencing in March 1967, has called for an investment during the first year of 5,000 million Afghanis. Afghanistan's economic development so far has been fairly satisfactory, but the execution of the third plan depends heavily on the availability of foreign aid, of which the required amounts have yet to be promised.

Each of the development plans has been forced to concentrate on the communications sector, in which Afghanistan was very poorly provided until the 1950s. Paved roads now link Kabul with Jalalabad and the Pakistani frontier in the Khyber Pass, and with Kandahar, Herat and the Oxus port of Qizil Qala. Afghanistan has no railways, and seems likely to remain without them, but air transport between the main cities has been developed by Ariana Afghan Airways.

In recent years the USSR and eastern-bloc countries have typically taken about 40 per cent of Afghanistan's exports and supplied about 35 per cent of her imports. Among the western countries, the United States has proved her most important export market, followed by Britain, India, West Germany and Pakistan. The USA again heads the list of non-Soviet suppliers, but Japan and West Germany have consistently exported more to Afghanistan than Britain or India. Britain's adverse balance is probably accounted for by the use of London as a market for *karakul* ('Astrakhan') lambskins, Afghanistan's most important single export to western countries. Cotton has accounted for the bulk of exports to Russia and dried and fresh fruit of those to India and Pakistan. Her imports have generally exceeded her exports, and Afghanistan has been generally forced to rely on foreign loans and grants to cover her current deficits.

BIBLIOGRAPHY

Afghanistan: das Land im historischen Spannungsfeld Mittelasiens, by Max Klimberg (UNESCO, Vienna, 1966) is the most recent general introduction to modern Afghanistan, and effectively replaces Donald Wilber's *Afghanistan* (Human Relations Area Files, New Haven, 1962). Sir Percy Sykes's two-volume *History of Afghanistan* (Macmillan, 1940) is the standard work in English: *Afghanistan, Highway of Conquest* by Arnold Fletcher (Cornell University Press, Ithaca, 1965) is briefer, but more up to date. In the field of economics there is as yet no English equivalent of *Die Wirtschaftliche Entwicklung Afghanistans 1880–1965* by Eberhard Rhein and A. Ghanie Ghaussy (Leske, Opladen, 1966), but the annual *Surveys of Progress* issued by the Ministry of Planning in Kabul give much useful information. There is only one published geographical study, J. Humlum's *La Géographie de l'Afghanistan* (Scandinavian University Books, Copenhagen, 1959).

PAKISTAN

Guy Wint

PAKISTAN was born out of the decision by the British Government that it could not compel the parts of India in which there was a Muslim majority to accept an All-Indian government which, reflecting the composition of the rest of the sub-continent, was predominantly Hindu. The decision was not reached in a hurry. For years there was discussion, and a long and painful attempt to reassure the Muslims by providing safeguards which would limit the power of the executive over them. Much of the most adroit political intelligence of England was directed for some years to this effort. The effort at conciliation was in vain, and in June 1947 the British Government accepted the demand of the leader of the Muslim League, Mr Jinnah, for a separate state.

Pakistan consisted of the North-West Frontier Province, Sind, Baluchistan, part of the Punjab, part of Bengal, and certain Muslim States.* Divided into two parts, West and East, with 1,000 miles of Hindu territory between, it was the part of the sub-continent in which the Muslims, according to the census reports, formed a clear majority. This fell short of Mr Jinnah's claims, which were roughly that it should include as the homeland of the Muslims all the territory ruled by Muslims before the coming of the British. By the settlement actually reached, a large section of the Muslims, over 30,000,000, were left in India. These lived in areas in which they were a minority, even though, as in the Uttar Pradesh, they had enjoyed an exceptionally favoured position in recruitment to government service. For this section the creation of Pakistan was no triumph. They were immeasurably weakened by the secession of the major part of the Muslim community to form their own state; they were forced to lower their claims, and to be satisfied by the tolerance accorded them by the Hindus.

The first result of the setting up of the new state was a violent explosion in the Punjab, due largely to the situation of the Sikh minority, which

---

*The idea of Pakistan was first invented by Rahmat Ali, a student at Cambridge, and was aired first in 1933. He explained the name as follows: 'The name "Pakistan" is composed of letters taken from the names of its component parts – Panjab, Afghans (inhabitants of the North-West Frontier Province), Kashmir, Sindh, and Baluchistan.' Rahmat Ali also derived the name from the word (*Pak*) (which means pure or clear). The word therefore means the land of all that is noble or sacred in life for a Muslim.

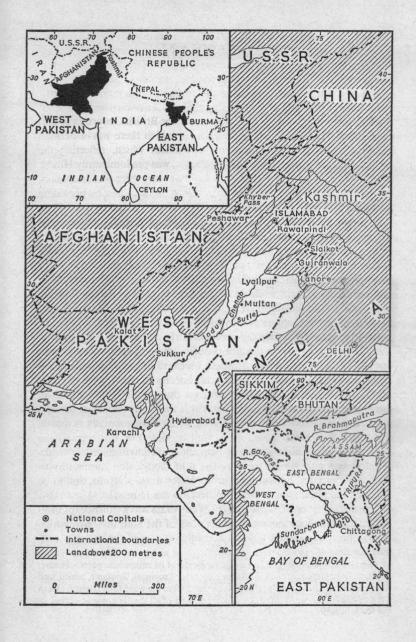

emigrated *en masse* to India. In the excitement caused by the movement of population, law and order broke down, old scores were settled, trains were ambushed, and there was mass plunder. The worst was over within a month. In the meanwhile, the civil servants had performed a remarkable feat in putting together the apparatus of a modern government. This was in spite of the fact that the number of civil servants who opted to work for the new state was far too small. They worked under great physical handicaps, having often no offices or furniture. But somehow they managed to bring order out of chaos.

GEOGRAPHY AND CLIMATE

In its ultimate shape Pakistan had a territory of 365,000 square miles. With its population of 100 million it ranks among the major powers. As the majority of the population are Muslim, Pakistan counts among the leading nations in the world of Islam.

The country consists of two geographically separate parts, West Pakistan and East Pakistan. The capitals of the two wings are almost 1,500 miles apart, and while Dacca can be reached by fast aeroplane from Karachi in three hours, it takes six days by sea to go from Karachi to Chittagong, the seaport on the Bay of Bengal.

West Pakistan borders in the west and north on Iran and Afghanistan and it is thus interested in the affairs of the Middle East; in the south it reaches to the shores of the Arabian sea; and in the east India is its neighbour. East Pakistan (East Bengal) borders in the west, north and north-east on India, in the south-east on Burma and in the south on the Bay of Bengal. It thus looks eastwards and its interests are closely tied to events and developments in West Bengal and elsewhere in South and South-East Asia.

West Pakistan absorbs some 85 per cent of the territory of the whole country, but only 45 per cent of the total population. Some of the country's internal difficulties derive from these disproportions in territory and population; whereas others are due to racial and linguistic differences. The chief language of West Pakistan is Urdu; in East Pakistan Bengali is spoken. English continues to be the medium of communication between officials and intellectuals of the two parts of the country.

The landscape of Pakistan varies from the mountainous regions in the north and north-west to the arid plains of West Pakistan and the alluvial plains of East Bengal. In the west the river system which embraces the Indus, Chenab, Jhelum, Ravi and Sutlej provides the irrigation without which the country would be barren. In the east the Ganges and Brahma-putra and their tributaries form an extensive network of waterways.

The interior of West Pakistan has a continental climate with cold winters and hot summers. Early in the year frost occurs whilst in mid summer temperatures up to 120°F are recorded. Some twenty inches of rain are the most that can be expected in the three summer months, not enough to sustain farming without irrigation. East Bengal has a sub-tropical climate with high temperatures and a degree of humidity which can be trying to the indigenous population, let alone to Europeans. During the winter months the rainfall is usually slight and temperatures are tolerable.

The geographical separation, following independence, of the two parts of the country called for two capitals. Karachi, at first the capital of the country, is to be replaced by a new capital which is being built north of Rawalpindi and which will be called Islamabad. In the interim Rawalpindi serves as the seat of government. In East Pakistan, Dacca will be replaced by Tejgaon, lying four miles outside the present administrative centre.

EARLY HISTORY: BREAKDOWN OF GOVERNMENT

The state was unfortunate to lose early its Governor-General and founder, Mr Jinnah; he died, exhausted, a year after setting it up. In the beginning the government was carried on by a Cabinet responsible to a National Parliament and Constituent Assembly which, in addition to members representing the Pakistan constituencies, included also the Muslim members from the former Parliament of India; those who chose to throw in their lot with Pakistan were provided with seats in the new Pakistan Parliament. Unlike India, Pakistan made slow progress in drafting its constitution. It was said that time was deliberately spun out by the representatives from the Indian constituencies, who were in danger of ending their career when the Constituent Assembly finished its work. The most serious issue of the time was the bid by the orthodox and the mullahs to gain a political privilege guaranteed by the constitu-tion. They agitated for boards to be set up consisting of Muslim divines, and these boards would have had the power to veto any legislation of either national or provincial legislature if they thought this inconsistent with the principles of Islam.

While these discussions took place, there was a serious deterioration in the standards of government; and corruption became a national scandal. The main cause of the malaise was alleged to be the nature of the political parties. The Muslim League, the militant party which had created Pakistan, began soon to break up, first in East Pakistan and then in the West, and totally failed to produce a vision or a leadership which could hold the state together. It had been obvious from the start that there would be tension between East and West. There was little bond of union except the glaring one of religion. The East, which considered itself more progressive because more practised in parliamentary government, resented the favoured position of the Punjabis in the civil service and armed services. Politics were haunted by the struggle between these two wings of the state, and this further frustrated the making of the constitution.

For these reasons, parliamentary government in Pakistan broke down. It was the first failure of the parliamentary system in the Commonwealth; its crash was therefore regarded as momentous. The country moved towards its crises by stages. There was an interval of highhanded intervention by the Governor-General, Ghulam Mohammed; then a return to the constitution, under which the parties lurched further onwards to discredit; gradually the public came to look to the Governor-General – or President, as he was when Pakistan followed India and became a Republic – as a more reliable repository of power than the Prime Minister, who was a shifting figure at the mercy of Parliament. In October 1958 the President, who at this time was Sikander Mirza, a former diplomat of the old Indian Political Service, declared that Parliament was abolished, and that Pakistan was to be governed by its civil servants, their authority guaranteed by the Army. The event which precipitated the crisis was a squalid brawl on the floor of the legislature in East Bengal, in which the Deputy Speaker was killed. The party system was discredited. Within a month Mirza was replaced by the Army Commander in Chief, Ayub Khan. Mirza himself was too much tainted with the corruption of the previous regime.

AYUB KHAN'S CONSTITUTION

It quickly became clear that the new system of government, though called a military dictatorship, was different from old-fashioned ones. After the first days the army was kept very much in the background. The Government turned its attention to urgent matters which had been scandalously neglected by its parliamentary predecessor, such as rehousing refugees from India who had been left in frightful squalor ever since the foundation of the state, and remedying the economic administration which had produced a foreign exchange crisis. The civil service was purged of those members who had made it corrupt. A modest land reform was carried out, important because of the excessive power of the landed class in North-West Pakistan. But after this start, the Government was preoccupied with the problem of the constitution: how this should be reformed so that some form of democracy could be resumed, but without the instability of government which the Westminster type of democracy seemed fatally to engender in Pakistan.

President Ayub Khan appointed a Commission which was instructed to review the constitutional issue by a fixed time. The drafting of the new constitution was the work chiefly of Mr Manzur Quadir, an able lawyer who had had no part at all in politics until he was invited into the Cabinet by President Ayub. It was published early in 1962. The guiding principle of the constitution was to prevent the continued existence of the political parties which according to the judgement of the regime had been responsible for the squalid life of the past. The constitution therefore prohibited political parties. There would be legislatures, both at the centre, and for the East and West halves of the state, and they were to be indirectly elected by 80,000 local councils called Basic Democracies. These local councils had been already brought into existence in the previous year. Candidates were to be chosen on a personal basis, and not as members of a party.

The elections were held in the spring. They went against the Government plan. For, though formally the candidates stood as individuals, and there was no mention of party ties, in fact many stood as the veiled supporters of the parties which had existed before the Presidential coup. The prospect opened up of a struggle between the President and Parliament, the issue being the legitimization of the parties.

In the result, President Ayub did not contest the coming to life of the parties. He abandoned the attempt to organize a parliament without parties. He accepted the fact that wherever there is a parliament, parties are bound to come into existence. He therefore concentrated on patching up parliamentary support in such a way as to guarantee the executive a long term of life, and to remove it from the danger of being made and unmade too frequently, in which he saw the root cause of all the weaknesses of the parliamentary system. In order to obtain influence in Parliament, he became a leader of one of the two parties into which the old Muslim League had divided.

The leadership of the politicians passed chiefly to Mr Suhrawardy, a former Prime Minister (and former Prime Minister of Bengal in the last days of the British Raj). His own party, the Awami League, was very small; but he had the best political head in the country, and the course of future events looked like taking the shape of a long political duel between him and President Ayub. Suhrawardy had, however, the handicap of being a Bengali, and the old regionalism of the country was likely to frustrate him. Broadly speaking the aim of the politicians was to sabotage the President, to compel elections held on the old party basis and with unrestricted franchise and to revert to the old constitution. Suhrawardy died in the autumn of 1963.

The Presidential government of Ayub Khan has been notable for efficiency, and for a humanity that is rare in military dictatorships. The Government realized that the threat of repression was enough to enforce its will upon a rather timid opposition: it did not need to employ coercive methods. Freedom of opinion was only half-heartedly controlled. Here and there the Government has been arbitrary. But it has been able to govern with few political prisoners. There has been little interference by the executive with the law courts. Ayub Khan's government has been especially notable for redressing the balance between the West Pakistanis and the Bengalis. The long-standing grievance of the Bengalis, that they paid an undue share of the cost of the state and received far too few of its benefits, has, in practice, been removed.

A Presidential election was held on 2 January 1965. The opposition parties were able to unite, and put up Miss Jinnah as a candidate. She was the sister of the founder of the state, and as such she enjoyed much of the veneration belonging to him. For a time her candidature seemed to endanger the popularity of Ayub Khan, and the election became a test of his regime since the call was raised for a reversion to the form of democracy which existed before. In the result, Ayub Khan was re-elected by nearly two thirds of the vote, though Ayub was defeated in the two main cities (Dacca, the provincial capital of East Bengal, and Karachi, the previous capital of Pakistan). His election, which was not seriously challenged as using unfair methods, considerably increased his prestige. In 1967 Miss Jinnah died.

FOREIGN POLICY

In foreign relations Pakistan, throughout its life, has been obsessed with the quarrel with India over Kashmir. The details of the dispute are set out elsewhere in this book. It can scarcely be said that Pakistan's concern was unreasonable. The greater part of the Indian Army was massed on its frontier, and leading Indian statesmen, such as Mr Krishna Menon, did not hesitate to describe Pakistan as 'India's enemy No. 1'; Mr Krishna Menon continued to say this even when fighting had begun between India and China on India's northern border. The need to woo the support of great powers against India led Pakistan to throw in its lot with both SEATO and the CENTO alliance (formerly the Baghdad Pact). In the times when public opinion could be expressed in the newspapers, it was made clear however that this policy was not popular and that there was a strong current of opinion in favour of Pakistan going neutralist. The Pakistan Government veered towards China in its dispute with India, and took advantage of China's cordiality to get a favourable settlement of the part of its border which used to be undemarcated.

Pakistan followed this by an exploration of its relations with China over the whole field, and caused anxiety in India that it would enter into an understanding with Peking which would be directed against India. Pakistan also caused anxiety in the United States, and doubts grew about the permanence of its membership of SEATO and CENTO.

In 1965 there took place a dispute over the Rann of Cutch, an area of marshland near the Arabian Sea. Its ownership had remained uncertain because it was uninhabited, and because it was totally flooded for part of the year. For reasons which are obscure the Pakistan army came into conflict with the Indian army over the frontier delimitation. For some days the situation was threatening, but eventually the dispute was settled judicially.

The military conflict which was thus narrowly averted in the Rann of Cutch broke out in the late summer in fighting in Kashmir. (For the Six Weeks' War, see pages 521–4.)

After rumours of high tension over Kashmir, which were often well founded, full-scale fighting between India and Pakistan became a reality on 7 September 1965. After a stubborn combat which lasted just over a fortnight, a United Nations order of a cease-fire was obeyed. It was the prelude to a general agreement between the two countries which was reached, under the good offices of Russia, at Tashkent in January 1966. This marked a return of Russian diplomatic activity in the relations of India and Pakistan. Russia sought in this way to counter the designs of China.

Ayub Khan, in agreeing to the cease-fire, had gone counter to the public opinion of the western part of the country (East Bengal was less stirred up, though it had been perfectly loyal during the fighting). The regime has therefore been partly weaker ever since, and this incident precipitated the resignation of Mr Z. Bhutto, the Foreign Minister, at that time regarded as Ayub's probable successor.

An agreement with India over the share-out of the canal waters of the

Punjab, one of the outstanding achievements of the regime, has remained intact.

Pakistan has a feather in its cap for its settlement of its quarrels with the tribal peoples of the North-West Frontier. During the British period this region was continually disturbed. The people of the Frontier were not directly administered by the Government. They were continually raiding the administered areas. The first act of Mr Jinnah was to withdraw the army with which the Government had been accustomed to overawe the tribal people, and to appeal to them on the score of a common Islamic attachment to live at peace with Pakistan. The success of this bold gesture surprised the former British administrators. It was backed up by an economic policy of aid to help the Pathans of the region in developing small industry. Reward for enlightened policy came later when Afghanistan tried to stir up the tribes in an anti-Pakistan movement (see page 535). By and large Afghanistan has had an extremely limited success.

Less satisfactory was Pakistan's record with its minorities in Bengal. The main trouble was relations with the Hindus. In West Pakistan these and the Sikhs fled the country in 1947; but in the East a very large Hindu minority remain, including the middle class which dominated the economic life. Subsequently it is hard to acquit the Government of deliberately squeezing out the Hindu inhabitants. There was in any case a popular feeling against them, and the Government did nothing to discourage this. Tension came to a head in 1950 when there were savage riots in East Pakistan (as there were corresponding riots in West Bengal in India). Opinion throughout Pakistan was bitterly roused, and there was serious danger of war with India. The Hindus interpreted the signs of the times, and most of the more prosperous members of the community migrated to India. In 1963 tension again rose, and there were savage riots in East Bengal, which caused equal savagery in Bihar in reprisal. The disorders rose out of the eviction of Muslims – who according to India had settled unlawfully – from Assam.

Pakistan's foreign policy may be divided clearly into separate phases. In the first years of independence it placed its trust in membership of the Commonwealth. It was disappointed when the Commonwealth was deaf to its appeal to rectify matters over Kashmir. There followed an attempt to exploit its position as the largest Muslim country in the world, and to align itself with the Muslim states of the Middle East. This move was rebuffed, partly because it was countered by skilful Indian propaganda, chiefly in Cairo. Pakistan, in its search for security against India, then availed itself of the offer by America of alliances with the countries which could give it a foothold on the Asian continent. But it sought to give the alliance an anti-Indian slant, while America tended all along to treat it as directed against Russia. It was fear that America was providing too great an arms supply for India, following on the invasion by China, that led Pakistan to reconsider its loyalties towards America.

Before events took this turn, Ayub Khan had made an attempt to come to terms with India, proposing a joint direction of their armed forces. The offer was made under the shadow of Chinese aggression. It was rebuffed by India.

THE ECONOMIC SITUATION

Pakistan, not unlike other countries in South and South-East Asia, is still a predominantly agrarian community, and it is likely to remain so for some time to come. Four out of every five Pakistanis live in villages, and three out of four are engaged in farming, forestry and fishing, which contribute half the national income. Agriculture supplies the chief subsistence crops: wheat in the west and paddy (rice) in the east of the country. Moreover, some of the principal commercial and export products are of agricultural origin; i.e. jute, cotton, tea, wool and hides. Before the war, East Bengal held the world monopoly in raw jute production. Since the partition of the sub-continent India has developed in West Bengal the cultivation of jute as a raw material basis of her jute mills, while East Pakistan has built mills for her raw jute so as to become independent of Indian processing.

The means of exploitation known in the 19th and early 20th centuries held out little hope that Pakistan would lend itself readily to industrial development. The means of transportation and modern machinery developed during the last war and thereafter, and Pakistan has enjoyed boom conditions, but it is still a poor country and problems of further development remain formidable. Pakistan does not appear to be endowed with rich mineral resources, though deposits of coal, iron, manganese, lead, chromite, tungsten, limestone and gypsum have been found. Natural gas has been discovered in large quantities. Some mineral oil is also produced and intensive oil exploration is carried out in various parts of the country.

At present less than half the country's energy requirements and only one per cent of its steel consumption are met from indigenous sources. The use of energy and steel per head of population may be taken as a measure of the distance which Pakistan has to go before she will rank among the industrial countries of the world. In Japan, the only industrialized country in Asia, the supplies of energy and steel per person are approximately twenty and thirty times respectively as large as in Pakistan.

While manpower and manual skills are not lacking, the high rate of illiteracy and the shortage of teachers and skilled technicians of all kinds present serious problems in any programme of development. Only one quarter of those eligible are enrolled in primary and secondary schools, and only a little over one per cent of the nation's income is spent on education (against 6 per cent in Japan and in the United States). Only 2 per cent of all students train in agriculture (against 10 per cent in Taiwan). As almost half the population is under fourteen or over sixty-five years of age (against 35 per cent in Britain) and many women are still in purdah, the active population accounts for one third only (against over half in the Soviet Union).

In an effort to overcome the inhibitions that stand in the way of progress, a National Planning Board was founded following the declaration of independence. A Six-Year Plan was formulated in 1950. The year 1965 saw the end of the second Five-Year Plan under which a total of Rs.19,000 million (£1,400 m.) was spent at the rate of 3:2 in the public and private sectors of the economy: 60 per cent of the expenditure was expected to be mobilized from indigenous sources and the remainder from overseas aid, foreign credits and investors. Foreign assistance has been made available multilaterally under the Colombo Plan, by a Western consortium, by the specialized agencies of the United Nations, and bilaterally by the United States (over $700 million), by Britain (nearly £40 million) and, more recently, by the Soviet Union ($45 million) and China ($60 million).

One of the chief objectives of the Plan was to attain self-sufficiency in food grains. Irrigation schemes, flood controls and multi-purpose projects (irrigation and electric power development) were designed to this end; so were plans to reduce the salinity of the soils in West Pakistan and to extend the fishing fleet as well as the marketing and procuring of fish as a major source of animal protein.

The contribution of industry and construction is still less than one fifth of the national income. Not unnaturally industries based on the traditional indigenous raw materials such as jute, cotton, sugar and leather are still in the forefront; but cement, paper and chemicals have been added in recent years. Hydro-electric projects and natural gas have provided industry with much-needed energy, but the fuel and power economy represents a bottleneck in the process of development.

The replacement of imports by domestically produced goods is a prime target of the Plan: by comparison, any scheme designed to contribute to international or intra-regional divisions of labour ranks low among the priorities of the Plan. The Pakistan Industrial Development Corporation (PIDC) has the task of promoting industries essential for the development of the country. It is supported by an Industrial Finance Corporation (PIFC) as well as an Industrial Credit and Investment Corporation (PICIC).

As a member of the sterling area Pakistan has been able to draw on her sterling accounts accumulated during the last war, but currency reserves have declined greatly and the balance of payments position is tight. Britain is still Pakistan's main export market, but the United States is her main supplier of imports. In 1955 Pakistan devalued her currency and this brought it into line with those members of the sterling area who devalued their currency, together with Britain, in 1949.

POSTSCRIPT

At the end of 1968 there were signs of a weakening of the regime. Ayub Khan was recovering from a severe illness. Mr Bhutto, who had left the Government in June 1966 and tried to form an opposition party, pro-Chinese and more anti-Indian than Ayub Khan, was imprisoned in the autumn. Simultaneously there was a clash between the Government and the students, who agitated for a return of the former constitution.

Relations with India continued to be bad. Pakistan gave more or less open encouragement to the Nagas. Over policy towards China, it showed the greatest hesitancy and uncertainty. The motive which governed it was to obtain more arms to use against India.

BIBLIOGRAPHY

J. Russell Andrus and Azizali F. Mohammed. *The Economy of Pakistan.* (Oxford University Press, 1958.)

L. Binder. *Religion and Politics in Pakistan.* (University of California Press, Berkeley and Los Angeles, 1961.)

Keith Callard. *Pakistan: A Political Study.* (Allen & Unwin, 1957.)

Robert D. Campbell. *Pakistan: Emerging Democracy.* (Princeton University Press, Princeton.)

Fazl Al-Rahman. *New Education in the Making in Pakistan.* (Cassell, 1953.)

A History of the Freedom Movement, 3 vols. (Pakistan Historical Society, Karachi, 1960.)

Sir William Ivor Jennings. *Constitutional Problems of Pakistan*. (Cambridge University Press, 1957.)

Mahbub ul Haq. *The Strategy of Economic Planning*. (Oxford University Press, 1963.)

W. N. Peach, M. Uzair and G. W. Rucker. *Basic Data of the Economy of Pakistan*. (Oxford University Press, Karadu, 1959.)

Rahinat Ali. *The Pakistan National Movement and the British Verdict in India*. (Pakistan National Movement, Cambridge, 1946.)

Ian Stephens. *Pakistan*. (Ernest Benn, 1963.)

Richard Symonds. *The Making of Pakistan*. (Faber & Faber, 3rd edn, 1951.)

The Second Five-Year Plan, 1960–65. (Government of Pakistan, Planning Commission, Karachi, 1960.)

Hugh Tinker. *India and Pakistan: A Short Political Guide*. (Pall Mall Press, 1962.)

L. F. Rushbrook-Williams. *The State of Pakistan*. (Faber & Faber, 1962.)

CEYLON

Bertram H. Farmer

CEYLON is a tropical island with a marked individuality and strong internal contrasts. Although its culture embodies many Indian traits, the survival and dominance of Buddhism is alone sufficient to mark it off from the mainland. Internally, the contrast between Wet Zone and Dry Zone has been of great significance throughout history. The Wet Zone of the south-west is liable to rain at all seasons; but the Dry Zone, which covers most of the lowlands in the north and east and extends in modified form into the eastern part of the central highlands, is subject to searing drought during the months from May to September, or longer, and to unreliability of rainfall at other seasons.

THE EARLY HISTORY OF CEYLON

In the closing centuries of the era before Christ the Sinhalese (who seem to have come from north India) established a high level of civilization in the Dry Zone, especially in the north-centre around Anuradhapura, and in the south-east. This was based on the skilful use of irrigation; and its surviving memorials, in the shape not only of irrigation works but of Buddhist shrines, are most impressive.

The Sinhalese Kingdom was often rent by internal dissension and troubled by the threat of the Tamils from South India. The first contacts of these Hindu people with the Sinhalese seem to have been peaceful; but from the second century B.C. onwards there were repeated armed invasions by Tamil rulers. The centre of gravity of Sinhalese settlement moved southward from the Anuradhapura region towards and eventually into the Wet Zone and the hills, whose thick jungles had been avoided in earlier centuries. The Dry Zone declined, its irrigation works fell into disrepair and decay, and (apparently) malaria came in for the first time; by the time of European contact in the 15th century it was a region of occasional malaria-ridden villages, except in the Tamil-occupied Jaffna Peninsula and along the east coast.

But Buddhist monks had written down the story of the ancient glories, as they saw them; and what they wrote has had a profound influence on the modern Sinhalese. Ceylon is seen as Sri Lanka, 'holy Ceylon', the island with a unique role in the preservation of Buddhism; and the

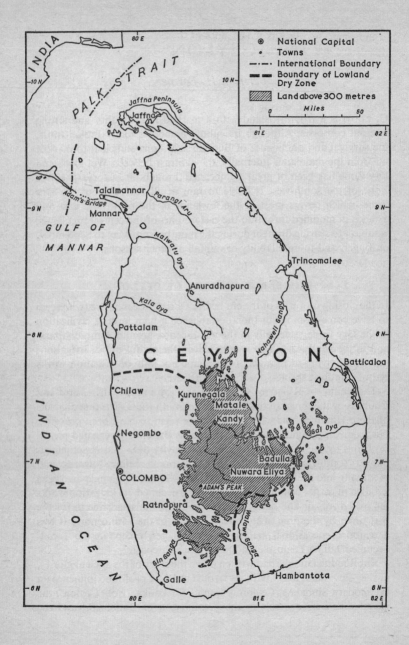

Tamils are identified as the enemies of the heroes of old and, even, as the destroyers of the glory of ancient Ceylon.

THE PORTUGUESE PERIOD

Ceylon has fallen during the last 450 years successively under Portuguese, Dutch and British rule. During the earlier part of their period from 1505 to 1597 the Portuguese maintained the fiction that the Sinhalese king was the sovereign, though increasingly he was their puppet. From 1597 until 1658, the King of Portugal claimed the sovereignty, though he never exercised it in the Up-country kingdom of Kandy. The Portuguese had a lasting effect on the maritime regions, beginning that process of differentiation which still sets the 'Low Country' Sinhalese apart from the 'Kandyans'. The Roman Catholicism which they implanted is still dominant in some coastal areas, especially among the Karava, the fisher caste. These and other formerly lowly castes owe to the Portuguese the beginning of their rise in status. The commercial influence of Portugal was less lasting.

THE DUTCH PERIOD

The Dutch East India Company had for some time been the ally of the Kandyan king before they finally ousted the Portuguese in 1658. From then till 1795 they held undisputed sway in the Low Country and in Jaffna, and in 1766 extracted from the Kandyan king (with whom they had been in conflict) the cession of the entire seaboard. The Dutch continued the concentration on the lowlands of the Wet Zone that had been a feature of Portuguese rule, though they were also interested in Jaffna; in their time, however, seekers after cinnamon penetrated into the Kandyan kingdom. The cinnamon trade was to the Dutch 'the great industry', and plantations were established. Castes such as the Karava (already mentioned) and the Salagama (cinnamon peelers) benefited greatly from this interest of the Dutch. The Dutch Company further encouraged the settlement of persons in its service, and there remains to this day a sizeable community of 'Burghers'. Roman-Dutch law is an important element in the legal system of Ceylon.

THE BRITISH PERIOD

The British, after one or two preliminary skirmishes, moved into Ceylon in 1795–6, mainly in order to deny Trincomalee and other bases to the

French during the Napoleonic Wars. After a period of uncertainty, Ceylon became a Crown Colony in 1802. The British soon succeeded where their predecessors had failed; for, in 1815, the Kandyan kingdom finally became British territory, a treaty being signed which guaranteed the integrity, laws and religion of the kingdom and which further differentiated the Kandyan from the Low-country Sinhalese.

The British period was one of revolutionary change, much of it centring on the introduction of plantations, first of coffee Up-country then of tea when coffee was stricken by disease, and later of coconut and rubber on rather lower ground (though still almost entirely in the Wet Zone, for climatic reasons). European plantations and enterprise were rapidly imitated by Ceylonese land-owners and small-holders who planted nearly all of Ceylon's million acres of coconuts. Great social changes were set in train and the economy of the country was transformed, so that it came to import much of its food and almost all of its manufactures in exchange for exports of plantation products.

With the development of plantations came the immigration of Indian Tamil labour, the construction of roads and railways, the improvement of the port of Colombo, the growth of towns, the spread of Ceylon Tamils from Jaffna into southern Ceylon, and apparently a rise in average living standards until the 1930s. But little of all this (apart from the construction of a road network) affected the Dry Zone. Something was done from 1870 on to restore irrigation works, but only locally did this have much effect on settlement until, after 1932, serious efforts were made to encourage colonization. But much of the effort here was made under the influence of Ceylonese Ministers, notably D. S. Senanayake, and success depended on malaria control with DDT.

The British period also saw the establishment of an educational system which was particularly potent in its effect on those who became the English-educated upper middle class, and the development of a modern administration and judiciary.

Ceylon is of course the classic case of a colony which slid gently and with very little disturbance through a sequence of constitutional changes to independence. It had by 1923 a Legislative Council in which unofficial members were in the majority. In 1931 under the so-called 'Donoughmore Constitution', universal adult franchise was introduced and Ceylonese Ministers were for the first time placed in charge of departments of government. There were further constitutional changes in May 1947, most of whose Westminster-style provisions have survived into the era of independence.

CEYLON SINCE INDEPENDENCE

During the first eight years of independence the United National Party (UNP) dominated the scene. The Party had been founded by D. S. Senanayake in 1945-6, and had won the elections under the Soulbury Constitution (1947) which provided the first Parliament of independent Ceylon. The UNP brought together Sinhalese who had been associated with Senanayake in the Ceylon National Congress, a number of Ceylon Tamils, the Ceylon Muslim League, and, until 1951, S. W. R. D. Bandaranaike's Sinhala Maha Sabha (Bandaranaike crossed the floor in that year), while in 1948 even G. G. Ponnambalam, leader of the Tamil Congress, joined Senanayake's Cabinet.

D. S. Senanayake died in March 1952 and the Governor-General called on his son, Dudley, who had been Minister of Agriculture and Lands, to form a Government. The UNP easily won the elections of May 1952. Dudley Senanayake resigned in October 1953, and was succeeded by his uncle, Sir John Kotelawala.

Under UNP rule, in spite of strikes and other troubles, Ceylon seemed to many western observers to have discovered not only how to maintain law and order and to work a Westminster-style constitution but also how to contain communal disharmonies. Such observers expected the UNP to continue in office after the elections of April 1956, but in the event that party limped home with eight seats only, decisively defeated by Bandaranaike's coalition, the Mahajana Eksath Peramuna (MEP). What had happened to the power and apparent stability of the UNP? Its defeat owed something to the untimely loss of D. S. Senanayake, to the personal unpopularity of Kotelawala (who was very insensitive to public opinion) and to the passing of the wave of sympathy that had helped to return Dudley Senanayake to power on the death of his father. It owed something to the feeling that the UNP had been in office long enough and had grown indolent if not corrupt; and to the tactical skill with which Bandaranaike brought into his MEP coalition not only his own SLFP but the Viplavakari Lanka Sama Samaja Party (VLSSP), the more extreme of Ceylon's two Trotskyite parties, as well as other smaller groups, and with which he engineered a 'no contest pact' with other anti-UNP groups, notably the Nava Lanka Sama Samaja Party (NLSSP, the other Trotskyite party), and the Communists.

But there was more to it than personalities, or the swing of the pendulum, or Bandaranaike's tactical skill. The UNP, unlike the Indian Congress Party, was essentially narrowly based, for all D. S. Senanayake's genuine desire to create a united nation and for all his efforts to weld other groups to his own. It was essentially the party of the English-educated affluent middle-class families who had formed the spearhead of the nationalist movement. Many members of this group had by 1956 lost whatever touch they had ever had with the growing urban working class, with the small but articulate intelligentsia, and with the social movement that was developing in the villages. This movement was, in fact, a complex social revolution compounded of a Buddhist revival and an associated resurgence of Sinhalese language and culture, largely in reaction against the West but stimulated also by *Buddha Jayanti* (the 2,500th anniversary of the Buddha's attainment of nirvana) and sustained by that sense of historic destiny to which reference has already been made; and compounded also of the frustration of vernacular-educated Sinhalese (especially Buddhist priests, school-masters, ayurvedic physicians and the like) who found that jobs went to the English-educated, and who felt hostile not only to the English-educated and to the UNP but also to the Tamils, who were alleged to have more than their share of Government jobs and who anyway were seen as the historic enemy. Bandaranaike, sensing what was abroad in the villages, was able to canalize these and other complex grievances and in doing so to amplify them. The UNP on the other hand adopted its Sinhalese-only policy too late. Bandaranaike's advent to power may have brought to the common man a new sense of purposeful involvement in politics. It was certainly followed by a period of instability compounded of much labour unrest; severe communal disturbances in 1956 and 1958 (following moves to implement the declared policy of establishing Sinhalese as the sole 'national language'); a number of periods of rule under a state of emergency; unprecedented Cabinet dissension which broke up the MEP coalition in 1959; the assassination of Bandaranaike on 25 September of the same year; a period of indecisive rule by a Cabinet rent by quarrels under his successor, W. Dahanayake; an election in April 1960, which very briefly returned Dudley Senanayake and the UNP to power; a further election in July 1960, which brought back the Sri Lanka Freedom Party (SLFP), Bandaranaike's own party and the main constituent of the former MEP, his widow being called upon to form the Government; an attempted coup by police and military early in 1962; the defeat of Mrs Bandaranaike's government in December 1964 (mainly because of the defection of some of her erstwhile supporters); the three months of uncertainty, re-alignment and increasing bitterness preceding the ensuing elections, which brought the UNP back to power, but only with the help, in coalition, of the Tamil

Federal Party; a second attempted coup in February 1966. Such is the catalogue of main events, and it does not need much imagination to sense the political instability and the inevitable shelving of major economic issues which lie behind it. But at least Ceylon can claim that it has never yet changed its Government except by due electoral process.

Not surprisingly, the reaction of a large proportion of the Ceylon Tamils to Sinhalese linguistic nationalism was to unite behind the most extreme of the Tamil parties, the Federal Party, which wishes a federal solution to the problems of the Tamil-populated northern and eastern provinces. The UNP, because it was forced into coalition with the Federal Party, can be and is represented as pro-Tamil. The Indian Tamils are mostly disenfranchised by Ceylon's citizenship legislation; but according to the so-called 'Sirima-Shastri Pact', agreed between Mrs Bandaranaike and the late Lal Bahadur Shastri in November 1964, 300,000 persons of Indian origin (mainly Tamils) would be absorbed by Ceylon, which would grant them citizenship, while 525,000 were to return to India, leaving 150,000 whose fate was to be decided later. There have, however, been moments of acute tension when it seemed that the Indian and Ceylon Tamils were about to make common cause. And the Sinhalese are aware, of course, that, although a majority in their own island, they face the Dravidian mass of south India across Palk Strait. Not surprisingly, then, but most unfortunately, no politician in Ceylon today can afford to neglect communal feeling. The poor showing of the NLSSP and the Communists in the 1960 elections, widely interpreted in the West as a defeat for the left, was in the main due to their support for parity in the language issue.

But polarization between left and right is of growing significance: the coalition between the SLFP and the NLSSP effected in May 1964 certainly increased the influence of the left until the fall of the Government (mentioned above) for reasons that included suspicion by some SLFP members of their leftist allies, among which anti-Marxism was certainly an issue in the 1964 elections.

ECONOMIC SITUATION

Ceylon became independent with an economy which, while narrow-based and hence very liable to booms and slumps, made possible an average standard of living higher than that of most Asian countries; and a start had been made with the agricultural colonization of the Dry Zone and with industrialization. In the years since independence booms and slumps have continued: in 1951, for example, came the post-Korean boom, while since 1961, Ceylon has suffered with increasing severity from low commodity prices and foreign-exchange problems. With these short-term problems (at least one hopes they are short-term) the coalition Government has been attempting to grapple, though, many would say, with insufficient vigour. But agricultural production is growing, as is industrial production behind a wall of controls.

The possibility of the nationalization of foreign-owned enterprises in Ceylon, and, in particular, of tea estates, is an aspect of Ceylon politics that has attracted attention. Nationalization has always formed part of the programme of the various left-wing parties in Ceylon, and Mr Bandaranaike, in engineering the coalition and the 'no contest pact' that brought him victory in 1956, followed suit, largely in order to win left support. He did, in fact, nationalize public road passenger transport, which had aroused a great deal of public dissatisfaction. He also nationalized the port of Colombo. But he left foreign estates well alone; and the same line had been pursued by his successors in office. Foreign enterprises have not escaped entirely, however, for in May 1961 a State Oil Corporation was formed and took over compulsorily certain installations previously owned by foreign oil firms.

And ever more insistent looms the shadow of a runaway increase in population: there were 5·3 million people in Ceylon in 1921, there were 10·6 million in 1963, there may well be 21 million by 1981. A considerable amount of thought has been given to the consequent economic problems. A Ten-Year Plan, 1959–68, whose cornerstone was progressive industrialization, resting, however, on the development of agriculture both for home production and for export, was overtaken by events, particularly the foreign exchange crisis already mentioned. But it is worth recording that agricultural yields seem to be rising (both in the export sector and in the traditional rice-growing sector) and a cash economy spreading, while a determined and largely successful effort is being made to increase food production, notably in the Dry Zone.

BIBLIOGRAPHY

Sydney D. Bailey. *Ceylon*. (Hutchinson, 1952.)
The Economic Development of Ceylon. World Bank mission report. (Cumberlege, London, 1953.)
B. H. Farmer. 'Ceylon', (in O. H. K. Spate and A. T. A. Learmonth (Eds.), *India and Pakistan*. (Methuen, 3rd edn, 1967.) *Ceylon: A Divided Nation*. (Oxford University Press for Institute of Race Relations, 1963.) *Pioneer Peasant Colonization in Ceylon*. (Oxford University Press for Royal Institute of International Affairs, 1957.)

Sir Ivor Jennings. *The Economy of Ceylon*. (Oxford University Press, Madras, 2nd edn, 1951.)

E. F. C. Ludowyk. *The Story of Ceylon*. (Faber & Faber, 1962.)

E. F. C. Ludowyk. *The Modern History of Ceylon*. (Praeger, New York, 1966.)

Donald R. Snodgrass. *Ceylon: an Export Economy in Transition*. (Irwin, Homewood, Ill., 1966.)

The Ten-Year Plan. (Planning Secretariat, Colombo, 1959.)

W. Howard Wriggins. *Ceylon, Dilemmas of a New Nation*. (Princeton University Press, Princeton, N.J., 1960.)

Central Asia

TIBET

George N. Patterson

TIBET A POWERFUL NATION

IT was in the 7th century that Tibet as a nation, and a powerful one at that, emerged from the realm of legend and entered history. A Tibetan king, Srong-tsen Gampo, conquered regions in north Burma and western China and exacted tribute from the Emperor of China, including the marriage of the Emperor's daughter. The same king was equally successful in his attacks on the Indian border, subjugating large parts of Nepal and taking a princess from that country also as tribute. These two queens were Buddhists and converted the king to their faith, and in the years that followed he extended the Buddhist religion throughout the whole of Tibet. Until this time Tibet had only had an oral language, derived from the same linguistic family as the Burmese; but Buddhist scriptures were now brought from India and a written character adapted from the Sanskrit to fit the Tibetan language.

PEACE TREATY WITH CHINA

In the 8th century Tibet became a great military power in Asia, reaching from the Chinese capital of Changan, which its armies had captured, to near the River Ganges in India, and from Turkestan to Burma. In the 9th century, after over 100 missions had passed between the two countries, a peace treaty was signed on the basis of equality.

In the 13th century Tibet became a vassal state of the Mongols under Genghis Khan, but later Kublai Khan appointed a favourite Tibetan priest as Priest-King of Tibet and constituted ruler of (1) Tibet Proper, comprising the thirteen states of U-Tsang Province; (2) Kham, and (3) Amdo. In the 17th century when the Great Fifth Dalai Lama visited Peking, Tibetan records claim that he was received as an independent sovereign.

CHINA'S CLAIM TO SUZERAINTY

After the death of the Sixth Dalai Lama there was a period of considerable intrigue. At one point the Chinese Emperor sent three armies into Tibet which were eventually successful in defeating the Mongols who were then in possession, and he installed a Seventh Dalai Lama of his

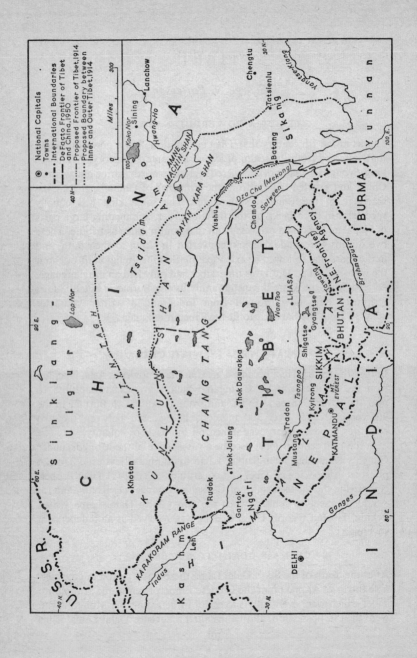

U. S. S. R.

C H I N A

Sinkiang - Uigur

Khotan

Lop Nor

KUN LUN A-LI-N LAGH

Tsaidam

A M D O

Koko Nor

Hwang-Ho

Sining

Lanchow

AMNE MACHIN SHAN

BAYAN KARA SHAN

Yushu

Chamdo

Dza Chu (Mekong)

Salween

Batang

Sikang

Tatsienlu

Chengtu

Yunnan

Yangtse-kiang

T I B E T

CHANG TANG

Thok Daurakpa

Thok Jalung

Rudok

Gartok

Ngari

Leh

KARAKORAM RANGE

Kashmir

Indus

LHASA

Nam Tso

Tradon

Mustang

Tsangpo

Kyirong

Shigatse

Gyangtse

Yatung

SIKKIM

MT EVEREST

KATMANDU⊙

N E P A L

Ganges

DELHI ⊙

I N D I A

BHUTAN

N.E. Frontier Agency

Brahmaputra

BURMA

own choice. China's claim to suzerainty over Tibet appears to date from this invasion. Following it, a Manchu resident and a garrison force of 3,000 Chinese troops were left behind and communication with China was kept open by stationing small detachments of troops along the Lhasa-Chamdo-Batang-Tachienlu 'road'. The new boundary between China and Tibet was demarcated by a pillar, erected in 1727 on the Bum-La south-west of Batang. (See map.)

TIBET RECOVERS 'GREATER TIBET'

The absolute rule claimed by the Chinese residents in Lhasa was not maintained. When inter-tribal war broke out in Kham Province in 1860, rapidly involving the whole of East Tibet, the inhabitants appealed to both the Chinese and Tibetan Governments for help. The former were in no position to help because of their involvement with foreign powers, but the Dalai Lama responded by sending a Tibetan Army which suppressed the fighting in 1863. The Tibetan claim to the re-conquered territory dates from this time, when the Chinese Imperial Court confirmed the claim. When the Younghusband expedition marched on Lhasa in 1904 the Chinese reacted to this threat to their interests in Tibet by appointing an 'Imperial Resident' in East Tibet. The Khambas revolted, the Chinese sent in an army under General 'Butcher' Chao Erh-feng, and he ruthlessly brought the whole country under the direct control of the Chinese Government. Chao was killed in 1911, but his assistant proposed that East Tibet should be converted into a new Chinese province to be called '(H)Si-kang', or 'Western Kham'. Following the revolution in China the Kham Tibetans again revolted, defeated the Chinese, but agreed under pressure from Britain not to invade west China.

THE SIMLA CONVENTION

In 1913 a Conference was held in Simla between China, Tibet and India, from which emerged an agreement to divide Tibet into two zones, 'Outer Tibet', nearer India, including Lhasa, Shigatse and Chamdo; and 'Inner Tibet', nearer China, including Batang, Litang, Tatsienlu and a large part of East Tibet. Chinese suzerainty over the whole of Tibet was recognized, but China agreed not to convert Tibet into a Chinese province. Two days after China had initialled the draft, she repudiated it, but it should be noticed that she objected to the boundary between 'Inner' and 'Outer' Tibet, and not to the rest of the agreement. Tibet and Britain recognized it as binding upon themselves, with China, having repudiated the Conference, entitled to none of the advantages which the Convention would have conferred upon her. The agreement included the fixing of the boundary between Tibet and India, known as the 'MacMahon Line'.

Little of major historical importance occurred in Sino-Tibetan relations between the Simla Convention and the Chinese Communist invasion in 1950. In the war between China and Japan Tibet maintained a neutral position. Following the end of the Second World War and the deteriorating political situation in China, arms and ammunition on a large scale became available to the East Tibetan leaders and brought the possibility of a successful revolt against the central Lhasa Government – a long-cherished ambition of the East Tibetans, or Khambas, as they are known – within reach.

CHINESE COMMUNIST 'LIBERATION' OF TIBET

On 25 October 1950, Peking radio broadcast that the process of 'liberating' Tibet had begun. However, it was still not publicly admitted to be a military action. At this time the Chinese were almost certainly sincere in their desire for a 'peaceful liberation'. As the historical record indicates, while there was some ground for Chinese claims to Tibet based on their conquests of the country at various times, there was an equally sound basis for Tibet's claim to independence through having ultimately expelled the Chinese from the country. It was this uncertainty as to Tibet's actual historical status which accounted for the early hesitation of the Chinese in their 'liberation' action, while at the same time loudly insisting on their 'right' to liberate. But when the Dalai Lama's brother dramatically escaped to the United States, and a copy of a top-secret American military briefing booklet was discovered to be circulating on the border disclosing alarming plans, the Chinese must have decided that 'peaceful measures' were no longer practicable.

On receiving the report that Chinese troops were entering Tibet the Tibetan Government approached the Government of India to raise the matter of China's aggression on Tibet's behalf in the United Nations, but the Indian Government advised the Tibetan Government to approach the United Nations directly. This they did on 11 November 1950, and an 'unofficial note' was circulated to members of the Security Council. On 17 November the El Salvador delegate formally raised the complaint against China in a letter to the Secretary-General. But both the Governments of the United Kingdom and India opposed the Tibetan appeal.

CHINA IGNORES SEVENTEEN-POINT AGREEMENT

The Tibetan Government appealed to the UN and prepared four delegations to proceed to Britain, the US, India and Nepal, to seek support. The appeal to the UN was shelved and the delegation discouraged from proceeding by the countries concerned. The Tibetan Government were forced by this isolation into submitting to the Chinese take-over of Tibet. The Chinese Government proposed that a Tibetan delegation be sent to Peking, and on arrival this delegation, according to their report and the Dalai Lama's later statement, were forced to sign a Seventeen-point Agreement, in May 1951. Armed with this 'Agreement' the Chinese authorities and occupation army proceeded to take over the whole of Tibet. However, they met considerable resistance from the Tibetan people at all levels and were forced into ruthless methods of coercion; this in turn caused sporadic outbreaks of protest and even armed revolt. A Report on Tibet published by the International Commission of Jurists in 1961 established that from 1950 to 1959 there were over 90,000 deaths in Tibet. Most were killed in the savage fighting, but some were killed after trials which were conducted in public for their opposition to Chinese measures. According to the Dalai Lama many were beaten to death, crucified, burnt alive, drowned, starved, strangled, hanged, buried alive, disembowelled, beheaded. Thousands were rounded up, imprisoned, taken to labour camps, or forcibly expatriated to China. To cope with the growing revolt the Chinese were forced to put more troops into Tibet until there were a reputed 250,000 in various parts of the country. In addition hundreds of thousands of Chinese 'settlers' were also sent to Tibet in a programme of enforced colonization.

Such a large and unexpected influx of people in the precariously balanced food situation which obtained in Tibet forced the Chinese to make drastic 'reforms' of Tibet's archaic methods of food storage, supply and distribution. As these methods were intimately connected with the rights of monasteries as granaries, landowners and tax leviers this inevitably resulted in protests and scattered riots. The policy of land reform was at first restricted to east Tibet. But while the remote character of this territory may have lent itself to facilitating an unwitnessed and rigorous enforcement of land reforms, the policy itself, in an area that was notoriously hostile to the Chinese, was bound to be an explosive issue. In 1952–3 widespread fighting of a sporadic character broke out in Kham and Amdo.

REFORMS AND DEMONSTRATIONS AND
FLIGHT OF DALAI LAMA

In Lhasa itself the Chinese proceeded much more cautiously, but even in the capital there were anti-Chinese demonstrations from as early as 1952. Many of the issues raised by the anti-Chinese groups were apparently inspired by feudal officials who wanted little or no change at all and were only using popular sentiment to oppose reforms of any kind. This feeling, to a great extent, was due to the irritating presence of Chinese troops in Tibet which, with the famine due to floods and other causes, roused resentment. Finally, the Chinese policy of imposing the Chinese language, dress and customs in the schools, and the enforced expansion of Communist Party cadres, sparked the Tibetans into revolt. The revolt began in Kham, in East Tibet, in 1956, but by mid 1958 20,000 Khambas, short of food and ammunition, had fallen back on central Tibet. Here Lhasa Government sympathizers had access to secret stocks of arms, ammunition and food never declared to the Chinese, and the fighting spread rapidly to south and south-west Tibet and the local revolts had become a national uprising. On 17 March 1959 fighting broke out in Lhasa, and the Dalai Lama and members of his Government left the capital secretly and fled to India. A few months later the Tibetan rebels ran out of ammunition and the revolt ended.

On his arrival in India the Dalai Lama repudiated the Seventeen-point Agreement of 1951 as being signed under duress. He was given asylum in India, but was not permitted to set up a Government in exile. However, a third attempt to raise the matter of Chinese aggression in the United Nations was successful, when Ireland and Malaya acted as sponsors, in 1959, and a mildly worded resolution was passed.

INSTITUTIONAL INTEGRATION WITH CHINA

Following on the ruthless suppression of the revolt in the accessible areas of Tibet – even by Chinese figures at least 20,000 rebels were still free in the inaccessible mountains – the Chinese authorities took over complete control. Hitherto, they had sought to retain a façade of control through the Dalai Lama, Tibetan institutions and officials; but now Chinese personnel were appointed over Chinese institutions reorganized on a Chinese pattern through Chinese heads of departments and

Chinese cadres, as in China itself. Towards the end of 1960 the Panchen Lama was so little in evidence at the many Chinese-organized public demonstrations that it was widely rumoured both inside and outside Tibet that he was either under strict house arrest or dead. For ten months he was kept in Peking before being permitted to return to Lhasa. In December 1964 the Dalai Lama was formally dismissed from his official position in Tibet under the Chinese regime and in January 1965 the Panchen Lama was also so dismissed.

In the meantime, the primary target of the Chinese was the monasteries and the complete destruction of all that pertained to the priestly feudal system. Tens of thousands of lamas were sent into forced labour. The monasteries were first of all denuded of their treasures, then used as centres of indoctrination. The monastic system which had dominated Tibet for centuries was broken up, and even in the event of the Dalai Lama and his Government returning to Tibet it is now unlikely that the priests will ever return to their former influence.

SHORTAGE OF FOOD

After the revolt, all Tibetans, both priest and lay, were given just adequate supplies of food if they completed their labour quotas, but after a few months even this was cut down and ration cards were issued. There seems no doubt that the initial starving was a punitive measure. But the growing food crisis in China, together with the new tactics of the Tibetan guerillas, who destroyed all crops within reach of the Chinese and blew up lines of supply, created a situation in which the Chinese troops might have mutinied. The Chinese retaliated by depriving the Tibetans of food in towns and villages under their control. This, in turn, drove these Tibetans to join the guerillas in their inaccessible mountain hide-outs with more attacks and local uprisings.

ECONOMIC SITUATION

In a desperate attempt to suppress another revolt the Chinese have ruthlessly reorganized the economy of the whole country. The 'Eight-Point Charter' for agricultural production used in China has been imposed in Tibet, but while this may look impressive on paper, in Tibet it has not solved any problems. Since 1959 Tibet has had good harvests, it is true, but this cannot be directly attributed to the 'Charter' since this was only introduced after 1959 – and, in any case, the food has been requisitioned under duress and sent to China. Confiscated estates have been taken from monasteries and landowners under a 'redemption policy' but promissory notes have not been honoured.

Every town and village in the country has been divided into four zones and each zone is supervised by a branch committee of the municipality organization of the Chinese Communist Party. Supply and market co-operatives were introduced into every district under Chinese jurisdiction and under the guidance of the state trading companies set up in urban centres.

Schools had already been introduced before the revolt, but after the revolt they were introduced on a large scale. In the three years since March 1959 Peking reported that 1,941 schools of all kinds had been set up, with an enrolment of 59,877. Peking did not mention, of course, the many thousands of Tibetan children who had been taken forcibly to China for 'education'.

Chinese reports also claim 157 medical institutions, with a hospital to every special administrative region. These have a reported staff of 560 professional medical workers and 643 spare-time health workers.

Surface mines are being opened in and around Lhasa, and small factories for tanning are springing up around large towns. Along the main China–Tibet highway the heavy military traffic has created the demand for garages and repair shops. In addition, small factories for farm implements and small tools are being encouraged and subsidized.

THE FUTURE

At one time it looked as if Tibet would have no future, but recently, with the widening breach between India and China, Tibetans have been hopeful that this will mean a relenting of India's previous policy of non-commitment. They see this in terms of supplies of arms, officially or otherwise, for the guerrillas, and in this event they are optimistic that what they almost succeeded in doing in 1959 with a minimum of arms they will successfully accomplish next time. Certainly, any influx of arms to the guerrillas will mean a long and costly engagement for the Chinese, with all the disadvantages on their side – plus the possibility of the revolt spreading into west China. The alternative to this is the absorption of the nation of Tibet and its consequent destruction within maybe twenty years.

BIBLIOGRAPHY

Sir Charles Bell. *Tibet Past and Present*. (Oxford University Press, 1924.)
Concerning the Question of Tibet. (Foreign Languages Press, Peking, 1959.)

TIBET

David Howarth (Ed.). *My Land and My People. The Autobiography of His Holiness the Dalai Lama (XIV)*. (Weidenfeld & Nicolson, 1962.)

A. Lamb. 'Tibet in Anglo-Chinese Relations'. (*Royal Central Asian Journal*, London, 1957–8.)

Thubten Norbu. *Tibet Is My Country*. (Rupert Hart-Davis, 1960.)

George N. Patterson. *Tibet in Revolt*. (Faber & Faber, 1960.)

H. E. Richardson. *Tibet and its History*. (Oxford University Press, 1962.)

The Question of Tibet and the Rule of Law. (International Commission of Jurists, Geneva, 1959.)

Chanakya Sen. *Tibet Disappears*. (Asia Publishing House, 1960.)

Sir Eric Teichman. *Travels of a Consulate Officer in Eastern Tibet*. (Cambridge University Press, 1922.)

Tsung-lien Shen and Sheng-ch'i Liu. *Tibet and the Tibetans*. (Stanford University Press, Stanford, 1953.)

L. A. Waddell. *The Buddhism of Tibet*. (W. Heffer, Cambridge, 2nd edn, 1934.)

MONGOLIA

Owen Lattimore

GEOGRAPHY AND HISTORY

MONGOLIA – the Mongolian People's Republic – is a little over 600,000 square miles in area; roughly the combined area of France, Germany, Italy, and Great Britain. It has a population slightly over one million, or double the number of half a century ago. In 1960 the death rate was 10·5, birth rate 43·2 per thousand. Its northernmost point – 52° 15′ N – is not quite as far north as Moscow, or Edmonton, Alberta; its southernmost point – 41° 32′ N – not quite as far south as New York city. An average elevation of 4,800 feet adds to the severe continentality of the climate. The highest mountain peak is over 15,000 feet. The average all-year-round temperature at Ulan Bator, the capital (population 160,000), is a little below freezing, with extremes of over 90°F in summer and below – 50°F in winter. The 'gobi' or desert regions in the south represent the zone of maximum aridity, not reached by precipitation from Siberia in the north or China in the south. In the north there is a considerable river system – Selenge, Orkhon, Tola (Tuul) and Kerulen – and here, with a rainfall approaching 20 inches per annum, wheat growing is possible and is being rapidly expanded.

The Mongolian People's Republic is considerably smaller than historical Mongolia. In the late 16th and early 17th century the Manchus conquered the eastern and southern fringes of Mongolia and used its tribal levies in the conquest of China (1644). This is the origin of 'Inner' Mongolia (meaning Mongolia nearer to the Great Wall of China), which today under the Communist government of the Chinese People's Republic survives in part as an Inner Mongolian Autonomous Area, but has partly been absorbed into several Chinese provinces. The Mongolian People's Republic is the historical 'Outer' ('more distant') Mongolia, finally conquered by the Manchus only in the 18th century. West of Inner and Outer Mongolia, also under Manchu rule, were Mongol tribal groups in Sinkiang province and in Tibet. The Kalmuk Mongols of the lower Volga, near Stalingrad (now Volgograd), were migrants from Sinkiang. Finally there are the Buryats, or Buryat-Mongols, of Siberia, mostly east of Lake Baikal, who were never conquered by the Manchus and were not fully integrated among the Mongol people even in the time of Chingis (Genghis) Khan.

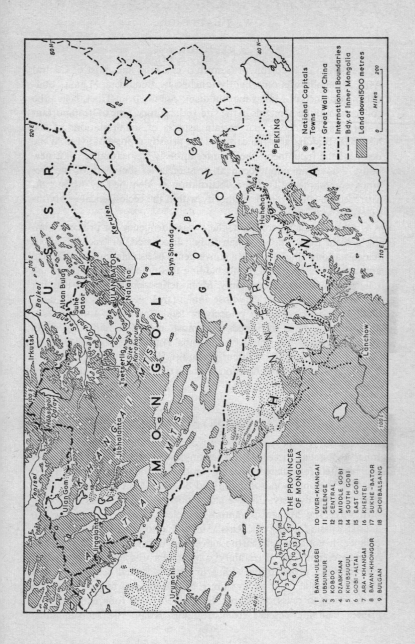

THE PROVINCES
OF MONGOLIA

1 BAYAN-ULEGEI   10 UVER-KHANGAI
2 UBSUNUUR   11 SELENGE
3 KOBDO   12 CENTRAL
4 DZABKHAN   13 MIDDLE GOBI
5 KHUBSUGUL   14 SOUTH GOBI
6 GOBI-ALTAI   15 EAST GOBI
7 ARA-KHANGAI   16 KHENTEI
8 BAYAN-KHONGOR   17 SUKHE-BATOR
9 BULGAN   18 CHOIBALSANG

National Capitals
Towns
Great Wall of China
International Boundaries
Bdy. of Inner Mongolia
Land above 1500 metres

0   Miles   200

RELIGION

In the period of the Mongol Empire over China and most of Central Asia, Mongolia was only lightly touched by Buddhism. 'Lama' Buddhism, a branch of Mahayana Buddism, coming from Tibet, began the conversion of the Mongols in the late 16th century. One of its important features is the theory that certain aspects or manifestations of the historical Buddha are 'reincarnated' in priestly representatives. At the death of the incumbent, the manifestation is 'reincarnated' in a new body, that of an infant born at or soon after the death of the previous embodiment. The new incarnation is identified by priestcraft, a procedure which retains authority within the ecclesiastical establishment.

Until the Manchu conquest, there was a tendency for princes claiming descent from Chingis Khan to be 'discovered' or 'recognized' as reincarnations, thus effecting a convergence of secular and ecclesiastical authority. The Manchus, by forbidding this practice, were able to use religion to prevent political unity. Monasteries were allowed to acquire, by endowment, territories whose inhabitants were under their jurisdiction. A dual system of princely or feudal authority and monastic authority was thus instituted. The most important reincarnation in Outer Mongolia was the Jebtsundamba Hutukhtu. His residence or 'household', *eruge* in written Mongol, *örgöö* in modern Mongol, 'Urga' in Russian pronunciation, became the capital of Mongolia (now Ulan Bator).

POLITICAL HISTORY – TSARIST PERIOD

In 1911, the year of the Chinese Revolution, Outer Mongolia (but not Inner Mongolia) succeeded in breaking away from China. The theory (only crudely formulated, since Mongolia had no international lawyers) was that the only bond of union had been the Manchu dynasty. With the fall of the dynasty, Chinese and Mongols were each free to go their own way. The Mongols, wanting complete independence, turned to Tsarist Russia for support. Russia, unwilling to upset the international balance, negotiated a tripartite agreement under which China was to have sovereignty (or 'suzerainty'), Mongolia was to have autonomy, and Russia a protectorate with – in effect – a dual veto: to prevent Outer Mongolia from adding Inner Mongolia, and to prevent China from trying to reassert control. Since there were four main lines of princes claiming descent from Chinghis Khan, the Jebtsundamba

Hutukhtu was recognized as simultaneously spiritual and secular sovereign, to prevent jealousy among them.

HISTORY – SECOND REVOLUTION

With the outbreak of the Russian Revolution in 1917 autonomous Mongolia lost its Tsarist support. A Chinese warlord of a Japanese-supported clique captured Urga and forced the Mongols to sign a renunciation of autonomy. Anti-Bolshevik Russians then retreated into Mongolia and the Chinese were ousted, but a reign of terror began under the 'mad Baron' Ungern-Sternberg. This led to a second revolution, now celebrated by the Mongols as their 'real' revolution, in 1921, led by an ex-soldier, Sukebator, and an ex-student-interpreter, Choibalsang, who was already in secret contact with Russian Communists. Partisans were organized who asked and received help from the Bolsheviks. Scattered bands of Chinese were driven out and Ungern-Sternberg captured and executed. Soviet troops were stationed at Urga (later withdrawn), but Soviet policy was restrained, in order not to force a crisis with China. The Hutukhtu was continued as a limited monarch, with real power in the hands of the revolutionaries.

Sukebator died in 1923 and the Hutukhtu in 1924. No successor was proclaimed, and Mongolia became, historically, the first of the 'People's Republics' outside the Soviet Union but within the Soviet sphere. The issue of international recognition of Mongolia's independence from China was still kept in the background. There was some contact with the more left wing of the Chinese Nationalists, but not with the Chinese Communists, who were geographically remote. Right wing and left wing tendencies alternated in Mongolian internal politics. Choibalsang, the Communist-oriented companion of Sukebator, achieved complete ascendancy only about 1935.

RECENT HISTORY

The dominating consideration was by then the danger of Japanese invasion. With Soviet support more openly proclaimed in successive declarations, and after severe border fighting in which Soviet forces took part, Japanese invasion was staved off. In 1945 Mongol troops joined Russian forces in routing the Japanese in Manchuria and Inner Mongolia. In 1946, pursuant to one of the clauses in the Yalta agreements, Chiang Kai-shek consented to a plebiscite in which the Mongols chose full independence in preference to federation with China, and

China then formally sponsored Mongolia's first application for membership in the United Nations. The next year this support was withdrawn, nominally because of a frontier dispute, and from then until 1961, through Chiang Kai-shek's influence with the United States, Mongolia's membership in the United Nations was successfully blocked.

PRESENT STATUS AND CONDITIONS

Besides being a member of the United Nations, and recognized of course by all nations of the Soviet-Chinese bloc, Mongolia has diplomatic relations with some twenty non-Communist countries. Victory of the Chinese Communists in 1949 made possible the demobilization of most of the Mongolian army, since Mongolia has frontiers with only two states, China and the Soviet Union. The resultant savings in manpower and budget speeded up economic development. Defence expenditure fell from 46·6 per cent of the budget in 1940 to 2·6 per cent in 1959, but increased again to 6·4 in 1960.

The Mongolian People's Republic (Bügd Nairamdakh Mongol Ard Uls) is a one-party state. Unlike China, no minority parties are even nominally recognized. Unlike Poland and several other countries, the single party, the Mongolian People's Revolutionary Party (Mongol Ardyn Khuv'sgalt Nam), was not formed by even nominal coalition with one or more previously existing parties. It began as a pre-Communist, nationalist revolutionary party which by successive changes in membership requirements transmuted itself into what is essentially a Communist Party. Choibalsang died in 1952, ending a period of personal supremacy now stigmatized as a 'cult of personality', though the condemnations have not been as severe as in the case of Stalin.

Two policies underlie present conditions. (1) The campaign against religion, which led to bloodshed and failure in the 1930s, was resumed successfully by persuasion and by organized provision of alternative occupations for priests. The number of lamas (priests) was reduced from about 100,000 to about 200, and most ex-priests are now married and several monasteries and temples are maintained as museums. One large monastery is now under state protection. (2) Education was pushed to the point where there is now virtually no illiteracy, though the proclaimed minimum 10-year (8–18) schooling has not everywhere been achieved. In 1921 there was only one elementary school; by 1960 there were 419, with 15 'secondary specialized schools'. A university was founded in 1947; it now has an enrolment of about 2,000, and there are seven other 'higher' schools, for medicine, agriculture, teacher training, etc.

ECONOMIC SITUATION

The economy is approximately 70 per cent pastoral, with an animal population of some 24 million, about 58 per cent sheep, 25 per cent goats, and the remainder horses, horned cattle (including yaks) and camels. Livestock has been historically subject to heavy losses, even more through storms than disease, but the increase of agriculture, to provide hay and fodder, the building of winter shelters, and a great increase in veterinary services, is remedying this instability. The pastoral economy is organized under co-operatives which have some of the features of Soviet collectives, but under complicated regulations which take account of small children and old people, families may privately own up to 75 head of stock. The former export economy of raw wool, hides, and live animals is being modified by a new industry of textile manufacture, tanning, bootmaking, and meat canning. Flour mills make it no longer necessary to import flour. Furs are an increasingly important export.

Existing industrial energy is supplied largely by the thermo-electrical generating stations at Ulan Bator and Darkhan – some 150 miles north of Ulan Bator, near the Soviet frontier. These are based on the coal mines at Nalaikha and Sharin Gol, both of which are highly mechanized. Ulan Bator, the political capital, is intended to remain the principal industrial centre. At Darkhan an electrical generating plant is being installed by the Soviet Union, a cement factory by Czechoslovakia, and a silica-brick factory by Poland. Electrical power from Darkhan is being supplied to Sukhe Bator in the north and also to Ulan Bator and will eventually be taken to collective and state farms. Near Darkhan there will be light industries based on local raw materials of animal origin. Construction of a third industrial centre at Choibalsan in the north-east has recently begun and will include a thermo-electrical generating plant and a large meat-packing plant, to be installed by the Soviet Union and Bulgaria.

An oilfield in the south near the Chinese frontier was successfully exploited for some years and the refineries there are still being used for the processing of crude oil imported from the Soviet Union. Geological and mineralogical exploration continues, but exploitation is confined to coal, wolfram and fluorites, possibly because of the limited development of rail and road communications. Other resources as yet under-exploited include fisheries and timber. In general, industrial development is limited by a factor rare in Asia – underpopulation. There is not a large surplus of manpower to be transferred at will from the traditional pastoral occupations to industry. At present many thousands of Soviet construction troops are engaged on industrial and municipal projects for the benefit of the Mongolian economy, as well as comparatively large numbers of Soviet and East European experts and technicians. Aid projects undertaken by Mongolia's partners in the Council for Mutual Economic Assistance invariably lay heavy emphasis on training Mongols to fill posts at all levels in the developing industrial economy. There is no question of permanent settlement in Mongolia by nationals of aid-giving countries. The creation of an industrial proletariat is one of the declared aims of the series of Five-Year Plans for economic and cultural development by which the Mongolian Peoples' Revolutionary Party reckon to transform their country.

Economic development is backed mainly by long-term, low-interest credits from the Soviet Union for the purchase of machinery and equipment and for engaging the services of technicians. Many of these credits have become outright gifts over the years. Aid from and trade with the Communist countries of Eastern Europe has become increasingly important, although still on a small scale in comparison with that offered by the Soviet Union.

Until about 1964 the Chinese People's Republic made important contributions to Mongolia's economic development, through both trade and aid. Chinese labour was used extensively for the construction of Ulan Bator and in other aspects of industrial development. Several thousand Chinese workmen, many of them highly skilled, came to Mongolia in the spring, worked through until the cold weather set in, returned to China for the winter, and came back to Mongolia in the following spring. This pattern was maintained, although with steadily diminishing numbers, until the winter of 1966 when the Chinese went home for the winter but did not return to Mongolia in the spring of 1967. The reduction of Sino-Mongolian trade to a trickle and the virtual cessation of Chinese aid is a reflection of the deterioration of Sino-Mongolian relations which has resulted from Mongolia's openly taking the Soviet part in the Sino-Soviet dispute. One aspect of this deterioration is the loss of income from the transit trade between the Soviet Union and China along the Trans-Mongolian railway.

Mongolia has practically no national minority problems, an advantage possessed by few other countries in Asia. Most Chinese fled or were driven out in the 1920s. Their descendants (usually Chinese father, Mongol mother) are now thoroughly Mongol. Less than 2 per cent are listed as 'Chinese'. Kazakhs (4·3 per cent) are the largest minority. They are pastoral nomads, Turkish by language, related to the Kazakhs of Chinese Sinkiang and Soviet Kazakhstan. There are a few Buryats (2·9 per cent), mainly in north-east Mongolia, and a few reindeer-herders, speaking a Turkish language, west of Lake Khubsugol.

BIBLIOGRAPHY

Gerard M. Friters. *Outer Mongolia and its International Position.* (Johns Hopkins University Press, Baltimore, 1949.)

Owen Lattimore. *Nomads and Commissars.* (Oxford University Press, 1962.)

Ivor Montagu. *Land of Blue Sky.* (Dobson, London, 1956.)

National Economy of the Mongolian People's Republic for 40 Years. (State Publishers, Ulan Bator, 1961.)

RUSSIAN CENTRAL ASIA

Geoffrey Wheeler

THE GEOGRAPHICAL BACKGROUND

RUSSIAN or Soviet Central Asia is the name usually given to the area bounded on the north by Western Siberia, on the south by Persia and Afghanistan, on the east by the Sinkiang-Uygur Autonomous Region of China and on the west by the Caspian Sea. It consists of the five Soviet Socialist Republics of Kazakhstan, Turkmenistan, Uzbekistan, Kirgizia and Tadzhikistan. Soviet geographers include only the last four in the term 'Soviet Central Asia', Kazakhstan being regarded as a separate geographical region.

The northern part of the area occupied by Kazakhstan consists of steppe and semi-desert bordered by a mountain belt in the south-east. To the south of this is a desert belt known as the Turan lowland and containing the two great sandy deserts of Karakum and Kyzylkum separated from each other by the Amu-Dar'ya (Oxus) river. Further south again there is another desert strip consisting of sandy steppes and oases which in the west runs along the Soviet-Persian frontier. The south-east consists of some of the largest, highest and most glaciated mountain ranges in the world – the Tien-Shan and Pamirs. The climate is dry and continental with hot summers and cold winters. Dry farming is extensively practised in the north, farming in the south being mainly irrigated. The most important economic asset of the area is cotton, mainly grown in the Fergana and Vakhsh valleys. Cereals are now grown extensively in Kazakhstan and many other crops in the semi-desert and desert regions. There are important mineral resources including iron, copper and lead.

The population of about 30 million is roughly 67 per cent Asian and 33 per cent European, mainly Russian and Ukrainian.

EARLY HISTORY

Since the 5th century A.D. Central Asia has been repeatedly invaded both from east and west. Turkic nomads swept over the whole area in the 6th century and remained in possession of Kazakhstan until the coming of the Russians. Transoxania, the land between the Amu-Dar'ya and Syr-Dar'ya rivers, was conquered in the 8th century by the Arabs who challenged and overcame paramount Chinese influence. During the 9th century most of Transoxania became part of the Persian Samanid Empire which had succeeded Arab rule. From the overthrow of the Samanids in 999 up to the Mongol invasion which began in 1220, the desert and oasis regions were mainly ruled by various Turkic Muslim dynasties, the most important being the Seljuks, who ruled the whole of Muslim Asia up to 1157, and the Khorezm Shahs, who reached the zenith of their power at the beginning of the 13th century. From 1137 to 1212 Transoxania and Semirech'ye (now West Kirgizia and the Alma-Ata and East Kazakhstan Oblasts of Kazakhstan) were dominated by a Tungusic or (possibly) Mongolian people, the Kara-Kitays, who came from the East and never embraced Islam although they were tolerant of it. The Mongol invasion and subsequent domination included the whole of the desert and oasis regions and a part of the Kazakh steppe. The greater part of the Mongol forces was composed of locally recruited Turks and the number of Mongols who settled in the area was negligible. By the middle of the 14th century all the Mongol rulers had become Turkicized and embraced Islam.

From the middle of the 14th to the beginning of the 16th century the desert and oasis regions, and particularly Transoxania, were under Timur (Timurlane) and his successors. During the 15th century the nomad Kazakhs began to embrace Islam and a part of them, the Uzbeks, came south to overturn the Timurid Empire and establish an Uzbek Empire which remained in power until 1510 when it broke up into various khanates of which the principal were Bukhara and Khiva.

THE COMING OF THE RUSSIANS

The first phase of Russian expansion in Asia had been a movement due east from the Urals to the Pacific, which began at the end of the 16th century. The second phase was the gradual spread over what is now Kazakhstan. This was begun by Peter the Great at the beginning of the 18th century. The third phase was the advance into the semi-desert and desert regions ending with the establishment by the end of the century of Russian rule over the whole area now occupied by the five Republics, with the partial exception of the Khanates of Bukhara and Khiva, which remained semi-independent vassal states until 1921. The Russian advance to the frontiers of China, Afghanistan and Persia and the establishment of Russian rule in Central Asia were motivated by political, economic and military considerations: it was desired to establish frontiers with 'properly constituted states', e.g. Persia, as

Petropavlosk

70°E

Omsk

80°E

R . S . F . S . R

Barnaul

E L I N N Y

Kokchetav

Pavlodar

Atbasar

K R A Y

Tselinograd

Semipalatinsk

Ust-Kamenogorsk

50°N

Karaganda

H S T A N

O U T H

Balkhash

K H S T A N

OZERO BALKHASH

Taldy-Kurgan

R A Y

Kuldja

Dzhambul

ALMA-ATA

Chimkent

FRUNZE Tokmak

Przheval'sk

C H I N A

ASHKENT

K I R G I Z I A

TYAN' SHAN

40°N

Namangan

Dzhalal-Abad

Andizhan

Leninabad

Kokand Osh

Fergana

Kyzyl-Kiya

Kashgar

Samarkand

80°E

N

T A D Z H I K I S T A N

DUSHANBE

Kulyab

rgan-Tyube

KASHMIR

ANISTAN

KABUL

70°E

PAKISTAN

	National Capitals
	Capitals of Union Republics
	Other Towns
	International Boundaries
	Boundaries of Union Republics
	Boundaries of Autonomous Republics and Krays
	Land above 1,000 metres
	Sand

Miles

0   100   200   300

distinct from the semi-barbarous khanates; the Russian Government and commercial firms wished to exploit the economic resources of the region and particularly its cotton, and to deny it both economically and militarily to Britain, whose hold on India and influence in Afghanistan were regarded as a threat to Russia.

Russian rule did much to ensure peace and security in Central Asia. Communications and irrigation were improved and extensive development was planned for the future. Little was done in education and discontent was caused by widespread colonization by Europeans. Before the Revolution some two million Russians and Ukrainians had been settled on the land. Little account was taken of nationality or nationalist aspirations and nothing was done to build up a trained indigenous civil service. On the other hand, there was little interference with established traditions and the local inhabitants were exempt from military service until 1916 when the introduction of labour conscription caused widespread revolt. This measure and the suppression of the revolt to some extent predisposed the population in favour of the Revolution of 1917.

THE REVOLUTION AND THE CIVIL WAR

In 1917, after the 'February' Revolution, the Muslims of Russia, entirely on their own initiative, had moved some way towards unity on the basis of their common culture. Various Muslim Congresses were created throughout the Empire, but although one of them, held in Orenburg in April 1917, raised the idea of territorial autonomy, most of the Muslim intelligentsia were concerned with cultural rather than political matters and were prepared to leave their political future to an all-Russian Constituent Assembly. The Soviet leaders were at first ready to treat the Muslims as a cultural and even, perhaps, as a political entity and one of their first acts (December 1917) was to declare the Muslim 'national and cultural institutions' free and inviolable in future. A Commissariat of Muslim Affairs was formed, and in June 1919 a 'Russian Party of Muslim Communists'. Shortly afterwards, however, this was dissolved and its functions taken over by a Central Bureau of Muslim Organizations of the Russian Communist Party. By the middle of 1919 the Commissariat of Muslim Affairs itself was dissolved and the whole concept of Islam was removed from Soviet political parlance, never to return.

During the Civil War there were some manifestations of political as distinct from cultural nationalism in Central Asia. Since, however, this nationalism was concerned mainly with getting rid of foreign influence, and particularly of foreign settlers, and was not interested in the class war and socialism, it was quickly suppressed by the Soviet authorities. This resulted in intense friction between the Muslims and Russian colonists. A purely Muslim Government created in Kokand was soon liquidated by Russian military force in January 1918, and in April an Autonomous Soviet Socialist Republic of Turkestan was created. After considerable resistance by a Social Revolutionary Government in Ashkhabad (now capital of Turkmenistan) the Tashkent Government, which was almost entirely Russian with only nominal Muslim participation, gained virtual control of the whole of Turkestan by the end of 1919, except for the Khanates of Bukhara and Khiva. But resistance to the Soviet regime now became widespread in the form of the Basmachi movement, which can best be described as the despairing reaction of the people to the inefficient and oppressive authority exercised by the Tashkent Government. A so-called Turkestan Commission despatched from Moscow to deal with the situation brought into being a number of palliative measures designed to humour the Muslims, and as a result of this the Basmachi movement began to collapse in 1922. By this time Khiva and Bukhara had become the Khorezmian and Bukharan 'People's Soviet Republics' and remained nominally independent until 1923 and 1924 when they became the Khorezmian and Bukharan Soviet Socialist Republics. In 1924 the administrative frontiers of Turkestan and Kazakhstan were re-aligned, the Republics of Turkestan, Khorezm (Khiva), and Bukhara were abolished, and the whole area was divided into the five Republics of Uzbekistan, Tadzhikistan, Kirgizia, Turkmenistan and Kazakhstan.

THE NATIONALITIES POLICY AND HISTORY TO 1962

The nationalities policy of the Communist Party can best be seen as an expedient designed to compromise between the total disruption of the Russian Empire, which would have deprived the Russian state of vital natural resources, and the formal perpetuation of that Empire, which would have run directly counter to the principles of Communism. By creating a so-called federal structure under the overriding control of the Communist Party it was hoped to ensure the economic and military security of the Empire, while at the same time giving world, and particularly Asian, opinion the impression that the non-Russian nationalities of the Soviet Union were being granted self-determination.

As stated earlier, the Tsarist Government had taken little account of nationalities in Central Asia. The social structure was in fact clan and tribal rather than national, the only peoples whose homogeneity and territorial concentration gave them any sense of national consciousness being the Kazakhs and Turkmens. Generally speaking the distinction was not as between nationalities, but as between nomads and settled peoples. As a result, however, of the nationalist sentiment aroused during the Civil War, it was possible to arrive at a more or less precise labelling of nationalities, largely on the basis of language. Ostensibly language was the deciding factor in the delimitation of 1924; but in effect any territorial division on the basis of language was and is impossible, particularly in respect of the Fergana and Zeravshan valleys, where the Uzbeks and Tadzhiks are culturally and historically one people. In the new delimitation the primary consideration was without doubt economic and administrative: by parcelling out the economic resources of the region as far as possible the Soviet authorities ensured that none of the Republics would have economic predominance. At the same time, by emphasizing what were in many cases very slight linguistic and cultural differences, the possibility of the various nationalities 'ganging up' against the Soviet regime was appreciably diminished.

After the collapse of the Basmachi movement active opposition to the new regime was only sporadic. In 1937 there occurred in Uzbekistan what was described by the authorities as a nationalist conspiracy. The Prime Minister and the First Secretary of the Uzbek Communist Party were accused of nationalism and of being British agents and were executed with a number of their alleged supporters. They admitted to having worked for the independence of Turkestan from Soviet rule but not to collusion with Britain, of which no proof was forthcoming. It has never been established whether there was a real plot; the numerous arrests and executions may simply have been part of Stalin's Union-wide purge of so-called enemies of the people. During the Second World War large numbers of Muslim prisoners and deserters fought for the Germans against the Soviet army.

As elsewhere in the USSR, post-war reconstruction was very rapid and the material condition of the people greatly improved. After Stalin's death there was some posthumous rehabilitation of the victims of his purges. Although the authorities continued to inveigh against 'bourgeois nationalism', survivals of the past and religion, there were no overt signs of active opposition to the regime. From about 1954 onwards there has been a steady stream of delegations from the independent Asian and African countries to the larger cities of Uzbekistan,

Tadzhikistan and Turkmenistan, delegations to Kazakhstan and Kirgizia being much less frequent. Up to 1967 foreign visitors were not free to visit rural areas.

POLITICAL STATUS AND SYSTEM OF GOVERNMENT

Under the 1936 Soviet Constitution, the five Republics are regarded as fully sovereign Soviet Socialist states forming part of the USSR. The system of government and administration is uniform, each Republic having a President, a Council of Ministers and an elected Supreme Soviet or Parliament. Overriding control of all political, economic and cultural activities is exercised by the Communist Party, either the First or the Second Secretary of each Republic Party always being a non-native, usually a Russian. Although the Republics are nominally self-governing, responsibility for defence and security, foreign affairs, communications and a large range of economic and financial subjects is vested in the Central Government in Moscow. The Autonomous Soviet Socialist Republic of Kara-Kalpakia is included in Uzbekistan and the Autonomous Oblast of Gorno-Badakhshan (the Pamirs) in Tadzhikistan. Conscription into the Soviet armed forces is universal. There are no national formations and conscripts are liable for service anywhere in the Soviet Union or abroad.

THE ECONOMY

Before the Revolution the economy of the whole region was almost entirely agricultural, industry being confined to cotton ginning and a small amount of copper and coal mining. Since the Revolution, and particularly since 1950, expansion in all branches of the economy has been very great, although many of the irrigation and other projects had been visualized by the Tsarist Government. Collectivization was introduced between 1928 and 1932 and resulted in a great increase in cotton (a mono-culture); it had disastrous effects on stock-breeding, mainly in Kazakhstan, and on the supply of meat and dairy produce. In 1954 the Virgin Lands campaign was launched and a vast area of virgin land was put under cultivation in Kazakhstan, the main crop being wheat. For this purpose hundreds of thousands of Russians and Ukrainians were brought in from the west of the USSR and the proportion of Kazakhs has now dropped to 29 per cent of the total population of the Kazakh SSR.

During the Second World War a large number of factories with their trained personnel were transferred to Central Asia from the west and this gave a great fillip to the industrialization of the whole region. The output of coal, oil, natural gas, lead and steel has enormously increased, and light industries such as food packing and textiles have been greatly developed. In a survey carried out during 1957 by the secretariat of the United Nations Economic Commission for Europe, it was established that while cultivation and export of raw cotton and silk naturally remained the mainstay of the region's economy, not only cotton ginning and the production of cotton-seed oil but also the manufacture of fertilizers, of cotton picking machines, and of 60 per cent of the Soviet Union's output of spinning machinery were among its major industries. Cotton spinning and weaving account for 4 per cent and 5 per cent respectively of the Soviet Union's total output. Both steel and an increasing range of engineering products are now made in Central Asia; and a wide range of industries producing building materials and light consumer goods show a share of total Soviet output that does not fall far short of the share of population. As a result, Soviet Central Asia can be characterized as a region equipped with a fairly broad range of consumer-goods industries producing for the local market, but dependent on imports for nearly all capital goods. The 1957 survey reported favourably on living standards which it found were 'on much higher levels than in the neighbouring Asian countries'; it estimated that the average living standards for the region as a whole were probably one fifth to one fourth lower than the Soviet average but found that this disparity could not be regarded as large compared with that found in other countries.

SOCIAL CONDITIONS

Although Soviet Central Asia has many affinities – ethnic, cultural and climatic – with the Middle Eastern and South Asian countries adjoining it, the Republics have no direct diplomatic, commercial or social contacts with them. The earlier Soviet policy of trying to attract to the Central Asian Republics people belonging to the same ethnic groups across the Soviet border – Azerbaijanis and Turkmens in Persia, and Uzbeks, Tadzhiks and Turkmens in Afghanistan – has long been discontinued. Whereas in Tsarist times there was continual movement across the Russian frontier by nomad tribes, traders and pilgrims to the holy cities of Persia and beyond, the frontiers are now firmly closed. Westernization in respect of living and work habits, general and technical education, the status of women and the break-down of the old tribal, clan and family groupings and loyalties has proceeded much further in Central Asia than in any other part of the continent. An important factor has been the enormous increase in white settlement since the Revolution. The number is now more than three times what it was in 1917 and the Russians (excluding the Ukrainians and Belorussians) are now the most numerous nationality in the whole region. Nevertheless, the white settlers tend to live side by side with rather than among the native population: there has been very little inter-marriage, that between Muslim girls and European men being virtually nil. In the arts, and particularly the theatre, music and painting, there is a tendency to hark back to the past and this evokes strong and constant criticism by the Soviet authorities.

CULTURE AND EDUCATION

After the Arab conquests of Transoxania in the 8th century, Islamic culture spread rapidly throughout the settled districts and by the end of the 10th century had obtained a firm hold, Bukhara and Samarkand becoming two of the most important theological strongholds of the Muslim world of that time. The effect of Islam on the nomad Kazakhs, Turkmens and Kirgiz was more gradual and much less marked; it gathered strength, however, under Tsarist rule, since the Russians regarded it as a stabilizing and civilizing factor. Although the actual conquest of Transoxania had been carried out by Arab forces, the administration of the region became to a large extent Persianized, and today the still predominantly Islamic culture of Central Asia and Kazakhstan is Iranian rather than Arab.

The main effects of Islam were on law, social customs and language. Muslim canon law (*shari'at*) and customary law (*'adat*) were already widely practised in the settled districts before the Mongol conquest. The canon law had little vogue among the nomads until the Russian conquests brought some degree of stabilization, but Muslim customary law began to take a hold during the 17th century. Before the Mongol conquest the written official and literary language had been Arabic and, to a minor extent, Persian, but during the 13th and 14th centuries under the Timurid Dynasty a written Turkic language called Chaghatay (after one of Chingis Khan's sons) was developed. This used the Perso-Arabic script, which remained the only script used for Central Asian languages until the introduction of a Latin in 1930, and later a modified Cyrillic alphabet from about 1940. From the Arab conquests up to the Russian Revolution of 1917 all the Central Asian languages borrowed extensively from Arabic and Persian, but hardly at all from Mongolian. Since 1917 borrowing has been confined to Russian and international words.

Unlike the Tsarist Government, which interfered little with native culture, religion and languages, the Soviet Government from the beginning pursued an active policy in all these matters. The arts have been greatly encouraged and largely remodelled on Soviet and Russian lines. Languages have been systematized and developed, and great efforts have been made to build up national literatures on standard Soviet lines. At first the tendency was to emphasize the often slight differences in native cultures and languages; but with the intensification of the declared official policy of uprooting all traces of nationalism, more emphasis has recently been laid on similarity and inter-resemblance than on differences. The Soviet attitude towards Islam, the prevailing religion, has been consistently hostile, particularly in respect of practices thought to interfere with economic productivity. Of the vast number of mosques which existed before the Revolution only a very few remain in operation and religious instruction has been totally excluded from education.

In education progress has been remarkable; illiteracy, which stood at over 95 per cent before the Revolution, has been virtually stamped out; in addition to the primary and secondary schools, each Republic has at least one university and large numbers of technological and other training colleges. Local languages are the medium of instruction in the primary and secondary schools, but the study of Russian is greatly encouraged since it is largely used in higher and technical education and training.

THE FUTURE

It is reasonable to expect that the great material progress achieved during the last 15 years will be maintained and extended. There is, however, no immediate prospect of the peoples of Central Asia attaining independence or self-government of the kind now enjoyed by such former colonial territories as India, Pakistan, and the Arab countries. Indeed, it is possible that even the nominal national status of the republics will eventually disappear if the present plans of the Soviet regime are realized. Up to Khrushchev's downfall in 1964 it was being increasingly emphasized that the present so-called federal structure of the Soviet Union was a temporary one from which a unitary multi-national state would ultimately evolve. There would be an intermediate phase known as 'getting together' (*sblizheniye*) in which national distinctions such as frontiers and languages would fade away to prepare for the final phase of 'fusion' (*sliyaniye*). Since 1965 there has been much less emphasis on the process of 'getting together' and hardly any mention of ultimate 'fusion'.

BIBLIOGRAPHY

A. Bennigsen and C. Quelquejay. *The Evolution of the Muslim Nationalities of the USSR and their Linguistic Problems.* (Central Asian Research Centre, London, 1961.)

Sir Olaf Caroe. *Soviet Empire.* (Macmillan, 1953.)

Nathaniel Curzon. *The Russians in Central Asia.* (Longmans, 1889.)

M. Holdsworth. *Turkestan in the Nineteenth Century.* (Central Asian Research Centre, London, 1959.)

Alexander Park. *Bolshevism in Turkestan 1917–1927.* (Columbia University Press, New York, 1957.)

Richard Pierce. *Russian Central Asia (1867–1917).* (University of California Press, Berkeley, 1960.)

Richard Pipes. *The Formation of the Soviet Union.* (Harvard University Press, Cambridge, Mass., 1954.)

E. Schuyler. *Turkistan* (2 vols.). (Sampson Low, London, 1876.)

F. H. B. Skrine and E. D. Ross. *The Heart of Asia.* (Methuen, 1899.)

N. A. Smirnov. *Islam and Russia.* (Central Asian Research Centre, London, 1956.)

Geoffrey Wheeler. *Racial Problems in Soviet Muslim Asia.* (Oxford University Press, 2nd edn, 1962.) *The Modern History of Soviet Central Asia.* (Weidenfeld & Nicolson, 1964.)

S. A. L. Zenkovsky. *Pan-Turkism and Islam in Russia.* (Harvard University Press, Cambridge, Mass., 1960.)

Map of Soviet Central Asia and Kazakhstan (four sheets and gazetteer, 60 miles to 1 inch). (Central Asian Research Centre, London, 1962.)

Central Asian Review. (London: quarterly since 1953.)

The Far East

CHINA

Geoffrey Hudson

GEOGRAPHY

CHINA today covers the same area as the so-called Chinese Empire at the end of the nineteenth century except for Outer Mongolia, which has become an independent state, and Tannu-Tuva, which has been annexed by the Soviet Union. The old Chinese Empire comprised within its borders both Chinese in the strict sense – speakers of one of the dialects of the Chinese language – and certain non-Chinese peoples of whom the most important were the Tibetans, Mongols and Turkis (now known as Uigurs). The Chinese were, and are, the overwhelming majority of the total population – over 93 per cent – but an ethnographic map shows more of a balance between the Chinese and other nationalities, because the Chinese predominate in all areas of high population density, whereas the non-Chinese elements prevail in vast areas of mountain and desert where population density is very low. The extent of the territories they occupy has thus made the non-Chinese peoples of China more important, both historically and at the present time, than their numbers would indicate.

Three thousand years ago the Chinese occupied only a small part of the area which they now inhabit. It was confined to the middle and lower basin of the Yellow River, including both the loess-soil uplands of Shansi and Shensi and the alluvial lands of the North China Plain. From this homeland they have expanded their ethnic range in historical times in three directions; the main one southward to the Yangtse, the south China coastlands, the West River basin and Yunnan; the second westward into the borderlands of Tibet and Turkestan; and the third north-eastern into Manchuria. There have also been scattered settlements further afield within the range of Chinese political authority, and in recent times the large emigration to the south beyond the confines of Chinese territory, which has produced the communities known as the Overseas Chinese. In this demographic expansion the Chinese, while retaining their language and strongly marked culture traits formed in their Yellow River valley homeland, have mingled with earlier inhabitants and adapted themselves to a variety of climatic conditions. The Yellow River basin is a region of relatively low rainfall and temperate-zone continental climate with hot summers and cold

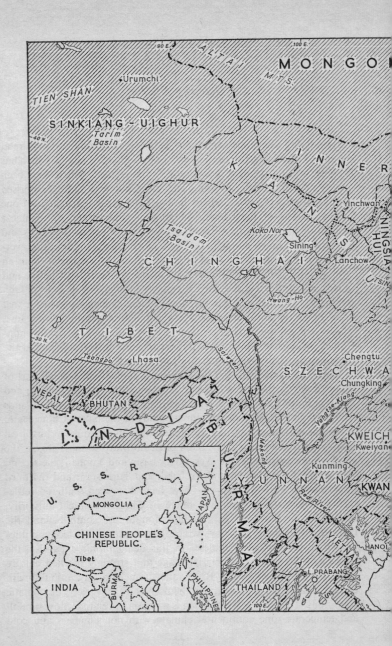

winters; Manchuria and the north-western borderlands are even drier with greater extremes of temperature; the Yangtse valley and south China, on the other hand, are regions of high rainfall and subtropical climate with mild winters and humid summers. The climate differences are reflected in the prevailing forms of agriculture; in the north wheat, millet and sorghum are the principal grain crops, whereas all China south of the divide between the Yellow River and the Yangtse is primarily a zone of wet rice cultivation.

The Chinese ethnic region has a coastline on the east side of Asia looking out towards the Pacific Ocean or rather the inner seas separated from the main ocean by the island chain made up of Japan, the Ryukyu Islands, Formosa and the Philippines. On the landward side the region is surrounded on the north, west and south-west by great tracts of mountain and desert which have in the past acted as barriers secluding China from close contacts with other main regions of civilization in South and West Asia and Europe. To the north is the arid plateau land of Mongolia, with a surface varying from uninhabitable desert (the Gobi or Shamo, 'Sea of Sand') through short-grass steppe suitable only for the pasture of animals to long-grass steppe which can be cultivated, but at the risk of producing 'dust-bowl' conditions. To the north-west is Sinkiang, or East Turkestan, as it used to be called – an even more arid region, but enclosed and traversed by high mountain ranges which feed fertile piedmont oases from their snows and glaciers. East Turkestan has more desert than Mongolia, but has always, nevertheless, had a more settled population because of the possibility of intensive agriculture in the oases. It has also in the past been the main avenue of overland trade between China and West Asia and even India (in spite of the roundabout routes involved); the ancient 'silk road' from China ran this way and Roman merchants from Syria used to buy Chinese silk at a place in the Pamirs, the mountains which mark what is today the western extremity of China's territory.

South of East Turkestan lies Tibet, a country of high plateau, much of it 15,000 or 16,000 feet above sea-level and uninhabitable because of the combination of aridity and altitude. The lower ground provides pasture for animals, and agriculture can be carried on in a few sheltered valleys, particularly in the south-east, but Tibet as a whole must be reckoned a desert country sharply contrasted with both China proper to the east of it and with India to the south and south-west. From India Tibet is separated by the great curving range of the Himalayas, which not only comprises many of the highest mountains in the world, but also divides two different climatic zones; the Tibetan plateau to the north of the range is almost entirely treeless, whereas the southern slopes of the Himalayas descending to the plains of India receive a heavy summer monsoon rainfall and are clothed with dense forest. Tibet is a very difficult country for anyone to enter or cross, but it is somewhat more accessible from China than from India – a fact which has helped to determine its history in modern times. It is a natural barrier and buffer between India and China, and formerly, even when it was controlled by China, it was hard for a government in Peking to exert power on the Indian border because of the inadequacy of communications; it is the penetration of Tibet by motor road and air transport which has made China a much nearer neighbour to India as a result of the recent reconquest than it was in the 18th and 19th centuries.

Finally, there are to the south-west of China, forming natural frontiers with Burma, Laos and Vietnam, mountain ranges which, although of low altitude as compared with the Himalayas, are for the most part covered with thick jungle and very difficult to cross. These mountains have in the past effectively separated China by land from the countries of South-East Asia – though less from Vietnam than from Laos and Burma – and communication with these countries has always been mainly by sea, so that they have come to be known collectively to the Chinese as the 'South Seas'. Sea routes from China in the days of sail led southwards to Cambodia and the Gulf of Siam, to the Moluccas, Borneo, Java and the Malay Peninsula, with further access onwards through the Straits of Malacca into the Indian Ocean. But the enormous distances by sea round Malaya from the ports of China to the Bay of Bengal or the Persian Gulf greatly reduced the possibilities of contacts with India, Persia or Arabia through maritime trade.

THE SHANG DYNASTY

The earliest Chinese civilization of which we have knowledge flourished in the plains of northern Honan close to the Yellow River in the second millennium B.C. It can be identified with the period of the Shang Dynasty, which was mentioned in ancient Chinese historical records, but was believed by critical Western scholars to be mythical until its material remains were revealed by archaeological excavation from about 1930 onwards. Shang society was based on intense agriculture and its capital was a town of some size. Since the Shang people lived in the midst of relatively primitive tribes and had no knowledge of any civilization as materially advanced as their own, they called their land

Chung Kuo or 'the Central Country', which remains to this day the Chinese name for China. The implications of such a name – that China is the centre of the world, a country of unique civilization surrounded by inferior peoples on the periphery – has never ceased to affect the Chinese outlook. Foreigners naturally were not inclined to accept this Chinese estimate of their own pre-eminence and tended to call their country by the name of the dynasty reigning over it when they first had knowledge of it. Thus the Arabs used the name of the Ch'in or Ts'in Dynasty which ruled China during the later part of the 3rd century B.C.; this passed into Latin as Sinae, and ultimately into English as 'China'. The Russians, on the other hand, who first became aware of the existence of China by overland trade routes during the Middle Ages, called it Kitai – the Cathay of Marco Polo and other medieval travellers from Western Europe – which was the name of a Mongol tribe dominant in north China in the 11th century A.D., and this is still the name used in Russian.

The Shang period in China is memorable particularly for the magnificent bronze vessels, which are often great works of art and exhibit a highly developed technique of working in metal. Most characteristic of the archaeological finds, however, are the so-called 'oracle bones'; these bones were used for divination and the questions and answers were inscribed on them. Thus we have specimens of the earliest forms of Chinese writing; this was a 'picture-writing' developing into an 'ideographic' script, similar in some ways to Egyptian hieroglyphics and other pre-alphabetic scripts of other ancient civilizations. But, whereas these comparable modes of writing were elsewhere superseded by alphabets, derived ultimately from a single model created in the region of the East Mediterranean, the Chinese have retained their ideographic script to the present day, though the individual signs have been so far altered from the forms of Shang times as to be usually unrecognizable. The Chinese system of writing has always indeed been one of the most characteristic features of Chinese civilization, and at the present day the question whether to retain it – in a simplfied form – or to discard it is still a matter of controversy in China, for the script is too cumbrous for an age which aims at streamlined efficiency, yet its total abolition would make too great a break with China's cultural heritage to be easily acceptable to those who – even if they are Communists – set store by China's separate national identity.

THE CHOU DYNASTY

The Shang period was followed by that of the Chou, a dynasty originally based on the Wei valley in what is now Shensi province to the west of the Shang country in Honan. The Chou kings ruled over a much larger area than the Shang and greatly increased it by the conquest of non-Chinese tribes round the fringes of the Chinese homeland; these conquered lands were settled by Chinese colonists who absorbed the native inhabitants and thus extended the territory of the Chinese race. The dynasty was unable, however, to govern so large an area effectively from a single centre and parcelled it out into fiefs, which, as central control was relaxed, developed into independent states, often at war with one another and paying only nominal allegiance to their suzerain. The period from 403 to 221 B.C. is known in Chinese history as the Era of the Warring States. In spite of the incessant warfare it was a time of economic expansion, as rival local rulers sought to increase their revenues, and of intellectual development, stimulated by the decay of old religious and social institutions and the quest for new norms of government and morals.

CONFUCIUS, TAOISTS AND LEGISTS

Among a number of philosophical schools which then arose three were outstanding. One was that of Confucius, which taught a humanist ethic not unlike that of Greek Stoicism; men should be educated in virtue in preparation for the public service, and the ruler who was himself virtuous would also be successful because his good administration would make his subjects contented and attract others to his side. In contrast to the Confucians, the Taoists held that wisdom and happiness for man came through a mystical inner illumination; politically they were anarchists and considered that the best thing a ruler could do for his subjects was to lead them back to a state of primeval innocence where they would not need any more government. The third school, that of the so-called Legists, shared the Taoists' disregard of the Confucian virtues, but taught that salvation lay, not in the reduction, but in the enhancement, of the power of the state; the ruler who, through rigorously enforced laws, strengthened his own state sufficiently would subdue all his rivals and establish universal peace through a universal empire.

THE CH'IN DYNASTY

The Ch'in state, which heeded the advice of the Legists, finally succeeded in destroying all the other Chinese states and creating a universal empire between the Tibetan border mountains and the Pacific coast in 221 B.C. The Ch'in ruler adopted a title rendered in English as 'emperor' and subsequently used by all Chinese monarchs, but hitherto applied only to gods. He governed his empire, which now extended from the plateau of Mongolia – where he built the Great Wall to stop the raids of nomadic tribes – southward to Canton, through a centralized bureaucracy of appointed officials, suppressing the hereditary aristocracy which had sustained the feudal system of Chou times. He persecuted the Confucians because of their association with the old political order, but failed to find any other moral or religious basis for the empire which he had established by the ruthless use of force. After his death his dynasty disappeared almost immediately in a series of political convulsions which convinced educated Chinese of the insufficiency of Legist principles.

THE HAN DYNASTY

The next dynasty, the Han, which, except for a short interval of usurpation, reigned for four centuries (206 B.C. to A.D. 220), established a compromise on which Chinese society and government continued to be based in essentials down to the overthrow of the imperial monarchy in 1912. The Han Emperors maintained the centralized bureaucracy created by the Ch'in for governing an even more extensive territory – to the Ch'in dominions they added what is now Sinkiang and also northern Vietnam – but instead of opposing traditional learning, they patronized it, and turned the Confucian school, which had become the equivalent of a religious sect, into a pillar of their rule. The Confucians accepted the autocracy of the Emperor, but held that he should administer the empire through officials who had been specially educated for their task through study of Confucian philosophical writings and other literature regarded by the Confucians as morally edifying.

ORIGIN OF THE CIVIL SERVICE

The test of qualification for office was thus some kind of examination which conferred an academic degree, and this was the origin of the system of public competitive examinations for the civil service which became the most distinctive social and political feature of Chinese civilization. The system was not perfected all at once; it evolved over many centuries. Its tendency was to substitute merit – though merit according to a special criterion – for birth or wealth as a qualification for administrative office, and it became possible for a man of the most humble origin to rise to the highest position in the state if he had the required ability and could acquire the necessary education. The latter condition was, of course, always a limiting factor, for the bulk of the population was too poor to be able to afford the education for its sons, except in so far as promising boys might be helped by charitable 'clan' or village endowments. But the numbers of those competing in the examinations grew ever greater as time went on, and from the 11th century was indirectly increased by the development of printing, which made books more easily available.

The 'scholar' class overlapped with the landowning class and the term 'gentry' is usually applied to that element of Chinese society which combined academic qualifications with landed property and was able, when not actually holding appointments in the imperial civil service, to live a life of cultivated leisure on income from rents and take part in local government, thus supplementing the work of the central bureaucracy and forming such 'public opinion' as existed under a monarchy not restricted by any kind of parliamentary or municipal rights. There were always, however, landlords who were not scholars, thus lacking the social status which belonged to the scholar class, and also scholars who had no landed or other property and made a living, when not in government service, as teachers, secretaries, clerks and even letter-writers for the illiterate. The number of qualified scholars was always much greater than the number of civil service jobs available for them, so that they had to rely on alternative sources of income; their aspiration, however, was to serve in the greater offices of state, as ministers of the central government or as governors of provinces; these were the 'mandarins', who lived in grand style and had great opportunities of acquiring wealth, but were always liable to dismissal, degradation or even execution if they incurred the displeasure of the Emperor.

The scholar class was officially Confucian, but its members, especially when they were living in retirement, were often addicted to the mystical practices of Taoism, which, when carried to an extreme, involved an ascetic life as a recluse in the mountains. Thus the Chinese cultural tradition has both a worldly side, in which the individual is subordinated to family duties and the service of the state, and an unworldly one, so often represented in Chinese art, in which he can achieve spiritual emancipation in a mountain hermitage – where, as a Chinese saying has it, the sage 'regards the affairs of the world as so much duckweed'. From the 1st century A.D. the Taoist opposition to Confucianism was reinforced by that of Buddhism, which was introduced into China from India by way of Central Asia. Buddhism, with its monastic ideal, its doctrines of reincarnation and *nirvana*, its subtle epistemology and its emphasis on personal salvation rather than on social duty, ran counter to Confucian philosophy, and Buddhism never succeeded in establishing itself as a state religion in China, but in its popular form it gained a strong hold on the masses of the people. Buddhism and Taoism – which had in the meantime developed into a popular religion with its own gods, ritual worship and magical beliefs – were rivals, but they also influenced each other and a product of this interaction was Ch'an Buddhism, better known under its Japanese name of Zen, which concentrated on a technique of meditation designed to produce an inner enlightenment. Educated Chinese often combined Confucianism, as a system of mundane ethics, with Ch'an Buddhism, as a means to spiritual illumination; and although the more orthodox Confucians strongly disapproved of both Taoism and Buddhism, there was a prevailing tendency in Chinese thought to regard them all as complementary rather than incompatible, and one of the stock themes of Chinese pictorial art represents Confucius, Lao Tzu and the Buddha engaged in an amicable intellectual discussion.

The Chinese upper class of landlords, scholars and government officials was sustained by rents and taxes from the production of the masses of peasants and artisans who made up the bulk of the population. In periods of good administration and freedom from external or civil war, when the pressure of population was not too great, these classes enjoyed tolerable conditions of life, but even at the best times China was exceptionally liable to famine brought on either by droughts, when the uncertain spring rains were insufficient to nourish the crops, or by floods, when the great rivers swollen by melting snows on the mountains of Tibet overflowed their banks in the flat plains and inundated vast areas of cultivated land. There were moreover two human factors which aggravated these natural conditions. The unchecked growth of population in times of peace tended to force a surplus of the peasantry on to marginal lands, to drive them into the towns as casual labour usually unemployed, or make them tenants of landlords who thus acquired more and more land. At the same time the decline of a dynasty, which so often followed its early period of energy and good administration, led to official corruption and abuses of power imposing additional burdens on the people. According to Confucian theory a dynasty reigned because it held the 'Mandate of Heaven', a divine commission to govern, but it lost this mandate if the descendants of the founder proved unworthy, and the displeasure of Heaven was manifested by an increase of natural calamities. This belief was more than the primitive idea that monarchs should be responsible for the weather; one of the symptoms of a breakdown of administration was that officials neglected the care of dykes and dams, so that floods, when they came, were far more devastating than when such public works were well maintained. In circumstances of over-population, governmental maladministration and widespread famine, the combination of social discontents with the belief that the reigning dynasty has lost its mandate has often in Chinese history been sufficient to cause large-scale popular revolts and a change of dynasty, a new dynasty being founded sometimes by the leader of the revolt and sometimes by a general who takes advantage of the disorder to install himself in power. Such upheavals were never, however, until 1912, real revolutions, for the political structure and methods of government remained in essentials the same from one dynasty to another.

THE HAN DYNASTY AND THE ROMAN EMPIRE

The Chinese Empire of the Han was contemporary with the Roman Empire in Europe and the lands round the Mediterranean, and the two great political units were roughly comparable in size and population, but their historical destinies were widely divergent. The Roman Empire broke up, never to be reconstituted in its original shape; even apart from its Asian and African lands, its European territories are today partitioned between seventeen sovereign states. On the other hand, all the territory held by the Han Dynasty, except for Vietnam, remains today within the frontiers of China. For most of the twenty-one centuries between the founding of the Han Dynasty in 206 B.C. and the fall of the Ch'ing in A.D. 1912 China was politically united under a single government, and even in periods of political division its cultural unity remained virtually intact. But if China thus excelled Europe in the stability and continuity of its civilization, it was the divisions and mutations of Europe which opened the way to more progressive modes of economic and intellectual life. In China the weight of ancient tradition, the prestige of the 'classics' and the authority of a conservatively indoctrinated bureaucracy were adverse to advance in the sciences and

143

to economic and political innovations. There were some remarkable developments of natural science and technology in China in the early centuries, but Confucian orthodoxy was unfavourable to scientific inquiry, and progress in this field had virtually ceased long before the great advances of Western science which ushered in the modern age of mankind. Similarly the vast Chinese Empire produced a flourishing internal commerce and a considerable foreign trade, but social and political conditions obstructed the rise of a genuine capitalist economy. The Chinese merchant might become rich, but politically he remained at the mercy of the imperial bureaucracy; he could give his son an education to enable him to complete in the civil service examinations, and himself could purchase a nominal degree which would admit him to the ranks of the 'gentry', but he had no municipal or parliamentary representation which would have given him political power.

The main factors in the history of Chinese civilization before the 19th century were internal, but there were two important external factors. One of these was Buddhism, which has already been mentioned; this was an entirely peaceful influence. But the other factor was the permanent threat of the nomadic peoples, few in numbers and spread out over vast expanses of steppe and desert, who were nevertheless highly mobile, and, accustomed as they were to herding on horseback, formed natural cavalry armies which under a capable military leadership could become potent instruments either for predatory raiding or for permanent conquest. To hold the northern nomads at bay was always the primary strategic concern of a Chinese government, but on several occasions in history the defence failed and a part or the whole of China was overrun.

THE MONGOL AND MANCHU CONQUESTS

The two most notable conquests were those made by the Mongols in the 13th century and by the Manchus in the 17th. The invasions of these plundering barbarians caused much suffering and humiliation to the Chinese people; nevertheless, the Chinese cultural tradition was little affected, for the northern nomads had no higher culture of their own and were unable to draw regular revenues from conquered China without employing Chinese civil servants, with the result that the conquerors became gradually assimilated to the civilization of the conquered. This happened especially to the Manchus, whose dynasty, the Ch'ing, replaced the native Chinese house of Ming in the imperial capital of Peking in 1644. The Ch'ing Emperors learned to speak and write Chinese, and the Manchu language fell into disuse; certain government posts were reserved for Manchus, but the Chinese element in the administration became more and more predominant, so that by the 19th century there was little to distinguish the Ch'ing from a pure Chinese dynasty. In one respect, however, it was more effective than a purely Chinese dynasty would have been. The military organization of the Manchus combined with the resources of China sufficed to add Mongolia, Sinkiang and Tibet to the Manchu–Chinese Empire; none of these three territories had been held by the Ming Dynasty, nor had any previous purely Chinese dynasty controlled Tibet. Thus the China that confronted Europeans in the Far East in the early 19th century was more than twice as large territorially as that which the Portuguese voyagers found when they first reached China in the 16th century.

BEGINNING OF WESTERN TRADE WITH CHINA

The voyage of Vasco da Gama, who reached India round Africa in 1498, had opened the Indian Ocean to European navigation, and after the Portuguese capture of Malacca in 1511 it could not be long before they reached China as well. The first voyage there was in 1516. At first there was little to distinguish the Portuguese in Chinese eyes from the Arab and Malay traders who had long visited Chinese ports; for their services to the Chinese Government in suppressing piracy they were granted the right to establish a trading settlement at Macao. But neither the Portuguese nor the Dutch, French and English merchants, who followed them to the China Seas, made any real impression on China until the second quarter of the 19th century. They were allowed to trade in certain ports – from 1757 only at Canton – but they were not permitted to travel in the interior or to have any contacts with the Chinese people except for merchants officially licensed to have dealings with them. Nor was the Chinese court willing to enter into diplomatic relations on a basis of equality with envoys of the European maritime nations; it would receive diplomatic missions only if they came to offer homage and tribute to the Chinese Emperor. Only with Russia was some sort of diplomatic contact established; this was because, while the other states of Europe had made contact with China only through merchant shipping, Russia had a land frontier with the Chinese Empire to the north of Manchuria and Mongolia, and negotiations were required in order to settle frontier disputes and keep Russia from aiding rebellious Mongol tribes. But neither the Russian outposts in Siberia nor the European traders coming to Canton impressed the Chinese as bearers of a civilization comparable to their own.

THE FIRST JESUIT MISSIONARIES

A stronger impression was made by the Catholic missionaries, especially the Jesuits, who penetrated into China from the beginning of the 17th century. They were respected by the Chinese for their mathematical knowledge and employed by the Government for certain purposes such as astronomical observations for regulating the calendar – a matter of great importance for Chinese state rituals – and geographical surveys. Their opportunities for making converts were, however, severely restricted, particularly after the Pope had decided against the Jesuit policy of accepting the Confucian cult of ancestors as a civil observance compatible with Christianity. The influence of the missionaries was thus a very limited one, and their presence in China did little to stimulate curiosity about the West in the minds of the Confucian scholar-officials, whose outlook had become imperviously ethnocentric and self-sufficient. Only a great shock, or series of shocks, could arouse China from the complacency of an immobile traditionalism in a rapidly changing world.

THE 'OPIUM WAR' AND THE TREATY OF NANKING

The first great shock was administered by defeat in the Anglo-Chinese war of 1839–42, the so-called 'Opium War'. The occasion of this was the action taken by a commissioner of the Chinese Government to enforce a prohibition of the import of opium which was being violated by British merchants with the connivance of the local authorities. But even without this particular issue an armed conflict was imminent because the British, as the principal European traders at Canton, were unwilling to put up any longer with the conditions imposed on the trade there. The fighting which then took place suddenly revealed the Chinese Empire as incapable of standing up to even a small expeditionary force of a European power, and the Treaty of Nanking which concluded the war was a great humiliation for China. Britain obtained the opening of additional ports, including Shanghai, a fixed customs tariff instead of arbitrary taxation on trade, rights of residence in the ports with extra-territorial jurisdiction of British consuls, and the cession of the island of Hong Kong. Other Western nations hastened to conclude similar treaties on behalf of their merchants. China could no longer be secluded from contact with the West; the Western 'barbarians' were now in Chinese ports no more on sufferance, but as of right which they had the power to enforce.

THE T'AI P'ING REBELLION

The loss of prestige suffered by the Ch'ing Dynasty, added to the factors which, as we have seen, tended to undermine all Chinese dynasties after the first few generations, produced the great T'ai P'ing rebellion, which began in 1851 under the leadership of a convert to Protestant Christianity. The rebels overran a large part of south China, captured Nanking and advanced as far north as Tientsin, but were driven back and finally crushed by forces loyal to the Ch'ing. The Manchu garrisons in China had proved incapable of resisting the rebels, but the religious fanaticism of the latter – the first manifestation of the new Western influence in China – set the Confucian scholar class against them, and this was their undoing. In the last phase of the civil war the Ch'ing cause was aided by the Western powers, whose trade was suffering from the extension of T'ai P'ing military operations into the neighbourhood of Shanghai, and the fame of General Gordon and his 'Ever-Victorious Army' led to a widespread popular belief in the West that his campaign had decided the issue of the civil war; but in fact the T'ai P'ing had already lost nearly all their territory outside Kiangsu province before the Western intervention took place. While the civil war was in progress Britain and France had carried on a war of their own against the Ch'ing Government resulting in new treaties which gave foreigners unlimited rights of travel in the interior of China and provided for the residence of foreign diplomatic missions in Peking and diplomatic relations with China on terms of equality – a concession which the Chinese court had hitherto denied on principle to 'barbarians'.

EXPANSION OF WESTERN INFLUENCE

British and French troops entered Peking in 1860 to enforce the demands of their Governments, but withdrew after the ratification of the new treaties. China remained an independent state – reunified after the collapse of the T'ai P'ing revolt in 1864 – but subject to servitudes on its sovereignty through extra-territorial rights of foreigners within its borders and to economic pressures which began slowly, but surely, to transform the basis of its social order. The foreign merchants brought with them their banks and insurance companies; their commercial operations were immune from the exactions of Chinese officials, and increasingly covered Chinese domestic as well as foreign trade; Western shipping predominated not only on the overseas routes but also in coastwise navigation and on inland waters such as the Yangtse river. Foreign capital was invested in harbour facilities and public utilities in the ports and found a new field with the beginning of railway construction in China. The general policy of the Chinese Government towards these innovations was to make concessions under pressure to foreign interests, but to obstruct economic development wherever possible. The first railway in China was constructed from Shanghai to Woosung in 1876, but in the following year the Government bought it, tore up the rails and demolished the rolling stock.

The new conditions nevertheless forced the government itself to open the door to the modern world, if only a little way. It needed men with knowledge of foreign languages and international law for the diplomatic service which it had been compelled to create; it needed men with mathematical and scientific qualifications in order to build the modern army and navy which after the defeats China had suffered were recognized as essential for national defence. It was believed by leading Chinese statesmen of the time that it was possible thus to train experts without damage to the Confucian ideology or to the existing structure of the state. But the young diplomats and officers drank in Western political ideas with their languages and sciences and became violently discontented with their environment. The vogue of Western education grew rapidly and a new Western-educated intelligentsia was formed.

THE PERIOD OF REFORMS

In 1895 China suffered a shock greater than any previously undergone. A war with Japan which began in the previous year ended in utter defeat for China. Such humiliation at the hands of the Japanese was a greater blow to Chinese pride than had been inflicted by the wars with Britain and France, because Japan had been a cultural satellite of China and her new naval and military superiority over China was manifestly due to the fact that she had modernized her whole state system on Western lines, which China had not tried to do. Patriotic indignation in China – further stimulated by extortions of leasehold territories and railway concessions by Germany, Russia, Britain and France – now took shape in an agitation for sweeping reforms which, through the advocacy of a scholar named K'ang Yu-wei, converted the reigning Emperor Kwang Hsu and caused him to issue a series of

Reform Edicts in 1898. But the reforms antagonized too many vested interests, and the Dowager Empress Tzu Hsi, whose sympathies were with the conservatives, carried out a *coup d'état*, whereby the Emperor was made a prisoner in his own palace and the reform party suppressed. The sequel was the rising of the so-called 'Boxers', a popular anti-foreign movement through which the emotions generated by China's degradation were diverted from the agitation for reform into attacks on foreign residents, particularly missionaries. Although the Boxers were supported by a Court faction and joined by part of the army, their attempt to drive the Western nations out of China by force was fore-doomed to failure; an international army composed of contingents from all the principal Western powers and Japan marched in the summer of 1900 to Peking where the legations had been besieged by the Boxers, and the Court had to flee from the capital. For the Ch'ing Dynasty and for the *ancien régime* this was the beginning of the end. Although the Dowager Empress continued to hold the reins of power for another eight years, she now accepted the inevitability of reforms, and entrusted her political henchman Yuan Shih-k'ai with the task of putting them into effect. His primary concern was with the reorganization of the army, but of even greater importance than his military measures was the abolition of the old system of examinations for the civil service. A Western education and not Chinese classical learning henceforth be-came the key to the public service, and this had the most profound effect on the Chinese mind, for the whole range of ideas and values on which Chinese society and government had traditionally been based was now discredited overnight. The monarchy itself only survived by six years the passing of the examination system. Republican ideas had already become current among young army officers, reflecting the pre-dominant American influence in Western education in China. In October 1911, at Hankow on the middle Yangtse, the garrison troops mutinied and proclaimed a Republic; other army units made common cause with them, and after some indecisive fighting the Regent for the last Ch'ing Emperor, then still a child, signed an edict of abdication.

THE CHINESE REPUBLIC

The Chinese Republic, which thus came into existence, was dedicated in theory to the principles of popular sovereignty and liberal democracy which the intelligentsia and young officers had imbibed from the West, but the reality of the new regime was something very different. Since the army had made the Revolution, effective power rested with the generals, and since revenue to pay the troops was raised on a provincial basis, the military governor of each province had an opportunity to exercise political power on his own. The masses of the people were bewildered and apathetic; they had lost faith in the old order of things, but the new ideas meant nothing to them. China was threatened with serious internal disorder and at the same time with the loss of the outer territories of the old empire, for Outer Mongolia and Tibet now declared themselves independent, claiming that their allegiance had been to the Manchu Dynasty and that they had no other ties with China. The Chinese garrisons in Outer Mongolia and Tibet were driven out, and the new Chinese Republic was unable to undertake the reconquest of these territories; it had its hands full with trying to restore the authority of the central government in the provinces of China itself. The leading personality of the new regime was Yuan Shih-k'ai, who, having abandoned the cause of the Ch'ing Dynasty, had been elected President of the Republic and proceeded to try to convert his office into a personal dictatorship. His real aim was to restore the monarchy in his own person and found a new dynasty, but his control over the army was insufficient; he had himself proclaimed Emperor in 1915, but was overthrown by a revolt in which the republican intelligentsia combined with generals whose only motive was jealousy of Yuan. The elimination of Yuan and his death in 1916 left China without any outstanding leader, and the forces of disintegration now gained the upper hand. The years from 1916 to 1928 are known as the 'warlords period' because of the predominance of the provincial military governors who tore China apart with their civil wars and intrigues; there was no longer a national army and the Government in Peking, composed of adherents of the strongest military faction, ceased to exercise more than a nominal authority.

SUN YAT-SEN AND THE KUOMINTANG

In opposition to the phantom government in Peking – which continued to be recognized internationally as the legal government, since it was established in the capital – a government of the Kuomintang Party was set up at Canton in the extreme south of China under the leadership of Sun Yat-sen, who had played an important part, though a far from decisive one, in the Revolution of 1911. The Kuomintang was a party of liberal and progressive ideas drawing its support mainly from the commercial middle class in Canton and Shanghai and also from 'Overseas Chinese' in Singapore, San Francisco and elsewhere. As a prophet of republican democracy, Sun had supposed that China could pass directly from the bureaucratic absolutism of the Ch'ing to a political system on the American model; he was sadly disillusioned by what actually happened after 1911 and came to the conclusion that a period of 'tutelage' or party dictatorship would be necessary to re-unify China, suppress the warlords and establish an effective central administration before liberal democratic institutions could function in China. It was no simple matter, however, to undertake such a task, for the Kuomintang had no army of its own and was dependent on pacts with the local warlords of south China. It was, above all, in the hope of obtaining military assistance that Sun was finally induced to turn for support to the Government of Soviet Russia, although he was not himself a Communist nor was his party a Marxist one.

The key to this development lay in the international situation in which China was involved after the First World War. China took no direct part in the war, but its indirect effects were far-reaching. The absorption of the Western powers in the mutual slaughter in Europe left Japan free to act in the Far East, and in 1915 Japan addressed to China the notorious Twenty-one Demands, which, if accepted in full, would have turned China into a Japanese protectorate. With encouragement from the United States, China rejected some of the demands, but accepted others, including a provision for transfer to Japan of the Germany-leased territory of Kiaochow in Shantung, which had been captured by a Japanese expeditionary force soon after the outbreak of war. Japan's claim was confirmed by Britain and France in secret treaties in return for Japanese naval assistance against German submarines in the later stages of the war. After the end of the war, however, there was an intense nationalist agitation in China against the transfer of Kiaochow to Japan, and a delegation was sent to the Paris Peace Conference – China having formally declared war on Germany – representing both the Peking and Canton Governments but acting less as a team of Government officials than as an agency of unofficial nationalist opinion. Britain and France supported Japan at the Conference; President Wilson protested at the secret treaties, but allowed the transfer of Kiaochow to be written into the Treaty of Versailles, which the Chinese delegation then refused to sign.

At the Washington Conference two years later Japan at length agreed to restore Kiaochow to China, but in the meantime Chinese sentiment had become extremely hostile not only towards Japan, but towards all the Western powers with the exception of the new Soviet Government of Russia, which had not taken part in the Paris Peace Conference and had demonstratively renounced as a matter of principle all extra-territorial rights and other concessions acquired by Tsarist Russia in China. Nationalist public opinion in China thus came to regard the new regime in Russia as China's only friend in opposition to Western and Japanese imperialism, and it was in these circumstances that the Chinese Communist Party was founded in 1921. Its following was at first mainly in Shanghai and Canton, the cities where the Kuomintang was already most strongly established and where there were larger numbers of industrial workers than anywhere else in China. The Chinese Communists adhered to the orthodox doctrine of Marxism-Leninism which held that only the urban proletariat could make a socialist revolution and concentrated their efforts on winning the support of this class in the places where it existed. They also, however, in accordance with Lenin's principle of a worker-peasant alliance, extended their activity to the countryside where conditions were ripe for an agrarian revolt. To an increasing congestion of population on the land had been added oppressive taxation by the warlords for the upkeep of their private armies and the rapacity of landlords who were the only source of credit for a peasantry living on the margin of subsistence. Among the peasant masses the preaching of Communism was unexpectedly successful, but as yet the party leadership had no inkling that the decisive action of the Chinese Communist Revolution was to take place entirely in rural areas.

While the Communists were building up their party in China the Soviet Government made direct contact with the Kuomintang. Joffe, its envoy to China, met Sun Yat-sen and agreed on terms of co-operation whereby the Soviet Union would render political and military assistance to the Canton government. In accordance with this agreement Michael Borodin was sent to Canton in the autumn of 1923 as a political adviser, and a little later General Galen (Blücher) went with a team of Russian officers to train cadets for a Kuomintang Party army at a military academy set up at Whampoa. The Kuomintang reached an agreement with the Chinese Communist Party for a united front against the warlords and foreign imperialism, and Communists were permitted to enrol individually as members of the Kuomintang. A certain Chiang Kai-shek was appointed Director of the Whampoa Academy with a Communist, Chou En-lai, as his deputy in charge of political education.

CHIANG KAI-SHEK AND THE KUOMINTANG

Sun Yat-sen died in March 1925, and three months later an incident in Shanghai, when International Settlement police under the command of a

British sergeant opened fire on rioting Chinese strikers from a Japanese textile factory, was used by the Kuomintang–Communist alliance to start a nation-wide agitation against British and Japanese imperialism. The foreign concessions in Canton were blockaded and Hong Kong was paralysed by strikes instigated from Canton. Meanwhile there was a struggle for power in succession to Sun within the Kuomintang and Chiang Kai-shek emerged as the supreme leader. In July 1926 he led the Kuomintang army, now officered by Russian-trained Whampoa cadets, northwards from Canton to the Yangtse. It won a series of easy victories over the mercenary armies of the warlords, the ardour and efficiency of the new Kuomintang military force being supplemented by the propaganda of the Communists which everywhere 'mobilized the masses' in support of the revolutionary drive. The Kuomintang captured Hankow, where the British Concession was overrun, and Nanking, where a number of foreigners were killed, and entered Shanghai, where British troops were landed to guard the International Settlement. The movement now reached a point of crisis. Further attacks on foreigners and their property would have involved open war with Britain and perhaps other Western nations. Chiang Kai-shek suspected that it was the object of the Russian advisers and the Communists to embroil him in such a way; he was also alarmed at the success of the Communists in 'mobilizing the masses' and feared that they would soon try to take over power from the Kuomintang. Moscow, on the other hand, wished to maintain the Kuomintang–Communist alliance as a means of pressure on Britain and Japan, and dissuaded the Chinese Communists from taking independent action. Chiang was thus able to move first, and in April 1937 he carried out a *coup d'état* against the Communists in Shanghai; this was repeated in other cities where the Communists had a following, so that the party was broken up and suppressed, with many of its members imprisoned or executed.

What survived from the wreck of the Communist movement was a peasant revolt which had broken out in remote rural areas of Kiangsi and Hunan provinces under the leadership of Mao Tse-tung, himself sprung from a Hunan peasant family. Mao had diverged from other Chinese Communist leaders in the importance he attached to the agrarian *jacquerie*; in a report he wrote in February 1927 he declared that the poorer peasants were providing seven tenths of the forces of the revolution. The party leadership, however, was reluctant to accept a situation which was so different from the Russian model in which the proletariat had made the revolution in Petrograd and Moscow and the peasants had been only auxiliaries in the civil war. They kept on trying to capture cities and provide the revolution with its proper proletarian base. But all these attempts failed, while Mao's peasant guerillas held their own in the mountains of south China and a large area of southern Kiangsi was brought under a 'soviet' administration.

The Kuomintang, after its break with the Communists, moved politically towards the right. It refrained from further direct attacks on foreign treaty rights in China and obtained international recognition as the *de jure* Government of China after its capture of Peking – which, however, it downgraded from its status as capital, making Nanking the new seat of government. It compromised with the warlord system, allowing several of the provincial generals to retain a private military power on condition of acknowledging the supremacy of the central government. All this was indeed an anti-climax after the intense revolutionary impetus of 1926. But there had been real progress; there was now a genuine national authority in China instead of the anarchy of the previous decade and a sense of purpose which had been lacking in the freebooting generals who had made the history of the warlord period. The Kuomintang aimed at creating an effective state administration and building up a modern industry in China; in foreign policy it hoped gradually to obtain revision of the 'unequal treaties' and get rid of extra-territoriality and foreign leaseholds by various forms of pressure, but without war.

Had twenty years of peace been granted to Chiang Kai-shek's government, it might have achieved much in unifying and modernizing China and raising the country's international status. But it had to cope with two great Japanese invasions, the first in 1931 which tore away Manchuria from China, and the second beginning in 1937 which brought vast areas of China from the Great Wall in the north down to Canton and the island of Hainan in the south under hostile military occupation. The loss of Manchuria deprived China of what was then its most industrially developed area; during the eight years of war which began in 1937 China was first partially, and then totally, blockaded by sea and six of her seven largest cities were captured by the enemy. Against these invaders, greatly superior in military organization and armaments, China could only fight a war of 'resistance', retreating into the interior of the country and trying to exhaust the enemy by a protracted opposition and refusal to accept dictated terms of peace. Such a struggle involved immense suffering, devastation and disruption of normal life for the Chinese people, and it was no wonder that the newly erected fabric of central government and reformed fiscal administration cracked under the strain. The currency went into high inflation, and it was only possible to maintain armies in the field by allowing generals to requisition supplies in their respective 'war zones' – a practice which inevitably revived the habits of warlordism. The commercial middle classes of the larger cities, who had provided the liberal element in the Kuomintang, fell under Japanese occupation or became refugees; the government became dependent on the co-operation of the landlords for carrying on its administration and its politics became increasingly reactionary. Meanwhile in the Japanese-occupied areas the Kuomintang officials either fled or collaborated with the enemy, and a political vacuum was thus created into which guerila resistance forces could infiltrate. Since the Communists were specialists in guerila tactics, it was they who were able to take advantage of this situation.

THE RISE OF COMMUNISM

From 1927 to 1937 the Communists, without ever being able to capture cities, had preserved a local independent state of their own, first in southern Kiangsi in south China, and then, after being driven out of that area by the Kuomintang, in northern Shensi in the north-west, which they reached by the famous 'Long March'. This Communist state within China, complete with government and army, schools and even a university, was always confined to rural territory; having expropriated landlords for the benefit of the peasants, it had the support of the latter, but it controlled no industrial areas, and was dependent for its arms on the most primitive kind of production supplemented by captures from the Kuomintang or the Japanese. Such an agrarian regime was obviously far removed from the original Communist idea of an urban proletarian revolution, but it was held that since the Communist Party was by definition the vanguard of the proletariat, peasants under Communist direction were really acting under the leadership of the proletariat even though the movement in the cities had almost ceased to exist. From this strange situation the idea later arose in the West that the Chinese Communists were not real Communists, but merely 'agrarian reformers'. But as far as their principles went they were orthodox Marxist-Leninists; their ruralism had been imposed on them by force of circumstances, not by their own choice. It did, however, have the effect of bringing to the top men such as Mao Tse-tung, who were best able to adapt themselves to the conditions imposed on the party by the course of events.

The civil war between the Kuomintang and the Communists went on simultaneously with the Japanese campaigns in Manchuria from 1931 to

1933, and after these were ended by the so-called Tangku Truce, Chiang Kai-shek concentrated his military forces against the Communists. But Japanese encroachments continued, and Chinese public opinion began to demand a cessation of the civil war and the formation of a national united front to resist Japan. On a visit to Sian at the end of 1936 Chiang Kai-shek was kidnapped by a local commander who insisted that he call off the struggle against the Communists and lead a united front. When Japan renewed the war in the summer of 1937 an agreement for joint action against the Japanese was reached by the two parties; operations by the Communist army were to be subject to orders from Chiang Kai-shek as supreme commander of all Chinese armed forces. In practice their operations were those of mutually distrustful allies rather than of components of a single national army, and it soon became evident to the Kuomintang that the war was working to the advantage of the Communists, because, as experienced guerillas, they were better able to infiltrate behind the Japanese lines. The Kuomintang, therefore – or rather the Chinese Government headed by Chiang Kai-shek in its war-time capital of Chungking, in the west of China – instituted a blockade of the Communists' territory to prevent them from obtaining supplies of arms. This met with strong objection from General Stilwell, who after the outbreak of war between Japan and America was sent by President Roosevelt as military adviser to Chiang Kai-shek. Stilwell wanted to send American arms to the Communists and use them for an offensive against the Japanese in north China; Chiang's opposition to the scheme culminated in a demand to Roosevelt for Stilwell's recall. Roosevelt complied and replaced Stilwell with another American general, Wedemeyer, who dropped the idea of arming the Communists.

CHINA POLICIES OF THE USA AND USSR

The war against Japan was brought to an end, not by the Chinese themselves, who in spite of their obstinate resistance were incapable of driving the Japanese from their territory, but by the Americans, who had destroyed Japanese sea-power in the Pacific and finally brought Japan to surrender with two atomic bombs, and by the Russians, who overwhelmed the Japanese army in Manchuria in a brief campaign in the last week of the war. It was with the aid of these two powers that China was now to regain her lost territory and take the surrender of the Japanese forces which remained on her soil. The political aims of the two powers, however, were divergent, and neither was free from contradictions. The Americans provided shipping and transport aircraft to enable Chinese government troops to take over Nanking, Shanghai, Peking, Tientsin and other cities from the Japanese, thus also forestalling the Communists, who but for this logistical support for the Kuomintang might have reached them first. The Americans were not, on the other hand, willing to back the Chinese Government in a new civil war against the Communists and put pressure on it to form a political coalition with them. The Russians, for their part, were ready to give limited aid to the Communists but not to repudiate Chiang's regime as the legal Government of China; they turned over to the Communists the stocks of arms they had captured from the Japanese in Manchuria and thus greatly strengthened the Communist army, but they continued to negotiate with Chiang and concurred in the American idea of a coalition. In December 1945 President Truman sent General Marshall to China as his personal representative to mediate between the two sides in what was again developing into a civil war. His task was doomed to failure from the start, for both sides aimed at dictatorial power and neither had any trust in the other; the Marshall mission achieved nothing except to bring odium on America for uninvited interference in Chinese internal affairs. The civil war was renewed and after a period of deadlock ended in the collapse of the Kuomintang arms and the decisive victory of the Communists. Chiang Kai-shek with the remnant of his army and a number of civilian Kuomintang supporters with their families took refuge in the island of Formosa, where they were for the moment safe, since the Communists had no fleet with which to pursue them. The whole mainland of China, however, submitted to Communist rule, and in October 1949 a new government, that of the Chinese People's Republic, was proclaimed in Peking. The Soviet Union hastened to extend *de jure* recognition to it, and Mao Tse-tung went to Moscow, where he concluded a treaty of military alliance with the Soviet Union.

THE KOREAN WAR

Of the non-Communist powers Britain extended recognition after a brief interval, partly in accordance with the British practice of recognizing any government which appeared to have stable control of a nation's territory, and partly in the hope of preserving British commercial interests in China. The American Government would have followed suit but for a crisis in domestic politics. The American people had long been accustomed to regard China as a special friend and ally of the United States and were dismayed at the emergence of a new Communist China allied with Russia; they were critical of the Truman Administration for what was considered its failure to give adequate support to the government of Chiang Kai-shek – a failure which was widely believed to be due to pro-Communist influences in the State Department. President Truman, therefore, decided to postpone recognition of the new regime in China until after the mid-term Congressional elections in November of 1950, but in the meantime the Korean War broke out, and before the end of the year the United States and Communist China were engaged in large-scale hostilities. Korea, liberated from Japanese rule by the Allied victory in 1945, had been divided into American and Russian zones of military occupation pending the establishment of an independent Korean state; in the outcome a Communist government had been set up in the Russian zone and an anti-Communist one in the American, so that when the Russian and American forces withdrew, the two rival Korean factions were left confronting each other, the Communists being the better armed. In June 1950 the North Koreans attacked, and Truman took a decision to send American forces to the assistance of South Korea. Since the elections which had been held in South Korea had been supervised by the United Nations, South Korea was in a sense a ward of the latter, and a decision of the Security Council in the absence of the Soviet Union (which was boycotting Council meetings at the time) turned the aid to South Korea into a United Nations war, but although fifteen other nations sent contingents to take part in the war, the bulk of the troops committed – and the casualties incurred – were always American. As a supplement to the action being taken in Korea – regarded in America as a war for the containment of Communism – the American Government sent a fleet to protect Formosa against a threatened invasion from the Chinese mainland. Chiang Kai-shek's government was thus not only secured in its possession of Formosa, but remained in full diplomatic relations with the United States and with American support retained China's seat in the United Nations.

Communist China intervened in the Korean war after the North Korean forces had been decisively defeated by the United Nations army, which then advanced to the Yalu river separating Korea from Manchuria. The Chinese drove the United Nations army out of North Korea, but were unable to dislodge it from a fortified line established across the middle of the peninsula close to the parallel of latitude which had divided the former Russian and American occupation zones. After three years of fighting – which cost a million military casualties for the belligerents and the lives of a similar number of Korean civilians – the war was ended by an armistice, but was followed neither by a peace treaty nor by any reconciliation between Communist China and the United States. The Chinese Communists now regarded America as their mortal enemy, the conflicts which had arisen over Korea and Formosa being in line with the ideological view that America, as the strongest capitalist power, must be the principal foe of the 'socialist' world. The Americans, on their side, were embittered by the war and convinced that the new China would try to extend its power all over the Far East unless firmly held in check; American defensive alliances were concluded with Japan, South Korea and Formosa to safeguard them against Communist penetration or attack.

CONSOLIDATION OF THE COMMUNIST REGIME

Internally the Korean war helped to consolidate the Communist regime in China, for it enhanced Chinese military prestige and enabled the Government to evoke patriotic emotions in the Chinese people over and above support for Communism; it also provided pretexts for a reign of terror in which great numbers of former supporters of the Kuomintang were put to death as alleged agents of America. After the war the Communist Government took in hand the economic and social transformation of China in accordance with its principles. It had already brought the whole country – except for inaccessible Formosa – under a firm central control, and through its omnipresent party organization and the universal use of radio loud-speakers extended its directives and exhortations into every village. By ending the civil war it had enabled agriculture and industry to revive and it had stabilized the currency; the war in Korea, which did not touch the territory of China itself or even its coastwise shipping – since the Americans in fear of Russian intervention had kept the war confined to Korea – did not reverse this progress. Socially the land reforms which the Communists had already carried out had eliminated the landlords as a class – and often physically destroyed them – but the Chinese bourgeoisie was not at first expropriated. From 1954 onwards, however, new measures were undertaken. Plans were formulated for raising national productivity and carrying out the long overdue industrialization of China in the shortest possible time. Together with the direction of the economy by the state to bring about rapid economic growth, private business was to be nationalized and the peasants induced to merge their individual holdings of land into collective farms. These aims were vigorously pursued during the mid fifties and met with remarkably little resistance; this success was mainly due to the tactical skill with which the measures were carried out. Owners of business enterprises received some compensation for the loss of their property, and the peasants were led on by stages to collectivization, the advantages of collective farming being demonstrated by the fact that agricultural credits and other state facilities were available only to collectives.

THE 'HUNDRED FLOWERS' AND THE 'GREAT LEAP FORWARD'

The Communists had more trouble, however, with the intellectuals; these had been generally sympathetic to Communism in the days of Kuomintang rule, but their addiction to ideas of personal and academic freedom caused them to chafe at the authoritarian controls now imposed in every sphere of Chinese life. The use of techniques of 'brain-washing' had only a limited success in converting the educated class to Communism, and in an attempt to conciliate the intellectuals and obtain their co-operation Mao Tse-tung proclaimed a new era of freedom of speech known as the 'Hundred Flowers' movement. But this produced so much criticism of the party that the policy was reversed and the critics persecuted for 'rightism'. This reaction coincided with an economic crisis; bottlenecks had developed in industrial production and economic growth was being slowed down. The answer of the Communists was to proclaim the 'Great Leap Forward' in which the mobilization of China's immense man-power – and woman-power – for urgent economic tasks was to make up for lack of capital and overcome all difficulties. The Great Leap was urged on with propaganda which gave it all emotional accompaniments of a religious revival and the whole Chinese people were stirred to extraordinary efforts. Groups of collectives were combined to form 'communes', work was carried on under a kind of military discipline, and steel was produced in backyard furnaces all over the country. But the pace could not be kept up, and the neglect of agriculture for the sake of high-speed industrialization exacted its penalty when bad weather produced crop failures in three successive years. The whole economic structure was threatened by food shortages and precious foreign exchange had to be used to buy grain abroad; priority had to be given to agriculture and new incentives found for peasants to produce more. The Great Leap Forward ended in something of an anti-climax; its results were quite disproportionate to its promises and the efforts it exacted, yet the economy was gradually developing and the time when China would be one of the great industrial nations was in sight.

FOREIGN POLICY: SINO-SOVIET AND
SINO-INDIAN DISPUTES

In foreign policy Communist China, without bettering its relations with America, began to have trouble with its Russian ally from 1958 onwards. The Chinese suspected – and not without reason – that the Russians were reluctant to give China as much aid as they could, particularly in the military field, because of a fear of the increase of Chinese power which would result if the most numerous people in the world were to attain their full strength. They were also alarmed at Russian attempts under Khrushchev to seek a *rapprochement* with America because they were afraid that China would be left out of any deal that might thus be concluded. Further, the Chinese resented the Russian favours shown to India, which, as a bourgeois and non-aligned power, the Chinese considered to be a dangerous rival for influence in Asia. The Chinese expressed their sense of grievance and their anxieties by an ideological campaign designed to convince the world Communist movement that any Russian deal with America would be a betrayal of the Communist cause, that 'imperialism' was incorrigible, and that Nehru was one of its stooges. The Russians replied by denunciations of 'dogmatism' and of those who would provoke nuclear war by provocative policies. The quarrel rose to its height at the time of the Khrushchev–Eisenhower exchanges of 1959–60, was allayed during the next year or so, and then flared up again in connexion with China's border disputes with India and the Chinese military campaign against India in the autumn of 1962. In July 1963 an attempt to resolve ideological difficulties by discussions between Russian and Chinese Communist Party representatives in Moscow failed completely, and in August Peking bitterly denounced the Nuclear Test Ban Treaty, which appeared to the Chinese to be an attempt to maintain an exclusive 'nuclear club'. The Chinese press also revealed that Russia had promised to help China produce nuclear weapons but had gone back on the promise at the time of Khrushchev's visit to the United States in 1959. It was clear that whatever the strains on the Chinese economy, and whatever China's weakness might still be in a conflict with a nuclear power, the rulers in Peking were resolved that China should play the part of a Great Power in world affairs and compensate for political isolation by a bold and vigorous self-confidence.

BIBLIOGRAPHY

Theodore H. E. Chen. *Thought Reform of the Chinese Intellectuals*. (Hong Kong University Press, Hong Kong, 1960.)

H. G. Creel. *Chinese Thought from Confucius to Mao Tse-tung*. (Eyre & Spottiswoode, 1954.)

C. P. FitzGerald. *China: A Short Cultural History*. (Cresset Press, London, revised edn, 1954.)

Geoffrey Hudson, Richard Lowenthal and Roderick MacFarquhar. *The Sino-Soviet Dispute*. Documents and Commentary. (*The China Quarterly*, 1961.)

Owen Lattimore. *The Inner Asian Frontiers of China*. (American Geographical Society, New York, 2nd edn, 1951.)

Mao Tse-tung on Guerrilla Warfare. Translated with an Introduction by Samuel B. Griffith. (Cassell, 1962.)

Edwin O. Reischauer and John K. Fairbank. *East Asia: the Great Tradition*. (Allen & Unwin, 1961.)

Benjamin I. Schwartz. *Chinese Communism and the Rise of Mao*. (Harvard University Press, Cambridge, Mass., 1951.)

Ssu-yu Teng and John K. Fairbank. *China's Response to the West. A Documentary Survey, 1839–1923*. (Harvard University Press, Cambridge, Mass., 1954.)

CHINA

The Contemporary Scene
1958 to the Present

Martin Bernal

IN a way the Great Leap Forward of 1958 can be seen as an attempt to
resolve the divisions or, to use Mao's own vocabulary, the major
contradictions within Chinese society. All tasks were to be shared and
there was to be no specialization. Industry was brought to the countryside and peasants and intellectuals took part in the industrial process of
making steel. Thousands of students and office workers were sent into
the country to do agricultural work and soldiers took on civilian tasks
while large sections of the population were enrolled into the militia.
The communes were an attempt to unite state and society. Agricultural
collectives, the chief economic units, were merged to form entities that
could be administratively effective. On the national scale administration
was de-centralized to the commune. Another administrative aspect of
the changes was a withering away of government at local levels. In all
Communist states power has rested on the tripod of party, government
and army. In most cases the party has been pre-eminent; however in
the Soviet Union and other countries, government ministries have
considerable power particularly over the economy and industrial
planning. Because China is an overwhelmingly agricultural country it
has always been subject to comparatively less government influence.
During the Great Leap Forward government structure was weakened
still further as bureaucrats were required to work in the fields or to concentrate their efforts in party or political work. This change was caused
partly by the millenarian atmosphere which demanded rounded personalities, the worker-peasant-intellectual, and the unification of state and
society, and partly by the long-standing difficulty for a country with
very few skilled administrators to maintain both a government and a
party hierarchy. Thus after 1958 the party seems to have replaced the
government at the local level.

The period from 1960 to 1962 was one of retrenchment; bad weather,
administrative confusion and the withdrawal of Soviet experts led to
severe economic difficulties. Investment in heavy industry was cut back

163

and emphasis was placed on agriculture and industries directly related to it. On the land the communes were divided up. In 1959 there were 24,000 but by 1963 the number had grown to 74,000. Furthermore smaller units within the communes – the production brigades and production teams – became increasingly important in the organization of work and the distribution of produce. At the same time considerable concessions were made to peasant individualism. Public kitchens established in many areas during the Great Leap disappeared and small private plots for growing vegetables and raising chickens and pigs, which had been abolished in 1958, were gradually restored. This together with the restoration of private marketing made it difficult to persuade the peasants to devote time and fertilizer to the public fields. However the changes coincided with a great increase of food supplies to the cities, and the situation improved still further with the good harvests from 1963 to 1966. Although no coherent economic statistics have been published in China since 1960 it seems that industrial investment and production increased with the agricultural progress and by 1965 there was relative prosperity throughout the country.

In 1958 China was on bad terms with most of her neighbours. There were armed clashes with India over disputed boundaries and doubts about her frontiers with Burma, Nepal, Bhutan and Mongolia. In the early 1960s China made considerable efforts to remedy the situation, signing what were considered to be generous border agreements with Burma and Nepal in 1960, Bhutan in 1961 and with Pakistan and Mongolia in 1962. However 1962 also saw considerable fighting between India and China along both the western and eastern sections of their frontier. The origins and rights and wrongs of this conflict were immensely complicated but the result was clearcut victory for China, which to the surprise of the rest of the world she did not pursue. Chinese forces retired to the positions they had held in 1959, leaving a situation which the Indian Government has preferred not to contest.

China has never challenged the legitimacy of her frontiers with Vietnam and Laos but she continues to be extremely interested in Indo-Chinese affairs. In 1961 the Foreign Minister Ch'en I made it clear that if the United States persisted in her attempts to turn Laos into a bastion of anti-communism, China might intervene, and soon after President Kennedy announced a major change of policy; support for Laotian neutrality and the reactivation of the International Control Commission whose activities America had previously opposed. China also cooperated with the USSR in the Geneva Conference on Laos in 1961 and 1962, which established a neutral coalition government that lasted until the right-wing coup of 1964.

China was also concerned with the increase of American forces in Vietnam. In 1961 she endorsed a North Vietnamese appeal to the UN Secretary General on the subject and during the American escalations of 1964 she joined in calls for a reconvention of a Geneva Conference on Laos with strong implications that it should consider Vietnam. However with the beginning of regular American bombing of North Vietnam in February 1965 China's position changed. Since then she has become increasingly opposed to any negotiations before an American withdrawal. China has consistently given moral support both to North Vietnam and to the National Liberation Front in the South, and since 1965 has sent a considerable amount of material aid to the North. However, while offering to send troops if they are asked for, she has been extremely wary of becoming militarily involved, repeatedly insisting that only the local people can fight effective revolutionary wars.

One neighbour whose relations with China did not improve during the early 1960s was the Soviet Union. Tensions between the two countries which had been developing during the late fifties had come into the open in 1960 with the withdrawal of all Soviet experts working in China. The quarrel has many causes, some traditional – such as the difficulties along the frontier – others modern, the basic difference here being the Soviet contention that in the atomic age the overriding issue is the avoidance of world war, while the Chinese maintain that the liberation of oppressed people should always have priority, adding that appeasement of the Americans is the surest way to bring about a nuclear catastrophe.

One of the bitterest aspects of the clash has been over atomic weapons. China seems to have begun the development of nuclear arms in 1957. The project received Soviet help until 1959 when the Russians broke their agreement, and refused to continue the aid. Since then China has gone it alone. In 1963 she refused to sign the Test Ban Treaty and in October 1964 she detonated her first atomic bomb. This impressive technological achievement was surpassed by the even more rapid development and testing of her first hydrogen bomb in June 1967.

ATOMIC POWER AND THE ARMY

There seem to have been several reasons for China's devotion of a large part of her national resources to nuclear weapons. Firstly the development of a hydrogen bomb can be seen as the start of a long-term programme to enable China to retaliate against any American attacks. Secondly it proved China was a major world power with both industrial strength and technological skill. Thirdly, expensive though it is, the atomic programme is cheaper than the cost of providing China's army of over two million men with sophisticated conventional weapons.

The refusal to provide the army with large quantities of conventional arms has a close relationship to some of the major tensions within Chinese society. In 1959 Marshal P'eng Te-huai, the Minister of Defence, was replaced by Marshal Lin Piao. It has since emerged that P'eng, who was the commander of Chinese forces in the Korean War, was only one among a very large number of military officers who argued that to defend China it was necessary to modernize the army. They maintained that to achieve this, equipment should be improved, specialist officers should be allowed power and responsibility and emphasis should be placed on military techniques rather than political work. The officers also implied that to obtain new equipment and specialist training it was necessary to maintain some links with the Soviet Union. Even after P'eng's dismissal a considerable struggle took place in the army between this faction and the more political group led by Lin Piao. Lin and those who think like him believe that 'men are more important than machines'. In a way this attitude, and the proposals that come from it, reflect a reversion to the tactics of the 1940s when the Chinese Communists used political methods and mass enthusiasm to check the Japanese and defeat the Nationalists, both of whom had overwhelming material and technological superiority. In another way Lin's attitude is a recognition of the fact that China cannot hope to compete with American wealth and weapons and that her only hope is to rely on revolutionary spirit.

Lin Piao's success was confirmed in September 1965 when it was announced that all army ranks and insignia were to be abolished. Even though the reform cannot have been total it obviously was a severe blow to army officers as a class. In the absence of formal military organization constant political meetings, in which speeches and articles were discussed and analysed, were used to inculcate a spirit of devotion and self-sacrifice. Worship of Mao and his writings replaced discipline as the most important cohesive force in the army. Soldiers were urged to follow the example of certain heroes. These models were all young soldiers from poor families with limited education. Filled with a desire to help others and a hatred for imperialism and revisionism they had died heroically for their comrades and their country, their last thoughts being on Chairman Mao.

Mao is the Lenin and the Stalin of the Chinese Revolution and it is hardly surprising that a cult of Mao as the omniscient leader should have existed since the early 1940s. During Stalin's lifetime and the years immediately after the de-Stalinization of 1956 there were limitations to the height to which he could be exalted, but to nearly all Chinese Mao is, and has been for over twenty-five years, the personification of the Chinese Revolution and the new China. In 1959 his replacement by Liu Shao-ch'i as President – he remained Party Chairman – may have lessened his political power but it did not harm his prestige. In the early 1960s Lin Piao carried through his persistent campaign to promote Maoism in the army until by 1965 Mao had become a deity and his portraits and copies of his collected works were attributed with miraculous powers. The army itself was described as a 'great school for the study of the thought of Mao Tse-tung'.

THE REAPPRAISAL OF SOCIETY

The split between China and the Soviet Union and the increased understanding between the latter and the United States led Mao to reassess the nature of Soviet society. First it was considered revisionist and then bourgeois. Mao explained this retrogression as the action of 'a handful of people in authority who have taken the capitalist road'. According to him this handful was able to overthrow the whole of Soviet society because the Soviet Communist Party had so ossified that the lower ranks had blindly followed orders from above simply through the habit of 'slavish' obedience. Through their luxurious life the top bureaucrats had become susceptible to bourgeois ideas. These ideas were available from the bourgeois culture in which the 'new class' had immersed Soviet society. Chinese leaders maintain that as the rigidity of the Soviet system had stifled the creation of a new proletarian culture, the Soviet Union had been forced to rely on pre-revolutionary art and literature. This had perverted the elite and sapped the revolutionary spirit of the masses.

Mao's belief in a Soviet retrogression made him modify some of his theoretical views. He now saw that the inevitable flow of history in Marxist historical-materialism had more important undercurrents than he had previously imagined. This meant that for the first time it was now theoretically possible for the Chinese Revolution to be defeated. In Marxist terms the Soviet backsliding was the overthrow of a socialist economic base by a bourgeois social and cultural superstructure. Although Marx and Engels admitted exceptions, in Marxism as it is generally understood, it is the economic base that determines the superstructure not vice versa. In the 1950s the Chinese leaders believed that once a socialist economic base was established the revolution would be secure. In the mid 1960s they were no longer so certain.

In general Marxists tend to lay emphasis on the overriding importance of impersonal economic forces. However, throughout the history of the Chinese Communist movement there has been a strong tradition of voluntarism; that is, belief in the power of individual will and effort to triumph over military, economic and social obstacles. The analysis of the 'betrayal' of the Soviet Revolution has brought out the converse of this faith; that lack of spirit can lose everything. Thus even though the Chinese Revolution has destroyed pre-revolutionary society and private property there is an increased fear that a failure of willpower, encouraged by the persistence of bourgeois culture and the growth of a 'new class' alienated from the masses, can wreck all that has been achieved.

Aware of China's tradition of a mandarin bureaucracy totally divorced from the people Chinese Communists had been concerned about the danger of such an elite for a long time. This fear seems to have been the chief reason for the 'rectification' campaigns of 1942 and 1957. Both campaigns began with the free publication of criticisms of bureaucracy and the abuse of power. Investigations were made and meetings called at which officials were criticized and made self-criticisms. After five or six weeks the situation was reversed and many critics were attacked and punished as 'deviationists' or 'rightists'. The movements of 1942 and 1957 were only the most widespread and far-reaching; smaller campaigns of a similar kind have frequently been carried out in different parts of the country.

Through these campaigns and the process of criticism many more people have become involved in political activity. Officials and cadres were made more circumspect and aware of popular feelings. On the other hand cadres have become demoralized and sometimes unwilling to make decisions or take responsibility. To some extent official morale may have been restored by the later repression of many of the critics, but this in turn has made ordinary people afraid to express themselves and cynical about the whole process of rectification.

One of the most important elements in these campaigns has been the relationship between politics and culture. From 1935 literature was under the firm control of a minor writer and major bureaucrat, Chou Yang. However Chou's position has never gone unchallenged. The first attack came in 1935 from Lu Hsun, the greatest writer of Chinese prose in the 20th century, and his student Hu Feng. Lu Hsun died in 1936 but Hu Feng and others continued their criticisms. The critics were not unified and literary battles were fought on many different grounds; however some general lines can be traced. One argument was on the creation of a new culture. Chou Yang and the establishment took the position that the counter-revolutionary and offensively feudal elements in traditional painting, literature and drama should be removed but that the rest should be tolerated and developed in a socialist direction. In the fifties there appeared to be no danger in this as the Chinese Revolution was seen as irreversible and culture was only part of the non-essential superstructure. Chinese tradition was seen as a collection of museum pieces, attractive, interesting and satisfying to national pride but unable to affect society. As a stock upon which to graft new shoots it also had the great advantage of being familiar and understandable to the people. The critics tended to argue that traditional culture was an integral part of a corrupt society and that a totally new society should have a totally new culture.

An even more important division between Chou Yang and his antagonists was on the question of authority. Chou maintained that the 'proletarian discipline' of the Communist Party required artists to work within the guidelines set down at any given time by the Party. Hu Feng and the critics contended that the truly revolutionary artist must be free to look for the truth as he sees it.

It is difficult to describe this conflict as one between right and left or moderate and extremist and, although the analogy is crude, the least unsatisfactory description is that of a struggle between catholic and protestant. Chou Yang and the establishment relied on revolutionary faith but believed in the need for a hierarchy with which to amplify instructions from above and filter criticisms from below. Lu Hsun and the critics, the 'protestants', believed that the only effective discipline was spontaneous and that to achieve the new society the topmost authority and the lowest revolutionary artist should be in direct communication.

The division between 'protestant' and 'catholic' ties in very closely with that between the officials and the critics or 'revolutionary masses' in the Rectification campaigns of 1942 and 1957. The latter was part of the Hundred Flowers campaign launched with the slogan:

> Let a hundred flowers bloom
> Let a hundred schools of thought contend.

At the time this campaign was seen in the West as a short spell of liberal freedom introduced either because Mao saw the need for a safety valve in order to avoid 'a Chinese Hungary' or from a Machiavellian desire to expose anti-Communists. This interpretation was given plausibility by the Party authorities' denunciation of the critics as 'rightists' or 'counter-revolutionaries'. In fact the most influential and disturbing criticisms and protests were not demands for the restoration of capitalism but calls for the free expression of revolutionary ideas and attacks on bureaucracy, privilege, cynicism and apathy among officials. In many respects it was an attack by the young on the middle-aged and old or by passionate idealists on experienced and somewhat cynical realists.

The most convincing explanation of the Hundred Flowers movement, and the Cultural Revolution that followed it, is that they were attempts by some people in high authority to break up the log-jam of middle-aged officials, to encourage young militants to become involved in politics, and to create a new atmosphere of vitality. The great drawback to their case is that it is impossible to give freedom to revolutionary 'flowers' without tolerating some 'poisonous weeds', and it was on the grounds that it was essential to uproot the latter that the officials suppressed all dissidence and freedom of expression in late 1957.

'THE GREAT CULTURAL REVOLUTION'

The term 'the Great Cultural Revolution' was first used in the autumn of 1965 in connexion with public attacks on certain writers who were accused of having published bourgeois or revisionist pieces. The most important of these was a play called *Hai Jui Retires From Office*. It was written in 1960 by Wu Han, an eminent playwright and the Vice-Mayor of Peking. Hai Jui was a distinguished official under the Ming Dynasty who was dismissed and punished for his forthright criticisms of the decadent administration. In 1965 Hai Jui was seen as a cover for P'eng Te-huai, and Wu Han's play as an attack on Government policies, and Lin Piao's reform of the army in particular. The most curious aspect of the campaign against Wu Han and others was that it was not launched in the usual way by the Peking press but by the Army newspaper *Chieh-fang chün-pao* and the Shanghai journal *Wen-hui-pao*.

During the winter of 1965-6 this campaign was merged with a movement to reform all the arts. Now there was to be only one literature, a 'proletarian' literature. Models for the new form, were biographies of the young army heroes. Peking and other local operas were finally purged of their traditional aspects. New drama made up of scenes depicting revolutionary fervour and heroic self-sacrifice all under the inspiration of Mao Tse-tung were performed instead. The Cultural Revolution also spread to the universities where many professors and other specialists were criticized, and denounced for their bourgeois and 'objective' – non-revolutionary – attitudes.

In May 1966, after an absence of several months in which there had been considerable speculation about his health, Mao Tse-tung was seen in public. Soon after this it became clear that the 'Cultural Revolution' was not purely cultural. It also became evident why initiative had come from the army, and from Shanghai rather than Peking, when the Communist Party leadership of the *People's Daily*, Peking University and Peking municipality were removed from office and denounced. Most of the men dismissed were not intellectuals with possible liberal tendencies but veterans of the Party organization. The First Secretary of the Peking Party, P'eng Chen, was one of the ten most powerful men in China, and his fall was made even more startling by hints that someone still more important was involved.

In China when official bodies are dismissed or suspended it is usual to replace them with 'work teams' – *ad hoc* groups of Party members brought in from elsewhere. To begin with this is what happened in 1966. However during that summer the pattern changed, and from within the institutions themselves new 'revolutionary' organizations emerged or were encouraged to emerge to take control.

In June the whole educational establishment was overthrown. Examinations were abolished and all academic studies were suspended in order to have time in which to create a totally new 'proletarian education'. Initially this was to be for six months but in fact students did not begin to return to work until the autumn of 1967. The students' time was now used to carry through the Cultural Revolution. People wearing smart clothes or with 'decadent' hairstyles were jeered at or attacked, old street signs were removed, statues and paintings were destroyed or covered with slogans, academics were denounced and persecuted – several committed suicide – houses were searched for bourgeois property: gold, jewels, embroidery, elegant furniture, books and so on. These were seized, some objects being destroyed and others being stored away in public buildings. Traditional culture had to be totally eradicated, as the Soviet example had shown that it could be used as the launching pad for a bourgeois restoration.

In July 1966 the Minister of Propaganda and his subordinate Chou Yang, the watchdog of literature, were dismissed and denounced as revisionists. At the same time Chou's old enemy Lu Hsun was proclaimed a 'pioneer of the Cultural Revolution' and Lu Hsun's firm stand for his own beliefs even when ordered to change them was raised as a model for all 'revolutionaries'. This change made clear the belief of Mao and his group that a proletarian culture capable of replacing the bourgeois one was only possible, if one allowed 'true revolutionaries' freedom of expression.

That same month the Communist Party Youth League was dissolved and new 'revolutionary' groups, most notably the Red Guards, took its place. The first group using the name Red Guards was formed in a Peking University early in June, but for some time it was not known whether or not it had higher approval. Nevertheless groups of Red Guards sprang up all over China and in August 1966 their position was confirmed when Mao Tse-tung himself put on a Red Guard armband. In many areas Red Guards and other 'revolutionary' groups began to hold meetings and to put up posters attacking local government and party officials. In this and in the fact that they were almost entirely made up of students and school children the new organizations closely resembled the 'rightist' groups of 1957, and many party officials acted accordingly. In some cities student agitation was suppressed by force but as it became clearer that the movement had higher backing local officials increasingly tried to create their own 'revolutionary' organizations to counter the attacks made upon them.

The situation was made still more confused by the fact that each institution formed its own 'revolutionary' group or groups. There were verbal and sometimes physical conflicts between students from different schools and even within institutions distinct and often hostile groups clashed on such matters as the degree to which local officials should be criticized. Mao and the small group around him, most notably Lin Piao, Mao's secretary Ch'en Po-ta and Mao's wife Chiang Ching who had never played any public role before 1965, now formed a semi-official 'Cultural Revolution Group'. The Group appears to have welcomed the widespread confusion as a proof of 'revolutionary' vitality. However in order to uncover false 'revolutionary' groups and to increase involvement and enthusiasm students were given free railway passes to travel round China to 'exchange revolutionary experience'. Despite some official harassment so many students took this opportunity that the national transport system was seriously affected and in the autumn of 1966 students were encouraged to travel on foot. The result of these mass migrations was to convince hundreds of thousands of students that Mao was behind the 'revolutionary' movement and that they really were expected to challenge all authority.

The mood that no one – of course excepting Mao himself – should be spared was strengthened as it became increasingly evident that 'the No. 1 person in authority taking the Capitalist Road' was Liu Shao-ch'i, the President of China.

Liu Shao-ch'i fell from number two in the hierarchy to number eight in August shortly after a plenary session of the Central Committee of the Communist Party. This plenum, the first to be held for four years, was the scene of a crucial power struggle which ended with victory for Mao and Lin Piao and legitimation for the Cultural Revolution. However even before the meeting Mao sent out directives to local parties. These were very much in the spirit of the Great Leap Forward. They were instructions for the de-centralization of power and the resolution of the 'major contradictions' of Chinese society. Industry was to be moved to the countryside and the towns were to produce their own crops. Workers were to become peasants and peasants workers, intellectuals were to work with their hands and toilers were to become 'proletarian intellectuals'. A convincing explanation of this attempt to return to guerrilla Communism was that it provided a way in which China could survive American bombing of her centres of communication.

This movement for an integrated society without divisions was part and parcel of the Cultural Revolution. Throughout the autumn of 1966 there were attempts to extend the 'Revolution' from educational institutions into industry. Students went to the factories and 'revolutionary' groups were set up to criticize authority. However in China as in the rest of the under-developed world industrial workers are a privileged elite with a vested interest in stability and the *status quo*. In 1957 they protected Party officials from 'rightist' students, and in 1966 they continued to resent student interference and disturbance. In October and November there were severe clashes involving serious bloodshed between groups of workers and students, in Canton, Shanghai, Nanking, Sian and several other cities.

By the end of 1966 China had been in confusion for twelve months and in chaos for six. All over the country young people were marching up and down chanting from the works of Mao and waving the little red book of his quotations as a talisman. Education had ceased and the cultural establishment was totally destroyed. Nevertheless in some ways the turmoil was only theatrical, agriculture was very little affected and exports of industrial goods were not significantly down. Many political leaders disappeared from public view and virtually every figure in Chinese life had been under some form of attack. Even so a surprisingly large number still held their posts, if only nominally. Liu Shao-ch'i, though denounced as 'China's Khrushchev', remained President of China.

1967 started with the 'January Revolution', when 'revolutionary' organizations overthrew the Shanghai Municipal Party and established a 'revolutionary' administration. Party officials were accused of having sabotaged the Cultural Revolution by attempting to bribe the workers. It is very likely that officials, trying to maintain order and consolidate support, did in fact increase wages. This was condemned by the Cultural Revolutionaries as imitation of the Soviet revisionist policy of material incentives as opposed to the political incentives advocated in China. In the early spring of 1967 political propaganda, especially the Thought of Mao Tse-tung, was used to try to involve the workers in the Cultural Revolution. The immediate result of this was a wave of strikes in factories, docks and railways which lasted until March.

At the same time plans went ahead for a consolidation. Revolutionary groups were urged to form 'revolutionary alliances', preferably 'triple alliances' consisting of the militia, the students, and the workers in any institution. Revolutionaries were also called upon to overthrow the 'capitalists in command' and to follow Mao's statement that: 'In the last analysis all the truths of Marxism can be summed up in the one sentence, "to rebel is justified".' Certain provincial governments were overthrown during 1967, but response was patchy, and by the end of the year only one out of the twenty-nine administrative regions was ruled by 'revolutionary committees'. and in some of the richest and most strategic provinces the administration remains unscathed.

Many 'revolutionaries' found it difficult to tell whether or not the experienced Communists who ran the locality were 'capitalist roaders', but in Hong Kong, unlike the rest of China, would-be rebels could have no doubts. Young militants there began agitation in a situation of great social inequality and tension made worse by the end of the building boom and a temporary failure in business confidence. In May 1967 economic strikes, followed by lockouts, turned into political demonstrations. Baton charges made by the unpopular police were widely believed to have been unnecessarily brutal. Tension mounted; there were widespread restrictions and curfews. Bombs were thrown, police raided Communist schools and publishing houses, and large numbers of militants were arrested in extremely harsh conditions.

The Chinese Government which gains a very large part of its foreign exchange through Hong Kong had every reason to maintain the delicate balance of power in the colony, and there is no evidence to suggest that it deliberately started the agitation. Nevertheless once the conflict had begun the Government was obliged to support the militants. Protests were made and there were demonstrations against the British Consulate in Shanghai. The office of the Chargé d'Affaires in Peking was broken into and British diplomats were assaulted and severely restricted in their movements. Reciprocal measures against Chinese diplomats in London resulted in a fight with the police outside the Chinese Embassy in Portland Place.

China's relations with other countries also deteriorated. In January 1967 Russian Embassy staff and their families were attacked by Red Guards. In July the Chinese Government gave moral support to Burmese Communist guerrillas for the first time. Chinese experts were withdrawn and exchanges with the Ne Win Government degenerated into a series of angry notes. China encouraged peasant revolts in India and in October 1967 there were skirmishes along the frontier. China also had differences with Mongolia, Ceylon, Nepal and for a while with Cambodia.

STABILIZATION

In July an attempt was made to resume school classes, but students did not begin to return until the autumn. Meanwhile the Cultural Revolution continued, with increasing emphasis on the importance of imitating the army and relying upon it to settle local disputes. In general the army seems to have restrained violence in the struggles that took place as 'revolutionary' groups fought among themselves or challenged Party leaders. In August the authorities in Wuhan detained two important leaders of the Cultural Revolution, who seem to have been released only by the personal intervention of Chou En-lai. In September Mao toured large areas of China, though not the whole country by any means, and declared that 'the situation was unprecedentedly good'. In fact the autumn of 1967 was relatively calm. The need for experienced administrators was admitted and emphasis was now put upon the rehabilitation of officials or cadres who had confessed their mistakes. There were condemnations of 'anarchism' and 'reckless criticism' and a new 'triple alliance' of the masses, the army and the cadres was recommended.

Even though there is a temporary lull the line dividing the forces involved is relatively clear and, as in the case of the literary struggle between Chou Yang and the critics, perhaps the least bad description of the two factions is of Liu Shao-ch'i and the officials as 'catholics' and

Mao and the Cultural Revolutionaries as 'protestants'. No one in China shouts 'down with Mao' or 'up with Liu'; everyone is more Maoist than thou. In fact it was Liu Shao-ch'i who created the Maoist cult, and the accusations that Liu is in any way right-wing are absurd. Both he and P'eng Chen were known for their extreme anti-imperialism. Where Liu differs from the Cultural Revolutionaries is in his emphasis on Party organization and on the total obedience of the lower ranks to higher orders. He and his supporters argue that 'proletarian discipline' and respect for revolutionary experience are what distinguish Marxism-Leninism from petty bourgeois populism or anarchism. They also maintain that industrialization requires rational planning that can only be carried out by the Party and Government.

Mao and the Cultural Revolutionaries could be called the 'protestants'. They want to destroy all hierarchies that fetter enthusiasm and separate the individual from the supreme being. For them all men are equal before Mao; if the youngest student or the simplest soldier reads Mao's works with an honest heart he should be considered as good as any high official with decades of revolutionary experience. Unless it came from Mao himself every order should be discussed, questioned and if necessary challenged. They argue that if this had been done in the Soviet Union the revisionists could never have succeeded. Rather in the way that freedom in Cromwellian England was reserved for the 'godly', in China it is restricted to the truly revolutionary. But this does not make the 'freedom' meaningless. Obedience to Mao's necessarily general and vague utterances allows much more scope than party directives that are amplified and made more precise as they pass down the hierarchy. Thus the aim of the Cultural Revolution is to create a society without specialization or divisions, not bound together by laws or institutions but united by a common goal, and a common faith in Mao Tse-tung.

Predictions at this point are extremely hazardous, but it would seem likely that after incorporating considerable numbers of the young militants who have emerged during the past two years the Communist Party will re-establish some sort of control. However the Cultural Revolution and the rectification campaigns that will undoubtedly come in the future will prevent the evolution of anything like a Stalinist Party. Whether or not the mass enthusiasm of the Cultural Revolution and its disdain for material and technical questions will be able to solve China's vast economic problems is another matter.

BIBLIOGRAPHY

Hans Granquist. *The Red Guard, A Report on Mao's Revolution.* (Praeger, New York, 1967.)

Jack Gray and Patrick Cavendish. *Chinese Communism in Crisis: Maoism and the Cultural Revolution.* (Praeger, New York, 1968.)

R. J. Lifton, *Revolutionary Immortality: Mao Tse-tung and the Cultural Revolution.* (Vintage Books, New York, 1968.)

THE CHINESE LAND FRONTIER

George N. Patterson

INTRODUCTION

THE vast, sparsely inhabited regions of China's land frontier, although linked many times in many centuries, were not truly integrated into the national life of China until the Chinese Communist military and political conquests of the country in the mid twentieth century. The clearly delineated boundaries drawn by the cartographers have more frequently than not been misleading, for in the mountains, deserts and steppes local chieftains and local loyalties have been far more important than national leaders and national loyalties.

China's long land frontiers run with twelve independent or protected States: Korea, the Mongolian People's Republic, the Soviet Union, Afghanistan, Pakistan, India, Nepal, Sikkim, Bhutan, Burma, Laos, Vietnam; plus the colonial territories of Macao and Hong Kong.

The Sino-Mongolian-Soviet border itself is about 4,000 miles long, roughly the same length as the frontier between Canada and the United States. Since the 17th century these areas have been an arena of see-saw conflict between China and Russia, and fifteen years after taking power in Peking, the Chinese Communists threatened once again to open the controversy. In addition, China has had border disputes and discussions with Tibet, Nepal, India, Burma, Pakistan and Afghanistan.

On 8 March 1963, the world was informed by all Peking news media that it was Communist China's intention to raise the question of the territories lost to Russia, as well as those lands lost to all other colonialist and imperialist powers. *China's claim amounted to over one million square miles of territory held at the time by the Soviet Union and certain other powers.* The situation in the disputed borders and territories is as follows.

KOREA

Korea – or 'Choson' to the Koreans, 'Chosen' to the Japanese – is a peninsula, with a broad mainland base. The mountainous east coast of the country borders the Sea of Japan, and the west coast borders the Yellow Sea. The northern land boundary, running from the north-east to south-west, separates, to a small extent, Korea from Russia and to a larger extent, Korea from Manchuria. The maximum north-south and east-west distances are about 450 and 170 miles respectively.

In the external relations of Korea, China and Japan played a larger part than Russia, whose interest only became strong in the late 19th century. The Japanese defeat of China in 1895, and of Russia in 1905, preceded the declaration of a Japanese protectorate over Korea in the latter year; annexation followed in 1910. But from the 17th century China had been claiming some sort of suzerainty over Korea. In the late 19th century the Chinese attitude was stated to be that 'in all that concerns Korea, the one point to start from is that Korea is China's tributary, and that China *will not only* fight anybody rather than give up her suzerainty, but will be forced to absorb Korea if troublesome scheming goes on there'. In the Treaty of Shimonoseki of 1895, however, China 'recognized definitely the full and complete independence and autonomy of Korea' together with the other provisions.

Nevertheless, over the decades which followed, conflicting ambitions inevitably led to incidents on the borders where the competing Japanese and Russian imperialisms met. These incidents increased in both numbers and intensity following the consolidation of the Bolshevik regime in Russia. The most serious of these was the 'Changfukeng Incident', which became known to the public in July 1938 when the Japanese Ambassador in Moscow demanded the withdrawal of Soviet troops from positions on the heights west of Lake Hasan near the juncture of Manchuria (then a puppet Japanese state), Korea and the Soviet Maritime Province. The Soviet Union rejected the demand, basing her position on maps published in 1886. On 31 July fighting broke out, and heavy artillery, tanks and even planes were used. A truce was finally negotiated to go into effect on 10 August and the fighting ceased. Russian losses were estimated at 300 dead and 600 wounded, while Japanese losses were reported in the press to be still higher.

Despite border incidents such as this and the general deterioration of Russo-Japanese relations during the Second World War, the Japanese continued to hold Korea with a minimum of Russian opposition until the closing days of the war in the Pacific. Ethnically Korean guerrilla forces under the then unknown leader Kim Il-Song (who had Russian citizenship) were trained by the Soviets, which allowed them to operate from bases on Russian soil.

After the Korean War of 1950–53, rivalry developed between Russia and China for influence over North Korea. China's troops had been relatively well disciplined and had established good relations with the citizens. Further, the Korean Communist leaders were well aware of the fact that it was the Chinese, and not the Russians, who had risked everything to keep North Korea Communist. Finally, in recent years Chinese economic assistance and technical aid to North Korea appears to have been more important than Russian aid, despite the problems faced by Peking. And while Korea has a common border with both countries, Peking is near and Moscow is far away. While North Korea tries to maintain a formal position of non-alignment in the Sino-Soviet dispute, she seems, like China, to regard the Soviet line as 'soft' and prefers the hard-line policies of China.

MANCHURIA

Manchuria – or 'the North-East', as it is now called by the Communist rulers in Peking – is the richest and most strategic of China's border-lands. It is situated in the north-eastern part of China, cut off from the eighteen provinces by the Great Wall.

During the Manchu period of Chinese history the Manchus restricted Chinese migration into their lands beyond the Great Wall, the original kingdom of the Manchu Dynasty, because they feared that the ensuing Chinese flood would overwhelm the native population. The Han Chinese were thus excluded from colonizing Manchuria as they had done in other parts. Manchuria included a total area of 365,000 square miles and, despite the severity of extremely cold winters and hot summers, was a most productive country. In addition to its tremendous agricultural productivity it was rich in timber and minerals, including coal, iron and gold. By 1900 the Manchu policy of keeping the Chinese south of the Wall had broken down and settlers had flooded in to reduce the Manchus to a minority. The economic development of the country is due, to a large extent, to the industry of those early Chinese immigrants. From almost every point of view, therefore, Manchuria became as much a part of China as the eighteen provinces south of the Wall.

By the late 17th century a common frontier had been established between China and Russia and this required an agreement regulating trade, so China made her first modern treaty with a Western State in 1689 with Russia. The successful Russian advance against weak semi-barbarian tribes was brought to a halt in Manchuria, and the Manchus signalized their success with the signing of the Treaty of Nerchinsk.

Treaty of Nerchinsk

This treaty was signed in unpropitious circumstances. It followed a period of several months' fluctuating fighting between Russian and Chinese troops. When peaceful negotiations were proposed the Chinese delegation arrived on the scene with an assemblage of some ten thousand men, which led the Russians to claim that the Chinese had come to make war and not to seek peace. Their fears were not unfounded for when Russia proved intractable over certain issues the Chinese leader of the delegation overtly deployed troops to make his point.

The Russians backed down, and the Treaty of Nerchinsk was signed in Manchu, Russian and Latin – with the Latin text being accepted as the official version – on 7 September 1689. The treaty consisted of six articles, the salient features of which were: the western boundary was to be the River Aigun; the northern boundary to commence at the River Gorbitsa and to extend to the sea of Okhotsk so that all the southern slopes of the Stanovoi mountains with the rivers flowing towards them from the Amur were to belong to the Chinese, and all the northern slopes with the rivers flowing north to belong to the Russians. Furthermore, all the Russian towns on the south of the River Aigun were to be removed to the north bank. The Russians were not permitted to navigate the Amur, and Albazin was to be destroyed. (The city of Albazin has been a constant source of friction between Russia and China since the 17th century when Russian troops first occupied it in reprisal against Chinese activities, then China laid siege to the city for some years.) Finally, commercial relations were to be restored and receive official protection from both countries. The Treaty of Nerchinsk was supplemented by that of Kiakhta in 1727, which delimited the Russo-Manchuria border westwards from the Aigun to the Sayan mountains, south of Lake Baikal.

The Treaty of Nerchinsk, the first that any Chinese emperor had signed with a foreign power, was observed until 1858. For more than 150 years the frontier between China and Russia was peaceful and without incident. Russia colonized the lands lying west of the Amur, while China made no further demands on the natives of the Amur except the customary tributes exacted every year. In 1846, however, the Russian Tsar, Nicholas I, ordered an investigation of the whole Amur as well as the adjacent territory to be made, and in 1847 he appointed Nicholas Muraviev as Governor-General of eastern Siberia. Muraviev was young, percipient and ruthless, and quietly noting China's plight in face of increasing foreign encroachments he sent many expeditions to what

181

became known later as the Maritime Province, as well as armed fleets up and down the Amur. This was contrary to treaty rights but the Chinese had no power to enforce them.

Treaty of Aigun

Muraviev paid little attention to treaty rights. When the Crimean War of 1854 weakened Russia's power in Europe it gave the ambitious Muraviev the opportunity he wanted to consolidate Russian power on the Pacific coast. On 16 May 1858, Muraviev, taking swift advantage of the chaos in China as a result of the wars with Britain and France, and the devasting effects of the Taiping Rebellion, compelled Prince Yishau, Commander-in-Chief of the Chinese Forces of the Amur, to sign what is known as the Treaty of Aigun. This military treaty set down in black and white what China had been obliged to permit through weakness, the surrender to Russia of all the territory on the left bank of the Amur, while the territory on the right bank as far downstream as the Ussuri was to be recognized as Chinese; the territory between the Ussuri and the sea was to be left undecided until a future date. Further, it insisted on the liberty of Russians to sail along the Amur and trade on both banks. This treaty, considered one of the most humiliating in Chinese history, secured for Russia a territory almost as large as France without any bloodshed. By an additional agreement in 1860, the territory east of the Ussuri was also brought within the Russian Empire, and Russia had extended her borders to the Pacific, the Korean border and the port of Vladivostok.

Treaties of Tientsin and Peking

At a critical time in her history, with widespread chaos caused by the wars with Britain and France, China was anxious to preserve normal relations with Russia. The opening of the five ports by the Treaty of Nanking, signed in 1842 and omitting Russia, had given fresh impetus to Russian expansionist ambitions, and China hoped to placate her by signing a fresh treaty. The Treaty of Tientsin was duly signed on 14 June 1858, and the five ports were opened to Russian trade as well. The treaty, however, while basically the same as the unequal treaties signed with other Western powers, gave Russia privileges which made Sino-Russian relations no longer those existing between equal powers, since it was almost completely a one-sided affair. Less than two years later, while China was again involved with Britain and France and the Taiping rebellion, Russia threatened to send the Russian fleet to Peitang if China refused to ratify the Treaty of Aigun, and also to cede the Trans-Ussuri, the Maritime Province of Primorsk. China had no alternative but to accede to the Russian demands and on 14 November 1860, the Treaty of Peking was signed in confirmation and elaboration of the Treaty of Aigun and the Treaty of Tientsin, reaffirming that the Amur should remain the frontier between China and Russia. In this way the Manchu Empire lost 400,000 square miles of territory.

While this was going on, hundreds of thousands of Chinese, because of the wars and famine, began the long trek to Manchuria where there was reported to be so much virgin soil waiting for hard-working peasants, and what beleaguered Chinese officials were losing at the negotiating tables the starving Chinese people were beginning to win back by sheer force of numbers in the fields and cities.

Treaty of Shimonoseki

Within a few years China was also involved in war with Japan, and in 1895 the Sino-Japanese war ended in China's ignominious defeat.

In 1895 a peace treaty was signed between China and Japan at Shimonoseki, in which China recognized definitely the full independence and autonomy of Korea. She was also forced to 'cede to Japan in perpetuity and full sovereignty (a) that part of Manchuria lying east of the River Liao (Liaotung) and south of a line from the junction of the River Anping and Yalu, by Fenghwang-cheng and Haichang, to Yingkow. . . .' The treaty advanced the Japanese position to that of equality of privilege with other Western states competing for interest in China but still did not leave her a primary force in the Far East.

But with the signing of this treaty Russia realized that her position in Asia would be jeopardized, or, at least, prejudiced, should Liaotung be turned over to the Japanese. Russia, with the help of the other powers, made a strong representation to Japan advising her to return Liaotung to China and accept a large sum as indemnity instead, and Japan was compelled to accept the offer.

Treaty of Alliance

Russian development in Manchuria went ahead rapidly under the able supervision of a Russian diplomat-economist, Count Sergei Witte. Witte's ambitions in Manchuria were mainly concerned with colonization and economic development. He advocated that Manchuria itself would repay any expenditure incurred by Russia, especially in his proposal for a projected railway to Vladivostok. Witte used the occasion of the coronation of Nicholas II as a wonderful opportunity to get China's elder statesman of that time, Li Hung-chang, to St Petersburg to discuss the project. Li Hung-chang at first objected but later agreed to the proposal. He telegraphed to Peking that he favoured the scheme, and stated that the building of the railway was beyond China's financial capacity, but if the concession were given to the Russo-Chinese Bank of Shanghai, China could secure the right of control and no difficulties would arise. Witte also insisted upon building a branch line to a seaport in south Manchuria, but while Li agreed to this, he stipulated that the branch line should be of standard gauge. Li also insisted that the contract must be with a private corporation.

The 'Secret Treaty of Alliance', as it was called, was then signed by Li, but the final text was not agreed upon until June 1896, and ratified by the Manchu Government on 26 August 1896.

RUSSO-JAPANESE WAR

One of the chief reasons for Russia's insistence on the return of Liaotung, in addition to her desire to limit Japanese expansion, was that she coveted this territory for herself. Having established Vladivostok as her naval base in the Far East she found that it had the same limitations as St Petersburg with its winter freeze-up. But at the southern tip of the Liaotung Peninsula were twin harbours – Port Arthur and Dairen-wan – admirably suited to serve as naval and commercial ports respectively. Russia requested the lease of the two harbours for a period of twenty-five years and a Convention was signed on 27 March 1898. This brought on a rush of demands by the other competing powers and Germany acquired Kiaochow, France seized Kwangchow-wan, and Britain secured the lease of Wei-hai-wei to maintain a balance of power at the expense of China. The lease of Port Arthur and Dairen to Russia, and her further intrusion into southern Manchuria, finally led to the Russo-Japanese war in 1904 through which Japan, by an overwhelming victory, recovered her lost influence in Manchuria. This part of the frontier continued to be the subject of negotiation until after the Communist revolution in China.

The 1950 Treaty of Friendship and Alliance

On 16 December 1949 Mao Tse-tung, Chairman of the newly proclaimed People's Republic of China, himself headed the first delegation to Moscow and personally conducted the ensuing discussions with Stalin. No details of the negotiations were made public but in a US State Department information release the conclusion reached was that the

Soviet Union, by obtaining control of the railways, by its military occupation of Dairen and Port Arthur and by its domination of industry and transportation, had 'placed the richest industrial area of China firmly behind the Far Eastern segment of the Iron Curtain'. But these provisions were very soon modified in China's favour.

SINKIANG

China and Russia meet in the Pamirs, a tangled knot of rugged peaks of 16,000 to 18,000 feet lying north of Kashmir and east of Afghanistan. Here Sinkiang adjoins the Tadzhik SSR and the boundary runs first northward into the Trans-Alay Range, then eastward into the Tien Shan. The Tien Shan, which cross Central Asia from east to west, extend for nearly 2,000 miles and divide the prairies of Sinkiang into two distinct halves.

The Tien Shan Range, together with the Pamirs and Kun Lun, were historically natural boundaries between Russia and China at the western end of their borders. The rich valleys of Dzungaria and the oases of southern Sinkiang attracted the nomad tribes roaming Central Asia in search of grazing lands. These tribes were seldom completely independent, and usually acknowledged the vague sovereignty of a more powerful nomadic people such as Huns, Turks and Mongols and paid tribute to powerful sedentary states such as China. The movement of these nomads meant a shifting of loyalties as they came under the shadow of one or another power.

About the middle of the 18th century the Kazakhs, a Turkic-Mongol nomad people, broke away from the Uzbeks and established themselves in the vast region stretching from the Pamirs and the Caspian Sea to the Russian steppes. The Kazakhs were divided into two groups, one falling under Russian influence and the other acknowledging Chinese superiority. On the basis of this relationship, Chinese territorial control was taken as extending westward beyond Lake Balkash nearly to the Aral Sea, and northward into the Upper Irtysh Valley to a point midway between Lake Zaisan and the present-day Semipalatinsk.

In 1741 the eastern Kazakhs came under internal Russian rule. Accustomed to plundering the settled communities as they moved from place to place, the Kazakhs had created a mounting antagonism among the local population in Turkestan, among them the Chinese officials, merchants and the families of garrison troops. To control these areas the Chinese placed pickets in certain places to limit the Kazakhs' use of pasturage. The controlled areas were in the lower Ili

Valley, the Dzungarian Gate and the northern and southern reaches of Lake Zaisan. The Kazakhs were permitted within the picket lines during the winter months, but were forced out again in the summer. The pickets were of two types; moveable watch towers placed on the extreme frontier and permanent pickets located near the towers. As sentries were withdrawn from the lonely outposts on the border and moved back to the Chinese towns, the pickets naturally contracted to the disadvantage of the Chinese claims. At the same time, the Russians began to assume more and more the mantle of protectors of the Kazakhs and to press claims to the pasture-lands as Kazakh – and therefore Russian – territory.

By 1759 Chinese troops had penetrated to Somotosh in the Alichur Pamir (now a part of the Soviet Union) and Russian historians and military leaders began to call attention to the military significance of the Ili Valley. The point was driven home a few years later in 1791 when a Chinese military expedition pushed Kalmuk tribesmen across the frontier and deep into Russian territory. Beginning in the early part of the 19th century, therefore, Moscow began sending troops into the area to 'regulate the affairs' of the Central Asian nomads and to control the strategic caravan routes. The Kuldja Treaty of 1851 opened the Ili Valley and Tarbagatao to Russian trade, and permitted Russians to reside in the area. This treaty was the outcome of negotiations between Tsarist Government officials and local leaders in the Kuldja region.

The Kuldja Treaty was followed very quickly by the Treaty of Tarbagatai (1864) which recognized Russian sovereignty over the Tien Shan region to the south of Lake Zssyk-Kul.

THE ILI PROBLEM

The Ili problem began when a Muslim rebellion broke out in Dzungaria and the Manchus were expelled from Urumchi. Inspired by the successes in the northern part of the province, similar uprisings took place in the Tarim basin, where a Uighur general named Yakub Beg seized control of Kashgar and the major oases. Moving north, Yakub Beg then defeated the leaders of the Dzungarian revolt and set up a separate state which included almost the whole of Sinkiang. The new regime was given qualified recognition by Russia and also by the British and Turkish Governments, both of which doubtless welcomed a development which might, presumably, lead to the establishment of a counterweight to the growing Russian power in Central Asia. Thus encouraged,

Yakub Beg began intriguing among the tribes north of the Tien Shan – implying a threat to Ili. The reaction of Kaufmann, the forceful Governor of the Turkestan Oblast, was swift. Acting independently of St Petersburg, he dispatched a Russian military force to occupy the entire Ili district as far as Kuldja. The Russian Foreign Office informed Peking that this was merely a temporary move, and that the Russian troops would be withdrawn when the Chinese proved themselves able to maintain order in the region.

The Chinese, now fully aware that all Central Asia might be lost to them, were not slow in taking counter-measures. Tso Tsung-t'ang, the Viceroy of Shensi and Kansu, who had distinguished himself during the Taiping Rebellion, was dispatched to crush Yakub Beg and restore Imperial control. Tso moved with the same sure thoroughness that he had demonstrated in dealing with the Taipings. By the end of 1877 Yakub Beg was dead, and all the major cities of the region – except those occupied by the Russians – were once again under effective Chinese rule.

In July 1878 Peking informed Russia that order had been restored and that China was in a position to take over the administration of the Ili district. Russia replied that the restoration of Ili could not be considered singly, but rather must be taken up in conjunction with the settlement of 'other outstanding issues' between the two states. After a period of protracted negotiation, a treaty was signed, on 2 October 1879, at Livadia on the Black Sea, where the Tsar was on holiday.

The Livadia Treaty required the Chinese to cede to Russia the city of Kuldja, together with the Tekkes Valley and the passes controlling Central Asian access to the Tarim Basin. The balance of the territory in the Ili district occupied by Russia was to be evacuated upon payment by the Chinese of an indemnity of 5 million gold roubles 'to cover the expenses of the Russian occupation'. In addition, a further seventeen articles regulated Sino-Russian trade in the region, usually to the advantage of the Russians, and Russian consulates were to be opened in seven cities.

The details of the treaty gave rise to amazement in Europe and caused consternation in China. It was pointed out that, if ratified, all western China would be left open to Russian military occupation. On his return to Peking in January 1880, Ch'ung-hou, the Manchu plenipotentiary, was arrested and imprisoned, and the treaty was formally denounced by the Manchu Government. The Chinese attitude was further stiffened by the encouragement of several of the European powers, notably Britain, who had no desire to see the Ch'ing dynasty collapse completely, or to have the Russians assume so powerful a position in Central Asia. Both Russians and Chinese now began to increase their troops in the Ili area, and the Chinese once again demanded that Kuldja be returned to Chinese administration. Fresh diplomatic negotiations forestalled direct military action however, and on 24 February 1881 the Treaty of St Petersburg was signed.

The Treaty of St Petersburg represented something of an improvement for the Chinese. By its terms, China regained Kuldja and the Takkes Valley, including the passes into southern Sinkiang, but gave up the western Ili lands between the Ala Tau Range and the river, as well as the area east of Lake Zaisan, between the Irtysh and the Altai Mountains. In addition, the Chinese were forced to pay an indemnity of 9 million gold roubles and to consent to the opening of two Russian consulates in the region. Though onerous, the terms seemed the best that a weak China could hope for, and the treaty was duly ratified.

SINKIANG IN THE MODERN PERIOD

Following the overthrow of the Manchu dynasty in 1911, it seemed quite probable that most of Sinkiang would become an appendage of Tsarist Russia. Central Chinese power all but disappeared from the region, leaving a confused and confusing assemblage of local khans, emirs and minor potentates. The Russian population of the area was growing, and the Russian consuls, in that day of general extra-territoriality, exercised more and more the power of local governors. Evidence exists that Moscow seriously considered the outright annexation of the entire Dzungarian region, including the approaches to the Tarim Basin oases (which, however, would be left to China). These plans were frustrated by the First World War and by the Bolshevik Revolution. In the chaotic days that followed, revolts of varying duration and degree broke out in Russian Central Asia: the Kirghiz population rose in 1916 against Tsarist military conscription, while in 1920–21 the Soviet government had to send a military force under General Frunze to put down uprisings inspired by the Turkish nationalist, Enver Pasha.

Soviet control over their Central Asian lands was not generally re-established until 1923. In the following year agreement between Moscow and Peking led to an exchange of consuls. The Chinese opened offices in Tashkent and four other cities, while the Russians opened consulates in Urumchi, Altai, Chuguchak, Kuldja and Kashgar. As a result, Russian influence in Sinkiang increased once again.

Theatres and libraries were established by the Soviets as adjuncts of their consular offices, and quickly became centres of Russian propaganda among the native people of the area. By the early 1930s most of Sinkiang's foreign trade was in Russian hands, economic exploitation being materially assisted by the completion in 1930 of the Turkestan–Siberian Railway running south from Semipalatinsk to Alma-Ata.

Soviet economic control was soon followed by outright political control. In 1931, faced with a major revolt of Chinese Muslims (Dungans), the Chinese Governor called upon the Soviet Union for assistance. The revolt was soon quelled and in return the Soviet–Sinkiang Trading Agency, Sovsintorg, was established in eight key centres of the Province and given the right to exploit Sinkiang's mineral wealth. Small detachments of Red Army troops remained also. Two years later, in 1934, a still larger Muslim uprising took place under an adventurous cavalry leader, Ma Hung-kwei, this time directed against the new Chinese Governor, General Sheng Shih-ts'ai. Himself a Communist sympathizer and unable to secure assistance from the central Government, Sheng invited massive Russian intervention. By the end of the year, Sinkiang had become a Soviet puppet state ruled ostensibly by a Chinese Governor but in actual fact by the Soviet Consul-General at Urumchi. Further revolts in 1936 and 1937 served only to strengthen Russian control by emphasizing that Sheng could not hope to survive without the assistance of his Soviet allies. The uprisings were put down by the Soviet troops with great brutality.

Russia's increasing involvement with Nazi Germany in the early forties, to which the climax was Hitler's invasion in 1941, meant a distinct diminution in the level of Soviet support for Sheng. Aware that outside assistance from some quarter was essential if he was to continue as Governor, Sheng entered into secret negotiations with the Nationalist Government at Nanking, and finally, in 1943, after the withdrawal of the Soviet troops to fight on the German front, Sheng expelled his Russian advisers and openly embraced the Nationalist cause. Local Communists were ruthlessly suppressed, and Mao Tse-tung's brother, who had been the provincial Minister of Finance, was executed. Otherwise occupied, there was little the Soviet Union could do at the time. In late 1944, however, after the tide had clearly turned in the West, a new series of Muslim revolts broke out, encouraged and equipped by Moscow. By late November 1944 a large part of the Ili Valley from Altai to Manass was under rebel control and an 'East Turkestan Republic' was proclaimed. With the Soviets acting as mediators, the Nationalists were forced to acknowledge the local autonomy of the Ili district and to give their pledge not to send troops into the area, in return for the dissidents' recognition of Nanking's overall sovereignty.

THE CHINESE COMMUNISTS

Although units of the People's Liberation Army did not reach Kashgar in Western Sinkiang or the more remote regions of Northern Sinkiang until the mid 1950s, a Chinese Communist provincial Government was established in December 1949. The Russians tried to maintain their special position in Sinkiang to the last, and the Soviet Consul-General in Urumchi attempted to persuade the last Nationalist Provincial Governor, General T'ao Shih-yueh, to declare Sinkiang independent, on the precedent of Outer Mongolia; in which case, he said, the Russians would 'order the Chinese Communists not to continue their advance' into the province. T'ao, however, rejected the Soviet offer, and defected to the Chinese Communists together with his troops. With Chinese Communist victory now certain, Russia bowed to the inevitable, and permitted the re-integration into the province of the Soviet-sponsored 'East Turkestan Republic', which had controlled North-West Sinkiang since 1944.

The Chinese Communist position was immeasurably strengthened when Saifudin, a Moscow-trained Uighur who was then Minister of Education in the 'East Turkestan Republic', threw his lot in with Peking. Although supported by the Russians, the north-western revolutionary movement was in essence pro-autonomy: its original aim had been the expulsion of all Chinese from Sinkiang and full independence for the province as a whole. The ability of the Chinese Communists to attract support from these nationalists, therefore, was quite significant. Saifudin declared that the Ining 'revolution' had merely 'opened the way', and that the path of the Muslim peoples of Sinkiang would henceforth be close association with the regime of Mao Tse-tung in Peking. In return, Saifudin became the chosen instrument and spokesman for Chinese Communist policy in Sinkiang.

Led by Saifudin, who had visited Peking in August 1949, a delegation from Sinkiang took part in the Sino-Soviet discussions in Moscow in early 1950. On 27 March 1950 an agreement was concluded establishing two Sino-Soviet joint-stock companies for the province, for the exploitation of oil and non-ferrous metals. Capital, control and profits were to be divided equally between Russia and China; each side would provide in turn the chairman of each of the companies or, alternatively, the general manager; deputies were to be drawn from the other side; the positions were to be reversed every three years, but the first general managers were to be Russian. The agreement was to run for thirty years. A further arrangement, concluded at the same time, provided for the establishment of a Sino-Soviet Civil Aviation Company, and the opening of an air link between Peking and Alma-Ata, by way of Sian, Lanchow, and Urumchi. This agreement was to run for ten years, until 1960. The announcement of these arrangements was hailed in the Russian press as 'constructive' and 'non-exploitative', although Chou En-lai carefully pointed out that the Chinese remained, in effect, the junior partners. By 1954, however, the Chinese had advanced to the point where they were able to secure the dissolution of the joint-stock companies, and a Chinese government was paramount in Sinkiang for the first time in one hundred years.

Yet the Chinese did not find it easy to bring Sinkiang under control. As early as 1949 the Kazakhs had staged a mass exodus in protest against Chinese domination, and pockets of armed resistance, defying all efforts at pacification, persisted. Muslim unrest was, in fact, endemic. Some of it had roots in a traditional hatred of Han Chinese – grounded in centuries of economic exploitation – but much stemmed from the attempt to impose an alien ideology and way of life on fiercely independent people with a long cultural tradition of their own.

In 1949 Han Chinese had accounted for only slightly more than 200,000 of a total population estimated at approximately $3\frac{3}{4}$ million, and in 1953 for 300,000 – or just over 6 per cent – of a total population of approximately $4\frac{3}{4}$ million. This figure rose sharply from the beginning of 1956 with the completion of the 'first stage of socialization', marked by the creation of the Sinkiang Uighur Autonomous Region on 30 September 1955 under the chairmanship of Saifudin. By 1958 the total population had increased by almost $1\frac{1}{5}$ million over the 1953 figure, and by late 1962 it had reached 7 million, of which Hans accounted for nearly 2 million, or 30 per cent. By 1965, the number of Hans had increased to $2\frac{1}{2}$ million, or 36 per cent of the total population. During the sixteen-year Chinese rule ending in 1965, therefore, the total population of Sinkiang had doubled, but the Han Chinese population had increased more than twelve times. And the superior status of the Han component was supremely visible in government, state enterprises, education and increasingly even in agriculture.

The extent of local nationalist feeling became apparent in 1957 with the opportunity for free expression offered by the period of the 'Hundred

Flowers'. It was alleged that the ratio of Han to non-Han cadres was far too great, and that the system itself encouraged the abuse of personal power. Charges were also made against the People's Liberation Army which was said to have shown scant consideration for the interests or feelings of the local populace.

Although Peking attempted to minimize the opposition in Sinkiang as the work of a handful of dissidents, the situation was serious and stern repressive measures were necessary. From the Party point of view, one of the most disturbing features was that criticism came from Communist as well as non-Communist sources, and from the young no less than the old.

A few months later, in June 1958, Wang Enmao, First Secretary of the Chinese Communist Party in Sinkiang, admitted that clandestine support for the former 'East Turkestan Republic' still existed.

There is no doubt that Soviet influence, though certainly diminished by the closure of the joint-stock companies in 1954, was far from eliminated. Russia continued to give technical and economic aid, and Soviet advisers were present in force throughout the province. Most significantly, the ties of blood and culture which united so many of the Turkic peoples on both sides of the frontier remained in being, and for the majority of these tribesmen it was institutions on the Soviet side which seemed most worthy of emulation. Beginning in 1958, then, the Chinese began in earnest a programme of narrowing contacts between the peoples of Sinkiang and those of the Soviet Union. One of the earliest steps was the elimination of the Cyrillic alphabet for use in transliterating the several Turkic dialects of Sinkiang, and the substitution of the Latin alphabet in its stead.

Despite the Party purge and measures designed to bring to heel the intellectuals – largely those who had received an Islamic education – unrest continued throughout the province, and was sorely aggravated by the people's communes. According to one report, there were 60,000 guerrillas operating in various bands in Sinkiang in 1958. Nevertheless, the Party pushed ahead undeterred by this extreme opposition. By the beginning of 1960 it was claimed that 96 per cent of the rural population had been organized into 491 communes and that more than half of the province's nomadic population had been settled in houses or fixed encampments.

But Peking's attempts to deal with the situation in Sinkiang by greater and greater doses of socialism and by stepped-up attacks on local traditions and institutions seem to have only increased the opposition and hostility of the Kazakhs, Uighurs and other Turkic nationalities. The earlier public reticence soon gave way to uninhibited polemic, rich in charges and counter-charges, however, and these have been repeated up to the present time.

It seemed clear, late in 1968, that the various non-Han nationality groups of Sinkiang remained largely disaffected. Despite the intensive efforts of Peking over the previous sixteen years, these Muslim peoples were still filled with resentment at Chinese attempts to eradicate, change and supplant their traditional way of life, whether through a programme of language reform (designed in part to deny the younger generation access to the older literature), through a programme of resettlement of nomads (and thus make them more amenable to cadre control), or through collectivization. It seems equally clear that the USSR, which these tribal groups see as their natural protector and source of assistance against Han Chinese power, has not and will not reconcile itself to the control of Western Sinkiang and the Dzungarian Gate by an unfriendly power.

AFGHANISTAN AND PAKISTAN

Afghanistan, a primitive mountain state of some 250,000 square miles and a population of 10–12 million, became of considerable strategic importance during the 'great game' period between Russia and India. It became a possible Russian route to India.

Prior to this period it had been the policy of both great powers to leave the matter of frontiers to the Kashmir Government and local tribes. The lofty and formidable Pamir-Karakoram mountain boundaries extended for 2,500 miles from the sensitive 'meeting-point of three empires' at the Pamir Knot to the tribal frontier zone of Northern Burma.

The Pamir region, as a study of any map will show, is indeed a strategic one. To the south lies Afghanistan and beyond it, Kashmir, which is disputed between India and Pakistan. The Anglo-Russian agreement of 1895 on the Pamir boundaries with its wedge of 'neutral' territory produced a frontier of about fifty miles between Afghanistan and Chinese Sinkiang.

Although the Russians, both before and after the Bolshevik Revolution, crossed into Sinkiang for political and economic advantage, the international boundary has remained unchanged for about a century. However, according to contemporary Chinese maps, the delineation across the Pamir plateau is still to be determined. Earlier (pre-1953) Chinese maps had been drawn with the boundary several hundred miles to the west of the present location, thus including a large part of the plateau within Sinkiang.

The present Sino-Soviet boundary through the Eastern Pamir, as shown on Soviet maps, leaves the Soviet Pamir within the Gorno-Badakhshan Autonomous Oblast, a subordinate unit of the Tadzhik Soviet Socialist Republic.

Until recently there was no road through or into the Chinese Pamirs, but in the last few years the Chinese have built a road south-west from Kashgar to Puli, 200 miles distant. Puli is the capital of the Tash Kurghan Tadzhik Autonomous Hsien, a subordinate ethnic administrative area in Sinkiang. Known as the Pamirs Road it heads significantly in the direction of the Karakoram Passes and Pakistani Gilgit Agency.

Buttressing the Karakoram on the east, the Kun Lun Range encloses a desolate area of high plateau where Buddhist Ladakh marches with Sinkiang on the north and Tibet on the east. Two treaties defined Ladakh's frontier as 'anciently established', though without further definition. The first dated from 1684 when Ladakh was a major Himalayan kingdom and the second from 1842, after its subjection by Gulab Singh, himself a feudatory of the Sikh Empire. The frontier of Kashmir became a responsibility of independent India with accession of the Maharajah of Kashmir in 1947. The subsequent dispute with Pakistan left this eastern area of Kashmir on the Indian side of the cease-fire line.

When the Chinese People's Republic was established in 1949, Afghanistan was quick to offer recognition and Ambassadors were exchanged early in 1955. Two years later in a first visit to Kabul, Prime Minister Chou En-lai mentioned that there was a common border – the one created by the Anglo-Russian-Afghan Pamir settlement which the Chinese had frequently denounced as 'secret'. In August 1960 the Sino-Afghan Treaty of Friendship and Mutual Non-Aggression was signed in Kabul, but an actual settlement of the strip of frontier territory involved was not finally undertaken until November 1963, after China's dispute with the Soviet Union in Sinkiang.

China's frontier settlement with Pakistan involved a much larger area. There was the traditional claim of the Chinese Empire to the allegiance of Hunza, relating to a 150 mile border. Pakistan maintained that Hunza had not in 1947 been a tributary of Kashmir and was therefore not affected by the Kashmir dispute with India. The much larger border of Balkistan from Hunza eastwards to the Kashmir cease-fire line, which Peking wished to discuss with Pakistan and refused to discuss with India, was not at first regarded by Pakistan as appropriate for negotiations with China.

There were Chinese maps which claimed large areas in the region, one of which (September 1959) appeared to include almost 6,000 square miles in the Hunza and Gilgit area as Chinese. There were even reports of Chinese military invasions as early as 1953, intrusions by Chinese military aircraft and, after the Tibetan revolt in 1959, border incidents and accounts of Chinese subversion. It was not until 3 May 1962 that Peking officially announced that both countries had 'agreed to negotiate on the boundary question'. Both sides, it was added, had agreed that the resulting settlement would be provisional pending a solution of the dispute over Kashmir between Pakistan and India, and an Agreement in Principle was reached on 28 December 1962 as to the location of the border with China in Pakistan-controlled Kashmir. On 2 March 1963 a Boundary Agreement calling for the establishment of a joint Boundary Demarcation Commission was signed, which the Indian Government regarded as illegal 'since Pakistan has no border with Communist China'. China, on the other hand, acknowledged the provisional status of the agreement by providing for a re-opening of the negotiations with 'the sovereign authority concerned', after the settlement of the Kashmir dispute.

SOUTH-EAST ASIA

China's boundaries with Tibet, Nepal, Sikkim, Bhutan and the North-East Frontier Agency are discussed elsewhere in the *Handbook*. Here we move on to South-East Asia.

Long before Burma and Siam came into being, the two major civilizations of the Far East, India and China, had made their indelible imprint on the earlier states of South-East Asia, and by the Middle Ages – in Western terms – they had divided up the region between them. The 'Indianized' division was much the larger, consisting of what are now Burma, Thailand, Laos, Cambodia, Malaya and Indonesia. The Chinese-influenced division comprised Tongking, Annam and Cochin-China.

In the last four and a half centuries Europe made its own peculiar impact on the region, which also resulted in a vast change of attitudes. Then, because of events in Europe itself, transforming its own outlook and manner of life, this impact has had revolutionary effects in the 20th century.

Twentieth-century Communist China's attitude towards this area was made explicit in a book, published in Peking in 1952, reissued two years later in a second edition, and given world-wide publicity by India in 1962. The book, with its important map and documentation designed to show 'the Chinese territories taken by the Imperialists in the Old Democratic Revolutionary Era (1840–1919)', was *Brief History of Modern China*, by Liu Pei-hua. The southern frontier of China is indicated by a line representing the Chinese borders of 1840 which appropriated Nepal, Sikkim, Bhutan, the Indian State of Assam and a part of East Pakistan, the Andaman Islands, the whole of Burma, Thailand, Malaya and Singapore and the States of the former French Indo-China. The line goes on to include the Philippines.

The status of Annam (the name given to the combined states of Indo-China) is described in 1952 as 'captured by the French in 1885' (from the Chinese). Burma is said to have 'become a part of the British Empire in 1886' (after Assam had been given to Britain by Burma in 1826'). Thailand, or Siam, whose frontiers and neutrality had been jointly guaranteed by Britain and France, was 'declared "independent" under joint Anglo-French control in 1904'.

BURMA

Beyond the usual custom of an exchange of presents China had no historical evidence for regarding Burma as a 'vassal'. The Burmese Supreme Council of State declared in a memorandum of 1 January 1886 that 'Burma has never at any time, on any account whatsoever, paid anything in the shape of tribute to China'.

Burma, with a population of approximately 20 million inhabiting an area of some 250,000 square miles, is a rich, self-sufficient country (rice, teak, petroleum, rubies, silver). The mountainous and heavily forested terrain have kept Burma in isolation from her neighbours and from becoming unified as a nation. There are Talaings in the south, Mongoloid Burmese in the north, half Chinese Thai-Shans in the east, together with other tribes such as Kachins and Karens.

The tribal areas of Upper Burma were brought under control by 1890. At Burma's western apex the frontier with eastern Tibet – less than a hundred miles of extremely difficult country – formed the extremity of the MacMahon Line boundary fixed at the Simla Conference of 1914 and not challenged, in this respect, by the Chinese.

The Government of India began a series of boundary settlements with China in 1897 which lasted for forty years, until Burma was constitutionally detached from India in 1937. The agreement reached at this time allowed China to retain the greater part of the important mineral area in the Wa States which had been in doubt and dispute. When the boundary demarcation had been agreed upon in the Sino-British notes of 18 June 1941, it was stated by a leading Western historian that 'China now has, for the first time in history, a fully delimited southern frontier from the China Sea to Turkestan'.

Burma was not only the first Asian state to recognize the new Chinese Communist regime in 1949, it was also the first country to display concern about its frontiers with the new China. There was good cause for such concern. Only the previous year the Nationalist Government of China, hard-pressed as it was, had still found occasion to raise the matter of Chinese claims to some 70,000 square miles of Burmese-claimed territory.

The new Communist Government's response to Burma's suggestion regarding a frontier settlement was an undertaking that the Chinese Communist forces would not violate Burma's borders unless they found themselves under attack from Nationalist Chinese remnants based in Burmese territory. When Burma protested at Chinese Communist intrusions into the Myitkyina and Kava areas China admitted the location of her troops but disputed that these were Burmese territories. The Burmese Government was even more concerned at the appearance of maps issued under the Communist regime which showed the frontier – though shown as 'undemarcated' – as far south as Bhama and Saling in a large part of the Kachin States.

The official Peking explanation in reply to representations, was conveyed to Parliament by the Burmese Premier U Nu on 9 March 1957: 'The Chinese Government had no time to draw a new map and had reproduced the old one.' However, ten years later the matter had still not been rectified when a map officially released by Peking under circulation showed the Irrawaddy flowing through south-west China.

In April 1955, at the Bandung Conference, Chou En-lai declared, 'we have common borders with four countries', without explaining who were the unacknowledged states. The only border problem specifically cited was that with Burma and that was in the context of Chinese Nationalist aggressive activities in north-east Burma.

In November 1955 there was a serious clash with Burmese units in the Wa States on the Burmese side of the frontier. Peking challenged the boundary line at this part as having been approved by the Chinese Nationalists in 1945. The following year there were sensational newspaper reports in Rangoon about the Chinese intrusions of some 1,000 square miles. Finally, on 1 October 1960 a boundary agreement was signed in Peking.

LAOS AND VIETNAM

The modern acceptance of the frontiers of Laos and North Vietnam, from the Burma tri-junction to the sea, began with the 1885 Treaty of Tientsin between France and China. (This is not to be confused with the 1858 Treaty of Tientsin between China and Russia, cited in the *People's Daily* article of March 1963.) Frontier conventions in 1887 and 1895 completed a detailed delimitation which has remained undisputed through subsequent political changes.

The 265-mile section of this southern Chinese frontier that adjoins Laos has been demarcated, but it runs through rugged watershed country where minority peoples, not fully controlled, straddle the boundary. The same is true of the western and mountainous portion of the Sino-Vietnamese frontier, where there is the opening to the sea that provides the only railway-crossing and a few road crossings in China's entire 4,000-mile frontier.

The narrow strip of Burma-Laos-Vietnam, therefore, joins to form an intervening corridor of rugged mountains, dense jungles and primitive communications, where the most effective way of travelling is on horseback. There are roads of a kind from Yunnan through Burma to Chiengai, in Thailand, used by the opium-sustained Shan rebels, private armies and ex-K M T remnants, and also from Vietnam through Laos to Nongkai and Nakhon Phanom, in Thailand.

When the Chinese Communists assumed power on 1 October 1949, France had already accorded 'independence within the French Union' to Vietnam and Laos, and Cambodia followed in November. In January 1950 Ho Chi Minh requested and received recognition of his Vietminh State from Communist China and the Soviet Union.

In his report to the Central People's Government Council on 11 August 1954, Chou En-lai spelled out specifically the interpretation which China put upon the Geneva settlement and its implications for South-East Asia.

If, on the basis of mutual respect for territorial integrity and sovereignty, the three Indo-Chinese states develop friendly relations among themselves and with France and enter into peaceful co-operation with their neighbouring countries, then it will be possible to establish an area of collective peace in Indo-China and its surrounding countries.

Since then China has demonstrated her determination in Korea and other sectors along her boundaries to preserve a belt of territory beyond her frontiers from possible invasion by hostile forces. The Peking authorities have declared on many occasions that China would not shrink from full-scale war in the event of any attack on what she considers Chinese territory. Specifically in relation to Vietnam, if the forward zone of Chinese defence should be 'invaded' (i.e. by ground forces) China 'would not stand idly by' – a similar attitude to that previously announced in respect of the adjacent frontier country of Laos.

HONG KONG AND MACAO

Following the Cuban missile crisis Soviet Premier Khrushchev, addressing the Supreme Soviet on 7 December 1962, scathingly pointed out to the 'Chinese comrades' that they were scarcely in a position to reproach him for his 'weakness' in the Cuban situation, when they had failed to recover Taiwan, Hong Kong and Macao.

Three months later the Chinese leaders replied in their now famous 8 March editorial:

Inasmuch as some persons have mentioned Taiwan, Hong Kong and Macao, we are obliged to discuss a little of the history of imperialist aggression against China ... within this category are the questions of Hong Kong, Kowloon, Macao and the question of all those boundaries which have not been formally delimited by the parties concerned in each case. The Chinese people are determined to exercise our sovereign right to liberate our own territory ...

The treaties brought into question by the Chinese on 8 March 1963 had evidently been chosen so as to equate territorial grievances against Russia with the questions of Taiwan, Hong Kong and Macao – ones about which Khrushchev had taunted the Peking leaders with inaction: Nanking 1842, Lisbon Protocol 1887, Shimonoseki 1895, etc.

The 1964 *Concise Geography* by Jen Yu-ti, published in English for external information by the Foreign Languages Press in Peking, described both Hong Kong and Kowloon as 'part of Chinese territory' to be recovered 'when conditions are ripe'. With regard to Macao, a curious episode occurred in July 1965 when the Chinese delegation to the World Peace Congress found itself in the equivocal position of having to play down the subject of Macao's return to China demanded by fellow Communists and manipulate its deletion from the agenda as that of 'a different kind of colony', an internal affair to be resolved as and when Peking should determine.

That 'conditions were not yet ripe' for this move by Peking in 1966–7 was evident by the official reaction to the disturbances caused by the overspill of China's Cultural Revolution in both Macao and Hong Kong. Although Communist elements in Macao had reduced the Portuguese Government to such abject humiliation that they offered to hand over Macao to China, the offer was ignored by the authorities inside China.

And while Hong Kong was subjected to a campaign of, first, demonstrations, then riots, and, finally, spasmodic acts of terrorism, it was evident throughout that these were locally inspired and had only the absolute minimum of acknowledgement from Peking – and even that minimum possibly reluctantly conceded on the basis of misinformation. Certainly, food supplies never stopped arriving, Liberation Army soldiers took no action on the borders and, most significant of all, when the time for agreed water supplies from the mainland to Hong Kong arrived on 1 October, the agreement was honoured to the letter.

OUTER MONGOLIA

This concludes the survey of China's land frontier. There are, however, matters of concern to Russia and China which are larger than frontier rectification. One of these is the question of the attachment of the territory of Outer Mongolia to Russia or to China.

In 1957 the noted authority on Sino-Soviet affairs, Klaus Mehnert, had occasion to examine some maps published by the Chinese Communist Government. He wrote:

> There could be no doubt about it: the roughly 2,700-mile-long frontier with the Mongolian People's Republic was not recognized by the Chinese Government as final, while on Soviet maps it has been shown as a normal, valid frontier. And even the frontier indicated provisionally on the Chinese maps differed up to sixty miles or more from the one shown as final on the Soviet maps.

Outer Mongolia was for many years a persistent political and diplomatic issue between China and Russia. In 1912 a Sino-Russian agreement recognized Outer Mongolia as legally part of the Chinese Republic, but as *de facto* autonomous and exempt from Chinese troops or colonists. A Tripartite Agreement between China, Russia and Mongolia concluded in 1915 and in general confirming the foregoing terms was ended by the Russian Revolution of 1917. The Mongolian princes were then forced to renounce their autonomy, and sought to come back under Chinese domination. If the Chinese Government had been in a position to do so it could at that time have incorporated Outer Mongolia as an integral part of the Chinese Republic. But what with warlords besieging Peking, and White Russians planning a Pan-Mongolian Empire in Siberia, they were in no position to do anything.

The Sino-Soviet Treaty 1924

With the outbreak of the Russian Revolution, the continuing instability in China, and the see-saw of regional ambitions of the White Russians and provincial warlords, the status of Outer Mongolia fluctuated according to whoever had sufficient power to enforce agreements at any given time. Thus, it passed from the agreed autonomy recognized in the Russo-Chinese-Mongolia Pact to the control of Russia and back to the control of China again. In 1923 a secret treaty was concluded between the Soviet Government and the Government of Outer Mongolia in which no reference was made to China, and which included among other things that unclaimed lands in Outer Mongolia should be distributed to Soviet citizens, and that Soviet troops should be stationed in Outer Mongolia.

In the spring of 1924 relations between China and Soviet Russia were again strained when Russia received information that China was contemplating taking complete control of the Chinese Eastern Railway, and Russia sent a warning note about 'Chinese aggression'. Negotiations between the two countries were resumed and on 31 May 1924 the Sino-Soviet Treaty of Recognition was concluded. The treaty provided for the establishment of diplomatic relations, cancellation of Russian extra-territoriality, reward of concession privileges and renunciation of Tsarist treaties. China refused to recognize any treaties concluded by Soviet Russia which 'affected the sovereign rights and interest of the republic of China', but Soviet Russia did not express its support of this section of the treaty, thereby leaving untouched the Soviet-Mongolian treaty of 1921.

Yalta Agreement 1945

Soviet Russia sought to consolidate her control of Outer Mongolia by giving more formal shape to their relationship with a Pact of Mutual Assistance in 1936, but the Chinese Government continued to regard Outer Mongolia as part of China and the subject remained one of those in dispute between the Soviet Union and the Chinese Nationalist Government.

This issue was settled in 1945 by the provision in the Yalta Agreement that 'the *status quo* in Outer Mongolia (the Mongolian People's

Republic) shall be preserved'. Britain and the United States pressed the Chinese Government to accept the Russian claim that this implied the total independence of the country. In an exchange of notes between the Soviet and the Chinese Governments at the time of signing of the Sino-Soviet Treaty of 14 August 1945, it was agreed that the Chinese Government would recognize 'the independence of Outer Mongolia *in her existing boundaries*' (my italics) – an important phrase in view of the wide distribution of the Mongolian people – subject to a plebiscite. The plebiscite was held on 20 August 1945. 98·4 per cent of the electorate were reported to have voted, all of them voting for independence. On 5 January 1946 China accorded official recognition to the Mongolian People's Republic.

The Chinese Communist regime also 'fully guaranteed the independent situation of the Mongolian People's Republic as a result of the 1945 referendum'. However, that this view was later altered was evident from the famous interview recorded by Edgar Snow when Mao Tse-tung declared: 'When the people's revolution has been victorious in China, the Outer Mongolian Republic will automatically become a part of the Chinese Federation of their own will.'

Friendly relations between China and Mongolia began openly to deteriorate almost from the moment of signing the Sino-Mongolian Boundary Treaty in December 1962. Following on Mao Tse-Tung's highly publicized remarks to visiting Japanese journalists in 1963 about Russian attitudes and influence in Mongolia, both countries have reinforced their military positions on either side of the Sino-Mongolian frontier. There have also been a number of major reshuffles of personnel in Mongolia, in one of which, in 1964, three top officials were expelled for 'factional, anti-Party activities' and there was no attempt made to disguise the fact that the disgraced officials had links with the Chinese and had been encouraging anti-Soviet nationalism.

Tannu Tuva

The region of Tannu Tuva, at the northern apex of Mongolia, is inhabited by the Uriankhai Mongols and was formerly known by that name. It is separated from the rest of Mongolia by a range of mountains, the Tannu Ola Range, which makes it easy of access from Siberia. In 1914 Russia established a protectorate over the territory and in 1915 stationed troops there. Following on the Russian Revolution the area became Communist and in 1921 the Turinian People's Republic was set up under Soviet auspices. This was kept separate from the

Mongolian People's Republic and in 1944 it was announced that the area was to be incorporated into the Soviet Union as the Tuva Province of the Russian Socialist Federated Republic. The country is reportedly rich in minerals, and is of great strategic importance because of its proximity to the Kuznetsk.

BIBLIOGRAPHY

F. M. Bailey. *Report on the Exploration of the North-East Frontier*. (Simla, 1914.)

Max Beloff. *Soviet Policy in the Far East, 1944–51*. (Oxford University Press, 1953.)

Howard L. Boorman. *Moscow-Peking Access: Strengths and Strains*. (Harper, New York, 1957.)

A. Buchan (Ed.). *China and the Peace of Asia*. (Chatto & Windus, 1965.)

Cheng Tien-Fong. *A History of Sino-Soviet Relations*. (Public Affairs Press, Washington, D.C., 1957.)

J. L. Christian. *Modern Burma*. (University of California, Berkeley, 1942.)

George B. Cressey. *Land of 500 Million: Geography of China*. (McGraw Hill, New York, 1955.)

David J. Dallin. *Soviet Russia and the Far East*. (Yale University Press, New Haven, 1951.) *The Rise of Russia in Asia*. (Yale University Press, New Haven, 1949.)

D. J. Doolin. *Territorial Claims in the Sino-Soviet Conflict*. (Stanford University Press, Stanford, 1965.)

Sir G. Dunbar. *Frontiers*. (London, 1932.)

Lewis Fischer. *The Soviet in World Affairs*. (Princeton University Press, Princeton, N.J., 1951.)

Gerard M. Friters. *Outer Mongolia and its International Position*. (Johns Hopkins University Press, Baltimore, 1949.)

Elliot R. Goodman. *The Soviet Design for a World State*. (Columbia University Press, New York, 1960.)

Ho Ping-Ti. *Studies on the Population of China 1368–1953*. (Harvard University Press, Cambridge, Mass., 1959.)

Charles W. Hosler. *Turkism and the Soviets*. (Praeger, New York, 1957.)

G. S. Hudson and Marthe Rajchman. *An Atlas of Far East Politics*. (Faber & Faber, 1938.)

W. A. D. Jackson. *The Russo-Chinese Borderland*. (Van Nostrand, New York, 1962.)

Walter Kolarz. *Russia and Her Colonies*. (Praeger, New York, 1954.)

Alistair Lamb. *Britain and Chinese Asia*. (Routledge, 1960.)

Owen Lattimore. *Inner Asian Frontiers of China*. (American Geographical Society, New York, 1940–51.) *Nationalism and Revolution in Mongolia*. (Oxford University Press, 1955.) *Studies in Frontier History*. (Oxford University Press, 1962.)

Prince A. Lobanov-Rostovasky. *Russia and Asia*. (Wahr, Ann Arbor, 1951.)

Lionel Lyde. *The Continent of Asia*. (Macmillan, 1933.)

Manchuria, Treaties and Agreements. (Carnegie Endowment for International Peace, 1921.)

Franz H. Michael and George E. Taylor. *The Far East in the Modern World*. (Holt, New York, 1956.)

H. E. Morse. *The International Relations of the Chinese Empire*. (London, 1910-18.)

Harrison E. Salisbury. *To Moscow and Beyond*. (Harper, New York, 1959.)

Theodore Shabad. *China's Changing Map*. (Praeger, New York, 1957.)

Geography of the U.S.S.R. – a regional survey. (Columbia University Press, New York, 1954.)

I. C. Y. Shu. *Ili Crisis*. (Oxford University Press, 1965.)

Peter S. H. Tang. *Russia and Soviet Policy in Manchuria and Outer Mongolia, 1911-31*. (Duke University Press, Durham, North Carolina, 1959.)

Geoffrey Wheeler. *The Modern History of Soviet Central Asia*. (Weidenfeld & Nicolson, 1965.)

Alan S. Whiting. *Soviet Policies in China, 1917-1924*. (Columbia University Press, New York, 1954.)

Alan S. Whiting and General Sheng Shih-ts'ai. *Sinkiang: Pawn or Pivot?* (Michigan State University Press, East Lansing, 1958.)

Dorothy Woodman. *Making of Burma*. (Cresset Press, London, 1962.)

Aitchan K. Wu. *China and the Soviet Union*. (John Day, New York, 1950.)

TAIWAN

Richard Harris

TAIWAN presents many problems according to whether it is seen through Chinese eyes (mainland Communist or Nationalist), through American eyes or through the eyes of those other countries concerned with which government to recognize and with the rival claims of each government to occupy China's seat in the United Nations, a seat which includes permanent membership of the Security Council as one of the war-time five Great Powers.

In the Chinese mind Taiwan is primarily one of those territories lost to Chinese control during a century of weakness and humiliation, a century whose memory they are anxious to expunge. To the government in Peking Taiwan remains the outstanding territory in this task of restoration. The attainment of this goal is hindered in part by the Nationalist Government with its rival claim to be the Government of China, in part by American policy which supports that claim militarily and politically. In the early stages after 1949 Peking's hostility to the remnant force of their Nationalist enemy was as great as to the Americans, but time has concentrated this hatred wholly on the Americans. Proposals made or hinted at by Peking for a resolution of this issue – the restoration of Taiwan to mainland sovereignty – have gradually got more and more tolerant to the point of accepting as a first step no more than a recognition of Peking's sovereignty, leaving the Nationalist Government intact, though of course demanding as a counterpart of this temporary independence of the Kuomintang Government, a total American withdrawal from this piece of Chinese territory in which the United States has no business to interfere.

From the Nationalist viewpoint the unity of Taiwan and the mainland is also a sacred fact. While the Nationalists remain recognized by the Americans and others as the Government of China their *raison d'être* has to be maintained by annual declarations of a forthcoming return to the mainland where the Chinese suffering under the Communist yoke would, they claim, welcome them.

This consistent view of the Nationalist Government led by Chiang Kai-shek has lately been given an unexpected fillip by the turmoil of the cultural revolution on the mainland. Hopes that a real anti-Communist opposition to Mao Tse-tung might emerge were soon disappointed when men such as Liu Shao-chi (always, and with wild inaccuracy, the favoured pro-Russian man in the Chinese Communist hierarchy), Peng Chen and others were accused of disloyalty to Mao Tse-tung. Plainly none of them are anti-Communist.

The dependence of this government in Taiwan on the United States is still heavy enough to prevent Chaing Kai-shek expressing his resentment at American failure to provide the air and naval support which the Nationalists claim is all they need for an invasion. Despite the interest created by the cultural revolution this invasion does not seem to have become any more urgent. Of the refugee mainland population of about 2 million now settled on the island the *status quo* is as much as they can hope for. The population of Taiwan who are Chinese, though alienated by circumstances – as the brief history following shows – have little interest in the national issue and would probably prefer to be independent. The claim to independence was made by a Taiwan independence party exiled in Japan but the defection to Chiang Kai-shek's rule (from what pressures is unknown) of two leaders of this group have weakened its influence in the outside world. Nevertheless, with almost the whole of the Nationalist Government kept in the hands of the mainlanders (although 85 per cent of the island's population are native Taiwanese), and with an army in which Taiwanese provide 85 per cent of the rank and file but only 5 per cent of the officers, grounds for political discontent are quite strong enough to keep a solid sense of Taiwan loyalty alive.

One good reason why political differences do not burst out as they might is the undoubted progress Taiwan has made in economic growth. Its rate of growth is now second in Asia to Japan. Its *per capita* income at US $190 is a long way behind Japan's US $620 but much higher than anywhere else in Asia save Singapore. The benefits of this growth could easily be eroded by an uncontrolled birth rate but in the last three years this rate has begun to fall.

The outside world sees Taiwan in terms of recognition of one Chinese government as against another. But in this respect it is not to be compared with East and West Germany or other states divided in terms of the Cold War. For one thing the balance of territory under the control of each side is too small to sustain any Nationalist claim. In any case the situation in China was such in 1946–9 that Britain and other Western countries recognized the Communist Government set up in Peking in 1949. Many of the countries which still in theory recognize the Nationalist Government in Taiwan as the Government of China do so in deference to American policy which has since the

Korean War regarded a change by any government as something of an un-friendly act. The argument for the admission of the Peking Government to China's seat in the United Nations is a stronger and more active issue and of greater concern to the world than the issue of recognition, which is a matter for each government to decide. It is the American policy over this, rather than its choice of which government to recognize, which has caused such a prolonged crisis.

A separate issue is the future of the island itself, irrespective of its government; the question whether it should be independent of the main-land – as its inhabitants would probably prefer – or whether it is in-alienably part of China. International opinion on this varies from those who sustain Chiang Kai-shek's claim to be the Government of China, through those who while dismissing this claim and anxious to see the Peking Government seated in the UN would nevertheless argue that Taiwan has a claim for independence, to those who support not merely Peking's admission to the UN but the return of Taiwan to control by the mainland as a just concomitant of such admission. Even this last position would divide those who think this return should be peacefully arranged by international agreement and those – confined to China's Communist allies – who accept the Chinese argument that the return of Taiwan is their affair to be arranged as they think fit, including if needed an invasion to drive Chiang Kai-shek from power.

Before analysing all these various opinions, the facts on Taiwan must be set out. How just is the claim that it is a part of China and what have been the international events leading to the present position?

HISTORICAL SUMMARY

Taiwan was not appreciably populated by Chinese or ruled as part of China before the 17th century. Its aboriginal inhabitants had been raided from time to time, beginning as far back as the 7th century, from both the Chinese mainland and, in later centuries, from Japan. The Portuguese gave it the name of Formosa; the Dutch set up trading stations and built forts in 1624, being driven there by trading competi-tion from the Spaniards and Portuguese who were then in occupation of the Philippines and Macao. The Dutch in turn were driven out by the powerful Chinese sealord Chen Ch'eng-kung. He came of a Fukien family who created their own pocket of resistance to the conquest of China by the Manchus. He was known in Europe as Koxinga (from the local dialect pronunciation of his assumed name as a resistance leader, Kuo Hsing-yeh). Heavily pressed on the mainland he and his followers retreated to Taiwan as a base and thus considerably increased the Chinese emigrant population. For twenty years after 1662 he and his successors ruled the island. Eventually the established Ch'ing (Manchu) Dynasty ended this exiled opposition and in 1683 Taiwan came under Chinese rule.

Emigration from Fukien province and to a less extent from Kuangtung gradually filled up the island with Chinese settlers during the following centuries – a period during which it was administered loosely as a prefecture of Fukien. It was not until 1885 that the island became a Chinese province and not merely an adjunct of Fukien across the straits. Japanese aggression meanwhile had grown and concentrated on the island. After the war against China of 1894–5 the island was ceded to Japan. Under Japanese rule it was developed through improved agriculture and its inhabitants began to enjoy higher standards of living than those of the mainland. But they were of course Chinese, speaking the non-Mandarin minority dialects of Fukien province, even though by 1945 they had been somewhat alienated by time and circumstance from their Chinese past.

The present population is nearly 14 million of whom only about 200,000 of aboriginal stock remain.

Under the Cairo declaration of 1943 it was agreed that all territories occupied by Japan since 1894 should be given up. This was formalized in the Potsdam agreement in 1945 where it was laid down that Taiwan should be returned to the Republic of China. After the Japanese surrender the island therefore returned to the administration of the Nationalist Government under a provincial governor. If anything Taiwan suffered even more than the mainland from the exactions and misrule of these post-war years, though in the early stages there was some welcome from the Taiwanese for the mainland Chinese as liberators from Japanese rule. This soon changed when prominent Taiwanese were treated as collaborators, assets were seized and made government monopolies, and the economy of the island quickly reduced to ruin by carpet-bagging mainland officials. In February 1947 the despairing Taiwanese broke out in revolt but the provincial governor gave an assurance of reforms. A month later, when he had got sufficient reinforcements from the mainland, the leaders of the revolt were massacred and opposition was ruthlessly suppressed throughout the island; in all some ten thousand Taiwanese were killed. After American protests a new provincial governor was appointed and some reforms were introduced.

In 1948 Chiang Kai-shek began to prepare the island as a

retreat for his government and sent General Chen Cheng as governor. Martial law was re-established and members of the left-wing opposition were arrested and executed. While temporarily stepping down from the Chinese Presidency Chiang Kai-shek transferred assets to the island, including American military aid, and himself moved there in 1949, the Nationalist Government of China formally establishing itself in December of that year. Although American economic aid continued, in accordance with programmes already initiated, military aid declined with the end of the civil war on the mainland. Hainan island fell to the Communists in April 1950 and it was expected that an assault on Taiwan would soon follow. In addition the Nationalists had retained control of some islands off the mainland, the most important being Quemoy and Matsu. A hastily mounted assault on the former had already been beaten off at the end of 1949 when Communist armies were pushing southwards. In January 1950 President Truman declined any further involvement in the Chinese civil war and refused any further military aid. Chiang Kai-shek's precarious position was suddenly transformed in 1950 after the outbreak of the Korean war when President Truman ordered the American Seventh Fleet to prevent any attack on Taiwan from the mainland, at the same time ordering the Nationalists on the island to cease attacks on the mainland. He declared that the legal status of Taiwan must await a peace treaty with Japan. Although in theory this move was intended to be temporary, American military, political and economic commitment to the island and the chastened Nationalist Government steadily grew. A military advisory group was sent in 1951, pressures for reform were more readily accepted than they had been on the mainland and gradually the island's economy was restored. Continued recognition of the Nationalist Government as the Government of China was reaffirmed by Dean Rusk, Assistant Secretary of State, in May 1951. In 1952 President Eisenhower's new administration removed the restriction that had been put on Nationalist attacks on the mainland (though in the form of minor guerilla raids these had never ceased).

At the San Francisco conference of 1951 (to which neither the Peking nor Taiwan Governments were invited as participants) a peace treaty was signed with Japan by the Western Powers and in it Japan renounced all rights to Taiwan. Later a subsidiary peace treaty was signed between Japan and the Nationalist Chinese Government, though this did not cede any specified legal title to the island. In December 1954 a further measure of American alliance was a mutual security pact signed with the Nationalist Government, thereby ensuring American defence of the island (and the subsidiary Pescadores islands near the west coast) against any attack from the mainland. Heavy shelling attacks on Quemoy and Matsu from the mainland occurred in September 1954 and again in October 1958. American statements at the latter time implied that the defence of these offshore islands might be undertaken by American forces only if such an attack was considered to be preliminary to an attack on Taiwan itself. But apart from this ambiguous position no American commitment to defend these islands has been made.

Since the signing of the security pact in 1954 American military aid to the Nationalist army has given it modern equipment and efficient training. In spite of the Sino-American ambassadorial talks which began in 1955 and have continued in Warsaw, no agreement has been reached on the Taiwan issue which has been one item on the agenda. The Chinese argue that Taiwan being part of China any action there is an internal Chinese matter and that they cannot give an undertaking not to use force in a matter in which the United States has no rightful part.

Any change in the status of Taiwan will arise from one of two things: a change in American policy or a vote in the United Nations giving China's seat to the Peking Government.

TAIWAN AT THE UNITED NATIONS

Some change in American policy was foreshadowed with the election of President Kennedy but the impetus fell away, and under President Johnson's administration American involvement in South Vietnam precluded any possibility, in American eyes, of a new policy towards Peking. This may, of course, be forced on the United States if support for the administration of the Peking Government at the United Nations gains a majority. The United States had until 1961 always postponed discussion of the China issue at the United Nations by means of a moratorium on which it was able to get a majority vote. In 1961 – perhaps foreseeing that a majority vote would no longer be possible – the decision was taken to allow discussion of the issue, but to regard it as 'an important matter' thus requiring a two-thirds majority for any change. The procedural motion to define the issue as important was passed by 61 to 34 with 7 abstentions (Britain voting with the majority). A Soviet resolution was then submitted coupling admission of Peking with the expulsion of the Taiwan Government from the United Nations. This won 37 votes against 48 with 19 abstentions. A similar resolution, amended by neutral countries to cover only the admission of Peking, also failed to be passed. Britain voted in favour of both resolutions. The voting in the second case was 21 for, 41 against, and 39 abstaining. (Since the latter resolution made no mention of Taiwan, the Communist bloc countries all abstained.)

Early in 1965 shifts of recognition by some of the smaller African states had almost brought support for Peking level with support for the Nationalist Government in Taiwan but the postponement of the United Nations General Assembly prevented the matter being brought to the vote.

If and when a vote for the admission of Peking's representation looks like gaining the required two-thirds majority the future of the Nationalist Government will become a live issue. The admission of the Peking representative would not in itself demand a settlement of the Taiwan issue, but a solution much canvassed in the United States has come to be known as the 'two Chinas' policy. The aim is to have both governments in the United Nations, leaving the territorial *status quo*. The refusal of both governments to entertain it makes this policy highly unreal. If Peking's representative were admitted to the United Nations the possibilities would then be:

The dismissal of the Nationalist Government from the United Nations, thereby reversing the situation that has obtained for the past thirteen years. This would not mean any alteration in Taiwan's status though it is probable that many countries now recognizing Chiang Kai-shek's government as the Government of China would switch to recognition of Peking.

Or: a seat in the General Assembly could be reserved for the Taiwan Government – described as China – while giving the permanent seat on the Security Council to the Peking Government. (This amounts to the 'two Chinas' solution.)

Or: a seat in the General Assembly could be reserved for the Taiwan Government described as such and not as China. (This would probably be supported by many neutralist countries which would not accept the 'two Chinas' solution.)

If present attitudes are maintained, the Communist Government in Peking would not take its seat in the Security Council unless the Nationalist Government ceased to be represented at all. Equally the Nationalist Government would refuse a seat in the General Assembly if the Communists were admitted to the Security Council and would certainly refuse if they were described as Taiwan and not as China. No simple solution to the problem of United Nations seating is therefore likely, in so far as any fulfilment of the United Nations' declared wishes are concerned; nor is there any policy that looks like getting the necessary majority in the United Nations.

Apart from the issue as seen from the United Nations, however, we must consider as a separate political question the future of the Nationalist Government of Chiang Kai-shek. Once its claim to be the Government of China is no longer admitted by the United Nations and the majority of governments now so recognizing it, then its future as the Government of Taiwan naturally will come up for consideration. Among its mainland supporters there are no doubt those who would be willing to accept a share in ruling an independent Taiwan, though Chiang Kai-shek personally would refuse such a reduction of his status. But if an independent Taiwan was agreed to then the indigenous population would certainly press their claim to elect or nominate that government from among their own number. In any case, in the event of Chiang Kai-shek's death or retirement we may expect to see a gradual loosening of the cohesion of the Nationalist (Kuomintang) party and a gradual taking over of power by Taiwanese.

AMERICAN POLICY TOWARDS TAIWAN

The difficulty of the issue really stems from American policy towards China, which has in the past been highly emotional and which looks on China increasingly as the source of all revolutionary disorder in Asia. While these conditions continue, a wholly new policy towards China is unlikely. There has, however, in recent years been a distinct decline in interest in the Nationalist Government in Taiwan as a factor in this policy. During Mr Dulles's days it was admitted that Chiang Kai-shek was indeed maintained as an alternative government which might regain power one day on the mainland, and thus Peking could argue that a government dedicated to its overthrow was militarily supported by the United States. This threat had some substance in the years after the Korean war but it is no longer a reality on either side now. But there can be no settlement of the Taiwan issue while the *status quo* is maintained. American policy can only change step by step and the first step to break up the jam would be the withdrawal of American recognition from Chiang Kai-shek's government as the Government of China, while recognizing its continued authority in Taiwan. This would open the way eventually for a more widely supported government to emerge on the island and need not affect any American decision over the recognition of Peking.

Otherwise the prospect is that with the death of Chiang Kai-shek (who has now passed his eightieth birthday) the break-up of the Kuomintang as a party would begin; the prospect of any return to the mainland would then be formally and not merely tacitly dropped. At the same time there might be renewed offers from the mainland for an accommodation in the knowledge that a struggle for power in the KMT could revolve round such factors. Such tensions certainly exist in the KMT party but circumstances have not been favourable for the mainland's claim and it is impossible to tell what following it might be able to gather from the ranks of a crumbling Kuomintang. Equally there is no means of estimating what sympathy for a link with the mainland exists among the native Taiwanese. Nationalist rule has at least had the effect of ending their alienation from Chinese ways under Japanese rule. The national language (Kuo Yu or Mandarin) is taught in schools and the sense of Chinese nationalism is inculcated. But even with this advantage, conditions on the mainland, both political and economic, must confine support for their case to such few dedicated Communists as survive underground in Taiwan.

Certainly while China's present leaders remain there will be no dropping of the Taiwan issue. The determination to restore it to Peking's rule will be unaltered. On the other hand a change in Taiwan towards regarding Taiwan as Taiwan and not as a part of China could result from the retirement or death of Chiang Kai-shek or a change in American policy.

BIBLIOGRAPHY

W. G. Goddard. *Formosa. A Study in Chinese History.* (Macmillan, 1966.)

George H. Kerr. *Formosa Betrayed.* (Eyre & Spottiswoode, 1966.)

Mark Mancall (Ed.). *Formosa Today.* (Pall Mall Press, 1964.)

Robert P. Newman. *Recognition of Communist China?* (Macmillan, New York, 1961.)

HONG KONG

W. A. C. Adie

ORIGIN

HONG KONG sprang into being out of the clash between two worlds – Europe and China – which had developed civilizations that were self-sufficient, but so different that each regarded the other more or less as barbarians. The declining Manchu Dynasty was concerned to insulate its alien Chinese subjects from any contact with other foreigners, for fear that new ideas might subvert them. At the same time, the Emperors and their mandarins clung to an unrealistic, sinocentric view of the world. They could not conceive of the existence of independent foreign states with which diplomatic relations on a basis of equality could be possible, or trade relations desirable. Chien Lung wrote to George III that 'Our dynasty's majestic virtue has penetrated every country under Heaven, and kings of all nations have offered their costly tribute by land and sea . . . we possess all things.'

Although the Portuguese were allowed to settle in Macao in 1557, the main representatives of Europe eventually became the British, whose East India Company set up a trading post in Canton in 1715. Their ideology, as expressed by men like Wilberforce and Adam Smith, could not be reconciled with the feudal outlook of a Chien Lung; they were convinced that Christianity and commerce were the true creators of liberty and welfare for all races. But after 1757, foreign traders in China were confined to a sort of ghetto in Canton under severe restrictions – for example, no one was allowed to teach them Chinese, on pain of death. In fact, although the Manchu Government was able to frustrate diplomatic and cultural contacts, it could not prevent the spontaneous growth of commercial intercourse, which in the circumstances largely took the form of blatant smuggling with the connivance of the very officials who were supposed to restrict the foreigners' activities. After the expiry of the East India Company's monopoly of the China trade in 1834, the British Government became seriously concerned to find some way of normalizing the situation in Canton and controlling its own subjects' behaviour. But Lord Napier's attempt to establish contact with the Manchu authorities was frustrated, like all previous attempts, owing to their unrealistic beliefs about the world as described above. Shortly after this, the Emperor sent down the energetic and

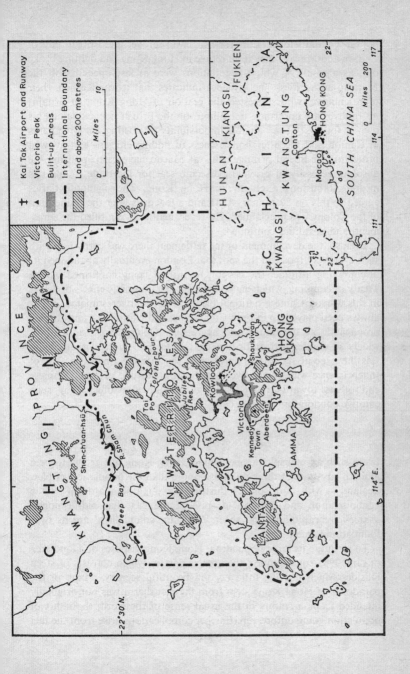

Legend:

Kai Tak Airport and Runway
Victoria Peak
Built-up Areas
International Boundary
Land above 200 metres

Miles 0 — 10

CHINA

HUNAN | KIANGSI | FUKIEN

KWANGSI

KWANGTUNG

Canton

Macao   HONG KONG

SOUTH CHINA SEA

Miles 0 — 200

KWANGTUNG PROVINCE

CHINA

Shen-ch'uan-hsü

Deep Bay

R. Sham Chun

NEW TERRITORIES

Tai Po

Tolo Harbour

Jubilee Res.

Kowloon

LANTAO

Victoria

Kennedy Town

Aberdeen

Shaukiwan

HONG KONG

LAMMA I.

22°30' N.

114° E.

24°

22

22

111   114   117

honest Commissioner Lin Tse-hsu, who drove the British out of Canton and Macao; they took refuge in Hong Kong and fighting broke out, as a result of which negotiations were at last opened with the Manchu authorities. The evidence indicates that it was Keshen, their representative, who suggested the cession of Hong Kong to Britain; his motives are uncertain, but Elliott, on the British side, explained his own as follows: 'The palpable impossibility of trusting our Merchants at Canton and the utter hopelessness of finding efficient and avowed protection or liberal arrangements at Macao have cast upon me the absolute necessity of providing a secure seat for the trade' – and this meant establishing a colony in Hong Kong. The plenipotentiaries agreed to this on 20 January 1841 and a few days later the foundation of the Colony was proclaimed. However, neither side ratified the agreement, and hostilities continued.

Even so, the development of the settlement there was carried on with such energy by those on the spot that London eventually abandoned its discouraging attitude, the cession to Britain being confirmed by the Treaty of Nanking, which ended the war. The traumatic effects of defeat in this war on Chinese national pride cannot be overestimated; it has always been played up in both Communist and Nationalist anti-foreign propaganda as the unjust and aggressive 'Opium War', and it was widely so condemned in Britain too; in fact, to pretend that opium was the issue at stake is as naïve as to say that the American War of Independence was fought over tea. But the attitude of many Chinese and others towards Hong Kong is undoubtedly affected by such emotive connotations to this day.

POPULATION AND LAND PROBLEMS

From such an inauspicious beginning, Hong Kong has grown to be a modern city state of three millions – more than the population of New Zealand – with flourishing industries and high standards of public administration and welfare, in spite of the fact that old-fashioned *laissez-faire* capitalism and sheer Victorian 'colonialism' are its twin foundation-stones.

To maintain its large population, Hong Kong disposes of a land area of only 398¼ square miles, the greater part of which consists of steep hillsides which provide little beyond beautiful scenery. Many of the paradoxes of Hong Kong stem from the fact that it was not originally intended to be a colony in the usual sense of the word, the influx of population being unforeseen. Further complications arise from the fact that 365½ square miles of its area – the New Territories, on the mainland – are only held on a 99-year lease granted by the Manchu Emperor on 1 July 1898, although they are very important for the colony's life. Almost all possible land in the New Territories (about fifty square miles) is under intensive cultivation, and in the last few years new industrial towns have been built there, partly on land reclaimed by tipping hills into the sea. Both in the city of Victoria on Hong Kong island and in Kowloon, which faces it across the harbour, there has been a spectacular building boom since the war; owing to the shortage of land, the ultra-modern blocks of flats, hotels, banks and offices must either cling to the cliffs or tower up from the strip of land reclaimed from the harbour. About 500,000 people, many of them immigrants from China, had been rehoused in eleven Government-built resettlement estates by the end of 1962 and about the same number by 1967. In 1962 the Government adopted a ten-year plan to build flats for more than 150,000. Nevertheless, many still live in improvised shacks on the hillsides or on the roofs of large buildings. Although the annual value of agricultural production is HK$200 million or more, and of fisheries HK$60 million, much of the food must be imported from China, and under an agreement signed in November 1960, China also sells 5,000 million gallons of water a year to Hong Kong. The provision of an adequate water supply has always been difficult because there are no large rivers or underwater springs. At present, the reservoirs can store 10,500 gallons of rainwater, and when the building programme now under way is completed, conventional sources of supply will be pretty well exhausted and the use of nuclear power to distil sea-water may have to be considered. Apart from the influx of refugees, Hong Kong's birth rate is the second highest in Asia, at 32·8 per 1,000.

HONG KONG'S INDUSTRIAL REVOLUTION

At the outbreak of the Second World War, Hong Kong's population was estimated at 1,600,000, of whom about a quarter were sleeping on the streets. Japanese occupation brought it down to about 600,000 but by the end of 1950 it had risen again to 2,360,000.

Next year the Korean War trade boom came to an end, and the embargo on export of strategic goods to China dealt a severe blow at Hong Kong's traditional entrepôt trade; trade with China was also considerably reduced because of the Chinese Government's own decision to cut imports of consumer goods, and import capital goods mainly from the Soviet bloc.

As a result, the refugees could not find employment in the declining entrepôt trade, while primary production – agriculture and fisheries and a little mining – could only absorb a few. But among them were many businessmen from Shanghai and Canton who brought with them their capital and experience. Thus, a new 'entrepreneurial élite', as described by W. W. Rostow, arrived ready-made to help prepare the 'take-off into economic growth' which all underdeveloped countries dream of. The necessary preconditions for industrialization – efficient administration and financial arrangements, an adequate infrastructure of communications, public utilities, education and welfare services, port facilities, the shipbuilding industry and so forth – had already been provided.

Among the factors contributing to Hong Kong's spectacular economic growth must be noted, first of all, the high quality of the managerial and labour force and the rarity of industrial unrest. This may be partly due to the fact that the trade union movement is split between Communists and Nationalists, but is mainly due to some characteristics of Chinese social structure, such as the prevalence of family firms and of the recruitment of the foreman's own clansmen as workers. Such factors also tend to limit bureaucratic wastefulness in business, and to reinforce the effects of traditional Chinese thrift, industriousness and skill. Savings have been high, and apart from remittances to relatives in China they have usually been ploughed back into equipment for further production. Compared to private capital formed locally or transferred from unsettled areas abroad, the grants from the Colonial Development and Welfare Fund have been negligible. Hong Kong has received no 'aid' under the Colombo plan, or any other such scheme.

A most important factor, however, has been the survival of *laissez-faire* capitalism in Hong Kong owing to its origin as a free port; while some of the inherent evils of capitalism have been mitigated by the Chinese social system or by Government action, economic planning and controls have been almost non-existent, and the much-maligned profit motive has reigned supreme.

THE PROBLEM OF THE REFUGEES

At the last census, in March 1961, the population was found to be 3,133,131, over 99 per cent of whom were Chinese; what has the industrial revolution done for them? Studies carried out by economists have shown that the standard of living of the average worker, low as it still is, is far higher than in mainland China (where industrialization started at about the same time) and compares favourably with other developing countries. The workers themselves evidently prefer Hong Kong, though they could return to China any time. Many of those who did leave to help 'build socialism' there have since trickled back to Hong Kong. It is still easy to find squatters without proper houses, and almost as easy to find people who look underfed; but this is not the fault of the Hong Kong Government, which has made superhuman efforts to keep up with the influx of refugees, and has resettled many hundreds of thousands in modern multi-storey blocks during the last few years.

When the island was ceded, a supplementary treaty provided that all Chinese would have unrestricted access to it; moreover the status of Chinese residents in Hong Kong has all along been ambiguous, since according to the Chinese principle of *ius sanguinis* they remain Chinese nationals even though they may be, from the British point of view, citizens of the United Kingdom and Colonies by birth. This situation has caused many complications; in May 1950 the Government was finally compelled to restrict entry from the mainland, except for local traffic to and from Kwangtung: China immediately protested. When a relaxation was tried in 1956, control had to be reimposed after three months because the inflow was again getting out of hand. An official quota of fifty a day is still allowed in. In May 1962 the Canton authorities relaxed their own border controls, and in a few days about 50,000 had crossed over illegally. If the flow had been encouraged, it would have swamped the Colony's resources entirely; for one thing, the precarious water situation was emphasized a few days later when the Chinese were obliged by the drought to cut off the water they were supplying across the border. Most of the escapees had to be sent back.

THE FUTURE

Although, in theory, the New Territories will revert to China in 1997, leaving only the ceded territory of Kowloon ($3\frac{1}{4}$ square miles) and Hong Kong island, building and investment continues apace and few appear to think that far ahead. At present Hong Kongites seem more worried about the limitations lately imposed by various countries on the imports of Hong Kong-manufactured goods, especially textiles.

Though Hong Kong's unique situation has so far precluded the normal colonial development towards self-government, it would seem that some political provision must be worked out to regularize its continued existence perhaps as a member of the South-East Asian

Federation and/or under international guarantee. Peking would probably not wish, for some time to come, to lose such a fruitful source of foreign exchange; while Hong Kong's potentialities as a 'shop window' of an alternative way of life, and for bridging the present artificial and dangerous political, cultural and ideological gulf which again yawns between China and the rest of the world could, if properly handled, prove increasingly important for world peace in the coming years – whether or not China's efforts to achieve Great (and nuclear) Power status are crowned with rapid success. It must be noted that by proposing the establishment of a Chinese Consulate in Hong Kong, Peking has clearly recognized British sovereignty; though since such a Consulate could claim authority over the majority of the inhabitants, these proposals have so far been turned down.

The interests of the world at large require that Hong Kong should on the one hand receive adequate outside assistance in solving its refugee problems, and on the other, that the anomalies in its status, and that of its residents, should be removed by suitable international arrangements and internal political development. Three million Chinese demonstrating the arts of democratic self-government might give Asia an example in the political field which would be even more instructive and valuable than Hong Kong's existing economic success.

BIBLIOGRAPHY

G. C. Allen and A. G. Donnithorne. *Western Enterprise in Far Eastern Economic Development*. (Allen & Unwin, 1954.)

Sir Charles Collins. *Public Administration in Hong Kong*. (Royal Institute of International Affairs, 1952.)

Maurice Collis. *Foreign Mud*. (Faber & Faber, 1956.)

S. G. Davis. *Hong Kong in its Geographical Setting*. (Collins, 1949.)

G. B. Endacott. *A History of Hong Kong*. (Oxford University Press, 1958.)

E. Hambro. *Hong Kong Refugees Survey Mission*. (Report to the UN High Commissioner for Refugees.) (Leyden, 1955.)

E. R. Hughes. *The Invasion of China by the Western World*. (A. & C. Black, London, 1937.)

E. V. G. Kiernan. *British Diplomacy in China 1880–85*. (Cambridge University Press, 1939.)

Sir F. Lugard. *Memorandum regarding the restrictions of opium in Hong Kong and China*. (Hong Kong, 1908.)

E. Luard. *Britain and China*. (Chatto & Windus, 1962.)

A. Mills. *British Rule in Eastern Asia*. (Humphrey Milford, London, 1942.)

M. Perham. *Lugard, The Years of Authority, 1898–1945*. (Collins, 1960.)

HONG KONG

G. R. Sayer. *Hong Kong: Birth, Adolescence and Coming of Age.* (Oxford University Press, 1937.)

E. F. Szczepanik. *The Economic Growth of Hong Kong.* (Oxford University Press, and Hong Kong University Press, 1958.)

A. Waley. *The Opium War Through Chinese Eyes.* (Allen & Unwin, 1958.)

See also Hong Kong Government Annual Reports. (H.M. Stationery Office, London, or Government Publications Bureau, Hong Kong.)

JAPAN

Richard Storry

EARLY HISTORY

THE remote ancestors of the present inhabitants of the four major and nearly three thousand minor islands of Japan almost certainly came from the mainland of Asia; from China, Manchuria, and Korea. It may be that there was also some immigration from the region of South-East Asia. But no records exist of these early movements of peoples. There is only a substantial and elaborate body of myths, suggesting that invaders from overseas gradually supplanted the existing inhabitants of Japan, the Ainu (of whom a few descendants survive in the northern island of Hokkaido).

Mythology alleged that the Japanese islands were created by the gods; that the grandson of the sun goddess came down, at her command, to rule Japan; that he was the progenitor of a line of semi-deities destined to be the Emperors of Japan, his own great-grandson being the first. Nothing more need be said about such legends, except to note two things: first, that this mythology was intimately connected with a cult of the sun; secondly, that the myths of national origin were taught in Japanese schools as factual history until soon after the end of the Pacific War, in 1945. Japanese nationalist sentiment rested squarely on a belief in this mythology; and for anyone to express public disbelief in it could lead to a popular outcry and, occasionally, to unpleasant consequences for the person concerned.

Japan, an intensely mountainous country, has two important plains. One is in the east, in what is known as the Kanto area. Here today are to be found Tokyo – the largest city in the world – and the conurbations of Yokohama and Kawasaki. The other main plain is in the west, in what is called the Kansai region, at the head of the Inland Sea. This area, in which have grown up the cities of Kyoto, Osaka, and Kobe, is the heartland of the historical Empire. The ancient capitals, changing with every new Emperor, were all in this Kansai area. A permanent capital was established in A.D. 794 at Heian-kyo, later to be known as Miyako or Kyoto. This city remained, in name at any rate, the metropolis until 1868.

In early times it was natural that the Japanese should have been profoundly impressed by the culture of China, the country that represented

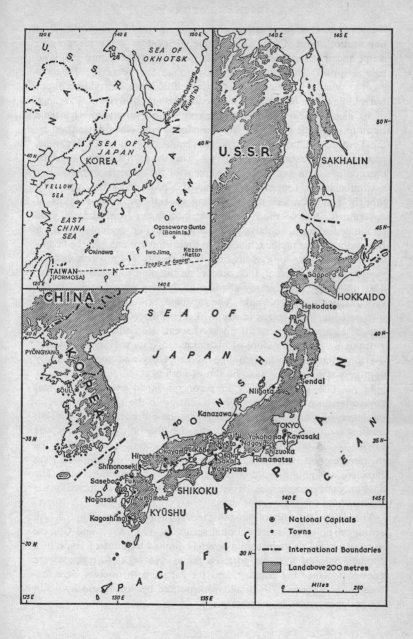

U.S.S.R.

SEA OF
OKHOTSK

KURIL'SKIYE OSTROVA
(Kuril Is.)

SEA OF
JAPAN

KOREA

YELLOW
SEA

EAST
CHINA
SEA

Ogasawara Gunto
(Bonin Is.)

Okinawa   IwoJima   Kazan
                     Retto

Tropic of Cancer

TAIWAN
(FORMOSA)

PACIFIC OCEAN

U.S.S.R.

SAKHALIN

Sapporo

HOKKAIDO

Hakodate

CHINA

SEA OF

JAPAN

PYŎNGYANG

KOREA

SŎUL

Sendai

Niigata

Kanazawa

TOKYO

Gifu Yokohama Kawasaki
      Nagoya
Kyoto   Shizuoka
Okayama Kobe Hamamatsu
Hiroshima Osaka
        Sakai
Shimonoseki   Wakayama

Sasebo Fukuoka

Nagasaki Kumamoto   SHIKOKU

Kagoshima KYŪSHU

H O N S H U

J A P A N

P A C I F I C   O C E A N

National Capitals
Towns
International Boundaries
Land above 200 metres

Miles
0   250

the very acme of civilization and power in the Asian world. Two importations from China deserve special mention – the ideographic script and the Buddhist religion. The former gave structure and style to the spoken language, although through the years the Japanese evolved syllabic ideographs of their own. Buddhism, introduced about the middle of the 6th century, dazzled minds and hearts with the range of its metaphysical beliefs and the colour and variety of its artistic traditions. All the same, the Buddhist faith, even when patronized by the Throne, did not supplant the indigenous religion of the Japanese, namely Shinto, bound up as this was with the myths surrounding the creation of Japan and the establishment of the Imperial dynasty.

Confucianism, too, entered Japan, with profound effects upon the thought and behaviour of succeeding generations. Chinese ideas of government, like so much that came into Japan from abroad, were remoulded along distinctively Japanese lines. For example, it was a basic concept among the Chinese that their Emperor enjoyed the favour of Heaven only so long as his rule was virtuous. If Emperors became vicious and incompetent, then others had the right to overthrow them. Thus the sometimes bloody changes of dynasty were justified in the eyes of sages and people alike. The Japanese, however, never saw their own hereditary sovereigns in this light. The Emperor of Japan was the Son of Heaven by virtue of divine descent. He could not fail to be virtuous by the very nature of his unique inheritance. So any idea of overthrowing the traditional line of Emperors and replacing it by another was so impious as to be almost unthinkable.

In practice, only very few Emperors of Japan exercised any real governmental powers. From the 8th century to the 12th these were in the hands of a gifted family of courtiers, the Fujiwara. From the 12th century until more than half-way through the 19th, government was carried on, in the Emperor's name, by a succession of Shoguns, or their representatives. The name 'Shogun' is an abbreviation of a long Japanese compound word meaning, in essence, 'generalissimo'. The Shogun's government was basically a military affair, conducted in the main by and for the warrior class.

The last great family of Shoguns, the Tokugawa, adopted in the 17th century a policy of strict national seclusion. The Dutch and Chinese were permitted to engage in a severely limited amount of trade in a confined part of a single port, Nagasaki. No other foreigners were allowed to enter the country; and the Japanese themselves were forbidden to go abroad. Christianity, introduced by Portuguese Jesuits in the 16th century, was suppressed.

JAPAN

ARRIVAL OF COMMODORE PERRY

The inevitable intrusion of the outside world occurred in the 1850s. Commodore Perry of the United States Navy, with a powerful squadron, was the first to compel the reluctant Japanese to open their doors. This happened in 1854. Within the next twenty years other powerful countries had followed suit and under the impact of their pressure a number of changes took place; and these were almost as revolutionary as those which followed Japan's surrender in 1945.

The Shogun's government was overthrown by a combination of feudal lords and their retainers from south-west Japan. The new masters of the country declared that the Emperor would be restored to the full dignity of sovereign ruler, and in what is known as the Meiji Restoration the reigning Emperor, a young man in his teens, moved from Kyoto to a new capital in the east, the modern Tokyo. The seclusion policy was wholly abandoned, the national aim now being to modernize Japan with all possible speed.

JAPAN AS PUPIL OF THE WEST

The small group of able retainers of the lords from south-western Japan carried out the policy of modernization with single-minded determination. They were indeed the founding fathers of modern Japan. Under their authoritarian direction a system of compulsory state education was established as the necessary basis of future progress. The machinery of government was reshaped on Western lines. A programme of industrialization was put in motion, as quickly as men could be trained in the use of new techniques. Railways, steamships, harbours, banks, printing presses, and post-offices – these and other typical appurtenances of Western industrial culture were soon established on Japanese soil. Needless to say, a modern army and navy also came into being; and by 1894 Japan was strong enough to engage in war with China. By the following year China, having suffered a series of defeats, signed a treaty of peace by which Japan obtained Formosa and other gains.

Only ten years later Japan inflicted defeat on Russia by land and sea; and thus in 1905, after this success, Japan was one of the Great Powers; a status confirmed after the First World War, when the Japanese obtained a permanent seat on the Council of the League of Nations. The Japanese Empire now included not only the Kurile Islands, South Sakhalin, Korea, Formosa, and part of South Manchuria, but also the former German islands in the Pacific north of the Equator. Such a rapid rise to world power, in terms of economic as well as military and political strength, had not been known in modern times. Even the history of Prussia and Germany in the second half of the 19th century seemed less impressive.

At first, Japan's rise to power was welcomed by most of the people of Asia. Here was an Asian country, after all, that had defeated Imperial Russia and thus exploded the myth of white invincibility. This was how millions in India, Burma, Java, and in China too, interpreted Japan's victory in 1905.

IMPERIALIST JAPAN

It was not long, however, before Japan began to be regarded as an imperialist nation as proud and overbearing as Britain, France, Holland, and the United States. This was due, in the main, to the course taken by Japanese-Chinese relations.

These had always been ambivalent. On the one hand the Japanese gave shelter and help to radical Chinese in their early struggles – to Sun Yat-sen, for example. On the other, the Chinese discovered that Japan regarded China, especially Manchuria and north China, as her sphere of political and economic influence. The Japanese, having consolidated their modernization, were in an expansive mood; and after 1905 China appeared to be the natural target for Japan's expansion. The confused state of China's polity after the collapse of the Manchu Dynasty in 1912 was in itself almost an invitation to the Japanese to take a hand, overtly or behind the scenes, in Chinese affairs.

Throughout the period of the First World War and the 1920s Japan's relations with China were always tense, often stormy, sometimes deceptively calm. The breaking point came in the 1930s.

In September 1931 Japanese forces in south Manchuria seized the city of Mukden and then set about the conquest of all Manchuria. This action, in its initial stages at all events, was carried out without the approval of the Japanese Government. But once the army was committed to its course of aggression the cabinet in Tokyo could do little to restrain it. For by constitutional practice the cabinet had no jurisdiction over the operations of the fighting services. This was the province of the Supreme Commander – in other words the Army and Navy General Staffs. Moreover the Army and Navy Ministers, invariably generals and admirals, always felt that their first obligation was to their respective services. It was unusual for them to be aware of any binding ties to their cabinet colleagues.

In defiance of a large body of opinion both inside Japan and outside – for Japan's action was condemned by the League of Nations and the United States – the army not only completed the occupation of Manchuria but also transformed the country into a nominally independent state, Manchukuo. In fact Manchukuo was wholly controlled by Japan.

FASCISM

There now followed a period which Japanese historians have labelled as 'fascist'; although the Japanese brand of fascism lacked a Duce or Führer, and there was never a single mass party in Japan, as in Italy and Nazi Germany.

In a sense it was a quasi-revolutionary period. The Great Depression had hit Japan very hard, bringing great distress to a large proportion of the farming community, which was drastically affected by the collapse of Japanese silk exports. The processing of silk cocoons was a vital household occupation for many hundreds of thousands of households.

Amid the general misery and discontent Japan's still weak parliamentary system, often disturbed by unsavoury corruption scandals, hardly showed to advantage. Confucian traditions, the strongly ethnocentric nationalist training implanted by school and family alike, the rigorous watchfulness of the ubiquitous police – these prevented grievances seeking an outlet in Marxist agitation. The eruptions took the form of ultra-nationalist militancy. No fewer than three Premiers and ex-Premiers were assassinated by nationalist fanatics in uniform between the spring of 1932 and the spring of 1936. Other public men were killed in the same period; and a number of bloody conspiracies failed only because of timely discovery by the police. Even so, in February 1936, a group of young officers at the head of over a thousand troops, after carrying out a series of assassinations, occupied buildings in the heart of Tokyo and only surrendered after four days of defiance. The city was fortunate in being spared the sight of Japanese soldiers fighting each other, the mutineers being persuaded to lay down their arms peacefully.

The views and purposes of these extreme nationalists were not always clear. But they claimed to be passionately loyal to the Emperor – this was somewhat ironic, since the Emperor was a quiet, liberal-minded scholar with no time for extremism of any sort – and most of them declared that the Emperor was given evil advice by selfish and corrupt courtiers and politicians, and that these must be liquidated in summary

227

fashion if Japan were to be saved from further ruin. There was a pronounced National Socialist flavour to much of this agitation. Many
young officers, sincerely concerned by the plight of the farming districts
from which most of them came, were bitterly hostile to the great
capitalist combines, the so-called *zaibatsu* ('financial cliques'), which
dominated the economy. The young officers despised the Diet, which
they regarded as little more than a stage for marionettes operated by
the *zaibatsu*. Some officers advocated the nationalization of all private
property in excess of a certain figure. Yet Marxism and orthodox
Socialism in general were suspect in their eyes. The ultra-Nationalists,
then, tended to be both anti-capitalist and anti-Marxist. On the conduct
of foreign policy their views were usually chauvinist in the extreme.

This kind of unrest enabled the leaders of the army to exert a form
of blackmail on the Japanese Establishment. For example, the Minister
of War would tell the cabinet that unless the army's wishes on some
matter of policy were adopted, he and the other generals could not
guarantee that their subordinates would behave themselves. In such
manner the already considerable political influence of the army was
greatly enhanced. Thus in 1937, when fighting broke out between a
detachment of Japanese troops and Chinese forces near Peking, the
cabinet felt unable to refuse a demand from the Minister of War that
reinforcements should be sent to north China.

In this way a local Sino-Japanese clash developed into a full-scale
undeclared war, the so-called 'China Incident'. This struggle outraged
both the British and the Americans, whose interests were destroyed,
purloined, or disrupted by the Japanese armies as these occupied the
coastal cities of China and advanced into the interior.

EUROPEAN ALLIANCE

Between Japanese militarism and European fascism there was a certain
climate of opinion in common and a growing identity of purpose. For
Germany, Italy, and Japan thought of themselves, in the horrible jargon
of the day, as 'Have-Not Nations'.

But it was not until September 1940 – after Germany's spectacular
victories in Europe – that the three formally allied themselves in the
Tripartite Axis Pact.

Thenceforward relations between Japan and the Anglo-Saxon Powers
became steadily worse; until in July 1941 a serious crisis arose after
Japan had persuaded the Vichy Government to permit the establishment
of Japanese military, naval, and air bases in the southern part of French

Indo-China. This move was interpreted in Washington and London as implying a clear threat to the security of both Malaya and the Dutch East Indies. Accordingly the United States Government placed a virtual embargo on trade with Japan. Similar action was taken by the Governments of Britain and Holland.

The Americans insisted, in talks with the Japanese at Washington, that they would raise the embargo only in return for a firm promise that Japan would withdraw from both Indo-China and China proper. The Japanese now faced a serious situation – one brought upon them by the folly and ambition of their own military nationalists. For imports from South-East Asia – notably oil from Dutch Borneo – were essential to Japan's economy, now being placed on a war-time basis.

The Japanese Premier of the day, Prince Konoye, was prepared to bow to Washington's demand. The alternatives, after all, were economic strangulation or war. But Lieutenant-General Tojo, the War Minister, was adamant in rejecting any idea of a military withdrawal from China. The result of this clash of views was Konoye's resignation in mid October 1941, Tojo succeeding him as Prime Minister. It had already been decided in secret, at a conference of the highest military and civilian leaders in Tokyo, that, if talks with the Americans were not successful by the late autumn, then war must come.

PEARL HARBOR

It came on 7 December 1941, when Japanese forces suddenly attacked the American Pacific fleet in Pearl Harbor, Hawaii, the British at Hong Kong, Malaya and Singapore, and American airfields in the Philippines. The Japanese assault preceded their declaration of war. They had adopted the same surprise tactics in their struggles with China in 1894 and with Russia in 1904.

For the next six months, until the early summer of 1942, the Japanese were overwhelmingly victorious. A vast area from the Indo-Burmese border to the Solomons Sea fell into their hands.

The tide turned very slowly at first. But the ebb quickened in 1944, with defeats for the Japanese in the Pacific, on the frontiers of India and Burma, and in the Philippines. Shipping losses and increasingly heavy and frequent air raids began to cripple the Japanese economy; and so by the summer of 1945 the situation was becoming desperate indeed.

In July 1945, the Japanese asked the Soviet Government to mediate for peace; but the response in Moscow was evasive. The Russians in fact were preparing to enter the war against Japan; for this had been agreed upon by secret accord with the British and Americans at Yalta at the beginning of the year.

HIROSHIMA

The dropping of the first atomic bomb over Hiroshima on 6 August 1945, followed within the next three days by Russia's attack and the dropping of a second atomic bomb over Nagasaki, enabled the Emperor of Japan to resolve a deadlock that had developed in the counsels of his military and civilian leaders. Half of them were ready to admit defeat. The other half maintained that the war must continue. Both sides turned to the Emperor, asking him in effect to give the casting vote. The Emperor, who had never acted except on the advice of his government or high command, now declared that Japan ought to accept the terms of the Potsdam Proclamation – by Truman, Churchill, and Chiang Kai-shek – which demanded the unconditional surrender of all Japan's armed forces. This decision was broadcast, in the Emperor's own words, on 15 August 1945.

THE OCCUPATION OF JAPAN

Although in name an Allied responsibility, the Occupation of Japan, which lasted for a little over six and a half years, was primarily an American affair. In fact General MacArthur, the Supreme Commander, would brook little interference from Washington or elsewhere with the way in which he and his staff conducted their business. They governed indirectly, through the Japanese cabinet, passing on to the latter a stream of instructions which were usually executed without cavil or delay.

In his official announcement of Japan's decision to surrender, the Emperor had admonished his subjects 'to beware most strictly of any outbursts of emotion that may engender needless complications'. Thus it was clearly understood by all officers of the state that co-operation with the Americans was now the national policy. Mr Yoshida, Prime Minister during most of the Occupation period, tells us in his memoirs that Admiral Suzuki, Premier at the time of the surrender, observed that while it was important to be a good winner in a war it was equally important to be a good loser. The Japanese as a whole seemed to be of this mind. Relations between the Japanese and the Americans, then, were remarkably harmonious.

Having disarmed Japan the prime aim of the Occupation authorities was to reform the social and political life of the country – or, in a word, to 'democratize' it. And under prompting from the Americans something not far short of a real, though bloodless, revolution took place during the Occupation years. The Japanese, dazed and disillusioned by their national collapse, were ready, often eager, to accept 'democracy' as the talismanic word of the new era.

The vote was given to all men and women of twenty-one and over. In a new constitution, drafted by MacArthur's staff, sovereignty was formally vested in the people, and the Diet became the 'highest organ of the state', the Lower House having much greater power than the Upper House. As for the Emperor, he became 'the symbol of the unity of the people'. Women were given full equality with men in such matters as property rights, inheritance, and divorce. Millions of tenant farmers were granted possession of the land they tilled. The oppressive, centralized authority of the police was radically curtailed. The teaching of Japanese history in schools came to a stop, pending the introduction of new text-books purged of ethnocentric bias.

With these and other reforms Japan became a free society almost overnight. Individualism began to outweigh community and family ties. Pacifism replaced belligerence. Samurai ideals of self-sacrifice gave way to hedonism. An entire structure of traditional ideas about the Emperor, about Japan and the Japanese race, about the obligations of the individual to society, came toppling down. In its place stood two modest but satisfying ideals – hard work and the pursuit of personal happiness.

On 8 September 1951 Japan signed a Treaty of Peace with forty-eight other nations in San Francisco. No doubt because war-time ill-feeling had to some extent subsided, and thanks to the foresight and resolution of Mr Foster Dulles as chief architect of the Treaty, the peace settlement was not ungenerous. No crippling reparations were imposed on Japan; no limitations were imposed on Japanese economy and trade. All the same, the treaty formally liquidated a colonial empire, from south Sakhalin to Formosa, already lost.

Together with the Treaty of Peace Japan signed another document, a Security Pact with the United States, whereby the latter could retain her forces in and around Japanese territory in order to protect it from attack. Moreover, the Americans continued to have jurisdiction over the Ryukyu and Bonin Islands immediately south of Japan.

The Peace Treaty came into force on 28 April 1952. Japan was once again, in an official sense, an independent nation.

JAPAN SINCE 1952

The most striking development since the Peace Treaty came into force has been Japan's economic growth. This is examined in another section of this book. But its important political and social effects should be mentioned here.

The rise in the standard of living, though unevenly spread, has immensely increased the number of those Japanese who regard themselves as belonging to the middle class, the bourgeoisie and petty bourgeoisie as opposed to the urban and rural proletariat. Indeed some sociologists claim that probably more than 70 per cent of the Japanese people feel that they are members of this broad middle class, since they now own property in the form of land or savings.

In political terms this has meant that in every general election since the Peace Treaty the Conservatives, represented by the present Liberal-Democratic Party, have contrived to win a majority of seats in the all-important lower house – the House of Representatives – of the National Diet. There have been seven of these elections between the beginning of 1952 and the middle of 1967. During that period of fifteen years the tendency has been for the Socialists to increase their percentage of the total number of votes cast; and this figure was just over 40 per cent in the election of January 1967. But they are still hardly within sight of winning power. In 1967, for example, the Conservatives held 277 seats in the House of Representatives. Their opponents on the Left held 175 seats.

Indeed, so far there has only been one Socialist cabinet in Japanese history, the Katayama administration, which held office – in coalition with a group of Conservatives, be it noted – from May 1947 to March 1948.

Yet the leading organs of the press and the greater part of the academic world, a very articulate section of Japanese society, favour the Socialists. The powerful trade union movement is also clearly tied to the main Socialist party. Furthermore, it is probable that younger voters, especially in the cities and towns, support the Socialists. But the countryside on the whole is Conservative. This is not so much because traditions are always stronger in country districts than in towns; rather, it is due to the Occupation land reform, and to the food and agricultural policy of successive governments which has meant that the farmers have had an assured market and a guaranteed price for rice, the staple crop.

The long years in opposition have been very frustrating for the

Socialists. Hence a certain bitterness in the tone, and an air of irresponsibility in the content, of many of their pronouncements and electoral manifestoes. Equally its continued success at the polls has often tempted the Government party to display an unedifying ruthlessness in the Diet, an almost flippant lack of consideration for the rights of the Opposition; and this has stunted the proper growth of the parliamentary spirit in Japan. For in response to such tactics by the Conservatives the Socialists have on many occasions resorted to a form of violence inside the Diet; one typical method being to sit on the floor of the corridor leading to the Lower House, thus preventing the Speaker from taking his chair. This produces inevitable counter measures from the Liberal-Democrats, who with the help of the Diet police set about the physical ejection of their opponents.

The most notorious of these 'battles' took place on 19 May 1960, at the crisis of the debate over the ratification of the revised Japanese-American Security Pact. On this occasion some five hundred policemen were called in to remove the far from passive 'sit-down' Socialists. The Conservative rump then hastened to ratify the new Pact, although the entire Opposition and even several Government supporters were absent from the chamber.

FOREIGN RELATIONS

These have been dominated by the Cold War. The Japanese as a whole would prefer to be committed to neither side in this great East–West struggle. Nevertheless they value their association with the United States. After all Japan's prosperity is based on a capitalist economy, and Japan's present political structure has been deeply influenced by American example. On the official level Japanese foreign policy is closely tied to that of the United States; and the economic bonds with America are multifarious and are intimately related to Japan's own standard of living. For example, the export of high-class consumer goods to America has greatly helped to promote the domestic demand for these commodities. Thus the Japanese home market has become increasingly Americanized. Any serious rift with the United States would be regarded as an almost unmitigated disaster.

Japan, then, is the ally of the United States – but a somewhat fearful and sometimes reluctant ally. The Japanese – perhaps even more than most people in the modern world – dread the prospect of nuclear war; and one of the most effective points that the Socialists make in their appeal to the Japanese people is that American bases may attract

Communist rockets. This particular fear lay behind the great demonstrations against the revised Security Pact that took place in Tokyo in May and June 1960.

In many respects the new Pact was an improvement, from the Japanese point of view, on the old. For the old Pact, signed together with the San Francisco Peace Treaty, had no limit set to its validity; and there were other elements in it which retained something of the flavour of the Occupation, when Japan lacked independence. For instance, American forces in Japan under the terms of the old Pact could be used to quell serious disorders on an invitation from the Japanese Government.

The revised Security Pact of 1960 is an agreement, formally at any rate, between two equal and independent powers. Its duration is ten years.

But this term is regarded as too long, not only by Japanese Socialists but also by some Conservatives. Furthermore, the revised Pact was negotiated and signed a few months before the U-2 incident; and the Americans were forced to admit that some U-2 planes were based on airfields in Japan, although it was asserted that these planes had been used exclusively for weather observations. The U-2 affair and the disruption of the Paris 'Summit' talks occurred before the revised Security Pact had been ratified by the Japanese Diet. It was only a few days after ratification by the Lower House, amid the rude violence that has been described, that Khrushchev warned Japan that American bases would be dealt 'a shattering blow' if they were employed for intelligence flights over Soviet territory.

The physical struggle inside the Diet, followed by the hasty and undignified ratification of the new Pact by the Liberal-Democratic rump, scandalized the Japanese public. Khrushchev's message thoroughly alarmed it. There followed the massive demonstrations in Tokyo that attracted the attention of the world. Moreover, an official visit to Tokyo by President Eisenhower was cancelled, only a very short time before it was due to take place, by the Americans at the request of the Japanese Government.

This was misinterpreted outside Japan, and especially in the United States, as the result of some skilfully organized Communist plot.

But it should be noted that the Pact was ratified by both Houses of the Diet, that although the Prime Minister, Mr Kishi, resigned – in July 1960, when the storm of agitation was already dying down – he was succeeded by Mr Ikeda, of the Government's party; and in the next general election, of November 1960, this party, as we have seen, obtained a substantial majority of seats.

Mr Ikeda diverted public attention from foreign affairs by promising to double personal income, in terms of real purchasing power, within ten years.

What, then, has been Japan's relationship with the Communist Bloc, with the Soviet Union and the People's Republic of China?

The Soviet Union refused to sign the Treaty of Peace at San Francisco; and there is still no formal and official peace agreement between the Soviet Union and Japan. But in October 1956, after long months of negotiations, the two countries agreed to resume diplomatic relations. Trade between the two has not reached formidable proportions; but Japanese businessmen hope that they may be able to contribute to the development of Siberia by furnishing industrial machinery and other manufactured products. There is in fact the possibility that at least some of this hope may be gratified, the Russians bartering oil for machinery.

As one would expect, the Soviet Union, as the country of Lenin and the pioneer Communist state, enjoys what is now almost a traditional prestige in the eyes of the far left. But it must be said that, except among the members of the Japan Communist Party and the ranks of its fellow travellers, the Soviet Union is an object of widespread suspicion and dislike in Japan; and such feelings are not unmixed with fear. For the Russians, in addition to extending their territorial waters from three to twelve miles, have for many years drastically restricted Japanese fishing in the seas north of Hokkaido. The Russians retain not only the Kurile Islands and South Sakhalin but also certain small islands geographically grouped with the Kuriles, which were administratively part of Hokkaido up to the summer of 1945. These particular islands, the Habomais and Shikotan, are very close indeed to Hokkaido. Yet their shores and near-by waters are entirely closed to Japanese fishermen.

The treatment of Japanese prisoners in Siberia after the War and the Soviet slowness to repatriate them – as late as 1957 it was alleged that there were still about 11,000 Japanese prisoners-of-war in Russian hands – caused deep resentment, as did the barbarous way in which Japanese residents were expelled from South Sakhalin in 1945.

Communist China, however, is not the object of comparable antipathy. Until the period of the Cultural Revolution Red China attracted a good deal of sympathetic interest in Japan. This was due to a variety of factors. First, every educated Japanese was aware of his country's cultural debt to China in the past. This, however, was no doubt a minor factor. Of more importance was the feeling, particularly strong among intellectuals, that a tradition of co-operation with 'progressive' Chinese had been shamefully betrayed by Japan's aggression against

China between the two World Wars and especially from 1937 onwards. Indeed everyone in Japan knows that the attack on China was accompanied by all manner of abominations; for these matters, heavily censored up to 1945, have been given great publicity through Japanese magazines and books in the post-war years. So among educated people there has been a feeling akin to guilt in their attitude to the Chinese. But China's nuclear explosions have done much to wipe out this sense of guilt on the part of the Japanese.

Ideology, of course, also plays a significant part. While it is true that in the left-wing student movement there is a substantial faction which criticizes Mao Tse-tung, Japanese intellectuals in general – teachers, students, artists, writers, actors, and journalists – are to some extent fascinated by the spectacle of the People's Republic, even if many of them disapprove of the restrictions on personal liberty that the regime has imposed, not to mention the excesses of the Cultural Revolution. For such people Communism in operation in China still has something resembling a moral appeal. Yet here we might note that when Japanese scholars write about the people's communes they rarely advocate this type of organization for Japan. The Japanese farmer, indeed, is very unlikely to be attracted to the idea of compulsory collectivization.

It is worth remarking, also, that in contrast to Soviet Russia the People's China adopted a lenient policy towards Japanese war criminals and was not slow to send back to Japan those Japanese in China whom the Nationalist Government had not yet repatriated before its exodus to Formosa.

But it is perhaps the pull of economic interests that makes Japanese of all shades of opinion keenly interested in what goes on in China. The Japanese business world is prepared to ignore ideology when it comes to the prospect of trade with Red China. For undoubtedly the Government's policy of doubling incomes within ten years will mean much larger imports of raw materials. This must lead to more persistent demands by Japanese businessmen for access to Chinese iron ore, coal, and other resources.

However, until very recently the Peking Government has made it plain that any enlargement of Sino-Japanese trade depends on a change in Japan's diplomatic policy towards the two Chinas. For Japan – thanks to American insistence during the winter of 1951–2 – recognizes the Nationalist Government in Formosa as the legitimate government of China.

So an official gulf separates Japan from the People's Republic; and, since China's foreign trade is controlled by a commission of the Peking

Government, commercial dealings with Japan can be cut off at any moment – as occurred in 1958 when, on the excuse of an insult given to their trade delegation in Nagasaki, the Chinese abruptly cancelled all outstanding contracts and severed economic relations with Japan.

Nevertheless the Chinese have welcomed various deputations from Japan. One of these, representing the Socialist Party, achieved some notoriety. The deputation was headed by the party's Secretary-General, Mr Asanuma. He was moved, while in Peking, to make a speech in which he referred to the United States as 'the common enemy' of Japan and of the People's Government. This was in 1959. In the autumn of the following year, at a public meeting in Tokyo and in full view of the audience and of a battery of television cameras, Asanuma was stabbed to death by a youth belonging to one of the small extreme right-wing groups that still poison the political atmosphere in Japan. The young man – who later committed suicide while in detention – declared that it was Asanuma's speech at Peking which made him a deserving victim of assassination.

An even nearer neighbour than either Soviet Siberia or mainland China is not yet on the best of terms with Japan. This is Korea, or more strictly South Korea. Here the many years of Japanese rule left a legacy of active dislike. This is to some extent reciprocated. For a minority of the Koreans in Japan, for years little esteemed by the Japanese among whom they lived, behaved with possibly pardonable arrogance, and sometimes with inexcusable lawlessness, as soon as Japan surrendered and the restraints imposed by the overbearing police were moved. There was no doubt greater resentment in Japan over the so-called Rhee Line, which denied Japanese fishermen access to waters within fifty miles of the Korean coast. Syngman Rhee himself, while he was in office, would allow no Japanese economic repenetration of his country; and it is only recently that the establishment of normal diplomatic relations between Japan and South Korea has done something towards bringing mutual amity.

With Britain and the Commonwealth Japan's relations have improved in slow, undramatic, solid fashion. Hydrogen bomb explosions over Christmas Island drew protests from Tokyo, in the form of diplomatic notes and large but orderly crowds in processional demonstration outside the British Embassy. In general, however, Japanese–British relations are cordial. British exports to Japan have been rising steadily, and in 1962 a Trade Treaty was signed by the two countries.

As for Asia outside China, Japan once again occupies the position, in terms of prestige, that she held for a few years after the defeat of

Imperial Russia in 1905. For the developing countries of Asia, and of Africa and the Middle East also, see in Japan an example of rapid economic growth achieved without revolution or the complete suspension of parliamentary government.

Yet, considering her status as the most technologically advanced country in Asia, and one of the most industrialized nations of the world, with her literate population of not far short of a hundred million, Japan has not played the part on the stage of world diplomacy – at the United Nations, for example – that her innate and potential strength might require. For one thing no really outstanding Japanese statesman has impressed his image on the world in post-war times, in the manner, let us say, of Nehru or Adenauer. The fact is that since the death of the last of those who created modern Japan in the 19th century Japanese leadership has been both collective and curiously undramatic. It has also been a shifting leadership – between civilians and soldiers (and sailors) before the War; between factions of Conservative politicians since. The one constant has been the energy of the Japanese people, harnessed or guided by a devoted and capable bureaucracy.

Japan's professional foreign service, for example, is an admirable organization which suffered greatly from its comparative impotence during the 1930s and during the Pacific War. The Occupation purges affected it much less than other branches of the bureaucratic machine, such as the Home Ministry. But the masterly conduct of foreign policy requires more than able ambassadors and Foreign Office officials. It needs the drive and inspiration that only a statesman of the first magnitude can provide. This figure has yet to make his appearance in post-war Japan.

DEFENCE

Article 9 of the Japanese Constitution clearly states that 'the Japanese people forever renounce war as a sovereign right of the nation and the threat and use of force as a means of settling international disputes'. It goes on to say that 'land, sea, and air forces, as well as other war potential, will never be maintained'.

There can be no doubt that this clause of the Constitution was generally welcomed when the people of Japan were introduced to it, and that it has retained great popularity ever since.

The Japanese have not shed their ethnocentric prejudices so thoroughly as to be indifferent to the charm of being thought unique in the world. To be the only nation without any armed forces would certainly confer a unique status on Japan. Armed neutrality, like that of Switzerland, is one thing; unarmed neutrality quite another.

However, under strong pressure from the United States Japan embarked upon a measure of re-armament even before the Peace Treaty was signed. This was the creation in 1950 of a body of infantry, some 75,000 strong, known as the National Police Reserve. The Peace Treaty itself specifically recognized Japan's right to self-defence in accordance with the principles of the United Nations Charter.

Today, Japan possesses an army, navy, and air force – known respectively as the Ground, Maritime, and Air Self-Defence Force. They are not equipped for offensive purposes. The Air Self-Defence Force has no bombers; and the Maritime Force contains no vessel larger than a destroyer. None of the services has nuclear weapons.

Still, it is difficult to see how this situation can be squared with Article 9 of the Constitution. Japanese governments have tried to get round this issue by a variety of legal fictions. They have argued that the requirements of the United Nations Charter, including the right of collective self-defence acknowledged in Article 51 of the Charter, must take precedence over a clause in a national Constitution. They have also contended that armed services without nuclear weapons and offensive aircraft do not constitute 'war potential'. It may be observed, however, that old Mr Yoshida, still powerful in his retirement, was reported to have stated in the summer of 1962 that Japan needs nuclear weapons for her defence; and since then his words have been echoed here and there by other Japanese.

THE JAPANESE ISLANDS

The Kuriles stretch, a long string of them, from the north-east of Hokkaido to the southern tip of Kamchatka. The Habomais are very small islands lying immediately north-east of the Nemuro Peninsula of Hokkaido; north-east of the Habomais, and close to them, is the island of Shikotan.

THE KURILE AND HABOMAI ISLANDS; SHIKOTAN

Until the 19th century even Hokkaido (then known as Yezo) was by no means well colonized by the Japanese; as for the Kuriles, few Japanese penetrated as far north in feudal times. All the same, it was generally recognized that Hokkaido and its adjacent islands were under Japanese jurisdiction. The local inhabitants were the unsophisticated Ainu, who were hunters and fishermen. The Ainu on the nearer Kuriles and in the southern part of Sakhalin would see Japanese traders and officials from time to time. Nevertheless the Shogunate did not become seriously concerned to exercise its authority in the northern islands until Russian penetration became manifest early in the 19th century. When in 1853 and 1854 the Russians tried to force open the doors of Japan – simultaneously with Perry's arrival in Yedo Bay – the Shogun's representative told the Russians that 'all the Chishima Islands of Yezo [the Kuriles] are Japanese territory. . . . In olden times our territory extended as far as Kamchatka, and it was inhabited only by the Ainu. It was only in later times that your country took possession of some of those islands.'

In 1855, however, the first Russo-Japanese Treaty recognized Japanese possession of Kunashir and Etorop, the two large Kurile Islands nearest to Hokkaido, and Russian possession of the other Kuriles stretching north-east to Kamchatka. The Habomai group and Shikotan were not discussed in the Treaty; for these clearly belonged to Japan. Twenty years later, by another treaty, Japan surrendered all claim to Sakhalin and in exchange obtained the rest of the Kuriles. Then in 1905, by the Treaty of Portsmouth, Japan, as part of her prize for her victory over Russia, obtained the southern half of Sakhalin.

Forty years later these arrangements were again disturbed. With Japan's surrender in 1945 Russian forces occupied not only South Sakhalin and the Kuriles but also Shikotan and the Habomais.

South Sakhalin and the Kuriles had been promised to the Soviet Union by secret agreement at Yalta in February 1945. Moreover, the Cairo Declaration of December 1943 had made it clear that after her submission Japan would be reduced to her four main islands and such minor islands as the Allies should determine. Again, by Article 2 of the San Francisco Peace Treaty, 1951, Japan renounced all claims on South Sakhalin and the Kuriles. Meanwhile, in 1947, the Russians had made the Kuriles, Habomais and Shikotan part of Sakhalin Oblast.

But the Japanese do not regard the Habomais and Shikotan as part of the Kuriles. Furthermore, they make a distinction between the South Kuriles and the rest of the Kurile chain. They tend to claim that the renunciation made in Article 2 of the Peace Treaty cannot properly apply to Kunashir and Etorop – still less to the Habomais and Shikotan – since these islands were recognized, by the Russians, as belonging to Japan as long ago as 1855.

It is not so much the islands themselves as the seas in their vicinity that are important to the Japanese. For in pre-war years these northern waters provided half of Japan's total catch of salmon and 30 per cent of the nation's crab fisheries.

Since 1945, however, the Soviet Union has placed stringent restrictions on Japanese fishing in these seas.

In recent years the Russians have hinted that they might be willing to consider returning the Habomais and Shikotan to Japan, provided the latter formally recognize Russia's legal sovereignty over the Kuriles.

THE RYUKYU AND BONIN ISLANDS (OKINAWA)

The long chain of 55 islands known as the Ryukyus extend from Kyushu in south-west Japan to a point about 100 miles off the north-east coast of Formosa. The largest island is Okinawa; and this contains the only substantial town, Naha, and 80 per cent of the entire population of the Ryukyus.

From the early 17th century onwards the ruler of the Ryukyus paid tribute not only to the Emperor of China but also the Lords of Satsuma in Kyushu, Japan. In 1879, however, the Japanese Government, ignoring Chinese protests, dethroned the ruler and incorporated the islands, as Okinawa Prefecture, in the national administrative system.

The Ryukyus fell into American hands during the last year of the Pacific War, when Okinawa was captured after a bitter and costly struggle lasting for two and a half months. American government of the Ryukyus was recognized by the San Francisco Peace Treaty.

Nevertheless, the Americans have acknowledged that Japan has residual sovereignty over the islands; and in 1954 the most northerly islands were restored to full Japanese control. Over the rest of the islands an American High Commissioner (the commanding general) exercises ultimate authority. This was slightly modified in 1962, when President Kennedy, by Executive Order, gave a measure of greater self-government to Okinawa Legislature (of 29 elected members). The President declared on this occasion that he recognized the Ryukyus 'to be part of the Japanese homeland', that he looked forward to the day 'when the security interests of the free world will permit their restoration to full Japanese sovereignty'.

The Bonins are four groups of small islands in the Pacific south of Japan, the principal island being Chichishima and the most famous, Iwojima. Sparsely populated – 'Bonin' is said to be a corruption of the Japanese expression, *munin* ('devoid of people') – the islands were formally annexed by Japan in 1876. In February 1945 the United States Marines fought a gruelling campaign for possession of tiny Iwojima (eight square miles in area) which the Japanese had heavily fortified. The Japanese garrison of over 20,000 died almost to the last man in its defence. Since 1945 the Bonins have been under American military administration.

A GLANCE AT THE FUTURE

Nothing is more uncertain than prediction. Only fools make guesses. But a few judicious and highly tentative speculations seem in order, even in the case of a people as volatile as the Japanese. Given two basic conditions – peace and economic well-being – the Japanese, though never safe from the natural hazards of earthquakes and typhoons, will surely not risk the artificial disasters that might follow the loss of a free parliament and a free press. For some years after the War there were many, in Japan as well as outside, who forecast that the free, almost licentiously free, society of the post-war era would not long endure. So far their forebodings have not been justified, in spite of pressures and threats from the extremes of right and left in political and social life. These have been resisted with success, and indeed with apparent ease.

It is doubtful, for example, whether a Conservative government will ever obtain the necessary two-thirds majority in the Diet to carry out a revision of the Constitution, in order to give the Emperor a more positive status and to bring Article 9 into closer touch with existing realities. Extremism, then, is not likely to prevail, provided that war or economic recession are avoided. It is the sudden pressure of an international crisis, such as the U-2 affair and its immediate aftermath, when the people of Japan feel the breath of the Third World War on their necks, that creates the panic in which a group, representing one political extreme or another, might see some chance of grasping power. Short of the sudden appearance of such turbulence the barometer for Japan appears to be set at Fair.

BIBLIOGRAPHY

Sir Esler Dening. *Japan*. (Ernest Benn, 1960.)

Donald Keene. *Living Japan*. (Heinemann, 1959.)

James Kirkup. *These Horned Islands. A Journal of Japan*. (Collins, 1962.)

John M. Maki. *Government and Politics in Japan*. (Thames & Hudson, 1962.)

George B. Sansom. *A History of Japan*. 3 vols. To 1334, 1334–1615, 1615–1867. (Cresset Press, 1958, 1961, and 1964.) *Japan, A Short Cultural History*. (Cresset Press, 1946.)

Richard Storry. *A History of Modern Japan*. (Penguin Books, 1960.)

Glenn T. Trewartha. *Japan, A Physical, Cultural and Regional Geography*. (Methuen, 1960.)

SOUTH KOREA

Walter Frank Choinski

HISTORICAL SUMMARY

THE Koreans trace their origin back some forty-three centuries, the year 1969 being 4302 on the Korean calendar.

Except for the mythical Tan-Gun, the earliest known Korean ruler is reputedly a former Chinese Minister of the Chou Dynasty who in 1200 B.C. migrated to north-west Korea as a result of political upheavals in China between the Shang Dynasty and the Chou Dynasty.

In 193 B.C. the Ki Ja Dynasty was overthrown, and succeeding governments interfered with overland trade routes between China and South Korea. Irritated by this interference, Chinese armies attacked and in 108 B.C. north-west Korea capitulated. Chinese power in the peninsula disintegrated rapidly and by 37 B.C. north-west Korea was once more under non-Chinese rule.

With the fading of Chinese control began the period of the Three Kingdoms which were to dominate the peninsula for the next 1,000 years.

The beginning of the 13th century saw the rise of Mongol power, and in 1208 Genghis Khan embarked on his imperialistic career. Initially, by virtue of having lent some aid to the Mongols, Koryo stood in a favourable position for an alliance. However, the opportunity vanished when the Koreans snubbed the Great Khan's friendly but uncouth envoys and made it clear that they wanted no association with the northern barbarians. This attitude led ultimately to a Mongol attack, and in 1252 the Koryo king fled to the island of Kangwha where he was safe from the invader, who had no boats. In 1240 the Mongols withdrew but returned in 1253 to invade the country more ruthlessly than before. Finally, with the capitulation of the Koryo king and his subsequent death in 1259, the occupation by the Mongols was complete. In 1260, Kublai Khan inherited the empire.

Rebellions in China during the last half of the 14th century signalled the wane of Mongol power, and the Ming Dynasty came to power in 1368.

The Ming Emperor recognized the new king and approved the name Chaohsien (Choson) for Korea. Yi selected Hanyang (Seoul) as his capital. The following 200 years were punctuated by border incidents

243

and Japanese pirate depredations, against both of which the Koreans were uniformly successful. Korean culture reached its highest point during the reign of Chong-jong (1506–44).

At this time, in Japan, a very capable military leader named Hideyoshi became Shogun, and immediately set out to satisfy his ambition to conquer China. This took the form of a request that Korea join Japan in attacking the Chinese. In the spring of 1592, a Japanese army landed in Pusan and Korea became a stepping stone to invasion. After a succession of sieges and bribed escapes, the Japanese were pocketed in the south in 1593, and a four-year truce was observed. In 1597 Hideyoshi launched a second invasion. Admiral Yi was reinstated, but too late to prevent the landing of the Japanese fleet. The year 1598 found the Japanese bottled up in the fortress of Ulsan, but once more they bribed their way out and set sail for home.

While the Koreans were still recovering from the destructive Japanese invasion, the Manchus to the north were growing in power and threatening China. Once again Korean respect for the Ming and her contempt for the uncultured Mongol barbarians led Korea into trouble. In 1619 a Korean army sent to aid the Ming Emperor was defeated, and in 1627 the Manchus, with their Mongol allies, invaded Korea. The Korean rulers unwisely maintained their attitude of contempt for the Manchus and thereby provoked a second invasion in 1636. The court was besieged in Namhan, the ancient Paekche capital seventeen miles south-east of Seoul, and Manchu troops again ravished the country. Finally the Koreans capitulated.

The Japanese, who in 1872 had managed to exchange envoys with the Koreans, in 1884 engineered a revolt by Korean aggressives who took over the palace. The Chinese supported the Korean conservatives and a conflict ensued which ended in the Tientsin agreement in 1885, with promises by both Chinese and Japanese to evacuate their military forces. This agreement was violated when, in 1894, Chinese troops were brought into the peninsula to help suppress a revolt in the south. This provoked the Japanese and a war between China and Japan started on Korean soil. In successive battles, the Japanese defeated the Chinese, concluding the war in a Japanese victory on Chinese territory in 1895. Following this victory, the Japanese adopted a stronger attitude towards Korea. For seven years the Russians and Japanese sparred for political domination of the Korean peninsula, and in 1904 Japan finally declared war. Korea was forced into the position of being Japan's ally. After the war, and in the flush of military success (1905), a Japanese Resident-General was established to rule the country. Two years later the king was forced to abdicate in favour of his feeble-minded son, and finally in August 1910 annexation by Japan formally ended Korean independence and the Yi Dynasty, which had ruled for over 500 years.

The Koreans did not accept Japanese annexation placidly, and for ten years Korean patriots carried on armed resistance which the Japanese sought to suppress with military force.

On 1 March 1919 thirty of the most prominent Koreans signed a proclamation of independence and sent it to the Governor-General. This is popularly known as the 'Mansei Uprising'. Arrest followed swiftly, and great crowds joined the demonstration irrespective of class, age, religion or sex; all had the single common bond of nationality.

The Japanese were infuriated that the subjugated people should dare to seek liberty from the benevolent imperial plan for their social and political salvation, and the Governor directed all the power at his command towards crushing the populace by force. In August 1919 a new Governor-General was sent out from Japan, and a plan of wholesale reform in the administration was inaugurated. With increased Japanese involvement in military 'incidents' economic pressure increased until, during the last years of the Second World War, every effort was made to force maximum Korean production for the war effort. The conclusion of the Second World War brought an end to Japanese rule.

In December 1943 the Cairo Declaration promised Korea its independence 'in due course'. A provisional Korean government was formed in Chungking in 1944 and at the Potsdam Conference in July 1945 the Allies declared that 'the terms of the Cairo Declaration shall be carried out'. The USSR committed itself to support the independence of Korea when it declared war on Japan on 8 August 1945. Russian troops entered Korea from the north on 12 August 1945, and United States troops from the south on 8 September 1945.

With the end of Japanese rule, a political vacuum existed in both the Soviet and United States zones. In South Korea, two separated political forces presented themselves to the United States Occupation authorities. The first, the Korean People's Republic, was proclaimed on 6 September 1945. It was Communist-dominated and was opposed to the United States Military Government. The other was the exiled Korean Provisional Government which returned to Korea from the United States and China after the Japanese surrender. United States authorities maintained the Military Government was the only government in South Korea. In February 1946, the United States Military Government created the Representative Democratic Council, an all-Korean body which was to act in an advisory capacity to the Commanding General of the American Forces. Syngman Rhee was made Chairman. This was replaced in October 1946 by the Korean Interim Legislative Assembly, which was created to give the Koreans control of their government with United States authorities retaining the power to dissolve the assembly and to appoint half its members.

The first effort to unite Korea came at the Moscow Conference of December 1945 at which the United States, the United Kingdom and the USSR (with China abstaining) agreed that the United States and USSR commands in Korea were to form a joint commission which was to make recommendations to the Four Powers regarding the organization of a provisional Korean democratic government. The 'joint commission' provided for by the Moscow agreement met from 20 March to 8 May 1946, but was unable to reach agreement. It reconvened a year later but the discussions were stalemated.

The United States referred the Korean question to the United Nations and, on 14 November 1947, the General Assembly adopted a resolution calling for elections throughout Korea under the observation of the United Nations Temporary Commission on Korea. The elections were to select a national assembly, to draft a democratic constitution, and establish a national government. The Soviet Command, however, denied the United Nations Commission entry to its zone.

Elections were held in South Korea on 10 May 1948, under the supervision of the United Nations Commission, and the National Assembly met for the first time on 31 May 1948 and elected Syngman Rhee Chairman. Subsequently, on 20 July 1948, he was elected President.

The Republic of Korea was inaugurated on 15 August 1948. On the same day the United States Military Government in Korea came to an end.

THE KOREAN CONFLICT

On 25 June 1950, well trained and experienced North Korean Communist forces invaded South Korea with massed armour and heavy artillery supported by tactical aircraft. It was the relatively small army of South Korea, immature, without trained and experienced leaders, operating under the untried government of an impoverished country, that bore the brunt of the sweep of the Red forces across the 38th parallel.

Overwhelmed by vastly superior Communist forces the South Koreans fought as best they could but were forced to retreat. However, less than twenty-four hours after the surprise attack, the Security Council of the United Nations (which the Soviet Union had boycotted at the time) branded the North Koreans as guilty of a 'breach of the peace' and demanded an immediate cessation of hostilities and with-drawal of North Korean forces. When the invader failed to comply, the United Nations Council called upon other member nations to give all possible help to the Republic of Korea to repel the attack and restore peace and security in the area.

On 27 June, President Truman announced that the United States would send air and sea forces 'to give the South Korean Government troops air cover and support', and on 30 June he ordered Occupation troops to be flown from Japan to Korea.

Material contributions to aid the Republic of Korea were made by more than forty countries, sixteen of which contributed ground, naval and air forces. A United Nations Command was created and General of the Army Douglas MacArthur was appointed Commander in Chief.

It was apparent by 5 July 1950 that only maximum support and effort by the United Nations could stave off the total collapse of the Republic of Korea. The ROK Army had been forced to withdraw so fast that vast quantities of arms and ammunition fell into the hands of the invaders, and resistance was offered only in the form of hasty road blocks and light defensive positions at the Han River. The announce-ment of United Nations aid and the arrival of American air and ground support from Japan brought new hope to the South Koreans.

By 1 October the situation was definitely in Allied hands. Seoul was again occupied by friendly forces, and most of the elements of the United Nations forces and ROK Army were on or north of the 38th parallel. Following the decision to clear all Korea of the Communist threat, a determined drive to the north was begun in all sectors, and by 7 October, the drive towards the Yalu River was begun. However, by this time Chinese Communist Forces (CCF). under the guise of volun-teer forces, were committed to assist the army of North Korea. The full effect of this intervention was felt on 26 November when the ROK forces collapsed completely under a direct frontal attack. All attempts to coordinate the defence of the area failed. The majority of the units were able to avoid annihilation by escaping through the mountains, but at the expense of their heavy equipment.

Late on New Year's Eve of 1950, the enemy began a general offensive across the entire front with an attack directed at Yonchon. As the drive gained momentum across the Imjin River, the Eighth United States Army, now supporting ROK forces, and the ROK forces were forced to withdraw until all reached Yongwol where the Chinese Communist forces' drive to the south was stopped dead.

Late in January 1951 the American Eighth Army began to launch limited offensives designed to inflict maximum damage to the enemy with a minimum of United Nations casualties. Operation Thunderbolt was the first of the offensives under the new doctrine. Playing a leading role in this attack were the ROK forces. United Nations forces were again on the Han River by 12 February and from then on friendly forces remained in a favourable position. A secure front, passing through Hongchon, was established across the entire Korean Peninsula by 15 March. By the end of April of 1951 the entire army was in line across 116 miles of commanding terrain, almost entirely north of the 38th parallel.

The long-awaited spring offensive of the Chinese Communist Forces came on 22 April. Although there were heavy losses in ground, the first attempt of the Communist-termed 'fifth phase offensive' was halted. By 1 June United Nations forces were again north of the 38th parallel, which, with minor changes, is the present United Nations defensive position.

The Soviet delegate at the United Nations, on 23 June 1951, proposed negotiations for a truce. The United Nations agreed to negotiate because its original objective – that of repelling aggression against the Republic of Korea – had been achieved. Truce negotiations began in July, were suspended first by the Communists, then resumed, suspended next by the United Nations delegation, resumed again, and finally brought to a conclusion two years later when an armistice was signed on 27 July 1953.

During those two years of frustrating, deadlocked negotiations, some of the hardest fighting of the Korean conflict took place, for both sides considered it necessary that military operations continue until an armistice agreement was signed. There were patrol clashes, raids and bitter small-unit struggles, and hard-fought battles involving many divisions. The air-war over Korea was intensified, and large-scale United Nations air attacks, naval bombardments, and strikes by carrier-based planes, as well as fierce ground fighting, finally convinced the Communists that they could not conquer the Republic of Korea.

The stumbling block to a truce was the question of the repatriation of prisoners of war. The Communists demanded that all P.O.W.s be returned to the countries from which they had come. The United Nations Command, which held about eight times as many P.O.W.s as the Communists, insisted on voluntary repatriation of prisoners, on the principle that no one who did not wish to return to his homeland should be compelled to return.

Finally, the Communists agreed to voluntary repatriation of prisoners, and the armistice was signed. Under the agreement, a demarcation line across the Korean peninsula was established along the final battle line. Most of it runs north of the 38th parallel, with a short dip below the parallel at the western terminal. The troops of both sides were withdrawn leaving a two-and-a-half mile demilitarized zone between them. The agreement provided for the reunification of Korea to be brought about through political negotiations. But the negotiations failed because the Communists refused, among other things, to agree to elections supervised by the United Nations.

In the Korean conflict, 58,000 Koreans were killed and 176,000 wounded, more than a million civilians were killed, and another million wounded or injured. The tides of war left 100,000 Korean orphans and more than 284,000 widows with 517,000 dependent children. About eight million South Koreans were driven from their homes.

The cost in lives, wounded, money and effort by United Nations forces reached monumental figures.

FIRST GOVERNMENT: PRESIDENTIAL SYSTEM

South Korea's first government had similarities to both the American presidential system and the British parliamentary system.

The Constitution provided for popular sovereignty, defined a separation of powers, but awarded the President a preponderance of authority, especially in time of economic 'crisis'.

Legislative power was vested in the National Assembly of which the House of Representatives was the only existing body. Each member represented approximately 100,000 people. A House of Councillors, or upper house, was specified in the Constitution as a part of the National Assembly, but was never formed.

Provincial government was an administrative subdivision of the executive branch of the Central Government. The nine provinces in the ROK, and Seoul as a 'Special City', were administered by the Ministry of Home Affairs. Provincial Governors and the Mayor of Seoul were appointed by the President. County administrators were appointed by the President of the Republic on recommendation of the Provincial Governor through the Minister of Home Affairs. Chiefs of ward offices in Seoul were appointed by the President of the Republic on the recommendation of the Mayor through the Minister of Home Affairs.

The cities, towns, and townships were governed by elected local councils, who in turn elected their own chief executives. These local councils had the power to enact and repeal local ordinances and also were required to carry out the tasks assigned them by the Minister of Home Affairs.

All policemen were appointed by the National Government and were under the supervision of their Provincial Governor, and were not subordinate to local officials.

All the above factors were instrumental in enabling the Syngman Rhee Government to control the outcome of elections and the enforcement, or non-enforcement, of legal provisions. As the time for the second election approached, in 1952, it appeared that incumbent President Syngman Rhee would not be re-elected. However, strong pressures were brought on the National Assembly by the executive branch and the elections, required on or before 23 June 1952, were postponed; martial law was declared and thirteen Assemblymen were arrested by the Government. After boycotts of the Assembly by various factions, the Assembly, on 4 July 1952, unanimously adopted four amendments to the Constitution: (1) the President should be elected by popular vote; (2) the National Assembly should be reorganized into a bicameral body; (3) Cabinet members should be appointed by the President upon the recommendation of the Prime Minister instead of by the President on his own initiative; and (4) the Cabinet may be dissolved by a vote of no confidence by the Assembly.

Syngman Rhee was re-elected on 5 August 1952, for a new term beginning on 15 August.

A second constitutional change was undertaken in November 1954. Three important points in the amendment were (1) the abolition of the office of Prime Minister and authorization for the President to preside directly over the State Council and appoint its members; (2) incumbent President Rhee was exempted from the constitutional limitation of two consecutive four-year terms; (3) provision was made for the Vice-President to succeed the President should the latter die in office.

Syngman Rhee was re-elected in 1956 and for the presidential race of 1960 the Liberal Party again nominated him for a fourth term. He was again elected President. On election night major demonstrations occurred throughout South Korea against the election results.

On 19 April and thereafter a very large demonstration by university and high school students occurred demanding the resignation of

President Rhee and the holding of new elections, and, as a result, the Cabinet resigned and President Rhee tendered his resignation.

NEW CONSTITUTION:
ASSEMBLY-RESPONSIBLE GOVERNMENT

On 15 June the House of Representatives adopted a new Constitution, substituting a straight parliamentary system for the previous presidential system. The post of President was continued, but it was transformed into a ceremonial position without executive authority. The executive power was placed in the hands of a State Council headed by a Prime Minister. The Prime Minister appointed his own Cabinet, and was required to resign if he received a vote of no confidence in the House of Representatives on a major issue.

Following adoption of the new Constitution, the old Assembly dissolved itself, designating 29 July as the date for a new general election. Provisions were made also, for the first time since the passage of the 1952 constitutional amendment, to elect the House of Councillors.

In the July election, the Democratic Party won a majority of seats in the House of Representatives. President Yun, under pressure, nominated Dr John M. Chang, Head of the Democratic Party, for the position of Prime Minister. He was elected on 19 August.

No sooner had the 25 million Korean people observed the first anniversary of the student-led uprising of April 1960 than another revolution struck the discontented country. On 16 May 1961, a closely knit group of younger generals and colonels overthrew the strife-torn but freely elected Government of Prime Minister John M. Chang. The new Government, under the title of 'The Revolutionary Military Committee', announced a six-point declaration of 'Revolutionary Pledges' which emphasized anti-Communism, observance of the United Nations Charter, strengthening of ties with the United States and other friendly nations, elimination of political corruption and social evils, advancement toward economic self-support, building up of national strength against Communism, and return of the governmental authority to 'new and conscientious' politicians upon completion of its 'revolutionary tasks'.

The military junta, which was renamed 'The Supreme Council for National Reconstruction', let it be known that there would be heavy punishment for any violations of the new regulations, declared an 'emergency' martial law and ordered the arrest of the Chang Cabinet, a blockade of the sea and air ports, freezing of banking, dissolution of the National Assembly and all local legislatures, press censorship, prohibition of assemblage, and a 1900 to 0500 curfew.

A Revolutionary Court and a Revolutionary Prosecution were organized in July to administer the revolutionary laws, mostly applicable retroactively. Close to 40,000 government officials were found to be corrupt, guilty of partisan politics, patronizing mistresses, or excessive use of foreign luxuries (which were banned).

General Park Chung Hee, who had remained in the background in the initial stages of the *coup d'état*, took over control of the SCNR on 1 July, arrested Lieutenant-General Chang Do Yung, and placed him under trial with forty other military officers on charges of being 'counter-revolutionary'. In December Park announced his intention to run as a candidate for election to the presidency, but in March of 1963 he renounced this intention and declared that he was going to extend his military regime until 1967.

Anti-Government demonstrations, without precedent as to violence, broke out in major cities in spite of an array of 150 admirals and generals avowing support of General Park. The American Ambassador informed the 'Military Junta' and General Park that they should 'work together' with major political groups on a procedure for transition from the incumbent military rule to a civilian government acceptable to the 'South Korean Nation' as a whole. The impression was left that the American Government might be inclined to consider withholding its economic aid.

General Park announced his agreement to the demands of existing political parties, stated that elections would be held within the year 1963, and that he would be a candidate, as a civilian. As Mr Park he was elected and formally inaugurated on 17 December 1963 as the first President of 'The Third Republic of Korea', and thus ended the 945 days of military rule in South Korea. His re-election as President and defeat of Mr Yun Po-sun of the New Democratic Party on 3 May 1967 by a huge majority caused little surprise, but the overwhelming victory of his party in the 8 June National Assembly election provoked a nation-wide political crisis. As a result of student demonstrations and the efforts of the opposition National Democratic Party, Mr Park announced the expulsion of eight of his party's elected candidates from the National Assembly.

South Korea is currently administered by Park's Democratic Republican Party which occupies 122 seats giving him a comfortable majority of more than two thirds of the 175-member one-house Parliament. There are in all twelve parties, the organization and functions of which are now regulated by law. Each promises the constituency the benefits of social security, long-range economic development programmes, adherence to the United Nations Charter, and unification of the two Koreas under United Nations-sponsored general elections.

The Democratic Republican Party, led by Park Chung Hee, is committed to revolutionary ideals, and a popularly elected president with powers to control the executive branch as provided by the Constitution drafted by the Military Junta. It is the strongest party, with a powerful secretariat, the first of its kind in Korean political history. The Minjung (Civic Rule) Party, led by Yun Po Sun, successor party of former Premier John M. Chang ousted by the Military Junta, has pledged revision of the Constitution to curb presidential powers. The Democratic Party, led by Mrs Park Sun Chon, ranked high in elections, perhaps owing to the fact that it is the successor to the Democratic Party ousted by the Military Junta Revolution of 1961. The Party of the People, led by Huh Chung, is a coalition of many pre-revolutionary groups now under the leadership of the man who was Premier for three months following the downfall of Syngman Rhee. The Liberal Democratic Party, led by Kim Do Yun, consists of dissidents who broke away from their pre-revolutionary associates. It presumes to share in the revolutionary objectives of the party in power. The Liberal Party, led by Chang Taik Sang, comprises a conglomeration of former Syngman Rhee liberals. The Chungmin Ho (Right Citizens) Party, League of Pyun Yung Tai (former Prime Minister), Chupung Ho (Autumn Breeze) Party and Society of Oh Jae Yung and Sin Heung (New Development) Party are splinter groups with great hopes of attaining political significance under a civilian government.

Considering the fact that in 1948 there were forty-eight parties which participated in the general elections supervised by the United Nations, it may be concluded that the Republic of Korea may be approaching a degree of political integrity.

PROGRAMME FOR ECONOMIC DEVELOPMENT

For the past several years the economy has been gradually sinking into a downward trend with the gross national product falling from 4 per cent in 1955 to 2·3 per cent in 1960. The outbreak of the April Revolution (1960) and the May Revolution (1961) aggravated the depression as a whole.

However, with the enactment of the Foreign Investment Encouragement Law and the devaluation of the currency (won), economic prospects began to recover until in 1964 they reached proportions not known since the establishment of the Republic. To make the plan more realistic, the 1962–6 Five-Year Plan was readjusted to the extent that the original 7 per cent annual growth rate was reduced to 5 per cent. The production of grains, coal, cement, power and industrial consumer goods has since advanced so far that South Korea now seems capable of permanent industrial development for home consumption and export.

Exports have shown remarkable increases in the last few years and, with industrial 'know-how' increasing, neighbour countries are looking to South Korea for low-priced consumer goods – the wage scale being about one half that of Japan. During 1964 approximately 50 per cent of South Korea's exports (about US $60 million) consisted of consumer goods. South Korea's prospects for extended private and US Government capital and markets, through its Industrial Development Agency, seem promising.

Now that Korea and Japan have returned to normal economic relations, a healthy and viable South Korean economy will compete for a share of world trade. Although the growth rate of South Korea's gross national product has risen to 9 per cent (1966) the increase of the population is such that the growth rate of the country's gross national product *per capita* is only 6·2 per cent.

If industrial ambitions are fully realized, the once under-developed 'Land of the Morning Calm' may yet become the 'Land of the Morning Smog'.

BASIC ISSUES

The major problem besetting the Republic of Korea is the military and political division of Korea into North and South. This separation colours and intensifies all other problems.

Korea had been developed by the Japanese on an agricultural pattern in the south, and on an industrial pattern in the north. Much of this pattern has continued to exist. The south is overpopulated, the north underpopulated. The division impedes the development of a self-sustaining economy in the south. In reaction to this artificial situation, unification has become the central theme of ROK politics. The division of Korea presents a formidable security problem to the Republic of Korea, requiring it to maintain an extremely large and costly army. In spite of this situation, the Communists are constantly seeking to infiltrate the Government, the police and the armed forces, and the Republic of Korea must be alert continually for espionage and subversion.

The north-south split divides families and natural trade areas, and perpetuates a state of suspended hostilities in Korea.

The Republic of Korea's problems are intensified by the task of remedying the destruction which occurred in the Korean War, in which 400,000 homes and many factories and mines were demolished, many agricultural fields and paddies damaged, and millions made refugees. This repair and rebuilding work has overtaxed the resources of the Government and the economy, despite the large amounts of aid given by the United States.

If the ROK is to cope with its 26 million population, it must have financial resources to continue rehabilitation, to expand factories and mines, to improve agriculture, and grant the people greater participation in the affairs of their Government. This the new Government promises to accomplish.

BIBLIOGRAPHY

Walter Frank Choinski. *The Republic of Korea*. (Military Assistance Institute, Arlington, Virginia, 1964.)

Chong-Sik Lee. *The Politics of Korean Nationalism*. (Berkeley University Press, California, 1963.)

Economic Statistics Yearbook. (Bank of Korea, Seoul, 1964.)

Korea, Its Land, People and Culture of all Ages. (Ministry of Public Information, Republic of Korea, Seoul, 1963.)

Military Revolution in Korea. (Supreme Council for National Reconstruction, Seoul, 1961.)

Miryok Lee. *The Yalu Flows: a Korean Childhood*. (Harvill Press, London, 1954.)

W. D. Reeve. *The Republic of Korea: a Political and Economic Study*. (Oxford University Press, 1963.)

Republic of Korea. (Far Eastern Economic Review Yearbook, Hong Kong, 1965.)

NORTH KOREA

Chong-Sik Lee

THE Democratic People's Republic of Korea, which is the official designation of the North Korean regime, is in firm control of the Korean peninsula north of the armistice line drawn in 1953. Like the Republic of Korea government in the south, the Pyongyang regime has claimed itself to be the only legitimate sovereign government in Korea, although in more recent years it has acknowledged the *de facto* power of the South Korean regime by proposing negotiations on unification.

North Korea, in theory, is still in the stage of the people's dictatorship. Thus the regime has kept its three 'major' political parties, i.e., the Korean Workers' Party, the Korean Democratic Party, and the Ch'ondogyo Youth Fraternal Party, and has been allocating a certain number of seats in the Supreme People's Assembly to the two latter groups. But, in fact, North Korea has long been under the complete control of the Workers' Party, particularly its supreme leader, Kim Il-song (born 1912).

Political developments in North Korea since 1945 have clearly manifested Kim Il-song's shrewdness and lack of any scruples in political engineering. Although the future premier did have some revolutionary record behind him, as a Communist partisan in Manchuria during the Second World War, he was a relatively unknown figure in 1945 when he returned to Korea at the tail of the Russian forces invading Japanese-occupied Korea. Since then Kim has been intent on establishing himself as the unequivocal leader of the Korean Communist movement. He was able to depend upon support from the Russian command in Pyongyang in the early stages of post-war political struggle. He was 'elected' premier in 1948.

In his struggle for the mastery over North Korean politics Kim used the tactics of amalgamation of rival groups, purges, and occasional violence. As is to be expected, massive propaganda accompanied each move.

FOUNDATION OF THE COMMUNIST PARTY

Thus in October 1945, soon after Kim's arrival in Korea, the 'North Korean Central Bureau of the Korean Communist Party' was created in Pyongyang and all the indigenous Communists were forced to submit to it. There were throughout Korea at this time numbers of Communists and Communist sympathizers organized by indigenous leaders who had emerged from their underground dormancy after the liberation of Korea but were independent of Kim Il-song. Having, with Russian help, established himself as the first secretary of the new organization, Kim proceeded to execute a sweeping purge in December to remove the 'undesirable elements' in the party. One of the strongest contenders for power against Kim, Hyon Chunhyok, had already been assassinated in broad daylight in September.

Six months later, in July 1946, the Central Bureau annexed the New People's Party, headed by Korean returnees from north-west China. The returnees, generally known as the Yenan faction because of their close association with the Chinese Communists in Yenan, included such prominent figures as Kim Tu-bong, Mu Chong, Kim Ch'ang-man, Ch'oe Ch'ang-ik and Han Pin among others, and added considerably to the prestige and strength of the Communist camp as a whole. The newly amalgamated party was named the North Korean Workers' Party, and the alliance of the two groups lasted a number of years.

Finally, in June 1949 the North Korean Communists absorbed the Communist 'exiles' from South Korea, merging the North and South Korean Workers' Parties into the Korean Workers' Party (Choson Nodong-dang). Pak Hon-yong, one of the few survivors from the earliest stage of the Korean Communist movement in 1921 and the leader of the South Korean Workers' Party in 1949, in effect surrendered himself and his followers from the south to the young leader who became the chairman of the new, united party of Korea.

The purge of the possible contenders for power against Kim Il-song continued during and after the Korean War. Thus in December 1950 the third plenum of the Central Committee of the Workers' Party dismissed Mu Chong from the command of the Second Army Corps on the grounds that his neglect of duties during the retreat inflicted grave damage on the army. The significance of this episode goes beyond the fact that one of the major leaders of the Yenan faction was purged. It shows Kim Il-song's political ingenuity and skill, in that Mu had been a close comrade of P'eng Teh-huai since the 1930s and that P'eng was in command of the 'Chinese People's Volunteers in Korea', who had just joined the Korean War in late October. Was there, perhaps, a fear on the part of Kim Il-song that Mu Chong might subvert his power in an alliance with P'eng Teh-huai, and was the purge merely a scheme to prevent this outcome? This hypothesis is substantiated partly by the fact that at least three known comrades of Kim Il-song from the partisan days, Kim Il, Yim Ch'un-ch'u, and Ch'oe Kwang, were purged or reprimanded at this conference on similar charges with Mu and were all reinstated shortly afterwards. Kim Il since then has attained the lofty position of First Vice-premier and Minister of Agriculture, in charge of carrying out the all-important collectivization programme; Yim Ch'un-ch'u was made ambassador to Albania and Bulgaria; Ch'oe was later promoted to be a full general in the North Korean Air Force.

Another major purge occurred in 1953 when Pak Hon-yong (Vice-premier and Foreign Minister), Yi Sung-yop (former Minister of Justice), Chu Nyong-ha (former ambassador to Russia and Vice-minister of Foreign Affairs), Kwon O-jik (former ambassador to China), and several other important leaders of the 'domestic faction' were implicated. Official charges advanced against them were that they had actively engaged in espionage for the United States occupation forces while they were in South Korea, furnishing information about North Korean political and economic conditions to enemy agents, and attempted to overthrow the existing government in North Korea. It has been surmised in the West, however, that the real reason for the purge was the discovery of an attempt to obstruct the armistice at Panmunjom, and that the Government may also have sought to put the responsibility for starting the war upon the shoulders of the purged group. Be that as it may, another significant segment of the Korean Workers' Party that posed a potential threat to Kim Il-song was eliminated.

The de-Stalinization campaign in Russia also had its impact on North Korea. Although Khrushchev's secret speech itself had not been printed in the North Korean papers, the regime made it known to the public that the twentieth congress of the Communist Party of the Soviet Union had denounced Stalin's 'cult of personality'. In these circumstances, it was natural for some of the leading elements to decide to bring about a change in Pyongyang similar to that in Moscow – for the cult of personality practised by Kim Il-song had gone to extremes.

An attempt was made by two leading figures in the 'Yenan faction', Yun Kong-hum, the Minister of Commerce, and Ch'oe Ch'ang-ik, the Vice-premier, in alliance with a 'Soviet faction' man, Pak Ch'ang-ok, Minister of Mechanical Industry, to denounce Kim Il-song. At the August 1956 plenum of the party's Central Committee, which had been called to hear the Premier's report on his visit to the Soviet Union and Eastern Europe, Yun Kong-hum criticized the authoritarianism of Kim and the 'anti-people' nature of Kim's policies. Other critics of the

Premier joined in support of Yun, and a major crisis developed at the plenum. The supporters of Kim, however, outnumbered the dissidents and branded the critics as anti-party reactionary elements. According to one source, the three major critics had been expelled from the Central Committee and stripped of their official functions when P'eng Teh-huai, the Chinese Defence Minister, and Anastas I. Mikoyan intervened and secured their restoration to the Central Committee.

PARTY PURGES

The last major purge known to the West was revealed at a plenum of the Korean Workers' Party in March 1958. The Premier stated that the sixty-nine-year-old Kim Tu-bong – the elder statesman of the Yenan group, who had been chairman of the presidium of the North Korean Supreme People's Assembly since its establishment in 1948 – together with Vice-premier Pak Ui-wan and the former secretary of the North Korean Communist Party, O Ki-sop, had conceived of (not actually plotted) overthrowing the party, although no evidence was 'as yet obtained' to prove that they had participated in an 'anti-revolutionary riot'. The Premier also stated that although the party had been 'patient in educating' these persons for the past year and a half, they were not earnest enough to confess their past mistakes and correct them. In the same speech Kim Il-song denounced Ch'oe Ch'ang-ik, Kim Ung (former general commander of the war front and Vice-minister of Defence), and others for engaging in sectarian activities. It has been asserted by independent observers that General Chang P'yong-san, one of the delegates at Panmunjom, and other influential military men of the Yenan faction were purged in May 1958 on account of an alleged *coup d'état* planned for May Day. The Yenan faction virtually disappeared from North Korean politics in 1958.

A review of political developments of the last two decades thus clearly reveals that the authoritarian leader of North Korea effectively squashed all his opponents and rivals and put the party and the regime firmly under his control. Kim Il-song did not hesitate to purge members of the domestic and Yenan factions, and even some of the Soviet faction, but he has been most dedicated to nurturing the strength of his personal followers. It is significant in this connexion that the histories published in North Korea after 1958 omit all mention of the Korean revolutionaries in North China (the Yenan group) and have nothing but contempt and invective for the Communist movement in Korea before 1931, in which year Kim Il-song allegedly started his revolutionary career. It is now stated that the illustrious Marshal Kim Il-song and his personal followers were the only true Communists Korea produced during the early, pre-Second World War years of the movement.

ECONOMIC PLANNING

The extremism and fervour with which the personal power of Kim Il-song was consolidated was reflected in the economic programmes adopted by the regime after the armistice that concluded the Korean War in July 1953. Three years of war had virtually ruined all industry and the country was plagued by severe food shortages. According to North Korean sources, the output of various industries in 1953 in comparison with the pre-war level in 1949 was as follows: electrical 26 per cent; fuel 11 per cent; metallurgy 10 per cent; chemical 22 per cent. Many mining and industrial facilities were completely destroyed. Damage to irrigation facilities and river dams affected some 900,000 acres of farm land and reduced the area of arable land by about 200,000 acres out of about 5·5 million acres normally cultivated. Grain production in 1953 was reduced to 88 per cent of the 1949 total.

At the conclusion of the armistice, the regime immediately began to reconstruct ruined industries and rehabilitate the economy as a whole. The Three-Year Plan (1954–6) aimed at the recovery of the pre-war production level. The first Five-Year Plan (1956–60) was designed to build the 'foundation of socialist industry', and the Seven-Year Plan (1961–7) was to turn North Korea into an 'advanced socialist industrial country'.

In the process of planning economic rehabilitation and development, the regime placed the main emphasis upon the reconstruction and further development of heavy industries. Thus during the three-year rehabilitation period the regime allocated approximately 49·6 per cent (or 39,900 million won) of a total investment of 80,600 million won to industry and only 7,400 million won, or 8·6 per cent, to agricultural reconstruction. Approximately 81 per cent of the funds for industry went to heavy industry. At the end of the Three-Year Plan, the Premier reported that machine production and metal processing had increased by more than three times the pre-war level, and construction materials by 2·8 times, while mining and metallurgy had reached the pre-war level, but the most essential electrical, fuel, and chemical industries were still below the pre-war level. At the end of the Five-Year Plan in 1960, however, the regime declared that even these industries had overtaken the pre-war level, electricity production having increased 1·5 times, fuel production twice, and chemical production four times. Allegedly, North Korea was in 1960 sufficiently industrialized and its economy so well diversified as to be totally rid of all the characteristics of a colonial economy.

The regime launched the Seven-Year Plan with great fanfares in 1961 and has continuously asserted that progress is being made on schedule to reach the heights of socialism. The following table taken from an official North Korean publication illustrates the volume of production and the rate of growth contemplated by the regime:

| | Production Goals for 1967 | |
	Physical Units	Times 1960
Electric power	17,000 million kw-h.	2·4
Coal	25 million tons	2·4
Iron ore	7·2 million tons	2·3
Pig iron	2·3 million tons	2·7
Steel	2·3 million tons	3·6
Hydraulic and thermal turbines	448,000 kw.	106
Tractors (in terms of 15 h.p. unit)	17,100 units	5
Automobiles	10,000 units	3·2
Chemical fertilizers	1·7 million tons	3
Cement	4·3 million tons	1·9
Fabrics	500 million metres	2·6
Underwear	65 million pieces	3·9
Footwear	40·7 million pairs	1·8
Grain	6,600,000 tons	1·7
Meat	350,000 tons	3·9
Eggs	800 million	6·4

The Seven-Year-Plan, however, proved to be too ambitious. The regime, therefore, announced a three-year extension of the plan in 1966. The prospect of fulfilling the original goals of the Seven-Year Plan by the end of 1970 is not very bright.

ECONOMIC ORGANIZATION

It must be noted in this connexion that North Korea suffered a heavy loss in population during the war due not only to war casualties, but also to the heavy outflow of refugees to South Korea. In order to bring about rapid industrialization and to meet the labour shortage, the regime moved large numbers of farmers to urban areas, requiring all these men and women to participate in industrial activities. Of the total population of 10,789,000 as of 31 December 1960 (48·4 per cent male), 38·3 per cent were classified as labourers and factory workers, 13·7 per cent as office (or 'white collar') workers, and 44·4 per cent as farmers. At the end of 1953, when the population was 8,491,000, farmers accounted for 66·4 per cent. The annual rate of population growth is reported to be approximately 3 per cent.

The regime has been requiring each worker to perform an incredible amount of work each day, and since April 1959 has used the system of *Chôllima* or 'flying-horse' teams granting awards for the over-fulfilment of assigned quotas. Instead of providing material incentives, the regime resorted to more indoctrination and discipline accompanied by occasional purges, to ensure the increase in production. The following quotation from Kim Il-song's speech of 26 February 1959 applies not only in the context of economic development, to which he was referring, but also in other spheres of life:

In some of the factories the social groups carry out few educational activities. Furthermore, even the party organizations neglect this, and hence the economic duties are performed through sheer coercion. What is done instead, day and night, is ideological investigation. The guiding group from the central party will investigate one's ideology, and so on. Nothing but complaints will result from these investigations.

The entire agricultural population in North Korea has been collectivized, being placed in co-operative farms as socialist workers. After a brief 'experimental stage' in 1953 and 1954, the party undertook a full-scale collectivization programme in November 1954. Within three years, by December 1957, 95·6 per cent of the farmers were organized into 16,000 co-operatives. In October 1958, only two months after the Chinese Communist regime launched its commune movement, the North Korean regime amalgamated the small co-operatives into 3,843 large co-operatives with an average of some 300 households each.

The farmers in each co-operative are organized in work teams, and their daily work is supervised and evaluated by team leaders who, in consultation with other officers of the co-operatives, issue points to the farmers at the end of the day. The farmers are paid (or given a share of the products) at the end of the year according to the total points they have earned. Available information indicates that the state and the co-operatives take a lion's share of the products in the form of various fees and 'common reserves of the co-operatives', allowing much less than a half of the products to the farmers.

The co-operatives have provided the regime with a convenient channel for regimenting and disciplining the people. The farmers in a co-operative are organized into a number of 'party-policy study groups' to receive proper Communist indoctrination in their spare time. Each co-operative is equipped with a number of 'Party history study rooms', 'agitators', and 'conversation leaders' to provide proper 'guidance'. North Korean sources indicate that 'concentrated guidance groups' from various party hierarchies make frequent rounds at the co-operatives and that the farmers receive their 'education' and indoctrination at their place of work during the rest period.

In spite of the official pronouncements to the contrary, there are signs of considerable strain in North Korean agriculture. For example, even the official publications admitted a drop in agricultural production in 1959, the first year after the agricultural co-operatives were merged into larger units. North Korean newspapers (which are under complete state control) also occasionally print articles written by reporters and letters from readers that severely criticize the 'mistakes and tardiness' of the local officials. In December 1961 the regime took the extreme measure of removing the agricultural co-operatives from the jurisdiction of the prefectural (*kun*) governments on the ground that the 'administrative methods of the prefectural people's committees could not smoothly guide the agricultural co-operatives'. The co-operatives are now placed under newly created 'management committees' at the prefectural level staffed by agricultural experts dispatched by the central government. Since the agricultural co-operative was, in fact, the only administrative unit of local government under the prefectural level in rural areas, and since the co-operatives are pervasive in their functions, the decision of December 1961 did not leave much to the prefectural governments. It is reasonable to surmise, therefore, that the regime was compelled to resort to this drastic action by some unexplained but serious defects in the co-operatives. Structural changes in the management and control of the farms failed to increase agricultural production in any significant degree. In October 1966 the regime announced the grain production in 1965 to be 119 per cent of 1960, which would be 4,525,000 metric tons. The regime had announced that the harvest in 1961 had exceeded 4·8 million tons and in the succeeding years it had claimed continued increase.

PROSPECTS OF UNIFICATION OF KOREA

Practically every political speaker in North Korea today ends his speech by referring to the goal of 'peaceful unification' of Korea. The Pyongyang regime has also conducted a ceaseless propaganda campaign in recent years to attribute all responsibility for the prolongation of the division of the country to the South Korean leaders and the 'American imperialists'. The North Korean proposals on unification have the air of reasonableness. First of all, so goes the argument, the Korean problem must be solved by the Koreans alone, i.e., without interference by the United Nations Commission for the Unification and Rehabilitation of Korea or by the United States. The North Korean regime demands, therefore, the immediate withdrawal of the United Nations agency and the United States military forces from South Korea (where there are two infantry divisions), as well as the cancellation of the mutual defence agreement between the Republic of Korea and the United States, as the first requirements for unification. When these conditions are met, the two Governments are to send their representatives to establish the 'Supreme National Committee', which will bring about a unified policy on economic and cultural developments while at the same time preparing for a 'free election' to be held throughout Korea. In the event that the establishment of the Committee should not be feasible, the North Korean Premier has proposed that a committee consisting of 'representatives of industry and commerce' shall be allowed to meet in order that they may agree on trade and 'assistance' matters.

The North Korean rulers, however, are obviously aware that it would be impossible for the United States to withdraw its troops from South Korea and to cancel the mutual defence agreement with the Republic of Korea Government. A mere hint of this nature on the part of Washington would create unrest in the South, and actual American withdrawal would probably cause another Korean War. In the face of such conditions, the Pyongyang regime seems to have adopted a basic tactic of steady propaganda (1) to influence the South Korean populace in order that they may turn against the United States and (2) to consolidate the 'democratic basis' in North Korea. Every economic measure taken in North Korea, therefore, is presented as being justified in the name of 'peaceful unification of the fatherland'.

The regime of Kim Il-song emerged in its early period under the auspices of the Russian army, but between 1960 and 1965 it was strongly identified with Communist China in the Sino-Soviet ideological dispute. North Korean literature attacking 'international revisionism' began to appear about 1958 and in the same year the agricultural programmes in China were also imitated. Later the Pyongyang regime consistently sided with China on such issues as the Sino-Indian border dispute and the arming of Cuba. The North Korean party has been attacked along with the Chinese and Albanian parties by some of the Eastern

European Communist parties. Although the causes and the meaning of the North Korean position in the current intra-bloc dispute are yet to be explored, some explanations are possible.

First, the North Korean Communists have always found it difficult to accept the principle of 'peaceful coexistence' advanced by the Soviet Union. As early as August 1953 the Premier had declared that it was dangerous and harmful to think that North Korea could coexist with South Korea. He accepted the correctness of the principle in the international sphere at that time, but one gained the impression that Kim Il-song was not fully convinced of the validity of the Russian argument. Full acceptance of the principle of coexistence would mean a reduction of intensity in the anti-American campaign which was an essential part of the 'peaceful unification' movement. It would also weaken the argument for radical economic programmes in North Korea, in that the construction of the 'democratic base' is an integral part of the 'peaceful unification' movement. Thus the desire for the rapid recovery and development of the economy of North Korea and the existence of anti-Communist regimes in Nationalist China and South Korea may have drawn North Korea closer to Peking. The latter factor would in particular draw the two regimes closer to attack 'American imperialism' as the prime enemy of the 'peace-loving peoples'. It is perhaps relevant to remind readers that the Korean War was launched in 1950 in the midst of the North Korean campaign for 'peaceful unification'.

These factors alone, however, would not justify and hence would not explain the extent to which Pyongyang has aligned itself with Peking. The present writer believes that the stronger cause for the seemingly sudden change in the North Korean attitude around 1958 lies in Kim Il-song's discovery that the anti-party plot by Ch'oe Ch'ang-ki and his group, i.e., the 1956 denunciation of the Premier, had received encouragement and support from Moscow. It would certainly be difficult to relegate the North Korean identification of the Ch'oe group with 'international revisionism' to a mere coincidence. It can be argued, then, that the North Korean leadership was united with the Chinese and Albanian comrades in their resentment of the Soviet interference in domestic politics.

The removal of Premier Khruschev from the position of leadership in the Soviet Union and mounting difficulties in economic and defence fields in North Korea precipitated considerable modification in the North Korean attitude toward the Russian and Chinese comrades. After 1965 the North Korean regime concluded a number of agreements with the Soviet Union to buttress its economic and defence posture.

Although the North Korean Communists still renounce revisionism, they would rather like to see the Communist camp reunited to fight against the common enemy, 'American imperialism'. So far, the Peking regime has withheld any official attack against the North Korean regime, but the wall posters in China have frequently attacked the North Koreans for taking an opportunistic line.

BIBLIOGRAPHY

Wilfred G. Burchett. *Again Korea*. (International Publishers, 1968, New York.)

The China Quarterly, April–June, 1963. A Symposium on North Korea.

Chong-Sik Lee. *The Politics of Korean Nationalism*. (University of California Press, Berkeley and Los Angeles, 1963.) 'Stalinism in the East: Communism in North Korea', in R. A. Scalapino (Ed.), *Communist Revolution in Asia*. (Prentice-Hall, Englewood Cliffs, N.J., 1965.)

North Korea: A Case in the Techniques of Takeover. (US Department of State, Washington, 1961.)

Philip Rudolph. *North Korea's Political and Economic Structure*. (Institute of Pacific Relations, New York, 1959.)

RUSSIA IN SIBERIA
AND THE FAR EAST

S. V. Utechin

THE BEGINNING

THE most significant feature of Siberia and the Russian Far East, under-lying all economic, social, and political developments, is that it has been an area of gradual Russian colonization since the late 16th century. The small and mostly primitive indigenous peoples were easily subdued by small Cossack detachments, which, within a few decades, occupied and annexed to Russia the whole vast territory from the Ural Mountains to the Pacific. The main attractions for the Russian colonists were at first the precious furs, then (from the 18th century) the lead and silver mined in the Altay area and in Transbaykalia, and from the 1830s also gold which was found in many places in central and eastern Siberia. There was little agricultural colonization in the early period except in so far as it was necessary to provide food for the Russian traders, miners and military and administrative personnel (the latter of necessity including a very considerable number of people engaged in transport and communications). Almost from the very beginning of Russian colonization, Siberia was used as a place of banishment for common criminals, religious dissenters and political offenders. Of the latter, two comparatively numerous groups played an important role in the intellectual development of the area – the Decembrists from the late 1820s and the Poles after the Polish uprising of 1863. Siberia never knew serfdom, but many of the mine-workers in the 18th century were state peasants who, together with their families, were compulsorily settled there to work in the mines; and in the 19th century the mines were partly worked by convicts.

The indigenous peoples were at first largely left alone, provided they paid tribute (later taxes) and did not interfere with the Russian colonists. In the 1830s a more ordered system of indirect rule was introduced, with either tribal or district assemblies electing headmen who had the double function of internal administration according to customary law and of representing their people with the Russian authorities. Assimilation was comparatively easy, since there was no racial prejudice on the Russian side, and the majority of the indigenous peoples were, at least formally, Christianized (though Buddhism was at the same time making headway among the Buryats).

The great reforms of the 1860s and 1870s, which profoundly transformed European Russia, did not affect Siberia to the same extent, partly because there were no serfs to be emancipated, but also because there was no local nobility either, and with this class lacking and the small educated stratum consisting mainly of banished revolutionaries the St Petersburg authorities were reluctant to introduce local government and the reformed judiciary. This was resented by the more enlightened among the merchants (especially in Irkutsk and Tomsk) and the more prosperous among the peasants, and a Siberian 'regionalist' movement developed from the 1870s. A similar tendency began to develop towards the end of the century in the Far East, where the Amur and Maritime areas had been annexed by Russia following the treaties with China in 1857 and 1860, and Vladivostok, founded in 1862, had rapidly developed into a prosperous port with a cosmopolitan (Russian, Chinese and Korean) population and wide trading contacts in the Pacific area.

THE RAILWAY

A new era in the life of Siberia and the Russian Far East opened with the construction of the Trans-Siberian Railway in 1891-9, the eastern section of which was at first formed by the Chinese Eastern Railway built by the Russians in Manchuria in 1896-1903. The immediate effects of the new ease of communications were twofold: a rapid increase in agricultural colonization, and a more intensive Russian involvement in Far Eastern affairs in general, especially as regards China and Korea. Colonization was now primarily motivated not by the needs of Siberia but by agricultural over-population in European Russia. This peasant settlement was put on a systematic and rational, though very bureaucratic, basis, the whole operation being directed from the Resettlement Board in St Petersburg. The tempo of colonization was further accelerated by the agricultural reforms of Stolypin in 1907. On the eve of the 1917 revolution the peasant population of Siberia and the Far East was not homogeneous, being divided on the one hand into the 'old inhabitants' and the 'new settlers', and the latter in turn into those who had done well and those who had not succeeded in creating viable farms. Dairy farming was the most profitable enterprise, and through a co-operative butter-making and marketing organization Siberian butter went as far afield as England.

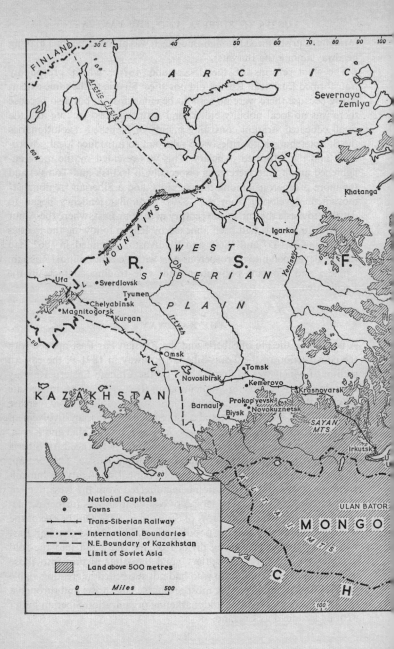

FINLAND

30 E   40   50   60   70.   80   90   100

A   R   C   T   I   C

Arctic Circle

Severnaya
Zemlya

60 N

Khatanga

MOUNTAINS

W   E   S   T
S   .   F.

R.   S   I   B   E   R   I   A   N

Ob

Igarka

Ufa
• Sverdlovsk

P   L   A   I   N

Tyumen

Chelyabinsk

Irtysh

Yenisey

Magnitogorsk   Kurgan

50

•Omsk

K   A   Z   A   K   H   S   T   A   N

Tomsk

Novosibirsk

Kemerovo

Krasnoyarsk

Barnaul•   Prokop'yevsk•

Biysk   Novokuznetsk

SAYAN
MTS.

80

Irkutsk

U

⊙   National Capitals
•   Towns
+—+—+   Trans-Siberian Railway
—•—•—   International Boundaries
— — —   N.E. Boundary of Kazakhstan
— — —   Limit of Soviet Asia
▨   Land above 500 metres

0   Miles   500

ULAN BATOR

M   O   N   G   O

MTS

C

H

100

O C E A N

120 130 140 150 160 170 180

Tiksi

S.   R

Magadan

Yakutsk

Lena

Lake Baikal

Chita

A

N

PEKING

KOREA

Anadyr

BERING SEA

Kamchatka Pen.

Petropavlovsk-Kamchatskiy

SEA OF OKHOTSK

Sakhalin

Komsomolsk

Blagoveshchensk
Birobidzhan   Khabarovsk

Yuzhno-Sakhalinsk

Kuril'skiye Ostroba

Vladivostok

J A P A N

TOKYO

THE REVOLUTION

Siberia and the Far East had their share of revolutionary events, during both the 1905 and the 1917 Russian revolutions, and in both cases it was the railwaymen and the soldiers who were the most responsive to the call of the revolutionary parties. During the Civil War the area was for the most part in the hands of various, usually ephemeral, anti-Bolshevik regimes, one of which was a Siberian Government formed in Tomsk in 1918 by the regionalists. In 1919–20 Omsk in Western Siberia was the residence of Admiral Kolchak, recognized by the other White Governments as the 'Supreme Ruler' of Russia. The Bolshevik victory in 1920 was socially a victory for the poorer elements among the 'new settlers', who now benefited most from the redistribution of land. Until the mid 1930s most of Siberia was ruled by the Bolsheviks as a single unit, first by the Siberian Revolutionary Committee, then by the Siberian Bureau of the Central Committee of the Communist Party, and at the end as one administrative area – the Siberian *kray* (territory). The Far East was not at once incorporated into the Russian Soviet Federative Socialist Republic, but a Far Eastern Republic was formed in 1920 (with Chita as its capital) as a kind of buffer state between Communist Russia and Japan. It was one of the first examples of a 'people's democratic' regime controlled by the Bolsheviks. The Far Eastern Republic existed until 1922, when it ostensibly dissolved itself and was admitted into the RSFSR as the Far Eastern *kray*. The indigenous peoples of the area, of which some of the larger tried to organize autonomous regimes of their own in 1917 and during the Civil War, were subjected to the usual Soviet policy of fictitious territorial autonomy (there are now three Autonomous Republics, three Autonomous Oblasts and six National Okrugs in Siberia and the Far East) and encouragement for the development of cultures 'national in form and socialist in content'.

COLLECTIVIZATION OF AGRICULTURE

Collectivization of agriculture in 1929–34 put an end to the class of prosperous Siberian farmers, and dairy farming was so severely hit that it has still not recovered. The peasants put up strong resistance to collectivization, and there were several uprisings, one of them (in the Altay area) lasting for four years. On the other hand, industrialization, which had begun with the construction of the Trans-Siberian Railway and had received some slight impetus from the First World War, was again taken up during the First Five-Year Plan period (1929–32), and the

Kuznetsk coal-mining basin became second in importance in the whole USSR. Throughout the period of Stalin's rule in Russia most construction projects in Siberia and the Far East, as well as timber-felling and the mining of precious metals, were largely worked by the forced labour of concentration camp inmates and 'special settlers' (people deported from European Russia and from the territories in the west which were annexed between 1939 and 1946). During the Second World War, when many factories were evacuated to Siberia from the west, and throughout the post-war period, Siberian industry has been growing very rapidly, especially in western Siberia. The Virgin Lands Campaign of 1953–6, and the emphasis in the current Seven-Year Plan on accelerated development of the eastern parts of the USSR, have created boom conditions in western and central Siberia: the cities are growing rapidly, Novosibirsk having reached the million mark; the Trans-Siberian Railway has been electrified as far as Irkutsk; a Siberian division of the USSR Academy of Sciences has been established which appears to be very vigorous and somewhat freer from ideological shackles than older academic establishments.

The Far East (including the Kurile Islands and the southern half of Sakhalin, which were annexed from Japan after the end of the war and from which all Japanese were expelled) has so far been little affected by this new expansion, and its rate of economic development in recent years has been lower than the USSR average, though it too has to some extent benefited from the freer conditions of the post-Stalin era – e.g. the Far Eastern University in Vladivostok, which had been closed in consequence of the Great Purge of the late 1930s, was re-opened in 1956, and there have been signs in the last year or two that there is some realization of the Far East's potentialities as a supplier of industrial goods to the under-developed countries of Eastern Asia.

THE GREAT PURGE

The Great Purge of 1937–8 affected Siberia and the Far East at least as severely as the rest of the Soviet Union. Among the people who were shot or died in concentration camps were the leading members of all the Party and administrative apparatus in the area, including Marshal Blyukher, who, as commander of the Soviet armed forces in the Far East, had for a decade exercised something like vice-regal powers. All the Chinese, and those Koreans who were not Soviet citizens, who for more than half a century had lived in Vladivostok and other parts of the Far East, were expelled from the USSR, while Koreans who were

Soviet citizens were deported to Kazakhstan and Central Asia. The Siberian and Far Eastern concentration camp areas, which included some of the most notorious in the country – copper and uranium mining in Norilsk on the lower Yenisey and gold, platinum and tin mining in the *Dalstroy* camp system in the extreme north-east centred on Magadan – were the scenes of some of the most important strikes and uprisings of camp inmates in 1953–5. Since the release of the prisoners in 1955–7, the industries of these areas have declined and now appear to be stagnant.

ECONOMIC PROSPECTS

The economic outlook for Siberia, especially its southern parts along the Trans-Siberian Railway, is bright thanks to its mineral riches, great rivers and abundance of forests. The known plans for the next two decades foresee the building of several huge hydro-electric and thermal power stations, a further great expansion of the iron and steel industry and engineering, and the creation of aluminium and chemical industries. These plans are likely to be fulfilled, provided, of course, that Siberia continues to enjoy the priority that has been given to its development in recent years. A difficult problem is that of labour, since the natural increase of the population will provide only a small fraction of what is required. Since the forced labour of camp inmates and the large-scale deportation of people to Siberia as 'special settlers' have now ceased, the authorities have to rely for attracting settlers from European Russia upon a combination of material incentives (which have to be very substantial, because of the adverse climatic and living conditions) and all sorts of pressures short of actual deportation. This last category of semi-volunteer labour consists mainly of young people who are recruited soon after they leave school, and they form rather an unstable element in Siberia. On the one hand they are often enthusiastic and selfless in work, caring little about the difficult conditions, but on the other hand many soon return home, unwilling to stick it out for long, while those who do remain are often difficult to handle and strikes occur frequently. The prospects for Siberian agriculture are much less promising than those for industry. The Virgin Lands Campaign has brought under cultivation large areas and western Siberia has become one of the chief producers of grain in the country; but mono-culture and bad management have already led to soil erosion, the yields, even at first not very high, are falling, and in view of the generally irrational agricultural policy of the Soviet leadership (under-investment and restrictions upon initiative) little improvement can be expected in the foreseeable future.

RACIAL ASSIMILATION

The native peoples, apart from the Mongol-speaking Buryats and the Turkic-speaking Yakuts (perhaps also the Tuvinians, whose country was quietly annexed in 1944), are expected to become assimilated, though this is not often stated openly. Far more important is the question of whether the Soviet Government (or any Russian government) will be able or willing to maintain the policy of exclusively white settlement in the Russian Far East pursued since the 1930s, or whether it will be forced (not least by the need for labour, which is already critical) to re-open the doors to Chinese immigration.

BIBLIOGRAPHY

J. P. Cole and F. C. German. *A Geography of the U.S.S.R. The Background to a Planned Economy.* (Butterworth, London, 1961.)

D. J. Dallin. *The Rise of Russia in Asia.* (Hollis & Carter, London, 1950.) *Soviet Russia and the Far East.* (Hollis & Carter, London, 1948.)

G. Kennan. *Siberia and the Exile System,* 2 vols. (The Century Co., New York, 1891.)

R. J. Kerner. *The Urge to the Sea. The Course of Russian History: The Role of Rivers, Portages, Ostrogs, Monasteries and Furs.* (University of California Press, Berkeley and Los Angeles, 1946.)

W. Kolarz. *Thr Peoples of the Soviet Far East.* (George Phillip, London, 1954.)

C. Krypton. *The Northern Sea Route and the Economy of the Soviet Union.* (Methuen, 1956.)

G. V. Lantzeff. *Siberia in the Seventeenth Century.* (University of California Press, Berkeley, 1943.)

E. Lipper. *Eleven Years in Soviet Prison Camps.* (Hollis & Carter, London, 1951.)

M. A. Novomeysky. *My Siberian Life.* (Max Parrish, London, 1956.)

V. Petrov. *It Happens in Russia, Seven Years Forced Labour in the Siberian Goldfields.* (Eyre & Spottiswoode, 1951.)

M. Raeff. *Siberia and the Reforms of 1822.* (University of Washington Press, Seattle, 1956.)

Y. Semyonov. *The Conquest of Siberia.* (Routledge, 1944.)

E. Thiel. *The Soviet Far East. A Survey of its Physical and Economic Geography.* (Methuen, 1957.)

D. W. Treadgold. *The Great Siberian Migration: Government and Peasant in Resettlement from Emancipation to the First World War.* (Princeton University Press, Princeton, N.J., 1957.)

South-East Asia

SOUTH-EAST ASIA

Saul Rose

LANDS AND PEOPLES

SOUTH-EAST ASIA, which stretches from Burma's western frontier to the most easterly island of Indonesia, consists of a peninsula of the Asian continent together with an archipelago lying between Australia and the China coast. These geographical features have given it the character of a crossroads. It has provided stepping-stones for the migration of peoples making their way down from the mainland, while through the Straits of Malacca – 'the gateway to the Pacific' – has lain the main sea route to the East.

Most of the population of the area, which is estimated to total more than 200 million, can be classified as belonging to the 'Indonesian' type. Their ancestors are believed to have originated from more northerly climes, and to have made their way southward in two major migrations between 2500 and 1500 B.C. Descendants of earlier inhabitants are still to be found in tribes such as the Sakai, which live in the jungles of Malaya; and there were later arrivals, notably the Annamites, the Thai and the Burmans, who also moved down from the north. Thence too came the overseas Chinese who are scattered about the region in considerable numbers, amounting to 12–13 million. As a result of these migrations the region presents a kaleidoscope of peoples, and each country is confronted with the problems of a 'plural' or multi-racial society.

CULTURAL INFLUENCES

In addition, the cultural pattern was strongly marked by external influences. South-East Asia has been an area of overlap between the Indian and Chinese spheres. In the first phase Indian influence predominated. Brahmanism and Buddhism were imported by Indian merchants, and the impress was visible in various forms ranging from styles of architecture to systems of government. Indianized kingdoms rose and fell during the first fifteen centuries of the Christian era. Some of them paid tribute to the Emperor of China from time to time, but the Chinese cultural impact was felt mainly in the area adjacent to the Empire, particularly in Annam.

In the 14th and 15th centuries Islam reached South-East Asia,

279

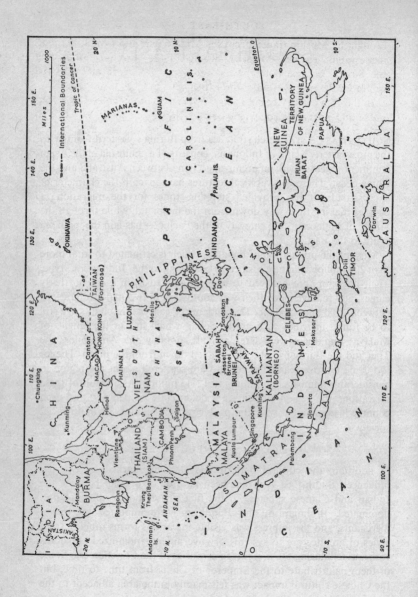

brought by Muslim traders from the Middle East and from India, and made rapid headway. Malacca, through its key position dominating the Straits, became both the main entrepôt for trade and also the centre for the propagation of the faith.

In the 16th century began the era of Western dominance. The Portuguese and Spaniards sought not only 'Christians and spices' but also political supremacy. The Portuguese captured Malacca in 1511 and secured control of the valuable Spice Islands, while the Spaniards established themselves in the Philippines. The Portuguese in their turn were ousted by the Dutch in the following century. The East Indies, despite British efforts to intervene, fell under Dutch control, and Portugal was left with the vestigial possession of half the island of Timor.

The wave of imperialism in the 19th century brought the British back on the scene. Burma was conquered; Singapore was founded and soon outstripped Malacca, which was acquired from the Dutch; the rest of the Malay peninsula was brought under British protection, which was extended to Sarawak, North Borneo and Brunei. The French established their ascendancy in Indo-China, and Siam was left as a buffer state between French and British spheres of influence, owing its survival to their rivalry. Then at the end of the century, after their victory over Spain, the USA took possession of the Philippines.

By 1900, therefore, almost the whole of the area had fallen under Western sway. Even Siam's nominal independence was subject to strong Western influence. This state of affairs lasted for forty years. It would have gone on considerably longer had it not been for the Japanese onslaught which overthrew the Western positions in a matter of a few months. From 1942 to 1945 the Japanese 'New Order' replaced Western dominance, but made very few converts. The interregnum, however, had two decisive effects: it showed that Western rule was not unalterable, and it encouraged the growth of nationalism in resistance to foreign domination from any quarter. Ironically the concept of nationhood was in many cases the result of colonial conquest. The political boundaries in South-East Asia are largely the result of accidents of acquisition. It was out of the idea of combined resistance to alien rule that the concept of common nationhood grew.

WESTERN WITHDRAWAL

At first the policy of the Western Powers, returning to South-East Asia as the end of the Japanese war approached, was essentially the restoration of the *status quo ante bellum*; but this was found to be impossible. The USA had promised independence to the Philippines, and fulfilled that undertaking in 1946. In the British sphere a process of decolonization set in, starting with the Indian Empire and spreading inexorably eastward. In the event the only question was whether the Western Powers would go gracefully or be ejected. Britain parted with Burma on friendly terms; and then Malaya attained independence, leaving the State of Singapore with a large measure of internal self-government and the dependencies of Sarawak, North Borneo and Brunei as the last outposts of empire. The Dutch, however, had to be expelled by the combined forces of the Indonesian nationalist movement and world opinion, although they retained Western New Guinea until 1962 despite continual complaints from Indonesia. The anti-Western movement was reinforced from 1949 by the Communist triumph in China. This was felt particularly in Indo-China; and the French, after a grim and costly war, were obliged to quit. Laos and Cambodia became independent states, but Vietnam was divided between a Communist regime in the north and an anti-Communist regime in the south.

The Indo-China crisis in 1954 led to the Western proposal for a regional defence arrangement, which was accepted by some of the countries in the area. The South-East Asia Treaty Organization, which was set up by Pakistan, Thailand, the Philippines, Australia, New Zealand, Britain, France and the USA, extended its protection to the Indo-China settlement reached at the Geneva Conference. While SEATO has proved effective in preventing any open Communist aggression, it has shown itself unable to cope with subversion in areas bordering on the Communist sector. Laos and South Vietnam have been subjected to infiltration and Cambodia has been under pressure. Communist guerilla activity was successfully combated in Malaya, but it had no direct line of communication with its main base in China and, even so, it took ten years of considerable military effort. The border zone is much more vulnerable to penetration.

COMMUNISM AND NATIONALISM

The spread of Communism elsewhere in the region has been inhibited partly by the unassimilated character of overseas Chinese society. Often unpopular because of their role as moneylenders and middlemen, they are sometimes regarded with suspicion as a potential 'fifth column' for Chinese imperialism. To the extent that Communism is now identified with China its appeal to the other communities is diminished.

The force of nationalism is still predominant. In the colonial period the Communists could exploit the nationalist movement for their own ends, since for both of them the immediate aim was to shake off the foreign yoke. Once independence was achieved, however, a Communist movement which showed itself subservient to alien control lost the support of nationalists. Even when the current of nationalism has run counter to Communism it has not led to a pro-Western stand, partly because the memory of the independence struggle dies hard, and partly because in some places Western rule still persists. So long as the Dutch held on to Western New Guinea President Sukarno could maintain a state of 'permanent revolution', with advantage to the Indonesian Communist Party and sympathy from his Asian neighbours. The Portuguese in Timor may not be left undisturbed much longer. For Britain a problem was posed by Singapore and the Borneo territories. The solution that was propounded was to merge them with the Federation of Malaya in a 'new Malaysia'. This project only became feasible after Malaya had attained independence and showed its capacity for self-government. The scheme was accepted by Singapore with its predominantly Chinese population; but in the Borneo territories, where public opinion had only rudimentary means of political expression, the situation was more obscure. The Sultan of Brunei declined to join. The two British colonies of Sarawak and North Borneo (now called Sabah) were incorporated in the new Malaysia in September 1963 after a UN commission of inquiry had found that most of the population favoured the project. But the new creation aroused hostility from neighbouring Indonesia, which embarked on a policy of 'confrontation' designed to intimidate and 'crush' Malaysia.

To the problem of insecurity is added the question of whether the countries of South-East Asia can be made politically and economically viable. Most of them adopted forms of Western democracy as their model, partly because of familiarity and partly because their claim to independence had been based on democratic principles. Whether Western-style institutions, even though modified, are suited to South-East Asian conditions is open to question. In South Vietnam, under constant Communist threat, they merely veiled the dictatorship of President Diem and his successors. President Sukarno instituted 'guided democracy' in Indonesia. Siam experimented briefly with a limited form of democracy until Marshal Sarit put a stop to it. In Burma a much more promising experiment has also been halted by the Army. In several countries the attainment of independence has been followed by an increase in communal tensions, previously overlaid by the nationalist movement, and a need has been felt for more discipline and cohesion, which the Army has been ready and willing to supply.

POLITICS AND ECONOMICS

Although there is a trend towards more authoritarian rule, this does not imply any abatement of the spirit of national independence. But Communism might find an opening if the new countries cannot supply the material needs of their peoples. They occupy an extensive and productive portion of the globe, comprising a land area of more than $1\frac{1}{2}$ million square miles. Although there are some dense concentrations, particularly on the islands of Java and Luzon and in the Red River delta of Vietnam, the region as a whole is not very thickly populated and has traditionally provided a surplus of food, particularly rice, for export. Among the other major products entering into international trade are rubber, tin, timber and oil. The region is 'under-developed' although the standard of living is generally higher than in China or India. The economy is mainly agricultural, and not greatly diversified. It is consequently vulnerable to economic fluctuations. There is competition between East and West in the supply of economic and technical assistance; but the new states are sensitive, and suspicious of 'strings' being attached. They are torn between the desire for foreign investment and their resolve to avoid any form of 'colonialism'. Economic development is subordinated to political considerations.

THE COLOMBO PLAN

In 1950 the Colombo Plan was launched, under Commonwealth auspices, with the aim of bringing assistance to the countries of South and South-East Asia, partly by mutual aid. This project was so successful that it was extended and expanded: it is still continuing and includes every country in the region except North Vietnam. But the amounts supplied are relatively small. Much greater quantities are being provided by the USA directly to individual countries through bilateral arrangements.

Partly through economic influence and partly for reasons of strategy the US role in South-East Asia has been enhanced while that of the European Powers has declined. America has assumed some of the responsibility – and also some of the odium – which previously attached to the Colonial Powers. Australia too is taking a growing part in the affairs of her 'Near North', while China under the new regime has clearly not lost her traditional interest in the 'Southern Ocean'. These attentions are unwelcome in some quarters, but they are unavoidable. Neither side can afford to relinquish the region to the other.

Several of the South-East Asian countries, for their part, refuse to be committed and prefer a policy of non-alignment. Similarly, in their domestic affairs, presented with a choice between Communist and Western models, they decline the option and are trying their own methods. These experiments may sometimes appear misguided, but they are a mark of independence; and perhaps there may emerge from them a new contribution towards solving the problems of South-East Asia.

BIBLIOGRAPHY

J. G. Brimmell. *Communism in South-East Asia.* (Oxford University Press, 1959.)

R. H. Fifield. *Diplomacy of Southeast Asia, 1945–58.* (Harper, New York, 1958.)

D. G. E. Hall. *History of South-East Asia.* (Macmillan, 1955.)

B. Harrison. *South-East Asia.* (Macmillan, 1955.)

G. McT. Kahin (Ed.). *Governments and Politics of South-East Asia.* (Cornell University Press, New York, 1959.)

BURMA

Hugh Tinker

ORIGIN

MORE than most countries, Burma is a complex of antitheses. A national unity and a tribalistic disunity; the cult of serenity and withdrawal, and the cult of force and violence; the worship of absolute authority, together with an absence of social barriers; relaxed and easy personal relations, constantly exploding into tension and schizophrenia: these are some of the attributes of this puzzling country. Burma has undergone invasion, colonial occupation, foreign economic exploitation, the ravages of 20th century war, the intoxication of a Socialist-style democracy, and the drab regimentation of military rule. While foreign observers have constantly predicted disintegration and collapse, Burma has survived all these experiences with the essence of its social and religious life unimpaired. This resilience is, perhaps, the key to this paradoxical, indeed Gilbertian, country.

Burmans are fond of recalling that their national unity predates the Norman conquest of England. King Anawrahta (A.D. 1044–77) ruled an empire that included most of modern Burma within its boundaries, from his capital, Pagan. The Burmese race had penetrated the northern and eastern mountain boundaries about the year A.D. 700. They gradually displaced earlier inhabitants, the Pyu and the Mons, though their settlements did not penetrate into the region of Lower Burma. The Burmese were followed by branches of the great Thai race, known in Burma as Shans. Between 1287 and 1531, the Shans dominated Upper Burma. All these peoples adopted wet-rice cultivation, using irrigation, and embraced (to greater or lesser extent) the teaching of the Theravada school of Buddhism, gained from Ceylon. They occupied the level lands of the Irrawaddy plain, and the valley country in east and north Burma. The hills remained the domain of tribes who largely practised shifting, dry-rice cultivation, and who remained Animists. Among the more prominent were the Kachins, the Karens, and the Chins. Remaining outside Buddhism, they did not acquire a literary culture and they did not imitate Hindu ideas of kingship, as did the plain-dwellers.

The Prime Minister of Burma between 1947 and 1962, U Nu, in his appeals for national unity constantly reminded his countrymen that

CHINA

BHUTAN

INDIA

EAST
PAKISTAN

DACCA

BAY OF

BENGAL

20 N.

Akyab

MYITKYINA

Bhamo

UPPER
BURMA

Lashio

Mandalay

BURMA

Magwe

Prome

LOWER
BURMA

Bassein

RANGOON

Moulmein

ANDAMAN

SEA

ANDAMAN
IS.

90 E.

Tavoy

Mergui

THAILAND

LAOS

Luang
Prabang

VIENTIANE

KRUNG THEP
(Bangkok)

GULF

OF

SIAM

10 N.

90 E

100 E

20

10 N-

100 E

INTERNAL
DIVISIONS

CHIN
DIVISION

KACHIN
STATE

BURMA PROPER

SHAN
STATES

KAYEN

KAREN

Miles

National Capitals
Towns
International Boundaries
Disputed Boundary
Land above 200 metres

0   Miles   200

Burma had never long sustained a unified polity. Nu recalled: '. . . the evil tradition of wresting power by force. Burmese history is full of instances where a king is overthrown by a contender by force, and who in turn is similarly ousted by a still more forceful rival. Except for the glorious period of Anawrahta, Bayinnaung and Alaungpaya, Burma has been a battlefield of warring states.' Bayinnaung reigned from 1551 to 1581; Alaungpaya from 1752 to 1760. Both unified Burma by military conquest, but neither created a unitary state. Alaungpaya's dynasty ruled until 1885, when Burma finally passed under British rule; but not even its most able kings created a regular system of administration, while under the worst the country degenerated into anarchy.

BURMA ANNEXED TO BRITISH INDIA

Burma was annexed to British India between 1826 and 1885; it was governed as an Indian province, and its administration, educational system, laws, and economic structure were largely conditioned by the Indian connexion. Immigration, much from south and east India, led to the growth of an Indian community of half a million, and the most important sectors of commerce were in Indian hands. The export-import trade was dominated by British and Indian companies. Whereas in India the experience of British rule created, virtually, a new class – a middle class with an all-India outlook who formulated a demand for political autonomy and independence – in Burma, no such transformation came about. The small professional middle class was drawn almost entirely from the small group of official families which had served the Burmese Kings. They failed to establish any kind of leadership, or contact with the peasant mass. In the aftermath of the Dyarchy reforms in India, Burma received instalments of political devolution: a legislature, ministerial government, and responsibility for many aspects of administration.

THE 'THAKINS'

But the middle-class lawyer-politicians remained cocooned in their own little world, and mass political leadership passed to itinerant monks (not unlike the hedge-priest, John Ball), of whom U Wisara was fore-most. Theirs was a crude, rabble-rousing appeal, and their programme was little more than preaching hatred of the foreigners and a return to the good old days. In the 1930s they gave way to an extremist group, the *Dobama Asi-ayone*, commonly called *Thakins*, or 'Masters'.

The Thakins attracted a following among a group of students at Rangoon University. Drawn from the rural lower middle class, for the most part backward in their studies, these rustic students decided to invest in political agitation. In 1936 they contrived a strike which involved about half the undergraduates. Under pressure from the Minister of Education, Dr Ba Maw, the university authorities capitulated. Thenceforward, the militant strike was the master-weapon in Burmese politics.

The 1930s in Burma opened with the Saya San rebellion, a primitive, messianic revolt, and with the anti-Indian riots; the decade closed with student riots and the formation of political private armies on the Fascist model: the Thakin Army was known as the Steel Corps. The Thakins linked up with Japanese agents, and thirty young men, headed by Aung San, the 1936 strike leader, went to Japan for military training. Early in 1942, they re-entered Burma with the Japanese invader. Having driven out the British forces, the Japanese granted a façade of independence to Burma. They appointed Dr Ba Maw as Head of State, *Adipati*, or Generalissimo. His principal lieutenants were drawn from the Thakins, with Aung San as *Bogyoke*, or chief of the Japanese-controlled 'Burma National Army', Thakin Nu as head of the Foreign Office, and Than Tun (a Communist Thakin) as Minister for Agriculture. Gradually, the Thakins became disillusioned with their Japanese masters, and they made contact with British military intelligence agencies. In 1944 the tide of war turned; the Japanese suffered their most severe military disaster in any theatre in an abortive advance into India; in the early months of 1945, British–Indian forces swept down into the plain of the Irrawaddy. Aung San led his Burma National Army into hiding and subsequently made his way to British military headquarters.

RECOGNITION OF AUNG SAN

After hostilities ceased, Burma came under British military government, and events were considerably influenced by the decision taken by Admiral Mountbatten as Supreme Commander to recognize Aung San and his colleagues as leaders of the 'Patriotic Burmese Forces'. In the post-war political settlement, Aung San successfully outplayed other contenders for power. He kept together his erstwhile soldiers in a quasi-military association, the 'People's Volunteer Organization' or PVO, and he held together a significant political following in the 'Anti-Fascist People's Freedom League' or AFPFL. This included the growing Communist movement led by Than Tun. Aung San's demand was nothing less than full control over the Government. Taking advantage of police grievances, he was able to launch a national general strike which immobilized all the public services. His demands were accepted, and on 9 January 1947 he came to London to negotiate an agreement with Mr Attlee, the import of which may be summarized as 'full independence within one year'.

Although there was much that was ignoble in his make-up, Aung San was a man of vision: he saw that an essential prerequisite of independence was national unity, and he realized that the Shans and the hill tribes still nourished ancient enmities, arising out of a thousand years of conflict. In February 1947 he negotiated an agreement with leaders of the frontier peoples which largely secured their confidence. In June, a constitution was introduced – which entailed Burma quitting the British Commonwealth – and then, in July, Aung San and most of his Cabinet were assassinated. At the invitation of the last British Governor, Sir Hubert Rance, Thakin Nu took his place as Prime Minister, and led his country into independence on 4 January 1948.

INDEPENDENCE AND AFTER

During the following months, the Union of Burma seemed unlikely to have any lasting duration. Revolts broke out on every hand. First, Than Tun and the Communists 'went underground'; they were followed by the now leaderless PVO; finally, in February 1949, a large section of the Karen minority joined the rebellion. Many of the Karens had become Christians, many had served in the Army, and they had formed by far the most effective war-time resistance movement; now they came close to capturing Rangoon, but they divided their forces in order to take secondary objectives, such as Mandalay, and their moment faded. In the hour of crisis, Nu was deserted by his Socialist colleagues in the Cabinet, Ba Swe and Kyaw Nyein; he was compelled to form a non-partisan Government of national emergency, in which his principal lieutenants were Justice E Maung (Foreign Minister) and the Commander of the Armed Forces, General Ne Win (Deputy Premier, Minister for Home Affairs and Defence). Gradually, the insurgents were thrown back; first, the principal towns were retaken, then, lines of communication were re-established; and at last the rebels were driven into the hills and the jungle. But they could not be completely finished off, as were the Communist guerrillas in Malaya.

GENERAL ELECTIONS AND THE AFPFL

The first general elections after independence took place in 1951. Because of continuing insecurity, they were staggered over the months June–October. The AFPFL, as the ruling coalition, secured 85 per cent of the seats in Parliament on 60 per cent of the popular vote. The only element of opposition came from a small group representing Arakan; which region considered itself underprivileged after independence. Following the elections, the AFPFL Government made strenuous efforts to further its programme for economic development. The philosophy of the AFPFL leaders was, originally, thoroughgoing in its Marxism. Soon after independence, measures of nationalization (that is, expropriation) of foreign-owned utilities were pushed through. The insurrections slowed down the process of nationalization, and the flight of foreign capital gave the Government food for thought. A team of American economists and technicians were invited to make a survey of Burma's resources and to prepare a blue-print for future economic development. This team presented a preliminary report in May 1952, and on its recommendations the Government launched a development programme (July 1952) under the slogan 'Towards a Welfare State'. In Burmese this was called *Pyidawtha* (literally, 'sacred-pleasant-country'). The next year, the American team presented a 2,000-page *Comprehensive Report*, which purported to provide a recipe for all Burma's problems, economic and administrative. There was to be an investment programme, to be completed by 1960, to cost 7,500,000,000 kyats, or £562,500,000. The attitude of those who drafted this plan is summarized in their declaration:

There is no known limit to possible improvements in materials, methods, and products. . . . Burma must become a progressive nation, so that her people not only live better in 1960, but look forward to continued improvement without limit.

All this was very much to the liking of politicians who had preached that their British rulers had deliberately kept them poor. Unfortunately, not one forecast made in the plan was ever implemented. A number of new industrial undertakings were launched: textile mills, a steel mill, a pharmaceutical plant. All swallowed up foreign exchange, all ran into difficulties, and none was made to run at a profit. During the same period, the international terms of trade shifted, to Burma's disadvantage. The world price of rice, upon which Burma mainly depended, came tumbling down; imports increased in volume, but receipts steadily fell. By 1955 Burma was suffering from an acute balance of payments crisis. Attempts to alleviate the position by a series of barter agreements with Communist countries proved highly disadvantageous. The industrialization programme was first curtailed, and then largely liquidated. All this was intensely frustrating to the Marxist-Socialist members of the Cabinet.

BUDDHISM AS SOLUTION TO THE NATION'S PROBLEMS

Meanwhile, Nu as Prime Minister was steadily putting more and more emphasis upon religion, upon Buddhism, as the solution to the nation's problems. Between 1954 and 1956 an international Buddhist Council held conclave at Rangoon, and much merit accrued to the Prime Minister and to Burma. A second general election took place in April 1956. Again the AFPFL was confirmed in power, but with a considerably reduced majority. Nu decided to take a year's sabbatical leave from the premiership, in order to reorganize and rejuvenate the AFPFL. Ba Swe, the Socialist boss, became Prime Minister *ad interim*. When Nu returned to office, it became clear that a breach was opening between his supporters and the Socialists. This became acute when, in January 1958, at an All-Burma Congress of the AFPFL, Nu delivered a long statement of policy in which he concluded 'the AFPFL rejects Marxism as a guiding philosophy or as the ideology of the AFPFL'. This was taken by Ba Swe and Kyaw Nyein as a direct challenge to their Marxist-Socialist position. On 4 June 1958 these two resigned from the Government, along with all their following. To confront the well-organized Socialist parliamentary faction, Nu had only the rump of the so-called 'Clean' AFPFL. He obtained reinforcements from the Arakanese bloc, and from ex-Justice E Maung and others. Faced with a Socialist motion of no confidence, he obtained a majority of seven. To break this near-deadlock, Nu announced that fresh elections would be held in November. But this was not to be.

THE ARMY TAKES OVER

On 28 October, Parliament was assembled, and Nu announced that he was handing over power to General Ne Win and the Army. Constitutional proprieties were observed, and the General secured the assent of Parliament to his actions. He announced his intention of restoring national order and stability, in order to create a situation in which fair elections could take place. The military regime carried through a number of reforms, but earned increasing unpopularity.

Elections were fixed for February 1960. Most observers favoured the chances of the Swe–Nyein group, called the 'Stable' AFPFL. They were known to have the support of influential Army leaders, such as Brigadier Aung Gyi, the Chief of Staff. Nu enjoyed the support of a handful of front-rank politicians, but behind them stood a raggle-taggle party. Undaunted, Nu flung himself into a political campaign reminiscent of Franklin Roosevelt in his prime. He made two sweeping promises: he declared that Buddhism should be declared as the state religion, and he undertook to extend the principle of separate state or regional autonomy, already enjoyed by the Shans, Kachins, Chins, and Karens, to two other minorities: the Arakanese and the Mons. When polling day came, Nu won a landslide victory; out of 250 seats in the Chamber of Deputies, his party won 166 seats; his Socialist opponents gained a mere 34 seats, and both Ba Swe and Kyaw Nyein were unseated.

General Ne Win promptly handed back the premiership to Nu, and withdrew his military men from the ministries and public corporations. Nu now named his party the *Pyidaungsu Ahphwe-gyok* or Union League, leaving to the Swe–Nyein group the discredited name of the AFPFL. His Government redeemed its pre-election promises circum-spectly, but showed no great readiness to tackle the problems facing the nation. One long-term problem was student unrest; the 1936 pattern of the militant strike was constantly repeated. A reforming Rector, Dr Hla Myint, attempted to tighten discipline and raise the lax aca-demic standards. Nu compromised and conciliated, and Dr Hla Myint resigned. Another urgent problem was the continuing suspicion of many of the frontier peoples of the policies of the central Government. The Shans, especially, included a section which desired to secede from the Union of Burma, as the 1947 Constitution entitled them to do. The Army had exercised a heavy hand in the Shan States, and in 1959 a new revolt broke out in the Shan hills.

THE REVOLUTIONARY COUNCIL

Among the Army leaders, an influential group had never accepted the desirability of a return to parliamentary government. This group became steadily more powerful, and eventually they prevailed upon General Ne Win to intervene. On 2 March 1962 the Army moved into Rangoon. The Prime Minister, the President, the Chief Justice, and a number of prominent persons were arrested. The 1947 constitution was abolished, and General Ne Win became chairman of a revolutionary council. With one exception, the new Government was drawn exclusively from the armed forces. The country's constabulary was absorbed into the Army. The Supreme Court and the High Court were dissolved. A draconian policy of national discipline was instituted; the only serious protest came from the student body. A riot on the usual model in July 1962 was suppressed by military force, with the death of fifteen student agitators. Measures to discipline the ebullient, pleasure-loving Burmese were accompanied by measures to control and exclude foreigners. Xenophobia, endemic in Burma, arose again. In the past Burma had many times slammed the door in the face of the outside world. But in the 1960s there was one power which Burma could not hope to shut out: Communist China. The conclusion of an agreement with China on 28 January 1960 over the disputed boundary was in many respects an achievement for Burma. In return for the transfer of about fifty square miles of territory to China, Burma secured a recognized frontier line, and China abandoned long-standing claims to all the country north of Myitkyina. But the tacit price of this concession was Burma's acceptance of a neutrality which allowed for no association with countries inimical to China, especially India.

THE BURMESE WAY TO SOCIALISM

The manifesto of the Revolutionary Council reflected this insistence upon development through an essentially 'Burmese Way to Socialism'. Foreign activity in the economic life of Burma was to come to an end, and the purpose of development was declared to be the good of the people as a whole, not merely the good of the elite – the educated, westernized middle class. In place of the competing political parties of the parliamentary period, one national 'rally' was formed, the Burma Socialist Programme Party, or *Lanzin*. This adopted the Communist Party model of an active cadre or core organization. The Secretary General of the Central Organizing Committee is Brigadier San Yu. Throughout the country, adherents are encouraged to associate themselves with *Lanzin* in categories known as 'candidates' and 'sympathizers'. Only a chosen few are accepted as members. These are expected to undergo a Marxist course of indoctrination at the Central School of Political Science. Civil servants, Army officers, and other leaders are also required to graduate from the School. The principal statement of ideology is called 'The Correlation of Man and his Environment'.

Those who are qualified as leaders are expected to identify themselves with the masses through labour, in the fields or on public works. Periodically, representatives of the people are invited to participate in workers' and peasants' seminars. Declarations have been made by General Ne Win announcing a new democratic form of government in which the people would take part through workers' and peasants' councils; but no actual constitution has emerged.

General Ne Win continues to receive the loyalty of the armed forces, despite a marked deterioration in the security situation throughout the country, especially in the Shan and Kachin areas. The only other prominent figure in the Revolutionary Council is Colonel Tin Pe, the most thorough-going Marxist among the leaders, who has carried through an economic policy leading to total control by the state of all economic activity, commercial, industrial, and agricultural. Burma's gross national product *per capita* is calculated at about £45; the second lowest in South-East Asia, and among the lowest in the world.

As a by-product of the Cultural Revolution in China, there were clashes in Rangoon in June 1967 between local Chinese youths performing as Red Guards, and Burmese objectors. There was damage to Chinese property, and subsequently a marked deterioration of Sino-Burmese relations. However, there was no attempt by the Revolutionary Council to resume closer relations with any other countries as compensation.

BIBLIOGRAPHY

J. R. Andrus. *Burmese Economic Life*. (Stanford University Press, Stanford, 1947.)

J. F. Cady. *A History of Modern Burma*. (Cornell University Press, Ithaca, New York, 1958.)

J. L. Christian. *Modern Burma*. (University of California Press, Berkeley, 1942.) Re-issued with additional chapters as *Burma and the Japanese Invader*. (Bombay, 1945.)

J. S. Furnivall. *The Governance of Modern Burma*. (Institute of Pacific Relations, New York, 1958.)

D. G. E. Hall. *Burma*. (Hutchinson, 2nd edn, 1956.)

W. C. Johnstone. *Burma's Foreign Policy: a study in Neutralism*. (Harvard University Press, Cambridge, Mass., 1963.)

Maung Maung. *Burma's Constitution*. (Nijhoff, The Hague, 2nd edn, 1961.)

Ba Maw. *Breakthrough in Burma; memoirs of a revolution, 1939–46*. (Yale University Press, New Haven, 1968.)

L. W. Pye. *Politics, Personality, and Nation Building: Burma's Search for Identity*. (Yale University Press, New Haven, 1962.)

Thakin Nu. *Burma under the Japanese*. (Macmillan, 1954.)

HUGH TINKER

H. Tinker (Ed.). *U Hla Pe's Narrative of the Japanese Occupation of Burma.* (Cornell Data Paper, Ithaca, New York, 1961.)

H. Tinker. *The Union of Burma: A Study of the First Years of Independence.* (Oxford University Press for Royal Institute of International Affairs, 4th edn, 1961.)

THAILAND

D. Insor

ORIGIN

THAI tribes started their migration from south-west China about a thousand years ago. Some advanced along the Salween river, others along the Mekong: these areas form the present-day Shan States of Burma and the Kingdom of Laos. Only the Thais, reaching the head-waters of the Menam Chao Phraya, finally penetrated to the sea.

In the 13th century the Thais drove out the Khmers (Cambodians), whose empire extended over much of the 'golden peninsula', and founded the Kingdom of Sukhotai. Ayuthaya became the capital of a new and powerful dynasty a hundred years later. This city, until its capture and total destruction by the Burmese in 1767, rivalled London in size and magnificence. In 1782 the victorious general Chakri founded the present ruling dynasty with its capital at Bangkok.

TWO REMARKABLE KINGS

From a remarkable line of kings two stand out. The wise and noble Mongkut – twenty-seven years a monk, he travelled the country, learned English and was devoted to astronomy – was succeeded in 1868 by Chulalongkorn, the 'beloved monarch', who in the forty-two years of his reign revolutionized, with the help of foreign advisers, the laws, administration and customs of the kingdom. It is a tribute to the reforms of these kings – and to the rivalry between Britain and France – that Siam (now Thailand) alone in South-East Asia was never a colony.

Free of foreign control the Thai people also preserved their independence at home. Land was made available to all who might farm it. No peasant wars have been recorded in Thai history – though invasion, forced resettlement, disease, slavery and the *corvée* (up to the end of the 19th century) exacted their toll. It is a peasant, and not a landlord, economy which accounts for the ease and stability of Thailand – the envy of less fortunate peoples.

RELIGION

The Thais, like their neighbours – except the Malays – are Buddhists. The influence of this compassionate yet reasonable and 'detached'

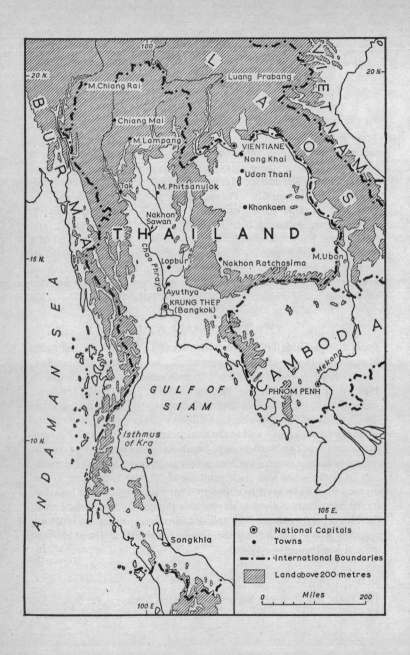

religion is deeply marked. There have been no Buddhist crusades and no Buddhist persecutions, either of heretics or unbelievers. Tolerance, acceptance of 'fate' (*karma*, the result of one's own actions), even non-violence, are characteristic. Thai people are cheerful, easy going, friendly, hospitable; sometimes quick-tempered, often indolent; for they live in a climate that is warm and relaxing, in a land generally fertile and well watered, suited to the traditional rice culture.

REVOLT AND COUNTER-REVOLT

The Thai people, more than 80 per cent of whom live in villages, are naturally conservative, either ignorant of politics or indifferent. Thus when in 1932 absolute monarchy was overthrown by a group of young civilians and officers, the people remained largely untouched and unmoved. Under the Constitution half the deputies were elected and half appointed, but few of the electors bothered to vote. The Army, which had defeated a royalist counter-revolt, gained more and more control over the civilians. Japan's role in the thirties had a strong attraction for the military leader, Colonel (later Field-Marshal) Pibun Songkram, who became Prime Minister in 1938. His civilian rival, Pridi Panomyong, a young lawyer, in succession Minister of the Interior, Foreign Affairs and Finance, was powerless to reverse the prevailing trend which, in 1941, culminated in virtual military dictatorship and alliance with Japan.

THE PRIDI REGIME

Thailand bowed to the inevitable. But Pridi secretly organized a 'Free Thai' resistance movement with the help of the Allies and of Thais in Britain and America. In 1944 Pibun was compelled to resign and Pridi took over behind the scenes. Thailand was spared the devastation of other countries of South-East Asia but suffered serious moral deterioration. Remarkably free of corruption (or brutality) before the war, the Thai administration at that time faced few complicated problems and had been strengthened by the numerous foreign advisers recruited by King Chulalongkorn and his successors. Severely hit by the inflation of the war and post-war years, officials, politicians, and later, soldiers, succumbed to the temptations offered by Government-controlled schemes, notably, in those years, the rice trade – Thailand's major export.

The Pridi regime might have endured the financial crisis, the responsibility of providing rice reparations to Malaya and the cession of parts of Burma, Malaya, Laos and Cambodia seized by Pibun, but for a tragic occurrence: the death in June 1946 of the young King. The mystery – whether it was accident, suicide or murder – has never been solved. But Pridi was blamed for failing to investigate promptly, and was even accused by his opponents of instigating the 'murder'. For over a year the parliamentary regime hung on until in November 1947 it was forcibly overthrown.

MARSHAL PIBUN'S TAKE-OVER

Thus failed the second attempt at democracy in Thailand. With the support of the Army, Marshal Pibun regained power for the next ten years. Police General Phao Sriyanond, Pibun's aide, controlled parliamentary elections, suppressed 'subversive' opposition, expanded the police and inaugurated – among other profitable activities – an opium-smuggling network. The Army crushed an attempted *coup d'état* by followers of Pridi in 1949 – Pridi had fled the country – and a revolt by the Navy in 1951. Later that year Pibun staged his own coup, in reply to a Communist 'plot'. Such plots were uncovered almost yearly, and hundreds of suspects, especially Chinese, were arrested. From 1950 the regime received economic and military aid from the United States. In 1954 Thailand signed the South-East Asia Collective Defence Treaty and SEATO Headquarters were set up in Bangkok two years later. The Thai Government sought security in commitment to the West.

Internally, Pibun tried to balance between the rival – and growing – power of the Army, led by Field-Marshal Sarit, and the Police. Attempting to secure wider support, Pibun turned in 1956 to a new-found belief in democracy. Political parties, trade unions, free speech (at a 'Hyde Park' by the Grand Palace), were duly authorized. But when elections were still framed, students demonstrated in protest. The Army also came out in opposition and a few months later (September 1957) the tottering regime fell. Pibun fled to Japan, Phao to Switzerland, where they later died.

DEMOCRACY ENDED

Democracy briefly flourished. Free elections were held in December 1957 and the opposition grew – Socialists in the impoverished north-east and the independent Democratic Party in Bangkok. Alarmed at the disintegration of authority Marshal Sarit descended on Bangkok (from convalescence, after a serious operation abroad) and carried out, not a *coup d'état* (he emphasized), but a revolution. The Constitution was abrogated, Parliament dismissed, parties and trade unions disbanded, Communist suspects rounded up and the country placed under martial law (as it still is). 'Evils and corrupt practices had multiplied,' declared Marshal Sarit.

Subversion of the Government was the order of the day. . . . The nation's economic situation was highly precarious, with thousands of millions of *baht* of debts. . . . The garb of democracy was weighing down Thailand. . . . Consequently the Revolutionary Party has to seize power.

MARSHAL SARIT'S REGIME

Six years of discipline and enforced political stability brought striking economic results. A six-year economic development plan begun in 1961 succeeded in raising national income at a rate of seven per cent a year. Large-scale irrigation and hydro-electric projects, including the Yanhee Dam, the biggest in South-East Asia, have been completed. Highways and feeder roads (to bring farmers' produce to market) were constructed. Wide streets, fountains, new offices, shops and hotels gave Bangkok a new air of prosperity.

Under Sarit, politics were kept under firm control. Under martial law what he said was final. Leftist politicians were put in gaol. Demonstrations were not permitted and the press was subdued. The Government formed under a provisional Constitution was headed by Sarit, the Supreme Commander of the Armed Forces. His Army deputies, Generals Thanom and Prapart, were Ministers of Defence and of the Interior respectively. Yet enterprising civil servants joined the Cabinet, notably Thanat Khoman, Minister of Foreign Affairs, and Sunthorn Hongladarom, Minister of Finance. And the monarchy was highly regarded – more so than in former times. On more than one important occasion the reasoned views of King Bhumibol Adulyadej prevailed. Although the Constitution was gradually taking form, Sarit was reluctant to jeopardize economic progress by an early 'relapse' into democracy.

THE NEW ERA

The death of Marshal Sarit in December 1963 marked the end of an era. With his heavy hand removed there were new stirrings towards democracy and away from arbitrary rule. Exposure of the amount of state funds – some £10 million – misappropriated by the late leader shocked the Thai people. General (now Field-Marshal) Thanom became the new Prime Minister. His position is not as secure as his predecessor's; his main rival is General Prapart, who as his deputy and Minister of the Interior controls both the Army and the Police. Thanom brought into his government the able and respected Pote Sarasin, Secretary-General of SEATO, as Minister of National Development, and hastened the drafting of the Constitution which gained approval in principle from the Constituent Assembly in 1965. Following widespread municipal elections in December 1967, a new Constitution was promulgated in June 1968, calling for the institution of a bicameral legislature with an elective lower house, and national elections were scheduled for early 1969.

COMMUNISM

Communism is the greatest danger, judging by ministerial pronouncements; Communists appear to be at the root of all disorders. In reality Communism has little appeal to most Thais, who are reasonably contented, Buddhist by religion and monarchist by inclination. It is true that some students, labour leaders, journalists and politicians have shown themselves susceptible to Communism, or at least neutralism – often, in Government circles, considered the same thing. But in general the Thais, unlike the large and industrious Chinese minority (about 2 million out of a total population of over 30 million), are simply not affected. The exception, and it is an important one, is the people of the north-east. This is the poorest, least fertile and most neglected area of the country. Its people consider themselves Lao, akin to the inhabitants of Laos just across the Mekong. Separatism, economic discontent, Communist propaganda and the influence of the Pathet Lao together form a major problem for Bangkok.

RELATIONS WITH NEIGHBOURS

The Government is urgently developing the north-east and improving the calibre of officials. But the disturbing situation in Laos is now recognized to be beyond its control. In return for the United States' commitment to defend Thailand without waiting for a decision by the other SEATO members, the Thai Government has reluctantly come out in support of America's 'neutralist' policy in Laos. Relations with Burma, the traditional enemy, are remarkably good; with Cambodia, bad (diplomatic relations were broken off in October 1961). Malaysia is a new friend, a partner with Thailand and the Philippines in the Association of South-East Asia for Economic and Cultural Co-operation. The Vietnam war, to which Thailand has committed 15,000 troops, dominates the nation's immediate outlook, while the resurgence of China's influence cannot be long delayed.

PRESENT AND FUTURE PROSPECTS

To sum up: the Government is not popular, especially among the intellectuals, but neither can it be called oppressive. The Thai people traditionally respect authority; most of them are not interested in politics and so long as they are left alone hardly object to the system by which they are ruled. The local Chinese, in particular, find the favourable opportunities for making money well worth the absention from politics. 'Sino-Thai co-operation' – the watchword of the Chinese Chamber of Commerce – takes the sensible form of Chinese directorships being offered to prominent Thai officers or officials in return for 'security of tenure'. But what the Chinese think privately, they keep to themselves.

What are the prospects for democracy? Ironically, the very success with which Thailand warded off colonialism in the past has contributed to the failure of democracy in the present. There was no colonial power to oppose, hence no national movement, uniting all sections of the population, could grow and develop. (Thailand, on the other hand, is pleasantly free from feelings of inferiority or prejudice towards the West. Encouragement of foreign investment and the constructive use of American aid are noticeable, at least compared with several other countries in Asia.) Democracy in Thailand started at the top, with the successful coup – precursor of many others – against absolute monarchy; it never took root. Popular indifference – the voting record ranged from 20 to 40 per cent of the electorate – and the influence of personality rather than policy, led to rule by isolated cliques. These could be – and were – easily overthrown by armed force.

The 'military group' is still dominant in the country even if its power is qualified – outwardly at least – by the promise of constitutional development. But, in the longer view, the economic progress sponsored by Sarit and continued by his successor must strengthen – in number, quality and effect – the very middle class (and even the richer peasantry) whose former instability and weakness permitted the military to take command.

303

D. INSOR

ECONOMIC SITUATION

From the sea, south of Bangkok, almost to the northern foothills near Burma and Laos, extends the great Central Plain of Thailand. The countryside is flat, paddy fields stretching to the horizon; only a few trees and clumps of bamboo indicate the occasional farmhouse, raised on stilts to avoid flooding during the five or six months of the rainy season. Villagers catch fish in the ponds and swamps; boats pass by along the rivers and canals; children tend grazing buffaloes. 'There is rice in the fields, fish in the water' – this is the way the people have expressed it since the days of Sukhotai.

Agriculture still accounts for almost half the national income and for 85 to 90 per cent of exports. Almost three quarters of the cultivated land is under rice. More than half the total crop comes from the Central Plain – which provides most of the yearly export of 1 to 1½ million tons – while less than one third comes from the same amount of land in the north-east. Rubber and tin from the southern peninsula, bordering Malaya, are major exports; also teak from the northern forests around Chiangmai; and, recently, upland crops successfully grown in the north-east – chiefly maize, jute and kenaf, and tapioca.

Thailand lacks the basic fuel and metal resources for heavy industry: there is no coal, a little oil, some lignite, and small deposits of iron ore. Less than one in ten of the active population works in industry. Up-country there are saw mills and rice mills – nearly all owned by Chinese, who also buy, transport and export rice. In and around Bangkok, cement, tobacco, spirits, soap and textiles are produced. At Sriracha, south-east of Bangkok, an oil refinery has been completed. New projects – encouraged by the Board of Investment – include a large oil refinery, a big textile works, a jute mill, various car assembly plants and a tin smelter in the south.

Much progress has been made in attracting industry, and developing power and communications, but for Thailand the needs of agriculture are, and will long remain, decisive.

BIBLIOGRAPHY

Wendell Blanchard (Ed.) *Thailand: Its People, its Society, its Culture*. (Human Relations Area Files Press, New Haven, 1957.)

John Blofeld. *People of the Sun: Encounters in Siam*. (Hutchinson, 1960.)

Noel Busch. *Thailand: an Introduction to Modern Siam*. (Von Nostrand, New York, 1959.)

Chula-Chakrabongse. *Lords of Life*. (Alvin Redman, London, 1960.)

THAILAND

Richard J. Coughlin. *Double Identity: The Chinese in Modern Thailand.* (Hong Kong Univeristy Press, Hong Kong, 1960.)

John de Young. *Village Life in Modern Thailand.* (University of California Press, Berkeley, 1955.)

W. A. Graham. *Siam,* 2 vols. (de la More Press, London, 1924.)

James C. Ingram. *Economic Change in Thailand Since 1850.* (Stanford University Press, Stanford, 1955.)

D. Insor. *Thailand: a Political, Social and Economic Analysis.* (Allen & Unwin, 1963.)

Alexander Macdonald. *Bangkok Editor.* (Macmillan, 1949.)

Donald E. Nuechterlein. *Thailand and the Struggle for Southeast Asia.* (Cornell University Press, Ithaca, New York, 1965.)

Robert L. Pendleton. *Thailand: Aspects of Landscape and Life.* (Duell, Sloan & Pearce, New York, 1962.)

A Public Development Program for Thailand. (Johns Hopkins University Press for International Bank for Reconstruction and Development, Baltimore, 1959.)

W. D. Reeve. *Public Administration in Siam.* (Royal Institute of International Affairs, 1951.)

William G. Skinner. *Chinese Society in Thailand: an Analytical History.* (Cornell University Press, Ithaca, New York, 1957.)

David Wilson. *Politics in Thailand.* (Cornell University Press, Ithaca, New York, 1962.)

W. A. R. Wood. *History of Siam.* (Siam Barnakich Press, Bangkok, 1933.)

CAMBODIA, LAOS AND VIETNAM

P. J. Honey

CAMBODIA

General

THE English name 'Cambodia' is a corruption of 'Kambuja', itself
derived from the Hindu 'Kambu', the mythical founder of the Khmer
people. The country was subject to strong Indian religious and cultural
influence through the Empire of Funan, between the 2nd and 6th
centuries A.D. The Khmer kingdom of Angkor was founded by
Jayavarman II in A.D. 802 and reached the zenith of its development
between A.D. 1000 and A.D. 1200, the period during which the un-
paralleled Khmer architectural masterpieces were constructed. Subjected
to continual Siamese military pressure from the 14th century onwards,
Cambodia was assailed on the other flank by the southward advance of
the Vietnamese in the 17th century. Much Cambodian territory was
annexed by the Vietnamese during the 17th and 18th centuries, and
she became the centre of Siamese-Vietnamese rivalries during the 18th
and 19th centuries. In 1863, following the establishment of French
power in neighbouring Cochin China, King Norodom placed
Cambodia under the protection of France, and her status of protectorate was recognized by Siam four years later. A further treaty of 1884
reduced the King's power and permitted the introduction of French
administrators. The two provinces of Siem Reap and Battambang
have long been the subject of disputes with Siam and have changed
hands several times, but they were finally restored to Cambodia in
1945.

Under Japanese pressure, Prince Norodom Sihanouk declared
Cambodia independent in 1945 but, in January 1946, concluded an
agreement with France whereby Cambodia continued to enjoy internal
autonomy but left foreign affairs and national defence in French
hands. During the Indo-Chinese war, a Cambodian resistance movement, the Khmer Issaraks, fought for full independence, but the
movement was small and lacked prestige because it was directed by the
Vietnamese Communists. The Geneva agreements of 1954 placed

CHINA

Mekong

Red River

Lao Kay

Tuyen Quang

Lang Son

Phong Saly

Dien Bien Phu

T O N K I N

HANOI

Hai Duong

Haiphong

Sam Neua

Nam Dinh

L A O S

Luang Prabang
Plaine
des Jarres

Xieng Khouang

NORTH
VIETNAM

Hainan

Vinh

VIENTIANE

ANNAM RANGE

Dong Hoi

17th Parallel

Savannakhet

Quang Tri

Hué

Danang

THAILAND

Pakse

A N N A M

SOUTH CHINA SEA

BANGKOK

Site of
Angkor
×

Qui Nhon

Battambang

Tonle Sap
(Great Lake)

Mekong

C A M B O D I A

Kompong Chhnang

Kompong Cham

Nha Trang

PHNOM-PENH

Dalat

GULF OF
SIAM

Sihanoukville

Bien Hoa

SAIGON

Cholon

Plain of
Reeds

My Tho

SOUTH
VIETNAM

10 N.

⊚ National Capitals

• Towns

—·—·— International Boundaries

▨ Land over 200 metres

0   Miles   200

110 E.

the whole country under King Norodom Sihanouk, although formal independence of France was not achieved until December of that year.

Political

Impulsive and unconventional by nature, Norodom Sihanouk clashed with the International Control Commission appointed to supervise the carrying out of the Geneva agreements when he sought to alter the electoral provisions of the 1947 constitution. In Shavian fashion, he abdicated in favour of his father, Norodom Suramarit, on 2 March 1955 and organized a political party, the Popular Socialists, which won an overwhelming majority in the September 1955 elections. Since then, Norodom Sihanouk has continued to play the dominant role in Cambodian politics and has shaped the country's policies irrespective of whether he was in or out of office. In December 1955 Cambodia was admitted to membership of the United Nations Organization.

Norodom Sihanouk has accorded recognition to Communist China and has established diplomatic relations with countries of the Communist bloc. Though professing neutralism, he has rejected the protection offered by SEATO and inclines his foreign policy to meet the wishes of China. Cambodia's refusal to accept further United States aid has subjected her formerly stable economy to severe strains. Her friendly relations with the Communist world have proved an added source of friction between Cambodia and her immediate neighbours, South Vietnam and Thailand, and have caused the severing of diplomatic relations with these states. They accuse Cambodia of providing Communism with a base in South-East Asia, and there is much evidence to show that the Communist insurgents in South Vietnam regularly operate from Cambodian territory.

Future Prospects

Cambodia is a small country, weaker than either South Vietnam or Thailand, and would certainly have been annexed by one or other of these states had it not been for the intervention of France during the 19th century. Since the departure of the French in 1954, she has survived, thanks to the balance of power between the Communist and anti-Communist forces in the world. Norodom Sihanouk has acquired prestige and influence far in excess of what the mere size and importance of Cambodia would seem to justify. So long as the equilibrium of world power remains undisturbed, Cambodia will certainly continue to make her voice heard in Asia. If, however, that balance is disturbed, or if Communist forces should prevail in South Vietnam or

Thailand, then, as Norodom Sihanouk admitted in a famous personal letter to the *New York Times* in May 1965, there is little likelihood that Cambodia would survive on her own as an independent state. Her own resources are totally inadequate for her defence, and she has made several attempts to secure an international guarantee for her frontiers with Thailand and Vietnam; none has been forthcoming. Native Communists, trained and controlled by North Vietnam, have increasingly menaced internal security, while Norodom Sihanouk's policy of using China as the country's ultimate protector against Vietnamese expansionism appears less and less likely to prove effective.

LAOS

General

A country of jungle-covered hills and valleys, with few roads and no railway, whose principal highway is the river Mekong, Laos is the least developed of the former states of French Indo-China. Most of its people – less than half of them are Laos, the rest being hill tribesmen – live by subsistence rice farming in the lowlands or by slash and burn cultivation in the hills.

Laotian history, recorded since the 14th century, is a story of internal dissension between rival princes and foreign interference or domination. Laos has enjoyed unity and independence only when there has been a power equilibrium between her neighbours or when these have been weak, and when she has been governed by a ruler powerful enough to impose his own control over all the regions. The country split into its constituent principalities in 1711 and, following the Siamese conquest of Vientiane in 1828, fell largely under Siamese control. French control replaced Siamese later in the 19th century and, in 1899, France reunited the kingdom. Present frontiers were established as a result of Franco-Siamese treaties between 1893 and 1907. King Sisavang Vong, acceding to Japanese pressure, proclaimed the independence of Laos in March 1945, but later revoked the proclamation after the return of the French.

War

A Laotian resistance movement, Lao Issara, defied the King and set up an independent government but, when it was defeated by French troops in March 1946, its leaders retired to Bangkok. There a split developed between the extremists, led by Prince Souphanouvong, and the moderates, who later returned peacefully to Laos. In 1949 France granted Laos independence within the French Union, and the Lao Issara was dissolved.

The key figure in subsequent Laotian disorders was Prince Souphanouvong. Although a Laotian prince, he was educated in Vietnam and France, worked as an engineer in Vietnam, and married a Vietnamese Communist. He has lived longer in Vietnam than in Laos and depends largely upon the Vietnamese Communists for support. Under Vietnamese direction he formed the Pathet Lao, nominally a Laotian resistance movement, but in fact comprising many hill tribesmen and Vietnamese as well as Laotians, and under Vietnamese Communist control. From its base at Sam Neua in northern Laos, the Pathet Lao declared itself the only legal government of Laos and its claim was, not unnaturally, supported by the Vietnamese Communists.

The Aftermath

The Geneva agreements of 1954, which ended the war in Indo-China, accorded sovereignty over the whole of Laos to the royal government. The Pathet Lao were, however, given temporary control of two provinces, Phong Saly and Sam Neua, pending their integration with the royal government. Foreign troops were to be withdrawn except for a small French military training group.

Imprecise wording in section 14 of the agreements was exploited by the Vietnamese Communists, not only to prevent Pathet Lao integration, but to strengthen and enlarge the movement. The United States provided aid on a massive scale to the royal government and the struggle for supremacy between the two rival Laotian parties assumed a Communist/anti-Communist aspect. Until December 1955 the royal government sought unsuccessfully to impose a military solution and then changed its tactics, attempting to form a democratic coalition government together with the Pathet Lao. This lasted until 1958 and was followed by a less tolerant attitude towards the Pathet Lao. After the *coup d'état* of Captain Kong Le in August 1960, a neutralist, Prince Souvanna Phouma, formed a government and civil war broke out.

The deposed right-wing government of Prince Boun Oum re-established itself in Vientiane while Souvanna Phouma's supporters joined forces with the Pathet Lao in the resistance. Communist North Vietnam and the USSR poured in aid to the Pathet Lao with the result that the military campaign went against Boun Oum's government and the Pathet Lao overran northern and much of central Laos. A fourteen-nation conference met at Geneva in the spring of 1961 and, after lengthy deliberations, reached agreement in June 1962. A neutralist coalition government, comprising the three rival factions, was set up but failed to function effectively. After disputes with the Pathet Lao, the neutralist faction joined forces with the right wing and fighting was resumed. North Vietnamese use of Laotian territory to supply the insurgents in South Vietnam has provoked American bombing of points along the route.

Future Prospects

Laos shares common frontiers with Communist China and Communist North Vietnam, both of whom materially support the Pathet Lao, the Vietnamese contributing regular military formations. Armed Communist take-over of the whole country has been prevented primarily by fear of United States and Thai intervention which might result. North Vietnam regards Laos as a secondary objective, the main one being South Vietnam. Consequently, the future of Laos depends upon the outcome of the war in South Vietnam. If Communism prevails there, it is likely to do so in Laos as well. Should Communist North Vietnam be forced to desist from her military efforts in South Vietnam, it is likely she would also withdraw her support from the Pathet Lao. The future prospects of Laos are therefore overshadowed by events in Vietnam.

VIETNAM

Chinese Domination

THE very early history of Vietnam is mythical and little is certain before 111 B.C., when Han Wu-ti captured the Kingdom of Nam Viet for China and renamed it the Province of Giao Chi. From then until A.D. 939 it remained part of the Chinese Empire and was profoundly influenced by Chinese civilization, still everywhere in evidence today. Chinese religions, philosophy, writing, social and administrative patterns, and much else besides were adopted by the Vietnamese people during this millennium of subjugation. Ngo Quyen drove out the Chinese in A.D. 939 to re-establish Vietnamese independence, which was maintained, with the exception of one short period (1407–27) of Ming domination, until the French conquest during the second half of the 19th century. Even Kublai Khan's Mongol hordes were defeated by General Tran Hung Dao in 1284 and driven back into China.

Independence

In the 10th century A.D. Vietnam occupied only the northern part of her present territory, but a relentless – if gradual – expansion southward engulfed the Kingdom of Champa and part of Cambodia until, by 1780, its frontiers reached the southern tip of Ca-mau in the Gulf of Siam. National unity failed to survive this territorial expansion and the country split into two mutually hostile states early in the 17th century, the dividing line being close to the present frontier between North and South Vietnam. Two centuries later, in 1802, the land was re-united under a single Emperor, Gia Long, the founder of the later Nguyen Dynasty which survived until after the Second World War.

French Domination

France attacked Vietnam in 1858 and established the colony of Cochin China in 1867. Under the treaties of 1874, 1884, and 1885, Annam and Tonking became French protectorates, thus completing French domination over the whole of Vietnam. Cities, roads, railways, bridges, and ports were constructed by the French, who transformed the archaic imperial system of government into a modern colonial one. Great changes took place in the Vietnamese social structure, system of education, and national economy. In 1940 the French colonial government submitted to Japanese might and Vietnam, Laos, and Cambodia, which together formed the Indo-Chinese Union, were brought under Japanese domination. The French continued to administer the territory under Japanese control until March 1945. After Japan's surrender to the Allies, northern Vietnam was occupied by Chinese Kuomintang troops and the south by British troops, but by then political change was already taking place.

War

Clandestine Nationalist political activity was prevalent during the 1920s and 1930s in Vietnam but most indigenous leaders, lacking training and experience, were ineffectual. Only Ho Chi Minh, a dedicated Russian-trained Communist, had these qualifications, but he devoted himself to the service of his ideology rather than his country. He formed the Vietnamese Revolutionary Youth League in China, indoctrinating young Vietnamese patriots at Whampoa Military Academy and returning them to Vietnam to form Communist cells. In 1930 he founded the Indo-Chinese Communist Party.

When Japan occupied Vietnam in 1940, the leading Vietnamese

Communists fled to southern China, where Ho Chi Minh joined them. There they formed the Viet Minh League, ostensibly a Nationalist coalition but in reality a Communist-dominated body, and induced the Allies to supply its guerrilla force inside Vietnam. Immediately following the Japanese surrender in 1945, the Viet Minh occupied Hanoi and proclaimed the independent Democratic Republic of Vietnam. The French were in prison, where they had been placed by the Japanese, and no other Vietnamese group was armed, so the Viet Minh encountered little resistance. The Emperor, Bao Dai, abdicated in its favour.

A period of confusion followed when the British released the imprisoned French in the south and the Chinese-supported Vietnamese Nationalists opposed the Viet Minh in the north. Following the withdrawal of the British and Chinese occupation forces, confusion was further confounded with the French, the Viet Minh, and the Nationalists all striving to win control of Vietnam. French efforts were baulked by the inability of France to send reinforcements, while the Nationalists proved no match for the Viet Minh. After inconclusive fighting and fruitless negotiations, the Viet Minh commenced open warfare in December 1946.

Despite American military aid and the support of a Nationalist government under Bao Dai, restored as Chief of State, to whom they granted increasing independence, the French were defeated. Communism's victory in neighbouring China enabled massive military aid to be given to the Viet Minh. In the spring of 1954, with a large French force besieged at Dien-bien-phu, an international conference met at Geneva to decide the future of French Indo-China.

Peace

The Geneva conference negotiated an armistice and split Vietnam into two at the 17th parallel, according control of the northern zone to the Communists and the southern to the Nationalists. The French withdrew and an International Control Commission (Chairman India; members Canada and Poland) was sent to supervise the truce. National elections and reunification were envisaged for July 1956, but these did not take place. Nearly a million refugees fled south from the Communists, and the frontier was closed.

South Vietnam – The Republic of Vietnam

Agriculturally rich but industrially poor, South Vietnam was given little chance of survival in 1954. Premier Ngo Dinh Diem faced a land ravaged by war, torn by internal dissensions between armed politico-religious sects, riddled with Communist agents, filled with penniless refugees, and defended by a defeated, demoralized army. With American financial aid he accomplished a seeming miracle by breaking the power of the sects – army morale and prestige were restored by these victories – establishing control over the whole territory, and resettling the refugees successfully. By 1956 he was ready to dispose of the absentee Chief of State, Bao Dai, through a popular referendum and to declare a Republic with himself as President. A democratic constitution was promulgated and a parliament was elected.

With order and peace restored, the countryside returned to normal and abandoned lands were reoccupied. New settlements were established in the uplands and, thanks to generous United States monetary and technical help, the foundations of a light industry were laid. But the Communist threat obliged the government to maintain very large armed forces, a big drain on the economy, and to impose strict security measures which generated increasing resentment among the population. The absence of full political freedom antagonized the educated elite in towns and cities, while the arrogance and corruption of many provincial administrations displeased the peasantry. Nevertheless, much real economic progress was made between 1956 and 1959 and agrarian reforms improved the lot of the poorer peasants. In mid 1959, however, Communist subversion commenced and spread rapidly.

During 1960, Communist terrorism and guerrilla warfare increased dramatically and some areas fell under the control of the insurgents. Terrorists and military supplies reached South Vietnam in ever larger numbers, infiltrated from the North through Laos, Cambodia, or by sea. Government forces encountered continuing setbacks and President Diem produced no new solution save the *agroville*, or large defended village, many of which were hastily built. In November three battalions of parachute troops rebelled in Saigon, almost overthrowing the government thanks to the inaction of the other troops there. Their declared object was to replace Diem with a more effective leader against the Communists, but the revolt was crushed.

American military help was increased during 1961, but the strength of the Communist insurgents also grew, so that it was not until early 1962, when helicopters and aircraft flown by United States pilots were used and United States officers accompanied army units on operations, that the military situation improved. Britain dispatched the Thompson Mission, comprising veterans of the Malayan emergency, while Australia sent army officers to train the Vietnamese in jungle warfare.

A programme of defending villagers from Communist insurgents inside strategic hamlets met with initial success, but the scheme was pushed ahead too quickly without sufficient preparation and lost much of its effectiveness. Increasing Communist infiltration and ever more stringent repression by the government created rising tension. An incident at Hué in May 1963 set in motion a series of anti-government demonstrations which could not be suppressed. Buddhist monks achieved most notoriety by their self-immolation, but the movement was nation-wide and embraced all religions. On 1 November the government of Ngo Dinh Diem was overthrown by an army *coup d'état* in which the President and his brother were murdered. During the months that followed, one military regime replaced another as rivalries among generals increased and political stability was eroded. In August 1964 agitation led by a clique of politically ambitious Buddhist monks began and, throughout the remainder of 1964, made stable government almost impossible. Nevertheless, the war against the Communist insurgents was waged with varying fortunes, though the scale of fighting escalated steadily.

By the end of that year the insurgents were able to assemble forces big enough to make surprise attacks on the garrisons of small townships. Units of the South Vietnamese army, rushed often by American helicopter from one to another as reinforcements, began to suffer such severe casualties in the resulting ambushes that whole regiments had to be taken out of the line. The momentous decision was taken in Washington in February 1965 to commit the United States army to the ground fighting, in the hope that its superiority in weapons and equipment could prevent a military collapse and, fairly quickly, reverse the balance of casualties and force the Communists to withdraw to North Vietnam. At the same time bombing by the United States air force and bombardment by offshore naval units began to be directed against North Vietnamese communications. These American measures had the effect in Saigon of stemming the factional in-fighting among the generals running the government, who rallied behind an administration presided over by Generals Nguyen Van Thieu and Nguyen Cao Ky for long enough to enable progress by rapid stages to the restoration of civilian government. The process was completed in the autumn of 1967 by the election by universal suffrage of the same two generals, as civilians, as President and Vice-President, with a third of the votes, against a field of ten rivals and, at the same time, the election of a bicameral legislature.

American forces rose above the half million mark and were augmented by a smaller contingent from Korea and token forces from the Philippines, Thailand, Australia and New Zealand, but the Communist side consistently matched these increases in spite of extension of American bombing to industrial plants as well as communications. Throughout 1966 and 1967 the military tide turned inexorably against the Communists, who suffered rising casualties and defections. Under the pressure of these developments, the Communists adopted a new strategy and mounted simultaneous surprise attacks on all South Vietnam's cities and towns at the end of January 1968, during a period of truce for the festival of Tet. The massive assault failed to achieve its objectives of inducing popular uprisings, overthrowing South Vietnam's government, and establishing a Communist-sponsored regime, though it caused enormous material damage and attracted world-wide publicity. The offensive proved costly to the Communists, who suffered dispro-portionately heavy casualties, as they again did during the second assault of Saigon in May 1968. Despite participation in bilateral talks with the United States in Paris, North Vietnam has evinced no willing-ness to abandon the struggle. In the United States the Democratic party was divided on the issue of Vietnam, one faction urging American withdrawal. Meanwhile, South Vietnam's armed forces have improved markedly in performance, giving rise to the hope in America that the United States force may be gradually reduced in size.

North Vietnam – The Democratic Republic of Vietnam

North Vietnam is largely mountainous and, although it possesses most of Vietnam's limited industry and almost all her mineral wealth – coal, apatite, metals – it is a densely populated food deficit area. When the Vietnamese Communist regime assumed control in 1954 it had three principal objectives: to impose Communism; to reunify Vietnam so as to acquire South Vietnam's rice surplus; to industrialize rapidly. Of these, the first was considered the most important since South Vietnam appeared likely to collapse under the weight of her own dissensions and industrialization would require some time to achieve. Conse-quently, Chinese-style agrarian reforms were carried out with great ruthlessness. The ferocity of the campaign and the numbers killed by the people's courts led to scattered revolts, so that a 'correction of errors' campaign had to be instituted. Nevertheless, a typically Com-munist regime was imposed upon the country, but Communism lost most of its popular appeal and prestige in the process. Since then, the unpopularity of the regime has continued to grow.

Great efforts were made to solve the food shortage by putting new

316

land under cultivation, but much of the benefit was lost through the rigid imposition of collectivization. This proved distasteful to the peasantry and adversely affected agricultural production. A series of good harvests up to 1959 enabled the population to be fed, albeit at a very low level, but between 1960 and 1964 harvests were poor and severe food shortages persisted. In some areas famine caused many deaths and the pressures for reunification so as to obtain access to South Vietnam's rice have become progressively greater.

Aid was provided by countries of the Communist bloc from 1954 onwards, with China the largest individual contributor. With its help war damage was repaired and a start was made on the programme of industrialization, but progress was far slower than the Vietnamese Communists had anticipated. The basic economic plan, reduced to its simplest terms, was to build factories for the production of manu- factured articles which would be sold abroad. The foreign exchange thus earned would be used to purchase rice to feed the population. Poor planning, bad management, and the lack of experienced personnel all contributed to the relative failure of this plan, with the result that industry has been unable to bridge the food gap and will not be capable of doing so in the foreseeable future.

Sino-Soviet differences in recent years have proved a source of great embarrassment to North Vietnam. Vietnamese Communist leaders remained acutely aware of the geographical proximity of China, Vietnam's traditional enemy, and they went to great lengths to avoid causing her any offence. Russia, on the other hand, and Eastern Europe are the only available sources of industrial equipment which North Vietnam so badly needs. Moreover, the Russian presence is regarded by the Vietnamese as a safeguard against possible Chinese encroach- ment, so that it was important to avoid offending Russia. Until August 1963, North Vietnam maintained a neutral position in the dispute and benefited economically from the attempts of the two Communist giants to woo her support. Refusal to sign the partial nuclear test ban treaty displeased Russia and aligned the North Vietnamese more closely with China. Differences over North Vietnam's conduct of the war later dis- rupted the close relationship with China. This factor, together with North Vietnam's increasing dependence on the Soviet Union for modern weaponry, moved the Vietnamese Communists closer to Russia than ever before. Significantly North Vietnam, in sharp contrast with China, supported the invasion of Czechoslovakia in August 1958.

Food shortages, the lamentably slow progress of industrialization, and the inability of the Communist countries to supply food all combined to persuade North Vietnam that the only solution to her difficulties lay in the annexation of South Vietnam. The campaign of armed subversion began in 1959 and its scale increased rapidly under the pressure imposed by a series of bad harvests. The ability of the South, thanks to American economic and eventually military support, to hold out, in spite of its bitter internal dissensions, against the Communist attack has tended to increase the dependence of the North for its part on support from Russia and China. The latter has supplied small arms, ammunition and the labour of her pioneer units, the former more sophisticated weapons and, since the commencement of the American bombing, anti-aircraft defences which have included surface-to-air missiles. China's internal disorders severely delayed overland deliveries of military aid, while the sea route from Russia was lengthened by the Suez Canal closure and made less effective by bomb damage to North Vietnamese ports. Internal transport routes were disrupted by air attacks, so that supply became a major problem for the North Vietnamese. These logistic difficulties, coupled with the failure of the Tet offensive to achieve its objectives in South Vietnam, persuaded North Vietnam to accept President Johnson's offer of 31 March to suspend all bombing north of the 19th parallel in return for bilateral talks between the United States and North Vietnam. The talks opened in Paris during May and still (January 1969) continue, though no progress has yet been made towards a negotiated armistice.

The future of North Vietnam depends upon the outcome of the war. If she were to fail in her bid for reunification of the whole country under her Communist regime, she would experience important repercussions in her internal affairs. Government stability has so far been ensured by President Ho Chi Minh, but he is now 78 and reported to be showing signs of senility; his retirement or death could well cause a power struggle. Industrial progress has been adversely affected by the dispersal of factories for security reasons and agriculture has suffered severely from the massive withdrawal of men to serve in the war. The annual population growth of 3·4 per cent – 3·7 per cent in cities – makes it imperative to expand production rapidly, but the war has prevented this. Even if peace were restored North Vietnam would have to rely heavily on external aid for many years.

The Economic Situation

North Vietnam possesses the bulk of the country's mineral resources, with coal and anthracite deposits estimated at 20 billion tons and iron deposits estimated at 250 million tons. The country is overpopulated in relation to available agricultural land – an imbalance likely to become greater as a result of rapid population growth – so that economic planning has aimed at industrialization. Planners hope to export manufactured products and to import food so as to bridge the existing deficit. Economic assistance, credits and technical aid have been provided by the Communist bloc, with China as the largest individual donor state, followed by the Soviet Union and the East European countries. Among the most notable of North Vietnam's industrial projects are the Thai-nguyen iron and steel complex, with a claimed production of 200,000 tons in 1965, the electro-chemical complex at Viet-tri, and the fertilizer industry centred about Lam-thao, which is supplied from large apatite deposits at Lao-kay. There are textile mills at Nam-dinh and Hanoi, a cement factory at Haiphong, and machine tools factories close to Hanoi. Heavy emphasis has been placed on the construction of thermal electricity generating stations to remedy the inadequacy of present electrical power supply. Even without the damage wrought by recent American bombing, progress in industrialization was already hampered by a number of political factors.

South Vietnam's large agricultural areas are capable of producing over 5 million tons of rice annually, enough to supply home needs and to provide a large surplus for export. The country's most valuable export is rubber, with a potential annual production of about 80,000 tons. Sugar and coffee are other important agricultural products. A large industrial complex was under construction at An-hoa, drawing its power from the coal deposits at Nong-son near by, until insecurity forced the suspension of most of the enterprises. Much of the invest-ment emphasis in recent years has been upon manufacturing, and considerable progress has been made, particularly in cotton fabric production from imported yarn; other manufactures include jute bags, wood products, brown sugar, paper, glass, pharmaceuticals and tobacco. But the necessity to prevent inflation and replace by customs duties the direct taxes no longer collected in the countryside has forced the government to flood the market with imported commodities, paid for from American aid, in competition with the manufactures of its own growing industrial enterprises, several of which have been driven prematurely out of business as a result. A 160,000 kw hydro-electric scheme at Da-nhim, given to South Vietnam by Japan as war repara-tions, had barely been completed when Communist insurgents wrecked first the transmission cables and pylons and later the turbines. Much disruption has been caused to agriculture by the Vietcong insurgents, who have interrupted communications, carried out sabotage, spread terrorism, and forced large numbers of farmers to seek safety in towns and cities. Whatever the outcome of the war, the social upheaval and economic dislocation will make the country deeply dependent on foreign aid for its recovery.

BIBLIOGRAPHY

C – Cambodia   L – Laos   V – Vietnam

C – Lawrence Palmer Briggs. *The Ancient Khmer Empire.* (*Transactions of the American Philosophical Society*, Vol. 41, Part 1, Philadelphia, 1951.)

V – Joseph Buttinger. *The Smaller Dragon: a political history of Vietnam.* (Praeger, New York, 1958.) *Vietnam: a Dragon Embattled.* (Pall Mall Press, 1967, 2 vols.)

C, L, V – G. Coedès. *The Making of South-East Asia.* (University of California Press, Berkeley, 1967.)

V – Allan B. Cole. *Conflict in Indo-China and International Repercussions.* (Cornell University Press, New York, 1956.)

L – Lucien de Reinach. *Le Laos,* 2 vols. (A. Charles, Paris, 1901.)

V – Philippe Devillers. *Histoire du Viet-Nam de 1940 à 1952.* (Editions du Seuil, Paris, 1952.)

L – Henri Deydier. *Introduction à la Connaissance du Laos.* (Imprimerie Française d'Outre-Mer, Saigon, 1952.)

V – Dennis J. Duncanson. *Government and Revolution in Vietnam.* (Oxford University Press for Royal Institute of International Affairs, 1968.)

V – Bernard Fall. *Le Viet-Minh, 1945–1960.* (Armand Colin, Paris, 1960.) *The Two Vietnams.* (Praeger, New York, 1963.)

C – Thomas FitzSimmons (Ed.). *Cambodia, its People, its Society, its Culture.* (Human Relations Area Files Press, New Haven, 1959.)

V – Ellen J. Hammer. *The Struggle for Indochina* (Stanford University Press, Stanford, 1954.)

V – Hoang Van Chi. *From Colonialism to Communism.* (Pall Mall Press, 1964.)

V – P. J. Honey. *Genesis of a Tragedy.* (Benn, London, 1968.)

V – P. J. Honey (Ed.). *North Vietnam Today.* (Praeger, New York, 1962.)

V – P. J. Honey. *Communism in North Vietnam.* (Ampersand Books, Allen & Unwin, 1965.)

V – Pierre Huard and Maurice Durand. *Connaissance du Viet-Nam.* (Imprimerie Nationale, Paris, 1954.)

V – Jean Lacouture and Philippe Devillers. *La fin d'une guerre: Indochine 1954.* (Editions du Seuil, Paris, 1960.)

V – Donald Lancaster. *The Emancipation of French Indo-China.* (Oxford University Press for Royal Institute of International Affairs, 1961.)

L – Paul le Boulanger. *Histoire du Laos Français.* (Librairie Plon, Paris, 1931.)

L – Frank M. Lebar (Ed.). *Laos, its People, its Society, its Culture.* (Human Relations Area Files Press, New Haven, 1960.)

V – Charles Robequain. *The Economic Development of French Indo-China.* (Oxford University Press, 1944.)

L – Katay D. Sasorith. *Le Laos, Son évolution politique: Sa place dans l'Union Française.* (Editions Berger Levrault, Paris, 1953.)

V – Georges Taboulet. *La geste française en Indochine,* 2 vols. (Maisonneuve, Paris, 1955.)

V – Virginia Thompson. *French Indo-China.* (Macmillan, New York, 1937.)

V – Gérard Tongas. *L'Enfer Communiste au Nord Vietnam* (Nouvelles Editions Debresse, Paris, 1960.)

MALAYSIA AND SINGAPORE

Derrick Sington

HISTORY

UNTIL the 19th century the world importance of the little kingdoms of the Malay Peninsula and North Borneo was only as stepping-stones on the great sea-route between India and China. Indian penetration began about 100 B.C. and superimposed Hinduism, Buddhism, and then Islam on the earlier animism of the Malay peoples who had come out of Central Asia in about 9000 B.C. and 2000 B.C. In the 8th century A.D. the Malay kingdoms were conquered by the Kings of Srivijaya in Sumatra; and in the 15th century Malacca conquered the whole peninsula and much of Sumatra. The Malacca dynasty fell in 1511 to Portugal, which lost the lucrative trade beyond India to Holland in the 17th century. Based on Java, the Dutch East India Company monopolized the trade in tin from the Malay west-coast kingdoms for 130 years.

Meanwhile the British East India Company in 1773 set up an outpost on Balambangan, North Borneo, which however was soon overrun by Sulu pirates. Thirteen years later Francis Light, a merchant sea-captain, got the East India Company to lease Penang Island from the Sultan of Kedah. In 1795 the Dutch asked British forces to take over Malacca to prevent it from falling into French hands. The scene was set for the establishment of the most successful of the Company's three Straits Settlements by the gifted Stamford Raffles, who had become Governor of Java (1811–15) when that island was taken from the Dutch, after Holland had fallen to Napoleon. Following the restoration of Java to the Netherlands Raffles, who burned to extend enlightened British rule, persuaded the Governor-General of India, against the wishes of the British Government, to allow him in 1819 to found Singapore.

He took advantage of rivalry to the throne of Johore, and an agreement was signed giving the East India Company rights to establish trading-stations in Singapore. By 1825 the trade of the port had quintupled as a result of Raffles's policy of 'opening it to ships of every nation free of duty'. Meanwhile Holland recognized Malaya as a British sphere of influence in return for British recognition of Dutch interests in Indonesia. Malacca was re-transferred to the British East

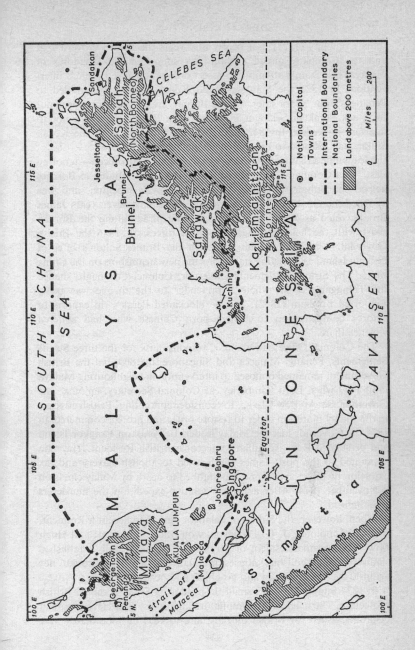

India Company (1824). For nearly fifty years the British Government and the Company aimed at non-intervention in the kingdoms of Malaya. But Siam's attempts to assert dominion caused limited intervention. In 1821 the Siamese seized Kedah (whose Sultan fled to Penang). Four years later, in the Burney Treaty, Siam promised not to attack Perak or Selangor in return for a British guarantee not to interfere in Kedah. In 1842, with British diplomatic help, the Kedah Sultan was restored to his throne by the Siamese.

Meanwhile (1839) an adventurous young British officer – ignoring East India Company policies of non-intervention – landed in Borneo, helped the Sultan of Brunei to quell a Dayak rebellion, and was awarded the Governorship of Sarawak. For twenty-seven years James Brooke ruled as White Rajah, suppressing piracy along the Borneo coast with the help of Singapore naval forces. In 1846 the British Government authorized him to accept the Brunei Sultan's offer of Labuan Island as a coaling station for the new steamships on the China route. The Straits Settlements Governor, Colonel Cavenagh, shelled the Trengganu coast, where a pretender to the throne was being supported by Siam (1862); and he blockaded Perak's tin exports to enforce compensation to Penang-born Chinese who had suffered violence there.

The Colonial Office had assumed responsibility for the three Straits Settlements, Penang, Malacca and Singapore, in 1869, but the British Government remained opposed to intervention in neighbouring Malaya until 1873 when Lord Kimberley, as Colonial Secretary, enjoined the Governor, Sir Andrew Clarke, to 'consider appointing' British advisers to the Malay States, in order to restore order and protect commerce. In 1874 the Governor met the Malay leaders of Perak on Pangkor Island and persuaded Raja Abdullah to accept a British Resident. The man appointed to the post, James Birch, tried to abolish slavery and tax extortion by direct action and was stabbed to death by Malay chiefs on 2 November 1874. After a British punitive expedition the murderers were hanged.

When, however, the Sultan of Selangor agreed to accept a Resident, the man appointed, J. G. Davidson, won Malay approval; and Hugh Low, who became Resident of Perak in 1877, successfully established 'indirect rule', abolishing abuses, gradually, by working through, not against, the Malay Sultan and his chiefs and headmen.

In 1874 Sungei Ujong, a small tin-producing State, accepted British protection. The neighbouring miniature kingdoms, after eleven years of disorders, asked for British officials, and in 1895 all nine States were merged under one king to form the State of Negri Sembilan, to which a British Resident was appointed. Pahang in 1887 accepted a British Agent, Hugh Clifford, and in 1888 a Resident. But his attempts to establish a rule of law and to stop chiefly extortions resulted in a rebellion which was put down after four years (1895). In 1896, Selangor, Perak, Pahang and Negri Sembilan were federated under a Resident-General, Frank Swettenham. The Malay Sultans remained rulers only in name and appurtenances. A modern central administration was built up in Kuala Lumpur. Economic development went ahead. Population in the Federated States increased by 60 per cent between 1891 and 1901. Revenue trebled between 1895 and 1905. But Malay – and European business – opposition to the power of the Resident-General of the Federation grew. In 1909 a Federal Council was set up under the Governor of the Straits Settlements.

In the same year Siam, no longer expansionist, ceded Kedah, Perlis, Kelantan and Trengganu to British control. But the Rulers of these States and of Johore preferred to remain outside the Federation. Each Unfederated State accepted a British Adviser. The great transforming force of Malaya, rubber, was brought from Brazil and planted experimentally in Singapore in 1877. Two hundred tons of it were exported from Malaya's 50,000 acres in 1905. By 1920 Malaya exported 196,000 tons, or 53 per cent of total world production. During the 1890s large-scale excavation techniques developed in tin-mining. Malaya's tin exports almost trebled between 1890 and 1930. She produced half the world output.

The 1930s saw a shift of power from the Federal Government to the governments of the individual States, whose Malay Sultans had continued to urge this. Control over agriculture, education, health and public works was given to the States. But the Federal Council retained the purse-strings. The four Unfederated Malay States were more loosely controlled and, with the exception of Johore, less developed economically. The three Straits Settlements, largely Chinese-populated, remained under a British Governor and Residents, with Legislative and Executive Councils composed of officials and nominated unofficials. Thus no democratic representation had come to Malaya by the time the Japanese erupted into the territories in 1942. Racial antagonism was still dormant because of the presence of the ruling European power.

In the reign of Sir Charles Brooke, the second White Rajah of Sarawak, between 1868 and 1917, piracy was finally put down and tribal head-hunting reduced. Revenue rose from about £14,000 to £200,000 a year, through orderly conditions, improved communications, and increases in trade and production. Sir Charles Brooke could not prevent the Brunei Sultan from making over large tracts of North Borneo in 1877 to the Austrian Baron Overbeck who was financed by Alfred Dent. Overbeck leased other areas of North Borneo from the Sultan of Sulu. In 1881 Dent secured a Royal Charter from the British Government, to form the North Borneo Company. In 1888 North Borneo, together with Brunei and Sarawak, came under British protection. Fifteen years later much land was leased to companies and smallholders for rubber-planting. The Japanese invasion of 1942 devastated many of the towns of North Borneo. Sarawak suffered less. In 1941 the third Brooke abrogated his absolute powers in Sarawak and set up an advisory council.

WAR AND CIVIL WAR

The rapid Japanese conquest of Malaya in 1942 broke the confidence of the inhabitants in the invincibility and permanence of British rule; it also stimulated Malay nationalism, because the Japanese tried to join Malaya with Sumatra, thus helping forward a Pan-Malay movement linked to Indonesia. But Japanese rule awoke inter-racial antagonisms in Malaya. It evoked armed resistance by the Chinese Communist Malayan People's Anti-Japanese Army (MPAJA) which fought a tough guerrilla war from the jungle. Before the British returned in 1945 the MPAJA tried to take over areas of the country, with consequent clashes between Chinese elements and Malays, many of whom had 'collaborated' with the Japanese. The British Military Administration restored order. But the Malayan Union which Britain then tried to create, based on equal citizenship for all races, and on centralized control of the nine Malay States, aroused bitter Malay opposition, which crystallized around Dato Onn bin Ja'afar and his United Malays National Organization (UMNO). In 1948 a looser Federation was substituted, in which the Malay States retained important powers. Singapore was excluded because of Malay fears that the accession of its million Chinese would mean Chinese domination of the country. Malayan citizenship was made available to all races, but under stiff qualifications so that even many second-generation Chinese did not qualify.

The resultant Chinese disappointment provided a favourable moment for a Chinese-led Communist insurrection, launched in June 1948. At first the revolt looked like disrupting the machinery of government. It was conducted by about 7,000 men from deep-jungle bases. They had support from 50,000 Chinese peasants who supplied them, and they tried, by intimidation, assassination and destruction, to wreck the Malayan tin and rubber industries. At the peak of the insurrection some 30,000 troops and 60,000 police were deployed against the rebels. They were gradually mastered, largely as a result of the systematic cutting off of their supplies through General Briggs's planned resettlement of half a million scattered Chinese 'squatter' cultivators. By the time the British High Commissioner, Sir Henry Gurney, was ambushed and killed in 1951 the Communist leaders had realized that their terror tactics could not bring victory, especially since the Malay half of the population hated and feared this Chinese bid for power. But only after General Templer's energetic period as High Commissioner (1952–4) was it clear that the Communist rebellion had failed.

Ultimate fiasco that it was, the Communist insurrection none the less indirectly brought independent nationhood to Malaya. It sharpened nationalist feeling; and it caused the British Government to seize courageously the opportunity of appealing to a nationalism which was inevitably Malay-led, but which constituted a counter-force that was too strong for the Communists. This involved taking a considerable risk. Although Malcolm Macdonald, as British Commissioner-General in South-East Asia, had successfully brought the leaders of the different races together in a Communities Liaison Committee, no democratic election had yet been held in Malaya. On the other hand, an attempt by Dato Onn to launch an all-races nationalist party had come to grief. The Malay leader had overestimated the extent to which Malays and Chinese were prepared to bury their differences within a single organization. Later Tungku Abdul Rahman, Onn's successor as UMNO leader, succeeded in forming an Alliance between UMNO and the Malayan Chinese Association. In 1954 a Malayan-British committee drafted a plan for a largely elected assembly. The first general election was held in 1955, and the victors were the all-races Alliance which immediately pressed for full independence.

PARTY POLITICS

From their position of nationalist strength Abdul Rahman and his colleagues met the Communist guerilla leader, Chin Peng, and offered him an amnesty in return for surrender and the abandonment of Communism. The offer was rejected, and the Malayan leaders then secured a promise of independence from the British Government at a London conference (1956). A Commonwealth commission, including Australian, Indian and Pakistani representatives, under Lord Reid, drafted a constitution. Malaya became a sovereign independent nation on 31 August 1957. Under the Reid Constitution qualifications for citizenship were much eased, but Malay predominance in the civil service was safeguarded. In a second general election, in 1959, the Alliance won again, but with a reduced majority. The Communist rebellion had petered out.

Singapore, with its 75 per cent of Chinese, had progressed to self-government by easier stages. Already in 1953 the legislative council was one-third elected. But the ferment of Chinese Communism was strong in the trade unions and the Chinese schools. The first Chief Minister, David Marshall, and his successor, Lim Yew Hock, had to face violent rioting, in 1955 and 1956, which could only be put down by British troops. The risk of a Communist take-over was considered too great, both by the British Government and by neighbouring Malaya, for an independent Singapore to be contemplated. And the Malay leaders were adamant against the incorporation of the politically unstable territory into Malaya. Lee Kuan Yew's anti-colonialist, non-Communist Socialist People's Action Party (PAP) easily won the Singapore elections of 1959, and he became the first Prime Minister under a self-government constitution which left foreign policy and defence under British, and internal security under a mixed council of British, Malayans, and Singaporeans.

The PAP Government set about eradicating Chinese Communism and chauvinism in Singapore by educating the people to live with, and understand, the neighbouring races. But Lee Kuan Yew warned the Malay leaders that the Singapore political danger would only pass if the island were integrated with independent Malaya. His warning was suddenly re-inforced in 1961. Three 'ex-Communists' in the PAP, including Lim Sin Siong, whose release from detention Lee had insisted on – believing them converted from Communism – campaigned against the PAP candidate at a by-election, and caused Lee a reverse. In a political landslide thousands left the PAP and joined a new 'Socialist Front' formed by the Communist front-man, Lim Sin Siong. The Government's majority in the Assembly dwindled to one. Seeing the 'red light', Tungku Abdul Rahman decided that Malaya would be safer with Singapore inside it than if she stayed separate. In August 1961 Lee and Abdul Rahman agreed that Singapore should join Malaya, sending fifteen members to a parliament of 119, and retaining autonomy in Labour and Education. But the Malayan premier stipulated at the same time that Sarawak, Brunei and North Borneo must also join Greater Malaysia since, with their large non-Chinese majorities, including Dayaks, Melanaus, Kayans, Dusuns and Muruts, these territories would counterbalance the accession of Singapore's 1¼ million Chinese to the new State.

The Singapore Socialist Front denounced the Malaysia plan as a 'sell-out' of Singapore to a 'reactionary, British-manipulated' Malayan leadership. But the British Government assented to the Malaysia project (November 1961), resigning itself to the consequent transfer of the Singapore base to a sovereign Malaysia. This would subject the base to the Anglo-Malayan Defence Agreement of 1957 which, literally interpreted, precluded its automatic use for the purposes of the South-East Asia Treaty Organization of which Britain was a member.

SOVEREIGNTY AND FEDERATION

In August 1962 the British Government agreed with the Prime Minister of Malaya to transfer sovereignty over Singapore, Sarawak and North Borneo to the new Malaysian Federation by 31 August 1963. Detailed constitutional arrangements for the accession of the Borneo territories were to be drawn up by an inter-governmental committee. The Brunei Protectorate was expected to accede as well. The Cobbold Commission, which had visited the Borneo territories in February 1962, had found misgivings among the tribal majority about coming under a predominantly Malay government, and there were some local Chinese mercantile objections to joining Malaysia. An indefinite transition period was therefore arranged during which as many British administrators as possible were to stay for as long as possible in Sarawak and North Borneo.

On 1 September 1962, in a referendum, the people of Singapore voted, by a large majority, in favour of the PAP Government's proposals for joining Malaysia. The arrangements under which the referendum was held had been denounced as undemocratic by the Socialist Front. The provisions for a separate Singapore citizenship inside Malaysia, which had been insisted on by the Malayan leaders in order to prevent left-wing Singaporeans from standing for parliamentary election outside Singapore, were likewise bitterly attacked by the Socialist Front.

The final negotiations between the Governments of Singapore and Malaya over the structure of Malaysia, held in Kuala Lumpur and London in 1963, were tense and long. Having accepted disproportionately low representation for Singapore in the Malaysian Assembly, Lee Kuan Yew bargained hard, and successfully, to ensure that provision for a Malaysian Common Market – essential for Singapore's industrialization – should be incorporated in the Federal Constitution. There was also stiff bargaining over Singapore's contribution to Federal revenues and to the economic development of the relatively backward Borneo territories. The former was eventually fixed at 40 per cent of the island's tax-receipts, and the latter took the form of a £17·5 million loan. (Malaya was committed to providing £60 million over five years for the development of the two Borneo territories.) The final agreements to set up Malaysia were signed in London on 8 July 1963. On 21 September Lee Kuan Yew's People's Action Party won a decisive victory in Singapore's elections, securing thirty-seven out of fifty-one seats in the new Assembly.

But during 1964 and 1965 tension grew steadily between the Chinese leadership in Singapore and the Malay leaders in Kuala Lumpur. Lee Kuan Yew's fielding of nine PAP candidates on the Malayan mainland in the Federal elections of April 1964 made the Malays fear that the forceful Chinese of Singapore were bent on capturing power at the Federal centre. Prolonged recriminations followed, with Lee Kuan Yew decrying the outworn feudalism of Malay leadership and the Malays accusing him of racism. In August 1965 the short-lived original Malaysian Federation broke up. Singapore seceded, leaving a rump Malaysia which, however, still included Sarawak and Sabah, though the former had become a somewhat uneasy member of the federal partnership.

THE BRUNEI REBELLION

The winter of 1962 produced sharp surprises. Unexpectedly, in the tiny British-protected Sultanate of Brunei, an insurrection broke out against accession to Malaysia. The population of Brunei was only 83,000, with Malays numerically the largest race. But the oil which had been struck in 1929 meanwhile yielded some 5 million tons annually and accounted for 92 per cent of the Sultanate's exports; and Brunei's financial surpluses had, for years, been so great that it could, if necessary, have lived entirely on the interest accumulated from investment abroad. Since 1955 the Sultan, Sir Omar Saifuddin, had been under considerable pressure from the Ra'ayat Party, led by A. M. Azahari, to democratize his state and make a bid to become the constitutional monarch of a smaller federation of the three Bornean territories. In 1959, after talks in London, the Sultan promised indirect elections for a central legislature within two years. But he retained a nominated majority in the

Assembly, and the elections were postponed repeatedly before they were held in August 1962. By that time Tungku Abdul Rahman's Malaysia project had been agreed with Britain; but Brunei's accession to Malaysia depended on her Sultan. However Azahari's Ra'ayat Party won all the elected seats in the Brunei elections, fighting on a platform which was opposed to a link-up with Malaya in a Malaysian Federation. (In 1961 there had already been violent demonstrations in Brunei against certain Malays from the peninsula who had been appointed as officials. The Ra'ayat Party had been able to convince Bruneians that these Malays were coming in to monopolize key posts and to appropriate the wealth from Brunei's oil.)

However, Tungku Abdul Rahman had won the Sultan of Brunei over to his Malaysia plan; and, after it became clear that the Sultan intended to take Brunei into Malaysia, Azahari withdrew to Manila in the Philippines and launched his rebellion on 8 December 1962. But the revolt was doomed when the rebels failed to secure the person of the Sultan. Nor did the peoples of North Borneo and Sarawak support the 'Northern Borneo National Army' as Azahari had hoped. By 14 December the revolt had been virtually suppressed. Altogether 3,000 British troops had been involved. Several hundred insurgents escaped into the jungle near the Brunei-Sarawak border. On 20 December the Brunei Sultan suspended the 1959 Constitution and appointed an Emergency Council.

It soon became known that the Brunei rebels had been trained in Malinau and Tarakan in neighbouring Indonesia. On 19 December President Sukarno urged Indonesians to support the Brunei rebellion; three weeks later an Indonesian Government spokesman said that requests by Azahari for help in men and arms would be seriously considered. Finally, on 11 February 1963 the Indonesian Foreign Minister declared that the creation of a Malaysian Federation would be resisted by all means short of war. Indonesian leaders criticized the Malaysia project as 'neo-colonialist' (British bases would remain to protect it). Also during the 1958–61 insurrection in Indonesia the anti-Sukarno rebels had bought arms and supplies through a large illicit trade with Singapore and Malaya. Indonesian rebel leaders had found asylum in Malaya. Yet President Sukarno's threats did not prevent the birth of Malaysia. The London agreements of 8 July took Sarawak and North Borneo into the new Federation but with special safeguards against Malay domination. They retained a veto on immigration, had their own heads of state, controlled for a period their own education systems and public service appointments, and retained English as the official language for ten years. North Borneo and Sarawak were to have no state religions. The Sultan of Brunei, however, decided not to take his state into Malaysia.

Indonesia's hostility had placed the Malaysia project squarely in a wide international context. It was clear that, without resorting to direct aggression, Indonesia could foment guerrilla war in Northern Borneo from her own adjoining territory. Indonesia's two-million-strong Communist Party was evidently eager to do this. Since the Indonesian forces were largely Russian armed and aided, this would obviously have Great Power repercussions. More unexpected than the Indonesian political intervention was the unanimous resolution by the Filipino House of Representatives in April 1962 asking President Macapagal to claim North Borneo from Britain. The claim, lodged in June, was based on the contention that the Sultan of Sulu had not been sovereign, but subject to Spain, when he had leased North Borneo to the British business concern of Alfred Dent in 1878; or, alternatively, that this lease of North Borneo had been revocable and not a cession of sovereignty. The British Government rejected the claim in 1962 and during talks with the Vice-President of the Philippines in London during January 1963. But the claim continued to be pressed.

In January 1963 the United Nations Secretary-General, U Thant, expressed concern over the Malaysia situation, and his willingness to help diplomatically. His chief political adviser, Mr C. V. Narasimhan, visited Malaya, Indonesia and Borneo, and suggested tentatively that referendums might be held in Sarawak, North Borneo and Brunei to settle the issue of joining Malaysia. Following diplomatic activity by Britain and Australia, Indonesia and the Philippines became more conciliatory. President Sukarno and Tungku Abdul Rahman met in Tokyo in June and declared that they would try to settle their differences in a spirit of neighbourliness. But after the London signing of the Malaysia agreements (8 July) Sukarno declared that the Malayan Prime Minister had broken a promise made at Tokyo to consult the peoples of Borneo before creating Malaysia. The Indonesian and Filipino Presidents and the Malayan Premier met in Manila (30 July–6 August) and decided to set up a concert of their three nations to be known as Maphilindo. The Filipino claim to North Borneo was to be taken up after Malaysia had come into being. A postponement of the creation of Malaysia was agreed on, so that the United Nations Secretary-General could ascertain the wishes of the people of North Borneo and Sarawak. A nine-man United Nations Commission visited the two territories and confirmed that elections held in North Borneo (December 1962) and Sarawak (June 1963) had represented a free and fair vote on the Malaysia issue. The Indonesian and Filipino governments refused to accept this verdict; and when Malaysia was launched on 16 September they declined to recognize it. Indonesia broke off commercial relations with Malaysia (25 September).

INTERVENTION AND CONFRONTATION

On 18 September the British Embassy in Jakarta was burned down by a mob; and British firms in Indonesia were seized, though allegedly only as a temporary measure. Indonesian-fomented guerrilla activity in Sarawak increased. Britain, Australia and New Zealand remained committed under the 1957 Defence Treaty to help protect the Borneo territories; and by January 1965 some 12,000 Commonwealth troops and considerable naval forces were committed to Malaysia. In March 1964, following mediation by the late Senator Robert Kennedy, the Indonesian, Filipino and Malaysian Foreign Ministers met in Bangkok but failed to reach agreement. A summit meeting of the three took place in Tokyo in June and, although there was a declaration in favour of setting up an Afro-Asian commission of inquiry, the talks broke down. Indonesia insisted that further withdrawals of Indonesian forces from Malaysia should be geared to the progress of political talks. President Sukarno's aim seemed to be to force Malaysia out of its special relationship with Britain and to secure new plebiscites in Sabah (North Borneo) and Sarawak on the Malaysia issue.

From August 1964 onwards the Indonesians staged raids on the Malayan mainland both by sea and air. These were militarily ineffective, and Malaysia took the matter to the UN Security Council where a Norwegian resolution deploring the Indonesian landings was only frustrated by the Soviet veto. In July and September 1964 serious race riots broke out in Singapore, provoked, so the Malaysian Government alleged, by Indonesia. More and more it seemed that, under these pressures, harmony between Malaysia's main races was absolutely essential to the survival of the new Federation.

It was not, however, inflammation of the Malaysian masses by Indonesian propaganda which caused the break-up of the Federation in 1965, but rivalry and suspicion between the Kuala Lumpur and Singapore leaders. In October 1965 a severe setback occurred to Sukarno's rule in Indonesia. A revolt of left-wing officers and Communist party members was nipped in the bud. The sequel, within eight months, was the ending by new military leaders in Jakarta of

Sukarno's hostile confrontation of Malaysia. The Kuala Lumpur and Singapore leaders thus had one problem the less to face. But their own mutual mistrust remained unabated.

In March 1968 Britain announced her intention of withdrawing her garrisons from South-East Asia in 1971, and so abandoning the Singapore base. Agreement was however reached on economic assistance to cushion the effect of the withdrawal.

Relations with Indonesia rapidly returned to normal. In March 1967 a treaty on joint security arrangements in the border regions was signed and liaison offices were set up to implement it. Goodwill missions were exchanged and Indonesian prisoners repatriated. Full diplomatic relations at ambassadorial level were resumed in August.

Trouble developed with the Philippines over her claim to Sabah (North Borneo). Delegations met in Bangkok in June 1968 to discuss the claim, but without result. Both countries withdrew their senior diplomatic representatives, and Malaysia abrogated the anti-smuggling agreement. In September the Philippines legislature passed a bill incorporating Sabah, and made threatening military gestures. Demonstrators in Manila attacked the British Ambassador's residence, but a strong British protest elicited a quick apology from the government. President Marcos expressed a desire for reconciliation with Malaysia, and both countries continued their co-operation in ASEAN (Association of South-East Asian Nations).

BIBLIOGRAPHY

F. Spencer Chapman. *The Jungle is Neutral.* (Chatto & Windus, 1950.)

H. P. Clodd. *Malaya's First British Pioneer (Francis Light).* (Luzac, London, 1948.)

Reginald Coupland. *Raffles of Singapore.* (Oxford University Press, 1946.)

C. D. Cowan. *Nineteenth Century Malaya.* (Oxford University Press, 1961.)

Rupert Emerson. *Malaysia, A Study in Direct and Indirect Rule.* (Macmillan, New York, 1937.)

Emily Hahn. *James Brooke of Sarawak.* (Arthur Barker, London, 1953.)

D. G. E. Hall. *A History of South East Asia* (Macmillan, 1958.)

Brian Harrison. *South East Asia* (Macmillan, 1954.)

J. Kennedy. *A History of Malaya 1400–1959.* (Macmillan, 1962.)

John Lowe. *The Malayan Experiment.* (A Fabian Pamphlet, London, 1960.)

C. Northcote Parkinson. *British Intervention in Malaya.* (University of Malaya Press, Kuala Lumpur, 1960.)

Robert Payne. *The White Rajahs of Sarawak.* (Robert Hale, London, 1960.)

Victor Purcell. *The Chinese in Malaya.* (Oxford University Press, 1948.)
Malaya Communist or Free? (Victor Gollancz, 1954.)

MALAYSIA AND SINGAPORE

T. H. Silcock. *The Economy of Malaya*. (Donald Moore, Singapore, 1956.)

Sir Frank Swettenham. *British Malaya* (Allen & Unwin, 1948.)

K. G. Tregonning. *North Borneo*. (H.M.S.O., 1960.)

Paul Wheatley. *The Golden Khersonese*. (University of Malaya Press, Kuala Lumpur, 1961.)

Sir Richard Winstedt. *Malaya and its History*. (Hutchinson, 1948.)

C. E. Wurtzburg. *Raffles of the Eastern Isles*. (Hodder & Stoughton, 1954.)

INDONESIA

Leslie Palmier

ORIGINS

THE earliest Indonesians were the last group of migrants from the Asian mainland, the Malays. Before A.D. 200 they had evolved the highly productive technique of swamp rice cultivation. Their subsequent history shows control of the archipelago oscillating between states based on sea-trade with foreign ideologies, and land-based states with local adaptations of the ideologies.

Thus, the Hindu–Buddhist trading empire of Srivijaya, based on south Sumatra, 670–1350, was succeeded by Mojopahit centred on eastern Java, 1294–1500, whose Hindu–Buddhism had much more Javanese content, and whose power was based on production of a surplus of rice. Similarly, the coming of Islam led to the rise of Malacca as a major trading centre from about 1400; but the next major Islamic state was the Javanese inland empire of Mataram, established about 1580.

THE WEST

An era of sea-based power opened in 1511 when the Portuguese captured Malacca. They lost it to the Dutch, however, and by 1667 the latter had complete control of the spice-bearing Moluccas.

With the passage of time the Dutch shifted their interest to the produce of Java. That island was briefly in British hands from 1811 to 1815, when Stamford Raffles attempted to institute reforms; they would have created a market for British manufacturers. The Dutch needed rather to develop the island's produce to meet their financial exigencies. Their solution was the famous (or notorious) *cultuurstelsel* or forced cultivation system, instituted in 1830. The wealth it produced gave rise to a strong middle class in the Netherlands, who made the government abandon forced cultivation in favour of free enterprise. From the 1870s both estate agriculture and mineral resources began to be developed.

It was only at the turn of the century that Western enterprise turned to develop the islands round Java, with the government simultaneously extending the area of its administration. These 'outer islands' have therefore had a relatively short period of exposure to Western influence.

Western enterprise in the Netherlands Indies, however, was insulated

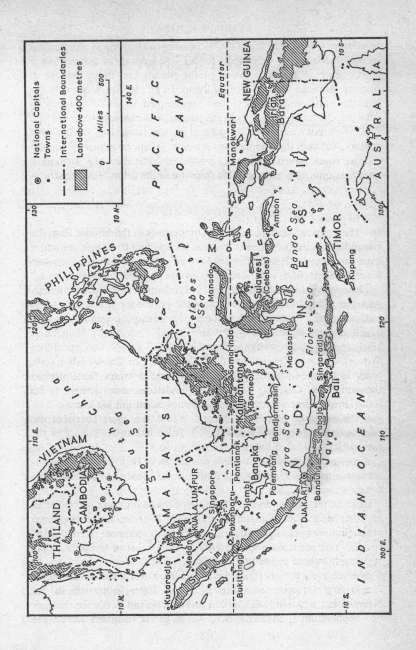

in enclaves. The way of life of the Indonesian cultivator was unimproved by any modernizing influences. Indeed, the growth of population, a consequence of the pacification of the islands and improvements in hygiene, lowered his standard of living. In an attempt to remedy the situation, an 'ethical policy' was inaugurated in 1900, designed to fulfil a moral obligation to help the people of the Indies.

Western education was introduced in the latter half of the 19th century, but very few Indonesians acquired it, and many of those who did were not given the social positions commensurate with their qualifications. They naturally felt resentful at the colonial dispensation.

NATIONALISM

In addition, new ideas from Muslim modernists in the Middle East, the rise of nationalist movements in Asia, the spectacular Japanese victory over Russia in 1905, and after 1917 the influence of Marxism-Leninism from the Soviet Union, all helped to arouse political interest.

The establishment, beginning in 1903, of urban and district councils on which some Indonesians sat, provided experience in politics. It was only a matter of time before modern organizations began to develop. The first to do so was the *Budi Utomo* (High Endeavour), founded in 1908; it aimed at revivifying Javanese culture and further spreading Western education. Somewhat similarly, in 1911 modernist Islam took shape in Indonesia in the form of the *Muhammadiyah*, which adopted the methods of Christian missions and undertook much social welfare work. In the same year, the first mass movement among Indonesians, and the only one before the Second World War, was founded: the *Sarekat Islam* (Muslim Association). It faded into insignificance in the early 1920s, disrupted by its Marxist faction.

A *Volksraad* (People's Council) was set up in 1918, but the Government did not treat it seriously, and so led Indonesians to despair of constitutional methods.

In 1920, the customary, or *adat*, law of the islands was revived; this had the effect of emphasizing the division between Westernized and other Indonesians. In addition, Indonesian political activity was strongly restricted. As a result, the new nationalist movements of the 1920s were limited to the Westernized.

The leaders of these movements emerged from the *Perhimpunan Indonesia* (Indonesian Association), a student organization in the Netherlands, which in 1922 turned to advocate independence through non-cooperation with the Dutch. Many of its members joined the

338

Bandung Study Club, organized in 1925 by Sukarno, which became the nucleus of the Indonesian Nationalist Party (PNI) founded in 1927, and had the same aims as the Association.

At the end of 1926 the Communist Party (PKI), which had come into being in 1920, attempted a revolt; the Dutch had no difficulty in crushing it. They then took a strong line against all non-cooperative and revolutionary organizations. Sukarno was arrested in 1929, released in 1931, and re-arrested in 1933; he was set free only by the Japanese in 1942. In his absence the non-cooperative Nationalist groups, disunited, had little influence, while many Nationalists began to co-operate with the Government. It is perhaps from this period, if not earlier, that one may date the opening of the bitter breach between co-operators and non-cooperators.

JAPAN INTERVENES

In February–March 1942 the Japanese Army overran the Indies. To ensure their control, the conquerors played off against one another the civil servants, the Nationalists, and the fervent Muslims (whose strength the Japanese built up through a village-based organization known as the Masjumi). Then, in October 1943, the Japanese created an Indonesian Army; it was to render invaluable service to the Nationalist cause.

Japan surrendered to the Allies on 15 August 1945; and on 17 August the Indonesian Nationalist leaders proclaimed independence. Sukarno was named President of the new Republic. From the end of that year to late 1949 it was in conflict with the Dutch, who sought to re-establish their dominion. The Republic was most strongly based in central Java, as well as in some parts of Sumatra. Despite two military actions against them, in 1946 and 1948, the Republicans remained unsubdued, and survived two internal revolts, left-wing in 1946, Communist in 1948.

THE DUTCH DEPART

The Dutch were however able to establish states in the areas not controlled by the Republic. Those Indonesians who served in their administrations came to be known as Federalists and were branded by the Republicans as co-operators.

Finally, at the Round-Table Conference at The Hague, held between August and November 1949, the Dutch agreed to leave. The only issue left undecided was the government of Western New Guinea. Sovereignty over the territory, as over the rest of Indonesia, went to the new state, the *Republik Indonesia Serikat*, or United States of Indonesia, composed of the Republic of Indonesia based on central Java, and the Dutch-created states. It was agreed that for one year Western New Guinea would be governed by the Netherlands and discussions would be held to decide its political future. Since Western New Guinea lay in their area, this agreement lowered the standing of the Federalists who had co-operated with the Dutch.

TRIUMPH OF THE UNITARY STATE

The United States of Indonesia's life was ill-starred. The Republicans, mostly Javanese, considered the Federalists, who were all non-Javanese, as little short of traitors. Yet the latter were drawn from the richer areas of Indonesia, which in the aggregate held the majority of the population. The Javanese homelands are Central and East Java. These are deficit areas, for which food itself has to be bought from the proceeds of the sale of non-Javanese produce. Thus, though the Javanese were dominant politically they were dependent economically, and lived in fear of losing their control. However, though in a slight minority in the population, they were united; the other Indonesians consisted of several disparate peoples.

Javanese history and culture have emphasized the role of the state; other Indonesians have much more sympathy for, and ability in, private trade. In addition, the Javanese are considerably more xenophobic than other Indonesians. So ideological differences compounded conflicts of interest.

Post-independence politics in Indonesia may be divided into three phases. First, the conversion of the state from federal to unitary, thus giving the Republicans dominance. Second, attempts at co-operation between the Javanese and the other-Indonesian factions. (The term faction indicates all those, whether of the ethnic group indicated or not, who supported its aims. Within either faction there were some of the same ethnic origin as those in the opposite camp.) Third, the establishment of an authoritarian state which would maintain Javanese control.

Indonesia's first three cabinets were either formed by the *Masjumi* (Islamic) party alone, or by a coalition between the *Masjumi* and the PNI (Nationalists). The latter was predominantly a Javanese party, but the *Masjumi* then also included the *Nahdatul Ulama* (Muslim Scholars), or NU, who were largely based on east Java.

JAVANESE LEADERSHIP

With the fall of the third Cabinet on 1 August 1953, the first attempt at co-operation ended. The N U had withdrawn from the *Masjumi* in mid 1952, and thereafter that party, as the 1955 elections were to show, spoke mainly for the other-Indonesians, and no party spoke for both factions. Politics became a battle in which the Javanese factions, consisting of the President, the P N I, the N U, and the P K I (Communists), sought to keep the *Masjumi* and the small but able P S I (Socialists), the main voices of the other-Indonesian faction, out of power.

The next Cabinet included only the Javanese faction; the *Masjumi* was in opposition. Despite manifest ineptitude and widespread corruption, the Cabinet enjoyed Presidential support and remained in office. It used its patronage to cripple the *Masjumi*'s chances in the forthcoming elections. Its main positive contribution was the holding of the Bandung Conference of Afro-Asian nations. The President, whose influence in government increased considerably, exerted himself to build up the Communist Party to offset the village-level support enjoyed by the *Masjumi*. His unsuccessful attempt to impose a chief of staff on the Army led to the fall of the Cabinet on 12 August 1955.

Indonesia held its first elections towards the end of that year; they gave a clear majority to the three major Javanese parties. One, however, was the P K I, and the threat it represented led to another attempt at co-operation. A Cabinet composed of the major non-Communist parties took office at the end of March 1956.

GUIDED DEMOCRACY

The exclusion of Communists from government was not to Sukarno's liking, and he called for a 'guided democracy', in which the Cabinet would include all major parties, and there would be a National Council, representing every organized interest in the community, to 'advise' the Cabinet. The Javanese faction supported these proposals, the other-Indonesians did not, and on 1 December 1956 Mohammed Hatta, who came from Sumatra, resigned his Vice-Presidency.

The favouring of Java by the Government had long been resented by the people of the other islands, as well as by their military units, who often found themselves without pay or food. As a result, in mid 1956 military commanders began to barter copra and rubber from their islands with Singapore. After Hatta's resignation, army-led councils took over provincial governments in Sumatra, Sulawesi, and Kalimantan. The Cabinet declared martial law and resigned.

The next Cabinet represented principally the Javanese faction, and was Sukarno's instrument. The National Council was established in May 1957. A National Conference, organized in November, failed to bridge the gulf between the two factions, and an attempt was made on Sukarno's life on 30 May.

REVOLT OF THE NON-JAVANESE

The previous day, the United Nations had rejected Indonesia's demand that the Netherlands be compelled to discuss Western New Guinea with her (transfer being a precondition). In December Dutch concerns were taken over and their personnel ejected from Indonesia; this assured the Javanese faction of support. Some in the other-Indonesian faction protested against the irrationality of the measures taken; they were threatened and beaten up. A number fled to Central Sumatra, where they formed a Revolutionary Council. In February 1958 they issued an ultimatum to Sukarno insisting that he abandon 'guided democracy'. When this was rejected, they declared a Provisional Government. They received little support, however, and by September Government forces had subdued all organized resistance. In August the President dissolved the *Masjumi* and the PSI.

The Constituent Assembly had been sitting since its election in 1955, and seemed on the point of reaching a decision in favour of a bicameral constitution, with the upper house reserved for regional representation. This would, of course, have safeguarded the other-Indonesians against Javanese hegemony, and did not please Sukarno. He therefore asked the Assembly to accept the still-born Constitution of 1945, which enshrined a strong Presidential Cabinet. When it refused he sent it home (on 5 July 1959); and decreed the 1945 Constitution. He then formed a Presidential Cabinet, and also went through the formality of re-christening the National Council as the Supreme Advisory Council provided for in the new Constitution.

SUKARNO'S CONSTITUTION

Sukarno's ideas involved the creation of governing bodies which included several major groups, but no formal opposition. The groups were to be 'regional and functional'; the latter including the armed forces, farmers, labour, religious groups, and co-operatives. Since the

342

functional groups had a predominance of Javanese, the formula ensured their majority. All such representatives were in any case directly or indirectly selected by the President. One may regard this either as a means of ensuring Javanese dominance, or as a recognition of the fact that the Javanese were the most advanced people in the archipelago.

This formula was applied in the creation of various new governing organs. In March 1960 the elected Parliament was replaced by a 'Mutual Help' Parliament. Half its seats were allotted to members of political parties, the remainder to members of functional groups. Only parties of the Javanese faction were given seats: the *Masjumi* and the PSI were excluded. (Indeed, a year later Sukarno ordained that only eight political parties were to exist; the *Masjumi* and the PSI were not among them.) No votes were to be taken; the President himself would decide in case of disagreement. The following year Regional Assemblies were established on the same basis as the Parliament.

A People's Consultative Congress was set up as supreme body. Parliament was included as one of its 'functional groups'. It met for the first time in November–December 1960, after conferring the title of 'Great Leader of the Revolution' on Sukarno, and decided to form a National Front to arouse the populace about Western New Guinea.

Sukarno also introduced a number of slogans, including USDEK, MANIPOL, and NEKAD, in which Indonesians were indoctrinated. MANIPOL is the Political Manifesto, in which Sukarno explained 'Guided Democracy'. USDEK stood for the initial letters of its five statements of principle, namely: return to the 1945 Constitution, Indonesian socialism, guided democracy, guided economy, Indonesian identity. Similarly, NEKAD represented maintaining the unitarian form of the Republic, socialist economy, restoration of security, supporting religious faith and loyalty to democratic principles.

RELATIONS WITH THE CHINESE

The expropriation of the Dutch was simply the first step towards 'Indonesian socialism'. The next to be dispossessed were the KMT (Nationalist) Chinese in September 1958; the following year Chinese engaged in rural trade, many of whom followed the Communist star, were deprived of their livelihood. Urban firms and plantations thus acquired were taken over by the state; rural trade was handed over to co-operatives. Friction with Communist China ensued, but in January 1960 the two countries finally exchanged ratifications of the 1955 treaty regulating citizenship of those of Chinese descent. The process did not stop with the foreigners. Both imports and exports were taken over by the state, forcing some 3,400 out of the 4,000 Indonesian importers out of business.

THE NEW ORDER

After all these changes, three centres of power were visible in Indonesia, none in the constitutional bodies. They were the President himself, whose position depended upon a strong personal following, and upon his ability to play off the other two centres of power against one another. These were the federation of military units known as the Indonesian Army, under the Chief of Staff of the Armed Forces, General Abdul Haris Nasution; and the Communist Party, the Secretary of whose Politburo was Dipa Nusantara Aidit.

The new order now set itself three priority goals: restoration of security; incorporation of Western New Guinea; and provision of enough food and clothing. It achieved its first task. By the end of 1961, most of the 1958 rebels had 'returned to the Republic'; in some instances this meant that they replaced Government forces as the legitimate authority in their areas. In mid 1962 the surrender was announced of the Darul Islam rebels, active since 1949. The Indonesian Army was thus able to concentrate its energies on the Western New Guinea Campaign.

THE WESTERN NEW GUINEA DISPUTE

The dispute between Indonesia and the Netherlands over the western half of the island of New Guinea arose from the Round Table Conference held at The Hague in 1949. The Dutch were prepared to agree that a new Federated Republic of Indonesia was to receive sovereignty over the Netherlands Indies only if Western New Guinea were excluded. The Indonesians refused to accept sovereignty over anything less than the whole of the Dutch colony. Eventually, both sides accepted an ambiguous compromise to the effect that whilst sovereignty over the whole of the Indies was to be transferred to Indonesia, the Netherlands was to continue to govern Western New Guinea for a year, during which its political future would be settled by discussions between Dutch and Indonesians.

This ambiguity permitted the Dutch to believe that since government was to remain in their hands, so was sovereignty unless the discussions concluded otherwise; and the Indonesians to hold that sovereignty was theirs, but that the Dutch were permitted to govern the territory for a year, during which talks would take place about its future government.

The discussions held in 1950 came to nothing. The incorporation of Western New Guinea thereafter became Indonesia's main aim. It seemed to her rulers that to permit one part of the former Netherlands Indies to remain outside its recognized successor would invite other parts to secede. In addition, animosity to colonialism helped to silence critics of Javanese dominance in government, and to divert the people's attention from their continuous impoverishment.

Western New Guinea consists of some 60,000 square miles of extremely mountainous and barren terrain, providing a bare existence to some 700,000 Stone-Age tribesmen. Strategically it has no value without command of the sea.

The Dutch initially thought that control of Western New Guinea would enable them to remain a world power, as well as to provide both a home for the Eurasians from Indonesia and a field for missionary endeavour. Though they were disappointed on all counts, they still refused to transfer the territory, but instead decided to prepare it for independence; a Representative Assembly was set up in 1961.

Faced with Dutch obduracy, Indonesia in 1956 abrogated the Netherlands-Indonesian Union formed at the Round-Table Conference, and repudiated her debts to the Netherlands. She tried to gain the backing of the United Nations Assembly for her claim, but could not muster the necessary two-thirds majority in her favour. After her third failure, in 1957, she expropriated all Dutch firms and expelled nearly all Netherlands nationals. From 1959 she proceeded to acquire large quantities of arms, mainly Soviet. In 1962 Indonesian and Dutch naval craft clashed in the waters of Western New Guinea, and Indonesian paratroops were dropped in coastal regions.

At about the same time the United States intervened, and in March talks between Netherlands and Indonesian representatives began outside Washington, with a former American ambassador to India, Mr Ellsworth Bunker, acting as third party. Agreement was reached on 16 August. From 1 October, Western New Guinea was administered by the United Nations, which handed the territory over to Indonesia on 7 May. Indonesia promised to hold a plebiscite before the end of 1969 to enable the Papuan inhabitants to decide the future status of Western New Guinea.

MALAYSIA

The incorporation of Western New Guinea came too late to heal the rift in the Indonesian body politic. The Javanese faction were firmly in the saddle. To their need for an external enemy was now added the interest of the Army (in which the Javanese were of course the largest single component) in justifying its large size and its great share of the national budget.

With the dispute over Western New Guinea settled, President Sukarno opposed the plan to form a Federation of Malaysia from Malaya, Singapore, and the British Borneo territories. However, he met the Prime Minister of Malaya, Tungku Abdul Rahman, and President Macapagal of the Philippines in Manila in August 1963 and they all resolved to ask for, and to accept, a United Nations verification of whether the people in British North Borneo and Sarawak wanted to join Malaysia. The UN accordingly carried out a survey and on 14 September announced a positive finding. Two days later, when the new State came into existence, Sukarno refused to recognize it. Malaysia therefore broke off diplomatic relations with Indonesia. Indonesian troops were moved to the Indonesian frontier with Sarawak and engaged in hit and run fights with Commonwealth troops; they achieved no great success.

Both the United States and the Philippines attempted a settlement of the dispute: though Sukarno promised much, he fulfilled little. A meeting with Tungku Abdul Rahman in Tokyo in June 1964 failed when Sukarno refused to end hostilities. The next month Anastas Mikoyan, then Soviet Deputy Prime Minister, visited Indonesia. He reaffirmed Soviet support for Indonesia, and a series of landings by sea and air of guerrillas began on the Malayan Peninsula proper (which Indonesia had recognized as independent since 1957). With the assistance of the local population, the invaders were quickly killed or captured.

Malaysia complained of Indonesian aggression to the Security Council, which in September voted in favour of a Norwegian motion deploring the Indonesian action; the Soviet Union, however, exercised its veto. Both Britain and the United States suspended all aid to Indonesia, with the sole exception of the latter's surplus farm products. The Indonesian government expropriated British firms and forcibly closed all branches of the British Council.

In August 1964 the Communist Party's Deputy Chairman was appointed to the Presidential Cabinet, which thus finally embodied Sukarno's conception of NASAKOM, or Nationalism, Religion, and Communism. The new policy was expressed a few months later in a statement by Subandrio, the Foreign Minister, that the revolution could not be accomplished without the Communists, who therefore belonged to the whole nation.

Indonesian foreign policy acquired a new intransigence, and in the first week of 1965 Sukarno announced Indonesia's withdrawal from the United Nations, consequent upon Malaysia's taking her seat in the Security Council (an arrangement made a year earlier). He then attempted to launch a rival international organization, the New Emerging Forces (NEFO), in his view all the poor countries of the world, which could gain no advantage from collaboration from the West. The organization was to be based on Djakarta, a conference was planned for 1966, and work was begun on a hall for it.

However, virtually the only support Sukarno obtained came from Communist China and its satellites, North Korea and North Vietnam. This new alliance was confirmed by Subandrio's visit to Peking in January 1965. The joint communiqué issued at its conclusion expressed support for the foreign policies of both countries.

As a natural consequence of the new foreign policy attacks were organized on the libraries and cultural centres of the United States Information Agency, which therefore closed them in March 1965. At the same time, relations were being improved with Pakistan, which had recently moved closer to China. After a visit by Sukarno to Rawalpindi in September 1964 and a conference in Karachi seven months later, finally in August 1965 an Organization for Economic and Cultural Co-operation was created between the two countries. When the Indo-Pakistan war broke out in September, Indonesia immediately accepted the Pakistani request for help against India, and a mob wrecked the Indian Embassy and the Air-India office in Djakarta.

Hostilities against Malaysia continued. Indonesian regular and guerrilla forces mounted sporadic attacks on the border with Sarawak, sea-borne landings were attempted, and occasional naval actions took place. Against the Malaysian forces stiffened by contingents from Britain, Australia and New Zealand, the Indonesians met continual failure. For the first time since the declaration of independence, the spread of Djakarta's power was checked.

ECONOMIC DECLINE

To failure on the foreign front was added incompetence in the economic field, making nonsense of the regime's promise to provide enough food. This was despite the fact that agriculture employs some 70 per cent of the population and provides more than half the national income and nearly two thirds of the exports. Before the Second World War, the islands were self-sufficient in food; since then, population has increased more quickly than rice. The government proved incapable of improving matters.

The bulk of export crops, of which rubber is the most valuable, are produced on estates. Both these and the small-holders have been adversely affected by war, insecurity, and political instability, and production has still to reach the level prevalent before the war.

After rubber, the principal foreign exchange earner has been crude oil, of which Indonesia is the largest producer in South-East Asia. From November 1960 the three foreign oil companies acted as contractors to the Government (the term 'contractor' being considered less offensive than 'foreign investor'). Almost alone among the economic indices, that for petroleum showed a steady rise.

The country's extreme dependence on these two sources of foreign revenue has accentuated the 'colonial' character of her economy, despite the promises of successive governments to diversify it. And in any case most of the other exports are primary products. Among them is tin, of which Indonesia is also a major producer. The industry is government-owned, and has long been neglected, so that production has shown a continuous decline. Only the high prices obtaining in the early 1960s induced the belated re-equipment of the mines.

Large and small industries in Indonesia account for about 10 per cent of the national product, but the amount of foreign exchange allocated to them has not been enough for growth. In consequence, they have not been able to clothe the population.

In an attempt to arrest the economic deterioration, in January 1961 an Eight-Year Development Plan was launched. It aimed at spending over the period 1961-8 Rp.240,000 million (about $5,400 million), of which it was hoped that a quarter would be provided in foreign aid. The chief object was to increase the national income by 12 per cent over the Plan period. Nearly half the amount allocated was to be spent on increasing production, and a quarter on improving distribution (including communications).

For the plan to work would have required the government to halt its reckless inflation, initially brought about by the Western New Guinea campaign. With the decision to commence hostilities against Malaysia, however, the inflation accelerated, the plan became obsolete, and the economy continued to go down. The Consumer Index in the capital, Djakarta, rose twenty-one times between 1958 and April 1964. Matters were no better in the countryside. In February 1964 the Deputy Governor of Central Java estimated that one million people were starving.

Sukarno's creation of a Supreme Economic Directorate in August of the same year did nothing to improve matters; even less did the seizure of American-owned rubber plantations in Sumatra in February 1965, the placing under government supervision of the three foreign oil companies the next month, or the expropriation of all remaining foreign property in April. Then, in August, Indonesia withdrew from the World Bank and the International Monetary Fund and so wantonly abandoned two economic life-lines.

THE FALL OF SUKARNO

Inability to achieve victories abroad or provide food at home went far to weaken the regime. It received the fatal blow on 1 October 1965. In an attempt to overthrow the Army leadership, the Commander of the Palace Guard, a Lt-Col. Untung, with the help of some troops and Communists killed a number of generals, including the Army Chief of Staff, and narrowly missed General Nasution but murdered his daughter. On hearing of this coup, which received the support of the Communist newspaper, fellow-conspirators in central Java attempted to seize power. However, order was very rapidly restored by General Suharto, a close associate of Nasution's. A national pogrom against the Communist Party then began. Fighting ensued, especially in Central and East Java, the Javanese homelands where the Communists had most support. In the event, the Party was totally destroyed, between two and five hundred thousand (the exact number is unknown) of its adherents, including Aidit and other leaders, being killed.

The Army under General Suharto, now Chief of Staff, became the dominant force. President Sukarno's actions at the time of the attempted coup had been somewhat ambiguous; nevertheless Suharto chose not to press the question, and for some time Sukarno proceeded much as before. In February 1966, however, he attempted to reshuffle the Cabinet in order to dismiss Nasution from office. This proved his undoing. For the next three weeks, Djakarta students and school-children rioted against Nasution's rejection. They stormed the Ministries of Education and of Foreign Affairs as well as the offices of the New China News Agency and the Chinese Consulate-General. Sukarno's orders to desist were ignored by the rioters and not enforced by the military. Finally, under the threat that the Army would not be able to ensure his personal safety, Sukarno handed over effective political power to General Suharto. With little delay, the Communist Party was banned and Subandrio and fifteen other Ministers were detained. The Sultan of Jogjakarta became First Deputy Prime Minister, and Adam Malik Minister of Foreign Affairs. Lt-Col. Untung was tried before a special military tribunal and sentenced to death in March; he was executed in September 1967.

LESLIE PALMIER

In May 1966 fifteen prominent political prisoners, who had been kept in custody for many years without trial, were released. Most of them were members of the *Masjumi* and the PSI, which Sukarno had dissolved. Two months later the People's Consultative Congress deprived him of his title of 'Life President'. It also decided to outlaw Communism, abolish the Djakarta-Peking axis, end hostilities with Malaysia immediately, and rejoin the United Nations and the other international organizations from which Indonesia had withdrawn. These decisions were all put into effect over the next few months.

More student demonstrations against Sukarno took place in September and October. In the latter month one of his leading supporters, Subandrio, was condemned to death; another, Air Vice-Marshal Omar Dani, implicated in the Untung coup, met the same fate in December. Two months later Sukarno was compelled to transfer all his powers to General Suharto, remaining titular President only. He did not enjoy this for long: at its meeting in March the People's Consultative Congress dismissed him from the Presidency and appointed General Suharto Acting President until the general elections for a new Congress in 1968. So ended, in this ignominious way, Sukarno's twenty-two year term of office.

Meanwhile, the new regime had been anxiously repairing the devastated economy. Already in April 1966 it had accepted a British offer of aid to the value of £1 million. A team from the International Monetary Fund visited Indonesia in January 1967 to assess the situation, preparatory to Indonesia's rejoining the Fund the following month. Conferences were held with Indonesia's Western creditors in Tokyo, Paris and Amsterdam (the last in February 1967), as a result of which some $250–300 million of Indonesia's debts were consolidated, and the beginning of repayment postponed to 1971. This laid the basis for further assistance. Indonesia also decided in April to return all foreign estates seized during the hostilities against Malaysia.

BIBLIOGRAPHY

B. Grant. *Indonesia.* (Penguin Books, 1967.)
B. Harrison. *South-East Asia.* (Macmillan, 1957.)
G. McT. Kahin. *Nationalism and Revolution in Indonesia.* (Cornell University Press, Ithaca, New York, 1952.)
G. McT. Kahin (Ed.). *Major Governments of Asia.* (Cornell University Press, Ithaca, New York, 1958.)
J. M. van der Kroef. *The Communist Party of Indonesia.* (University of British Columbia, Vancouver, 1965.)

THE PHILIPPINES

Walter Frank Choinski

GEOGRAPHY

THE islands comprising the Republic of the Philippines are at the crossroads of intercontinental and regional travel lines, off the southeast coast of Asia. They stretch from 5° to 22° north latitude, and from 117° to 127° east longitude. The island chain is in the form of a sprawling triangle, 1,152 miles from north to south, and 688 miles from east to west at the base. The irregular coastline of 10,850 miles is twice as long as that of the United States. The immense archipelago consists of 7,107 islands and islets, of which only 2,773 are named. The total land area is 114,830 square miles.

The eleven main islands have a land area exceeding 1,000 square miles each. Luzon is the largest with 40,814 square miles. Manila Bay, which has an area of 770 square miles, is one of the finest natural harbours in the world.

ETHNIC ORIGIN AND MINORITIES

The official census of the Philippines places the population of the Republic at 33·4 million persons. The Philippines may truly be referred to as an oriental melting pot, where all races and nationalities steadily mingle with the original inhabitants.

The Indonesians who migrated to the Philippines in two waves from about 8,000 to 3,000 years ago were of Mongoloid stock with Caucasian strains. They are of slender build, with light complexion, thin face, high aquiline nose, broad forehead, and deep-set eyes. The Ilongots of the Sierra Madre and the Carballo Mountains in central Luzon are descendants of the early Indonesians.

Following the Indonesians were the Malays, who came to the Philippines in several waves, starting about 200 B.C. The Malays are brown, of medium height, with slender bodies, flat noses, black hair, and brown eyes. Before coming to the Philippines the Malays had extensive cultural contacts with India, China, and Arabia.

About 58 per cent of today's population of the Philippines are descended from the Indonesians and the Malays. Europeans and Americans contribute only about 3 per cent to the population. It is estimated that there are about 250,000 Chinese in the Philippines.

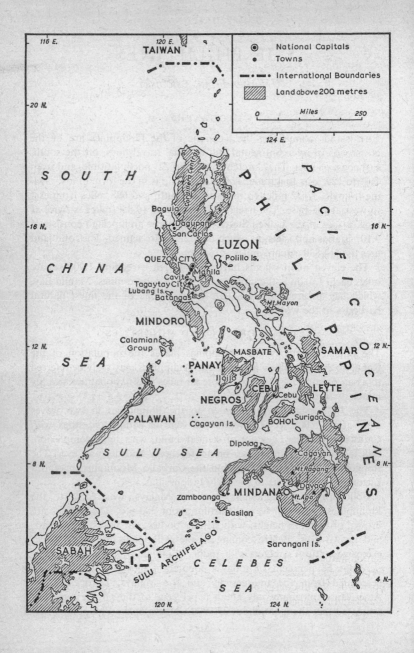

TAIWAN

National Capitals
Towns
International Boundaries
Land above 200 metres

Miles
0   250

S O U T H

P H I L I P P I N E S

Baguio

Cordillera Central

Dagupan
San Carlos

LUZON

QUEZON CITY
Polillo Is.
Manila
Cavite
Tagaytay City
Lubang Is.
Batangas

C H I N A

Mt.Mayon

MINDORO

Calamian
Group

S E A

MASBATE

PANAY
Iloilo

SAMAR

CEBU
Cebu

NEGROS

Surigao

PALAWAN

Cagayan Is.

LEYTE

BOHOL

Dipolog

P A C I F I C

O C E A N

S U L U   S E A

Cagayan
Mt.Ragang
Davao
Mt.Apo

Zamboanga
MINDANAO
Basilan

Sarangani Is.

SABAH

SULU ARCHIPELAGO

C E L E B E S

S E A

RELIGION

The Republic of the Philippines is unique in that it is the only Christian nation in the Far East. Christian Filipinos constitute 93·3 per cent of the population, while of the remaining 6·7 per cent a considerable portion are Muslims, and the rest pagans. Roman Catholics make up 82·9 per cent of the Christian population, the remainder belonging to the Filipino Independent (Aglipayan) Church, or Protestant churches of various denominations.

The Muslim faith is the principal non-Christian religion of the country. The Muslim Filipinos (commonly called Moros) are concentrated in the Sulu Archipelago, southern and western Mindanao, and southern Palawan. The solidarity of this group results in their having a considerable influence in national affairs.

Rituals vary among the pagan groups. Basically animistic, they have little influence on the national scene.

LANGUAGE

The Philippines is commonly referred to as the third largest English-speaking country in the world, next only to the United States and Great Britain. It is the language of the leading newspapers and magazines, and most of the radio stations. It is the language of government, trade, and commerce. It is used as the medium of instruction in all the schools (with some exceptions in the primary grades in the provinces) and hence must be considered as the leading language, despite the fact that only about one third of the population speaks English.

Tagalog, the official Filipino language, is spoken by about one third of the population. It is being taught in all schools.

In all, there are sixty-eight known dialects spoken in the Philippines, though only eight dialects provide the language for 90 per cent of the people. In addition to Tagalog, the leading dialects are Hiligayon, Cebuano, Bikol, Samareno, Ilocano, Pampanga, and Pangasinan.

HISTORICAL SUMMARY

Although the existence of the Philippines was known to the Portuguese through their trade contacts for many years before the arrival of the Spaniards, the discovery of the archipelago is traditionally credited to Ferdinand Magellan, the Portuguese explorer in the service of Charles I of Spain. On 17 March 1521, Magellan landed on an uninhabited islet south of Samar and shortly thereafter sailed westward to Cebu. He was slain on 27 April 1521, less than six weeks after his arrival, by Lapulapu, who recently has become a symbol of Philippine independence and is hailed as 'the first Filipino to have repelled European aggression'.

It was not until the arrival of Legaspi, in April 1565, that the actual conquest of the islands began. On 8 May of that year what is now Cebu City was founded and served as a hub for further exploration and expansion, which resulted in the selection of the Moro-dominated town of Maynila, renamed Manila, as the permanent centre of operations on 24 June 1571.

As education progressed and as contact with other nations increased, the dissatisfaction of the Filipinos with their colonial status became increasingly evident. The most significant events prior to independence took place between the years 1872 and 1899, when strong undercurrents advocating reform and independence first rose to the surface. The Cavite revolt of 1872, although quickly and ruthlessly suppressed, became a popular symbol and resulted in a propaganda campaign against the Spanish Government which grew with the years. Perhaps the best known of all Filipino heroes is José Rizal, who, although stimulated by intellectual activities, was saddened by the general apathy towards Philippine issues which he found among his intellectual countrymen. While completing courses at the Central University of Madrid for his doctorate in philosophy and letters, Rizal wrote his first political novel, *Noli Me Tangere*, which was more than well received by the Filipinos, but not by the Spaniards. Against the advice of his associates in Europe he returned to the Philippines in 1887. A year later he left for Europe, and in 1889, in Paris, he formed a group of Filipino patriots; he then moved to Madrid and Biarritz where he finished his second novel, *El Filibusterismo*. In 1890 he went to Hong Kong, whence he founded a colony within the territory of British North Borneo for dispossessed Filipinos.

Rizal returned to Manila in June 1892 with a draft constitution for a Liga Filipina which had as its aim the unification of the Filipinos. The Liga was formed on 2 July 1892, and four days later Rizal was taken into custody, imprisoned at Fort Santiago, Manila, and ordered into banishment to 'one of the islands in the south'. He went to Dapitan, Mindanao, but left for Spain in September 1896. As the steamer entered the Mediterranean he was placed under arrest by the ship's master and returned to the Philippines and Fort Santiago, where he was tried before a military court for sedition and rebellion. One and a half hours after he was married to Josephine Bracken, at 0700 hours on

30 December 1896, he was executed, ironically, by four Filipino soldiers.

Spanish reaction to this movement was so inflexible that its place was soon taken by another, still stronger movement, that advocated, not reform, but independence – the Sons of the People, better known as the Katipunan. This organization, formed in 1892 under the leadership of Andres Bonifacio and Aguinaldo, first raised the cry of Philippine independence on 26 August 1896.

Successes in the south by Aguinaldo led to a rivalry between him and Bonifacio which weakened the movement. It was not resolved until May of the following year, when Bonifacio, having refused to recognize the leadership of Aguinaldo, was executed by Aguinaldo's orders as a traitor to the revolutionary cause. By June 1897, Aguinaldo's forces were confined to an area around Biak-na-Bato. It was here, on 1 November 1897, that the Biak-na-Bato Republic was proclaimed, with Aguinaldo as the first President. A constitution was adopted with a preamble stating the intent to establish a Philippine Republic separate from Spain.

The military campaign, however, continued to favour the government troops, and on 14 December, following a series of negotiations, an agreement was signed which brought the revolution temporarily to an end. Under the terms of the agreement, Aguinaldo and approximately 40 of his companions were exiled to Hong Kong. The revolution ended on 31 December 1897, following the arrival of Aguinaldo in Hong Kong.

As an action in the American war against Spain, an American fleet under Commodore George Dewey destroyed the Spanish fleet in Manila Bay on 1 May 1898. Aguinaldo and his companions returned to the Philippines on 19 May aboard the American warship McCulloch. The Filipinos drove the Spaniards from many provinces and besieged Manila itself. Aguinaldo recalled many of his officers and generally co-operated with the American forces in suppressing Spanish authority. At this juncture the American military authorities concluded an understanding with the Spanish military commander to stage a mock battle for Manila, which surrendered on 13 August 1898.

On 10 December 1898 the United States Congress ratified the Treaty of Paris, under which Spain ceded the Philippines to the United States. Misunderstandings arose between the Americans and the Filipinos, and an incident at the San Juan Bridge in Manila touched off hostilities on 4 February 1899.

Under Aguinaldo's leadership a republic had been proclaimed on 23

January 1899. The open phase of the insurrection lasted approximately nine months, although guerrilla activity continued for nearly another year. The major fighting ceased with the capture of Aguinaldo on 23 March 1901. Organized Filipino resistance collapsed in 1902 with the surrender of the Philippine General Miguel Malvar to American forces.

Upon the surrender of Manila, the Americans established a military government with General Wesley Merritt as the first Military Governor. Local government was immediately organized in those towns that had fallen into American hands. In 1900, however, the Spooner Amendment was passed by the United States Congress authorizing the President to establish civil government in the Philippines. On 4 July 1901, William Howard Taft was inaugurated Civil Governor of the Islands.

In 1931 Senator Sergio Osmena and Speaker Manuel A. Roxas led a mission to the United States, which secured the passage of a law granting independence to the Philippines ten years after the establishment of the Commonwealth. This was called the Hare-Hawes-Cutting Law. It was adopted by the United States Congress in 1932, vetoed and passed again by Congress over the veto on 17 January 1933.

However, Senate President Manuel L. Quezon, the Filipino leader, objected to some of its provisions. The law was rejected by the Philippine legislature. Quezon led another mission to the United States and in 1934 secured the passage of a new independence law (the Tydings-McDuffie Law) more favourable to the Philippines.

This law provided, among other things, for the establishment of a Commonwealth of the Philippines preparatory to the granting of complete independence. An American High Commissioner was to reside in Manila to represent the President of the United States during the life of the Commonwealth.

A Constitutional Convention was called to frame an organic law. It met from 30 July 1934 to 19 February 1935, when it adopted the Constitution of the Philippines. President Franklin D. Roosevelt approved this Constitution on 23 March 1935. It was then submitted to the Filipino people for approval. In a plebiscite held on 14 May 1935, the Constitution was ratified by the Philippine electorate. Four months later, Manuel L. Quezon was elected President.

The Commonwealth of the Philippines was inaugurated on 15 November 1935.

On 8 December 1941, the Philippines were invaded by Japanese forces. The outnumbered Philippine-American forces fought a series of heroic battles culminating in the historic defence of Corregidor and Bataan. On 9 April 1942, Bataan fell and on 6 May Corregidor was overrun.

On 20 October 1944, the American forces under General Douglas MacArthur landed on Leyte Island. On 23 October, the Commonwealth Government was re-established on Philippine soil under President Sergio Osmena who had succeeded to the Presidency upon the death of Manuel L. Quezon on 1 August 1944. The liberation of Manila started on 3 February 1945, when the first United States forces entered the city. Public administration was transferred to the Commonwealth Government on 27 February 1945.

After the war, the Philippine Government was saddled with crushing problems of rehabilitation and reconstruction. In the elections that followed the liberation of the Philippines, President Osmena was defeated by Senate President Manuel A. Roxas. Roxas became the first President of the Republic of the Philippines, which was inaugurated on 4 July 1946.

President Roxas died in office in 1948, and was succeeded by Vice-President Elpidio Quirino.

In the elections of 1953, Quirino was defeated by the former Secretary of National Defence, Ramon Magsaysay.

Under the energetic leadership of President Magsaysay, the Filipino people embarked on a concerted effort to achieve peace and prosperity at home as well as security from external dangers.

The untimely death of President Magsaysay in a plane crash on the island of Cebu on 17 March 1957 was a great blow to the Republic. He was widely loved and admired as a man of the people, and a true leader. Vice-President Carlos Garcia was sworn in as President the next day, and in the November elections was chosen to retain that post.

Under President Garcia, the Republic continued to face numerous problems, the outstanding of which were basically 'personal economy' and corruption. Although the gross national product rose steadily throughout his administration, the economic level of the Filipino worker was such that three out of four 'barrio' people had but a cash earning of about P100 per year (US$24), while the wealth of the country concentrated around Manila and fell to those who managed to be 'in on the deal'.

It was no surprise then that when the national elections were held on 14 November 1961, President Garcia was defeated by Vice-President Diosdado Macapagal in what may be considered a landslide vote in his favour. Macapagal has expanded public housing facilities and reduced unemployment by 2·4 per cent but has failed to implement the land reform programme, improve workers' wages or stabilize the peso.

Widespread corruption, uncontrolled smuggling and the failure of the government to be more responsive to the needs of the people cost Macapagal the presidency in the elections of November 1965. The successful candidate, Senate President Ferdinand Marcos (Nacionalista), is dedicated to improving the lot of the average Filipino and to the moral regeneration of his country.

POLITICAL PARTIES

Although embryonic political parties appeared in the Philippines prior to the Spanish-American War, it was not until 1906 that viable political parties began to emerge.

Before the establishment of the Commonwealth in 1935, the two major parties active on the political scene were the Nationalist Collectivist Party led by Manuel Quezon and the Unipersonalist Nationalist Party of Sergio Osmena, Senior. Following the Nationalist Collectivist victory in the 1922 legislative elections these two parties joined to form the Nacionalista Consolidada Party. In 1935, after Quezon and Osmena were elected President and Vice-President, respectively, of the new Commonwealth Government, the party assumed the name of the Nacionalista Party, which, under Quezon's leadership, retained firm political control until the evacuation of the Government to the United States in early 1942 under the threat of Japanese occupation.

The Commonwealth Government under the Nacionalista Party returned to the islands in October 1944 and remained in office until 1946, when it was unseated by the newly formed Liberal Party under Manuel Roxas. The Liberals remained in power until the 1953 elections, when the Nacionalistas, led by Ramon Magsaysay as their presidential candidate, swept into office once more. Although weakened by the sudden death of President Magsaysay in 1957, the Nacionalista Party, under the leadership of President Carlos P. Garcia, former Vice-President under Magsaysay, was successful in the November 1957 campaign and dominates Philippine politics today.

There are five significant political parties functioning in the Republic at present: the Nacionalista, Liberal, Democratic, Nationalist-Citizens, and Progressive Parties. In addition, there are a number of minor political splinter groups, including the officially outlawed Communist Party, which have only a slight influence on the political scene.

The Nacionalista Party initially gained predominance in Philippine politics owing to its outstanding leadership and to its maintenance of a practical monopoly of the independence issue. Out of office during the period from 1946–53, its return to power was attributable primarily to the broad popularity of its 1953 candidate, Ramon Magsaysay, actually a Liberal turned Nacionalista for election purposes. Under President Magsaysay, and under President Garcia, the party had been concerned mainly with internal problems which centred around the weak Philippine economic base. It is generally pro-Western in its international orientation although it maintains considerable flexibility in its approach to problems of primarily Asian concern.

The Liberal Party was formed in 1945 from among members of the Liberal wing of the Nacionalista Party. Under the leadership of Manuel Roxas, the party offered the electorate a new and vigorous approach to the many post-war problems. It also answered the public's desire on the collaboration issue stemming from Philippine relations with Japan during the Japanese occupation, and easily unseated the Nacionalista Party in the 1946 election. President Roxas died on 15 April 1948 and was succeeded by Vice-President Quirino. Opposition charges of graft and corruption were used effectively in the defeat of the party in the 1953 campaign, and the party continues to suffer politically from such charges.

The Democratic Party was organized from a Liberal Party faction which unsuccessfully sought the presidential nomination for Carlos P. Romulo in 1953. In the campaign which followed, the Democrats supported the Nacionalista Party and have continued the support, with only minor variations, since that time.

The Nationalist-Citizens Party was formed by Senator Lorenzo Tanada of the Liberal Party in 1947 under the name of the Citizens Party. Initially a small and ineffective group politically, it gained somewhat by its support of the Nacionalista Party in the 1953 campaign. This gain was more than offset by losses incurred in supporting Senator Claro Recto for President in 1957, during which time its name was changed to the Nationalist-Citizens Party to indicate Senator Recto's Nationalist-oriented programme.

The Progressive Party is the newest political party in the Republic. It was formed shortly after President Magsaysay's death from a nucleus of the 'Magsaysay-for-President' movement active in the 1953 elections.

A possible 'third force', the Party for Philippine Progress, led by Senators Manuel Manahan and Raul Manglapus, campaigned during the November 1965 elections on the promise to overcome the shortcomings of the existing 'two-faction-one-party system' but failed to make a creditable showing.

PRINCIPAL INDUSTRIES

Primary economic gains appear to be possible in the expansion of firms engaged in producing goods for domestic consumption and in expanding facilities for further processing of materials in the extractive industries of the country before these goods are placed in the export market. However, cheap electric energy is lacking. When hydro-electric power becomes available in quantity and at a low price, metal ore concentrates may be smelted domestically, adding considerably to the unit value of such exports. A basic steel industry does not appear economically feasible at the moment, since coking coal and other necessary agents are lacking.

A further problem in Philippine industrial expansion is created by the reluctance of those with savings to invest in industrial ventures in which gains might be small and long in coming, and in which the risks are relatively high. Land, particularly agricultural land for tenant farming, is preferred as a high-return investment. Recent trends in national legislation towards Filipinization of certain sectors of the economy (Retail Trade Nationalization Act) have not encouraged needed investment from abroad, although an awareness of this problem has given rise to discussion in the national legislature of the problem of foreign investment funds.

INDUSTRIAL DEVELOPMENT

Principal impediments to industrial development in the Philippines have been the general shortage of managerial and technical know-how, shortage of power facilities in certain areas, some fear of competition from government-operated enterprises in certain lines of production, lack of basic information for planning new enterprises, and lack of domestic capital for financing new industries. Domestic investors have been reluctant to venture into the relatively new field of manufacturing, preferring to invest their capital in trade and real estate as in the past. The same preference has been displayed by the commercial banking system in its lending operations.

The Government has gone ahead with plans to establish an integrated steel industry at Iligan (Mindanao), where it now has some steel mills which produce a limited variety of products using ingots made from local scrap. The projected iron and steel complex is to include facilities for making most types of steel items and a large smelter to supply pig iron, produced from domestic ore. Some tentative contracts have been awarded for equipment, and the Philippine Republic is looking abroad – primarily in the United States – for assistance in financing the project.

BASIC ISSUES

Since the inauguration of the Republic of the Philippines on 4 July 1946, the pattern of development has been similar in many respects to that of any other new nation. There have been numerous social, economic, and political issues which have required adjustment and change, and which in general have been met and resolved successfully. There are certain recurrent aspects which in a basic sense have had, and probably will continue to have, considerable influence on the national development.

The widespread destruction and devastation of the islands during the Second World War have presented formidable problems. These have been met primarily by an ambitious development programme which has as its goal a viable national economy with strong growth potential. In many respects, the results have been remarkably good, but in other respects it is evident that further adjustments remain to be made. This is particularly true in the matter of Government control procedures designed to channel development into worthwhile efforts that will aid in stabilizing and balancing the economy.

Certain minority groups continue to require considerable understanding and effort. In the southern part of the country, particularly in the Sulu Archipelago area, the Moro minority is a proven source of irritation and concern. Because the Moro element is largely indifferent to customs regulations, the national Government is constantly involved in anti-smuggling drives to halt the illegal trade which continues between this area and the islands of Indonesia.

The Chinese minority element in the Republic, which is centred in the Manila area, for many years has been one of the dominant influences on the business life of the islands. In many respects, the Chinese represent a stabilizing group financially, which is beneficial to the national Government. Inherent Filipino distrust of this element continues to result in Government action to encourage Filipino participation in parallel business ventures, thereby curtailing Chinese opportunities for investment and growth. This problem will require a reasonable solution if the Government is to avail itself of the proven business and trade acumen of the 250,000 Chinese resident in the Philippines.

Communist influence, formerly a serious threat to the Government and to the welfare of the people, has been reduced greatly. The Hukbalahap (Huk) military potential is no longer considered to be a threat to the Government, although the extent of infiltration into the various political, social, and economic areas of Philippine society, particularly the school system, may prove to be a matter of concern in the future. Rather than operate as a 'liberation army', the Huks are now involved in all types of nefarious business and have assumed political aspirations under the guidance of prize-fighter Faustino Del Mundo and Luis Taruc's cousin Pedro. It is believed that these two have the support of half a million farmers whose votes may be cast *en masse* in favour of candidates for the offices of mayor, municipal councillor and national congressman. These followers of Sumulong ('to go forward'), the nickname of Del Mundo, adopt typical subversive tactics.

BIBLIOGRAPHY

T. A. Agoncillo. *Malolos, The Crisis of the Republic.* (University Philosophical Review, Quezon City, 1960.)

José Maminta Aruego. *Philippine Government in Action.* (University Publishing Co., Manila, 1953.)

Conrado Benitez. *History of the Philippines.* (Ginn, Boston, 1954.)

Howard Boyce. *The Philippines.* (Military Assistance Institute, Arlington, Virginia, 1964.)

Carlos Quirino. *Magsaysay of the Philippines.* (Alemars, Manila, 1958.)

The Philippines 1965. (Far Eastern Economic Review Yearbook, Hong Kong, 1965.)

PART TWO

GENERAL

Religion

HINDUISM

K. M. Panikkar

OF all the great religions of the world Hinduism is the least known outside India. It is also only recently that its claim to be a great religion has come to be recognized in the West. Formerly, while Indian philosophy was generally accepted among scholars and students as an independent and valuable contribution to the thought of mankind, Hindu religion was considered as a complex of superstitions, irrational customs, primitive beliefs and magical formulas, with innumerable divinities, grotesquely figured with many heads and arms, and even with animal shapes. Apart from the worship of images, always a difficult matter to understand for those professing religions of Semitic origin, the wider prevalence of the worship of the mother goddess (Kali) with rituals involving animal sacrifice gave the impression that Hinduism was one of the lower religions, which, it could be assumed, would break down with the spread of modern knowledge. Not much interest was, therefore, taken in it, except in an anthropological sense.

The fact that Hinduism was able to resist the onslaught of Islam for over 750 years, and has emerged stronger after over 150 years of challenge by Christianity, has now made the West realize that what it had previously considered to be no more than primitive superstitions, held together by a strange system of social organization which was termed 'caste', must have some inherent values of high significance. The Hindu religion has thus for the first time come to be studied as a religion, with a desire to understand its teachings and to discover its essential values.

Many factors add to the difficulty of understanding the Hindu religion. Unlike most other religions it has no founder. No Buddha, no Christ, no Mohammed taught a definable set of Hindu doctrines, at least to start with. Consequently it has no beginning. The Hindus define their religion as *Sanatana Dharma* or eternal truth. Secondly there is no scripture, no authoritative text to which the inquirer can turn. The Vedas (circa 1500 B.C.) are a collection of hymns, some philosophical, some ritual, which throw much light on the religious practices of early Indians, and also on the origins of their philosophical thought. But they provide no consistent body of doctrine, which may be formulated as a creed. The *upanishads*, which constitute the next great group of religious writings, deal with some of the major problems of religion, the nature of *Brahman* (the ultimate power), of *atman* (the soul) etc. But here also, though a consistent philosophical system is taught in many of the texts, the characteristics of a religion as the West understands it do not emerge. Again the popular religion preached in the *puranas* (another set of sacred writings) would seem to the outsider to be at variance with the high philosophical teachings of the *upanishads*. When it comes to later times Hindu religious thought sub-divides itself into many sects, varying from the worship of minor local deities to the two great philosophical forms of Saivism and Vaishanavism, with numerous sub-cults of their own. No wonder that an outside student is confused and troubled, as there is neither a church to declare, define and teach the faith, nor a universally accepted scripture which could be studied as authoritative.

It is the historical and evolutionary character of the Hindu religion that makes it look like a tropical jungle to one who views it from outside. During the last 3,500 years of its existence every generation has left a sediment of ideas, opinions and practices in Hinduism. Nothing was ever totally discarded. The rituals and the *yajnas* (sacrifices) prescribed in the Vedas and the worship of gods long since forgotten are still followed with the same meticulous regard for details, by different groups in different parts of India. The upanishadic doctrines continue to be taught and contemplated upon. The stories in the *puranas* of demons with many heads and kings with many hands are accepted as miracles, side by side with the highest speculations and the deepest religious feelings. Also, one can see in the popular religion everywhere the survivals of primitive religions and totemic practices. This diversity makes Hinduism difficult for the outsider to understand.

DOCTRINE

With such a confusing variety of sects, doctrines, and practices the question may well be asked whether Hinduism is a religion. It was a commonplace in European writing in the past to say that the only possible definition of a Hindu is one who has been born of parents claiming to be Hindu. It was generally said that no definition of Hinduism on the basis of dogmas or beliefs was possible. Belief in Christ was a minimum requirement for a person to claim to be a Christian. It was necessary for all Muslims to believe in Allah as the sole God and Mohammed as his prophet. But no such dogma could be postulated for Hinduism. A formulation, however widely made, would exclude groups of sects which are recognized as orthodox. Similar is the position in regard to Hindu social structure. Often it is held that caste is a characteristic of Hinduism and yet there are recognized sects like the Lingayats, the Arya Samaj and the Brahmo Samaj which do not accept the caste system and openly deny the superiority of the Brahmins.

However, in spite of this extreme diversity there is a framework of ideas and doctrines which could be considered as characteristically Hindu. It is within this framework that the different sects and creeds flourish and they are generally accepted as a common background for all Hindu systems. These ideas and doctrines may be broadly divided as falling within three categories: (1) conceptions relating to God and man's relations with God; (2) conceptions relating to the world; and (3) conceptions relating to man's life in society. In respect of all these Hinduism has an attitude which is different from that of all other religions.

The Hindu conception of God is on three planes: as the Absolute – *Brahman* – the supreme Reality which is undefinable, without qualities, beyond prediction; as *Isvara* or God with qualities, all powerful, all merciful, etc., conceived generally as Brahma, Vishnu and Siva, representing the three aspects of creation, maintenance and destruction; and as *Ishta Devata*, the God of choice, a representation according to one's special aptitude, as Krishna, Kali, Durga, Hanuman, Ganes, etc.

The only Reality that Hinduism accepts is the undefinable Absolute – *Nirguna Brahman* – or *paramatman*, a force which comprehends everything and to which no qualities could be assigned. *Neti* (not like this) was the way in which ancient teachers tried to convey the idea of Brahman. The whole universal *samsara* is but a reflection of this one Reality through the veil of *Maya. Maya* is generally translated into Western languages as illusion. It actually means the veil which conceals the Absolute. The phenomenal world is that veil, but it is no illusion. It is an empirical reality: something which exists but is subject to decay, death and transformation. Its true nature could only be understood in relation to the Supreme Reality, and that understanding is the ultimate object of human endeavour.

The *paramatman* – the universal soul, Brahman – is reflected in every sentient being as *jivatman* or the individual soul. This is the meaning of the supreme thought of Hindu religion, *Tat tvam asi, That art Thou*, which puts in a nutshell the doctrine of the relationship of the universal soul with the individual. The identity of the two is concealed by the enveloping veil of *Maya* and once that is penetrated the duality ceases to exist and the individual attains realization.

Brahman is without qualities, and therefore, judged by the conceptions of other religions, it may even be denied that it has anything to do with the idea of God. But the conception of *Isvara* meets this point. Brahman manifests itself as *Isvara*, possessing *gunas*, or qualities. The creation of the world, its maintenance and its continuous renovation are the primary functions which are associated with the *Isvara* conception. Though these are considered the separate attributes of Brahma, Vishnu and Siva – the Triad of Hinduism – it is always emphasized that they are merely three aspects of the same Brahman viewed as endowed with *gunas* or qualities. The function of Brahma is creation; of Vishnu is the upholding of the world; of Siva is the work of destruction and renovation. Brahma as the god of creation is not worshipped. But Vishnu and Siva are the 'gods' of Hinduism in the popular sense of the word. They are the manifestations of Brahman, whose worship leads one to the realization of the ultimate truth.

Another conception, which is most significant for the understanding of Hinduism, is that of *Ishta Devata*, or the God of Choice. Hinduism offers a variety to choose from, but the most popular are the various aspects of Devi (the mother goddess) and Krishna. Though the Devi cult may have had a non-Indian origin and may be connected with the worship of Ishtar, Isis and other goddesses of ancient times, in India it is well integrated with the rest of Hindu thought. The Devi, in whatever form conceived, represents *prakriti*, or energy, which, operating through *purusha*, or matter, sets in force all the activity in the world. All *Ishta Devatas* are conceived as involving this dual principle, of *prakriti* (energy) and *purusha* (matter) expressed in terms of male and female counterparts. This is the doctrine behind Hindu ideas of gods and goddesses in combination, an idea which leads to a great deal of misunderstanding in the Western world. Every manifestation of god, as *Isvara* or *Ishta Devata*, has its male and female counterpart; Siva and Parvati, Vishnu and Lakshmi, Brahma and Sarasvati, Krishna and Radha. In fact this conception is carried to its logical conclusion in the idea of Siva as *Ardha Narisvara* or god who is half man, half woman.

The doctrine of *Ishta Devata* has a special significance in Hinduism as it enables the worshipper to identify himself with a special aspect of god, with which he is in sympathy, to develop qualities of devotion, *bhakti*, and cultivate a sense of personal relationship.

This triple approach to God is the special characteristic of Hinduism, it being always emphasized that the worship of *Ishta Devata* is only a method of realizing union with *Saguna Brahman* or the ultimate God, of identification with Brahman or the Supreme Reality.

THE INDIVIDUAL AND THE WORLD

The Hindu view of life is as a succession of rebirths based on the idea that till the individual soul obtains its release by cutting through the bonds of *Maya*, and attains realization with the Absolute, it must be born over and over again. The chains of birth (which is a doctrine which Hinduism has in common with Buddhism) is determined by our individual *karma*. Karma literally means action. In this context it means the cumulative effect of a man's actions. The Hindu doctrine is that every action must have its effect, and the cumulative effect of a man's actions shapes his life. This is not a doctrine of fatalism for it is open to a man to change his future by shaping his *karma*. As *karma* is a continuous process, man is building up his own future. In order to break the chain of rebirth, man has to control his *karma* by a discipline of the mind and body, which is defined in Hindu philosophy as his *dharma*.

This discipline is the division of life into four *asramas*: study and preparation, life in society, life in retirement and finally renunciation. According to Hindu religion this is the ideal way of life. Every man must prepare himself for life by proper education and training (*brahmacharya*). Then he should fulfil his obligations to society (*grihastha*). The third stage is of retirement when he makes way for younger people contenting himself with advice and guidance, and he finally renounces the world and its activities. This division into four stages is no doubt only an ideal, but it is a universally accepted ideal among the Hindus, though but a few may follow it in practice.

Complementary to this idea of *asramas* is the definition of the objects of worldly life. The ultimate object is of course deliverance from the chain of rebirth and the attainment of union with the Absolute. But in life, there are three objects a man must seek to achieve; *dharma*, righteous conduct, *arth*, the acquisition of economic welfare, and *kama*, life in senses. A right balance between these three objects is what men should aim at. Both *artha*, economic welfare, and *kama*, worldly pleasure, should be subject to righteous conduct, as otherwise it will only accumulate evil *karma* and thus prevent the final objective of liberation. A text in the Mahabharata declares that *artha* and *kama* to exclusion of *dharma* should be shunned; but *dharma* without *artha* and *kama* is also not desirable. A proper harmony of these three objectives is what is taught as the ideal life in Hinduism.

'DHARMA'

Artha and *kama* are easily understood. The first is the life of earthly prosperity, the second the life of enjoyment. But *dharma*, which is to govern both and is the basic religious and ethical conception of Hinduism, is not so easy to define. One of the difficulties of defining *dharma* is the various meanings in which the word has come to be used. *Dharma* means duty, law, religion, ethical obligations, moral principles. The *dharma sastra* of Manu, for example, deals with law and morals; *rajadharma* means the duties of kings; *stridharma* means the duty of women. Each sect in a way elaborates the *dharma* a little differently. Broadly speaking, from the point of Hindu religious thought, *dharma* means the moral order. Now this conception of moral order is complicated by two ideas of *varna* and *guna* – caste and inherited qualities. *Varna*, which the West translates as caste, is a notional division of society in four orders, the Brahmins, Kshatriyas, Vaisyas and Sudras, based as Krishna says on *guna*, and *karma*, i.e. inherent qualities and actions. The four-fold division is theoretically on the basis of those devoted to intellectual, mental and spiritual pursuits (Brahmins); those concerned with upholding social order, leaders in temporal life – the arms of society (Kshatriyas); those concerned with economic welfare (Vaisyas); and the working classes. This broad division is expressed allegorically in the Vedas in a famous hymn which says that the Brahmins emerged from the face, the Kshatriyas from the arms, the Vaisyas from the stomach and the Sudras from the feet of *Purusha*. This division was originally not based on birth, but in due course came to be considered hereditary, though at all times there have been Brahmins who were engaged in non-intellectual professions, and Sudras who were scholars, saints and statesmen. The division was effective only in a broad sense and in the *samskaras* or rituals.

The doctrine of *varna* or caste however had a great influence on the conception of *dharma*. Normally speaking, the *varna* or caste was said to decide a man's *dharma*, or duties in life. *Svadharma* or the individual's duty came to be interpreted in terms of his caste. The Brahmin's *dharma* was theoretically to lead a disciplined religious life. The Kshatriya's *dharma* of upholding society authorized him to do many things which would be sinful for a Brahmin to do: killing in battle, taking of life in hunting, to mention only two examples. Similarly in the case of Vaisyas and Sudras. This was a popular and widely accepted view of *dharma* which provided a theoretical justification for caste.

'GUNA'

Apart from the idea of *dharma* based on *varna*, there is also the doctrine of *dharma* based on *guna*. The doctrine of *guna* is one of the basic notions of Hindu thought and pervades every aspect of it. Briefly stated, it means that there are three basic qualities – *satva, rajas* and *tamas* – which constitute human personality. *Satva* may be defined as harmony of qualities, an even balance; *rajas* where the egoistic characteristics predominate; *tamas* represents evil qualities. These are compounded in different proportions in all individuals, as a result of one's *karma*, inherited qualities, environments, etc.

This conception of *guna* affects all Hindu thought. Only the Ultimate, the *Brahman*, is without *guna*, and the highest expression of Hindu religion is in terms of *Nirguna Brahman* – that is *Brahman* without qualities. But when he manifests himself as *Isvara* – as God – he is endowed with *gunas*. The gods who are worshipped are necessarily conceived as having *gunas*.

'AVATAR'

There is one further conception in Hinduism which also differentiates it from all other religions: that is the doctrine of *avatar* or incarnation. In essence this doctrine is simple. At every critical stage in human history God incarnates in this world to serve mankind. Such incarnations may be for specific purposes or limited objectives but may also be for the general uplift of mankind. The theory of *avatars* is stated by Krishna himself in the *Bhagavad Gita* in the following verses:

> Whenever there is a decline of *dharma* and rise
> of *adharma* [unrighteousness] I incarnate myself.

> For the protection of the good, for the destruction
> of the wicked and for the establishment of
> righteousness, I come into being from age to age.
> (*Gita*, IV – Verses 7 and 8.)

The god of *avatars* is Vishnu, the sustainer of the world in the Hindu Triad. There are no *avatars* of Brahma or Siva as the functions of creation and destruction *ex hypothesi* do not require incarnations. Vishnu's *avatars* include such unlikely manifestations of divine power as fish, tortoise, boar, man-lion, etc., each of which was, however, only for a specific purpose. The only full *avatar*, i.e. the incarnation of God with the totality of divine powers, is Krishna himself, who, therefore is an object of worship. The Buddha, it may be mentioned, was also included among the *avatars* at least by the 10th century A.D.

The doctrine of *avatar* has, however, undergone a very significant evolution, which may be traced to the text in the Gita quoted above. When it is assumed that when *dharma* declines, and *adharma* is powerful, God will show himself in every age for the reorganization of society, this easily lends itself to the view that every major reformer of religion is in a sense an *avatar*. As Hinduism holds that every individual has a spark of the divine in him, it is but logical to assume that some have it in a greater degree and that others by spiritual discipline leading to greater realization of God may become the instruments of His Will. Thus the Hindus accept without serious question the prophets of all religions as manifestations of God, as *avatars* for re-establishing *dharma*. The Hindu attitude to Christ, Mohammed and other founders of religion is governed by this idea of *avatars*.

Also, the number of minor *avatars* in Hinduism has no limits. Sri Ramakrishna Paramahamsa (19th century) and Sri Aurobindo (died middle of the 20th century), to mention only two among others, are looked upon by their followers as *avatars*, and according to the doctrine of God manifesting Himself to rescue faith in times of degeneration, the claim could only be judged in the light of their success in their mission.

VARIETY AND TOLERANCE

It is this general body of beliefs that provides the framework of Hindu religion. Within that framework the greatest variety is permitted. Primitive beliefs and doctrines are easily adjusted, for the local gods and saints of tribes and racial groups come to be looked upon and accepted as manifestations and *avatars* of the supreme Godhead. There is no doctrine, except that of a complete denial of God and the *atman*, that could not be fitted within Hinduism.

One consequence of this is the wide tolerance that Hinduism teaches. Tolerance of other faiths is not with the Hindus a question of convenience; it is an article of faith, for has not Krishna himself said it: 'I give to each one according to his belief.' A higher belief may be recommended but worship of God under any form is considered by the Hindus as leading to a knowledge of Truth.

BIBLIOGRAPHY

Sir Edwin Arnold. *The Song Celestial* (verse translation of the *Bhagavad Gita*). (Kegan Paul, Trench, Trubner, 8th edn, London 1897.)

G. Morris Carstairs. *A Study of a Community of High-Caste Hindus.* (Hogarth Press, 1957.)

Paul Deussen. *System of Vedanta,* trans. Charles Johnstone. (Open Court Publishing Co., Chicago, 1912.)

Sir Charles Eliot. *Hinduism and Buddhism.* (Edward Arnold, London, 1921.)

John Farquhar. *An Outline of the Religious Literature of India.* (Humphrey Milford, London, 1920.)

P. D. Mehta. *Early Indian Religious Thought.* (Luzac, London, 1956.)

Sir Sarvepalli Radhakrishnan. *The Hindu View of Life.* (Allen & Unwin, 1927.) *Indian Philosophy,* 2 vols. (Allen & Unwin, 1923.)

Swami Nikhilananda. *Hinduism: Its Meaning for the Liberation of the Spirit.* (Allen & Unwin, 1959.)

Yadunatha Simha. *A History of Indian Philosophy,* 2 vols. (Simha Publishing House, Calcutta, 1956.)

ISLAM

Peter Partner

THE religion of Islam (which means 'submission') derives from the teaching of Muhammad, in the third decade of the 7th century, to the tribes of Arabia. It is in essence a prophetic revelation, revealed not continuously through an historic church, but once and for all through an historic personage. There is however some element of continued revelation in the development of Islamic law, which allows a certain discretion in the interpretation of the revealed laws transmitted by the Prophet in the Koran.

HISTORICAL

There is no distinction in Islam between the community of believers, the Dar ul-Islam, and the state. The society brought into being by the Muslim conquests, which in the early Middle Ages embraced half of the world known to Europeans, was a theocracy. The Caliph of Islam was not a sort of Pope, but the main prayer leader of a society whose entire organization was, in theory, religious. There was therefore no distinction between religious law and any other kind of law; the *sharia* embraces the whole life of man.

The great handicap of Islamic society was that its universality depended on its political supremacy. When the Islamic Empire began in the high Middle Ages to break up, to disintegrate into warring caliphates and to suffer defeat at the hands of Christians and Mongols, the religious prestige of the theocratic society suffered a corresponding depression. When the Arab Empires finally disintegrated in the late Middle Ages, and were replaced by the Ottoman Turkish, Mogul and Safavid Empires, the institutions of Islam suffered changes which were not compatible with the religious idealism of their origins. When, finally, in the modern period, these Empires in their turn succumbed in the face of Western technical progress and imperialism, Islam was left to become the religion of the conquered instead of that of the conquerors.

MODERN ISLAM

The institutions, the law, the outlook of Islam all derived from an Islamic past of conquest and theocratic rule. Contrasting this with their present state, modern Muslims have sometimes become disorientated and bewildered. 'Why' (to quote the title of an influential pamphlet) 'have the Muslims become backward?' The reaction of modern Muslims has taken two principle forms. On the one hand there has been a return to the sources: an attempt to cleanse and renew the fundamental tradition and law of Islam. On the other there has been a complex attempt at mimesis, sometimes in the shape of direct imitation or 'Westernization', sometimes by seeking parallels from Islamic history and tradition in the Western world, and so covertly importing Western things into a supposedly Islamic synthesis. Of this last tendency 'Islamic social justice' and 'Islamic democracy' are important examples.

Measuring the external characteristics of Muslim movements by their apparent distance from Western culture, Westerners have described some as 'extreme' or 'fundamentalist' (e.g., Muslim Brethren in Egypt, Jamaat-e-Islami in Pakistan, Dar-ul-Islam in western Java); others as 'Islamic moderate' (Masjumi party in Indonesia); and others as 'Westernizing' or 'secularist' (the ruling groups in Pakistan and Indonesia). Such classifications are useful for following the political rough-and-tumble. But as soon as one comes to any single major Islamic thinker they tend to break down. Naturally enough, most of the more important figures in Islamic thought of the past century have spoken both of an inward spiritual renewal which looks back to classical Islam, and of coming to terms at least in some degree with Western culture. Muhammad Iqbal in India, Muhammad Abdu in Egypt, the leaders of the Muhammadiyah movement in Indonesia, have all looked both ways. Plainly, some Islamic thinkers are more Western in outlook than others. But plainly also, Islam should not be judged or measured only by the degree to which it manages to approximate to Western ideas. Just as useful, and more interesting, than a spectrum of Muslim opinion which runs from 'fundamentalist' to 'Westernizer' would be a spectrum related to *ijtihad* or the faculty allowed by Muslim doctrine to the community of believers to interpret Muslim law. This faculty is not claimed in a wholesale or indiscriminate way save by a few; for most the exercise of *ijtihad* is reserved to a small group of those learned in the law, and the most conservative would claim that the gates of *ijtihad* are closed, and no further modification of Islamic law allowable. Such a spectrum would be very different; Muhammad Iqbal, whose philosophy is often regarded as Westernized, is on the whole conservative as regards *ijtihad*.

It is a paradox that Islam, this universalist religion, should have contributed so powerfully to the setting up of new national states. The Islamic revival stands behind Pakistani and Indonesian nationalism, just as it does behind Arab nationalism. But this association does not mean identity. The religious reformer Sayyid Abul Ala Maududi asked before Pakistan was brought into existence: 'Why should we foolishly waste our time in expediting the so-called Muslim national state and fritter away our energies in setting it up, when we know that it will not only be useless for our purpose but will rather prove an obstacle in our path?' At the other extreme Sukarno warned his nationalist followers that: 'It is useless to wait for help from an airplane from Moscow or a caliph from Istanbul.'

PAKISTAN

In Pakistan, the child of Islam, the demand for an Islamic state has so far been disappointed. The Muslim League was the party of Indian Muslims and not the party of north-west India and East Bengal; in 1945 Jinnah sacrificed the possibility of compromise in order to maintain just this principle. But when Pakistan was set up it became apparent that there was a great gulf between the Muslim League politicians, who thought primarily in Western political terms, and the orthodox Muslim *ulama* or religious leaders; and that operating on both these political forces there was regionalism which no one knew quite how to control.

The 1949 Objectives Resolution of the Muslim League announced as an objective of the future constitution of Pakistan that: 'Muslims shall be enabled to live their lives in the individual and collective spheres in accord with the teaching and requirements of Islam as set out in the Holy Koran and the Sunna' (Sunna means 'prophetic tradition'). This was cautious, but it opened the door to a movement for imposing Islamic law upon the state. Seven years of wrangling followed, in which the *ulama* to achieve this end became more and more deeply involved in national and regional politics. The disastrous riots which the *ulama* abetted against the heretical Ahmadiyah sect in the Punjab in 1953, and the involvement of the religious leaders in the regionalist demands of East Bengal, both contributed to the breakdown of parliamentary government in Pakistan. By that breakdown the movement for an Islamic state has been the loser. The 1956 constitution went far towards satisfying the *ulama*'s desires in the 'repugnancy' clause which declared that no law be enacted which is contrary to the injunctions of Islam, and that existing laws be made to conform with these injunctions.

The bureaucracy and the Army, which have ruled Pakistan for the past few years, have been hostile to the idea of a religious state. President Ayub Khan has pronounced himself in favour of the separation of religion from government, just as General Iskander Mirza did earlier. There is only a very evasive equivalent to the 'repugnancy' clause in the constitution of March 1962, and the Council of *ulama* and Muslim scholars for which it provides has a merely advisory function. For the moment the viewpoint which prevails is that expressed by the Pakistan Judges in 1954: 'The sublime faith called Islam will live even if our leaders are not there to enforce it ... our politicians should understand that if Divine commands cannot make or keep a man a Musalman, their statutes will not.' It would be wrong to say of Pakistan that the Islamic state has been defeated by Westernizers; perhaps it would be more correct to say that the Islamic state has proved to be a source of division rather than a principle of unity. Whatever solution is found for Islam in Pakistan will closely influence the 40 million Muslims in India – the largest Muslim minority in the world. Although the Indian state protects the rights of this great but depressed group, their condition is inevitably precarious, and affected by the relations of Pakistan with India.

INDONESIA

Indonesian Islam is the heir to a syncretist tradition, in which Islam has lain rather lightly on earlier Hindu and Buddhist elements, and in which mysticism has from the earliest times been more important than law. As compared with Pakistan, which looks back ultimately to the authoritarian Abassid Caliphate, Indonesia has a looser and less monolithic inheritance. Islam was adopted in the East Indies in the 15th and 16th centuries by a plurality of local rulers. Islamic law has been confined in the area largely to the law of personal status, and indigenous custom, *adat*, has – as in Malaya – always been more important than the *sharia* or body of Islamic law. Thus although Islam is probably the religion of nine out of ten Indonesians, and is in an important sense the great unifying force of the tribal and regional particularisms of this huge area, it is not a religion which has ever been imposed on the islands in a single and unified manner. When the modern Indonesian nationalists have sought a national myth, they have gone back beyond the Muslim period to the Hindu Kingdom of Majapahit and the Javanese pre-Islamic social ideal of 'Ratu Adil' (righteous king).

Nevertheless, Indonesian nationalism cannot be separated from Islamic revival. Although the Sarekat Islam party was Islamic in the political sense of representing Muslims as against Dutch or Chinese, and not in the religious sense, it would not have been so important had it not been for the currents of Islamic modernism which were circulating in Indonesia early in this century. Having already been influenced by the Arabian Wahhabi movement, Indonesia was early and profoundly influenced by the Egyptian 'Salafiyah' school of modernism, whose leader Muhammad Abdu also stood behind much of the thought of Arab nationalism. The instrument of Salafiyah ideas in Indonesia was the Muhammadiyah movement, which became a wealthy educational and social reformist force, with some two thousand schools and many other cultural institutions under its control. In this environment of the Muhammadiyah the group later known as 'Religious Socialists' formed their ideas.

In the Second World War the Islamic organizations were an important part of the Japanese scheme for penetrating Indonesian society and using it for their own ends. The Muhammadiyah, the Council of *ulama* and the Council of Muslim Associations were merged into a single Council supervised by the Japanese Religious Affairs Office. In the later stages this Council was involved in the 'Independence' movement sponsored by Japan. Thus the religious bodies were involved from the very beginnings of the setting up of a national Indonesian state.

Sukarno attempted to preserve a bridge between secular nationalism and Muslim feeling. His Five Points (Pantja Sila) included 'Faith in God', but he interpreted this in a sense which seemed merely to include Islam among the other religions. The Ministry of Religion set up by the Indonesian Government might also be described as a Ministry of Religions, in that it was concerned with religious freedom and the relations between the religious communities, besides Muslim law and *waqfs* (charitable foundations).

Relations between the Government and the Muslim groups have not been good. In the mountains of Western Java the Dar-ul-Islam movement maintained itself by terrorism and military action for many years. The doctrine of the Dar-ul-Islam differed only in degree from that of the *ulama*; what kept it in being seems to have been social and regional rather than religious forces. More important was the rebellion led by some of the Religious Socialists of the Muslim Masjumi party (heir of the Muhammadiyah) in Celebes and Sumatra in 1958–61. The *ulama* on the other hand have remained loyal to the government. Here as in the case of Pakistan it seems that the great obstacle to Muslim unity and progress is not ideological nationalism but regionalism.

OTHER ISLAMIC COMMUNITIES

Islam has penetrated less deeply into Malayan society than into that of Indonesia, and Islamic law has been operative in Malaya only in matters narrowly concerning personal status. India and Indonesia have influenced Malayan Islam in the modern period, but not profoundly, and although the Ahmadiyah sect and the Indonesian Muhammadiyah have made some impact on Malaya, there has been so far no development in depth.

Twenty million Muslims live in the USSR, about three quarters of them in the six Union Republics of Azerbaidjan, Turkmenistan, Uzbekistan, Tadzhikistan, Kirgizia and Kazakhstan. The attitude of the Soviet Government towards these Muslims is determined partly by the official hostility of Communist doctrine to all religions, but far more by the problem of the subject nationalities, and of the period of Russian colonial history which preceded the Revolution. At the time of the Revolution there was a short period of cautious collaboration between the Communist party and both the Islamic and the minority movements (notably the Turkic one). This was over by 1920, but even after this Sultan Galiev was able to get a hearing for his doctrine of an alliance between Communism and Pan-Islamic nationalism, based on a Muslim state on the middle Volga, and even for an alliance between Communism and eastern 'bourgeois' nationalism. This doctrine was condemned by Stalin, and although some of its elements have in practice been present in Russian policy in oriental countries since the war, the doctrine itself has never been rehabilitated. On the whole the temptation to use the Russian Muslim minorities as a bridge to Muslims outside the Soviet Union has been resisted because of fear that it might awaken the minorities against Russian rule. There has been a notable softening of the official attitude to Islam in the past ten years, but it has not gone far.

The Chinese Muslim minority ('Hui') numbers about ten millions, of whom roughly half are in the province of Chinese Turkestan or Sinkiang (now called the Sinkian Uighur Autonomous Region). It is made up of several ethnic groups, of which the most important are the Uighur and Kazakh. Chinese policy towards the Muslims has in late years been conciliatory; religious lands have escaped confiscation in Sinkiang. Like the USSR, China thinks to use the Muslims as pawns in foreign policy in Asia and the Near East. A Chinese *imam* accompanied Chou En-lai to Bandung in 1955.

PETER PARTNER

BIBLIOGRAPHY

A. Bennigsen and Chantal Lemercier-Quelquejay. *Islam in the Soviet Union.* (Pall Mall Press, 1967.)

Leonard Binder. *Religion and Politics in Pakistan.* (Cambridge University Press, 1961.)

G. McT. Kahin. *Nationalism and Revolution in Indonesia.* (Oxford University Press, 1952.)

W. Z. Laqueur (Ed.) *The Middle East in Transition.* (Routledge & Kegan Paul, 1958.)

Louis Massignon. *Annuaire de Monde Musulman: 1954.* (Paris, 1955.)

Wilfrid Cantwell Smith. *Modern Islam in India.* (Gollancz, 1946.) *Islam in Modern History.* (Oxford University Press, 1957.)

C. A. O. Van Nieuwenhuijze. *Aspects of Islam in Post-Colonial Indonesia.* (W. Van Hoeve, The Hague and Bandung, 1958.)

Geoffrey Wheeler. *Racial Problems in Soviet Muslim Asia.* (Oxford University Press, 1960.)

S. A. Zenkovsky. *Pan-Turkism and Islam in Russia.* (Oxford University Press, 1960.)

BUDDHISM

Edward Conze

SLIGHTLY more than a century ago the great bastions of Buddhism first experienced the ruthless onslaught of modern civilization. The Buddhist religion, quiescent since about A.D. 1400, initiated nothing of its own between 1850 and 1960, remained on the defensive and constantly retreated before hostile forces. The societies in which it flourished, notably China, Tibet and Japan, had for a time sought safety in withdrawing upon themselves. The Buddhists have on the whole maintained the old behaviour pattern and prefer to ignore the new and unwelcome developments.

To appreciate their feelings we just have to look at the blows which this ancient religion has had to endure. In China, soon after the Opium War in 1842 forced the Manchus to admit the foreign invader, the 'long-haired Christians' of the T'ai P'ing rebellion between 1850 and 1864 destroyed countless temples and monasteries, and Chinese Buddhism has been a shadow of its former self ever since. In Japan the threatened American invasion of 1853 was followed about 1870 by the disestablishment of the Buddhist Church and the burning or confiscation of innumerable temples, while the actual invasion of 1945 brought financial ruin through MacArthur's 'land reform' of 1947–50, and led to a 'general trend towards profanity' and to rather widespread religious apathy. In Tibet the day of reckoning came only in 1950, and in 1959 the Dalai Lama was forced once more to flee the country. In Mongolia between 1935 and 1937 Soviet troops demolished the lamaseries and killed most of their inhabitants. Less openly brutal, the English in Ceylon and Burma did immense damage to the Buddhist Order. Unwilling to take over the ecclesiastical functions of the native kings they promoted indiscipline in the monasteries, drove monks into politics and disorganized monastic finances, while in addition the temple schools could no longer provide a socially advantageous education. These are only a few of the more dramatic blows which have reduced Buddhism to impotence. They are as nothing compared with the slow-working antagonistic forces which grind it down from day to day.

For there was little to attract Buddhists in the amalgam of ideas which the gunboats, soldiers, traders and missionaries from Europe and North

America forced so assiduously upon Asian lands. Militarism, the back-bone of the whole system and the only reason for the presence of these intruders in Asia, was extremely distasteful to them, as involving the deliberate, habitual and large-scale taking of life. Commercialism like-wise displeased them because it increases greed and makes people discontented with what they have got. Modern medicine has its conveniences, but the wholesale multiplication of suffering and dissatisfied human beings is a doubtful boon. And to systematically increase the wants of the poor means to kindle an all-consuming furnace of discontent which is bound to destroy established authority everywhere beyond repair. Nor was the message of salvation through Jesus Christ presented to the Buddhists in a way likely to win their hearts. Missionaries remained profoundly ignorant of even the elementary tenets of the doctrine. To modern scholars their misconceptions seem almost grotesque, and yet they normally used the most offensive language when speaking of Buddhist beliefs and practices, or of monks and particularly nuns. To a Buddhist the way of life of these 'Western barbarians' could only appear as a complete abomination, as a fulfilment of the worst prophecies about the Kali Yuga – a complete lack of serenity and contentment, of beauty and charm, of manners and deportment, of peace and quiet, of respect for holy men and sacred things.

The present situation of Buddhism is the outcome of the deadly and irreconcilable conflict between Buddhist tradition and the main forces of the modern age. The pressure of modern life is threefold, and affects: (1) monastic institutions; (2) doctrinal integrity; and (3) the co-operation between monks and laity.

MONASTIC INSTITUTIONS

Monastic institutions are the powerhouses which generate the thought-force that sustains the Buddhist community. In their absence the religion must die, as it has nearly done in Nepal. History has everywhere shown that congregations of contemplatives must first be suppressed before 'progress' can really begin. Once the 'needs' of the 'masses', as interpreted by their capitalist or bureaucratic sponsors, set the tone of society, monks must appear as mere idlers, 'useful' in no way whatsoever. And monks are, of course, very vulnerable, and can be eliminated by removing either their physiological or their economic basis. Direct slaughter was the method adopted in Mongolia and Tibet. In China and Japan economic pressure sufficed. China has preserved a number of monasteries as 'living museums'. In Japan many thousands of priests survive, but they could not protect their sanctuaries from invasion by the turmoil of the outside world. It is only in the Theravada countries that the state has taken concrete measures to further the dignity and security of the monks, and to assist the dissemination of their message among the population.

DOCTRINAL INTEGRITY

The doctrinal integrity of the Buddhists is subjected to many pressures, of which it will be sufficient to mention four.

(a) Although Asian *nationalism* is an inevitable reaction to many years of humiliation and ill-treatment, it does not go very well with Buddhism. On closer consideration it must appear slightly ridiculous to compensate for one's own sense of inferiority by boasting about the achievements of one's ancestors. Nevertheless, in taking this detached point of view, Asian Buddhists would lose touch with their supporters. So we find them often buying survival by howling with the wolves, and in Ceylon, Burma and Japan they habitually recommended their religion for reasons of national pride. This is a departure which, if unchecked, must in due course degrade a universal religion into a conglomeration of frantic tribal cults.

(b) Basically the *cold war* is a matter of indifference to Buddhists. Nevertheless political issues seem at present in Asia to be so much more urgent than religious considerations that many Buddhists have become willing tools of the rival forces. The primacy of politics has nearly ruined the 'World Fellowship of Buddhists'. Thai monks sprinkle holy water on American tanks. After 1950 both the USSR and China have regularly sent high dignitaries on propaganda tours into Asia. Numerous prominent Buddhists have proclaimed the compatibility of Buddhism and Communism, while others have as vociferously demonstrated their incongruity. In other words, on these issues Buddhists have forgotten how to speak with a voice of their own.

(c) The corroding effect of *modern science* on the Buddhist faith has barely begun. Minor frictions have arisen from European geography, and Buddhist monks feel uneasy and embarrassed when asked to find Mount Sumeru or the land of Shambala on a modern globe. Likewise the prestige of science has undermined traditional beliefs by making a surprising number of Asian Buddhists ashamed of the magical elements in their religion. But up to now the deadly challenge has been so little understood that

Asian Buddhists like to indulge in euphoric statements to the effect that Buddhism is the only religion which has nothing to fear from science. The future will bring a sad awakening.

(d) The concern for the *standard of living* and the urge to constantly increase the consumption of industrial commodities is also none too helpful to the Buddhist way of life. There is no more deadly poison to spiritual insight than bodily comfort. All this preoccupation with material possessions and social position must seem a complete misdirection of energy which keeps people so busy that they have not much time left for religion. In consequence in all industrialized countries people eschew doctrinal complications, and prefer simple and 'straightforward' doctrines, such as that of the Jodo Shinshu in Japan.

MONKS AND LAITY

The new age furthermore presents the monks with some technical problems. In the village communities their mass support was assured, but now they have to find it in the big cities. New institutions must therefore be evolved, such as the Young Men's Buddhist Association and so on. Much more important, however, is the fact that the monks' social ideals are out of date. Religious bodies are intensely conservative, and dislike it if one social system suddenly replaces another. Perfectly adjusted to feudalism, the Catholic Church has made gigantic intellectual and organizational efforts to adapt itself to an industrial society, and yet it has succeeded only imperfectly. For over two millennia Buddhism has subsisted within a relatively stable society, agricultural or nomadic, headed by an absolute ruler who was consecrated by the monks in return for his obedience to the Dharma, and who established a harmony between society and the cosmic and spiritual forces on which its prosperity depended. None of this makes much sense in the modern world, and generally speaking the Buddhists have watched the change of events in a kind of stupor, without producing men like Lamennais or Marc Sangier, or documents like the encyclical *Rerum Novarum*. The one exception is U Nu, the one ruler who is also a sage, and who has tried to temper economic progress with an insistence on Buddhist values.

FUTURE PROSPECTS

As to the future prospects of Buddhism, the short-term outlook is extremely bad. Not one aspect of the present situation favours it as a religious force. If industrialization, militarization and national self-assertiveness are the three most powerful factors in Asian society at present, then the first two are uncompromisingly hostile to everything that Buddhists stand for, and the third favours them only on condition that they become untrue to themselves. Whether Buddhism be persecuted by the State or not, for quite a time to come increasing inanition will be its fate.

The long-term prospects are slightly better. And this for three reasons: (1) Modern communications have re-established contact between the various branches of Buddhism which had been separated for so long. Narrow sectarianism will therefore be slowly worn down, some cross-fertilization will take place, and a deeper understanding of the Buddha's message will thus emerge. (2) In the Communist countries Buddhism will in due course profit from the astonishing similarities which exist between dialectical materialism and Mahayana philosophy. Many observers have commented on these analogies, and over the heads of both priests and commissars a new synthesis may well be created within the next century or so. (3) The glory of Asia is bound up with Buddhism as a cultural force. Everywhere the finest periods were precisely those in which it was in the ascendant. Once the threat from the outside world is removed, once Asia is either united or tolerably secure, Buddhism may well recommend itself as the most suitable ideology. So many Asian empire-builders have in the past turned to it as the ideal cement of vast societies. A religion which has tamed the descendants of Genghis Khan need not necessarily fail with the successors of Mao Tse-tung.

It must be borne in mind that Buddhism has never sought survival through self-assertive competitiveness. Though it has endured many persecutions, it has never resisted, and yet it is still there. Spiritual trends operate on levels too deep for historians to reach, and we must always be prepared for surprises. Some of them may be triggered off by something as intangible as the recent revival of Buddhist meditation.

BIBLIOGRAPHY

Bhikku Amritananda. *Buddhist activities in socialist countries.* (New World Press, Peking, 1961.)

Charles Bawden. 'Mongolia Revisited.' (*Journal of the Royal Central Asian Society*, London, XLVII, 1960.)

Buddhists in New China. (Chinese Buddhist Association, Peking, 1956.)

W. K. Bunce. *Religions in Japan.* (Charles Tuttle, Tokyo, 1955.)

P. Carrasco. *Land and Polity in Tibet.* (University of Washington Press, Seattle, 1959.)

Edward Conze. *Buddhism. Its Essence and Development.* (Oxford University Press, paperback edn, 1960.) *Buddhist Scriptures.* (Penguin Books, 1959.) *A Short History of Buddhism.* (Chetan, Bombay, 1960.) *Buddhist Thought in India.* (Allen & Unwin, 1962.)

W. L. King. 'An experience in Buddhist meditation (in Burma).' (*Journal of Religion,* XLI, 1961.)

W. Kolarz. *Religion in the Soviet Union.* (Macmillan, 1961.)

C. McDougall. *Buddhism in Malaya.* (Donald Moore, Singapore, 1956.)

E. M. Mendelson. 'Religion and authority in modern Burma' in *The World Today.* (Oxford University Press, 1960.)

D. E. Pfanner and J. Ingersoll. 'Theravada Buddhism and village economic behaviour. A Burmese and Thai comparison.' (*Journal of Asian Studies,* New York, XXI, 1962.)

E. Sarksiyanz. *Buddhist Backgrounds of the Burmese Revolution.* (1965.)

D. E. Smith. *Religion and Politics in Burma.* (Oxford University Press, 1965.)

D. C. Vijayavardhana. *Dharma-Vijaya or The Revolt in the Temple.* (Colombo, 1953.)

O. H. de A. Wijesekera. *Buddhism and Society.* (Bauddha Sahitya Sabha, Colombo, 1954.)

A. Winnington. *Tibet: Record of a Journey.* (Lawrence & Wishart, 1957.)

RELIGION IN CHINA

C. P. FitzGerald

THE history and state of religion in China differ profoundly from the European and Western Asian experience. In the regions now Christian or Muhammadan these universal creeds have superseded the ancient paganism which preceded them, not only in its popular polytheistic manifestations, but also in its refined and sophisticated ethical and philosophical schools. In China nothing has finally perished: the ancient cults and the classical school of Confucian ethical teaching persisted side by side, until very recent times, with the new universal religion of Buddhism: new, that is, to China, about 1800 years ago.

In broad general terms it might be said that the people were both Buddhist and followers of the old polytheism which came to be known as Taoism: the scholars were Confucians. The ordinary, often illiterate, pepple both in the country and in cities worshipped indiscriminately at Buddhist monasteries and Taoist temples. To them there was no clear distinction between Bodhisattvas and the Gods. The fact that the theology of Buddhism conflicted sharply with many of the beliefs grouped under 'Taoism' was either unrealized or ignored. Ancestor worship, or reverence to the spirits of the dead, who were at least in theory believed to have both survival in another world and influence upon the fate of their descendants, continued as perhaps the most widespread and persistent religious cult. Yet the belief in a link between the dead and their living descendants is quite incompatible with Buddhist theology which teaches the transmigration of souls and the unimportance of the earthly condition.

CONFUCIANISM, BUDDHISM AND TAOISM

Popular religion was thus confused and inchoate, lacking any accepted overall theology, or central organization. 'Three Ways to One Goal', the common saying has it, meaning that the Goal is not Eternal Life, or Salvation, but the Good Life here on earth, and the three ways, which are equally valid approaches to this end, are rational ethical Confucianism (with ancestor worship as a kind of auxiliary rite), Buddhism, and Taoism.

For several centuries, since at least the 10th century of the Christian era, the Confucians, the educated class of scholars, have had no God at all. Ancient, classical Confucianism as taught by the Sage himself and his disciples, did indeed admit the existence of the gods, and acknowledged in a vague way the primacy of T'ien, 'Heaven', who had in high antiquity been a sky and weather deity. But when the Sung Confucian philosophers in the 10th century and later began to reshape Confucian doctrine to meet a more sophisticated age, they pruned away every vestige of theistic belief, leaving only Moral Law as the impersonal prime mover of the Universe. Chu Hsi, the greatest of the Sung philosophers (1137–1200 A.D.), said in reply to a question 'there is no man in Heaven judging sin'. Confucianism since his time has borne the deep imprint of his thought, and the view he held has been the accepted teaching of the scholars.

As such it can hardly be claimed that Confucianism is a religion at all in the Western sense; it is an ethical system to which were attached some very ancient imperial ceremonies, the worship of Heaven by the Emperor, the ancestral rites practised by most Chinese families. The imperial rites fell into disuse with the fall of the monarchy in 1912; ancestor worship has continued until the present time; but under the People's Republic the rapid social changes which are replacing the old Chinese great family of many relations living together by the small 'biological' family of parents and children, and the constant spread of state education teaching Marxism-Leninism as the only form of ethical instruction are, no doubt, quickly eroding the active practice of ancestral rites. Confucian ethical teaching is also at a discount; it is 'reactionary', 'feudalistic' and outmoded: the modern intellectual is brought up as a Marxist.

Buddhism was not in origin a Chinese religion; it was introduced to China in the 3rd century A.D. from India, and its first teachers in China were Indian monks. It was only very gradually that the new religion took hold amongst the Chinese people. A long and laborious process of translation from Sanskrit to Chinese – two very different languages – was necessary before the Chinese could read the Buddhist scriptures or master the theology. By the 5th century Buddhism had won a large following both among the educated class and the common people. New schools, some of Indian origin, others evolved in China, arose and active disputes among them stimulated intellectual interest. But these ideas did not reach far down; the people had never abandoned their own ancient cults, the gods of the wind, the sea, the mountains and rivers, of war and wealth. Innumerable and ancient, local and various, these cults took refuge under the umbrella of Taoism, which has in origin been the quietest philosophy of profound minds. Later Taoism turned increasingly to alchemy, magic, and the pseudo-science of astrology, making contact with the old popular polytheism, and, in open competition with Buddhism, adopting a monastic order. During the 6th and 7th centuries, when Confucian teaching was much neglected, the two popular creeds gained great power and influence, but never ousted Confucianism nor resolved their contest by the victory of one religion.

Thus the 'Three Ways' became coexistent, and gradually the fire and dynamism went out of them. After the T'ang period (7th to 9th centuries A.D.) Buddhism fell into a slow decline; while Taoism at the same period, the early Sung, was reorganized as a state cult in which every deity was given rank and function in a heavenly hierarchy modelled closely on the imperial civil service, and ruled, as on earth, by the Jade Emperor, a divine absolute monarch. The Chinese ruling class, themselves agnostic or atheist Confucians, were deeply distrustful of any popular religion which seemed to be gaining many converts and inspiring them with faith and zeal. Such movements all too easily turned from religious to political ends, engendered rebellions and stirred up unrest among the peasantry. It was thought better to extend imperial patronage to the two officially recognized religions of Buddhism and state Taoism, subsidize their great shrines, permit their great festivals, and keep them under surveillance and control. When, as happened from time to time, the Emperor himself, or the ladies of the Palace, became ardently addicted to Buddhism, the Confucian officials strongly remonstrated and recalled the monarch to his duty. Such memorials are treasured among the gems of later Chinese literature.

Thus the condition of religion in imperial China, down to the end of the 19th century, was almost the exact opposite of that with which the European peoples were familiar either at home with Christianity or among their traditional antagonists the Muslims. Agnosticism, instead of being a rare and unpopular attitude only safely adopted by the rich and powerful, was the acknowledged and proclaimed view of the ruling class, the basis of higher education, indeed of all education. Popular religion was not under the guidance and inspiration of dedicated men of learning, but left to persons of little education and often of less probity. A few unworldly men of letters retired, often after an active life as Confucian officials, to the peace of a mountain Buddhist monastery. A few retired scholars studied the works of the ancient Taoist philosophers. The two religions themselves had sunk into a mutual and apathetic tolerance, no longer attempting to instruct their followers in the niceties, or even the principles, of their theologies, and accepting the offerings and the worship of all indiscriminately.

THE CHRISTIAN MISSIONS

To the early Christian missionaries who began to reach China from the middle of the 17th century this seemed a wide open field. Here was the same degenerated paganism, the same detached, perhaps devitalized, philosophy as the early Christians had overcome in the late Roman Empire. What was needed was to find a Chinese Constantine and the triumph of the Church would be assured. The Jesuits laboured assiduously at both the Court of the Ming and then the Manchu Dynasty to achieve this aim. Portents for a time seemed favourable. Jesuits, men of great learning, were employed in the Government service. They reformed the calendar. They improved the Chinese artillery, they made some distinguished converts. But they did not convert an Emperor. In the middle of the 18th century a violent dispute between Jesuits and Benedictines, known as the rites controversy, ruined the chances of the Roman Catholic missions. The Emperor K'ang Hsi, incensed to find foreign priests appealing to distant Rome to settle the religious practices of some small minority of his subjects, forbade further missionary work.

Just as the Chinese Government had always suppressed Buddhist sects which became dangerously popular and active, so now when the Christian missionaries strayed beyond the field of their immediate usefulness to the Court, the tolerance of their mission was abruptly terminated. Catholicism languished for a century, retaining a hard core of faithful converts, but making no progress.

In the mid 19th century, the Protestant nations, led by Britain, and allied to Catholic France, defeated the Chinese in war and imposed on her the first 'Unequal Treaties'. Among the provisions of these instruments were some which obliged the Chinese Government to permit the free preaching of the Christian religion, the free movement of missionaries, and their right to build churches, establish residences, schools, and hospitals wherever they chose. The era of great missionary activity had begun. It lasted almost exactly one hundred years, until in 1950 the Communist Government of the People's Republic, having won total power in China, put into effect policies which led to the withdrawal of all Protestant missionaries and the expulsion of all foreign Catholic priests and missionaries.

During this century the number of Protestant Christian converts, of many separate sects, attained a maximum of about 2 million, and the number of Catholic Chinese also reached approximately the same figure. By the end of the missionary era the total population of China was 600 million. From these figures it is evident that although the influence of the Christian Chinese, by reason of their connexions with the outside world and the high educational average of the Protestant community, was out of proportion to their numbers, they still remained a tiny minority among the Chinese people, the vast majority of whom were wholly ignorant of Christian doctrine and belief, and not at all attracted to a religion which was deemed 'foreign'. Buddhism, after nearly two thousand years of life in China, still suffers from this stigma in the eyes of the Confucian scholar.

POLICY OF THE PRESENT GOVERNMENT

It is with a realization of the marginal importance of the Chinese Christian Churches to the nation as a whole that the policy of the present Government towards them must be considered. That policy is simply to confine religious activity purely to ritual observance and acts of worship. No social activity whatever, no schools, hospitals or orphanages, no active evangelism can be conducted or controlled by a Christian Church. Citizens of the Republic are, according to the constitution, permitted freedom of religious worship and belief. The Churches have had to sever all connexions with foreign churches or missionary societies. The Chinese Protestant Churches have since tended to amalgamate, encouraged to do so by the Government, and to ignore or slur over the doctrinal differences which separated Anglican from Presbyterian or Baptist from Methodist.

The Catholic Church resisted this policy until all the hierarchy had in consequence been put in prison, or if foreign, expelled. The uncompromising anti-Communism of the Vatican left the Church in China no alternative. Many of the lower clergy preferred, or were by the pressure of their flock induced, to submit to Government control, and a schismatic Church has now arisen which while in doctrine conforming with Rome accepts the authority in all lay matters of the Chinese Government. Since no bishops remain in China to ordain new priests, and since those whom the Vatican might appoint would not be accepted by the Chinese Government, there is no apparent end to this situation other than in interruption of the Apostolic Succession. It would appear that in general while a reduced number of Christians still practice their religion under these conditions in the cities, the rural mission churches in villages where the converts were few have been closed. The Catholic villages which existed in some parts of China continue under priests who are in the view of the Vatican schismatic.

Islam in China was always a small sect, and recognized as an alien religion. There are about 10 million* Muhammadans, now treated as a national minority; although in origin, in the 8th century, of Western Asian descent, they have intermingled with Chinese and are Chinese in speech and custom, apart from religion. Mainly concentrated in the north-west and south-west of the country, Muslim communities are found in all parts, and formerly specialized in certain trades such as caravan transport, eating-houses and the curio trade. Respected and permitted to live their own religious life as a national minority, they make no converts and exercise little influence as a community, except in the few areas where they are a local majority.

The present state of religion thus in some ways resembles the position under the Emperors. Buddhism is tolerated as a popular religion with, it is estimated, about 50 million ardent followers, and many more occasional supporters. Christianity is strictly controlled, but is a very small minority. Islam is given local special status; and the ruling class, although acknowledging a new ethic, Marxism, as their guide, remain, as before, openly atheist.

BIBLIOGRAPHY

K. S. Latourette. *A History of Christian Missions in China.* (Society for Promoting Christian Knowledge, 1929.)

Moslems in China. (Foreign Languages Press, Peking, 1953.)

W. E. Soothill. *The Three Religions of China.* (Oxford University Press, 3rd edn, 1929.)

A. F. Wright. *Buddhism in Chinese History.* (Stanford University Press, Stanford, 1959.)

A. F. Wright (Ed.). *Confucianism in Action.* (Stanford University Press, Stanford, 1959.) *The Confucian Persuasion.* (Stanford University Press, Stanford, 1960.)

* This estimate is controversial. Sometimes a much higher figure is given. (G.W.)

RELIGION IN JAPAN

Carmen Blacker

SINCE the beginning of historical records in Japan the religious life of the Japanese has been dominated by two cults, diverse but inter-mingled. The loosely connected complex of cults and practices that now goes under the name of Shinto was the native religion, stretching back into the remote prehistoric period when the present Japanese race was formed. On to the strong background colour of this folk religion was imprinted, from the 6th century A.D. onwards, the doctrines of Buddhism in various of the Mahayana sects. Although Buddhism is universally acknowledged to be a religion of an altogether 'higher' type than early Shinto, it has never attempted, as did Christianity in Europe, to stamp out the older folk cults. A commingling of the two has therefore, with brief interludes, been the religion of the great majority of Japanese for some thirteen centuries.

EARLY SHINTO

In its earliest form Shinto seems to have been largely a recognition of the mystery, power and 'otherness' manifested in those things which lie beyond the competence of primitive man. The coming of spring, the onset of the rains, the growth of crops, the fertility of animals and women, the unaccountable effect which something beautiful has on the mind, a man with extra majesty and skill – all these are beyond his control and understanding and operate in ways utterly mysterious. The mystery which inhered in these things and which seemed to betoken a more powerful world beyond his own, was shadowily personified and called *kami*. There were thus myriads of *kami*, who were given long names but who had no shape of their own. In order to manifest them-selves they had to be 'called down' into an object – usually a tall thin shape such as a tree or a stone or a banner – or even better into a human being trained to act as a medium. Thus summoned, they could be invoked for help and advice on problems which are usually humanly insoluble. The purpose of the *matsuri* or festival, celebrated in all villages on certain fixed days, was to call down the god, to feast him and entertain him, and then if possible persuade him to pro-nounce, through an appointed medium, on the prospects during the coming year for the rice harvest, the rains, the storms, the epidemics.

But the power of these superior beings was not uniformly benign. If they could grant blessings when duly reverenced, they could also blast with curses (*tatari*) when offended. Broadly, they were offended by death and blood. Anyone who had been in contact with a corpse, with a woman in childbirth, a wounded man or any other of the recognized sources of pollution, was considered contaminated and must undergo a ritual isolation from his fellow men for a stated period, and for an even longer time refrain from approaching a shrine. Any violation of these rules could incur the danger of a sudden *tatari,* striking in the form of sickness, madness, accident or fire.

In this early period such injunctions towards ceremonial purity were all that was required in the way of 'moral' conduct in the sight of the *kami. Tsumi,* the modern word for sin, indicated anciently only this physical pollution. The development of an ethical code in Shinto came only later, with the influence of Buddhism and Confucianism from China. Indeed, scarcely any Japanese word for moral qualities, with the exception of a single term meaning something like 'sincerity', is of native origin. Benevolence, justice, propriety, compassion – words for these qualities appeared in the Japanese language only with the arrival of the Confucian classics and Buddhist scriptures.

BUDDHISM

When in the course of the 6th century Buddhism made its first appearance in Japan from Korea, it is scarcely surprising that a religion so remote from such beliefs as those of early Shinto should have been at first misunderstood. The *kami* had after all been regarded as a superior source of power capable of bestowing worldly benefits beyond human grasp – a good rice harvest, recovery from sickness, easy childbirth, male children. The Buddha had taught that worldly prosperity, the accumulation of what seem to be the blessings of this world, was in the long run of little account. The world as experienced in the ordinary human manner was invariably full of suffering. Only by a profound internal transformation of consciousness achieved through meditational disciplines and moral purification could one arrive at the illumination which comes from knowledge of the reality lying behind the veil of appearances.

It was some time, therefore, before the Japanese understood Buddhism to be anything more than a new version of their old religion.

The figure of the Buddha and his attendant Bodhisattvas were seen not as images symbolizing a different state of consciousness, but as potential bestowers of worldly boons. The sutras too, the Lotus Sutra, the Large Prajnaparamita Sutra, the Suvarna-prabhasa Sutra, were during the early centuries used not as guides to an internal transformation revealing the vanity of the world, but as spells for rain, for the Emperor's recovery from sickness, for the birth of a male heir.

In the course of time the true purport of Buddhism was understood by a minority of Japanese, who inaugurated a distinctive and powerful spiritual tradition as well as a noble and moving school of Buddhist art. But even today it is still true that for the average Japanese Buddhism has but two main functions, neither of which finds any place in the original teachings of the Buddha.

The first is the disposal of the dead and the pacification of ghosts and spirits. The ancient Shinto cult, with its abhorrence of the pollution of death, had provided no means for the repose of the dead, and little in the way of a comforting eschatology. From the burial mounds of the pre-Buddhist period it is clear, indeed, that the dead were greatly feared. All dead spirits were apparently potentially harmful, but especially those that had died a violent or untimely death. It was Buddhism which came to provide the special requiem masses necessary to enable the spirit to settle down and join the benevolent ranks of 'the ancestors', to whom offerings were daily made in household shrines to ensure a constant benign protection. Although in the early Buddhist doctrine in India such steps were irrelevant, since the dead person was believed to be soon reborn in the state prescribed by his past karma, Japanese Buddhism has always provided the means, so insistently demanded by the folk religion, for the living to help the dead to final peace.

The second main function of Buddhism in Japan is still to provide magical spells for the production of mundane benefits. Even as new sects of Buddhism found their way during the medieval period from China to Japan, this stress on productive magic still persisted. The Tendai and Shingon sects, dominant from the 9th to the end of the 12th century, answered this need very well with their Tantric derivations, providing spells for warding off plague, fire, drought and malevolent ghosts. Indeed today it is only the Amidist Jodo and Shin sects which require from the faithful a complete self-surrender to the mercy of Amida Buddha, and which, together with the Rinzai sect of Zen, entirely eschew spells for worldly benefits. Even in the Soto sect of Zen the richest and most renowned temples are not those which shelter a wise teacher capable of guiding disciples towards spiritual illumination, but those which enshrine an image reputed to be efficacious in granting, for a stated sum of money, such boons as prosperity in business, harmony in the family or freedom from traffic accidents.

On a less popular level the Buddhist sects which have taken root in Japan have fallen roughly into two categories. The *tariki* or 'other strength' sects rely completely on the overwhelmingly superior power of Amida Buddha to enable all beings who call on his name to be reborn in his Pure Land, a paradise where eventually they can be sure of attaining the Buddhist goal of nirvana. The Jodo and Shin sects, which arose in Japan during the 13th century, thus deny the efficacy of any effort which the disciple himself may make towards his own enlightenment. All that is required of him is complete faith and trust in Amida, expressed in recitations of the sacred invocation *namu Amida Butsu*.

The *jiriki* or 'self strength' school, on the other hand, is eminently exemplified by the Rinzai sect of Zen. Here the disciple is taught that through strenuous *zazen*, sitting and struggling with various meditational exercises designed to lead the mind to hitherto unsuspected depths, he can by his own efforts, aided by the guidance of a qualified master, bring about in himself successively deepening experiences of illumination. It is here that we find the most profound and distinctive indication of Japanese spirituality. The Zen sect, with its unique and practical teaching towards 'sudden enlightenment', has deeply influenced much of the best of Japanese art.

STATE SHINTO

Until the Meiji Restoration in 1868 inaugurated a new era of contact with the West, most Japanese had without difficulty subscribed to both Shinto and Buddhism. Various philosophical amalgamations of the two religions had at various times been proposed, but the solution most generally accepted was that the Shinto *kami* acted as local guardians or occasionally as temporary manifestations of Buddhist deities. Hence every Buddhist temple invariably contained also a Shinto shrine, and in most people's minds the two supernatural orders were only vaguely distinguished. This was a true *shimbutsu-shugo*, joining of gods and Buddhas.

The policy of the Meiji Government in the early 1870s however was to foster a spirit of national identity and enthusiasm centring on the Emperor. They hence set about a drastic policy of forcibly separating Shinto and Buddhism (*shimbutsu-bunri*) and of persecuting Buddhism as a foreign and undesirably other-worldly creed. Buddhist temples were converted into Shinto shrines. Monks and nuns were forced to return to lay life. At the same time the Meiji Government was concerned to stamp out those aspects of the old Shinto which seemed primitive and 'uncivilized' – which in effect meant a great deal of the folk religion. All those cults in which Shinto and Buddhist elements were indissolubly mixed, such as the mountain cult of the Shugendo, together with survivals such as the *miko*, women who made themselves mediums for deities or spirits to speak through their mouths, were suppressed.

In their place a largely artificial cult of State Shinto was fostered, wherein the Emperor, who had hitherto lived a revered but shadowy existence in the confines of his palace in Kyoto, was elevated to the position of focal point of loyalty and blind reverence. At the same time the exceedingly ancient myths contained in the early chronicles, which for centuries had remained in virtual oblivion, were resuscitated to the position of divine scriptures, and forced to yield the exhilarating doctrine of the divine destiny of Japan to pre-eminence over all other nations.

With the promotion of the cult of State Shinto to its climax in the final catastrophe of the war went an increasingly severe policy of repression of all other religious cults. Those attempting to found new cults, whether in sympathy with State Shinto or not, were flung into prison and their organizations dissolved. It was only in 1945 when the American occupation dis-established State Shinto that the Japanese were for the first time since the early 1870s granted complete religious freedom.

THE POST-WAR SCENE

The immediate result of the removal of restrictive legislation was the extraordinary upsurge of what are known as the *shinko-shukyo*, the new religions. All over the country new cults sprang up, until by 1951 the number reached the remarkable figure of 720. With the weeding out of obviously fraudulent cases and the collapse of others through the death of the original founder, the number has now dropped. But the new cults are still a striking feature of the post-war religious scene in Japan, and their increasing wealth, converted into huge concrete cathedrals and powerful networks of propaganda, is in marked contrast to the increasingly dilapidated state of many temples of the more traditional Buddhist sects.

Undoubtedly these new sects have arisen to fill the void which resulted from the collapse of the reputedly invincible State Shinto. In most cases they are messianic in character, promising to the faithful a millenarian rain of divine blessings and worldly favours. Those crushed by defeat, poverty and total loss of any directing purpose in life were roused to ardent faith, hope and sometimes charity by powerful figures claiming unique divine revelation and promising unique divine rewards. Such figures as the founders of these new cults are not new in Japanese religion. Their counterparts can be traced back to the 7th and 8th centuries. What is new, of course, is the appearance of modern methods of propaganda and organization, so that we find the curious combination of religious cults in shape and inspiration of great antiquity, adorned with vast concrete edifices of bizarre modern design, missionary tours to Hawaii and California, private broadcasting stations, huge rallies reminiscent of an American football match. Most of the new cults are tolerant and innocuous, providing genuine comfort, fellowship and hope in otherwise humdrum lives. Only Soka Gakkai, with its intolerance, its militancy, its ruthlessly threatening methods of propaganda and its obscure political ambitions, strikes an increasingly fanatical and sinister note.

It should be noted, however, that these cults seldom appeal to Japanese with claims to academic or intellectual respectability. For them, as for most university students, a slightly melancholy agnosticism seems to be the approved order.

Christianity, it may be remarked, has largely failed to make much mark on the post-war scene. Perhaps one of its most moving triumphs was the discovery after the war of small communities in Kyushu who since the beginning of the persecution in the 17th century had succeeded in remaining 'hidden Christians', undiscovered and unsuspected by either the persecutors of the feudal regime or by the later and more virulent inquisitors of State Shinto.

BIBLIOGRAPHY

W. G. Aston. *Shinto*. (Longmans, 1907.)

W. T. de Bary (Ed.). *Sources of the Japanese Tradition*. (Columbia University Press, New York, 1958.)

Sir Charles Eliot. *Japanese Buddhism*. (Edward Arnold, London, 1935.)

D. C. Holtom. *The National Faith of Japan: a Study in Modern Shinto*. (Kegan Paul, 1938.) *Modern Japan and Shinto Nationalism: a Study of Present-day Trends in Japanese Religions*. (University of Chicago Press, Chicago, 2nd edn, 1947.)

RELIGION IN JAPAN

Ichiro Hori. *Folk Religion in Japan.* (University of Chicago Press, Chicago, 1968.)

Philip Kapleau. *The Three Pillars of Zen.* (Weatherhill, Tokyo, 1965.)

Joseph Kitagawa. *Religion in Japanese History.* (Columbia University Press, New York, 1966.)

D. T. Suzuki. *Essays in Zen Buddhism,* 3 vols. (Reprinted by Rider, London, 1950.) *Zen Buddhism and its Influence on Japanese Culture.* (Eastern Buddhist Society, Kyoto, 1938.)

Harry Thomsen. *The New Religions of Japan.* (Charles E. Tuttle, Tokyo, 1963.)

CHRISTIAN MISSIONS IN ASIA

David M. Paton

CHRISTIANITY in Asia, considered relatively to the antiquity of its cultures, is a newcomer; and, relative to the population, Christians are few. There are of course exceptions. Outside the Near Eastern homelands of Christianity (where the Churches today are the sadly attenuated but direct descendants of those planted by the apostles), the Christians of Malabar in South India trace their origin to one of the twelve, St Thomas; and although this claim is not usually conceded by historians, it is likely that Christianity arrived there in the second or third century. But Nestorian Churches which once stretched from modern Iraq to the China Sea have died out.   Recent archaeological evidence shows them to have been more widespread in China than was suspected. The missionary work of the Franciscan John of Monte-corvino and others in India and China in the Mongol period was also without permanent result. Living Christianity today largely descends from the work of Roman Catholic missionaries which started in various places around the year 1500 but was not on a large scale till the 19th century; or of Protestant missionaries beginning in India in 1706, in China in 1807, and in Japan in 1859. The much smaller Russian Orthodox effort, most successful in Japan, began there in 1861. South India apart, Christianity in Asia is usually not more than one hundred and fifty years old, and may be much younger. If there were Christian communities before, today's Christianity is not connected with them, but is the result of a fresh impetus from outside Asia.

CHRISTIAN COMMUNITIES COMPARED

Christian communities in Asia are usually very small. The figures for selected countries (extracted from the *World Christian Handbook*, 1962) in the table opposite tell their own story.

Except in the Philippines, in the most Christian parts of South India, in parts of Indonesia, and in Korea, Christians of all sorts taken together are normally a tiny fraction of the population – seldom more than 5 per cent, often less than one per cent. Moreover, for purposes other than statistical they usually cannot be 'taken together', because of the divisions between them. Most of these have been imported from the West; and if there have been Asian additions, it is also the case that the most significant project in Christian reunion – the Church of South India, inaugurated in 1947 – originated in Asia.

Country	Population	Roman Catholics	Protestants and others	Christians (% of Pop.)
Burma	23,735,000	183,713	1,137,084	6·4
Cambodia	4,845,000	52,632	46,000	2·0
Ceylon	9,388,000	737,259	92,533	8·9
China	669,000,000	3,266,000	1,000,000	0·6
India	402,750,000	5,620,054	8,875,336	3·6
Indonesia	89,600,000	1,176,693	6,231,803	8·3
Japan	92,740,000	266,262	676,719	1·0
Korea	31,400,000	413,485	2,687,451	9·9
Malaya	6,515,000	151,565	124,453	4·2
Pakistan	86,823,000	304,561	416,265	0·9
Philippines	24,718,000	17,397,000	3,228,150	83·5
Thailand	21,881,000	110,000	33,598	0·7

There are also between two and three million Orthodox Christians in Asia, for the most part of different race and culture from the bulk of the population. This qualification applies also to certain other Churches and Christian denominations, e.g. in Malaya the Christians are mostly Chinese or Indian, not Malay, and in Burma not Burman but Karen or Chin.

DOUBTFUL PROGRESS

Christianity in Asia shares with certain other aspects of Western culture the stigma of being the result of the imperialist expansion of the West in what Sardar K. M. Panikkar has called 'the age of Vasco da Gama'. Dr Panikkar has concluded from his review of Asian history that the Christian missions in Asia have 'definitely failed'. He is not alone in this judgement, which appears to be common form among Asian intellectuals. Churchmen in the West – Fr Gabriel Hebert SSM, for example, in God's Kingdom and Ours – have made considerable use of his Asia and Western Dominance in their analysis of missionary weaknesses without necessarily accepting either his presuppositions or his conclusions. It may well be that there are Asian Christians who come to much the same conclusion in practice – Christianity is their religion, but they do not believe that it will conquer and they are not certain it is true. If they so think, their thoughts run on lines very much like those of many respectable English Christians.

This is not the place to argue the Christian case (which is, pace Dr Panikkar and Dr Toynbee, inevitably 'exclusive'). One may, however, note that a Christian may have a clear-sighted, even disillusioned, view of the present condition and immediate prospects of Asian Christianity, and at the same time maintain a matter-of-fact and cheerful confidence in the future.

CHRISTIANITY AND THE ASIAN RELIGIONS

A recurring theme in the writings of Asian Christians concerns the necessity of a dialogue with the great Asian religions. Christianity has been present in the homelands of Hinduism, Buddhism and Islam for several centuries, and has not been without its effect on them; yet no real meeting between the religions has yet taken place. All the signs are that this encounter is about to begin. In the West, Christians will have to face Hindu and Buddhist missions from the East, and argue afresh about the 'scandal of particularity' involved in the incarnation of the Son of God. In the East, Asian intellectuals will have to consider that same 'scandal' when it is put to them, free of its association with 'Western notions of superiority', by fellow intellectuals, also Asians, who are fully orthodox Christians. Preparing for this encounter is the principal preoccupation of institutes for the study of religion and society (such as that at Bangalore, presided over until his death by Paul Devanandan and now by M. M. Thomas).

This intellectual activity will include, for virtually the first time, profound theological effort. In the days when the Asian Churches were wholly dependent on Western missions, theology tended to be laid down by missionaries and accepted by nationals. Today – China is the extreme example of a general trend – the Church is coming to the realization that it is itself responsible both for the purity of the Church's faith and the intelligibility with which it communicates that faith. Out of this double concern is born theology – a theology which is no more simply a copybook learning of other people's formulations but a struggle to express the truth of God in terms that writer and reader can make their own. In a sense, it is the enemies of Christianity who are the midwives of a truly Asian, truly Christian, theology.

Another prime concern is about the proper social role of Christians in Asia. Once upon a time, they were, in the Chinese phrase, 'running dogs of imperialism'. From this situation they must escape. But Christians cannot legitimately escape from subservience to the West merely to climb on to a nationalist bandwagon – there are too many awful warnings in the recent history of the West of the results of bestowing an uncritical blessing upon nationalist aims.

Voices can be heard now of leaders, of men and women committed to the quest for a Christian Church which is united or at least moving purposefully towards union and away from the multiplicity of Western-originated denominations. They are leaders who seek for such an indigenous Church and as part of its self-hood a new relationship with the nation. They seek for the same reasons to remain a true part of the world Christian community, building on the foundations bequeathed from the old era of dependence on the mission a new relation of mutuality and interdependence. They want Christianity in Asia to be a genuinely Asian Christianity.

This new reformation of the Asian Churches is expressed organizationally for the non-Roman Churches in the East Asia Christian Conference. There are similar stirrings on the Roman Catholic side. Bishops from Asia and Africa spoke and voted on the 'progressive' side in the Vatican Council. Protestant and Anglican leaders, however, must also reckon in some countries with an influx of independent and often sectarian missionaries, and with new division caused by the profound suspicion entertained by 'fundamentalists' of the theological and political reliability of the ecumenical leadership; the division between 'liberals' and 'fundamentalists' is at its deepest and most bitter in parts of Asia. This evangelical zeal may sometimes become united with a nationalist suspicion of the missionary and result in independent churches; in China one of these, known as 'the Little Flock', was reported a few years ago to be larger than any of the Protestant Churches founded by the Missions.

The Churches can also be caught by the internal divisions of the nations. The revolt of the Nagas in north-east India (many of them Christians) was grist to the mill of parties such as the RSS whose line is a militant Hindu nationalism. In Indonesia, on the other hand, one result of the turmoil of 1966 has been, especially in Central Java, a vast increase in the numbers of those seeking to join the Churches. All political developments, whether superficially 'favourable' or 'unfavourable' to the prospects of the Churches, raise delicate problems which can put a severe strain on both the inner fellowship of Christians and their outer relations with their neighbours.

FUTURE PROSPECTS

The majority of Asian Christians may be assumed to be preoccupied with more immediate matters. Many, perhaps most, so fear absorption into the dominant religious culture – be it Hindu, or Buddhist, or Islamic, or Maoist – that they are tempted to retire into a nostalgic self-enclosed Christian world, ready to be incapsulated in the larger society as a sub-caste in a ghetto. Dr D. T. Niles, of Ceylon, has recorded his belief that this ghettoism is a more pressing danger to the Church in Asia than the syncretism that is more feared.

The detached modern observer, especially if he be of humanist cast of mind, may concede that some Churches in some Asian countries may survive perhaps for centuries in this socially uncreative manner: he is not likely to expect any brighter future for Christianity in Asia. A Christian must needs be a more emotionally committed observer, but he must recognize that Christianity has not yet engaged the soul of Asia, and that what happened to Nestorian and Franciscan could happen in our time also. He need not accept that it *will* happen – indeed, if he remains a Christian he will not.

More than any others, Asians have explored the nature of religion. Now Asia moves with the rest of us into a world where religion is at a discount – a world 'come of age' in which men are 'religionless' (the phrases are Dietrich Bonhoeffer's). What in the depths of her being Asia will do with this secular world and what part Christianity (in whose bosom the modern world originated, and which is not *primarily* a religion for men to practice, but a message from the living God) will play in the drama does not yet appear. As usual the facts allow of several interpretations; and the prophecy any observer makes is likely to be determined as much by his prior assumptions as by his empirical analysis.

BIBLIOGRAPHY

P. D. Devanandan. *The Gospel and Renascent Hinduism.* (S.C.M. Press, 1959.)

John Fleming (Ed.). *This We Believe: Asian Churches Confess Their Faiths.* (Taosheng Press, Hongkong, 1968.)

K. S. Latourette. *History of the Expansion of Christianity*, 7 vols. (Eyre & Spottiswoode, 1937–45.)

D. T. Niles. *Upon the Earth.* (S.C.M. Press, 1962.)

K. M. Panikkar. *Asia and Western Dominance.* (Allen & Unwin, 1953.)

David M. Paton. *Christian Missions and the Judgment of God.* (S.C.M. Press, 1953.)

M. A. C. Warren (Ed.). *Christian Presence Series.* (S.C.M. Press, 1959.)

H. R. Weber. *Asia and the Ecumenical Movement.* (S.C.M. Press, 1966.)

Political Affairs

PAN-ASIANISM

C. P. FitzGerald

PAN-ASIANISM is neither an old nor an indigenous Asian idea. It is not ancient, since the very concept of the continent of Asia is not an Asian, but a European idea, formulated by the Greeks, taken over by the Romans, and handed down to modern Europe. To the Greeks it was natural to divide their world into the three regions which lay west, east and south of the Aegean Sea. So Europe originally meant mainland Greece and countries west and north of it, Asia meant what is now Turkey and Syria, Africa meant Egypt and Libya. Nothing beyond these regions was really known or named. The Macedonian conquest and the later Roman conquests enlarged the idea of Asia; it now stretched away to the confines of India and to whatever lay beyond, of which only imperfect knowledge percolated to the West. Africa was enlarged until it came to mean what it does today, although almost all the southern three quarters of the continent was still unexplored.

These geographical concepts were thus formed in Europe by Europeans; they were not familiar to the peoples of Asia, who did not divide their known world in this way. In ancient times the Chinese were not aware of what countries lay far to their west. When they gained some knowledge of them they distinguished India, known as Shen Tu, then Yin Tu; Persia, known as An Hsi, later P'o Ssu; and the Roman Orient, first known as Ta Ts'in, later as Fu Lin. In still later times these divisions came to correspond very broadly with the regions of Hindu, Persian, and Arabian Muslim cultures. Indians also saw the world as India in the middle, a Chinese world to the east, and a Muslim world to the west.

After the rise of Islam, Muslims tended to see the world as divided into three parts, Islam, the Christian West, and the infidel East. The spread of Buddhism throughout the Far East did not lead to any great change in these ideas. The Chinese saw Eastern Asia as either influenced by their culture, and thus in theory 'tributary' to the great central Empire, or barbarian, as were the nomad peoples to the north and the mountain and jungle peoples to the south and west. South-East Asia became predominantly a region of Buddhist religion, but as part of the area, the old Annamite Kingdom, was under Chinese cultural influence, while the rest was inspired by Indian, at first Hindu, culture, Buddhism, when it first replaced Hinduism, tended to take the colour of the underlying civilization, whether Chinese or Indian, and did not unify these countries in a new synthesis.

There was very little unity at all in what the Europeans thought of as 'Asia'. Chinese and Indians were (and are) as far apart in culture and in outlook as either were from the European peoples. The nomadic North, Mongolia, Siberia, and Turkistan, remained a world apart, the reservoir from which destructive invaders poured out upon the civilizations of the South. The Muslim West felt no unity with the infidels of the East, who were not even 'People of the Book' – the Bible – which although seen by Muslims as an incomplete revelation, was none the less held to be the Word of God. The idea that some bond united all these peoples in opposition, or in contradistinction, to the peoples who lived north of the Mediterranean and Black Seas was utterly strange and unknown to Asians before the 19th century.

ORIGIN OF PAN-ASIANISM

The origin of the notion of Pan-Asianism may perhaps be traced to the first European peoples who came by the sea route to southern and eastern Asia, the Portuguese and Spaniards. Both nations had had a long history of conflict with the Muslims: when they rounded the Cape, or crossed the Pacific to the Philippine Islands, they found in these new lands of Asia both Muslim rulers and also pagan peoples. It was natural to distinguish them sharply from Christian nations at home in Europe. The Muslims were traditional enemies, the pagans should be won for Christ. Since the Portuguese maritime empire touched upon many diverse peoples from Indians at Goa, Sinhalese at Colombo, Malays at Malacca right round to the Chinese at Macao, the newcomers tended to see them all as 'Asians'. Very gradually the Asian peoples themselves came to adopt this classification.

The idea was rather new, even in Europe. In the Middle Ages, during the Crusades, the Franks, struggling to maintain their precarious Kingdom of Jerusalem, had been very willing to seek allies beyond the Muslim world which hemmed them in. Envoys from the lay rulers and also from the Pope attempted to get into touch with the still pagan Mongols who had swept through Asia to the borders of Europe and Africa. There is no evidence that Western Europeans thought of these strangers from the Further East as having anything in common with the Muslims of the Near East. They were pagan, so could perhaps be converted to Christianity and become invaluable allies. Had they been converted they would have become part of Christendom.

In the early centuries of growing contact between the non-Muslim part of Asia – India and China – and Europe, the Western world did not conceive of itself as superior in any respect, except religion. The manufactures and luxuries of the East far surpassed those of the West. The huge Empires of Ming China and Mogul India were states beside which the greatest kingdoms of Europe were but small. The civil service of China represented a degree of state organization and control which no European power had attained since the fall of the Roman Empire. The one comforting defect about these great states and peoples was that they were pagan, or infidel. All their glory was overshadowed by the darkness of unbelief. The European enterprise in the East became a double one, to purchase the luxuries and refined products of the Asian world for resale at a handsome profit at home, and to win these peoples for Christ.

This situation did not outlast the 17th century. The Mogul Empire declined, and even if the Chinese Empire under the early Manchu rulers remained apparently very strong, it became evident in many parts of Asia that the Europeans had the upper hand in wars. Technical innovation, fostered perhaps by the important role of sea-borne trade in the European world, soon outstripped the level attained in Asia, which had a few centuries earlier been higher than that of Europe. By the middle of the 18th century the men who voyaged to the East had acquired the idea that European civilization was superior in other ways than possession of religious truth. The increasing European impact coincided with, and in part caused, a period of decline and confusion in the great communities of Asia. India fell into weakness, which facilitated European encroachment. China had passed the peak of the Manchu Dynasty's power and vigour. In South-East Asia division and political incoherence gave advantage to the sea-borne invader.

The 19th century saw the Europeans turn from trade to conquest. The process had begun in India after Plassey, and gathered momentum in the next century. It was partly, but only partly, inspired by the old 'dream of empire', the inheritance which the West had derived from the conquests of Alexander and the Roman proconsuls. Much more was it due to the simple necessity of imposing order on chaos, or the protection of trading ports. Most of the European nations expanding into the Asian countries would have preferred empires of the Portuguese type, a chain of fortified ports dominating the trade but not the administration of vast hinterlands. The decline of the Asian kingdoms and empires made this development impossible. In India, Malaya, Indonesia and Indo-China the Western powers were led step by step into annexation and the imposition of protectorates, which latter expedient steadily became in practice indistinguishable, except in form, from outright annexation.

This policy soon created a growing dilemma. The Asian lands were vast; militarily they had become insignificant antagonists, but for the colonial powers they still presented formidable administrative problems. When the British had absorbed India, they shrank from conquering China also; the decline of the Turkish Empire was as much an embarrassment as an opportunity. For while the nations of Western Europe had intruded by the sea route into Asia in search of trade, and stayed to rule, the Russians had expanded into Northern Asia, not as traders, but as conquerors and settlers. Russian conquests followed the old Roman pattern. Before the second half of the 19th century was much advanced the Western Europeans became more afraid of ultimate Russian ambitions than of the remnant strength of the independent Asian states.

THE RISE OF JAPAN, REVOLUTION AND NATIONALISM

The reaction of Asia to this double invasion, by sea and by land, was slow and confused. Up till nearly the end of the 19th century it found no positive or concrete expression. The main centres of such resistance as existed were negative: the Asian peoples did not respond to missionary zeal; conversion to Christianity remained statistically very small even in the 'pagan' societies; in Muslim lands it was microscopic. The second, more unfortunate, form of resistance was the slow response to Western technical superiority. It is true that the new colonial empires did not actively encourage economic progress or technical advance except where it showed a profit to them, or made political control easier. They built railways, but did not foster heavy industries. Yet in those parts of Asia, such as China, which remained independent, progress was if anything slower than in the colonial empires. Only Japan met the challenge by an all-out effort of modernization. This Japanese reaction was to a great extent an application of the American political adage, 'if you can't beat them, join them'. Japan sought to win recognition as an equal of the Western powers by adopting their techniques in industry and warfare, and by making such more superficial changes in her political system as would entitle her to 'join the club'.

The Japanese were really anxious to escape the growing stigma of being classed as an Asian people, except in the inescapable geographical sense. Yet it was their example and success which inspired the Pan-Asian movement. Up to the end of the 19th century no Asian people had successfully withstood a European people in arms. There had been local successes, heroic resistances, but always final defeat. It had become an axiom that the West must always win. The policy of the few remaining independent states was to walk a tightrope between the conflicting ambitions of the Western powers – 'playing off one barbarian against another' was the Chinese version, far from successful. The able King of Siam, Chulalangkorn, followed a plan of balancing French and British power while permitting some cautious modernization. His success was in part at least due to his own personal quality. Where such leadership was absent the results were usually fatal. Persia survived because Russia and Britain could not agree upon how to divide the spoil. Afghanistan survived for much the same reason. The break-up of Turkey would have precipitated a European war, and was consequently undesirable. The partition of China, frequently threatened, was avoided more by the daunting magnitude of the task and the certainty of inter-European rivalry than by the feeble defence policy of the declining Manchu Court.

In 1905 Japan went to war with imperial Russia and won a resounding victory. It is true that Russia, fighting at the end of an immense line of communications, menaced by internal unrest, and lacking effective sea power, fought at great disadvantage. This made no difference to the effect produced, which went far further than Japan herself either wanted or expected. The Japanese hoped, rightly, that their victory would make them finally and for ever accepted as a Great Power. They did not want the leadership of Asia in an anti-European movement, they wanted to be counted among the Great Powers, who were in fact all Western peoples. But elsewhere in Asia the result was seen in other terms. The Asians could 'do it' if they only acquired the means and the skill to carry on modern warfare. The means were modern armaments, the skill could be learned, the obstacles were lack of money and an inefficient and outworn political system.

Thus the first result of the victory of imperial Japan was an immense impulse to revolution in Asia. The old dynasties must go, either in favour of reformed monarchy or republic; opinions varied, but there rapidly appeared a new solidarity among revolutionary parties in different parts of Asia. The Congress movement in India included both Hindus and Muslims, and Hindus later gave support to the purely Muslim Khalifat movement, intended to save Turkey from partition by the European powers. There were contacts, slight but not without importance, between young Turks and Chinese republican plotters. The Young Turkish revolution of 1908 was by some Chinese regarded as a model.

The Asian intellectual of the early 20th century was now more often a 'returned student' than one who has been educated only at home in his native land. He was returned from England, America, France, Germany or Japan. There he had met and mixed with other Asian students, Chinese, Indians, Indonesians, Malays, Egyptians and many others. He had found that they saw their own problems just as he saw his. The enemy was Europe, but Europe was also the teacher. The Europeans in spite of their divisions and rivalries stood together, particularly in respect of colonial problems and unrest. It seemed obvious that cohesion and co-operation among Asian nationalists would be more effective than isolated and independent movements. Moreover the Asian countries were very large; most of them had not in the past had clearly defined sensitive frontiers, as in Europe, nor minorities from a neighbouring nation who could divide the loyalties of the nascent nationalist movements. It seemed that Indians and Chinese, Indonesians and Indo-Chinese could co-operate without any fear of rivalry. So the idea of Pan-Asia was born in these circles, essentially an emigré idea matured in foreign surroundings, under the strong influence of an alien culture and political system.

This is no doubt the main reason why Pan-Asianism has always been a theory rather than a practical policy adopted by governments. Asian nationalists spoke in favour of Pan-Asia; they acted, when they came to power, in furtherance of their national interests without finding Pan-Asianism much help in the task. The problems of the early Chinese Republic were not usefully related to the problems of Indian nationalism, Indonesian nationalism, or Arab independence. The enemies might all be Europeans but they were of different nations, with differing policies. For China it was soon Japan, not any European nation, which presented the most menacing front.

It was while the nationalist movements in Asia were still far from power and victory that Pan-Asianism made its greatest appeal to their members. Then all were equally among the dispossessed and despised. As they came to power they found that the actual problems of achieving complete independence were not closely connected with events in other Asian countries. In the period between the two wars the rise of Communist movements in Asia further weakened the Pan-Asian concept. The Communist parties opposed the Pan-Asian idea; it was un-

Marxist. It was the solidarity of all workers, the black, the brown, the white, and the yellow in opposition to all capitalists, of whatever colour or race, which they preached as the solution for the problems of Asia, just as much as for the problems of Europe, South America, and any other region. Pan-Asianism was divisive and therefore reactionary; the toilers of Asia needed to be freed from their own aristocratic or bourgeois exploiters as much as from European masters, and the working class of the West was in the same state of servitude.

THE DEFEAT OF JAPAN AND THE DECLINE OF PAN-ASIANISM

The policy of Japan in the Second World War was the last positive attempt to use Pan-Asianism as a political factor, and the failure of that policy and the defeat of Japan gravely discredited the whole theory. The Japanese Co-Prosperity Sphere was based on the idea that the Asian peoples freed from European colonial rule could be induced to accept Japanese leadership if it was dressed up in this Pan-Asian garb. Japan would lead Pan-Asia; for was it not Japan who had first upset the tradition of Western military victory, and was now following this up with further, shattering blows against the European domination in Asia? There can be no doubt that for a while this policy met with some success. Nationalists did co-operate with the Japanese, in Burma, in Indonesia, in Indo-China, and to some extent in Malaya also. The extreme wing of the Indian movement did the same.

But there was always one awkward exception, and of the largest size. China was the enemy of Japan, the ally of the West. In vain the Japanese tried to represent their puppet regime in Nanking as the true Government of China, their opponents, whether Nationalist or Communist, as 'Asian traitors'. The mass of the Chinese people both at home and overseas made it quite clear that they were utterly unconvinced, and felt no solidarity with the friends of Japan.

The defeat of Japan ended the Co-Prosperity Sphere, and all outward manifestations of Pan-Asianism. It was now the United States of America which emerged as the champion and friend of the newly liberated Asian peoples. American intervention brought an end to Dutch attempts to delay or arrest the independence of Indonesia. American opinion undoubtedly hastened the British into giving India and Pakistan, Ceylon and Burma, self-government or independence. America took over from France the protection of the new states of Indo-China, but upheld their right to national independence.

At the same time the real division of opinion in Asia became fixed on new lines. There were those who believed that colonialism could best be rooted out by destroying capitalism: the Communists. There were those who sought both to oppose Communism and to gain national independence at the same time: the Nationalists. The issue is still in debate; colonialism has almost wholly vanished, but its disappearance has not solved the problems in the way the ardent revolutionaries expected.

THE BANDUNG CONFERENCE

The latest, probably the last, Pan-Asian occasion was the Conference at Bandung in Indonesia in 1955. All Asian states, Communist and non-Communist, sent delegations. Some of the outstanding leaders of Asia, Nehru, Chou En-lai, Nasser, attended in person. No Western power sent a delegation, or was invited. President Sukarno of Indonesia delivered the opening address, speaking in English, with great eloquence. It was a passionate denunciation of colonialism, at the same time a paean of triumph that the dragon was slain. In the course of his speech he had occasion to refer to the assembled delegates as 'we of the coloured peoples'. It was evident from their startled movement that the Turkish delegates had never thought of themselves in this light. When it came to passing resolutions which could have a political implication, the conference could not give effect to any unanimous opinion. Colonialism was condemned, easily, because all had once suffered from it, but suffered no longer. But between Communists and anti-Communists, between non-aligned states and the allies of the United States of America, there could be no real meeting place. Thus the conference concluded with an air more of an Irish wake than a meeting to draw up a blue-print for the future. The funeral of colonialism was joyfully celebrated, but the heirs to the estate had no common plan for their inheritance and were in some cases sharply divided in their views as to how the assets should be allocated.

Since Bandung, Pan-Asianism, under any other name, is seldom mentioned. The Afro-Asian bloc in the United Nations Organization is a wider grouping, and is far from a solid bloc. The division between Communist, non-aligned, and Western-allied Asian states constitutes the reality of present Asian international relations. These three groups have little in common, are composed of diverse peoples from widely separated parts of the continent, not even closely corresponding to the ancient divisions between the Chinese Far East, the Hindu South, and the Muslim West of Asia. Pan-Asianism was a reaction against a

European attitude, itself outmoded. It has therefore withered as the concept to which it was opposed has also faded from the minds of European men.

BIBLIOGRAPHY

K. M. Panikkar. *Asia and Western Dominance*. (Allen & Unwin, 1959.)

G. B. Sansom. *The Western World and Japan*. (Cresset Press, 1950.)

Benjamin Schwartz. *In Search of Wealth and Power – Yen Fu and the West*. (Harvard University Press, Cambridge, Mass., 1964.)

POLITICAL
INNOVATIONS
IN ASIA

Guy Wint

SINCE the end of the war, the experience of the countries of Asia in handling political institutions has been imitative rather than creative. It has been remarkable what skill has been shown in adapting Western institutions for their needs. But the Asian countries have not used much ingenuity or imagination in the creation of new ones.

The Communist states have sought to copy Russia. In China, it is true, Mao Tse-tung has faced quite different problems from Russia, and has sought, usually without admitting what he is doing, to give the machinery of state a different twist from the Russian. Formally Mao, for all his achievements, cannot yet be regarded as a great innovator. It is possible that new political systems will emerge from the crucible of the Great Cultural Revolution. But this will become plain only in the future. Similarly, neither in North Korea nor North Vietnam has there been any novel development.

Among South-East Asian states the model has been the free world. The Philippines has a constitution borrowed from the United States; Malaya borrows from Westminster, though it has had to adjust this to provide for a form of federation. No constitution deserves special attention, except the one of South Vietnam which, rather like Kuomintang China of the past, combines a veneer of liberal institutions familiar in the West with the reality of single-party dictatorship.

In 1962 Burma passed under the dictatorship of Ne Win, and ceased to be governed by an imitation of the Western parliament. Ne Win is said to be so much concerned about the possibility of a nuclear war that he wishes to detach Burma from the influence both of China and of the West. Burma is ruled by a hierarchy of councils in which popular elections play a part; but the chairman of each council, the man who effectively controls their action, is always an army officer. The details of the operation of this political system are obscure.

In general the absence of political writing in the other countries is as remarkable as the absence of political innovation. They are thrown back on other models – Russian or Western – because they have not generated their own ideas.

There have however been significant innovations in the institutions of three governments, those of India, Pakistan and Indonesia. There has also been interesting speculation in Ceylon.

INDIA

In India the outstanding event has been the great success (up to the time of writing) of the system adopted in 1947. That in turn was the elaboration of the system which was devised by the British, and was embodied or forecast in the Government of India Act 1935. In one respect however India is making a notable advance. This is in the so-called Panchayet Raj. It is an attempt to give the peasant actual control of the lower reaches of administration, the part which comes closest to him. The Panchayet is the village council, and this is directly elected. The development of the system has been hastened by the considerable success and influence of the Community Development Projects, which are an attempt to stimulate rural development by making grants of capital available for projects in which the people as a whole show genuine interest, and which they are willing to further by personal sacrifice and effort. For this purpose the Panchayet obviously forms a very useful executive instrument. It will be some time before the whole of India has its Panchayets.

India is the place where a very considerable change was meditated in the years preceding independence, but, because of the way in which independence was in fact achieved, did not actually come about. When Mahatma Gandhi was the dominant figure in Congress, the nationalist view was that parliaments and the parliamentary type of government did not suit the needs of India. A complete new system, of village councils genuinely expressing the will of the people, was to be put in their place. But when the time came, Gandhi had ceased to be the controlling force (though he remained the keeper of the country's conscience) and the party leaders of Congress found it convenient to maintain their sophisticated political machinery. After the death of Gandhi the Gandhians, though they continued to exist as a wing of Congress, lost ground at first. But in time two forces appeared among them which seemed likely to give Gandhism a new lease of life and to make it influential in India's political development. One was Vinoba Bhave and his Bhoodan movement. The other was the ideas of Jaya Prakash Narayan.

419

Vinoba Bhave was in Gandhi's lifetime one of his most dedicated disciples. He lived as austerely as Gandhi, and like him refused to possess any property. Like him too he was a firm believer in non-violence. In the years after independence he became extremely depressed at the spread of Communism, and with it the cult of violence among the poor. He discovered that his way of life gave him immense power with the people, and he initiated a scheme of land gifts by the well-to-do to the poor. This was followed by a scheme of gifts of service. Thereby a great network was built up of people who were pledged by vow to a form of service, and in this he saw the best antidote to Communism. And so it was, but the weakness of the enterprise lay in the organization. There was no adequate scheme for settling the gifts of land upon the poor, or in fact of sorting out the genuine gifts from bogus ones, such as other people's land or waste land, which many landlords donated freely.

Jaya Prakash Narayan is the former leader of the Indian Socialist Party. He had a distinguished fighting record during the war-time clash of the Socialists with the government. He resigned from the Socialist Party to join Vinoba Bhave because he felt that at the time India needed missionaries of ideas rather than men of action. Jaya Prakash is the son of a peasant and the first major political leader who came neither from the Westernized intelligentsia nor from the administrative classes in the Princely States. He has prepared long manifestoes attacking at all vulnerable points the present system, and he has proposed a drastic recasting of the country's policy. He argues that India and the West are different worlds, and that institutions which may suit the West are not suited to India, either to its psychology or its present needs. He criticizes the parliamentary system of government on the grounds that it necessitates nation-wide political parties, which, by their nature, divide the country and carry new and unnecessary conflicts into society, especially the villages. These parties, he says, are creations of the towns, in which only 20 per cent of the Indian people live, and they know little of the realities of the Indian village. To the villager, the structure of parliamentary democracy is something remote and unmanageable.

In the place of the present system of government, Jaya Prakash Narayan proposes a new constitution which would tilt the focus of political activity from the town to the villages. Rather infelicitously, he calls this 'communitarianism'. The basic unit would be the village community with a village council directly elected by the suffrage of all inhabitants. Villages would be grouped into units of about 150 villages;

the councils for these, to be called the Panchayet Samithi, would be indirectly elected by the basic village councils. In Jaya Prakash's view, a very surprising amount of the ordinary business of government could be transacted by these councils. His hope is that the established political parties could be deterred, either by the law or agreement, from contesting the elections for the councils.

Jaya Prakash, though urging a sweeping change, is not an irresponsible anarchist, and accepts that superior units of government must exist, both provincial governments and a central government. The central government would maintain the army: Jaya Prakash is less of a pacifist than Gandhi. But the powers of the superior organs would be devolved upwards from below, and would be limited by law.

Jaya Prakash has recently lived aloof from day by day politics. But his ideas have been making headway. He enjoys great esteem in the public opinion polls which show the popularity of leaders in India.

PAKISTAN

Pakistan has had a more restless and troubled political history than India. From 1958 it was under military government; it has now ended, but the search for a stable constitution is still in progress. Pakistan began its political history in 1947 with a constitution of the Westminster type. In course of time this broke down, partly because the political parties proved unstable and lacked strong leadership. (In Asia, generally, parliament only thrives where there is a strong political party.) Serious concern was felt for the state and its economic system: corruption became widespread. The parliamentary regime was finally discredited by a squalid fracas on the floor of a provincial legislative assembly which resulted in the death of the Deputy Speaker. The army struck, and declared parliament abolished and the parties prohibited.

In form the new regime was a military dictatorship. But it was very unlike military juntas of the classical type. After the first few days the army was little in evidence. It existed as a sanction and a threat in the background. Under its protection Pakistan was ruled by its civil servants. It was very like the system of government in the heyday of British power in India. The army insisted on certain reforms, and they were executed, including the purge of the Civil Service, which thus redeemed itself from corruption. Reform took place in all branches of the government and social organization. But sooner or later the regime had to face the task of achieving a long-term settlement and giving the country a new constitution. The principal figures in this venture were President Ayub Khan and Manzur Quadir, his Foreign Secretary. Mr Quadir had had no previous experience of politics until he was brought into the government by President Ayub. He had been a fashionable lawyer, and was noted as a rather eccentric thinker about social problems.

These two men started, like Jaya Prakash Narayan, from the principle that the root evil in their system of politics was the parliamentary party; it was this which determined all features of politics, and determined them in a way which had little relation to the needs of the country as a whole. It brought to the top such undesirable elements as had reduced Pakistani politics to contempt, and bred inefficiency and corruption. It divided the country into factions fighting over issues with which they had no intimate concern. In place of the previous party system, they set themselves to produce politics of a new type, served by a new type of politician. To this end, they decreed the formation of what they called Basic Democracy, local councils handling local affairs. No less than 80,000 were brought into being. In the election of these councils, political parties were to be allowed no part, and in this way Ayub Khan and Manzur Quadir sought to exclude the old-style politician and also to foster a type of politics redolent of the countryside more than of the town. Candidates were to be local men, known intimately to the voters.

In 1962 President Ayub went a step further and tried to regularize the system by crowning it with a national parliament elected by the basic democracies. This, however, led to difficulties which are not yet overcome. His intention was that the candidates should be as independent of party as those which form the basic democracies. But, in fact, though candidates pretended to be independent, it was an open secret that many of them represented the former political parties. When they came together in the parliament, they acted together as cohesive groups, and Ayub had little choice except to recognize the reconstitution of the parties. At least, he did not decide to make an issue of it and to fight the parliament over the parties' existence.

Thus the political party had edged itself back into the centre of politics. The next move was an attempt at the restoration of the full parliamentary system. In January 1965 there took place a presidential election. The old-style political parties combined and put up Miss Jinnah as a candidate. At first her popularity was evidently more than President Ayub had expected. But the election took place in two stages. The first was the election of Basic Democrats; these then proceeded to elect the President. In the result, President Ayub's calculations proved correct; the constitution had been so made that a quite different result was produced from what might have been produced by direct election. President Ayub won comfortably. The next election of a President was planned for 1970.

INDONESIA

The following passage was written before the change in political direction in Indonesia which led to the eclipse of President Sukarno. The system described here has been discontinued. Nevertheless the account of it seems to be worth retaining since it appears to have been a genuine innovation, and may be revived in some future period.

The other country where there has been innovation is Indonesia. The system is called 'Guided Democracy'. This replaced in 1957 the previous type of government which had been the parliamentary system. President Sukarno was dissatisfied with cabinets created by the manoeuvres of the parties in parliament. He argued that they led to great waste of talent, since the majority parties excluded the minority ones. He wanted to have permanent representation in the cabinet of all the interests which he thought it in the public welfare to have recognized. And this representation was to be on a permanent or slowly changing basis, and not as evanescent as the fortune of parties in parliament. He therefore set up an executive consisting of representatives of all the parties and freed it from the liability of overthrow by the national parliament.

That was the theory of the 'Guided Democracy'. In practice it worked out to strengthen greatly the power of the President. Sukarno included in his cabinet only the representatives of the parties – and groups – which he favoured. The principal constituents were the Nationalists and the Communists. The great Conservative party of the Muslims – the Masjumi – was excluded, and indeed, was forbidden to function.

The Indonesian experiment, though great claims had been made for it, was really less radical than the innovation in Pakistan, which struck at the political party, and made that responsible for the shortcomings of politics. But the Indonesian system was based on the party. It was an attempt to make the government more representative and more lasting by building upon the party structure. But it freed the parties from the danger of eclipse or of defeat by their competitors at the polls and their consequent exclusion from office and their being doomed to running a fractious opposition.

CEYLON

There remains Ceylon. This has not actually made any innovation at all. It is governed, more or less regularly, by the parliamentary constitution which was given to it by the British at the time of independence. But its political life has not been a happy one, as is shown by the turmoil, the communal riots, and the extreme demagogy that have occurred since the fall of the UNP party in 1956.

A popular Prime Minister, Mr Bandaranaike, who ended by being murdered, proposed before his death a scheme of reform. This was less drastic than it seemed, and also less novel, because in some respects it looked back to the constitution of Ceylon which had actually been in force for a time, and is associated with the Donoughmore Commission; but it is none the less interesting. He wanted parliament divided into committees rather than parties, each committee having executive powers to carry out parliament's decisions. He believed that the parliamentary system was immensely wasteful in leaving at least half the members in opposition; and he sought to provide work for all members. Every individual member of parliament would take an effective, active role in the government of the country. The whole parliament would divide up into committees, to which would be allotted the administration. The composition of these committees would be determined by general agreement, or by drawing of lots. As a result, representatives would be known by their individual capacity and their importance would not be estimated by their attitude as party men.

Here again is an attempt at reforming the party system. It was cut short by the fall of the government after defeat at a general election. The party was reinstated in respectability. It is this which most Asian thinkers have taken as the vital element, the pivot on which the whole political system turns. It is still the same with most other countries though there is a growing disillusion with the party system. The most probable centre of change is at present India, which is hardly likely to continue for long with its present constitution intact.

BIBLIOGRAPHY

Sydney D. Bailey. *Parliamentary Government in Southern Asia.* (Hansard Society, 1953.)

A. Gledhill. *Fundamental Rights in India.* (Stevens, London, 1955.)

G. McTurnan Kahin. *Nationalism and Revolution in Indonesia.* (Cornell University Press, Ithaca, New York, 1962.)

POLITICAL INNOVATIONS IN ASIA

Beatrice Lamb. *India: a World in Transition.* (Pall Mall Press, 1963.)

Leslie Palmier. *Indonesia and the Dutch.* (Oxford University Press, 1962.)

R. L. Park and Irene Tinker. *Leadership and Political Institutions in India.* (Princeton University Press, Princeton, N.J., 1959.)

The Burma Socialist Programme Party, The System of Correlation of Man and his Environment. The Philosophy of the Burma Socialist Party. (Rangoon, 1963.)

Hugh Tinker. *India and Pakistan.* (Pall Mall Press, 1962.)

Tarzie Vittachi. *The Brown Sahib.* (André Deutsch, 1962.)

L. Howard Wriggins. *Ceylon: Dilemmas of a New Nation.* (Princeton University Press, Princeton, N.J., 1960.)

THE ROLE OF
THE MILITARY IN ASIA

Aslam Siddiqi

ASIAN nations have emerged independent in a troubled world. Political subordination was a great humiliation; they are therefore keen to win international acceptance and respect. One way to do this is to adopt the democratic form of parliamentary government and set up a liberal welfare state. Other aspirations, ideological, traditional and social, are not lacking. The nations of Asia thus generally set themselves a difficult task to fulfil.

These undertakings usually prove too onerous. Asians lack the experience to organize political parties which is so necessary to run a parliamentary government. Their raw administrations deteriorate and public affairs suffer. The liberal welfare state proves a mere dream. The people soon get frustrated and learn to disbelieve and disrespect their leaders.

The main reason for this failure lies in the constitution of the Asian societies. They are conglomerations of closed primary communities spread out in numerous villages. They have, in varying degrees, what Ibn-i-Khaldun calls 'Asabia' (clannishness). It ensures their continued existence but also gives them a narrow outlook and parochial loyalties. The people thus have communal but no public spirit. They organize themselves around individuals. Such organizations inevitably lack a national outlook. Besides, there are intrinsic flaws. These political organizations lack practicable programmes, public support and funds. Their leaders, and politicians, are constantly jockeying for positions and abusing their influence. When in power, they manipulate economic controls in order to buy support. Rapid industrialization puts too much money into circulation. The result is general deterioration in administration and serious political dissensions.

The liberal State is in principle so constituted that it is always on the very verge of disintegrating. Its constituent elements must for ever threaten to secede, to cut their ties and found their own true church. It tends for ever to degenerate either into a state of anarchy (thus inviting its totalitarian re-unification) or into a state of paralysis (thus inviting programmes for totalitarian activism). The spectre which haunts it is civil war. Ideally it tolerates but that bare minimum of cohesion, unity and consensus that enables hostilities to be suspended.*

To live with such a spectre demands national cohesion and discipline which the emergent nations do not have. The opposition parties take advantage of these 'states of anarchy and paralysis' and thus add to the enormous difficulties of the governments. They indulge in much irresponsible talk, critical and even abusive, of other parties and the government, but show little competence for action. The concept and the role of the loyal opposition is little known and less appreciated. They take full advantage of ugly situations. All the tactics used against the colonial powers are again adopted. Some of the Communist techniques are also employed. Subversion starts working silently and ceaselessly. Like Communists they look around for 'nation-wide crises' and for 'the ruling classes, passing through governmental crises' so that they may 'overthrow the government'. Law and order thus pose a grave problem for the Asian governments. To control the situation, military equipment and personnel become more necessary. Training in the use of new military equipment puts the military in the stream of the modern technological age, and thus much ahead of the politicians in their methods and attitudes. Initially the military forces are called in to control situations of emergency; but soon they feel constrained to stay on, wishing to remove the chronic national maladies in order to build a firm base for economic development and national security.

The Asians hold national independence very dear. Political chaos seems to jeopardize it. They try almost every political combination within the parliamentary system and government to set things right. But none succeeds. They seek to gain stability by concentrating on economic development. This is possible only by accepting the laws of industrial economy. For Asia, this choice amounts to a social revolution. The Asians have to adapt themselves to the new economy and in the process face the inevitable crises. Otherwise they must remain subservient to other powers economically and politically. They thus have to accept the economic revolution. The Asians are thus confronted simultaneously with economic, political and social revolutions. They feel the intense pangs of transformation but have no political philosophy to tackle the desperate situation.

Such a dangerous situation cannot last in any society. Somebody

*Henry S. Kariel, *In Search of Authority* (The Free Press of Glencoe, New York, 1964, p. 245).

has to take control. The Asian nations have, in fact, to select elites (leaders) in the economic, political and social fields, ensure their circulation and discover a position of balance. This is not easy to accomplish. The parliamentary system has already failed to produce leaders of the requisite calibre. In their desperation, they behave like Le Bon's crowds. 'The type of hero dear to crowds will always have the semblance of a Caesar. His insignia attracts them, his authority overawes them and his sword instils them with fear.'* They thus willingly choose military leaders who have on numerous occasions demonstrated their competence.

RIVAL MILITARY DOGMAS

Asia provides a battleground for the encounter of civilizations – Western democracy and Communism. The ancient civilizations of Asia are not mere spectators. They are already trying to pick and choose. How far they succeed, only the future can tell. The military has, however, a key role in this process. Asians are determined to stay independent, internally and externally. This demands efficient military forces. They can be secured only by adopting new techniques. Certain consequences follow. The Western military technique is the thin end of a wedge which cuts asunder every historic culture pattern. The broken pattern inevitably tends to reconstitute itself into an organic whole in the modern environment which raises all sorts of problems. The military thus becomes the instrument of modernity helping a broken civilization discover a new organic whole. What dogma of war the military adopts is of paramount importance for it will largely determine the future pattern of the Asian cultures.

The Western dogma of war is based almost entirely on weapons. The West has therefore concentrated on war technology and produced such deadly weapons that they are hardly usable. This has resulted in a balance of terror and also brought into question the role of military power in world affairs. Apart from their destructiveness, several other considerations inhibit their use. Offensive weapons are technologically superior to defensive weapons so that the destruction of contestants is far more assured than victory. There is lack of experience in the use of these new sophisticated weapons so that the element of uncertainty in planning military action is vastly increased. Moreover, no part of the globe is safe against nuclear weapons so that there are no secure bases from which to launch military attacks. War has thus ceased to be

* Gustave Le Bon, *The Crowd* (The Viking Press, New York, 1960) p. 55.

an instrument of policy so far as super-powers are concerned. Pressure may however be applied against lesser powers. But the danger of escalation and possible confrontation of super-powers always exists. Poor defence, great uncertainties and the immense destructiveness of nuclear weapons have thus brought the Western dogma of war almost to a dead end. The military power has lost very considerably in political utility.

No Asian lesser power can buy these prohibitively costly weapons; it may, however, beg and borrow. But this leads to dependence, which the Asians hate. A vicious circle is thus set up which there is no way to break. Moreover, Western weapons and war techniques have lost flexibility. In the words of General Maxwell D. Taylor they constitute 'the uncertain trumpet' which would not inspire the people to fight. Asians also find them unsuitable. In November 1962, Nehru ascribed the Indian collapse in the Sino-Indian clashes in the Himalayas to inefficient British techniques and unsuitable weapons. India has, therefore, raised the armed militia as a part of the regular armed forces. This marks a break with the Western war dogma.

The dogma of the protracted war, propounded by Mao Tse-tung, has, however, great fascination for the Asians. They feel hopeful when he declares,

Weapons are an important factor in war but not the decisive one: it is man and not material that counts. The contest of forces is not only a contest of military and economic power, but also one of the power and morale of man. Military and economic power must be controlled by man.*

The speed with which Mao captured China in 1949 astonished all, including Stalin. In the Korean War in 1952, the Chinese acquitted themselves quite well. Lieutenant General James M. Gavin writes,

The real tragedy of Korea was that this great nation, with its scientific resources and tremendous industrial capacity, had to accept combat on the terms laid down by a rather primitive Asiatic power.†

He deplores that the fighter-bombers failed to provide effective tactical air support and that 'even horse cavalry divisions were able to move the length of North Korea and participate in the battles'. In the Sino-Indian clashes in 1962, 'swift attack and withdrawal', 'swift concentration and dispersal' and 'quick decision', resulted in the collapse of the Indian forces. In Vietnam, this dogma is again being tried quite success-

* On the Protracted War (Peking, 1954) p. 56.
† War and Peace in the Space Age (Harper, New York, 1958) p. 123.

fully. On the result of this war will largely depend the course of future history in Asia.

Guerrilla warfare admirably suits Asia's primary societies. The members of such societies are bound by loyalties which the strains of war strengthen. The Asian nations can produce or procure only rudimentary weapons which are good enough for the guerrilla fighter. Their battles are mostly defensive which helps build morale. Nationalism is another morale builder. The large populations of Asian nations provide an adequate number of superb man-weapons. Their quality in general is such that according to General Alfred M. Gruenther it takes ten men in conventional forces to nullify one guerrilla fighter. In fact, they alone would be able to operate after a nuclear holocaust. The protracted or guerrilla warfare has clear advantages. But there is a fly in the ointment. As Clausewitz pointed out, the people's war is 'a state of anarchy declared lawful which is as dangerous as a foreign enemy to social order'. This view may not be quite valid in these days of total war. But it does constitute a danger to those military leaders who do not possess anything other than force to hold the loyalty of the people. This underlines the necessity of discovering political objectives which coincide with the aspirations of the people. In fact, the military leaders have to find for their people a political philosophy which probably eludes their grasp.

The adoption of this dogma of the protracted war has consequences not confined to the battlefield alone. It creates an attitude of mind and is responsible for what Klaus Knorr calls 'the David and Goliath Act'* in Asian history. The guerrillas feel a sense of righteousness in fighting Western powers and of working for the greater cause of humanity. They are convinced, in the words of the UN resolution (No. 1653), that 'the use of nuclear and thermo-nuclear weapons is contrary to the laws of humanity and a crime against mankind and civilization'. The converse of this conviction is contempt for those draped with nuclear weapons and always brandishing them. The transference of this attitude to other, more desirable aspects of Western civilization is so easy; and so full of ominous consequences.

LIMITATIONS OF MILITARY METHODS

To the Asian nations, the military leaders do provide stability and, in a restricted sphere, functional competence. The immediate problems are so obvious. They are also easy to handle. In all the emergent

* On the Uses of Military Power in the Nuclear Age (Princeton University Press, Princeton, N.J., 1966) p. 74.

nations corruption, bribery, smuggling, black marketing, hoarding, tax evasion and such other social evils are common. They have to be eradicated, and this is easily done. Drastic measures are immediately adopted. This clean-up operation is undertaken with a fanfare. Numerous regulations prescribing action in various fields are issued. Penalties are enhanced and martial law courts enforce the law rigorously. In the beginning, these measures prove fairly successful. But stray cases of unnecessary hardship inevitably occur. Some people are harassed and even punished without any valid reason except the hostility of neighbours. The quick and ready methods of the martial law have no time for deeper scrutiny of petty complaints. People fear a sort of witch hunt, and conform to the letter of law through fear which brings forth the baser traits of human nature. Thus even in this clean-up operation the military rule sows seeds of discontent. People therefore feel apprehensive and low in their morale.

This low morale is something which the military leaders dread. For such a development means collapse of the national base which they seek to preserve and strengthen. Their first constructive step is therefore to control all the information, news and views which adversely affect national morale. A sullen silence descends upon the people. But the military leaders have a different view of the situation. They are quite clear in their minds and consciences. They welcome freedom of expression provided it contributes to national morale. They cannot tolerate it at the expense of national morale and stability. Where to draw the line is difficult for anyone to decide. In their impatience, they enforce a control on the freedom of expression and thus hamper creative thinking, without which no nation can prosper.

It is, however, wrong to conclude that the military leaders are afraid of ideas or their expression as such. Their strong point in fact is familiarity with new ideas and new techniques. They are the apostles of modernity. They are much ahead of their people. What they resent is that some ideas which are vigorously propounded, are hardly relevant to the national situation, create confusion in the public mind and tend to lower the national morale. Theirs is like Plato's attitude towards poets whom he honours and respects but would like to have driven out of his 'well ordered state' for 'manufacturing images'. The military leaders have respect for the pedlars of ideas; but are intolerant of their activities which create suspicions and doubts in the public mind and lower national morale.

For the same reason, they enforce discipline in all political activities. The trappings of the normal political institutions are maintained but they are so worked that their verdicts are mostly in confirmation of decisions already taken. The new government has thus the semblance of the parliamentary democracy; but its essence is that of the military parade.

Decisions by debate are unwelcome. Such a process brings out different viewpoints which seem to indicate disorder and disunity. They are presumed to lower national morale. The converse of this process is very much appreciated. If decisions are taken with complete or near unanimity, then national unity is given a public demonstration which boosts national morale. This is an advantage which military leaders cannot miss. General elections are therefore discouraged; they inevitably lead to rival viewpoints being presented to an ill-informed public, creating confusion. Instead, referendums and plebiscites are encouraged. Here no viewpoints are to be canvassed; the people have only to express approval or disapproval of the decisions presented to them. They demonstrate collective thinking or monolithism, so near the heart of the military leaders.

The same attitude is adopted towards political parties, assemblies and other institutions. Formation of several political parties is discouraged. Political activity is monopolized or restricted to very few parties. This helps collective thinking and therefore national morale. Assemblies are intended to ratify decisions, already taken. Their sessions do not provide occasions for searching analysis of national problems or even debate and constructive criticism of national policies. They are no more than ceremonials and are intended to boost national morale.

Difficulties are inevitable in manipulating public life. In their impatience some military leaders use force. But

stringency begets resistance and every now and then you are forced to tighten the screw. The result is an extreme form of oppression. ... Whenever terrorism, particularly political terrorism, starts in a country, you can never eradicate it from the bones of the people. It provides an outlet for man's most primitive and animal instincts.*

The mistake of using force is, however, often made. Nations get divided and so do the military forces. The sword again proves the arbiter; and the strong men have to yield place to the stronger or craftier men. Nations blighted by such leaders are lost.

But the military leaders who understand and respect the limits of the military power, may prove saviours of the Asian nations. The

*President Mohammad Ayub Khan, *Friends Not Masters* (Oxford University Press, 1967), p. 80.

primary societies of Asia are on the move. Internally, they have to face the strains and stresses of national transformation; externally, the environment is not too friendly. They do need protection which military leaders promise to provide. Their success consists in giving this protection the form of institutions, acceptable to the people at large. 'My anxiety was to establish conditions and institutions so that people acquire a sense of participation in their own affairs.'* But institutions are coercive rather than enacted and they gain recognition only gradually. They have to fit into the institutional complex of a particular society before they become established. This is a difficult and time-consuming process. Experiments like the system of basic democracies or the guided democracy have therefore to be given time to grow and also sympathetic consideration before being condemned as political ruses. If the military leaders can additionally reconstitute that part of their culture which they have selected into an organic whole and adapt it to contemporary conditions, then they have amply justified themselves. This phenomenon however is not frequent.

The role of the military in Asia is thus a transitory and also a precarious one. The situation is such that risks have to be taken. The military leaders only symbolize the urgent need of providing steadiness to the Asian societies in the course of economic, social and political transformation. If helped in their venture, Asian nations may go forward and fulfil the large task they have set themselves. Otherwise they will fall by the roadside and prove sources of chronic danger to world peace.

BIBLIOGRAPHY

President Mohammad Ayub Khan. *Friends Not Masters*. (Oxford University Press, 1967.)

Brian Crozier. *South-East Asia in Turmoil*. (Penguin Books, 1965.)

William Gurtteridge. *Armed Forces in New States*. (Oxford University Press, 1962.)

Richard Harris. *Independence and After*. (Oxford University Press, 1962.)

Henry S. Kariel. *In Search of Authority*. (The Free Press of Glencoe, New York, 1964.)

Klaus Knorr. *On the Uses of Military Power in the Nuclear Age*. (Princeton University Press, 1966.)

Mao Tse-tung. *Selected Military Writings*. (Foreign Languages Press, Peking, 1963.)

Survival. Journal published by the Institute of Strategic Studies, London.

Hugh Tinker. *Ballot Box and Bayonet*. (Oxford University Press, 1964.)

*ibid.

THE MILITARY SITUATION
IN ASIA TODAY

David Wood

IT is very tempting to consider the overall Asian military situation
from a viewpoint of China's expansionist or aggressive intentions and
other Asian countries' reactions to such a threat. China has after all
over a third of the total population of Asia and has traditionally
considered herself to be the greatest of its powers. China is moreover
the first Asian country to have a limited nuclear capability, even if her
means of delivery for such weapons are not yet in existence. Finally,
in their statements of policy the Chinese leaders are firmly wedded to
the concept of spreading the Communist revolution throughout Asia,
and China has a small number of neighbour states who share these
ideological views.

However, there is much to indicate that the conditions which
applied in Western Europe soon after 1945, namely a monolithic
Communist bloc threatening a more loosely knit alliance of non-Communist states, simply do not apply to Asia today. In the first place, not
one but two major Communist powers have strategic interests in
Asia, and these powers, the Soviet Union and China, have recently
made no major attempt to co-ordinate their policies. Indeed, at
present, they are in direct competition with each other in many spheres.
Secondly, both of these powers have chosen for the most part to
pursue their aims by political manipulation or by promotion of
insurgency warfare rather than by the deployment of field armies.
Finally, the emergence of many newly independent or newly formed
states in the Asian area and the much earlier stage of political evolution
reached in many of them (when considered in Western terms) means
that there are many more extant territorial claims and local power
rivalries than in the Europe of the 1940s and 50s.

CHINA

However, any assessment of the military situation must start with
China. She has, with 2,700,000 regular troops and a civilian militia of
many millions, the largest standing armed forces in Asia. She has land

borders with two major powers (the USSR and India), and with seven smaller powers (Mongolia, Afghanistan, Nepal, Burma, Laos, North Vietnam, and North Korea), and a long coastline bringing her into maritime contact with a third major power (Japan). Her forces have – and this is a factor of great importance in an increasingly disarmed world – recent experience of sustained combat operations in the campaign against the Nationalists (1946–9), the Korean War (1950–53) and the invasion of India (1962). All these factors enable China to conduct military operations outside her borders if she chooses to do so. How has she exploited her advantages?

We find when we examine the Chinese armed forces more closely, that the equipment is of poor quality by European standards and in many respects inferior to that of neighbours such as India, Japan and Indonesia. In tanks and aircraft for instance, China is at least a generation behind the Soviet Union, and certainly that much behind the American and European countries. Her Navy is negligible by great power standards, consisting of twenty obsolescent escort ships and roughly the same number of ageing submarines. Her one* missile-firing submarine does not have any missiles. One of the greatest difficulties facing the Chinese Army is its lack of adequate motor and rail transport. As compared with the Soviet Army, the Chinese appear to have very few armoured personnel carriers, and their facility for lorry transport is restricted by the state of the road system. Although the railway system is adequate in the Peking area and in Manchuria, it is weak in other areas, particularly on the border with the Soviet Union.

China makes up for these deficiences to some extent, by her numbers, but it may be argued that she has that many more potential fronts to fight on, and that much of her armed forces have become engaged in the last two years either in internal security duties or in taking over some of the duties of the civilian administration. It is hard to see, to take one example, how China is fit to engage the Soviet Union on the broad open spaces of Central Asia. Out of a total of 120 Chinese regular divisions, only four are armoured, whereas the Soviets have over forty tank divisions in an army of the same size, and would outgun the Chinese at almost every level. Again, although the Chinese Air Force, with about 2,500 aircraft, is often described as the fourth largest in the world, it consists mostly of obsolescent types, and could not at this stage provide effective defence of the main Chinese strategic targets against a determined bomber attack either by the USA or the Soviet Union (not to speak of a strategic missile attack). China's

* Recent reports state that a second is being built.

own strategic bombing capability against defended targets outside China is similarly negligible. Although China is still primarily an agricultural country, there is a small number of large and important towns or industrial complexes which would be vulnerable to aerial bombardment. One thinks of cities like Peking, Shanghai, Canton, Wuhan, Mukden and Harbin, and there are obvious industrial targets such as the Ta-Ching oil-field and the iron and steel plant at An-Shan. In addition, the nuclear production and test sites at such places as Paotow, Lanchow, Kokonor and Lop Nor are obvious and very vulnerable targets.

One may assume from this that the military role of the Chinese armed forces is still seen by its leaders as one to be played inside China (i.e. in defence of Chinese territory) or to bring aid to a threatened ally with a common border (North Korea, and conceivably North Vietnam) or on rare occasions to strike at the exposed positions of a weak opponent (northern and north-east India). Certainly the current deployment of the Chinese Army with its preponderance in the Peking–Manchuria region and in the coastal belt from Shantung to Hong Kong shows it is still preoccupied with the need to guard against an invasion from Taiwan, and to a lesser extent the resumption of hostilities in Korea. A similar build-up of forces in the southern area near the border with Vietnam has not been observed.

How does China's acquisition of a nuclear capability fit into all this? China has carried out a series of nuclear tests, culminating in the explosion of a thermo-nuclear device on 17 June 1967. This means that she almost certainly has built up a stockpile of perhaps forty nuclear bombs with yields of up to thirty kilotons, and that she is on the path to possessing a similar stockpile of thermo-nuclear bombs with much heavier warheads (perhaps between two and seven megatons). It does not mean that she has an operational stock of H-bombs now, and she certainly has not the means of delivering them.

After building bombs, a prospective nuclear power must have either long-range bombers, inter-continental or at least intermediate-range missiles, or long-distance missile-firing submarines to deliver them. China's only strategic bombers are twelve twenty-year-old Tu-4s with a maximum range of 3,000 miles which would undoubtedly be shot down by any modern air defence. She is building perhaps two G-class submarines which are equipped for firing missiles from the surface, but two submarines do not make up a deterrent force and the missile-launching equipment had not been operationally tested by late 1967. All the indications are, in fact, that China intends to base her delivery system on missiles to be launched either from land or at sea. The nuclear test carried out in October 1966 was, it is claimed, carried out by means of a guided missile, but the range of this cannot have been much more than 400 miles.

China clearly has far to go in establishing an operational squadron of missiles with over 2,500 miles range, the point at which MRBMs and IRBMs become ICBMs. At present she carries out missile firings in Sinkiang, but at over 1,500 miles range she will run out of land space. The Soviet Union is unlikely to offer her facilities, and the Indians will not take kindly to Chinese missiles using Indian air space on their way to a splash-down in the Indian Ocean. China will have to carry out such tests in the Pacific, and this will mean, apart from other diplomatic considerations, that she will have to greatly expand her conventional Navy if only to organize the tracking and collection of missiles.

Taking all these considerations into account and assuming a normal development of the nuclear and missile programme in China, it is possible that China may have a small number of medium-range missiles with low-grade nuclear warheads that can reach targets in India, Vietnam and Japan by late 1968 or early 1969, and that by 1970 her missiles may be able to reach farther targets such as the Central USSR and American island bases in the Pacific. It is unlikely, however, and this is the view expressed by the retiring American Secretary of Defence, Mr McNamara, that she will have an operational stock of ICBMs of the range that the USA and the Soviet Union now possess (5,000–10,000 miles) until the mid 1970s. Even if she produces the weapons, she will have the major problems of guidance and targeting to deal with, and it is unlikely that she will receive any help in this field from the Americans or the Russians.

CHINA'S NEIGHBOURS

Of the nine sovereign states with which China shares a common border, four have Communist Party governments, (Soviet Union, Mongolia, North Korea and North Vietnam), one pursues neutral policies but has a left-wing government (Burma) and a further three pursue anti-Communist policies and maintain ties of various degree with Western governments (India, Nepal and Laos). In all these countries, the Soviet Union competes actively with China for power and influence, and at the risk of some generalization, it can be said that she has had the upper hand in three of these countries (Afghanistan, North Korea and North Vietnam) while Mongolia is virtually a Soviet satellite. Only in Nepal, Burma and Laos has China's influence been perhaps stronger. The most remarkable aspect of this situation is that in the two Communist countries closest to China's borders (North Korea and North Vietnam), and furthermore two of the militarily strongest countries in the area, Moscow's influence both at the ideological and military assistance level seems to be greater than Peking's.

Certainly China has not succeeded in constructing a formal alliance system of the Communist countries on her borders in the same way as the Soviet Union has with the Warsaw Pact. If there are formal defence commitments between China and such countries as North Korea and North Vietnam, they have not been made public. China's participation in the Korean War can be seen now as a reaction to the military threat to her own borders, rather than as a demonstration of ideological commitment to the Pyongyang regime.

North Korea maintains regular forces of nearly 400,000 men. Almost the entire equipment of Army, Navy and Air Force is Soviet in origin, and item by item it is superior to that of the Chinese. The North Korean Army has probably more modern tanks than the Chinese Army, and like the North Vietnamese it operates SA-2 surface-to-air guided missiles whose presence in the Chinese air defence system has not yet been confirmed. The North Korean Air Force is believed to have been given two squadrons of MiG-21 supersonic fighters by the Russians, whereas the Chinese are only now beginning to manufacture these aircraft for themselves.

A similar situation exists as regards North Vietnam's armed forces. The North Vietnamese Army has, it is true, received a proportion of their light arms from China, and the Navy has received some patrol boats and gunboats, but the vast majority of the heavier equipment, including a few tanks, about 120 jet fighters of the MiG series and the all-important anti-aircraft guns, radar control systems and surface-to-air guided missiles have been supplied by the Russians. A Soviet aid and training mission of perhaps 1,500 men aids the North Vietnamese war effort, but no Chinese. The only concrete contribution by China to the Vietnam war is their stationing of 20,000 railway engineer troops along the railway lines from Hanoi to China with a further 20,000 anti-aircraft artillery men to protect these engineers.

Until recently, most of this Soviet war equipment came into North Vietnam by rail and thus through China, and one could argue that China's contribution was to make this supply link possible. During 1966 and 1967, however, following the ideological rift between Moscow and Peking and Soviet allegations that China was appropriating some of the supplies for her own uses, it appears that the Soviets have been bringing most of the material in by sea via the port of Haiphong. Thus China's material contribution to the North Vietnamese war effort seems even less.

The basic deployment and capability of China's forces, coupled with the fact that she cannot count her immediate neighbours as true allies but rather as fellow-Communist states owing allegiance to her ideological rivals, argues that militarily China is in a defensive rather than an offensive posture. This is borne out even more clearly when we consider the situation on her long land border with the Soviet Union. This border is split into two sectors by Mongolia, which from a political point of view is heavily under Soviet influence. The USSR renewed a defence treaty with Mongolia in 1966, and there are indications that the treaty has provision for the presence in Mongolia of Soviet troops.

The border between Mongolia and China was demarcated by treaty in 1962, and the Chinese have recently complained of frontier violations. It seems that a large number of Khazakh tribesmen fled into Mongolia from Sinkiang soon afterwards, and the Chinese authorities then accused the Soviet authorities of abducting them. In February 1967 the Chinese Foreign Minister stated that the Russians had transferred thirteen divisions from Germany to the Far East, and were building up their Air Force there.

It is probably true that the Soviet Union has reinforced its Far Eastern Army in the last two years, but there is no evidence of such drastic denuding of the forces in Germany. What probably happened was the rotation of individual divisions, and this would at least have the effect of moving some of the best Russian armour to the China front. The most likely estimate of Soviet forces in the Far East is about fifteen divisions east of Lake Baikal and eight divisions in that part of Soviet Central Asia opposite the border with China – a total of about 250,000 men, including four armoured and two airborne divisions, and a Strategic Air Force of about 200 medium bombers.* Mongolia itself, which forms the link between these two sectors, provides only one division with cast-off Soviet equipment, but the USSR could undoubtedly deploy troops in its territory if hostilities broke out.

Significantly, China does not seem to have attempted a similar type of build-up on her side of the border. Current strength is estimated at

* Malcolm Mackintosh, 'The Soviet Generals' View of China in the 60s', in *Sino-Soviet Military Revolutions*, edited by Raymond L. Garthoff (Praeger, New York, 1966).

five regular divisions in each of the Sinkiang and Inner Mongolian Military Regions, with six divisions of less well equipped border troops strung out along the whole border. The main armour reserve (in so far as China has one) remains in the Peking area. It is probable that the Chinese leaders have concluded that it is not in their interest to confront the Soviets in this theatre, and they are undoubtedly justified in this belief from a military standpoint since the open terrain would be greatly to the advantage of the Soviet armour and tactical airpower.

The only offensive military actions which China has taken in the last two years have been on the frontier with India, and these have been only minor border incursions. It would seem that when China invaded India in 1962, she had sensed a weak point in the Himalayan defences and after fully exploiting this weakness, halted her advance when she could have gone on further. Since the débâcle of 1962 the Indian mountain defences have been considerably strengthened, and Chinese policy on this frontier seems to be to keep the Indian defence effort at full stretch by occasional pin-pricks. There is no evidence that China is planning another full-scale invasion of Indian territory.

As regards the Chinese military commitment to North Vietnam, the Chinese Prime Minister has in the past stated that China will not attempt to provoke a war with the United States over this issue, but that an invasion of North Vietnam would be regarded as an invasion of China. No further clarification of this policy has been made, in particular as to how American entry into the northern part of the demilitarized zone (a move which has been advocated recently by some American military circles) would affect the situation. Certainly the Chinese Army in its present deployment would have considerable logistic difficulties in bringing military support to an invaded North Vietnam. Communications between Vietnam and the neighbouring provinces of Yunnan and Kwangsi are not good, and comparatively few regular troops are stationed in this border area.

THE VIETNAM WAR

The military situation in the area immediately to the south of China is of course dominated by the Vietnam War, which has been in progress in its present intensified form for nearly five years. From a strict viewpoint of the overall strategic situation in Asia, the conflict in Vietnam is irrelevant since it is basically a struggle for political power in South Vietnam in which various factions of the Indo-Chinese peoples are engaged. What has made the war so dominant a feature of the Asian, and indeed the global scene, is the gradual involvement, for ideological and strategic reasons, of the two super-powers and of five Asian powers (Thailand, the Philippines, South Korea, Australia and New Zealand) – Cambodia and Laos being counted as Indo-Chinese countries more directly engaged. However, the United States is the only major outside power to have become directly involved in the fighting, and so it may be worthwhile to consider at this point the real military interests and commitments of the United States in Asia, and how this has affected or led up to her present heavy military involvement on the Asian mainland.

There have been American commercial and diplomatic interests in such areas as China, Japan and the Philippines ever since the 19th century, but the current military presence dates from the capture during the 1945 war by American forces of the territories occupied by Japan during that war, including eventually Japan itself. After 1945 the latent military threat from Japan was seen to have died away, but the emergence of a Communist regime in mainland China, and the American decision to support the Chiang Kai-shek regime, gave the American forces new responsibilities. In 1951 America signed a security pact with Australia and New Zealand, which recognized that these countries would in future look to the USA rather than to Great Britain for military aid.

FOREIGN COMMITMENTS

American participation in the Korean War resulted from a joint call by the United Nations rather than a specific American commitment to South Korea, but a mutual defence assistance pact between the two countries was signed in August 1953 immediately after the armistice, and since that time America has maintained two divisions in South Korea and is pledged to resist any aggression from the North. The Japan–USA security treaty of April 1952 gives America the right to maintain armed forces and bases in Japan, and a similar treaty in December 1954 between the Chinese Nationalist Government and the USA committed America to defend Taiwan and the off-shore islands. Finally in September 1954, Australia, France, New Zealand, Pakistan, the Philippines, Thailand, the United Kingdom and the USA signed the Manila pact which eventually set up the South-East Asia Treaty Organization (SEATO). This treaty committed the member nations to build up collective economic and military strengths and to consult with a view to joint defensive action in the event of direct or indirect aggression against a signator, or against the so-designated 'protocol' states of Laos, Cambodia, and South Vietnam.

The SEATO treaty was mainly conceived in the light of the Dulles strategy of 'containment' of Communist expansionism, both Soviet and Chinese, but provision was also made for joint action against such 'indirect' aggression as the type of guerrilla or insurgency warfare popularized by Mao Tse-tung and Vo Nguyen Giap. This type of war had already been practised by the Huks in the Philippines, by the nationalists in Indonesia and by Communist jungle-fighters in Malaya as well as in China and Vietnam, and apart from the Korean War, was to be the main pattern of warfare in Asia until the Vietnam conflict assumed its current scale. But it will be seen from this survey that by the late 1950s America had taken on military commmitments to no fewer than seven independent Asian countries, and this figure becomes ten if one includes the three Indo-Chinese countries subject to the separate protocol of the SEATO treaty.

America had, however, stationed very few troops on the soil of her allies after 1954. Apart from the two divisions in South Korea and large advisory and training missions in countries such as Japan, Taiwan, the Philippines and Thailand, and the possession of naval and air facilities in these countries, the USA kept the bulk of her Pacific theatre forces either in the USA or on Hawaii or in such American-controlled territories as Okinawa, Guam, and Midway. Britain, together with Australia and New Zealand, deployed probably a greater number of troops at this time at her garrisons in Malaya, Singapore, Borneo and Hong Kong. President Kennedy sent troops to Laos at the time of the 1961 crisis but these were withdrawn after an agreement was reached. It was not until the gradual build-up in Vietnam after 1963 that American combat troops were committed in any large numbers to the Asian mainland, beginning first with South Vietnam and in the last two years to Thailand also. There are still no American ground forces in Cambodia or Laos.

The determined support given by American regular forces to the South Vietnamese Army led other Asian countries to commit combat forces to this theatre – first the South Koreans, then the Australians and New Zealanders, finally the Filipinos and Thais. Although in the case of Australia and New Zealand, the Philippines and Thailand, this support could have been given under the 'indirect aggression' clause of the SEATO treaty, it does not seem that the treaty was invoked in this respect. The same consideration applies of course to the USA, but only in retrospective justification for America's Vietnam policy has the SEATO commitment sometimes been mentioned by its leaders; the original military support to South Vietnam was arranged on a strictly bilateral basis.

The military situation in Vietnam in July 1968 was that regular and irregular armed forces of the six countries mentioned above plus those of North and South Vietnam were taking part in the fighting, which was both of a guerrilla and conventional nature. There was no precise front-line between the combatants and large areas of South Vietnam are disputed for political control between the insurgents and the South Vietnamese government. Four other countries (China, the Soviet Union, Laos and Cambodia) either supply arms and equipment or allow their territories to be used to provide base facilities. No country involved has declared war on any other. All ground fighting has taken place within the borders of South Vietnam or in the demilitarized zone between North and South Vietnam. Bombing raids have been conducted against targets in both South and North Vietnam by the United States, and in the South by her partners.

South Vietnam maintains regular and para-military armed forces of about 750,000 men. The para-military forces and about half of the regular divisions are employed in a static defence role, and are equipped only with infantry weapons. The mobile striking force of the South Vietnam Army (ARVN) is mainly confined to the Airborne Division and the Marine Brigade (about 40,000 men). American, South Korean, Australian, New Zealand, Philippine and Thai forces operating in South Vietnam are employed both in the static defence and in the mobile retaliatory roles.

The regular armed forces of North Vietnam total about 450,000 men; there is in addition a regionally organized armed militia of at least 500,000. The Frontal and Coastal Security troops and the People's Armed Security Force total another 20,000. The regular Army provides the equivalent of thirteen infantry divisions (as opposed to the eleven divisions of the South Vietnamese Army), and of these perhaps eight (equivalent to 120,000 men) have been identified fighting in South Vietnam or deployed in the demilitarized zone north of the 17th parallel. A further 40,000 regular troops are operating in north and eastern Laos in support of the Pathet Lao forces. It is clear from these figures that a major part of the North Vietnamese Army has still not been committed to military operations outside North Vietnam itself.

The territory of South Vietnam is divided into four Corps areas;

American and other allied forces share this Corps organization with the ARVN. American ground forces in South Vietnam in July 1968 totalled 480,000; there were, in addition, 65,000 Air Force personnel. There were also 48,000 South Korean, 8,000 Australian, 2,500 Thai, 2,200 Philippine and 550 New Zealand ground and support forces.

American air strikes on North and South Vietnam have been made from aircraft carriers stationed in the South China Sea, from air bases on Guam and in Thailand, and from South Vietnam itself; the Royal Laotian Air Force has made air strikes against suspected North Vietnamese concentrations inside Laotian territory. There are 60,000 American ground and air personnel in Thailand. Coastal supply bases have been constructed by the Americans at Qui Nhon, Nha Trang, Cam Ranh, and Vung Tau in South Vietnam, and at Sattahip Bay in Thailand. The United States Seventh Fleet, now operating mostly off the Vietnam coast, includes some 80,000 Navy and Marine personnel, some 200 ships (including five attack carriers) and about 700 aircraft (including 250 light bombers).

Communist regular and irregular forces in South Vietnam totalled about 270,000 in July 1968; these consisted of about 150,000 organized in battle units, 150,000 in small guerrilla units and 170,000 in logistical support units and political cadres. Of the 270,000, about 85,000 were North Vietnamese regular troops, the remainder having been recruited in South Vietnam. Troops and supplies from North Vietnam are brought in through parts of Laotian and Cambodian territory (the 'Ho Chi Minh Trail'), and by sea as well as directly across the 17th parallel. Communist forces maintain no air forces in the territory of South Vietnam.

South Vietnamese regular and irregular forces have had about 70,000 fatal casualties since 1962; in the same period over 30,000 civilians have been killed, 70,000 wounded, and 40,000 reported missing as a result of insurgent action. American and other allied forces have had over 28,000 killed and 175,000 wounded in the same period. Communist fatal casualties in South Vietnam since 1962 are estimated at about 300,000. The American forces have lost over 3,800 aircraft in five years as a result of military operations in Vietnam. This figure comprises 2,200 fixed-wing aircraft and 1,600 helicopters, and includes aircraft destroyed in accidents or by ground attacks on airfields. About eighty North Vietnamese aircraft have been destroyed in the air or on the ground in North Vietnam.

VIETNAM – THE STRATEGY

This is not the occasion to make a detailed analysis of strategy in the Vietnam War, but the following very broad conclusions can be made from the five years of intensified activity following the American decision to reinforce their small combat element in 1962.

1. The American bombing of targets in North Vietnam has failed to break the will of the Hanoi government to continue supporting the insurgency in South Vietnam, or their ability to transfer men and equipment to the fighting area.

2. The key to the security of South Vietnam lies, as it has always done, with the ability of the Saigon government to extend its writ over the *whole* territory of South Vietnam, and of the South Vietnamese Army to obtain and preserve complete military control over the areas for which it is given responsibility.

3. The American armed forces, whatever their numerical strength, can only support the South Vietnamese authorities in this task. Local military successes, by themselves, do not ensure pacification of particular areas.

4. Just as the Americans and other allied contingents cannot win the war on their own, neither is it likely that, at their present level of strength, they can be dislodged from the areas for which they are responsible, by force of arms of the Viet Cong or the North Vietnamese Army.

5. The Soviet Union will increase its supply of war material to North Vietnam, but is unlikely to send troops, either overtly or under the guise of 'volunteers'. The Chinese government is unlikely to become militarily involved in the Vietnam War unless the Americans choose to invade that part of North Vietnamese territory close to the Chinese border.

In this context, the establishment of a constitutional government in Saigon in the summer of 1967 undoubtedly strengthened the hand of the South Vietnamese government. Many observers have always felt that the indifferent performance of the South Vietnamese Army ever since the departure of the French was the real reason for the continuation of insurgency in Vietnam, and the existence of a stronger government has enabled some of the inefficient and corrupt provincial governors and military chiefs to be dismissed. The Americans have also paid more attention to training and re-equipping of the South Vietnamese Army, and a real measure of progress from Saigon's point of view will be seen as ARVN units take over the combat military role from

DAVID WOOD

American and other allied units that have previously performed this task.

One of the most interesting aspects of the Vietnam War is the way in which other non-Communist Asian countries have become involved. The size of the contingents which the governments of South Korea, Australia, New Zealand, the Philippines and Thailand have sent may be small compared both to their total armed forces and to the American and South Vietnamese forces engaged, but for all these countries the actual commitment of combat troops has had important political effects. In South Korea, for instance, it seems that the widely admired performance of her troops in Vietnam has greatly increased national self-respect and confidence and has contributed to the stability of the Park government and economic prosperity.

BREAK-UP OF COMMONWEALTH LINKS

In Australia and New Zealand, the token commitment has driven home to the public the break-up of the traditional British Commonwealth defence ties in the area and emphasized the increasing allegiance of these countries to American defence commitments as suggested by the existence of the ANZUS and SEATO Pacts. Australia and New Zealand still contribute an infantry battalion each to the 'Commonwealth Brigade' stationed at Terendak in Malaya. This in turn forms part of the Commonwealth Strategic Reserve, which has an undefined commitment to SEATO. Other elements of this strategic reserve are the British Far East Fleet and Air Force based on Singapore, as well as approximately six British battalions remaining in Malaysia/Singapore. With the British government having taken its decision to withdraw most of its land forces in the area by the early 1970s and with the Malaysian government not showing any interest at this stage in filling the vacuum, it seems that the Commonwealth Strategic Reserve will gradually be allowed to fade away. Australia and New Zealand, who may find it convenient in the near future to co-ordinate their defence forces into a single entity, will presumably concentrate on defence of their own territory (including Papua) and fulfilment of commitments to any allies in the Asian area.

AMERICA'S ALLIES

The contribution of the Philippines and Thailand to the Vietnam War reflect rather the American desire that the non-European members

446

of SEATO should play a larger part in countering Communist aggression in the SEATO area. The decision to commit combat troops was reluctantly taken by the Manila government, but the Philippines has had enough experience of 'People's War' with the Huk rebellion (now seemingly resurgent) to know where their true interests lie. Philippine armed forces are very small for a population of nearly 33 million, the Army contributing only one combat-ready division with a further four in cadre form. From the point of view of its own defence, the Philippines benefits from having such big American naval and air bases as Subic Bay and Clark Field on its territory, but from a professional military point of view also it must profit by giving some of its troops actual combat experience in Vietnam.

Thailan d is in a position of being more directly threatened by any spread of Communist 'insurgency' movements through North Vietnam and Laos, and certainly some acts of terrorism have been reported in its north-eastern provinces, but it is a moot point whether the big American military build-up in Thailand has been as a result of or has led to the Communist threat to Thailand. Although this build-up has most recently been associated with obtaining better facilities for bombing raids on North Vietnam (Thailand's eastern border is nearer North than South Vietnam), the Americans originally moved stores and facilities into Thailand as a second line of defence should Laos fall completely under Communist control; it was in this area that the 'domino' theory was especially held to apply.

Laos (which lies in a narrow strip between Thailand and North Vietnam, with Cambodia immediately to the south) has been militarily a divided and unstable country ever since the Viet Minh and Pathet Lao forces invaded the territory in April 1953. Although minor insurgency and counter-insurgency operations are continuing all the time, and there have been spasmodic outbreaks of fighting, a major flare-up with the participating troops from outside countries has up to now been averted. The Americans supply the Royalist forces with light arms, light strike aircraft and a large military mission, but there are no American troops in Laos. The Soviet Union and China have similarly supplied military equipment to the Pathet Lao, but not any troops. North Vietnam has, however, had a sizeable contingent of its regular army operating in the Communist-dominated area for some years.

The military situation in Laos is that the Pathet Lao with North Vietnamese support control the north and most of the eastern part of the country including the Plain of Jars and most of the frontier with Vietnam. Part of the 'Ho Chi Minh Trail' from North to South Vietnam runs through this area, and the North Vietnamese clearly have an interest in expanding and improving this road network. The Royalist forces maintain uneasy control over the rest of the country, but where-ever the Pathet Lao put in determined attacks the Royalists normally have to give ground.

Cambodia, lying to the south of Laos and to the west of South Vietnam, has managed up till now to keep itself free from direct military operations. This is partly due to geography but also to the determinedly neutral policies pursued by Prince Sihanouk. The ruler has accepted arms from France, the Soviet Union and China (light tanks from France, medium artillery, anti-aircraft guns and jet fighters from the Soviet Union, light arms from China) but has kept free from military entanglements with the Americans. He has not gone in for heavy, prestige equipment but has concentrated on building small, mobile units especially equipped for border defence and counter-insurgency operations.

BURMA

Burma, which lies immediately to the west of Thailand, occupies in many ways a unique position in Asia from a strategic point of view. She has a short frontier with China and politically has enjoyed fairly close relations with the Peking government, yet most of her military equipment has come from Western (mostly American) sources. On the other hand, Burma belongs to no military alliance such as SEATO, or political grouping such as the British Commonwealth, as do in one form or another all her non-Communist Asian neighbours. Burma's main military preoccupations have been those of internal security, with the Karen and Shan tribesmen carrying on a running fight with the government authorities ever since independence was attained in 1948.

Recently, relations between Burma and China have taken a turn for the worse. Chinese technicians embarked on a £20 million economic aid programme in 1964, but it soon became clear that the completion of one of the projects, the bridge over the river Salween at Kunlong, would enable the Chinese to command a perfect invasion route into north-west Thailand. The Burmese leader, General Ne Win, gave assurances that Burma would not support such a threat to Thailand, and the Chinese have retaliated by encouraging the Burmese people, including a small Communist Party, to overthrow the Ne Win regime, Marxist though it may be in many respects. As a result of this attempted subversion, Burma may be expected to consolidate its military ties with non-Communist countries and especially the USA.

THE SUB-CONTINENT

The military situation in the Indian sub-continent concerns two separate areas, the border between India and West Pakistan, where Indian and Pakistani troops have continued to confront each other, especially in the Kashmir-Punjab sector, since the fighting of September 1965, and the Himalayas where 100,000 Chinese troops in Tibet (now a province and Military Region of China) have continued to threaten both India and its 'protected' States of Sikkim and Bhutan. Although the military aspects of operations in these two areas are quite separate, there is now a strategic connexion in that China has started to give economic military aid to Pakistan.

This is an ironic situation, in that Pakistan is a member of the two 'Western' military alliances, the Central Treaty Organization (CENTO) and SEATO, and had previously received all its arms and much military training from America. Pakistan's reaction to the fighting of September 1965 was to increase her armed forces from the comparatively modest level of 220,000 to the present 325,000, and to seek the necessary equipment for these units as well as replacing her war losses. Since the Americans would not supply any further arms, and both Britain and France were traditional suppliers to India, after the war Pakistan turned to China and her request was accepted. China is believed to have delivered to Pakistan the material to equip two new infantry divisions, as well as about 50 T-59 medium tanks, 70 MiG-19 jet fighters and possibly a squadron of Il-28 light jet bombers. The most remarkable aspect of this transaction is that the T-59s and MiG-19s must be in very short supply inside China's own armed forces, yet they have not hesitated to make them available to a non-Communist country.

China clearly hopes that its help in expanding and re-equipping the Pakistani forces will increase India's defence commitments. India's problem is that its armed forces must be organized and equipped to fight on two separate fronts, moreover fronts which require different types of units and of equipment. Following India's defeat by China in 1962, plans were made to almost double the size of the Army and Air Force, with particular relevance to units equipped for mountain warfare, and this expansion now seems to be complete with a total of nine mountain infantry divisions, and light tanks and transport aircraft specially suited to the demands of mountain warfare. However, the response to the fighting with Pakistan of 1965 seems to have been to strengthen the conventional infantry divisions and armour correspondingly, so that the Army with approximately 900,000 men is now well over its previously sanctioned level of 825,000. To this extent, the supposed Chinese strategy may be said to have succeeded.

Not being a member of SEATO or having any defence pact with the USA, India did not receive any major military equipment from the Americans, and her traditional suppliers were Britain and France. India has begun a limited arms-producing industry of her own, and is now able to produce most small arms, a medium tank, light warships and some types of jet aircraft under licence. However, with her recent rapid build-up of units, she has needed outside suppliers as much as Pakistan has, and when Britain suspended aid in September 1965, India turned even more to the Soviet Union from whom she had previously bought transport aircraft, helicopters and some light tanks. Although Britain announced the resumption of arms supplies in March 1966, India by then had found herself more than satisfied with her Russian equipment and the Soviet Union has now become the major outside supplier of arms to India. It is believed that she has delivered T-54 tanks (the equivalent of the Chinese T-59), SA-2 surface-to-air guided missiles and two submarines, and the Indian authorities are now assembling Russian-designed MiG-21 jet fighters under licence arrangements.

India is bound to view China's growing nuclear capability with concern, since cities like Delhi and Calcutta lie uncomfortably close to the likely missile launching sites in Sinkiang. Of all the world's non-nuclear major powers, India is the one that could, if she so decided, start to produce a small stock of atomic bombs from her own resources soonest, but like China, she has no acceptable means of delivery at present, and has not even started on the long path of producing such delivery vehicles. Although it is the current policy of the Indian government not to embark on the production of nuclear weapons, a debate on whether this policy should now be changed has been continuing in official and press circles for some years. Official Indian statements regarding the proposed treaty of Non-Proliferation of Nuclear Weapons have made it plain that India is unlikely to renounce the option of developing nuclear weapons unless there appears to be a much more hopeful outlook for the extension of great power agreements on arms control.

The alternative for India, if the Chinese nuclear threat becomes more concrete, is to obtain some form of guarantee from one of the existing nuclear powers against aggression by China. Britain's ability (her willingness apart) to give such a guarantee has depended on the maintenance of a British military presence in the Indian Ocean area, either by means of aircraft carriers carrying light bombers, or medium bombers operating from island bases, or conceivably of *Polaris*-equipped submarines. At the time of writing Britain's effective aircraft-carrier force will not last after 1971, her whole East of Suez presence (including the island bases) seems in jeopardy and the *Polaris* force will never be large enough to operate both in Atlantic and Indian waters. There remains only the USA, and although in normal times (i.e. without the excessive demands of the Vietnam conflict), the American Navy and Air Force clearly has the capacity to take on this extra commitment, the American government has made it clear that it would prefer not to undertake new responsibilities in the Indian Ocean area. Apart from the military complications, the acceptance of a nuclear guarantee from the USA would presumably mean that the Indian government would have to give up its present diplomatic policy of non-alignment.

JAPAN

Another Asian country that has the technical capacity to manufacture nuclear weapons but has so far refused to contemplate such a policy, is Japan. Japan is richer and more industrially advanced than either India or China, and could probably even outdistance China in developing a delivery system if she chose to do so. Indeed it is one of the ironies of the present Asian situation that the most prosperous country in Asia (with a current GNP of $107 billion, Japan comes fourth only to the USA, USSR, and West Germany in the world) should currently devote the smallest proportion of its resources (approx. 1·2 per cent) to national defence. By the terms of the 1947 constitution, Japan is not allowed to refer to her armed forces as Army, Navy and Air Force, but rather Ground Self-Defence Forces, Maritime Self-Defence Forces and Air Self-Defence Forces.

One reason why Japan has not needed to expand her armed forces to a level commensurate with what she can afford is of course the protection given to her by the sizeable American forces stationed both on Japanese soil, and in neighbouring areas such as South Korea, Okinawa, Taiwan, and Guam, and by the terms of the American-Japanese security treaties of 1951 and 1960. There has also been a genuine pacifist feeling at all social levels in Japan since 1945, and great care has had to be taken with the expansion and strengthening of the Self-Defence Forces even within the limits of the 1947 constitution. The

Defence Agency, which is responsible for the organization and equipment of the Self-Defence Forces, has still not been raised to Cabinet status. Its function is described as being to defend Japan against aggression from the outside, both direct and indirect.

In 1966, the Defence Agency submitted to the Government a new five-year plan calling for annual defence expenditures of $1,500 million (the current rate is $1,058 million). The plan, which calls for only a small expansion of manpower from the current level of 245,000, put emphasis on air defence, and proposed introducing new aircraft and surface-to-air missiles. The Air Self-Defence Force is now operating equipment such as the *Starfighter* jet interceptor, some of which are being manufactured in Japan under the designation F-104J, and *Nike-Ajax* surface-to-air missiles with non-nuclear warheads. The Maritime Self-Defence Force has also been improving its equipment, with several new Japanese-built destroyers joining the fleet, one of which is armed with *Tartar* surface-to-air missiles. Such developments as these will reduce to some extent Japan's present heavy dependence on the United States for her defence.

The Army (or Ground Self-Defence Force) is the largest of the three services with a sanctioned strength of 171,500, but is clearly cast in a defensive role. The twelve infantry divisions are each allotted to a particular defence area, and the armour reserve consists only of one mechanized division with obsolescent American tanks. Japan is currently manufacturing her own tank, the type-61, but this is not suitable for an offensive role. One object of all these plans is clearly to develop a force capable of defeating a local attack while leaving nuclear deterrence to the Americans. To this end, all American ground forces have now left Japan, and only air force units and naval facilities remain.

MALAYA AND INDONESIA

Moving to the south of Japan, the state of armed confrontation between Indonesia and the Malaysian Federation came to an end in June 1966. By that date, Indonesia had not succeeded in establishing her forces in any part of Malaya, Sabah, Sarawak or Brunei. Following the end of hostilities, Britain started to withdraw her troops in North Borneo, so that by December 1967 the only unit left was a battalion of Gurkhas (Nepalese citizens who have enlisted in the British Army) stationed in the independent state of Brunei. Malaysian Army units have moved into the British positions in North Borneo, and by the end of 1967 their approximate strength was two brigade groups.

Malaysia has continued the military build-up which was put under way at the time of confrontation. Her total armed forces have increased from about 22,000 in the autumn of 1964 to the present 33,000, and her defence expenditure from about $50 million to $128 million. Her army consists of about fourteen battalions especially equipped for fighting in jungle territory and does not include any notable armour. At the same time, Malaysia is building up a navy of coastal escorts and patrol craft, and by her purchase of CL-41 jet training aircraft is acquiring a limited air strike capability.

When Singapore seceded from the Malaysian Federation in August 1965, she took with her the two infantry battalions previously part of the Malaysian Army. These two battalions are the nucleus of Singapore's own independent defence forces, and may be increased to six, but for naval and air defence, Singapore relies entirely at present on British naval and air units stationed on Singapore Island.

There is no doubt that the complete failure of President Sukarno's 'confrontation' policy was one of the reasons for the strong reaction on the part of the Indonesian military leaders to the abortive Communist *coup d'état* in September 1965. There is a good deal of evidence for supposing that the professional military, especially in the army, were never fully committed to implementing 'confrontation', believing then as they do now, that the army's chief role in Indonesia is to maintain internal security throughout the three thousand islands of the Republic.

By the start of 1966 most of the blood-letting that followed the attempted coup was over, and the military junta under General Suharto moved steadily and carefully to consolidate its power and discredit President Sukarno and his policies. After Sukarno in February of that year started to try and divide the senior Army command, Suharto took the steps that have gradually led to his becoming President of Indonesia today. His subsequent policies have led to many military officers being appointed to senior positions in the government and administration, but they have not led to any expansion in military strength. Suharto realizes that the wasteful military expenditure on prestige equipment such as cruisers and jet bombers not only contributed to the debilitation of Indonesia's economy but also added nothing to the real military potential of the armed forces.

The Indonesian Army has been fighting against armed rebels in such areas as Northern Sumatra, the Southern Celebes and the Molucca Islands since independence until very recently, and it is never really known whether resistance has died down in some of the outlying areas. It is probable that about half the infantry battalions in the 290,000-strong army are employed on internal security duties in areas outside Java and Sumatra, though such internal security may often be combined with 'civic' action duties as the army is often the only effective form of administrative organization in such areas. It is also necessary for any Indonesian government to keep a strong reserve of the best-trained troops (the so-called KOSTRAD) stationed near Djakarta in case of internal threats to the regime. In the same way, the small Armoured Corps, with its French AMX-13 and Russian PT-76 light tanks, is kept close to the tank-training school at Bandung, and is seldom deployed to outlying areas.

Both the Indonesian Navy and the Indonesian Air Force, who for differing reasons were probably more closely identified with Sukarno and the 'confrontation' policy, have suffered from having to digest the vast stock of modern Soviet ships and aircraft which were pressed on them in the years 1958–64. In both cases, neither training capability nor maintenance facilities have been adequate with the result that neither service can effectively operate more than about a third of its supposed inventories, and will undoubtedly not be ready for any effective military operations until they have completely rethought their commitments and reorganized their structure and choice of equipment. Most of the Soviet advisory personnel have now left Indonesia, and without committing themselves to any military alignment, the Indonesian leaders are now showing themselves more willing to consult the military staffs of such countries as Australia, Malaysia and India.

The current military situation in Asia can therefore be seen as one in which, with the obvious exception of the Vietnam War, most military establishments are cast in a non-aggressive role. They are mostly committed to a policy of consolidation and re-equipment of their armed forces, without any glaring examples of expansion. The conflict in Vietnam, which has remained localized in a comparatively small area of Asia, serves to focus the military energies of at least eight Asian nations and two non-Asian nations with strong interests in the area, but almost all these countries show every sign of wanting the war to be confined to the Vietnam theatre.

APPENDIX
The Armed Forces of the Major Asian Nations

AUSTRALIA

Total armed forces: 80,300.
Defence estimates 1967–8: 1,118 million Australian dollars ($1,378,000,000).

Army
Total strength: 43,300.
8 infantry battalions, including 1 battalion group in Malaysia and 3 battalion groups in Vietnam.
1 tank regiment with *Centurions.*
2 battalions of the Pacific Islands Regiment.

Navy
Total strength: 16,500.
1 light fleet carrier (used for anti-submarine warfare).
1 submarine.
5 destroyers.
4 destroyer escorts.
25 other vessels.

Air Force
Total strength: 20,500; 200 combat aircraft.
40 *Canberra* light bombers.
80 *Mirage 111–0s* jet fighters (with *Matra* air-to-air missiles).
60 Australian *Sabre* fighters.

CHINA

Total armed forces: 2,700,000.
Defence expenditure: approx. $8,000,000,000.

Army
Total strength: 2,500,000 (including railway engineer troops).
The ground forces consist of about 120 line divisions (i.e. infantry, cavalry, armour and airborne) and supporting arms and services.

The 120 line divisions include 111 infantry, four armoured, three cavalry and two airborne divisions. There are normally 12,000 men in a Chinese infantry division, and rather less in armour and artillery divisions. The supporting arms and services include 20 artillery divisions and 5 anti-tank artillery regiments, 66 engineering regiments, 34 motor transport regiments, 2 signal regiments and 11 divisions of railway engineers (who, in the People's Liberation Army, are uniformed troops). There are also some desert cavalry and mountain units.

Heavy equipment consists of items supplied earlier by the Soviet Union,

455

such as artillery up to 152 and 203 mm. and the JS–2 heavy tank. Medium armour consists of the T–34 tank and the T–54 tank, which is produced in China under the description of T–59. Some 50 or more T–59s have been exported to Pakistan. Heavy field engineering equipment and heavy and self-propelled artillery, as well as motor transport, are all in short supply, while radar and electronic communications equipment is generally less sophisticated than modern Western or Soviet types.

Navy
Total strength: 136,000 (including 15,000 Naval Air Force).
4 destroyers.
5 destroyer escorts.
11 frigate escorts.
1 G–class submarine.
23 W–class submarines.
7 other submarines (ex-Soviet).
150 motor torpedo boats.
200 other vessels.

There are about 500 naval aircraft, including up to 150 I1–28 torpedo-carrying jet light bombers and substantial numbers of MiG–15 and MiG–17 fighters. These fighters, though under Navy command, are fully integrated into the air defence system of China.

Air Force
Total strength: 100,000; 2,500 aircraft.
There are up to 12 Tu–4 medium bombers (a copy of the B–29), and about 150 I1–28 light bombers. The remaining aircraft are chiefly early model MiG–15s and 17s, with a lesser number of MiG–19s and MiG–21s.

There is a small air transport fleet which includes some I1–18s and MiG–4 helicopters.

Para-military forces
Security and border troops number about 300,000. The border troops include 17 infantry divisions and 21 independent regiments permanently stationed in the frontier areas in addition to the 'line' divisions already there. There is also a People's Armed Police Force, and a civilian militia claimed by the Chinese authorities to be 200,000,000 strong.

INDIA

Total armed forces: 977,000.
Defence estimates 1967–8: 9,694 million rupees ($1,292,000,000).

Army
Total strength: 900,000.
1 armoured division with *Centurions*.

12 infantry divisions.
9 mountain divisions.
1 parachute brigade.
There are tank regiments of *Shermans* and *Vijayantas* with most of the infantry divisions; other divisions have reconnaissance regiments with AMX–13 *Stuart*, or PT–76 light tanks.
About 1,000 armoured vehicles in all, including 800 tanks.

Navy
Total strength: 17,000.
1 16,000-ton aircraft carrier.
2 submarines (ex-USSR).
2 cruisers.
3 destroyers.
3 anti-aircraft frigates.
5 anti-submarine frigates.
5 escort frigates.
20 other vessels.

Air Force
Total strength: 60,000; 500 combat aircraft.
45 *Canberra* B(1) light bombers.
8 *Canberra* PR.57 reconnaissance aircraft.
60 MiG–21 interceptors.
150 *Hunter* F–56 fighter/ground attack aircraft.
120 *Gnat* Mk. 1 interceptors.
60 *Mystère* IV fighters.
35 C–47, 9 *Super Constellation*, 75 C–119, 22 Il–14, 22 An–12, 30 *Otter* and 18 *Caribou* medium transport aircraft.
Some surface-to-air missile batteries with *Guideline–11* missiles.

Para-military forces
About 100,000 internal security troops in the border regions.

INDONESIA

Total armed forces: 352,000.
Defence estimates 1967: 20,325,000,000 new ripahs ($203,000,000).

Army
Total strength: 290,000.
16 infantry brigades formed from about 100 infantry battalions.
The KOSTRAD (Strategic Strike Command) consists of approximately 4 brigades.
Approximately 4 tank battalions with either AMX–13 or Russian PT–76 light tanks, and *Saladin* armoured cars.

Navy

Total strength: 40,000 (25,000 regular navy, plus navy air forces, and the 14,000 strong Marine Commando Corps).

1 heavy cruiser (ex-Soviet *Sverdlov* class).

12 submarines (ex-Soviet W–class).

7 destroyers (ex-Soviet *Skoryi* class).

11 frigates (of which 7 ex-Soviet *Riga* class).

12 *Komar*–class missile boats.

100 other vessels.

A small naval air arm including Il–28 *Beagle* and Mi–4 helicopters.

Air Force

Total strength: 22,000; 140 combat aircraft.

Over 60 MiG interceptors including 18 MiG–21s.

25 Tu–16 medium bombers, some with air-to-surface missiles.

18 B–25 *Mitchell* and B–26 *Invader* piston-engined light bombers.

20 F–51D *Mustang* light strike aircraft.

About 60 transport aircraft, including Il–14, C–130B, C–47 and An–12.

Para-military forces

The police force numbers about 110,000 and includes a para-military force (Mobile Brigade) numbering approximately 20,000.

JAPAN

Total armed forces: 246,000.

Defence estimates 1967–8: 380,900,000,000 yen ($1,058,000,000).

Army

Total strength: 171,500.

12 infantry divisions.

1 mechanized division.

1 airborne brigade.

380 M–4, M–24, M–41 and type 61 tanks.

Navy

Total strength: 35,000.

22 destroyers (1 with *Tartar* guided missiles).

17 frigates and other escorts.

7 submarines.

170 other ships.

Air Force

Total strength: 39,500; 480 combat aircraft.

200 F–104J interceptors.

265 F–86F day-fighters.

15 RF–86F reconnaissance aircraft.

2 *Nike-Ajax* surface-to-air missile groups (72 launchers).

MALAYSIA

Total armed forces: 33,200.
Defence budget 1967: M$393,000,000 ($128,000,000).

Army
Total strength: 27,600.
10 infantry battalions.
4 Ranger battalions.
2 reconnaissance regiments with *Ferret* armoured cars.

Navy
Total strength: 3,000.
1 ASW frigate.
6 coastal minesweepers.
27 other vessels.

Air Force
Total strength: 2,000. No combat aircraft.
20 CL–41 light jet strike and training aircraft.
20 *Twin Pioneer*, 8 *Herald* and 4 *Caribou* medium transports.

Para-military forces
Total strength: 23,000.

NORTH KOREA

Total armed forces: 368,000.
Defence expenditure 1967: about 1,182 million won ($460,000,000).

Army
Total strength: 340,000.
18 infantry divisions.
About 500 Soviet medium tanks and 450 armoured vehicles.
SA–2 *Guideline* surface-to-air missiles.
Reserve units total a further 110,000 men.

Navy
Total strength: 8,000.
2 submarines (ex-Soviet).
2 coastal escorts.
10 minesweepers.
80 small patrol craft (including 21 MTBs).

Air Force
Total strength: 20,000 men; 460 combat aircraft.
40 Il–28 jet light bombers.
25 MiG–21 jet interceptors.
400 MiG–15 and MiG–17 jet fighter-bombers.

Para-military forces
Total strength: 25,000.

NORTH VIETNAM

Total armed forces: 450,000.
Defence budget: approximately $500,000,000 equivalent.

Army
Total strength: 440,000, including at least 85,000 serving in South Vietnam,
and 40,000 in Laos.
13 infantry divisions.
A few T–34 medium tanks and PT–76 reconnaissance tanks.
About 6,000 anti-aircraft guns, including 37 mm., 57 mm., 85 mm., and 100
mm.
Some 50 surface-to-air missile sites for SA–2 *Guideline* missiles.

Navy
Total strength: 3,500.
3 coastal escorts (ex-USSR).
22 ex-Chinese motor gunboats (67 tons).
9 ex-Soviet motor torpedo boats (50 tons).

Air Force
Total strength: 4,500; 125 combat aircraft.
8 I1–28 light bombers.
24 MiG–21 interceptors.
90 MiG–15 and MiG–17 fighters.

Para-military forces
There is a regionally organized armed militia of about 500,000.

PAKISTAN

Total armed forces: 323,000.
Defence estimates 1967–8: 2,195,000,000 rupees ($458,000,000).

Army
Total strength: 300,000.
13 infantry divisions (one in East Pakistan).
2 armoured divisions with M–47 *Pattons*, M–48 *Pattons* and Chinese T–59
tanks.
About 900 125 mm., 150 mm., and 175 mm. guns.

Navy
Total strength: 9,000.
1 submarine.
2 large destroyers.
3 destroyer escorts.
2 ASW frigates.
15 other vessels.

460

Air Force
Total strength: 14,000; 240 combat aircraft.
8 Il–28 light jet bombers.
20 B–57B light jet bombers.
100 F–86F *Sabre* fighter-bombers.
70 MiG–19 *Farmer* jet fighters.
20 F–104A *Starfighter* interceptors.
About 40 *Bristol, Dakota* and *Hercules* transports.

SOUTH KOREA

Total armed forces: 612,000.
Defence estimates 1967: 48,000 million won ($180,000,000).

Army
Total strength: 540,000 (including 46,000 in South Vietnam).
18 front-line infantry divisions.
10 tank battalions with M–47 and M–48 *Pattons*.
10 reserve infantry divisions.
Hawk surface-to-air missiles.

Navy
Total strength: 17,000.
1 destroyer.
7 destroyer escorts.
15 coastal escorts.
46 other vessels.
30,000 marines.

Air Force
Total strength: 25,000; 200 combat aircraft.
30 F–5 tactical fighters.
60 F–86D all-weather interceptors.
100 F–86F fighter-bombers.

SOUTH VIETNAM

Total armed forces: 410,000 (regular).
Defence expenditure 1967: equivalent $193,000,000.

Army
Total strength: 370,000.
10 infantry divisions.
1 airborne division.
3 independent infantry regiments.
7 Marine battalions.
20 Ranger battalions.
10 tank squadrons with M–41 and AMX–13 light tanks.

Navy
Total strength: 24,000.
9 coastal escorts.
3 coastal minesweepers.
22 motor gunboats (less than 100 tons).
36 other ships.

Air Force
Total strength: 16,000; 150 combat aircraft.
4 B–57 light bombers.
105 A–1E *Skyraider* light bombers.
20 F–5 tactical fighters.
About 100 C–47, C–123 and *Beaver* transports.

Para-military forces
Total strength: 320,000.
Regional Forces: 140,000.
Popular Forces: 150,000.
Civilian Irregular Defence Groups: 30,000.

TAIWAN

Total armed forces: 547,000.
Defence expenditure: approx. $300,000,000.

Army
Total strength: 400,000 (including 80,000 on Quemoy and Matsu).
15 infantry divisions.
2 armoured divisions with M–47 and M–48 tanks.
2 armoured cavalry regiments.
6 light divisions.
Honest John rockets and *Hawk* surface-to-air missiles.

Navy
Total strength: 35,000.
5 destroyers.
6 frigates.
27 coastal escorts.
45 landing ships.
105 other vessels.
27,000 marines.

Air Force
Total strength: 85,000 men; 435 combat aircraft.
45 F–100 *Super Sabre* fighter-bombers.
300 F–104G and F–86F interceptors.
50 F–5A and F–84F tactical fighters.
100 C–46, C–47, C–119 and C–123 transports.

There are several American Air Force formations on Taiwan, equipped with jet fighters and tactical missiles.

THAILAND

Total armed forces: 126,500.
Defence expenditure 1967–8: 2,618 million baht ($125,000,000).

Army
Total strength: 85,000.
3 infantry divisions (including 3 tank battalions).
1 regimental combat team.
Armoured cars and light tanks.

Navy
Total strength: 21,500 (including 3,500 marines).
4 ASW frigates.
1 anti-aircraft frigate.
1 escort minesweeper.
52 other vessels.

Air Force
Total strength: 20,000; 125 combat aircraft.
45 F–86F fighter-bombers.
15 F–84G day-fighters.
About 65 T–6 and T–28 light strike aircraft.

Strategic Studies in Asia

The study of defence and military matters in universities and specialized institutes (as opposed to the normal military and staff colleges) has not reached the same level in Asia as it has in the United States and in some European countries, but it is beginning to make progress. Up till now, the main Asian countries where defence studies have been established as a specialized discipline are Australia, India, Japan and South Korea; no information is available on the development of such studies in Communist countries.

AUSTRALIA. In August 1966, the Australian National University established a Centre for Defence and Strategic Studies in the Research School of Pacific Studies. Its scope is considerably wider than that of the previous Defence Studies Project, since it will deal with Southern and South-East Asian security problems in their entirety. A senior scholar of the University will be in charge, with a Research Fellow and several assistants. The Centre will sponsor research, conduct conferences, and provide other facilities in the field.

The Australian Institute of Political Science, organized by the Department of Government, University of Sydney, is an important forum among the business, political, and academic communities for the discussion of national security problems.

463

INDIA. At the University of Poona, a Department of Military Studies was started in 1962 under the directorship of Major-General Y. E. Pranjpe. Professor P. C. Chakravarti of the Department of International Relations, Jadavpur University, is working on a study of India's northern borders. A series of courses in military history, given by R. K. Nehru, was initiated at Allahabrad University in 1966.

Official institutions concerned with strategic studies are (a) the United Services Institution, King George's Avenue, New Delhi, which is essentially an armed forces institution, whose object is to promote interest and knowledge in the art, science, and literature of the defence services. It offers opportunities to serving officers for strategic study.

(b) In September 1966 the Indian Government set up an Institute for Defence Studies and Analyses, 1, York Place, New Delhi. Its first Director is Major-General D. Som Dutt. The staff will comprise serving officers and civilians.

JAPAN. Studies connected with war have been unpopular in university circles in Japan. As a result, despite the advocacy of several prominent scholars, no Japanese university, state or private, has as yet a chair or lectureship in strategy, and the only appointment to an international relations chair is at the new Kyoto Industrial University, Kyoto.

Strategic studies are therefore confined to the Ministry of Foreign Affairs, the Defence Agency, the National Defence College (13, Mita, Meguro-ku, Tokyo), and three Armed Forces Staff Colleges. Of these, only the National Defence College publishes its studies and has its own journal. In 1966 the Kajima Institute of International Peace, a private research institute, was established.

The *Asahi Shimbun*, a leading newspaper, set up an intramural study committee on national security early in 1965. The *Mainichi Shimbun*, another newspaper, set up an Asian Affairs Research Council in September 1964; its President is former Prime Minister Shigeru Yoshida. In spring 1967 the newspaper *Yomiuri Shimbun* co-sponsored with the Institute for Strategic Studies, London, an international conference on Asian security.

Periodicals, which in the past had generally refused contributions on strategic studies, began to carry articles on national security following China's first nuclear test.

SOUTH KOREA. Until recently there were no research activities in the field of strategy and national security.

In 1966 the National War College was established. It organized a series of seminars on strategic issues, which met with considerable public interest, particularly within the armed forces. Since then a number of outstanding foreign books and articles on the subject have been chosen for translation into Korean.

Similarly, the universities now take an active interest in military problems as part of the wider field of international relations. In particular, the Asiatic Research Centre at Korea University, under the directorship of Professor Kim Jun Yop, has a sizeable research programme on the Communist bloc and current Asian problems. It publishes various journals and monographs on Korea and Asia.

A group of students of military strategy held monthly meetings on strategic studies from 1960 to February 1965, when the Korean Institute for Strategic Studies was formally created. This institute conducts independent research into problems of strategy, Communism, and international relations in the Far East.

BIBLIOGRAPHY

Alastair Buchan (Ed.). *China and the Peace of Asia.* (Chatto & Windus, 1964.) *A World of Nuclear Powers?* (Prentice Hall, Englewood Cliffs, N.J., for the American Assembly, 1966.)

William Chapin. *The Asian Balance of Power: an American View.* (Institute for Strategic Studies, London, 1967.)

D. Som Dutt. *The Defence of India's Northern Borders.* (Institute for Strategic Studies, London, 1966.) *India and the Bomb.* (Institute for Strategic Studies, London, 1966.)

Raymond L. Garthoff (Ed.). *Sino–Soviet Military Relations.* (Pall Mall Press, 1967.)

John Gittings. *The Role of the Chinese Army.* (Oxford University Press, 1967.)

Samuel B. Griffith. *The Chinese People's Liberation Army.* (McGraw Hill, New York, 1967.) *Peking and People's Wars.* (Pall Mall Press, 1966.)

Sisir Gupta. *Kashmir: A Study in India–Pakistan Relations.* (Asia Publishing House, 1966.)

Morton H. Halperin. *China and the Bomb.* (Praeger, New York, 1965.) *China and Nuclear Proliferation.* (University of Chicago Center for Policy Study, Chicago, 1966.) (Ed.). *Sino–Soviet Relations and Arms Control* (MIT Press, Cambridge, Mass., 1967.)

Anthony Harrigan. *A Guide to the War in Vietnam.* (Panther, 1966.)

D. E. Kennedy. *The Security of Southern Asia.* (Chatto & Windus, 1965.)

Alastair Lamb. *Crisis in Kashmir, 1947–66.* (Routledge & Kegan Paul, 1966.)

Mao Tse-tung. *Basic Tactics.* Translated and with an introduction by Stuart R. Schram. (Pall Mall Press, 1967.)

The Military Balance, 1967–68. (Institute for Strategic Studies, London, 1967).

Douglas Pike. *Viet Cong: The Organization and Techniques of the National Liberation Front of South Vietnam.* (MIT Press, Cambridge, Mass., 1966.)

Sibnarayan Ray (Ed.). *Vietnam Seen from East and West: An International Symposium.* (Pall Mall Press, 1967.)

John Rowland. *A History of Sino–Indian Relations: Hostile Co-Existence.* (Van Nostrand, London, 1967.)

DAVID WOOD

Michio Royama. *The Asian Balance of Power: a Japanese View.* (Institute for Strategic Studies, London, 1967.)

A. B. Shah (Ed.). *India's Defence and Foreign Policies.* (Manaktala, Bombay, 1966.)

Sir Robert Thompson. *Defeating Communist Insurgency: Experiences from Malaya and Vietnam.* (Chatto & Windus, 1966.)

COMMUNISM IN ASIA

Richard Harris

HISTORY OF COMMUNISM IN ASIA

COMMUNISM in Asia now has a history of nearly fifty years, but during that time it has made far less progress there than in Europe. It is doubtful if there ever was any hope that Communism would spread through cultures so different as those of Asia. Today the chances of success for Communist parties are small save in those countries of East Asia – China, Korea and Vietnam – where Communist parties were able to offer themselves as exponents and not simply as allies of nationalism.

In the last ten years the effects of the Sino-Soviet dispute, followed by the hysterical tone with which China has addressed the world during the cultural revolution, have combined to force Communist parties all over the continent to look to their own national problems and follow their own national paths. The end of Russian domination of the world Communist movement has not been followed by Chinese Communist leadership in Asia; nor does it seem likely that it ever will be so when China's own Marxist formulations have been made so distinctively national under the leadership of Mao Tse-tung.

The only generalization that could be made about Communism in Asia was to do with its origins. Just as imperial rule brought to these countries the political and economic outlook of the West, so the new Western political doctrine of Marxism was imported, either by Asians who went to study in the West and became associated with the Communist movement there, or by Western revolutionaries who went to the East as missionaries for their revolutionary faith. In the early days these European Communists were as much leaders as the imperial rulers themselves. Communist parties in Asia thus began, to borrow a Communist term, as semi-colonial parties, led by Asians whose impulse towards Western ways divorced them from their own country, advised by Westerners who had no knowledge of or sympathy for the conditions facing these countries in their own revolutionary course.

The first Communist party in Asia to escape from this Western tutelage and rebuild itself on native foundations was the Chinese, which was one, though only one, of the reasons for its final success. No other Communist party achieved this shift before the war and thus no party, with the exception of the Vietnamese, was able to catch the tide of anti-imperialism and ride to power with its backing. The refounding of these parties has come since the war; in India gradually and still far from complete; in Indonesia after the total failure of the revolt at Madiun in 1948. In Burma and Ceylon splits in the parties have weakened them; Malaya, with its strong Chinese element, remains a special case.

The post-war new-style Communist party differs from the old-style Comintern party. Its emphasis is national rather than international. It must have leaders who are not over-Westernized and divorced from their own culture. It recognizes that the peasants can be a revolutionary force in Asia if properly harnessed and it accepts the corollary that Communist victory can never be achieved through an urban proletariat. Finally Communism must accommodate itself after some fashion to the country's religious and cultural traditions. It must not seem opposed to the national spirit. Only then has it any hope of gaining a mass following.

Any further generalization about Communism in Asia is dangerous and indeed misleading since its growth depends on factors that differ from country to country, factors which favour its growth far more in some countries than in others; factors such as climate, population pressure on resources, the balance of religious and secular interests in society, the legacy of Western rule, the intellectual energy within the culture and so on.

The only useful distinction to be made is between the Communist doctrine and outlook in the relatively coherent civilization of East Asia.

EAST ASIA

East Asian civilization includes China, Japan, Korea and Vietnam. These countries are linked to China by the influences they have derived from its civilization over two thousand years; through China's direct rule or suzerainty, as in the case of Vietnam and Korea, or from the direct borrowings and exchanges with Japan. Chinese learning was the classic base for all these countries. Chinese philosophy moulded their political thought, especially when the Chinese language was accepted as the fundamental equipment of the scholar. And although there were profound differences as well, it may be said that Chinese political institutions and Chinese political thought have been part of the inheritance influencing these countries today.

This coherence in East Asian civilization, a coherence established by doctrines to which the convenient label Confucianism has been given, impelled it to resist the incursion of Western power with more vehemence and more confidence in its own superiority – above all in China's case – than South Asia did. And since its own state systems, if not directly Confucianist, were by tradition authoritarian, looking to an emperor or to a bureaucracy as a source of political and ideological authority, the influence of the West was difficult to incorporate piecemeal. In China in this century, Communism could seem a total substitute for Confucianism as a system for the organization of man in society. It is therefore in its claim as a total philosophy, as a new creed on which to refound these societies, that Communism has an appeal. It is a new system to replace the old, though a system to be translated into East Asian terms. In none of these countries is religious tradition or a religious hierarchy strong enough to be a barrier to the import of Communism. In a society where intellectual leadership has always operated through an authoritarian system East Asian Communism is a creed that appeals because it offers a central truth. A country that orders its society in accordance with prescribed truth about the nature of man and his relationships in society expresses its Communist faith in accordance with these traditions. Communism in East Asia has a total, ideological appeal; in South Asia its appeal is pragmatic and piecemeal. With these general observations we can turn to the state of East Asian Communist parties.

JAPAN

Just as Japan differs more from the East Asian pattern than the two smaller countries which grew up in China's shadow, so the Japanese Communist Party differs from the others. For one thing, the modernization of Japan after the Meiji Restoration of 1868 was a partial but, within its limits, wholehearted acceptance of Western ways. The Japanese Communist Party, which was founded under direct stimulation from the Comintern in 1922, was thus too late to play in Japanese life the same role as the Chinese Communists in China, as thinkers who offered a resolution of the conflict between East Asian and Western values. In large part Japan had already taken that choice and the Communists could thus make little headway with national sentiment. In so far as a national sentiment tried to assert itself in reaction to this Westernization there grew up the spurious creed which justified militarist expansion, veneration of the Emperor, the Shinto religion and other supposedly hallowed Japanese beliefs. This pre-war blind-alley phase in Japan's development naturally militated against Communist success, quite apart from the brutal suppression of Communists by most Japanese governments before the war.

With Japan's defeat the Communist Party could expand again in an atmosphere in which all Western ideas were equally welcome. Some of its leaders had been in exile, among them Sanzo Nosaka, the present Chairman of the Party, who had been with the Chinese Communists in Yenan. Under the American Occupation the Party was free to enter political life and by 1949 its membership had grown to 230,000 and it won thirty-five seats in the lower house of the Diet. But it had still not, like the Chinese Communist Party, been transformed into a native model. Land reform and economic progress under the Occupation reduced even further the possibility of any mass movement from below. Progressive Westernization – and the existence of the Japanese Socialist Party – removed its chances of offering a compact ideology for Japan's post-war renewal. Besides this, or perhaps because of it, the Japanese Communists still suffered from internal differences. One struggle was between the use of violent as against parliamentary methods; another was the conflicting traditions in the party between its Comintern-dominated past and those of its leaders influenced by a Chinese out-look. During the fifties membership fell sharply.

The growth of the dispute between the Chinese and Russians gradually brought the Japanese Communists on to China's side. A small breakaway to the Russian side in 1965 was followed by the main body of the Party in the spring of 1966 when discussions with the Chinese could not reach agreement on common Communist support under Russian leadership for the Vietnamese. Although a small group later broke away from the main body to come back to the Chinese side again the result was to leave the JCP sundered and isolated; indeed, the largest body of support for China in its Maoist revolution-ary phase now came from the pro-Chinese wing of the Japanese Socialist Party.

Japan has gone so far along the Western path, not merely in advanced technology and in Western-style institutions, but into acceptance of Western ideas, as to leave extremism and a total ideological solution no chance. Attempts to revive the right-wing ideology in numerous small parties are no more likely than Communism to be an answer to Japan's problems. Such parties still exist while the country moves uneasily from an East Asian into a wholly Western pattern. And there is always still the possibility that an accommodation with China could again bring Japan back into an East Asian world of thought. Otherwise the prospects for Communism in Japan seem poor.

KOREA

Korean Communism grew up in the 1930s largely among exiles opposed to the Japanese occupation of their country. Some were with the Chinese Communists in Yenan, a few in the West, but most in the Soviet Union. It was thus possible for the Soviet-trained Kim Il-song to be raised to power at the head of the Korean Laodong Party in the northern part of the country occupied by the Russians. The assault on South Korea showed the Stalinist character of the Party and its defeat after UN intervention much reduced the chance of Communism ever gaining a following in the south. Since the armistice the government in the north has restored its devastated territory and rebuilt its industry. Conflicts within the Party have necessarily reflected affiliations with either China or the Soviet Union. As the split between these two developed the Koreans slowly came down on the Chinese side, though trying not to offend the Russians. The extremism of the cultural revolution then drove the North Korean Party away from China and partially back to their Russian sympathies; but only partially. The effect of the Sino-Soviet split was to hasten on the same move towards independence and an attempt at a national identity which has occurred elsewhere in Asia.

VIETNAM

The Vietnamese Communist Party was founded in 1930 and enjoyed the leadership of the only man of comparable political stature to Mao Tse-tung in China – Ho Chi Minh. The party was severely repressed under French rule, began to build up its cells in the countryside during the war years, and, as the dominant element in a nationalist coalition, the Vietminh, was able to proclaim itself as a provisional government at the end of the war. In South Vietnam its strength was not enough to resist the allied reoccupation, but in the north the French negotiated with Ho Chi Minh's government. Eventually after a long struggle negotiations at Geneva led to the partition of Vietnam into a Communist North and an anti-Communist South. Under a declaration of the conference elections to unify the country were to be held by 1956, but the government of Ngo Dinh Diem, supported by the Americans, was unwilling to enter into discussions with the North and no elections were held. In 1957 and 1958 there were signs of revolt from Communist cells surviving in the South which expanded, after a repressive campaign by Diem, into full-scale guerrilla warfare in 1959. By 1960 this came under the political direction of the North and the war had reached a critical point with talk of negotiations early in 1965.

All through the Sino-Soviet dispute the Vietnamese did their best to avoid taking sides. The pressures to conform with the Chinese were strong, but as the war in Vietnam escalated the need for Russian aid kept the Vietnamese on good terms with Moscow. The excesses of the cultural revolution which went virtually unmentioned in Vietnamese propaganda may also have cooled relations with China. Despite the rigours of the war from the bombing of the North and the fighting in the South it cannot be said that Communism as a doctrine has lost its appeal for the Vietnamese. Nor has any rival doctrine emerged to dispute its claims to order the future Vietnamese society in North and South.

CHINA

Founded in 1921, the Chinese Communist Party grew slowly, wasted its energies in fruitless strikes and armed actions, was thrown out of the alliance by the Kuomintang and only began to gain strength when guerrilla armies set up liberated areas with the backing of peasant revolutionaries. Of such areas the largest and most successful was led by Mao Tse-tung in Kiangsi province. The evacuation and concentration of these liberated areas in north-west China (1934–6) gave the Chinese Communists a base from which they spread during the war years and won victory in the civil war in 1949.

Before it ever came to power therefore Chinese Communism had won confidence in itself as an independent military force and as the ruler of nearly 100 million peasants; above all, in the view of Mao Tse-tung and his colleagues, it was able to interpret Marxism-Leninism creatively in Chinese terms. When it took power in 1949 it was a largely home-grown movement, able to capture Chinese patriotic loyalty.

In the first decade of its rule the Chinese Party seemed united under Mao Tse-tung's leadership, but with the development of the Sino–Soviet dispute and especially with Mao's initiation of the 'Great Leap Forward' in 1958, serious differences of policy began to emerge. All through the 1960s Mao Tse-tung's dominance, leading to an exaggerated personal adulation, brought matters to a head in the 'great proletarian cultural revolution'. This convulsion led Mao personally, backed as he thought by the army under Lin Piao, to carry out an assault on his own party. He believed it had been poisoned by revisionism and would go the same way as the Russians. In the crises and conflicts engendered in 1966 and 1967 more than half of the old political bureau and of the central committee fell out with Mao Tse-tung. Liu Shao-chi, Teng Hsiao-ping, Peng Chen, Chu Te, Ho Lung and others who had been with Mao for thirty years or more were castigated as revisionists and traitors.

The damage this movement has done to the Chinese Communist Party still remains to be assessed. Nevertheless it seems probable that the Party will reconstitute itself after Mao Tse-tung leaves the scene in China, or alternatively that even Mao's remodelled Party will not, after a year or so, look very different from the old, or follow policies so very different from those attributed to the 'revisionist' Liu Shao-chi.

A further outcome of the cultural revolution has been to end China's peaceful coexistence with most of her neighbours, to add to her enemies, and to postpone for many years the time when Chinese influence of any kind will make itself felt in Asia. While it seems improbable that Maoist policies will survive the death or retirement of this powerful leader, the future of Chinese Communism after his death will probably bring to the top men of whom nothing now is known.

The belief that its influence will be great in Asia needs sceptical examination. For one thing its attitudes and methods are alien to those of South Asia. It has never had any close association with the Indian Communists; its cultivation of the Indonesian Communists will not necessarily mean stronger Chinese influence in Indonesia. The adherence to the Chinese line of such small parties as the Burmese and Thai adds little to Chinese power; indeed, during their dispute with the Russians the Chinese have shown rather more interest in the competition for the allegiance of nationalist-revolutionary movements than in Communist parties as such.

SOUTH ASIA

South Asian Communism still has more in common with European Communism than it has with East Asian Communism. It began with the same handicaps of semi-colonial status and while the international character was still dominant in 1948 began attempts to gain power by violence in India, Burma, the Philippines, Malaya and Indonesia. The relics of this warfare still drag on in some countries but for the most part their Communist parties have now come out in new colours. They are self-consciously 'national' parties, unwilling to allow that they are in any way bound to the dictates of international Communism. They are ready to accommodate themselves to regional, linguistic, religious or caste differences, as the Indian Communist Party shows. The tendency is for these parties to accept the argument for peaceful change wherever a democratic system allows them to function and this may continue in spite of Chinese arguments favouring violent revolution. It might be said that the Communists of South Asia represent themselves to the electorate as just like any other party, only more devoted to the electors' interests, more dedicated and uncorrupt and more efficient and progressive.

It may be a long time before this appeal goes very far. In many of these countries the early years of independence have been succeeded by a reaction, natural enough in countries severed by imperialism from much of their past, towards religion, language, culture and customs that modify the accepted progressive, Western standards with which they began their independent lives. This militates against Communist success and at most, Communists can hope only for regional success. A preference for friendship with the Russians – as against East Asian Communists – seems likely to survive.

INDIA

Even after twenty years of independent India the Indian Communist Party still retains traces of its old dependence on Western or other Communist parties. Since the Sino-Soviet split the Party has broken up into two wings. But with the Chinese attack on the Indian north-eastern frontier in 1962 any close attachment on the part of the more revolutionary wing became impossible. The Party has been most successful in those states where it has been best adapted to regional needs and allied itself with suitable caste factions. In the 1967 elections the Communists were easily returned to power in Kerala and dominated the coalition formed in West Bengal. Neither the right nor the revolutionary wing of the party – which has already split into bureaucratic and Maoist revolutionary wings – seems likely to be powerful on a national basis in India. In those states where the Communists have roots they will, like other parties, also develop regional loyalties. Even then any real growth in Communist strength in India seems doubtful.

INDONESIA

Rebuilt after the disaster of the Madiun revolt in 1948, the Indonesian Communist Party (PKI) quickly grew under a young leadership. By 1965 its membership was close on 3 million under the effective leadership of D. N. Aidit, leaning towards the Chinese in the dispute with the Russians but not attacking the Russians as the Chinese did. Then on 30 September 1965 a coup that was only briefly successful brought catastrophe to the Party. Left-wing army officers were responsible but elements of the Communist youth movement and of the women's movement took part. Though no evidence suggests that the PKI as such was associated with the coup the reaction in Indonesia was to let loose a campaign of slaughter which led to the death of Communists and their sympathizers to a total variously estimated from 300,000 upwards to half a million or more. From this catastrophe, involving the death of all the leaders, there is little sign – and little chance – for the PKI to recover, especially since the fall of President Sukarno.

MALAYSIA

Communism in Malaysia now seems to have little future. In Malaya itself the survivors of the emergency of the 1950s retreated to the Thai border and have held out there. Lately they have revived somewhat with the emergence of guerrillas in Thailand itself. But their influence in Malaya is small and is likely to remain so. This has come about partly because the cultural revolution in China has reduced the appeal of a Communism fired by Chinese example. In Singapore and Malaya political independence and the prospect of economic advance leaves little room for Communism. Only in a backward area like Sarawak has a largely Chinese guerrilla force survived from the period of Indonesia's confrontation to retain some kind of an influence on the politics of the state.

On the other hand the aftermath of the Indonesian confrontation has brought about brutal massacres of overseas Chinese in some parts of Indonesia, reflected in some incidents in Malaya, notably in Penang. It is conceivable that a Communism that has always been Chinese led and inspired could again expand in the absence of adequate non-Communist leadership among the overseas Chinese. For there are now more threats to their chances of assimilation and a peaceful livelihood in the Muslim area of South-East Asia than at any time in the past century. Demonstrations in Singapore and elsewhere imply that Maoism has its following among the young. But such a close link with Peking does not seem likely to strengthen the Communist case as a whole.

BUDDHIST SOUTH-EAST ASIA

The belligerent policies followed by Mao Tse-tung in the Sino-Soviet dispute and in the cultural revolution have led China to more open support for Communist guerrilla activity anywhere in South-East Asia. This has made these parties – in Laos, Cambodia, Thailand and Burma – clients of the Chinese more than before. While Laos remains a problem, with the Pathet Lao supported mostly from North Vietnam, and in Thailand guerrillas in the north-east of the country have had some successes, China's relations with Burma and Cambodia have been damaged by her support for the Communist elements in both these countries. This change in policy has gone beyond recall in Burma but may be stabilized in Cambodia if Prince Sihanouk's friendship is still valued in Peking.

In none of these countries – Laos included – does it seem likely that a Communist movement of any strength could develop.

CONCLUSION

Pan-Asian feelings have died away as Asian countries revert to their own individuality. The great gulf between East Asia and South Asia has been made dramatically obvious by the dispute over the India-China border. A Communism continually moulded by East Asian tradition will survive in China, Korea and Vietnam, detached from the Communism of Eastern Europe. In South Asia, as and when political conditions allow it, Communist parties will stand for election and may gain a solid following. In no one country do they seem likely to achieve power in this way (still less in any other way) in the foreseeable future.

Communist Parties in Non-Communist Countries in Asia

Country	Name of Party	Membership	Pro-Soviet	Pro-Chinese
India	Communist Party of India (CPI)	165,000 (split)	*	*
Nepal	Communist Party of Nepal	3,000 (split)	*	*
Pakistan	Communist Party of Pakistan	2,500		
Ceylon	Communist Party of Ceylon (CCP)	2,000 (split)	*	*
Taiwan	—	negl.		
Hong Kong	Communist Party of Hong Kong (section of Chinese CP)	unknown		*
Japan	Communist Party of Japan (JCP)	150,000		
South Korea	—	negl.		
Burma	Communist Party of Burma— Red Flag (CPB)	500		*
	Burma Communist Party— White Flag (BCP)	1,000		*
	National United Front (NUF)	unknown	*	

COMMUNISM IN ASIA

Country	Name of Party	Membership	Pro-Soviet	Pro-Chinese
Thailand	Thai Communist Party	unknown		*
	Chinese Communist Party (Thailand)	unknown		*
Cambodia	Pracheachon Party	100		*
Laos	Workers' Party (Phak Khon Ngan—PKN)	100		*
	Neo Lao Hak Xat (NLHX)	3,000		*
	Pathet Lao (armed forces)	20,000		*
South Vietnam	National Front for the Liberation of South Vietnam (NFLSV)	unknown		*
	People's Revolutionary Party	unknown		*
Malaya	Malayan Communist Party (MCP)	500		*
Singapore	Malayan Communist Party (MCP)	2,000		*
Sarawak	The Communist Organization (CCO)	1,000		*
Indonesia	Indonesian Communist Party (PKI)	unknown		*
Philippines	Filipino Communist Party (PKP)	2,000		

BIBLIOGRAPHY

J. H. Brimmell. *Communism in South-East Asia.* (Oxford University Press, 1959.)

Michael Edwardes. *Asia in the Balance.* (Penguin Books, 1962.)

P. J. Honey. *Communism in North Vietnam.* (MIT Press, Cambridge, Mass., 1963.)

Ruth T. McVey. *The Rise of Indonesian Communism.* (Cornell University Press, Ithaca, New York, 1965.)

Gene D. Overstreet and Marshall Windmiller. *Communism in India.* (Cambridge University Press, 1959.)

L. W. Pye. *Guerrilla Communism in Malaya.* (Oxford University Press, 1956.)

Stuart R. Schram (Ed. and Trans.). *The Political Thought of Mao Tse-tung.* (Pall Mall Press, 1964.) *Mao Tse-tung.* (Penguin Books, 1966, revised edn, 1967.)

Benjamin I. Schwartz. *Chinese Communism and the Rise of Mao.* (Oxford University Press, 1951.)

THE SOUTH-EAST ASIA
TREATY ORGANIZATION

Hugh Morley

THE South-East Asia Treaty Organization is an alliance of states located in or having interests or responsibilities in South-East Asia, formed in 1954 after the end of the Indo-China War as an earnest of continued Western resistance to the spread of Communism in the area. The nations concerned are the United States, Great Britain and France by reason of post-colonial obligations, the Philippines, Thailand and Pakistan by reason of location, and Australia and New Zealand by reason of propinquity. Although it remains in 1968 a useful organ of defence co-operation, policy disagreements between its Western members in recent years have reduced its credibility. This development has to some extent been counteracted by bilateral arrangements between certain of its members.

WAR IN INDO-CHINA AND THE GENEVA CONFERENCE, 1954

1954 was an anxious year for the West in the Orient. The war against Communist insurgency was only beginning to be won by the British in Malaya. The Communist grip on North Korea had been confirmed by the outcome of the Korean War in 1953. Communist insurgency was still rampant in the Philippines. The United States, moral and material backers of the French in Indo-China ever since Communist Chinese recognition of the Viet Minh in 1950, were to be saved only by their hard-headed Congressmen from US Air Force intervention to avert a French defeat at Dien Bien Phu. It seemed to many that the consequences of that defeat, the surrender of North Vietnam to Communism and of the other newly independent Indo-Chinese states to neutralism, would lead to the progressive collapse of freedom throughout the region. Mr Dulles, the United States Secretary of State, found neutralism immoral. 'The loss of Indo-China,' said President Eisenhower, 'will cause the fall of South-East Asia like a set of dominoes.'

These were the circumstances in which, on the eve of the Geneva Conference of 1954, Mr Dulles began to promote the idea of a collective arrangement 'within the framework of the United Nations, to assure the peace, security and freedom of South-East Asia and the Western Pacific'. France in the agony of her defeat raised no objection. Britain, who was to assume with Russia special responsibilities with regard to Indo-China as co-chairman of the Geneva Conference, sought to ensure that Mr Dulles's initiative should not prejudice either a peaceful settlement at Geneva or the chances of the Colombo Powers – India, Pakistan, Burma, Ceylon and Indonesia – joining in the proposed collective arrangement.

Preliminary discussions took place during the Conference itself. The agreements on peace in Indo-China with which it ended in July 1954 confirmed Mr Dulles's worst fears, although the price demanded for peace was less than the French had expected and was considered reasonable by the British. The Communists were, however, clearly not prepared to participate on practicable terms in any reciprocal guarantee of what had been agreed. It was the more urgent to underwrite the settlement as soon as possible with a definitive treaty.

Differences of view on the importance of associating the Colombo Powers in the new pact had meanwhile been part cause of some disharmony between Britain and the United States during the Conference. The United States never wholly accepted the British view that a South-East Asian defence organization without these nations could not be fully effective. In the event Mr Nehru, who welcomed the Indo-Chinese settlement but wished to do nothing to antagonize the Chinese, expressed uncompromising opposition. Partly for this reason Pakistan, alone of the Colombo Powers, became a member of the South-East Asia Treaty Organization when it was founded in Manila on 8 September 1954.

TERMS AND FUNCTIONS OF SEATO

The treaty came into force after due ratification on 19 February 1955. It was conceived as a regional organization under the terms of the UN charter. The area it covered was defined as the general area of South-East Asia and of the South-West Pacific south of latitude 20° 30′ north – a provision which excluded Formosa and Hong Kong – with the addition, of course, of the territory of Pakistan. The signatories agreed 'separately and jointly, by means of continuous and effective self-help and mutual aid' to 'maintain and develop their individual and collective capacity to resist armed attack and to prevent and counter subversive activities directed from without against their territorial integrity and political stability' and to co-operate in developing their economies to promote economic progress and social well-being. In the event of armed attack against any of their territories in the treaty area, or against the territory of any state designated by protocol to the treaty whose government invited or consented to their intervention, each signatory agreed that it would 'act to meet the common danger in accordance with its constitutional processes'. The states designated in the protocol were Laos, Cambodia and South Vietnam, who were regarded as being under the protective umbrella of the new alliance though they themselves could not join it.

The governments of member nations agreed that they would be represented on the Council of SEATO, as it soon came to be called, by their Foreign Ministers. The first Council meeting took place at Bangkok in February 1955, and it was at Bangkok that in the following year the permanent secretariat of the Organization was established. It was agreed that the Council would meet once a year or more often if necessary and that its decisions would be taken by unanimous agreement. The Thai statesman Mr Pote Sarasin took office as Secretary-General in 1957. He was replaced by Mr Konthi Supramongkhol in 1964 who was succeeded by Lieutenant-General Jesus Vargas of the Philippines in 1965.

Between Council meetings continuing consultation was maintained at Bangkok by permanent representatives who are member nations' ambassadors to Thailand and a specially designated representative for Thailand itself, and a parallel body, the military advisers, was made responsible to the Council on military matters. A permanent military planning office was set up at Bangkok in 1957. Its work includes the development of defensive plans, the planning of military exercises, the standardization of service procedures, and specialist meetings dealing with intelligence, counter-subversion, logistics, communications and cartography. The Asian members have received considerable military and civil training assistance under the treaty both by bilateral arrangements and through specialist schools set up in their countries.

Three other specialized committees work at Bangkok under representatives of the Council. The Intelligence Assessment Committee regularly reviews the situation in the treaty area and keeps the security authorities of member nations in contact. A committee of economic experts reviews for members the economic implications of their defence commitments under the treaty. A committee on information, cultural, education and labour activities provides expert advice in these fields. Public Information, Research Services and Cultural Relations Offices have also been established.

UNSOLVED PROBLEMS

The political and military situation in Indo-China caused, as we have seen, the formation of SEATO. It continued to be its chief preoccupation, for the three Indo-Chinese states, Laos, Cambodia and Vietnam, each left the Geneva conference-table with an unsolved problem. Laos had been cast for the role of neutral buffer between Thailand and North Vietnam, a role which her internal instability made it impossible for her to play. Cambodia, whose internal problem was quickly mastered by her royal national leader Prince Sihanouk, feared the revival of the dual threat from Thailand and Vietnam which had been quiescent during French colonial rule. Vietnam, partitioned into Communist North and non-Communist South, was left to reunify herself by free general elections in 1956, a solution never accepted by South Vietnam or by the United States.

The situation in Laos was of immediate concern to SEATO because of the long open border between Laos and Thailand. The threat to Thailand had, indeed, always been SEATO's central issue. In the summer of 1954, before the Organization came into existence, Thailand had notified the Security Council of the United Nations of her anxiety at the approach of the North Vietnamese to her frontiers by their invasion of Laos, and had subsequently accepted substantial assistance from the United States in order to double her military forces. Thailand's fears had deep historical roots. They rested in the ancient, bitter enmity between the closely related Thai-Lao and Thai-Siamese peoples and the Vietnamese, which in its turn was founded on the confrontation between Indian-influenced and Chinese-influenced states in Indo-China which has been going on for almost two thousand years.

When the French came to Indo-China in the second half of the 19th century, this ancient conflict had reached the point where Thailand – which had absorbed Laos – had become the protagonist of the Indian-influenced side, and faced the Chinese-influenced Vietnamese in a long struggle for power over Cambodia. France restored the integrity of Cambodia and rescued a small part of Laos from Thailand. Five sixths of the Lao population, however, and most of the old Laotian territory, remained in Thailand. In compensation, French Laos was given areas in the mountains to the east which had long served as a neutral buffer between Thailand and Vietnam, or whose people had other traditional objections to domination by the Lao. The potentially anti-Lao population in the hills was a little more numerous than the Lao himself, who inhabitated the more easily accessible valleys.

While France held the ring, the innate instability of Laos did not matter. But as French power finally departed, the ethnic contradiction built into the fabric of the country by the accidents of history made it impossible for Laos to achieve the internal harmony which the neutral role assigned her by the Geneva Conference demanded. The North Vietnamese were able to use the fears and suspicions of the anti-Lao hillmen to prolong their hold on northern Laos. The Lao population in their turn looked to the influence of the 7–9 million Lao in Thailand. The United States and then SEATO took up position on the side of Thailand; the Communist world was automatically ranged on the other. Laos could not be an effective buffer; it needed only the occasion to become a full-scale battleground. This was the root cause of Thailand's anxiety in 1954; not her anti-Communist sentiment, but the ingrained mutual hostility between her people and the Vietnamese.

UNDECLARED WARS

Matters came to a head in May 1962, when in spite of limited United States and Thai help to their friends in Laos, substantial Vietnamese support seemed likely to bring the Communist faction to the borders of Thailand at a moment when a new Geneva Conference was attempting to re-establish Laotian neutrality and stability. Although French disagreement prevented SEATO action as such, owing to the unanimity rule, other SEATO powers under the leadership of the United States responded individually to Thailand's appeal for help by moving troops and aircraft to the threatened area. These forces were withdrawn within a few months, but their presence and the implication that effective SEATO action was no longer prevented by the unanimity rule did much to reassure Thailand during the subsequent difficulties in Laos.

By the end of 1964 the complexities of the still unsolved Laotian problem were becoming more and more entangled with that of North and South Vietnam. This too had become critical, for South Vietnam's rejection of reunification, and the oppressive misgovernment of President Ngo Dinh Diem, had been followed by a peasant rebellion under Communist leadership, soon to be backed by North Vietnam. The increasing strength of the Vietcong, as it is called, had led to ever greater involvement of the United States in support of the non-Communist South Vietnamese government. Finally in February 1965, when over twenty thousand United States advisers and immense financial support failed to stem the Vietcong tide, United States aircraft began to attack targets in North Vietnam. A massive commitment of American troops to ground operations in South Vietnam followed. The United States thus took into her own hands the issue of peace or war in East Asia. SEATO is deeply concerned with the outcome.

Meanwhile, however, the nature of the SEATO alliance had changed in several ways. In 1957 Malaya, which under the British had both enjoyed the protection of SEATO and provided some of the bases for Commonwealth action in support of the alliance, became independent. This substantially reduced SEATO territory. Malaya did not join SEATO but the bases remained available for SEATO purposes subject to the veto implicit in Malayan sovereignty. The much more important Singapore base remained available under similar conditions when Singapore attained independence in 1963. But Singapore too stayed outside SEATO. Thus the undeclared war waged by Communist-inclined Indonesia on the newly integrated Malaysian state from 1963 to 1966 was also none of SEATO's concern, although effective Commonwealth participation in SEATO was clearly bound up with Malaysia's survival, and although three SEATO members became actively engaged on one side and a fourth, the Philippines, inclined to sympathy with the other.

Events on the Himalayan border between India and China in 1962 had led at the same time to changes in the attitude of Pakistan. When Pakistan became a member of SEATO in 1954 she was in little danger from Communist China in spite of her Himalayan border, and the danger from Russia through Afghanistan was remote. She was however deeply concerned with the threat from India, with whom she was still bitterly at odds over Kashmir. Although in ratifying the SEATO Treaty the Americans stated their view that SEATO was an anti-Communist alliance and that it was only against Communist aggression that the United States was committed, Pakistan's membership was motivated partly by her wish for allies in case of a war with India.

CENTO BETWEEN SEATO AND NATO

The Pakistani decision in September 1955 to adhere to the Central Treaty Organization (CENTO), then known as the Baghdad Pact, was more clearly directed towards the threat from the Communist world. CENTO was the third of the great regional pacts to come into existence, binding together Turkey, Iran, Iraq, Pakistan and Britain in terms somewhat similar to those of NATO and SEATO, with the backing of the United States. Turkey provided a link to the west through her simultaneous membership of NATO, and Pakistan to the east as a member of SEATO. The Iraqi revolution in 1958 led to the withdrawal of Iraq from CENTO and to the removal of the headquarters from Baghdad to Ankara, where in March 1959 bilateral agreements for mutual security and defence were signed by the United States with Iran, Pakistan and Turkey.

Through her two great alliances Pakistan was provided with ample assurance against attack by Russia and China, but in her quarrel with India over Kashmir she had always felt alone. In 1962 India's long-smouldering border disagreement with China burst into flame. The Indians were sharply defeated and turned to the West for help. Britain and the United States responded promptly and the pro-Chinese slant of India's non-alignment was at an end. For Pakistan the important point was that India, without being a member of SEATO or CENTO, had received substantial Western help which she might use against Pakistan. In 1965 Pakistan saw her worst fears realized. Nor did SEATO help her in the short, bitter, war with India. Her reaction was to mend her bridges with China: at the SEATO Council Meeting in 1967 she was represented only by an observer.

From the changed position which followed the return to power of General de Gaulle in 1958, France, too, no longer viewed the South-East Asian problem in the old simple terms of containment of Communism. The formation of SEATO in 1954 had followed hard on the heels of the Viet Minh victory over France in Indo-China, a war in which China materially supported the Viet Minh. It was natural that the French should view Communist China as an enemy. Ten years later, however, General de Gaulle, ever more critical of United States handling of the situation in Vietnam, gave point to his criticism by a cordial rapprochement with China. His new attitude did not yet entail a withdrawal from SEATO, although his refusal to act with SEATO in the successive Laotian crises, and his decision not to be represented at the SEATO Council Meeting in 1967, show how far circumstances have changed. The West, he said, should leave the people of the area to settle their quarrels themselves, and also to settle freely the question of their relations with China. This implied agreement to the Chinese claim to a natural hegemony in South-East Asia was not at all to the taste of SEATO as a whole.

SEATO IN CHANGED CIRCUMSTANCES

Nevertheless, there is no doubt that the nature of the threat to SEATO is different from what it was in 1954. When SEATO was founded it was assumed that China would seek by all means to spread Communism throughout South-East Asia, and that she would be backed by Russia in this aim. Now that the Sino-Soviet dispute seems to have invalidated this assumption, the short-term military threat from China has become less credible, in spite of her recent acquisition of a nuclear capability. Some Chinese have even shown a more immediate preoccupation with their border with Russia than with what they see as the threat to themselves in the south.

In these circumstances it may well be asked what useful purpose SEATO serves. The area concerned has recent experience of three wars in which its members have been engaged. SEATO has been formally involved in none of them, although its name is used by some members to justify their presence in Vietnam. Two of its members have entered into cordial relationships with the Communist power against whom the organization was constructed.

The answer lies partly in intangibles. Much has been achieved at the grass roots of international co-operation. The day-to-day work on common problems at Bangkok, the liaison, the training and intelligence exchanges have had immense value. The close collaboration between intelligence services and border control officials, the adoption of common police methods, the examination and analysis of propaganda techniques, the lending of experts, have been and will continue to be of great importance. The possibility of disagreeing without necessarily being disagreeable, the forum of discussion and compromise that membership of a great organization brings, are themselves contributions to stability.

The capital fact is, however, the substantial degree of unanimity that remains, exemplified by the recent adoption of a common attitude to the war in Vietnam by all the members of SEATO except France. As the widening Sino-Soviet rift leads statesmen to re-examine the foundations of their policies in the Orient, the measure of agreement within SEATO is perhaps as significant as the differences of view.

BIBLIOGRAPHY

Collective Defence in South-East Asia. (Royal Institute of International Affairs, 1956.)

Brian Crozier. *South-East Asia in Turmoil.* (Penguin Books, 1965.)

Saul Rose (Ed.). *Politics in Southern Asia.* (Macmillan, 1963.)

The South-East Asia Treaty Organization. (Central Office of Information, R. 5569, London, April 1963.)

CHINA'S 'ALGEBRA OF REVOLUTION'

W. A. C. Adie

THE BANDUNG CONFERENCE AND THE TEN PRINCIPLES

In April 1955 the first attempt was made by the leaders of some 'non-aligned' Asian and African countries to formulate a political platform acceptable to all of them. They met at Bandung, Indonesia, and drew up Ten Principles of Peaceful Coexistence as a code of international behaviour for developing nations. Several of these Principles referred to the Charter of the United Nations. The emphasis of this first Afro-Asian Conference, originally proposed by the non-aligned Colombo Powers, was mainly on economic co-operation among the participating countries on the basis of mutual interest, respect for mutual sovereignty, and non-alignment *vis-à-vis* the Great Powers.

By April 1965, when the tenth anniversary of the Conference was celebrated in Djakarta, much of the original concept had been transformed. Of the sixty countries invited to Djakarta only thirty-six were represented at the opening ceremony; delegates included only one foreign head of state (Prince Sihanouk of Cambodia) and three Communist prime ministers: Chou En-lai, Kim Il-song of North Korea and Pham Van Dong of North Vietnam. As the Japanese Kyodo news agency put it, these celebrations were meant to 'steal the thunder' of the second Afro-Asian Conference to be held in Algiers. President Sukarno called for a reconsideration of the first of the ten Bandung principles – respect for the purposes and principles of the UN Charter; this set the tone for the Sino-Indonesian approach to the Algiers meeting.

During the celebrations Sukarno laid the foundations for a building to house the Conference of New Emerging Forces (CONEFO) and he made clear that this conference, which he hoped to convoke in August 1966, was backed by China. Chou En-lai, whose diplomacy contributed so much to the success of the first Bandung Conference, also called for alteration of the Ten Principles and suggested that CONEFO could become a revolutionary and progressive alternative to the United Nations. During the preparations for the Second Afro-Asian Conference, the order of priorities adopted by the first was reversed; practical economic co-operation came last after subjects like decolonization and prohibition of nuclear tests.

The considerable shift in alignments since the doctrine of non-alignment was first adopted has largely been due to the attempts of the Communist Powers, especially Russia and China, to take over the whole idea of Asian, Afro-Asian and non-aligned movements and conferences and use them for their own purposes. Thanks to the cold war and the schisms in the Communist bloc, the emergent nations' movement towards solidarity and mutual co-operation has disintegrated and has become split between nations supporting the ideals of the 'non-aligned' conference of Belgrade and Cairo and nations in alignment with Peking.

POLICIES OF CHINA AND THE SOVIET UNION

China, for reasons connected with its own revolutionary history, reiterates that emancipation and economic development for emergent countries can never come from international organizations or big powers, and that disarmament and relaxation of international tension will not increase aid and produce world peace, that on the contrary permanent peace can be won only by purging the world in mass revolutionary war and building on the ruins. The Peking leaders cast Asia and its African and Latin American allies in the same role, on a world scale, as that performed by the peasant masses in China's revolutionary war: as the Chinese villagers were then united under the leadership of Mao Tse-tung in and by struggle against 'imperialism and its lackeys' in the towns, so now the 'world countryside' is to be united under the leadership of Mao's China in and by the struggle against 'United States imperialism and its lackeys' in the highly industrialized countries – including the 'revisionist' Soviet Union.

Just before the First Afro-Asian Conference at Bandung, Madame Sun Yat-sen published an article called 'Five Cardinal Principles' which claimed that the Soviet Union and China based their relations with each other on these 'Five Principles'. First invoked in 1954 to set Nehru's seal on Mao's occupation of Tibet, the Principles were: mutual respect for each other's territorial integrity and sovereignty, mutual non-aggression, mutual non-interference in each other's internal affairs, equality and mutual benefit, peaceful coexistence. At that time Stalin's successors had reappraised their policy towards such 'national-bourgeois' leaders as Nehru, Nasser and Sukarno; China was assigned a leading role in drawing them by diplomacy and example into a sort of economic co-prosperity sphere relying on Soviet weapons for defence; eventual economic, administrative and social Sovietization was the aim.

In order to harness the neutralist and pacifist sentiments of the emergent peoples of Asia and Africa for the new stage of the cold war – a great outflanking movement through the 'world countryside' – the World Peace Council (WPC), the Communist front organization for the exploitation of anti-European policy and national liberation movements, set up 'Afro-Asian Solidarity Committees' at a so-called 'Asian Nations conference for the relaxation of international tension' held in New Delhi. These later developed into the Afro-Asian People's Solidarity Organization (AAPSO). The Communists publicized this conference as a preparation for the Asian-African Conference; it was attended by a large Chinese delegation and by Soviet members of the WPC bureau, although Russia was not invited to Bandung. The Indian Government issued a denial that this meeting had any standing in relation to the Bandung Conference.

At Bandung, Chou En-lai radiated reasonableness, eclipsed Nehru and charmed Nasser; the AAPSO headquarters were set up in Cairo, not Delhi, and trade and diplomatic relations were established between Cairo and Peking. It looked as if China was indeed playing her part in a combined operation to harness the 'Bandung Spirit'. But after 1956 it became clear that Moscow and Peking were projecting rival interpretations of this 'spirit' which reflected ideological conflict underlined by rivalry for control of the territories, resources and subject peoples of Central Asia and the 'Third World'.

In Moscow, Khrushchev emphasized that the Soviet Near and Far East had a special part to play in his plans for attracting other countries of the East to his 'world economic system of socialism'. In Peking, Liu Shao-chi and others assigned a similar task to the minority areas of China. They emphasized the importance of their independent strategic resources. They also stressed the close connexion between United Front work in the non-Chinese areas within China's frontiers and the work of extending China's 'international united front' beyond them. In South-East Asia, it was hoped that Buddhist and Islamic organizations and the overseas Chinese would act as a link to promote this front.

At this time Mao Tse-tung probably still hoped to solve his problems, including Formosa, by kid-glove methods, assuming that he enjoyed overwhelming popular support. His followers' task was to 'help' the non-Communist Chinese to 'raise their ideological level'; they would accept Communism with a minimal use of violence on either side.

Similarly with the rest of the world; Chou En-lai and his colleagues have often said that '90 per cent of the world's population want revolution', and that it is China's 'special destiny' to help all those who are not yet 'liberated' – this includes all independent countries which have 'bourgeois-nationalist' governments, such as Indonesia.

Like the Russians, the Chinese handle their relations with the Afro-Asian world as an extension of their drive to 'help' the minority areas of Central Asia, and changes in the nature of the United Front within China have been closely linked with changes in relations with outside countries, notably India and the Soviet Union itself. These in turn have affected the whole atmosphere of Asian relations. With the 'sharpening of the class struggle' against supposed counter-revolutionaries in China, both the international Communist movement and the movement for Asian solidarity have been split in two. The main reason for this has been the nature of the Chinese revolution. In Mao's 'algebra of revolution' armed struggle is indispensable in order to have a 'main enemy' against whom others (secondary enemies) must willy-nilly join the Communists in a United Front; then the stress of enemy pressure and alternate doses of 'unity' and 'struggle' are used to assimilate these allies to the Communist core.

When the Chinese and then the AAPSO established themselves in Cairo, the AAPSO became the scene of an inconclusive struggle for control between the Chinese, the Russians and the Egyptians who supplied the Secretary-General. It soon became clear that the Chinese regarded their links with the Arab countries as primarily a means of access to areas where armed struggle could be encouraged, especially Algeria; the Arab leaders, Nasser's friend Tito and the Soviet leaders were opposed to the escalation of armed struggles in the area.

During the Middle East crises of 1956, 1957, and 1958 and in Iraq in 1959, the Chinese appeared eager to embroil the Soviet Union in an 'anti-imperialist war' and to encourage local armed risings. Nasser declared a 'holy war' against Communism and Khrushchev dissociated himself from China's militant talk of 'volunteers'. The Peking press told Nasser that if he wanted to promote Arab unity he should support 'the people of Algeria, Jordan, Oman, etc. now under direct imperialist aggression' – that is, promote armed struggles – and hinted that otherwise he would end up like Chiang Kai-shek. *Red Flag* denounced the UAR's slogan 'neither East nor West' as a 'step towards going over to the enemy'. During the CPC 10th Anniversary celebrations in October 1959, Peking published an attack on Nasser by the Syrian Communist leader, Bakhdash, which described him as a reactionary dictator and tool of the Bank of Egypt, if not of 'imperialism'. The Egyptian Foreign Office sent word to the twenty-five nations of the Bandung Conference suggesting that they reduce their representation at Peking to that of chargé d'affaires as a mark of protest against Chinese aggression against Tibet, India, Laos 'and now the UAR'.

In fact, by this time the original 'Bandung Spirit' had largely evaporated. Nehru had revealed China's activities on the Indian border and shortly afterwards a Tass communiqué dissociated the Soviet Government from China on this issue too. China had also faced Nepal and Burma with border claims, and quarrelled with Indonesia over her discrimination against the overseas Chinese; the Chinese press called this 'currying favour with US imperialism'.

These accusations of 'going over to the enemy' reflected Peking's recasting of the international united front. It was not a mere reappraisal of the neutralist leaders but a practical operation of revolutionary algebra to change their standpoint. Under struggle, they must move closer to China or be 'exposed' as stooges of the enemy, like the Dalai Lama. This operation against the neutralists abroad was the corollary of the tougher measures taken for the ideological transformation of non-Communist Chinese and of the Tibetans and other minority peoples, after the 'hundred flowers' period of free speech in 1957 had revealed an unexpectedly serious opposition to the Communist Party's rule within China.

Having carried 'struggle' to the extreme and thereby brought about Chinese international isolation, Peking now switched towards emphasis on 'unity' in both internal and foreign policy and rapidly mended its fences with Burma, Nepal and Outer Mongolia; but the reconciliation with Indonesia, sealed by the visit of Ch'en Yi to sign a treaty of friendship, soon acquired a wider significance. The joint communiqué issued after his talks with Sukarno called for 'a second Asian-African Conference in the shortest possible time'. Peking now began to use Djakarta more and more, as Moscow had originally tried to use Peking, as a catspaw for operations in the Afro-Asian world. Like Mao, however, Sukarno had his own purposes.

In 1960 the Chinese leaders began to consider Africa, especially tropical Africa, as the centre of the world revolution. They failed to have the AAPSO secretariat moved to Conakry, but after the fact-finding tour of Africa by a Chinese delegation to the AAPSO meeting there in June 1961, Peking increasingly used its Asian contacts, especially Indonesia and Ceylon, as a means of extending its influence in the continent. China's entry on the African scene was marked by the massacre of Arabs in the Zanzibar revolution. Although China probably had little to do with that event, she has profited from it since. But it is not clear whether her purpose is to supplant the Arabs, Indians, Soviets and Europeans in Africa or to secure valuable raw materials. As the *Peking Review* has pointed out, the Congo produces many minerals used to make thermonuclear and other weapons.

Soon after the opening of the Sino-Soviet cold war in April 1960, Mao Tse-tung began to edge the Soviet Union out of Asian and African organizations, with the help of his Indonesian allies. Battle was openly joined at the Afro-Asian writers' conference in Cairo. Soviet delegates told Asians: 'The Chinese pretend America is the enemy, but really it is ourselves.' The Chinese told the Africans: 'These Europeans are all the same.' In April 1963 Sino-Soviet polemics disrupted the AAPSO conference at Moshi, Tanganyika; and President Nyerere warned against the neo-colonialist tendencies of socialist as well as capitalist countries. In the same month a conference held at Djakarta set up an 'Afro-Asian Journalists Association' to rival the Soviet-controlled 'International Organization of Journalists'. In June the Sino-Indonesians took over the Afro-Asian Writers' Bureau; they have subsequently taken over the permanent bureau of the Afro-Asian Lawyers Conference in Conakry and tried with varying success to organize Front organizations for scientists, youth, workers, lawyers, 'peace-fighters', etc. The ultimate aim is to establish an 'Afro-Asian Permanent Secretariat' in Djakarta to replace the AAPSO and its subsidiaries the Afro-Asian Economic Seminar and Women's Bureau.

CAIRO CONFERENCE, 1964, AND SECOND AFRO-ASIAN CONFERENCE

All this activity was in preparation for a Second Bandung Conference and ultimately, perhaps, for CONEFO, which were expected to embody the 'great unity' of Afro-Asian and Latin American peoples under China's leadership, much as the Chinese People's Political Consultative Conference embodies the 'great unity' of China's people with Mao Tse-tung. In the last two years it has become increasingly clear that these conferences are seen by the Chinese as both a means and an alternative to the transformation according to Peking's requirements of the world Communist apparatus (now represented as a tool of the Soviet revisionists) and of the United Nations (still allegedly manipulated by the American imperialists).

At the end of 1963 Chou En-lai made a seventy-two-day tour of ten

African countries, Burma, Pakistan and Ceylon; on his return he reported that the tour had served to prepare for the second Afro-Asian meeting, at which 'concrete measures must be taken for the liberation of nations still under colonial rule'. At that time most of Chou En-lai's hosts were more interested in the coming second non-aligned conference in Cairo (5–11 October 1964) to which forty-seven countries sent substantial delegations. The conference adopted nine principles of co-existence and called on all nations not to produce, acquire or test nuclear weapons. China exploded her first atomic device six days later, and a *People's Daily* editorial welcomed Sukarno's demand for 'confrontation' instead of coexistence.

China's militant attitude again reflected her internal situation; a return to the tense political atmosphere of 1958–60 had followed concessions to 'capitalist' economic methods which arrested the economy's downward spiral but encouraged ideological deviations. With the escalation of the war in Indo-China, China multiplied her military preparations while Chou En-lai made strenuous efforts at the Bandung anniversary celebrations to cement the international Communist front. The postponement of the Second (Algiers) Afro-Asian Conference in 1965 was a setback to Chou En-lai's diplomacy, soon followed by the fall of Sukarno and Nkrumah and the US build-up in Vietnam. These events contributed to the division of the Party's leadership which was revealed in the erratic course of the 'Great Proletarian Cultural Revolution' during 1966. In 1967, China's foreign relations and trade suffered considerable damage thanks to the reckless provocations of extremist opponents of Chou En-lai and his foreign minister, Marshal Chen Yi; after the foreign ministry and several embassies had been sacked by Red Guards, relations even with such friendly countries as Cambodia and Burma deteriorated and Peking openly supported insurgent groups dedicated to the overthrow of most Asian governments, having apparently abandoned all hope of 'uniting' with them.

ASIAN POLITICAL CONFERENCES, 1946–65

1946 – Conference at Delhi convened by Jawaharlal Nehru for discussion of Asian affairs. Pan-Asianism given a trial run, but not regarded as a practicable ideal. Conference notable for clash between India and Kuomintang representatives of China over rival views on status of Tibet.

1949 – Conference of Asian countries called at Delhi to give moral support to Indonesians after Dutch attempt to suppress Indonesian Republic.

1954 – Conference of Colombo Powers (India, Pakistan, Burma and Ceylon) at Colombo. Stormy discussions between India and Pakistan over Kashmir. Conference led to widening of idea of Asian conferences and produced the Bandung Conference.

1955 – 'Asian Nations Conference for the relaxation of international tension' convened in Delhi before the Bandung Conference by WCP, an organization dominated by Soviet and pro-Soviet Communists. Recognized as an attempt to exploit Bandung idea for Soviet purposes, and repudiated by India and Indonesia.

1955 – Bandung Conference of Asia and African powers. Conceived as an international demonstration in favour of non-alignment. Struggle for primacy between India and China; China entered on period of respectability and diplomatic initiative. Soviet Union excluded from conference as being a non-Asian country. Anti-Communist front by Ceylon and Turkey proved on the whole a failure.

1961 – Conference at Belgrade of non-aligned powers. Held in the shadow of resumption of atom tests by Soviet Union. Western hopes that conference would roundly condemn the Communists were disappointed. Nehru and Tito dominant figures.

1964 – Cairo Conference of non-aligned countries; forty-seven participants adopted nine principles of coexistence and called on all nations not to produce, acquire or test nuclear weapons.

1965 – Algiers Conference, planned for July, postponed to November owing to revolution in Algiers. This conference intended as the sequel to Bandung; but whereas original Bandung Conference stressed loyalty to the Charter of the United Nations, this conference was expected to be a demonstration against the United Nations. Of special interest was attempt by China to exclude Soviet Union once more, and counter-attempt by Soviet Union to gain admittance. Indonesia, which played a leading part in making arrangements for the conference, tried to exclude Malaysia.

Minorities and Disputed Areas

MINORITY GROUPS IN ASIA

Edmund Leach

ALMOST without exception the frontiers of the present-day sovereign states of South and South-East Asia are the product of political bargains and administrative arrangements made by the European colonial powers during the 19th and early 20th centuries. Such frontiers pay scant regard to the ethnic peculiarities of the populations which they contain. For example, at least sixty quite different languages are spoken by the inhabitants of modern Burma and some of these correspond to cultural differences quite as radical as those which separate an Englishman from a Turk.

As British experience shows, the political problems which such ethnic differences entail are not easily predictable. The English ultimately assimilated the Cornish and achieved a political synthesis with both the Welsh and the Scots yet failed altogether to come to terms with the Irish. Similar puzzles present themselves all over Asia. A great variety of factors may be relevant, the numerical size of the 'minority' and the level of its political sophistication being among the more obvious. As to the latter, the incompatibility of Buddhist Sinhalese and Hindu Tamils in Ceylon or the relations between Chinese and Malays in the Federation of Malaya are issues of quite a different order from those posed by the tribal minorities of Burma or by the Nagas of Assam in relation to the Government of India. It is the circumstances of 'tribal' minorities of the latter kind which I wish briefly to consider in this essay.

MINORITIES

Several general points need to be stressed. In the first place this problem of the tribal minorities is no minor matter. Minorities of this kind exist in every Asian country; they number, in all, many millions of individuals; and in many countries, Burma, Thailand, Malaya and Indonesia for example, the map area inhabited by the tribal peoples is substantially greater than that occupied by the politically dominant majority.

Secondly it must be understood that within these tribal areas the number of distinguishable linguistic groups is very large. If each group is to be considered as a separate ethnic unit deserving special attention on its own then certainly the problems posed by the tribal minorities become insuperable. But that is not really how things are. All over Asia the smaller linguistic groups are ceasing to be distinguishable as separate entities; they are either disappearing altogether by assimilation with the dominant majority or else they are coalescing into self-conscious minority nations. In the borderlands of Burma and Assam the minorities which really matter are those which appear in news reports under such labels as Naga, Kachin, Chin, Karen. Originally these terms were merely category labels used by foreigners to describe a mixed collectivity of very small culturally distinct groups; it is only the political accidents of the past twenty-five years which have moulded the populations concerned into incipient nations. Thirty years ago there were no Nagas; there were only Angami, Ao, Rengma, Sema, Konyak and so on, all busily engaged in perennial mutual hostilities. Today the inhabitants of the Naga Hills are aware of themselves as Nagas and on that account they constitute a genuine political force of serious dimensions. In the essay which follows it is with tribal minorities of this latter scale that I am concerned.

At this level the common assumption that the adjective 'tribal' is equivalent to 'primitive' or 'backward' needs to be treated with caution.

It is true that, in general, the tribal peoples occupy inaccessible parts of the country, and on that account they are, quite literally, 'backwoodsmen'. A certain primitiveness follows automatically from the lack of communications; these are people who exist on the margins of the world economic system; compared with those of even the least sophisticated townsman their standards of life are elementary; by suitably selected photographs journalistic propaganda can readily make it appear that the typical tribesman is a naked savage. Even so it does not follow that such tribesmen are ill-qualified to take advantage of changing political and economic circumstances. The quality of the educated elite among the tribal peoples is often as good as or better than that on which the central government has to rely.

History is relevant here. When the European colonial regimes were first elaborated during the 19th century the tribal peoples of East Asia appeared pre-eminently 'primitive'. Precisely on this account, they received a disproportionate amount of charitable aid. Most colonial governments paid exaggerated respect to local religious prejudice. But 'religious' in this context referred only to the acknowledged major religions – Christianity, Hinduism, Buddhism, Islam. The religions of the tribal minorities were deemed to be mere superstition and deserved no protection. The great surge of 19th-century Christian missionary endeavour was therefore diverted towards the primitives. In the eyes of the administration the Christian conversion of a Buddhist or a Muslim might entail all sorts of unforeseeable political consequences, but surely the conversion of a cannibal or a headhunter could only be for the good? Maybe; yet in the long run this too had political consequences. The well-financed schools of the Christian missions often provided an education vastly superior to anything contained in the traditional system of the 'civilized' major groups.

Today the leaders of the tribal minorities are almost invariably mission-trained Christians of considerable educational attainment. They frequently display an almost European contempt for the ignorant stupidity of their 'heathen' political overlords. In consequence, the cultural gulf which now separates the tribal minorities from their nominal masters is much wider than it was in the original pre-missionary phase of colonial expansion. The prospect is lamentable. The opposition of Christian versus Buddhist or of Christian versus Muslim offers truly formidable obstacles to any attempted cultural synthesis or assimilation.

Another relevant historical detail is that in some (but not all) cases the colonial authorities systematically recruited military police from the 'tribals' rather than from the majority population. In Burma, for example, before 1940, locally recruited military and military police were drawn from the Kachin, Chin and Karen tribal minorities but none at all from the majority Buddhist population of Burmese and Shans. Similarly in Indonesia the bulk of the Dutch colonial army was recruited from the Eastern Islands in the vicinity of Amboina where most of the population are of Papuan extraction and converts to the Dutch Reformed Church. Government policy was plainly designed to range these dark-skinned Christians in opposition to the Indonesian Muslim population which is heavily concentrated in the Island of Java.

QUESTIONS OF SOVEREIGNTY

Although the successor governments are less dependent upon the loyalty of tribal soldiers, the military competence of tribal minorities still has widely ramifying political implications. For example the paradox by which Indonesia pursued a chauvinistic policy towards Western New Guinea at a time when the government's control over Indonesia proper was only notional was certainly influenced by the potential threat which an otherwise unemployed Amboinese soldiery might offer to the internal security of the state. Or again there is the Burma case.

At the coming of independence the Commander-in-Chief of the Burma Army was a highly qualified Karen graduate of the British Military Academy. His later dismissal coincided with the disbandment of a substantial (Karen) section of the Burma Army. This in turn helped to perpetuate the insurrectionist movement among the Karen minority, but it also increased the dependence of the central government upon the loyalty of the other main tribal minorities (Kachin and Chins). The semi-autonomous Kachin and Chin regions were then provided with lavish budgetary assistance from central funds. This admittedly was a temporary phase. After the military *coup d'état* which abolished the office of President of the Burma Union relations between the central government and the minorities tended to deteriorate. It is however a mark of the political importance of the minorities that prior to this event a Kachin had been appointed President and titular Head of State.

Yet although education and military advantage often place the leaders of the tribal minority on a par with the leaders of the political majority there are basic problems which remain unresolved. These stem from a fixed belief that the tribal minorities are, in their very essence, both primitive and inferior.

Despite all the fine talk of Asian freedom and 'emancipation from the slave mentality of the colonial epoch' the central governments of countries such as India, Burma, and Indonesia have tended to inherit the prejudices and administrative habits of their British and Dutch predecessors. Colonial administrators treated tribal peoples with ruthless severity. The military punitive expedition seldom achieved any useful purpose but it was the stock response of all colonial governments to any form of 'trouble' in tribal areas. The successor governments tend to react in an identical manner with equal lack of effect. Indeed the indications are that, over the past few years, certain governments, that of India in particular, have been *more* prone than their colonial predecessors to resort to military sanctions against the tribal peoples of their border zones.

The issue of national frontiers is very relevant here. The tribal peoples are frequently located in mountainous regions lying between the major states – the sub-Himalayan area between Assam and west China is a case in point. During the colonial period many such regions were left 'unadministered', that is to say they were designedly treated as buffer zones, a tacitly neutral no-man's-land which the Great Powers could conveniently leave alone. In such circumstances the tribal peoples enjoyed, in practice if not in theory, a large measure of independence.

In contrast, the successor states are preoccupied, to an exaggerated degree, with questions of sovereignty. Because of this, the precise details of political frontiers have come to assume an ominous importance. The territorial claims of the Indian government in the North-East Frontier are no different from those of the previous British Raj but, whereas the British were often enough satisfied with a notional frontier on a notional map, the Indians have felt themselves obliged to establish effective administration up to the very limits of their territory to the clear detriment of the tribal peoples concerned.

It is true that closer administration brings benefits in the form of better communications, medical services, education, trade and so on, but this is true of all colonial enterprise. In any particular case these advantages have to be weighed against the countless difficulties which ensue from the intensification of ethnic solidarity. The Indian Government may plead in all honesty that its attitude towards the tribal peoples is one of high moral purpose, that it aims to bring civilization and economic development to the primitive peoples of Eastern Assam. But this is an old story. The vices of paternalistic colonialism are not a peculiarity of white-skinned rulers and nationalist consciousness pays no heed to good intentions.

The currently existing nations of Southern Asia have proudly achieved their statehood by throwing off the shackles of colonial domination. Yet, in respect to the tribal peoples, they have simply taken over the role of the former colonial powers. *Vis-à-vis* the tribal minorities most of the central governments continue to act as if they themselves were colonial imperialists. Good works are imposed by force. Yet one may predict that where administrative policies of tutelage and apartheid depend upon military sanction then in the long run political nemesis is certain. In any tribal situation a policy of military coercion has the automatic consequence of consolidating a nationalist opposition out of the confusion of pre-existing tribal loyalties. In such circumstances (unless, as in Russia, the central authorities are prepared to be quite exceptionally ruthless) the long-term advantage seems to lie with the advocates of political independence even when economic factors seem to indicate precisely the opposite. The fact that an independent Naga State would be an economic absurdity does not necessarily imply that such a state will never come into being.

The Balkanization of Asia into a vast array of petty independent sovereignties seems undesirable from almost every point of view, yet the existence of the tribal minorities offers a constant threat of this kind of development. How far such Balkanization proceeds will depend in part upon how well the civilian politicians of the existing state manage to keep their military under control. Every act of military suppression postpones still further the prospect of cultural assimilation. This comment needs to be considered against the background fact that in non-Communist Asia in 1967 Pakistan, Burma, Indonesia, Thailand, Vietnam, and Taiwan were all military dictatorships.

If the tribal minorities are to play their part in a larger statehood they must be treated with respect. Military restraint is not enough; it is also necessary that the civil administrators of such regions learn to behave as civil servants and cease to parade themselves as imitation European nabobs and pukka sahibs. The problems posed by the minorities would largely disappear if the central governments concerned devoted their energies to civilizing the administration instead of civilizing the population.

THE SCALE OF THE MINORITY PROBLEM

The official census statistics for Asian countries are neither satisfactory nor comparable. Figures relating to 'minority' communities are especially defective. There are various reasons for this. Minorities tend to be located in inaccessible areas to which census enumerators do not penetrate; there is no agreed principle according to which minorities should be classified; figures are falsified outright for political reasons. The figures cited below are not comparable with one another but give some indication of the dimensions of the problem.

India 1951 Census. Nine major language groups accounting for 325 million out of a total of 356 million. Forty-seven other language groups were listed in which the speakers numbered more than 100,000 per group. 720 language groups were listed in which speakers numbered less than 100,000 per group. 1961 Census gives less detail. Grand total 439 million: this includes 30 million 'scheduled tribes' and 64 million 'scheduled castes'.

There is no way of assessing the total of those who might rate as 'tribal minorities' in the terms of this essay. Supporters of the controversial Nagas claim that they number 'about a million'; the census admits only that they number more than 343,000.

Indonesia 1953 Census. Of a total of 88 million, 52 million are concentrated in the politically dominant islands of Java and Madura. The remaining 36 million are divided into about 100 different major culture groups dispersed over hundreds of different islands.

Malaya 1957 Census. Population classified as 3 million 'Malaysians', 2·3 million Chinese, 0·7 million Indians and Pakistanis. The term Malaysian is here a very wide category including a number of substantial minorities who are not Malays in any ordinary sense.

Thailand 1960 Census. Claims that 94 per cent of a population of 26 million are of Thai culture, 1·8 per cent Chinese and 4 per cent Malay. Apparently the tribal minorities of the northern hill country were not enumerated at all. (For discussion see Kunstadter (1967) Vol. 1, pp. 369–75.)

Burma 1956 Estimate. Of a total of 20 million roughly 60 per cent Burmese, 6 per cent Arakanese, 7 per cent Shan, 9 per cent Karen, 10 per cent Mon, 6 per cent Kachin, Chin, etc. (See also Kunstadter (1967) Vol. 1, p. 87.)

Ceylon 1953 Census. Roughly: 5·5 million Sinhalese, 1 million Ceylon Tamils, 0·5 million Ceylon Muslims, 1 million Indians (without Ceylon citizenship).

Laos and Vietnam. All published figures must be discounted as items of political propaganda. In Laos the numerical total of the numerous tribal minorities appears to be at least equal to that of the politically dominant Thai.

BIBLIOGRAPHY

F. G. Bailey. *Tribe, Caste and Nation.* (Manchester University Press, 1960.)

Verrier Elwin. *A Philosophy of NEFA.* (Sachin Roy, Shillong, 1959.)

Julian F. Embree and Lilian O. Dotson. *Bibliography of the Peoples and Cultures of Mainland South-East Asia.* (Yale University Press, New Haven, 1950.)

Raymond Kennedy. *Bibliography of Indonesian Peoples and Cultures,* 2 vols. (Yale University Press, New Haven, revised edn, 1955.)

Peter Kunstadter (Ed.). *Southeast Asian Tribes, Minorities and Nations,* 2 vols. (Princeton University Press, Princeton, N.J. 1967.)

Edmund Leach. 'The Frontiers of "Burma"'. *Comparative Studies in Society and History*, Vol. III, No. 1. (Mouton, The Hague, 1960.)

H. N. C. Stevenson. *The Hill Peoples of Burma.* (Burma Pamphlets No. 6, Longmans, Calcutta, 1944.)

B. Ter Haat. *Adat Law in Indonesia.* (Institute of Pacific Relations, New York, 1948.)

P. D. R. Williams Hunt. *An Introduction to the Malayan Aborigines.* (Government Press, Kuala Lumpur, 1952.)

THE PROBLEM OF KASHMIR

Matinuzzaman Zuberi

THE State of Jammu and Kashmir has five political divisions – Jammu, the Kashmir Valley, Ladakh, Baltistan, and Gilgit. It has a population of over 4 million, an overwhelming majority of whom are Muslims; Hindus are mainly concentrated in Jammu and Buddhists in Ladakh.

HISTORY BEFORE THE PARTITION OF INDIA

Kashmir was the largest of the Princely States of India before partition. The Maharaja was an absolute autocrat. A system of forced labour combined with a complete lack of any means of expressing their grievances had reduced the people of Kashmir virtually to serfs. Muslims were especially discriminated against, being almost entirely excluded from Government posts and the State Army. In 1931, when the restlessness of the people found expression in a State-wide revolt led by Sheikh Mohammad Abdullah, who had just returned from the Aligarh Muslim University, thousands were thrown into prison without trial.

In 1932 Abdullah founded the All Jammu and Kashmir Muslim Conference. He realized, however, that if the struggle against Dogra princely rule were to succeed, it needed positive support from all sections of the people. Abdullah was brought into contact with the Indian National Congress and realized that the struggle of the Kashmiris was gradually becoming an integral part of the wider struggle for freedom in India. Accordingly, the movement was renamed the All Jammu and Kashmir National Conference and in June 1939 was thrown open to all communities. In 1944 it formulated the 'New Kashmir' plan, which advocated the abolition of landlordism and the convening of a Constituent Assembly based on adult franchise to frame a new constitution for the State.

When the movement became intercommunal in character, Ghulam Abbas, formerly one of its prominent members, parted company with Abdullah and in 1944 revived the Muslim Conference which was drawn towards the ideology of the All India Muslim League. In the same year, the National Conference became a member of the All India States Peoples' Conference, a sister organization of the Congress whose aim was to secure political rights for the people of the Princely States. Thus,

504

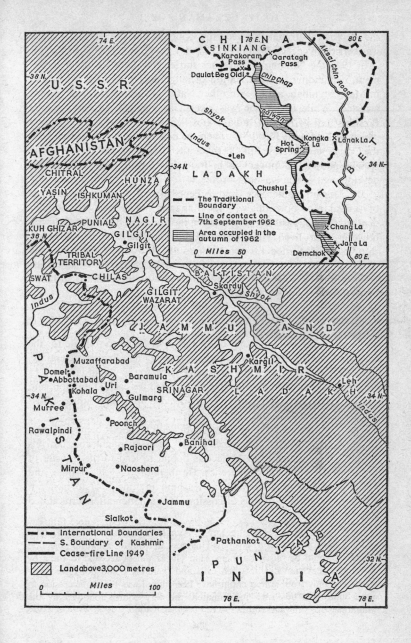

U.S.S.R.

38 N.

AFGHANISTAN

CHITRAL

YASIN   ISHKUMAN

KUH GHIZAR

36 N.   PUNIAL   NAGIR

HUNZA

GILGIT
•Gilgit

TRIBAL
TERRITORY

SWAT   •CHILAS

Indus

GILGIT
WAZARAT

74 E.

CHINA
SINKIANG

Karakoram   Qaratagh
Pass   Pass
Daulat Beg Oldi   Chip Chap

Shyok   Galwan

Indus   Kongka   ×Lanak La
                     Hot ×× La
34 N.   Spring
                          ×   34 N.
LADAKH
•Leh

•Chushul   T
                      I
                      B
The Traditional   E
Boundary   ×Chang La   T
Line of contact on
7th. September 1962   ×Jara La
Area occupied in the Demchok
autumn of 1962
0   Miles   50   80 E.

BALTISTAN
•Skardu   Shyok

JAMMU   AND

P   •Muzaffarabad   KASHMIR   •Kargil
U   Domel•   •Leh
A   •Abbottabad •Uri Baramula   L A D A K H
K   Kohala•   •Gulmarg SRINAGAR
34 N.   34 N.
I   •Murree   Indus
S   Rawalpindi•   •Poonch
T   •Rajaori   •Banihal
A   Mirpur•   •Naoshera
N   •Jammu
     Sialkot•
                              B
               •Pathankot   J   A

International Boundaries   M
S. Boundary of Kashmir   P U N   M
Cease-fire Line 1949   I N D I A   U   32 N.
Land above 3,000 metres

0   Miles   100

76 E.   78 E.

the ideological struggle between the Congress and the Muslim League was carried over to Kashmir.

In 1946 the National Conference started the 'Quit Kashmir' movement, demanding the termination of autocratic rule in the State, and in May, Abdullah, along with other National Conference leaders, was arrested. While in jail, he was elected as Nehru's successor to the Presidentship of the All India States Peoples' Conference, a position which he held until July 1948, when the organization was merged with the Congress. The close links between the National Conference and the secular nationalist movement in India have profoundly affected the development of the Kashmir problem.

The Muslim Conference tried to benefit from the temporary eclipse of its rival by co-operating with the Maharaja and opposing the popular demand for responsible government in the State. Such co-operation was, however, short-lived. Having arrested the National Conference leaders the Maharaja turned his attention to the Muslim Conference, and Abbas and his supporters were arrested on a charge of violating the law prohibiting mass demonstrations. Such was the political situation in Kashmir on the eve of partition.

KASHMIR AND THE PARTITION OF INDIA

The Indian Independence Act of 18 July 1947 failed to provide for the future of the Princely States, merely stating that British suzerainty, together with all treaties and engagements in force, would lapse on 15 August. A separate State Ministry was created for each Dominion, and by 15 August only three States had not decided upon their future status; one of these was Kashmir.

The Maharaja of Kashmir was in a difficult position: being a Hindu, he must have realized that accession to Pakistan might cost him his throne, while accession to India was bound to lead to the transfer of power to the National Conference. He therefore played for time, and when Lord Mountbatten went to Kashmir in June 1947 to hasten a decision, he avoided serious discussion. Mountbatten afterwards stated publicly in Britain:

Had he acceded to Pakistan before 15 August 1947, the future government of India had allowed me to give His Highness an assurance that no objection whatever would be raised by them. Had His Highness acceded to India by 14 August, Pakistan did not then exist and therefore could not have interfered. The only trouble that could have been raised was by non-accession to either side, and this was unfortunately the very course followed by the Maharaja.

On 12 August the Maharaja, in an attempt to maintain the *status quo*, sent identical telegrams to the new Governments of India and Pakistan asking for the conclusion of 'Standstill Agreements' with both countries. On 15 August a Standstill Agreement was concluded with Pakistan, providing for the continuation of the administrative arrangements for communications, supplies, posts and telegraphs. No formal agreement was concluded with India, although it was given effect in practice. However, these arrangements did not create the rights and obligations arising from an act of accession. The absence of a formal agreement with India was interpreted by Pakistan as an indication that Kashmir would ultimately accede to her, and it was later even assumed that the Standstill Agreement somehow covered defence and external affairs. That the Maharaja could simultaneously have asked both India and Pakistan to enter into arrangements involving control of defence and external affairs can certainly be dismissed as impossible. Pakistan's assumption of Kashmir's final accession to her was partly based on the fact that her lines of communication lay through Pakistan, while she had no all-weather road links with India.

Relations between Pakistan and Kashmir deteriorated rapidly. Kashmir complained of a shortage of essential supplies guaranteed by the Standstill Agreement. Refugees in thousands were pouring across the new frontiers of India and Pakistan, and Jammu became a refugee highway.

Amidst this chaos there occurred the Poonch Revolt. Poonch had been ruled by a Hindu Raja who had, after a lawsuit, been deposed by the Maharaja of Kashmir. Subsequently, the much more oppressive Kashmiri taxation system had been extended to Poonch and the people had risen in a no-tax campaign. When Dogra troops were sent to repress it, the militant Poonchis (traditional recruits for the Indian Army) crossed the frontier and returned with arms supplied by their Pakistani supporters. Thus, the movement flared into a full-scale rebellion to overthrow Dogra rule – the 'Azad (Free) Kashmir' movement – and set in motion a series of incidents culminating in the invasion of Kashmir.

INVASION AND ACCESSION

Realizing that he could no longer cope with the situation in the State without the help of the National Conference on 29 September, the Maharaja released Abdullah. The latter declared: 'Our first demand is the complete transfer of power to the people of Kashmir. Representatives of the people in a democratic Kashmir will then decide whether the State should join India or Pakistan.' While a delegation of the National Conference was trying to enlist the support of Pakistani leaders for Abdullah's demand for 'freedom before accession', full-scale invasion of Kashmir started on 22 October.

Tribesmen from the North-West Frontier Province of Pakistan marched across West Punjab and advanced rapidly towards Srinagar. They were joined by Pakistani soldiers 'on leave' under the leadership of Major General Akbar Khan, later Chief of Staff of the Pakistan Army. Looting, burning and abduction took place, claiming both Muslim and Hindu victims, and on the evening of 24 October the Government of India received a desperate appeal for help from the Maharaja. V. P. Menon, Secretary of the Indian States Ministry, flew to Srinagar to clarify the situation. Mehr Chand Mahajan, who became Prime Minister of Kashmir on 15 October, summed up the situation in his book *Accession of Kashmir*: 'We had decided by the 25th evening to go to India if we could get a plane or else to go to Pakistan for surrender.' Menon reported to the Defence Committee that military help was urgently needed. Mountbatten took the view that as Kashmir had not yet acceded to India, it would be improper to send Indian troops there. If, on the other hand, the Maharaja acceded to India, Kashmir would become an integral part of India and Indian troops could then be sent to defend it from further aggression. Mahajan and Abdullah also implored the Indian Government for immediate military assistance.

Menon next flew to Jammu accompanied by Mahajan. He advised the Maharaja, who had left Srinagar in unseemly haste, to offer accession to India. The Maharaja in fact did so, enclosing an Instrument of Accession with a letter to Mountbatten in which he asked for military aid from India. Mountbatten accepted the accession.

In a separate letter, Mountbatten told the Maharaja that it was his Government's wish that 'as soon as law and order have been restored in Kashmir and its soil cleared of the invader, the question of the State's accession should be settled by a reference of the people'. This letter has been the subject of great controversy. Pakistan has maintained that it makes Kashmir's accession conditional upon the verdict of the people and that as the Indian Independence Act did not envisage conditional accession, it is null and void, and that anyway the Maharaja had no authority to execute an instrument of accession after his flight from Srinagar. India, on the other hand, insists that it was a personal letter from Mountbatten in reply to the Maharaja's covering letter and does not form part of the acceptance of the Instrument of Accession, that that document is in no way different from those executed by some 500 other States in India, has no conditions attached to it and does not state that the accession is provisional, and is therefore a document complete in itself.

The Indian view is that legally the document had to be signed by the Maharaja; but it was supported by the largest political organization in the State, the National Conference, which occupied a position similar to that of Congress in India and the Muslim League in Pakistan. Constitutionally India was under no obligation to commit herself to ascertaining the wishes of the people of Kashmir, but with her declared hostility to feudal arbitrary rule and her close links with the popular movement in Kashmir, did not relish the idea of finding herself in a position where she became an ally of the Maharaja against his people. She therefore made this unilateral offer and insisted that despite critical conditions in the States popular rule should be established immediately. Accordingly, an Emergency Administration headed by Abdullah was established, thereby bringing about a revolutionary transfer of power from the Maharaja to the people, the first popular government that the State had ever had. India also maintains that her unilateral offer to seek the will of the people, which in no way affected the legality of accession, was to be implemented only *after* the expulsion of the invaders and the restoration of law and order in the State.

With the constitutional accession of Kashmir, a contingent of Indian troops flew into Srinagar on 27 October, just in time to halt, at the very edge of the airstrip, an advance party of the invaders. During the critical days between 22 and 27 October the National Conference maintained a remarkable degree of order with the help of a local militia. Thus the invaders, who certainly did not want Kashmir's accession to India, not only forced the hesitant Maharaja to make up his mind, but also acted as a catalytic agent in bringing about the overthrow of autocratic rule and the establishment of a popular government.

Pakistan suspected elaborate planning behind the Indian airlift and Jinnah ordered his Commander-in-Chief, General Gracey, to send Pakistani troops to Kashmir immediately. This Gracey was not prepared to do without the approval of Field-Marshal Auchinleck, who was responsible for superintending the partition of the former Indian Army. Auchinleck told Jinnah that such an act of invasion would involve the immediate withdrawal of every British officer from the Pakistan Army, whereupon Jinnah withdrew his order. As for the hastily improvised airlift of Indian troops, the three British Commanders-in-Chief of the Indian Army, Air Force and Navy have denied that it was planned.

On 30 October the Pakistani Government issued a statement alleging that Kashmir's accession to India was 'based on fraud and violence'. On 1 November Mountbatten conferred with Jinnah, who repeated the charge. The rest of their discussion is best summarized by Mountbatten's press attaché in his book *Mission with Mountbatten*: 'The argument then got into a vicious circle. Mountbatten agreed that the accession had been brought about by violence but the violence came from the tribes, for whom Pakistan, and not India, was responsible. To this Jinnah would retort that in his opinion it was India who had committed violence by sending in the troops.' When Mountbatten told Jinnah that the prospect of the tribesmen entering Srinagar was now remote, the latter suggested that both sides withdraw simultaneously. Mountbatten asked how Pakistan could ensure the withdrawal of the tribesmen, to which Jinnah replied: 'If you do this I will call the whole thing off.'

KASHMIR AND THE UNITED NATIONS

On 1 January 1948, after months of futile negotiations, India submitted a formal complaint to the Security Council under Chapter VI of the Charter. She requested the Council to ask Pakistan 'to prevent Pakistan Government personnel, military and civil, from participating in or assisting the invasion of Jammu and Kashmir State' and to deny to the invaders access to and use of her territory for operations in Kashmir. Pakistan lodged a series of countercharges and emphatically denied any complicity in the invasion of Kashmir, claiming that the Pakistani Government had 'continued to do all in their power to discourage the tribal movement by all means short of war'.

On 17 January the Council called upon India and Pakistan to desist from any action which might increase tension and to inform the Council immediately of 'any material change in the situation'. Three days later the Council authorized the appointment of a three-member Commission, one member each to be nominated by India and Pakistan, the third selected by the nominees, to investigate the situation and to mediate. Later the Commission was enlarged to five members. India nominated Czechoslovakia, Pakistan Argentina, and the Council appointed Belgium, Colombia and the United States. Had the Commission, proposed in January, been despatched without delay instead of reaching the sub-continent as it did only at the beginning of July, it might have succeeded in bringing about an early cease-fire in the snow-covered regions of Kashmir; by the time it arrived the snow had melted and the big spring offensive had already started.

THE UN COMMISSION AND THE RESOLUTIONS OF AUGUST 1948 AND JANUARY 1949

The Commission was informed by the Pakistan Foreign Minister that the Pakistan Army had at the time three brigades of regular troops in Kashmir, and that troops had been sent into the State during the first half of May. This action, it was claimed, was taken as a measure of self-defence. The Governor of the North-West Frontier Province told the Commission that the movement of the tribesmen into Kashmir had in fact to be canalized through his province in order to avoid the serious risk of outright war within the territory of Pakistan. It was further admitted that the Azad Kashmir forces were under the overall command and tactical direction of the Pakistan Army. The Commission was now confronted with a situation not visualized by the Security Council during its debates – a clash between the regular armies of India and Pakistan. Its failure to inform the Council immediately of this alarming development and to request fresh instructions had been the cause of many obstacles to settlement of the Kashmir problem.

On 13 August, the Commission adopted a Resolution consisting of three parts. Part I dealt with the establishment of a cease-fire. It did not mention the Azad Kashmir forces; responsibility for implementing the cease-fire was put exclusively on the High Commands of India and Pakistan. Part II set out the principles of a Truce Agreement, beginning with the recognition that the presence of Pakistani troops in Kashmir constituted 'a material change in the situation since it was presented by the Government of Pakistan before the Security Council'. It accordingly provided that (1) all Pakistani troops as well as tribesmen and other Pakistani nationals were to be withdrawn from Kashmir; (2) the territory thus evacuated was to be administered by 'the local authorities under the surveillance of the Commission'; (3) when the Commission had notified that the tribesmen and Pakistani nationals had withdrawn, 'thereby terminating the situation which was represented by the Government of India as having occasioned the presence of Indian troops' in Kashmir, and that Pakistani forces were also withdrawn, India would 'begin to withdraw the bulk' of her forces 'in stages to be agreed upon with the Commission'; (4) pending acceptance of the conditions for the final settlement India was permitted to 'maintain within the lines existing at the moment of the cease-fire' a minimum force which in agreement with the Commission was considered necessary to assist local authorities in the maintenance of law and order. Part III stated that after acceptance by India and Pakistan of a Truce Agreement, both countries would 'enter into consultations with the Commission' to determine conditions for the free expression of the will of the people of Kashmir.

India accepted the Resolution on 20 August with the following reservations to which the Commission gave its unqualified acceptance: (1) that the sovereignty of the Jammu and Kashmir Government over the area evacuated by Pakistani troops would not be brought in to question; (2) that no recognition would be given to the Azad Kashmir authorities; (3) that the time when the withdrawal of Indian forces was to begin, the stages in which it was to be carried out and the strength of the Indian forces to be retained in the State would be decided only by India and the Commission; (4) that the size of the Indian force to be retained in Kashmir should be conditioned by the need to ensure its security against external aggression; and (5) that Part III of the Resolution did not in any way recognize the right of Pakistan to have any part in the plebiscite. With regard to the strategic Northern Area of Gilgit and Baltistan, which had not been covered by the Resolution, Nehru requested that, after the withdrawal of Pakistani forces, the responsibility for the administration of this region (from which he was prepared to exclude Gilgit) should revert to the Kashmir Government and that for its defence to the Government of India. The Commission assured him that this question would be considered.

Pakistan, unenthusiastic, demanded clarification, her main objective being to bring about a 'balanced and synchronized' withdrawal of Indian and Pakistani troops without the disbandment of the Azad Kashmir forces. The Commission concluded that Pakistan was 'unable to accept the Resolution without attaching certain conditions beyond the compass of this Resolution, thereby making impossible an immediate cease-fire and the beginning of fruitful negotiations'. The Commission submitted its first report to the Council in November 1948 but the problem was not really explored. Another opportunity for a complete reappraisal of the problem was, therefore, lost and the Council merely asked the Commission to proceed with its efforts to bring about a cease-fire in Kashmir.

On 11 December the Commission drafted proposals for a plebiscite which were supplementary to the August Resolution. Their main feature was that the United Nations Secretary-General was to nominate a Plebiscite Administrator who would be formally appointed to office by the Government of Jammu and Kashmir.

India's acceptance of these proposals was based on a series of assurances received from the Commission. These were: (1) that India could not be expected to discharge any of her responsibilities regarding the plebiscite until there was satisfactory evidence that Pakistan was carrying out her obligations under Part II of the August Resolution; (2) that the Commission did not contemplate that the Plebiscite Administrator should undertake any administrative functions in regard to the plebiscite until Parts I and II of the Commission's Resolution of 13 August had been implemented; (3) that, in view of the fact that the Azad Kashmir forces now consisted of thirty-two armed battalions under the operational command of the Pakistan Army, there would be 'large-scale disarming' as well as disbanding of these forces; (4) that 'any political activity which might tend to disturb law and order could not be regarded as legitimate'; it was made clear that this assurance precluded any appeal to religious fanaticism; and (5) that should the Plebiscite Administrator find a plebiscite to be impracticable, the way would be open to consider other methods for ensuring the free expression of the will of the people of Kashmir.

Pakistan accepted the proposals after her fears regarding the selection and appointment of the Plebiscite Administrator had been removed by the Commission's assurance that Pakistan, along with India, would be consulted in his selection, and that he would be exclusively responsible for the organization of the plebiscite.

With the acceptance by India and Pakistan of these proposals, a Cease-fire Agreement came into force on 1 January 1949. An agreement on the demarcation of the cease-fire line was finally reached on 27 July. A group of United Nations Military Observers has been patrolling the cease-fire line ever since.

The December proposals were embodied in the Commission's Resolution of 5 January 1949. The very first sentence of these proposals reaffirmed the August Resolution. The manner in which this crucial Resolution was accepted by India and Pakistan had far-reaching consequences during the Truce negotiations. While India had accepted it on the basis of precise written assurances, Pakistan had imposed conditions which amounted to rejection and had later subscribed to it only indirectly. In its anxiety to bring about a cease-fire which depended upon Pakistan's adherence to the August Resolution, the Commission failed to clarify the nature of Pakistan's eventual 'acceptance' of it.

Its reports reveal that Pakistan continued to insist on her own interpretation.

On 24 March 1949 the United Nations Secretary-General nominated an American, Admiral Chester Nimitz, as the Plebiscite Administrator, an unfortunate choice in view of later developments. India had in fact proposed the appointment of the President of the International Red Cross to this post, a proposal favoured by the Colombian member of the Commission, but other delegations had 'explicit instructions' to urge that the Plebiscite Administrator should be a United States citizen. A diplomatic 'victory' virtually undid all the work the Commission had accomplished.

NEGOTIATIONS FOR A TRUCE AGREEMENT

Three interrelated problems presented insurmountable difficulties and wrecked the efforts of the Commission and all the United Nations Mediators to bring about a Truce Agreement: (1) disposal of the Azad Kashmir forces, (2) withdrawal of the regular forces, and (3) the Northern Area.

Disposal of the Azad Kashmir forces. The Resolution of 13 August, while taking note of the presence of Pakistani troops in Kashmir, did not mention the Azad Kashmir forces. The Commission had unanimously agreed that 'it should avoid any action which might be interpreted as signifying *de facto* or *de jure* recognition of the Azad Kashmir Government'. India relied on the assurance that 'large-scale disarming' of Azad forces would take place as a prerequisite to the holding of a plebiscite. She pointed out that these forces, hardly distinguishable from the Pakistan Army, now consisted of thirty-two battalions, which, according to the Commission's own Military Adviser, represented 'a formidable force'. This had changed the military situation since the Resolution was accepted by India; she, therefore, insisted that the phasing of the withdrawal of the 'bulk' of Indian troops from Kashmir depended on the progress made with the disarmament of Azad Kashmir forces. Pakistan, on the other hand, maintained that this question was not relevant to the Truce negotiations and that any disbandment of these forces was conditional upon a reduction in the Kashmir State forces and a withdrawal of Indian troops beyond that of the 'bulk' authorized by the Resolution. The Commission rejected her contention that the main objective of the proposed Truce Agreement was to create a military balance between the forces on either side. It stressed the crucial importance of the disposal of the Azad forces in relation to

514

the withdrawal of Indian troops and concluded that if it had been 'able to foresee that the cease-fire would be prolonged throughout the greater part of 1949 and that Pakistan would use that period to consolidate its position in the Azad territory', this question would have been dealt with in Part II of the Resolution.

Withdrawal of regular forces. India maintained that the timing and staging of the withdrawal of the 'bulk' of her forces and the strength of her troops to be retained in the State were matters for settlement between herself and the Commission only. Her stand on this crucial issue was based on the terms of the Resolution and the Commission's assurances. Pakistan, on the other hand, wanted the withdrawal of her forces to be synchronized with that of the 'bulk' of Indian troops, and in support of her stand she referred to an assurance that such a synchronization could be arranged between the respective High Commands and the Commission. But the Commission explained that its reference to synchronization was meant to ensure 'the establishment of a time sequence' for the two withdrawals after the acceptance of Truce Terms; it could not accept the Pakistani contention that the withdrawal of her forces was conditional on her agreement to the Indian withdrawal plan because this would have been incompatible with its Resolution.

The Northern Area. India relied on the Commission's assurance that although this area was not mentioned in the August Resolution, her demand to re-establish control over it could be considered in its implementation. Pakistan, on the other hand, maintained that as her forces effectively controlled it when the Resolution was drafted, the region did not require any special treatment and that Part II of the Resolution applied equally to all parts of the State where the armed forces of India and Pakistan faced each other. But the Commission was inclined to the view that Pakistan had consolidated her military control over the area between August 1948 and January 1949. It conceded that the Indian demand was 'based on legal claims', but in view of the changed military situation it could not be a party to an arrangement which would have resulted in an extension of conflict.

The deadlock was now complete. The greatest single obstacle to a Truce Agreement was the reorganization of the Azad Kashmir forces into thirty-two well-equipped battalions; it transformed the military situation and made the withdrawal of regular forces more difficult to achieve within the framework of the Resolution. The Commission had to admit that 'the situation in the State has changed; the Resolutions remain unchanged'. Abandoning its mediatory role, the Commission finally proposed compulsory arbitration by Admiral Nimitz on all points of dispute regarding the Truce Terms. Pakistan accepted the proposal but India maintained that the issues at stake were primarily political in character and did not lend themselves easily to arbitration, and that the main issue of the disbandment of the Azad Kashmir forces was 'not a matter for arbitration but for affirmative and immediate action'. The Commission admitted in its final report to the Security Council in December 1949 that its ambiguous clarifications and sometimes contradictory assurances had partly contributed to the deadlock.

THE DIXON REPORT

Even at this stage the Security Council failed to discuss the substance of the Kashmir problem. After an 'informal mediation' by General McNaughton, the Canadian member of the Council, which tended to eliminate the Commission's assurances regarding the Azad Kashmir forces and the Northern Area, the Council asked Sir Owen Dixon, an Australian jurist, to bring about the demilitarization of Kashmir and to make any suggestions which might contribute to a solution.

Dixon stated in his report that 'when the frontier of the State of Jammu and Kashmir was crossed on ... 20 October 1947, by hostile elements, it was contrary to international law, and ... when, in May 1948 ... units of the regular Pakistan forces moved into the territory of the State, that too was inconsistent with international law'. This statement by a jurist of international repute implied a recognition of the Indian case that Kashmir was constitutionally a part of India and that she had been a victim of aggression; but Dixon drew no practical conclusions. He proposed several schemes for the demilitarization of Kashmir which were unacceptable to India as they ran counter to the Commission's assurances. Concerned to avoid another refugee problem, he then suggested a combination of partition and plebiscite in the Valley. This was presented in two forms: (1) a plebiscite by sections and the allocation of each section according to the result of the vote, or (2) regions where there was no doubt about the will of the people should be allocated to India or Pakistan without any vote being taken, the plebiscite to be 'confined only to the uncertain area'. India was willing to discuss the second variation of Dixon's scheme with one addition – that the demarcation proposed in it should pay due regard to geographical features and to the requirements of an international boundary, and the Indian Prime Minister was prepared to attend a conference with his Pakistani counterpart to discuss such a settlement. Pakistan, however, refused to accept a proposal which went back on the idea of a plebiscite for the entire State. In order to obtain Pakistan's acceptance to his partition and plebiscite proposal, Dixon suggested the establishment of an administrative body under the Plebiscite Administrator in the limited plebiscite area; but then India could not agree to the supersession of the Government of the State for the duration of the plebiscite.

THE GRAHAM REPORTS

The Security Council did not explore the possibility of implementing Dixon's new proposals, but instead in April 1951 appointed Dr Graham, of the United States Ministry of Labour, as the new Mediator. Graham tried to bring about the demilitarization of Kashmir 'in a single, continuous process' within three months; but the three months became two years of fruitless negotiations. Between 1951 and 1953 he submitted to the Security Council five reports, the last of which recommended negotiations between the two countries. The main cause of Graham's failure was the fundamental conflict between India and Pakistan over their obligations under the Resolution of August 1948. While the Security Council tried to reconcile these differences at five-yearly intervals, the Kashmir situation, both in its local and international aspects, was completely transformed. The deadlock is now as complete as it was at the beginning of the Truce negotiations in 1949.

DEVELOPMENTS WITHIN KASHMIR

Abdullah's new Government, which replaced his Emergency Administration in March 1948, embarked upon a programme of economic and social reforms. The Instrument of Accession was superseded by Article 370 of the Indian Constitution which preserved the special status of Kashmir and prescribed a flexible procedure for the gradual application of the Constitution to the State. In accordance with the 'New Kashmir' plan of 1944, a Constituent Assembly was convened on 31 October 1951 which further clarified Kashmir's constitutional relationship with India. The Security Council took the view that the decisions of the Assembly could in no way affect the international commitments of India regarding the future disposition of the State. India, however, maintained that so long as Kashmir was constitutionally an integral part of Indian territory, the convening of the Assembly was a purely internal matter; her international commitments simply meant that in case the verdict in a plebiscite went against India, Kashmir would be relieved of its constitutional links with her.

The Assembly proposed the termination of hereditary rule and the abolition of landlordism without compensation. These sweeping reforms profoundly affected the interests of the Hindu landed aristocracy of Jammu. The Praja Parishad, a party representing these vested interests and having close links with Hindu communal organizations in India, accordingly started an agitation for the complete integration of Kashmir, demanding the total application of the Indian Constitution, which makes it obligatory for the State to compensate for compulsory acquisition of property. The Delhi Agreement of 24 July 1952, however, sanctioned the abolition of Dogra rule and preserved the special status of Kashmir, enabling the agrarian reforms to be implemented. Abdullah, the chief architect of the Agreement, triumphantly declared: 'This is not a paper agreement but a union of hearts which no power on earth can loosen.' On 14 November 1952, Karan Singh, son of the last Maharaja, was unanimously elected by the Assembly as the first Head of State for a period of five years. The Parishad revived its agitation with greater intensity. Abdullah, rumoured to be leaning towards an independent status for Kashmir and to have found encouragement from foreign powers, delayed full implementation of the Delhi Agreement. This led to a split in his Cabinet; three of his colleagues accused him of deliberately trying to rupture Kashmir's relationship with India. On 9 August 1953 Abdullah was arrested and Bakhshi Ghulam Mohammad, his Deputy since 1948, formed a new administration. In May 1954 further provisions of the Indian Constitution were applied to Kashmir. The State Constitution, which came into force on 26 January 1957, declares that Kashmir 'is and shall remain an integral part of the Union of India'. Bakhshi remained in power for a little over ten years; his present successor, Ghulam Mohammad Sadiq, has proposed the elimination of the remaining symbols of Kashmir's special status in the Indian constitutional framework.

But on the other side of the Cease-fire Line Pakistan has consolidated her position, directly administering Gilgit and Baltistan and indirectly controlling the Azad Kashmir area. There has been a great increase in the number of incidents along the Cease-fire Line.

KASHMIR, THE UNITED NATIONS AND THE GREAT POWERS

The period immediately following Graham's fifth report began hopefully. The Prime Ministers of India and Pakistan entered into direct negotiations and on 21 August 1953 issued a joint communiqué declaring that the question of Kashmir should be settled in accordance with the wishes of the people of the State. They agreed that the Plebiscite Administrator should be appointed by the end of April 1954; and that committees of experts should be set up to advise the Prime Ministers on the best way of bringing about the demilitarization of Kashmir. But differences immediately appeared. India pressed for the appointment of an Administrator from a small country so that the Kashmir problem could be isolated from Big Power rivalries. The whole question was radically altered in Indian eyes when Pakistan signed a Mutual Defence Assistance Agreement with the United States in May 1954 and later joined the Western-sponsored military pacts. Admiral Nimitz himself resigned in September 1954 from an office which he was never able to exercise.

The mediation of the United Nations in Kashmir was almost entirely based on the initiative of the Western Powers. While not formally committing themselves on the substance of the question, they were generally more favourable to the Pakistani point of view. The strategic importance of Kashmir in the context of the cold war and the growing divergence between the foreign policies of India and Pakistan furthered these tendencies. The one-sided character of the intervention of the United Nations in Kashmir was underlined by the non-participation of the delegates of the Soviet bloc in the Security Council debates. Apart from raising some procedural points, they invariably abstained from voting on the Council's Resolutions. The first major Soviet intervention came in January 1952 when the Soviet delegate suggested that the people of Kashmir should be given an opportunity to decide the question of the State's constitutional status by themselves without outside interference. Soviet policy was finally clarified when Khrushchev said in December 1955 that the question of Kashmir 'as one of the States of the Republic of India' had already been decided by the people of Kashmir. Since then the Soviet Union has maintained that Kashmir is 'an inalienable part of the Republic of India'.

The Kashmir problem has been further complicated by the direct involvement of China as a result of the construction of the strategic road in Ladakh linking Tibet with Sinkiang. While not formally clarifying her stand on the Kashmir question, Chou En-lai gave the impression on a number of occasions that China accepted India's basic position in Kashmir. After the Chinese attack on India in the autumn of 1962, however, Sino-Pakistani relations improved considerably. Having gained a third of the State in Ladakh, China was now willing to exploit Indo-Pakistani differences to her advantage. Pakistan, disenchanted with her Western allies who rushed military assistance to India and never questioned her sole responsibility for the defence of Ladakh which is, after all, part of Kashmir, was only too eager to make India's difficulty her opportunity to redress the Kashmir account. On 2 March 1963 Pakistan and China signed an agreement providing for the demarcation of the border of the northern area of Kashmir. This agreement proved fatal to the Indo-Pakistani ministerial talks then in progress to settle all outstanding problems between the two countries.

The Resolutions of August 1948 and January 1949 still remain the basic terms of reference for the Security Council's attempts to settle the Kashmir problem; but its deliberations have been increasingly divorced from the rapidly changing situation in the area. Graham's fifth report, submitted in March 1953, was not considered by the Council until 1957, when it requested Gunnar Jarring, the Swedish delegate, to settle Indo-Pakistani differences. Like his predecessors, he too failed in his mission. Graham made another effort to resolve the deadlock. His report, submitted in March 1958, was not considered by the Security Council until 1962. The Council has always tended to reaffirm its previous resolutions without giving due consideration to the new factors brought to its attention by its own mediators. The reports of the Commission have been buried under a series of resolutions which, while endorsing the two basic Resolutions, have marked a retreat from them. The warnings about the effects of a bitter plebiscite campaign on the minorities in India and Pakistan have been completely ignored. The practical problem of reconstituting the Kashmir electorate of 1947 has been brushed aside. As exercises in sheer frustration the Security Council's records could hardly be improved upon. It has failed to take note of the Chinese occupation of Ladakh, a third 'partition' of the State which undermined the whole basis of mediation by the United Nations. With the barren hills of Ladakh humming with military activity, demilitarization of Kashmir has become a farce, and the Kashmir problem can no longer be considered in the context of Indo-Pakistani relations alone.

There is no obvious solution acceptable to both India and Pakistan. Kashmir being only one of a complex of issues which have plagued the two countries since independence, only a determined effort to forge new ties of friendship will be able to heal the old wounds of partition. The Kashmir problem is linked with the fate of the minorities in India and Pakistan, and any disturbance in the *status quo* would not only have widespread domestic repercussions but would also add to Himalayan tensions.

BIBLIOGRAPHY

C. B. (Baron) Birdwood. *Two Nations and Kashmir*. (Robert Hale, London, 1956.)

Michael Brechner. *The Struggle for Kashmir*. (Ryerson Press, Toronto, 1953.)

Alan Campbell-Johnson. *Mission with Mountbatten*. (Robert Hale, London, 1950.)

A. Das Gupta, Research Fellow at St Antony's College, Oxford, 1965–8, teaches history at Presidency College, Calcutta. Author of *Malabar in Asian Trade, 1740–1800* (Cambridge, 1967). Writes on international affairs in the Indian periodical *Quest*.

Josef Korbel. *Danger in Kashmir*. (Princeton University Press, Princeton, N.J., 1954.)

M. C. Mahajan. *Accession of Kashmir to India (The Inside Story)*. (Institute of Public Administration, Sholapur.)

V. P. Menon. *The Story of the Integration of the Indian States*. (Longmans, 1956.)

Sheikh Mohammed Abdullah. 'Kashmir, India and Pakistan'. (*Foreign Affairs*, April, 1956.)

Publications by the Government of India: *Jammu and Kashmir* (1947). *Twelve Months of War in Kashmir* (1948). *Pakistan's War Propaganda Against India* (1951). *Indo-Pakistan Relations* (1951). *Kashmir* (1954).

Publications by the Government of Pakistan: *India's War Propaganda Against Pakistan* (1951). *India's Threat to Pakistan* (1951).

Reports of the United Nations Commission for India and Pakistan: S/1100, November 1948; S/1196, January 1949; S/1430, December 1949.

Reports of the United Nations Mediators (1950–58): S/1453, 1950 (Report of General A. G. L. McNaughton). S/1791, 1950 (Report of Sir Owen Dixon). S/2375, 1951; S/2448, 1951; S/2611, 1952; S/2783, 1952; S/2967, 1953; S/3894, 1958 (six Reports of Dr Frank Graham). S/3821, 1957 (Report of Gunnar V. Jarring).

EVENTS SINCE SEPTEMBER 1965

A. Das Gupta

India and Pakistan fought a limited war over Kashmir in August–September 1965. Indian determination to treat the problem of Kashmir as closed had, by this time, brought Pakistan to desperation. In the last weeks of Nehru's life there had appeared a glimmer of hope. In January 1964 large-scale disturbances took place in Kashmir after the theft of a holy relic from the Hazratbal shrine at Srinagar. Early in April 1964 Sheikh Abdullah was released and, with Nehru's blessings, attempted to bring about discussions between Pakistan and India, possibly to consider some form of condominium over Kashmir. After the death of Nehru on 27 May 1964 he abandoned these efforts. In March 1965 he flew to Algiers where he met the Chinese prime minister Chou En-lai and discussed Kashmir with him. On his return to India he was again arrested and, as before, detained without trial on 8 May 1965. Following this arrest serious disturbances broke out again in Kashmir. Out of this phase of unrest in Kashmir, 1964–5, emerged the Awami Action Committee under Maulana Faruk, pledged to bring about the unification of Kashmir with Pakistan. The government of Pakistan came to believe that an anti-Indian revolt was brewing in Kashmir.

In the meanwhile Pakistan's hopes that India, now dependent upon America to equip her armed forces against China, would be persuaded to reopen the Kashmir question, were disappointed. Not only did the Indian government stand firmly by its previous policy, but it proceeded to take away further from the 'special status' granted to Kashmir by article 370 of the Indian Constitution. In December 1964 the Indian parliament enacted legislation to extend the Indian president's emergency powers over Kashmir and took away the title of 'prime minister' from the head of the Kashmiri Cabinet. The military balance on the subcontinent continued to swing steadily against Pakistan. She thus knew that India was, more than ever, determined not to give up Kashmir; she thought that the Kashmiris were now ready to fight on her side and she feared that soon the ratio of power would move irrevocably against her.

Indians in the meanwhile had been alarmed and angered by Pakistan's growing friendship with China. In March 1963 Pakistan concluded a boundary agreement with China relating to the part of Kashmir she controlled. Exactly two years later President Ayub Khan visited Peking where he obtained some support for Pakistan's case regarding Kashmir. Z. A. Bhutto, foreign minister for Pakistan, had made it clear in a speech delivered to the Pakistani parliament on 17 July 1963 that Pakistan expected help from China in the event of an attack from India. On 4 September 1965, when hostilities between India and Pakistan had already begun, Marshal Chen Yi, the Chinese foreign minister, had discussions with Bhutto at Karachi. These, among other factors, convinced the Indians that Pakistan and China were planning a joint attack on their country.

To this we must add the fact that ever since the conclusion of the military alliance between America and Pakistan there had been some apprehensions in India about the striking power of Pakistan's armed forces, reinforced by Patton tanks and supersonic fighter aircraft. The defeat of the Indian army against the Chinese in 1962 was followed by its unimpressive performance against Pakistan in the Rann of Cutch, early in 1965. It was widely believed in India that Pakistan was thus probing India's ability and will to fight. This, together with the Sino–Pakistani axis, came to be recognized as a mortal danger to India, which transcended all local conflicts.

The first wave of Pakistani attack came between 5 and 10 August 1965 when, according to United Nations observers, over a thousand lightly armed commandos crossed into Indian Kashmir from the Pakistani side. This infiltration continued through August and Indian estimates put the final total of the intruders at around 5,000. Pakistan's aim, presumably, was that the commandos would fan the 'rebellion' already in progress within Kashmir and assist the rebels by local acts of terrorism and demolition. There does not appear to have been any rebellion among the Kashmiris and most of the intruders were, after a time, rounded up by the Indian Army. To cut off the main routes of infiltration, the Indians also struck across the cease-fire line at Kargil, Tithwal and the Uri-Poonch sector and occupied strategic positions within Pakistani Kashmir. This Indian gesture was meant to be purely defensive, but the positions occupied in the Uri–Poonch sector in particular brought the Indian army within striking distance of Muzaffarbad, capital of Pakistani Kashmir. The Pakistani's probably feared that a larger offensive might develop from this and in their turn struck at the Indian lines of communication on 1 September 1965 at Chhamb, immediately to the north of Jammu. This was a serious escalation in two ways. First, the Pakistani army, intervening openly for the first time, threw its American armour into the assault and the Indians called for air-strikes to stop the advancing tanks. From this point onward tanks were freely used by both sides but the air war never developed beyond close supporting action. Secondly, the Indians had for long realized the danger of a Pakistani offensive in the Chhamb area. The terrain here did not allow the Indian army to deploy in strength and there was little the Indians could do to protect their vital line of communications which lay along the strategic Jammu-Srinagar road close to Chhamb. They had come to recognize, therefore, that a Pakistani thrust at Chhamb could only be met by a counter-thrust at Lahore. By 5 September the Pakistani Pattons were in the outskirts of Akhnur, a vital centre of communications. Had this attack been successfully pressed the Indian military position in Kashmir would have become untenable.

Faced with a possible disaster in Kashmir, the Indians attacked across the international borders in the Punjab at several points on 6 September 1965. The major strategic aim clearly was to relieve the dangerous pressure in the Chhamb sector, but it is impossible to tell what the tactical objectives were in the Punjab itself. Indian infantry units reached the outskirts of Lahore, the second city of Pakistan, but were then either repulsed or recalled. Similarly the Indians approached to within a few thousand yards of the city of Sialkot in an encircling movement but had not cut it off when the fighting stopped. Indian military circles later maintained that it had never been their intention to capture either Lahore or Sialkot. Pakistanis believed however that they had fought off these attacks. The Indian strategic objective was certainly achieved as Pakistan at once withdrew her armour from Chhamb to defend her frontiers in the Punjab. The Patton tanks were not however very skilfully handled and the Indian Centurions certainly held their own in the furious tank-battles which followed.

It is much to be doubted whether the two armies could have fought on for long. Britain and America, on whom they depended for much of their spare parts, suspended all aid and military supplies immediately after the outbreak of hostilities. The Chinese gave no actual support to Pakistan but sent a dramatic ultimatum to India on 16 September calling on her to dismantle some military positions she was said to have established in Chinese territory to the north and east of Sikkim. It is possible that they thus pinned down several Indian divisions which might otherwise have been used against Pakistan. The ultimatum was otherwise ineffective and it was the peremptory 'demand' of the Security Council which brought hostilities to a close on 23 September 1965. The penetration of either army into the other's territory was slight and they held on to the gains they had made in their initial attacks, the Pakistanis in the Chhamb area and the Indians in the Lahore-Sialkot sector.

The disengagement of the armies and their withdrawal to their pre-war boundaries were brought about by a brilliant feat of diplomacy on the part of Alexei Kosygin, the Russian prime minister. He persuaded Lal Bahadur Shastri and Ayub Khan to meet at Tashkent on 3 January 1966 under his chairmanship. India and Pakistan then agreed to military disengagement and to seek solutions to their problems through continued bilateral meetings. The sudden death of premier Shastri, the day after the Tashkent declaration had been signed, appeared to throw a halo of sanctity around it and the two countries in a relatively chastened mood proceeded to implement the clauses relating to military withdrawal.

THE PROBLEM OF KASHMIR

The state of tension normal between India and Pakistan has since been restored. Through the war in 1965 India has demonstrated to Pakistan that she has the will and the power to hold Kashmir. Neither diplomacy nor war appears to promise anything further to Pakistan. Within Kashmir, politics continue to be mildly restive. Sheikh Abdullah, again a free man, continues to be active and is obviously still the most popular man in Kashmir. He is however coming under pressure from younger men, especially students, to adopt extreme anti-Indian positions. On the other hand liberal opinion in India, as represented, for example, by Jaya Prakash Narayan, wishes him to settle for autonomy within the Indian Union. It is important to note that Narayan, previously sympathetic to Pakistan in the Kashmir problem, now believes that Pakistan has put herself out of court by her attempt to solve it by force. Pressure from right-wing M.P.s however continues in the Indian parliament for the abolition of article 370 of the Constitution altogether, and the total integration of Kashmir within India.

FURTHER READING

An angry statement of the Pakistani case is in G. W. Choudhury, *India–Pakistan Relations 1947–1967*. (London, 1968). A more restrained presentation of the same point of view, with considerable sympathy for China as well, is in Alastair Lamb, *Crisis in Kashmir, 1947–1966* (London, 1966). The Indian case is argued with a wealth of documentation by Sisir Gupta, *Kashmir, A Study in India–Pakistan Relations* (Asia Publishing House, 1966) and J. B. Das Gupta, *Jammu and Kashmir* (The Hague, 1968). Also see A. N. Noorani, *The Kashmir Question* (Bombay, 1965) which incorporates two articles by Jaya Prakash Narayan on the subject written in 1964. The best account of the war so far is in Russell Brines, *The Indo–Pakistani Conflict* (London, 1968). Mr Brines is strongly sympathetic to India but is not always unfair to Pakistan.

THE NAGAS

Khushwant Singh and A. Das Gupta

THE north-eastern frontier of India is inhabited by a large number of Indo-Mongoloid tribes of whom the Nagas are the most important. The Nagas are not one people but over a dozen different tribes speaking different languages. Dr J. H. Hutton, an acknowledged authority on the subject, says:

> It is generally assumed in a vague sort of way that those tribes which are spoken of as Nagas have something in common with each other which distinguishes them from the many other tribes found in Assam and entitles them to be regarded as a racial unit in themselves. . . . The truth is that, if not impossible, it is exceedingly difficult to propound any test by which a Naga tribe can be distinguished from other Assam or Burma tribes which are not Nagas.

It is assumed that the conglomeration of what have come to be known as associated Naga tribes number almost one million people living in India (Assam-NEFA, Nagaland proper, and Manipur) and in Burma. The majority of the Nagas, between 60 and 80 per cent, are Christians (very largely Baptists); the remainder are Buddhists or Animists.

The origin of the word 'Naga' is obscure. Sanskritists believe that it is derived from *naga* – meaning hill – and therefore refers to the 'people of the hills'. (It has no connexion with *naga* – snake.) The late Dr Verrier Elwin, the Indian Government's expert on Indian tribes, was of the opinion that it is derived from *nok*, meaning people in several Tibeto-Burman dialects.

The world has known little about the Nagas' customs and manners except their practice of head-hunting. The introduction of Christianity and the spread of literacy has brought about revolutionary changes. No cases of head-hunting have been reported since 1958. Naga boys and girls attend schools and colleges in ever-increasing numbers; many have gone abroad for further studies or research to British and American universities.

HISTORICAL BACKGROUND AND BRITISH OCCUPATION

The earliest records of Nagas go back to the 13th century when a Shan chief subjugated their territory. The Ahoms (the dynasty from which

Assam derives it name) extended their sway over the Naga tribes and took tribute from them. The Nagas rose against the Ahoms several times during the 16th and 17th centuries, but later entered into matrimonial alliances with them by giving their daughters in marriage to Ahom princes. A Mogul chronicler who visited Assam in 1662 wrote that although the Nagas did not pay taxes to the Assamese ruler, 'yet they accept his sovereignty and obey some of his commands'.

The first contact with the British was in 1832 – eight years after the termination of the Anglo-Burmese war. That year the Raja of Manipur again subjugated the Naga tribes and occupied Kohima. The British, who were unhappy about the Manipur incursion, conceded that the Raja had some sort of *de facto* control over the hills.

The Nagas resisted British intrusion into their regions with the same determination they had shown towards other outsiders. They raided British-occupied areas and had to suffer retaliation – destruction of their villages, granaries, and standing crops. The British Government's attitude towards the Nagas vacillated between an aggressive 'mission of civilization' and a policy of 'leave well alone' to preserve the tribes as museum pieces. The chief determining factor was always finance.

In the latter half of the 19th century a cautious forward policy was resumed. In 1866 an outpost was established at Samaguting with a school and a dispensary. In 1877, Kohima was established as the headquarters of the administration with a sub-headquarters at Wokha. A police force was established and house-tax levied. This was the beginning of effective administration which in 1881 was regularized as the Naga hills district. In 1888 yet another sub-headquarters was opened among the Aos at Mokokchung. By and large the Nagas accepted the Pax Britannica with good grace.

THE NAGAS DURING THE WORLD WARS

The Nagas remained loyal to the British during the World Wars. In the First, about 2,000 men (half of them Semas) volunteered for the Labour Corps in France. In the Second, Naga partisans worked for the Allies behind enemy lines after the Japanese had over-run Naga territory. Field Marshal Slim paid them handsome tribute in his book *Defeat into Victory* as

the gallant Nagas whose loyalty, even in the most depressing times of the invasion, never faltered. Despite floggings, torture, execution and the burning of their villages they refused to aid the Japanese in any way or to betray our troops. Their active help to us was beyond value or praise. They guided our columns, collected information, ambushed enemy patrols, carried our supplies, and brought in our wounded under the heaviest fire – and then, being the gentlemen they were, often refused all payment.

However, a small number which included Mr A. Z. Phizo (an Angami Naga and later the President of the Naga National Council) collaborated with the Japanese invaders and the Indian National Army of Subhas Chandra Bose and were with them in the capture of Kohima.

THE NAGA DEMAND FOR AUTONOMY

In the 1920s the Nagas started becoming politically conscious and began to talk of independence. The Indian National Congress, specifically Mahatma Gandhi, encouraged the Naga freedom movement. In 1929 a delegation representing the 'Naga Club' presented a memorial to the Simon Commission demanding to be 'left alone' to determine their own future whenever the British decided to quit India. In 1930 southern Naga tribes rose in revolt under Jadunam of Zeliang. Jadunam was captured and hanged but his sister 'Rani' Gaidilu continued the struggle. She was arrested and spent eighteen years in gaol. She was freed by the Indian Government and granted a life-pension.

When transfer of power from British to Indian hands seemed imminent, the Nagas reconsidered their position. One section was for some form of association with India. The Naga National Council, a radical section consisting largely of Christians, formed in February 1946, was pledged to the establishment of an independent, sovereign Naga state. Its leader was Mr Phizo.

Negotiations were started between the Indian Government and representative Naga organizations. The spokesman for the Government was the governor of Assam, Sir Akbar Hydari. In June 1947 a nine-point Ten-Year Agreement was signed between the Government and the Nagas. The preamble stated:

That the right of the Nagas to develop themselves according to their freely expressed wishes is recognized. . . . The general principle is accepted that what the Naga National Council is prepared to pay for, the Naga National Council should control. The principle will apply equally to the work done as well as staff employed. . . .

The provisional terms of the Ten-Year Agreement stated that the judiciary, agriculture, the legislature and Tax, Education, and Public Works Departments, all came under the supervision and control of the Naga National Council.

The ninth point of the Agreement dealt with the all-important right of self-determination. It read:

The Governor of Assam, as the Agent of the Indian Union, will have a special responsibility for a period of ten years to ensure the due observance of the agreement; at the end of this period the Naga National Council will be asked whether the above agreement is to be extended for a further period or a new agreement regarding the future of the Naga people arrived at.

The clause was interpreted differently by the Indians and Naga moderates on one side and the Naga radicals on the other. The moderates and Indians believed that association with the Indian Union was implied; the radicals did not read that into the clause. A Naga delegation of radicals met Mahatma Gandhi on 19 July 1947 and later Prime Minister Nehru. While the Mahatma in his usual conciliatory language gave the Nagas assurances of independence, Mr Nehru in his equally forthright language stated that 'independence' meant no more than autonomy and the right to continue their way of living without outside interference. The moderates who later re-grouped themselves as the 'Naga People's Convention' agreed to co-operate with the administration.

The attitude of the Naga radicals and the Indian bureaucracy hardened towards each other. Mr Phizo became the undisputed leader of the Naga National Council. He was arrested. And as could have been anticipated, he came out of gaol with enhanced prestige amongst his own people and greater bitterness against his gaolers. In May 1951 Mr Phizo organized a plebiscite on the issue of an independent Naga-land and later announced that the Nagas had recorded a 100 per cent vote in its favour. The Indian Commissioner in charge described the plebiscite as a farce. Relations between the Naga supporters of Mr Phizo and the Indian Government became worse. Mr Phizo's supporters abstained from going to Indian schools, colleges, and hospitals. They boycotted the general elections of 1951. The match was applied to this inflammable situation by an incident at Kohima in October 1952. A procession of Naga demonstrators clashed with the police; casualties resulted on both sides. Amongst the dead was a judge of the Angami Tribal Court. A commission of inquiry exonerated the police officer concerned. This further angered the extremists. When Mr Nehru came to visit Kohima in March 1953, the Deputy Commissioner declined permission for a memorial to be presented to him; the Nagas demonstrated their resentment by walking out of the meeting arranged in his honour.

The Assam authorities proceeded to take action against the supporters of the Naga National Council. Fighting broke out in 1955. The rebels succeeded in importing arms from neighbouring states or capturing them from Indian patrols. They almost succeeded in overwhelming the local militia. Regular units of the Indian Army were sent in. While the Army was under instructions to take limited action, the rebels were able to muster their strength. Under the command of 'General' Kaito they raised and trained a volunteer militia of over 40,000 men. Whatever else the Indian Army did to suppress this revolt, it was unable to check gun-running across the borders.

The fighting continued with increasing bitterness and became particularly acute in 1956 and 1957. The Indian Army demanded a freer hand. The rebels complained of atrocities against non-combatants. In 1958 Mr Phizo escaped from India and in the summer of 1960 made a dramatic appearance in London. He succeeded in eliciting the support of the influential Sunday paper the *Observer* and the Reverend Michael Scott, who was held in great esteem by the Indians for his excellent work for the coloured peoples of South Africa. In his turn, the Reverend Scott elicited the support of Mr Jayaprakash Narayan, one of the most outspoken and honest of India's contemporary statesmen.

The Indian Government realized that it had allowed local bureaucrats to take matters too far. Mr Nehru took personal interest in the Naga problem. On 1 August 1960 he announced in the Indian Parliament that the Nagas would be given complete autonomy and Nagaland would become the sixteenth state of the Indian Union. He said: 'Our policy has always been to give the fullest autonomy and opportunity of self-development to the Naga people, without interfering in any way in their internal affairs or way of life.'

THE STATE OF NAGALAND
AND THE NAGA NATIONAL COUNCIL

In June 1962 an autonomous Nagaland came into existence with Mr Shilo Ao as the Chief Minister. Nagaland is 6,236 square miles with a population of about 400,000 Nagas belonging to thirteen tribes. The Naga National Council boycotted the Shilo Ao Government and intensified its underground activities. Hostilities continued unabated with all the ghoulish atrocities connected with guerrilla warfare. Ultimately a three man 'Peace Mission' consisting of the Chief Minister of Assam, Mr Badri Prosad Chaliha, the Reverend Michael Scott and Jayaprakash Narayan made contact with some of the fighting Nagas and arranged a cease-fire (25 May 1964), which was subsequently renewed on several occasions. Negotiations between the Naga National Council and the Indian Government were resumed under the auspices of the Peace Mission.

The differences between the Indian point of view and that of the Nagas in revolt were defined. The Indian Government contended that Naga territory had always been geographically a part of India and was inherited by them from the British; that Nagaland is too small to be economically or politically viable as an independent state: that it is strategically important to India in its defence against Communist China; and that the present recalcitrant attitude of a section of the Nagas is due to anti-Indian propaganda of Christian missionaries, the English who now have no responsibilities in the region and the active support of Communist China and Pakistan, both inimical towards India. The rebels refute Indian contentions. They claim that they are a Mongoloid race with nothing in common with any of the Indian races, and that being largely Christian they have little in common with the idolatrous Hindu; that they were never a part of India and were able to maintain autonomy even during British rule; that as an independent people they will be in a better position to safeguard the frontiers of India. The Peace Mission did commendable work in narrowing down differences between the Indian and the rebel Nagas' point of view. It proposed a formula whereby the Nagas should 'of their own volition decide to participate in the Indian Union', while the Indian Government would consider 'to what extent the pattern and structure of relationship between Nagaland and the Government of India should be adapted and recast so as to satisfy aspirations of all sections of Naga opinion'. Although this formula paved the way for negotiations, it could not resolve the fundamental question of sovereignty. While talks were going on, violence re-erupted. The Indian army demanded (and often used) strong-arm methods. Under directions of the Home Minister, Mr G. L. Nanda, Indian administrators tried forcible re-grouping of scattered Naga villages, armed anti-Naga tribes and sowed dissension between rival Naga factions. The rebels reorganized their forces, accusing India of genocide and tried to take the issue to the United Nations. The Peace Mission was dissolved in 1966 when its chief architect, the Reverend Michael Scott, was deported from India. In October 1967 the rebel Naga delegation broke off negotiations and accused the Indian Government of 'duplicity'. Whilst it is realized by both parties that the resumption of hostilities will have disastrous consequences, a settlement of the dispute is not yet in sight.

In spite of the cease-fire agreement, which has been renewed several times and is still in force, sporadic incidents continue in Nagaland. A major encounter occurred on 7 June 1968, when the Indian army attacked a Naga camp at the village of Jetsoma, six miles to the south of Kohima. It was said at the time that a large number of weapons, manufactured in China, had been recovered from the camp. Later disclosures in the Indian Parliament showed the quantity to have been extremely small. However, several documents and photographs, proving the connexions between China and the rebel Hagas, were also seized in this attack and on the strength of all this India protested strongly to China for its involvement in Nagaland. The murder of 'General' Kaito Sema in the first week of August 1968 introduced a bizarre complication in the situation. 'General' Kaito, who built up the underground army, had fallen out of favour with the underground after the cease-fire in 1964. Recently he had been following a policy of his own and had gathered some support among the dissatisfied members of the underground. His murderers are at the moment undetected, but it is being said that the rivalry between the Sema and the Angami tribes may have had something to do with it. Kaito was also known for his outspoken opposition to the pro-Chinese elements within the underground and his ebullient personality may well have made enemies for him.

On 28 February 1966 a revolt similar to the one in Nagaland broke out in the Mizo Hills district in the extreme south of Assam. This revolt was organized by the Mizo National Front under its chairman Mr Laldenga. The district was declared a 'disturbed area' by the Government of Assam in March of that year and the Mizo National Front was banned. The Indian Army was quick to establish its control over the towns in the district but stray incidents in the countryside have continued. The Government of India have decided to merge the three other hill-districts of Assam into a separate state called Meghalaya, with its capital at Shillong, to which the Mizo Hills district would be free to adhere after it had ceased to be a 'disturbed area'.

BIBLIOGRAPHY

Verrier Elwin. *Nagaland*. (Adviser's Secretariat, Shillong, 1961.)
Karl Eskelund. *The Forgotten Valley*. (Alvin Redman, London, 1959.)
Sir Edward Gait. *A History of Assam*. (Thacker, Spink & Co., Calcutta and Simla, 2nd edn, 1926.)
Ursula Graham Bower. *Naga Path*. (John Murray, 1950.)
C. von Fuerer-Haimendorf. *The Naked Nagas*. (Methuen, 1939.)

THE NAGAS

J. H. Hutton. *The Angami Nagas*. (Macmillan, 1921.) *The Sema Nagas*. (Macmillan, 1921.)

George N. Patterson. 'The Naga Revolt'. (*Royal Central Asian Journal*, London, January 1963.)

R. Reid. *History of the Frontier Areas bordering on Assam from 1883–1941*. (Shillong, 1942.)

L. W. Shakespear. *History of Upper Assam, Burmah and North Eastern Frontier*. (Macmillan, 1914.)

David Snellgrove. *Himalayan Pilgrimage*. (Bruno Cassirer, Oxford, 1961.)

Michael Scott. *The Nagas. India's Problem – or the World's?* (Mackay, New York, 1966.)

D. R. Mankekar. *On the Slippery Slope in Nagaland*. (Manaktalas, Bombay, 1967.)

PAKHTUNISTAN

Guy Wint

PAKHTUNISTAN has become one of the areas of debate in Asia. It is the region inhabited by Pathans – Pashto speakers – which lies on the borders of Pakistan and Afghanistan. Its area has never been defined exactly. Its claim to autonomy has been put forward since the war ended by various Pathan leaders in the area, and they are backed by the Afghan Government, but no maps exist with hard and fast boundaries. The claims put forward often grotesquely exceed the area in which Pathans are in a majority; and at the same time they usually omit any part of the Southern province of Afghanistan, in which there reside Pathans who are racially exactly the same as the Pathans of Pakistan.

The problem of the Pathans has been inherited from British days. Under the British the Afghans recognized an international line dividing Afghanistan from British territory called the Durand Line. On the British side of the line the Pathans who were tribally organized were divided into those of administered and unadministered territories. The administered territory formed six districts of the North-West Frontier Province. With some exceptions these districts were governed in the same way as the districts of the Punjab on to which they abutted. The unadministered Pathans lay between these settled districts and the Durand Line. In these no organized magistracy existed and there was no collection of revenue. The Government limited its interest to imposing peace along the roads. For the rest it relied on its influence with the tribespeople, exerted through the tribal chiefs.

The system underwent certain changes with the setting up of Pakistan in 1947. Previously there had been a constant state of war along the frontier. The unadministered tribespeople raided the settled areas, and intermittent military operations had to be undertaken to repress these raids. Pakistan, acting on the ideas of Mr Jinnah, sought a *rapprochement* with the tribal people, emphasizing that there was now no religious difference between them and the new Government. A military withdrawal was ordered from all the posts the Government occupied in the tribal region. The Government promised to respect the independence of the unadministered area, to continue the payment of subsidies which had been paid by the British Government as a kind of danegeld and began a scheme, which only reached a substantial size in the late fifties, for economic development. On the whole the policy has been extremely successful. The region has been quieter – and richer – than at any time within historical memory.

However, in spite of such an enlightened policy, the Pakhtunistan movement developed. It was fomented by Afghanistan which, in 1947, had refused to recognize the Durand Line. It put forward the demand that the Pathans should be independent; in the long run it doubtless wished that they should be annexed to itself, and it advanced the claims of the Pathans to include as wide a stretch of Pakistan territory as was possible. In appealing for support of the movement it made much of the historical tension which has always existed between the Pathans and the Punjabis.

It was argued on behalf of the Pathans that in a plebiscite which had been held in 1947 before the independence of India to decide on their future they had been called on to vote for Pakistan or India. They had not been given the opportunity to vote for an independent Pakhtunistan.

The Afghan Government has continued to support the movement, chiefly by backing ambitious or disgruntled tribal chiefs; the principal among these is Abdul Ghaffar Khan, a former Gandhian leader. It has smuggled in arms, conducted propaganda, dispersed large sums of money, and has kept up a radio war. In 1961 it sent into Pakistan an armed force of volunteers, though the fact that these were regular troops was camouflaged. On the whole these efforts have failed. Nothing was more striking than the lukewarm support which the Afghan leaders received. Pakistan's rule, its respect for tribal independence, and its economic policy are popular. They have attached the tribal territory to itself. Pakistan is vigilant, but the number of political prisoners is not high.

The Afghan backing of the movement has led to constant ill-feeling between Pakistan and Afghanistan. At one stage, the Pakistan embassy was burned in Kabul. In 1961 Pakistan broke off diplomatic and trade relations with Afghanistan on the grounds that Afghan officers stationed in the frontier region were openly inciting the people to revolt. In 1963 there was a change of government in Afghanistan which promised a milder policy. Mediation by Iran brought Pakistan and Afghanistan together again and Pakistan improved matters by releasing Abdul Ghaffer Khan from prison, but it is too early to say whether Afghanistan has given up promoting the cause of Pakhtunistan.

THE OVERSEAS CHINESE

Lois Mitchison

NUMBERS AND ORIGIN

THERE are about 17 million overseas Chinese, and this figure is only exact to around the nearest million. Some individuals and some countries count a man with one Chinese grandfather as Chinese and not belonging to the nationality of any of his other ancestors, and some do not. In countries with strict but ineffectively enforced immigration laws, Chinese who are illegally smuggled into the country are not declared in the national censuses.

There are small communities of overseas Chinese in the United States, the Caribbean, Peru, Britain, India, and Australia, but much the biggest groups are in South-East Asia. Hong Kong with a population of between three and four million is virtually a Chinese city. Three quarters of the citizens of Singapore, over 1,400,000 of them, are Chinese. In the Malaysian peninsula the 3 million Chinese make up 40 per cent of the population. Elsewhere there are proportionally smaller, but still sizeable, Chinese communities. In the North Borneo parts of Malaysia over a quarter of the population is Chinese (nearly 400,000 in a total population of a million and a half). In Thailand more than one person in ten is of Chinese origin ($3\frac{1}{2}$ million out of a total population of about 32 millions). In Indonesia there are about 3 million Chinese, almost half of whom are now Indonesian citizens, In South Vietnam there are about 1,400,000 Chinese, in North Vietnam about 40,000; 38,000 in Laos, 321,000 in Cambodia, at least 400,000 in the Philippines, and about 350,000 in Burma. Everywhere Chinese families tend to be large and are generally well cared for. The Chinese population increases at about 3·5 per cent a year, faster than that of most of the indigenous South-East Asian peoples.

Nearly all the Chinese ancestors of the present overseas Chinese have come from the four southern provinces of Kwantung, Kwangsi, Fukien, and Hainan island. During the 19th and early 20th centuries the land shortage and political troubles in the south led to the large-scale emigration of young men.

ECONOMIC POWER

The overseas Chinese have an economic power out of proportion to their numbers. Some of them first reached South-East Asia in 'the pig trade' – as indentured, poorly paid, and badly treated labour for colonial mines and plantations. But the colonial powers found that it suited their interests to foster the economic growth of Chinese middlemen standing between their own merchants and the local communities. The Chinese themselves were ambitious and generally harder working than the local peoples. They were also able to use and then spread further the network of relations and men from the same home district that they found in their new countries.

Everywhere in South-East Asia the Chinese have become crucially important as traders, industrialists and the skilled men of most trades. Outside Singapore, Malaysia, and Hong Kong they have taken little direct part in government or politics, and few Chinese are farmers unless they grow crops like rubber or pineapple which need greater skill and steadier labour than the local population will provide. The majority of Chinese settled in towns, often in special Chinese quarters. But itinerant merchants, village shopkeepers and cross-road garage mechanics kept before country people's eyes an enviable picture of greater Chinese education, business acumen and success.

ASSIMILATION

Like the European colonialists the Chinese did not assimilate easily into the countries where they settled. For at least the first generation the loyalties and interests of the new immigrants remained in China. They planned to return as soon as they had saved enough to buy a farm in their native village, and, meanwhile, they sent money to maintain wives and children or other relatives still in China. If they could not return alive the Chinese immigrants at least desired to have their coffins shipped back to their villages and be buried in their native soil. Where they could the immigrants married Chinese women, spoke Chinese, ate Chinese food, wore Chinese clothes, brought up Chinese families and had their children educated at special Chinese schools opened in the South-East Asian cities.

In the late 19th and early 20th centuries Chinese families in south China would not, in most cases, allow wives to emigrate with their husbands. Chinese men abroad, particularly in the tolerant Buddhist countries – Thailand, Burma and Cambodia – married local women.

Some of their descendants slid into the habits and language of their mother's nationality. Intermarriage was less common in Muslim countries. But in Malaya the best established Chinese families could trace their ancestry to traders who had first visited the country 300 years before, and these Malayan Chinese take great pride in their Malayan as well as their Chinese roots.

In the 1920s and 30s Chinese women were allowed to emigrate in large numbers, join their men, and set up completely Chinese families. Separatist feelings among the Chinese community were further fostered by more Chinese schools and a more concerned government in Kuomintang China.

Until recently a barrier to assimilation was the view held by Chinese law and enshrined in the minds of many Chinese and other Asians that 'once Chinese always Chinese': every child of a Chinese father, whatever the mixture of his ancestry and wherever the family's domicile, was Chinese and could not change his nationality. At the Bandung Conference of 1955 the Chinese government recognized in principle that overseas Chinese could opt for the nationality of the countries in which they lived. With considerable difficulty the Chinese negotiated a treaty with Indonesia giving a choice of nationality to local Chinese; but the Indonesians have failed to treat these Chinese as full citizens. Their difficulties have not encouraged other Chinese communities to seek a similar formal change of nationality negotiated between their domiciles and China. However changes of nationality recognized by the South-East Asian country but not by China are increasingly common among second and third generation Chinese.

CHINESE GOVERNMENT POLICY AND THE OVERSEAS CHINESE

Until the last years of the Empire the Chinese who went abroad without express imperial permission were officially disloyal Chinese whose emigration could earn them the death penalty when they returned to China. Overseas Chinese, victims of this law and ashamed of imperial weakness, were supporters of revolutionaries and notably of Dr Sun Yat-sen. In return his party the Kuomintang, when it became the government of China, protested on behalf of the overseas Chinese to the countries of South-East Asia, and provided Chinese schools abroad with teachers and textbooks. Chinese weakness between the wars, however, meant that Kuomintang protests were rarely effective.

Nearly all overseas Chinese have continued to feel proud of China's new strength and place in the world under her Communist government. Their approval of that government's actions in China has varied according to time and to the age and prosperity of the individual overseas Chinese. The young and poor have naturally been more sympathetic to internal Communist policies than their richer elders.

The Communist view of the overseas Chinese has also been ambivalent and has varied from time to time. On the one hand the constitution of Communist China pledges the Chinese government to protect all Chinese. The money the overseas Chinese remit to their relations in south China is particularly useful to a country short of foreign exchange. (Overseas Chinese remittances are currently (1967) estimated to run at more than £50 million a year.) Loyalty to China and discontent with their position in their adopted countries makes some young overseas Chinese likely recruits to the revolutionary movements which Peking – at any rate theoretically – wishes to see victorious in Asia, as in the rest of the world. Finally, if Peking should wash her hands of the overseas Chinese and their interests, the Kuomintang in Formosa are only too ready to take Peking's place, speak on behalf of the overseas Chinese, and collect their loyalties and their money.

On the other hand the overseas Chinese, most of them prosperous or aspiring bourgeois, are not Peking's ideal citizens, and their interests are not always those with which she is most concerned. They can also be an embarrassment to a policy of peace and friendship with China's Asian neighbours. Even in revolutionary wars Peking has seen that an entirely Chinese insurrection, like that in post-war Malaya, fails to prosper because it alienates local peoples.

At the time of the Bandung Conference and for some years thereafter the overseas Chinese appeared largely as an obstacle in the way of China's conciliatory policy in Asia. Overseas Chinese, particularly in the countries which had concluded alliances with China, were told by Chinese officials to learn the language of the country where they were domiciled, send their children to local schools, and adopt local customs. When Chinese were ill-treated by Asian governments, as in Indonesia, Peking was slow to protest, mild in the tone of its protests, and ready to evacuate Chinese refugees but to do little else for their protection.

However, in the drive to export during and after the Great Leap Forward of 1958 overseas Chinese merchants were useful to China. They were encouraged to sell goods made in China by favourable terms of sale or return on their consignments from the mainland, they received bank loans at low interest from local branches of the Bank of

China, and business help from Chinese consulates. Meanwhile universities and schools in China offered places to overseas students, elderly overseas Chinese were encouraged to retire to relatively luxurious settlements on the mainland, and both the returning overseas Chinese and their relations settled in China were protected from most of the recurrent pressures and hardships of ordinary Chinese life. This protection failed, but only temporarily, when the Red Guards molested visiting and retired overseas Chinese, and reproached them for their bourgeois appearance and possessions.

During the troubles of the cultural revolution it has not always been easy to separate riots caused by local leaders' unofficial over-enthusiasm, from riots that may have been caused by Chinese leaders' in Peking, or some Chinese leaders', deliberate exploitation of the overseas Chinese. Chinese rioted in Hong Kong in 1967. In North Borneo they formed local guerrilla units to fight against the Malaysian army. In Burma Chinese schoolchildren insisted with violence on wearing badges of Mao Tse-tung. Burmese crowds in retaliation killed Chinese schoolteachers and Chinese Embassy personnel. Peking has given verbal support to the young Chinese in these countries; but her words have not been backed by action. In Hong Kong the local Communist-owned newspapers have carried pointed articles on Hong Kong's duty to make her own revolution herself before the Red Army would cross the frontier.

POLICY OF THE ASIAN GOVERNMENTS

After the Second World War the new nations of South-East Asia and Thailand were acutely suspicious of the politics of their Chinese minorities and envious of their economic power. Restrictions were imposed on further Chinese immigration, and these restrictions, when they were not, as they proved they were in the Philippines, unreasonably strict, were on the whole successful. This was partly because emigration from south China was also effectively restricted by the new Chinese government.

There were less successful South-East Asian restrictions on the trades Chinese could engage in, on the use of the Chinese language, and on Chinese schools. When the economic restrictions were rigidly applied as in Indonesia and Burma the country's trade pattern was dislocated. As the Chinese merchants were driven out of the rice trade Burma ceased to be a rice exporting country, there was new poverty and unemployment, and the threat of economic and political chaos. In the Philippines laws making it difficult for Chinese to become Philippines citizens and restrictions of the use of the Chinese language added to the Chinese community's view of themselves as separate from the mainstream of Filipino life, and not always bound by patently unjust laws.

A relatively successful policy towards an overseas Chinese community was adopted by Thailand. There were restrictions on overseas Chinese occupations and trade, but Thai officials have turned a blind eye to the evasion of these restrictions providing it is not too blatant and includes a Thai partner, sleeping or otherwise, in the Chinese business. Chinese have been encouraged to opt for Thai citizenship, and Thai notables express public pride in their own Chinese ancestry and share in Chinese culture.

HOW POLITICAL ARE THE OVERSEAS CHINESE?

In spite of local persecutions, revolutions around them, and the occasional rebellion of the young, most established overseas Chinese are apolitical – apparently only wanting to live in peace and prosper. A Thai king, himself partly Chinese, once called them 'the Jews of the east'. Like the Jews they have much to contribute to the cultural as well as the economic life of the countries where they live if these countries will accept their contributions. And they are in general willing to accept the political slant of the countries where they live. In Thailand, which recognizes the Kuomintang as the government of China and is allied to the United States, Chinese homes and businesses give a prominent position to Chiang's portrait. In Burma until the recent troubles similar homes and businesses featured Mao Tse-tung. Where mainland Chinese consuls, banks and trading missions of any political colour exist the local Chinese are glad to avail themselves of their services. In countries where policy vacillates the Chinese community follows the government's lead. In Cambodia when China is in favour with Prince Sihanouk's government the receptions given by the Chinese Embassy are crowded. During the periodic chills the numbers of local Chinese able to accept invitations drop dramatically.

BIBLIOGRAPHY

J. H. Brimmell. *Communism in South-East Asia*. (Oxford University Press, 1959.)

Morton H. Fried (Ed.). *Colloquium on the Overseas Chinese*. (Institute of Pacific Relations, New York, 1958.)

D. G. E. Hall. *A History of South-East Asia.* (Macmillan, 1955.)

George McT. Kahin (Ed.). *Governments and Politics in South East Asia.* (Cornell University Press, Ithaca, New York, 1959.)

Lois Mitchison. *The Overseas Chinese.* (Bodley Head, 1961.)

Victor Purcell. *The Chinese in Southeast Asia.* (Oxford University Press, 2nd edn, 1965.) *The Chinese in Malaya.* (Oxford University Press, 1948.)

Lucien W. Pye. *Guerilla Communism in Malaya. Its Social and Political Meaning.* (Princeton University Press, Princeton, N.J., 1956.)

William G. Skinner. *Chinese Society in Thailand.* (Cornell University Press, Ithaca, New York, 1957.) *Leadership and Power in the Chinese Community of Thailand.* (Cornell University Press, Ithaca, New York, 1958.)

Virginia Thompson and Richard Adloff. *Minority Problems in Southeast Asia.* (Stanford University Press, Stanford, 1955.)

Lea E. Williams. *The Future of the Overseas Chinese in Southeast Asia.* (McGraw-Hill, New York, 1966.)

Asia and the World

THE INDIAN PERSONALITY

Raghavan Iyer

India will not lead the world in science, in industry, or luxury living, but she may well make invaluable contributions to mankind's understanding of itself and the human art of living. . . . In the past, light came from the East; in the future it will come again. But this time it will be a rainbow ray through a prism, one face of which was made in the West.

PERCIVAL SPEAR

PHILOSOPHERS today rightly debunk the notion of national character, as well as the dogma of historical inevitability. It can be both misleading and harmful to talk, for example, of the Israeli or the Irish or the Italian personality. The distortion and danger are even greater when we talk of the Indian personality, for at least two reasons. First of all, it has often been questioned whether India was ever a single cultural entity; much has been made of its bewildering diversity. Secondly, despite the emphasis on its vastness and variety, there has been a long-standing and deceptive mystique shrouding the sub-continent. Today, the traditional mystique wears a modern dress; the ancient land of Aryavarta has become a new nation, a sovereign republic after centuries of subjection by alien rulers. The emphasis abroad is now upon poverty, not riches; discontent, not fatalism; material uplift rather than spiritual exaltation; India's new international status instead of its age-old cultural stature. Fresh clichés are rife: the leader of the uncommitted world, the beacon of democracy in Asia, the alternative to China and its desperate rival, the exemplar of 'planning by consent'. Indians themselves are often the victims of the facile phrases coined by foreigners. But even the international personality of India is still peculiarly difficult for foreigners to comprehend. The new epithets, no less than the old, obscure the truth as much as they reveal it.

'The Indian personality' is both extremely old and very new; herein lies its distinctiveness and its perplexity. Traditional India, like classical Greece, is essentially timeless – one of the chief sources of human wisdom and inspiration. It was not merely the home of the Hindu-Buddhist religious heritage, the oldest philosophical schools and conceptual systems, a complete world-view and an exacting, rounded, way of life. It was, in fact, a world in itself, seemingly self-sufficient, smugly indifferent to the valuations of other peoples. It was ethnocentric in the strict sense; it was not aware of its insularity, especially as its image of itself enclosed and transcended the entire globe. Its dominating concepts were *moksha* and *tapas*, enlightenment and austerity, but it found place in practice both for the heroic outlook and the monastic ideal, enshrined in its two popular epics which even now live in the minds of millions of peasants. Society was split into compartments by caste and competition was anathema, but it was held together loosely and precariously by a shared concept of *dharma* or obligation under the Moral Law. Truth, love and compassion were incarnated respectively – as Vinoba has recently pointed out – in the personalities of Rama, Krishna and Buddha. Detachment and non-violence were held in high esteem and at times degenerated into apathy and passivity. *Satya* and *ahimsa*, truth and non-violence, were translated by Asoka in the 3rd century B.C. into practical applications of tolerance and civility. Even the worldly came to respect those who set the example of non-possession (*aparigraha*) and renunciation. These ideals and values were disseminated with the spread of Indian cultural influences by traders, missionaries and settlers in South-East Asia and the Far East. In India itself the impact of the Buddhist Reformation upon a decadent Hinduism was deep but short-lived. The weaknesses as well as the strength of Indian tradition were revealed as waves of Muslim invaders came into the country and created successive empires until the British unified the sub-continent and exposed it to the far-reaching impact of the modern West.

THE STRENGTH OF TRADITION

The strength of Indian tradition lay in its absorptive, assimilative character and in the elusive, essentially non-doctrinal and undogmatic nature of Hinduism, reinforced by the stability of small, self-enclosed village communities. There was a continuity of cultural life, though not as significant as has been claimed by some writers. Carlyle's 'everlasting yea' was the theme-song of Indian tradition, the basis of its genuine universality but also the main source of its weakness. Hard choices were evaded, immediate problems were shelved rather than solved, and the country suffered from its fatal inability to say 'No' to social abuses, anarchic tendencies, laxity in administration and in dispensing justice, internal feuds and violent intrigue. There were remarkable experiments in coexistence – between races, religions and languages – but also between universalism in theory and segregation in practice. The saving grace of tradition lay in that there arose from time to time exceptional individuals who displayed in their lives the potency of persisting ideals of detachment, gentleness, and concord. But these oases were few and far between in the spreading desert of indolence, cowardice and suspicion. Traditional India was too weak and divided to offer effective resistance to its invaders from afar, and it was considerably demoralized though not destroyed by centuries of alien rule.

During the nationalist movement against British imperialism, Indians were led to take pride in their ancient past and to stress the grandeur of their cultural heritage. Now that India has risen to take its place among the largest nation-states, the emerging national self-consciousness has almost freed the Indian personality from the burden, but also the spell, of bygone glory. The 'me-too'-ism and the messianic streak that were injected by the modernists and revivalists into the nationalist movement have diminished but not disappeared. These elements in the Indian personality are now focused upon the present and future achievements of a nation caught in the throes of economic and social change. Salvationist creeds secure acceptance more readily when they are couched in a secularist and utilitarian language. The gospel of progress – often presented in the naïve forms once fashionable in the West – suits the new nationalist temper. Dams, atomic reactors, military prowess, technical innovations, the rule of law under the Constitution, democratic planning, non-alignment – all these things matter more to the Indian intelligentsia than temples and monuments, epics and folksongs, *dharma* and *moksha*. But behind the modernist creeds that command enthusiasm there is a self-conscious eclecticism that comes easily to the inheritor of Indian tradition, however indifferent he may be to his national legacy.

It would be tempting to view the Indian personality as confused, insecure and schizoid, torn between an ineradicable pride in the past and a blinding obsession with the present status and advance of the new republic. Indians have no doubt not found as yet a balance between their desires and their limitations, their hopes and fears, the claims of tradition and the increasing demands for social change and economic growth. It is also true that the Westernized elites, alienated from the way of life of the rural masses and from the sources of Indian culture, hold the initiative today before a retreating orthodoxy and the divided, defensive traditionalists. Further, Mahatma Gandhi's reinterpretation of traditional concepts of *ahimsa*, *tapas*, *dharma*, *aparigraha* is less influential in moulding the thinking of policy-makers than Nehru's conception of a socialistic pattern of society, a casteless and egalitarian order in which the highest priority is given to 'modernization' and material advancement. Yet the very concern with the removal of rural poverty and the attempt to restore village panchayats owe their original inspiration to Gandhi. It would indeed be rash to conclude from the experience of a decade and a half that the seeming conflict between traditional values and 'modernization' has already been settled in favour of the latter. Nor is it meaningful to assert that the Indian personality has been rendered neurotic and schizoid by the complex and continuing interaction between indigenous and imported ideas, values and institutions.

If the Indian personality seems today to be distorted by its ambivalent response to the impact of the West, it could be differently viewed by placing it in the context of the cultural dialogue that began early in the 19th century and reached its high watermark with Gandhi and Tagore. The significance of this dialogue cannot be seen if we subscribe either to the 'sponge' theory of some Indian writers or to the 'historicist' dogmatism of some Western commentators. Both these attitudes express an essential truth but dilute its significance by effusive exaggeration and illicit inferences. The 'sponge' theorists are right to stress the assimilative power and the continuity of Indian culture but they ignore the high cost of assimilation. They also tend to overlook the fact of Indian resistance – to Buddhism and Islam, to the intrusion of alien influences,* and especially to the powerful inroads made by the West into the mental make-up and the self-awareness as well as the self-confidence of the modern Indian. The historicists are justified in asserting that the impact of the industrial civilization and secular culture of the West upon the life of traditional society is different in kind, and not merely in the degree of intensity, from that made by the earlier invasions of India. It is, however, naïve to think that the cultural deposit of thousands of years can be suddenly swept away by the factory system and the machine age, and that India cannot find its own way of preserving its soul while adapting its society.

DIALOGUE BETWEEN REFORMERS AND REVIVALISTS

It would be absurd to insist that the profound impact of the West has affected the Indian personality in the same way as it changed the Russian or the Chinese or the Japanese. The fact that India, unlike

* It was the power of Hindu resistance which made Nobili fail in India, whereas Ricci succeeded in making Christianity acceptable to the elite in China.

Russia, China, Japan or Turkey, came directly under Western rule and influence for over a century, resulted in a distinctive dialogue between the reformers and the revivalists. This dialogue was unique in that its leading participants, the Westernized and the traditionalists alike, had to come to terms with the source of strength and weakness of the Western impact as well as of Indian tradition. The reformers in India – Roy, Ranade, Gokhale, Tagore, Nehru – could not go as far as Westernizers in Russia like Chaadayev, for example, in actually despising their traditional society, despite its cultural decadence. Similarly, the revivalists in India – Dayananda, Vivekananda, Tilak, Bankim Chandra, Aurobindo – did not go as far as a Slavophile like Gogol, for instance, in debunking Western civilization or in denying that there was anything at all of any value in the impact of Western culture. Even Dayananda could freely concede the 'virtues of the Europeans'. There was an unreality and an extremist flavour about the dialogue between Westernizers and traditionalists in Russia or China which could not be found in 19th-century India directly under British rule. With Western education India imported the spirit of the European Renaissance and Reformation – critical, curious, and anti-authoritarian – which permitted a fresh look at traditional values and institutions and even facilitated a rediscovery of the Indian classics. As a result, the cultural dialogue in India for almost a century has been marked, on the whole, for its reasonableness and moderation, despite the occasional lapses into messianic dogmatism or romantic obscurantism. These two vices may still be detected in India today – among self-styled 'progressives' and very vocal communalists. But the pattern of the new Indian personality at its finest has already emerged – a few remarkable men and women, rooted in Indian culture, responsive to the best that the West has to offer, able and willing to appreciate the art and music as well as the literature and thought of India and the West.

In his perceptive essay on 'Hindu Protestantism', Ranade showed the importance for the modern Hindu of a selective approach and a reappraisal of his ancestral religion. Although this is a new attitude of mind, it may truly be said to be in the best tradition of Hinduism itself and perhaps even to be required among its sophisticated adherents. With the ending of imperial rule by foreigners belonging to a different, even a rival, religion, there is less need than ever to be defensive about corrupt Hindu practices or touchy about Hindu rituals. In general, the Indian is now freer than before to be as unorthodox or eclectic as he chooses in calling himself Hindu or Muslim, Buddhist or Christian, Zoroastrian or Sikh or Jain. Under the impact of the West, the religions of India have undergone a process of self-criticism and self-renewal, a process initiated by Western education and the challenge of foreign missionaries and intensified during the heyday of the Theosophical Movement in the eighties and nineties of the last century.

In the twenties Mahatma Gandhi introduced an ethical current into Indian life which has crucially affected the Indian personality. India began to experience, as Europe did in the 17th century, the consequences of a decisive shift in emphasis from the *via contemplativa* to the *via activa*, from *Moksha* to *Dharma*, from the cycle of withdrawal (*nivritti*) to that of involvement (*pravritti*). Gandhi also pointed out, in a celebrated controversy with Tagore, that Indians had to learn from the West to say 'No' to injustice, oppression, and exploitation in the political and social spheres. The habit of saying 'Yes' to everything sprang from a deep-seated universalism but it soon became a form of mental laziness, passivity and moral abdication. Tagore and Gandhi were agreed that narrow nationalism was a menace and that Indian freedom should be sought as an integral part of a new world order. The difference between them was a matter of emphasis, in regard to priorities and methods. Gandhi stressed that life is made up of affirmations and rejections and the latter are as morally significant as the former. Without non-violent non-cooperation in regard to despotism, however benevolent, there could be no genuine co-operation or goodwill to all men.

With the ending of alien rule and the martyrdom of Gandhi, a muddled mood of unreality, the old habit of wishful thinking, began to re-assert itself in the formulation of domestic as well as foreign policy. Nehru courageously and consistently said 'No' to casteism, provincialism, communalism as well as to authoritarian devices, thus laying the foundations of a secular State and a democratic polity. He also said 'Yes' to planning and socialism, liberal and egalitarian principles, and above all, to peaceful methods of social change. His concern was with securing a national consensus in regard to the immediate tasks and larger ideals of the new republic. In this he did achieve considerable success but only at the cost of by-passing, rather than removing, the divisive and separatist tendencies embedded in Indian society. He also tried to maintain the dynamism and tempo, the moral momentum of the national movement. Here his inevitable failure has been more apparent than such success as he undoubtedly achieved. The problems of poverty, inequality and factionalism are too intractable to be solved merely through committing the country to worthwhile social goals or to well-intentioned political and economic policies. The Indian personality today is deeply involved – intellectually and emotionally – in its fine affirmations and firm rejections, but it lacks the will to translate them into effective action. Further, with the ending of British rule, extremist and unreal attitudes towards the West are emerging both among the Westernizers and the traditionalists.

Nehru moulded the new international personality of India even more powerfully than its internal self-image. Behind the phraseology of his foreign policy – non-alignment, peaceful coexistence, *Pancha Shila* – there lay a recognition of the need to preserve the nation's effective independence; to create a climate and even an area of peaceful conduct in which to pursue national tasks; to learn from the experience of Western as well as Communist nations in transforming Indian society; to further the aspirations of other dependent and under-developed countries; to reduce the dominant influence of the Big Powers in the United Nations as well as to mediate between the ideological blocs in explosive situations. These concepts have influenced the attitudes of other new states to a remarkable degree, and even the two blocs have slowly come to accept their authenticity and force if not their validity and implications. Unfortunately, India has been far less successful in coming to terms with the fact that it has willy-nilly stepped into the shoes of a Big Power in its own geopolitical context. Further, while Nehru displayed a genuine Gandhian friendliness to all peoples, he did not show Gandhi's willingness to understand the attitudes of those inimical to India, and even more, he failed, unlike Gandhi, to take the proper measure of his foreign antagonists. Again, the fine affirmations of the Indian personality have become a substitute for an effective and coherent policy in regard to world affairs or the United Nations and especially in the matter of national defence. One of the odd consequences of an abstract faith in non-alignment is the concrete co-existence within the same government of politicians and officials who lean towards either of the two ideological blocs. This has hindered the formulation of an effective policy, especially in relation to India's neighbours.

GAP BETWEEN EXHORTATION AND EXAMPLE

All this points to inherent traits of the Indian personality – the tendency to mistake affirmations for achievements, the failure to face up to the implications of hard choices, the habit of regarding the promises of one's own or of others as tantamount to performance, exulting in the willingness of the spirit to the extent of overlooking the weakness of the flesh, a preoccupation with what might be or even with what ought to be unmatched by a careful examination of existing reality. In India the inherited faith in universal brotherhood and the concern with cosmic justice have all too often meant the neglect of the immediate neighbourhood. The higher the standards set, the more glaring the gap between exhortation and example. There is nothing surprising about this; what is sad is the apparent indifference to the growth of the gap, the same insensitivity with which Indians so often charged their former rulers. Again, it is not so strange that the Indian personality should be more concerned with Western opinion than with Asian opinion; this is the natural consequence of the hypnotic spell exercised by Western imperialism. It is also easy to see why the pan-Asian sentiments generated early in the century and repeated soon after independence should have rapidly evaporated with the emergence of SEATO and the developments in Communist China. What is more difficult to explain is the failure to appreciate the place of India in the immediate context of South Asia or the importance of its cultural and religious links with Tibet, South-East Asia and the Far East. Increasingly, in the coming decades the Indian cannot help focusing his vision eastwards rather than exclusively westwards.

Altogether, it would be only a superficial appraisal of the Indian personality that would merely stress its present predicament. Although it has its roots in the mature wisdom of a rich philosophical and cultural heritage, it has still not come of age in its new manifestation. If the Indian personality seems to be effervescent and volatile, tossed between abstract idealism and concrete cynicism, this is because it has still to gain the confidence that comes from experience in a new environment. It must find a way of recovering the toughness and the willpower that marked even the leading liberals of the last century and certainly the nationalist movement at its height in the decades before independence. The finest examples of the Indian personality in the present age are not visionaries or machiavellians, but practical idealists whose actions speak louder than their words – men like Gandhi and Vinoba and Karve. Such men have cared little for the cynicism of the outside world and incarnated their ideals while toiling at their chosen tasks. They did not mistake enthusiasm for idealism or cynicism for worldly wisdom. Their failures did not lead them to abandon their principles or their ideals, but only to a rigorous self-examination and a greater concentration of endeavour. Such men may be few, but their influence is far-reaching and will continue to be, as long as the acceptance of a *guru* remains a vital element in Indian life. The tradition of the *guru* has no doubt been much abused, but at its best it uniquely fulfils the function of transmitting ideals and providing ethical continuity to society.

As the inheritors of a living heritage, tested by time, Indians owe it to themselves not to succumb to the ephemeral fashions laid down by foreigners. Equally, as the citizens of a new republic, they owe it to the coming generations that they do not slavishly copy the patterns of thought and conduct that have emerged in the older states. If the Indian personality is to retain its distinctiveness and explore its hidden possibilities it must deepen its roots in its ancestral soil and mature its conception of the new society that could emerge in the foreseeable future.

BIBLIOGRAPHY

Mulk Raj Anand. *Contemporary Indian Civilization*. (Asia Publishing House, 1962.)

Vera Micheles Dean. *New Patterns of Democracy in India*. (Harvard University Press, Cambridge, Mass., 1959.)

Theodore de Bary (Ed.) and others. *Sources of the Indian Tradition*. (Columbia University Press, New York, 1958.)

Selig S. Harrison. *India – The Most Dangerous Decades*. (Princeton University Press, Princeton, N.J., 1960.)

N. V. Sovani and V. M. Dandekar (Eds.). *Changing India*. Essays in Honour of D. R. Gadgil. (Asia Publishing House, 1962.)

Percival Spear. *India – A Modern History*. (University of Michigan Press, Ann Arbor, 1961.)

Arnold Toynbee. *One World and India*. (Oxford University Press, 1960.)

THE CHINESE PERSONALITY

Richard Harris

ONE hesitates immediately at the very expression Chinese personality. In English the word personality has a roundness and definition which seems, the moment one tries to apply it to China, too extreme, too precise, essentially European. Of course the dictionary definition can be applied to the Chinese: they, too, have those 'qualities that make a being personal' – all seven hundred million of them; but as soon as one reflects on those distinctive qualities which we associate with the word then it is the self-definition, the individualism that first comes to mind; words such as conscience and soul and other similar ideas that have reverberated through European thought for the past five hundred years. As usual China seems to demand a different starting point.

Certainly one needs to insist that individualism and the cultivation of an individual psychology – much deepened in Europe by the Romantic movement – are practices totally alien to Chinese society. The lone man, the man thinking his own thoughts, guarding his conscience, responsible for his individual actions, taking all the choices that affect his own life, and acting individually in face of what is imposed upon him – all this, while not inapplicable to the Chinese, puts the emphasis wrongly for a civilization that has made a cult of harmony for two thousand years at least.

The Freudian approach applies, of course, and is interesting in itself, though understudied. A Chinese child's upbringing is, until the age of about seven, entirely permissive, with constant and close physical contact with the mother. The love of small children is so universal a Chinese characteristic that an adult Chinese can hardly pass a child without some gesture of affectionate admiration. Do small children cry in China? The Westerner sometimes almost doubts it: undoubtedly the Chinese child has a passivity that would astonish any European, not to mention an American.

Later in childhood Confucian traditions of discipline take over; the respect due to parents and above all to the father is firmly inculcated by the parents as well as by society. But to mention Confucian standards and the whole pattern of loyalty is to admit that after nineteen years of Communist rule any statements about the social formation of the Chinese personality must be set down with caution. For all these nineteen years, and never so relentlessly as during the cultural revolution, doctrine has been pumped into this society, above all in the minds of the formative, educated, urban classes. Even allowing for the survival of old standards in the early years of the revolution, one is forced to conclude that of late things have changed. The revolution within the revolution has damaged the psyche of many who had thought themselves moderately adjusted to change, who had found themselves places within the new order, had adjusted their personal and family lives to its rigours and who have, in the last three years, had to face new and violent shocks.

What change has all this wrought on what we might call the Chinese personality? The obvious answer is that we do not know and cannot know of a people so inured to dissembling in face of adversity. Even the most favoured foreign residents of China have not had enough contact with the Chinese people in their daily lives, or been party to their thoughts, or seen enough of their behaviour, to know how they have changed. Much that existed before may still survive, despite the Communist effort to displace the Confucian categories and obligations with new ones of their own. It may be that the temporary pressures that reached their peak in the hysterical phases of the cultural revolution will now recede, and that before long the new outline will be seen to share some lines with the old.

How much has Mao Tse-tung been imposed as a father-figure? How much deeper than before is the traditional Chinese tendency to form group associations as a means of finding personal security? None of these are questions that can be answered until the tensions of the Maoist era have begun to subside.

A more useful aim is thus to set forth in outlines that are very clear what one might call China's international personality. Whatever else China has done to the world since 1949 it has surprised it and shocked it – all of it, whether China's supposed allies in the Communist world, or her supposed brothers in poverty in the so-called Third World, not to mention the affluent imperialists whose actions in China over the previous century have done so much to stimulate the upheaval from which they are now the puzzled objects of hatred.

'Don't forget, China is a large country, full of Chinese . . .'. General de Gaulle's words to an Ambassador leaving for Peking make as good a starting point as any. These are the important things to remember about China and too few people even now apprehend their full implications. Start by realizing that China is unmatched anywhere else in the world – not in the historical sense, since many other civilizations preceded China's in antiquity, but in the continuity of ideas that have informed its civilization and the continuity of place in which that civilization has grown up. It is the largest area of the globe given coherence over a very long period of time by one culture, classical, medieval and now struggling to evolve a modern era that is not quite as much a rejection of the past as may seem or may even be proclaimed. Not least should one be aware why this civilization justifiably thought of itself as the centre and apex of the civilized world. For much of its history China had no reason to doubt the claim.

Thus no other people can look back over the kind of civilized past that the Chinese can. Of course they have been conquered; and to some extent they have been influenced by their conquerors. But for most of the time it is their culture that has been dominant. The ideas, the language, the literature, the myths, the festivals, the cosmology – these have persisted and given the Chinese their homogeneity. The visitor to China who finds himself faced with penetrating, patient, expressionless stares might think himself a new arrival from another world to have aroused such uncomprehending curiosity. The analogy is not so far-fetched: millions of Chinese live out their lives in a vast country, within a spreading and all-inclusive culture without ever seeing anyone but a Chinese. No wonder the first Westerners penetrating the country in any number – the mid-19th-century missionaries – found they could only make an impact by using the language, wearing the clothes and adopting some of the habits that were recognizably Chinese. They could act within China only in a Chinese context; they had to go through the gates to get behind the Chinese wall. The wall as a divide, the capacity to function on one side of it, and the differences in being on the other side of it – these are vital to an understanding of Chinese behaviour.

If we are to understand China's modern revolution, especially in the extremes of hysteria lately generated by the cultural revolution, it is best to start with the Chinese picture of a world on its own. The evolution of the Chinese personality in its current international manifestation comes from this long history lived behind a wall – metaphorically as well as actually. 'Within the four seas,' runs the Confucian epigram, 'all men are brothers.' But within the four seas was not Mercator's world but the cultural-zone of Chinese civilization. It was thus that the Chinese thought of themselves, as a civilization, as *the* civilization, not as one nation state among others. This European concept of the nation state was totally alien to Chinese thinking at the time when European power burst through the gates of the Chinese wall in the 19th century, and one might conclude that it is still not fully understood in the belligerent phase in which Mao Tse-tung is trying to galvanize revolutionary China.

This traditional sense of China, secure behind its wall, at least in the superiority of its culture, could be sustained because China had no direct contact with any comparable civilization or any kingdom of comparable power and size. So it was an attitude quite intact when European power was finally pressed against the closed gates of China in the early 19th century; indeed, the Manchu rulers of China installed 200 years earlier were themselves especially devoted to the sense of Chinese cultural superiority which they had themselves imbibed even before the conquest in the mid 17th century.

China's first reaction to the barbarians from the West was thus to domesticate and control them, making concessions where necessary to satisfy their avidity for trade, but assuming that in time they would be made sensible of the virtues of Chinese culture and would settle down as part of the Chinese culture-system, acknowledging the superiority embodied in the Emperor. When this attitude could no longer be upheld, and when the Chinese had gone through half a century of internal decline, the necessity of revolution could no longer be denied.

In this sense therefore China's revolution cannot be contained within the definitions we use elsewhere in the Third World. It was not simply a revolution to be explained by nationalism as in other ex-colonial territories. It was a revolution *against* the world; against the *whole* world; a revolution devoted to Chinese renewal as a necessity in itself to restore China's glory, but at the same time a revolution which by restoring China's strength would enable her to fend off, to deal with, at the very least to gain equality with, an outside world still fundamentally regarded as inferior to China.

For half a century after the Anglo-Chinese war of 1840 the unpleasant truths of decline and weakness were being brought home. For another half century – until a government capable of exacting Chinese demands and asserting Chinese rights at last came to power in 1949 – China was struggling towards an institutional and doctrinal stability. And from 1949 it may be at least another half century before China's equal confrontation of the outside world will even have fully demonstrated what problems of mutual accommodation still face both sides. We are concerned with a turning of the historical wheel lasting for 150 years.

This scale of change and the driving motives of Chinese renewal and self-assertion are still dimly comprehended in the outside world. Simply because of the belligerence of tone it is assumed that China's purpose can only be aggrandizement. The idea that all this could spring from a proud people, stung by the world's contumely all through the 19th century and much of this century – this tends to be underestimated. China's revolution is a great cry of vengeance and a demand for restitution. It is not a cry of conquest save in the sense that inherent in all cries coming from China there remains the assumption of superiority. But of course in the most hysterical phases of the cultural revolution the world can be forgiven for finding China an impossible member of the international community, ready to flout all rules, to despise all friends, to spit angrily at the world because it has not yet acknowledged China's rights and virtues.

The clues to understanding China's international behaviour become more visible if one starts from the assumption that the Chinese leaders may be rationally aware of the world in which they must now live but are yet instinctively, in the experience of revolution they have known, behaving as if their old world survived.

Chinese civilization has always been *indrawing* rather than outgoing, receptive rather than aggressive, peace-loving rather than militant, land-based in its ways of thinking rather than exploratory and adventurous in the way of maritime powers. Harmony has been one of its most cherished concepts, bargaining one of its most finely worked out practices, compromise a valued art rather than a sign of weak principle. And given the vast area of Chinese civilization, the Chinese saw the world of which they were the centre as one that paid tribute to Chinese superiority or else was too barbaric to be capable of appreciating what China had to offer. *Acknowledgement* was thus the key idea in China's relations with all her neighbours: once the acknowledgement was made where it was due – in the ceremony of the kotow to the Emperor – then harmony could be maintained, compromises effected where necessary, reason could rule. Naturally, then, the Chinese tried to impose these ceremonies and this acknowledgement on the missions that came from Europe, such as Macartney's in 1793, and equally naturally China's first real defeat was in 1860 when European power imposed on an unwilling China the admission of foreign diplomatic envoys to the Chinese court, envoys who came as representatives of states claiming equality with China and thus claiming the right of access to China's monarch. This was to strike at the very foundations of the Chinese system.

Observe how today this same pattern reproduces itself. The sense of self-righteousness in doctrine has again reasserted itself. At the end of the 19th century, when an unwilling Chinese hierarchy was making some concessions that distinguished European powers from those states in South-East Asia by which China had been surrounded, the slogan was current, 'Chinese thought as the base (*t'i*), Western thought for use (*yung*)'. The pure, as it were, and the applied; the philosophy and the technology. There was no need – it was assumed – to uproot the Chinese philosophy of society: only the need to add to this system of thought the technological expertise of the Western world which had contributed to its power and thus to China's defeat.

And so one sees today a new body of Chinese thought moved into position – the Thoughts of Mao Tse-tung – proclaimed to have exactly the same superiority, and demanding from the world, from him that shall see and be saved, the same kind of *acknowledgement* that was demanded in the past. True the emissaries from Paraguay or the Cameroons, clutching their little red books, now sit chatting to the Chairman over cups of tea and are not required to make obeisance; yet the acknowledgement is no less implicit, and the patronizing rewards are the same. China's righteousness has been restored. The moral superiority of China is manifest and all the country's servants act upon it.

Accompanying this sense of superiority is a readiness to spurn any who may be disowned because they fail in their acknowledgement or deny its validity. China has been at its best when most traditional, in the good relations of coexistence maintained with South-East Asian powers such as Burma and Cambodia, when something akin to the old tribute relationship could work on both sides. This instinctive attitude towards their smaller neighbours would probably be found in most of the men whose experience of the guerrilla hinterland of China has covered their most formative years. But to this must be added the peculiar and distinctive addition of Mao Tse-tung's personality as a revolutionary leader. His nationalism and his revolutionary zeal sometimes march together, sometimes conflict. Burma and Cambodia may also be spurned. The acknowledgement of China's greatness and superiority demands also the application of Mao Tse-tung's revolutionary thoughts.

The latest Maoist phase is therefore confusing, with Mao's personality cult raised to absurd heights, giving to Chinese pretensions an intolerable and at times laughable character. Yet the basic international personality is there and may be slow to change. Observe the delegations that have been going to China ever since 1949 from all parts of the world. What is required of them? They must learn, they must admire, they must *acknowledge*. And if a Chinese delegation ever does go to their country what does it do? It expounds, it publicizes, it explains.

China is all. The last purpose a visiting Chinese delegation conceives of is really to learn anything about the country it is visiting.

The same may be said of China's diplomatic mission. Not one of them, whether stationed in a Communist country, a Third World country, or a Western country, fulfils the normal functions of such missions. They are not exploring every aspect of the country to which they are accredited. They are not cultivating its leaders, they would be poor interpreters of its outlook: they are a lone island of Chinese righteousness embattled against aliens, spokesmen of a true and superior civilization. In every Chinese one meets the demand for acknowledgement.

Most Western knowledge about China has been acquired in the period of China's self-abasement. From the end of the 19th century until the middle of this century China was learning, was desperately looking for salvation. One sees in the Chinese view of themselves as it emerged in plays and films of the 1920s and 1930s the sense of suffering, of being ill-done by, that was the other face of the pride that has now asserted itself. (During the era of Chiang Kai-shek the pride only occasionally popped to the surface: the occasion for it, the doctrinal base, the *t'i*, was still being formulated and forged in the caves of Yenan.) This sense of suffering was easily married to the sense of Marxist progressiveness common among the young. In novels, in plays, in films, capitalists were evil toadies of the West, sellers of China's birthright: workers were strong, simple and good. Landlords were evil reactionaries, incapable by nature of coming to terms with the new truth: peasants were of the soil, soaked in Chinese goodness, the material of the future. Over all was the ethos of China's international suffering: the weak country forced to sign unequal treaties; a country violated, despoiled, thwarted by the outside world and prevented from assuming its true quality. As a doctrine it was pervasive: Mao Tse-tung could draw on it, he had no need to invent it.

The question that arises, of course, is how China is going to develop in the future. Granted that China has not yet been given the world's acknowledgement – not even in the formal sense of admission to the United Nations – granted that China's equality with the Western world in the development of her economy may take another thirty or forty years for even a superficial sense of attainment, is China then going to change? Or is China changing now? Is this indrawing civilization going to become outgoing; can China reverse her old habits; will China join the world's exchange in any cultural sense?

The only answer thus far can be that there is no sign of it. It may be noted that the Chinese have never shown much willingness or much ability to explain their own way of life and its virtues. Others must get behind the wall and find out. Even the many books written by Chinese expatriates in the United States are all written from the training and within the disciplines of American postgraduate work: none of them throw the faintest ray of *Chinese* light on China. Indeed, one might suggest that the Chinese personality becomes emasculated by being severed from a zone of Chinese culture. One reason why Chinese could never be good imperialists is that they could never function as lone rulers in lone outposts (if one could conceive of imperialism as the British knew it ever reproducing itself again).

It has also been noted that China has done little in importing the culture of others save to remake it in a Chinese form. What China once did to Buddhism China is now doing to Marxism. As for the trimmings, they do not exist. No collection of Western art, ancient or modern, exists in China. The Communist period has weakened what small foothold existed for Western music, literature or any other aspects of other cultures. Science, yes, that is *yung*, for use; but the base, the *t'i*, that must be Chinese and for the present it remains so.

Chinese culture and Chinese thought does not come to meet the foreigner half way; there is no crossing point of mutual exchange. There is an internal face of Chinese culture and for those foreigners who scramble over the wall and make themselves part of it, even to the merest foothold, it is visible. Other than that there is a Chinese face looking outwards, a face for dealing with foreigners who by definition live and have their being outside the Chinese world.

One answer to all the questions could surely be that after twenty years of confinement there might again be a new sense of curiosity in China about the outside world. And if China is really going to join the world's major economic powers how can she any longer remain enclosed and culturally immured? What applies to China applies *pari passu* to the rest of the East Asian world – Japan, Korea and Vietnam – which looks on China as the source of its own civilization and for whom China is the classical world, the Greece and Rome that is still alive and in business and is not to be ignored. That world of East Asia is one in which China may yet assume her place. Meanwhile the curious and puzzled world beyond will have to watch, and learn a little; even, perhaps, as it comes to reflect on its own past and present, to acknowledge that China's two thousand years of evolution does deserve a little more serious attention than the rest of the world has given it.

BIBLIOGRAPHY

Dennis Bloodworth. *Chinese Looking-Glass*. (Secker & Warburg, 1967; Penguin Books, 1969.)

C. P. FitzGerald. *The Birth of Communist China*. (Penguin Books, 1964.)

Mu Fu-sheng. *The Wilting of the Hundred Flowers*. (Heinemann, 1962.)

F. Geoffroy-Dechaume. *China Looks at the World*. (Faber & Faber, 1967.)

Robert J. Lifton. *Thought Reform and the Psychology of Totalism*. (Gollancz, 1961; Penguin Books, 1968.)

Roger Pelissier. *The Awakening of China, 1793–1949*. (Secker & Warburg, 1963.)

Victor Purcell. *China*. (Ernest Benn, 1962.)

Ssu-yu Teng and John K. Fairbank. *China's Response to the West*. (Oxford University Press, 1954.)

THE JAPANESE PERSONALITY

R. P. Dore

DELINEATING the personality of the Japanese people has been a favourite pastime of foreign observers at least since St Francis Xavier in the 16th century described those qualities which seemed to him to make the Japanese people 'the best of all among unbelievers' and the most ripe for conversion. The Japanese themselves have also been given to introspective analysis of the essential Japanese spirit, particularly at times when conflict with the outer world has given them reason to emphasize their unique Japaneseness.

It was a common assumption until the beginning of this century that the supposedly unique features of Japanese personality and culture were biologically determined; and leopards cannot change their spots. Thus the French sociologist Le Bon declared that although many a Japanese had acquired all the outward marks of Western civilization this was a mere 'varnish' which was 'quite superficial and has no influence on his mental constitution'.[*] It was with a sense of daring that Sidney Gulick, the missionary author of one of the first attempts at a full-length analysis of the Japanese character, started from the assumption that 'the main differences between the great races of mankind today are not due to biological but to social conditions'.[†] This however – except for the more fanatical Japanese nationalists of the thirties who claimed the benefit of direct descent from the gods – has been the assumption of most subsequent writers on the subject. There is, to be sure, no obvious reason for denying that, just as the basic physical similarity between, say, the average Japanese and the average Englishman is modified by marginal differences in stature, bone structure, pigmentation, etc., there might also – again in terms of mean values in the ranges of variation exhibited by the two populations – be marginal differences in those genetically determined dispositions which affect the development of temperament and character. But the presence in the United States of large numbers of sons and grandsons of Japanese immigrants no less 100 per cent American than the descendants of European immigrants should effectively dispose of any suggestion that biological heritage has a major importance in determining national differences.

[*] *The Psychology of Peoples*, 1898, p. 37.
[†] *The Evolution of the Japanese*, fourth edn, 1905, p. 21.

What, then, *are* the differentiating factors? Gulick, the American missionary, explained what he considered to be the typically Japanese personality characteristics simply as signs of 'backwardness' in the scale of evolutionary development. The suspiciousness, the fickle enthusiasm for current fads, the ambition and conceit, the submissive acceptance of fate, indirectness of speech and repression of emotions which he discerned in the Japanese were all the heritage of a feudal past which the forces of progress would – he hoped – soon eliminate. The pagan Lafcadio Hearn had a similar explanation for his rather different version of the Japanese 'race-character' – the charm, the kindliness, grace of manners, peaceable co-operativeness and loyal self-denial which would – he feared – disappear with rapid social evolution.*

THE PURSUIT OF DUTY

The anthropologists who made appreciations of the Japanese character for the guidance of American policy-makers during the Second World War worked with a different set of assumptions. The most whole-hog Freudian of them all, Weston LaBarre, had a simple key to the whole puzzle. The Japanese were the victims of 'severity and cruelty in treatment during the period of cleanliness training' in infancy. This resulted in their exhibiting as a people all the traits corresponding to the clinical description of the typical 'anal-compulsive' personality type – the secretive hiding of emotions, perseverance, conscientiousness, self-righteousness, fanaticism, perfectionism, ceremoniousness, ritual cleanliness, hypochondria, and of course sadomasochism.† Other writers were less obviously the victims of war-time tendencies to view the enemy as the devil incarnate, and less monocausal in their explanations. Geoffrey Gorer, for instance, also concentrated on the experiences of early childhood and ascribed somewhat similar results to toilet training, but he also stressed two other themes. The first was the nature of the child's emotional relations with his parents (which were supposed to give him a tendency to divide the world into the softer, yielding, feminine half towards which he can act aggressively with impunity and the male half which demands submissive compliance); and the second, the importance placed on bodily self-control and precise conformity to etiquette which was explicitly taught as a means

Japan: An Interpretation, 1904.

†'Some observations on character structure in the Orient', *Psychiatry*, 8 (1945), pp. 319–42, reprinted in B. S. Silberman, *Japanese Character and Culture*, University of Arizona, Tucson, 1962.

of avoiding shaming mockery from others and so retaining one's position as an esteemed member of one's group.* Ruth Benedict, the most subtle and urbane of these war-time writers, followed some of the same themes, but gave greater importance to the explicit ethic taught in schools and enshrined in proverbs and the everyday language of moral discourse. Her book† was, in effect, an elaboration of the epitomization of the Japanese character given in Nitobe's pre-war version of the 'international prize competition for an essay on the elephant' story. (According to Nitobe, the Japanese entry bore the title, 'The duties and domestication of the elephant.') Thus, in Benedict's interpretation the Japanese character was in large measure the product of explicit training in the need for self-sacrificing pursuit of duty – of duty towards the Emperor, the nation, the family, status superiors and personal benefactors, and of the duty to maintain one's good name in order to retain the esteem of one's group – a preoccupation which made shame rather than guilt the major moral sanction. Since the duties were particular duties relating to particular spheres of conduct and particular social relations, large areas of life were left free for innocent sensual enjoyment, untroubled, if there was no conflict with duty, by any sense of guilt. And this dichotomy was exemplified and reinforced by the discontinuity of childhood training – the indulgence of early childhood contrasting with the sudden requirement of conformist responsible behaviour later on. The Japanese had, in short, with their stress on particular duties rather than generalized principles of conduct, a 'situational ethic' which made them a well-disciplined moral people in familiar situations, but lacking in guidelines for behaviour when – as in war-time – they were faced with new ones.

Clearly the evolutionists struck closer to the truth than the 'potters and weaners' in their explanation of Japanese national character, if only because the latter jumped too easily to false conclusions about how the Japanese wean and pot. (An anthropologist who made a study of toilet training in a Japanese town in 1952 came to the conclusion that there was such individual variety of method as to make generalization impossible.‡ Consider, for instance, one aspect of the Japanese noted by many observers as differentiating them from Anglo-

---

*'Themes in Japanese culture', *Trans. New York Academy of Sciences*, Sect. II, 5, (1943), pp. 105–24. Repr. in Silberman, *op. cit.*

† *The Chrysanthemum and the Sword*, Houghton Mifflin, Boston, 1946.

‡ Betty Lanham, 'Aspects of child care in Japan', in D. Haring, ed., *Personal Character and the Cultural Milieu*, 1956, reprinted in Silberman, *op. cit.*

Saxons; a lesser willingness to take individual initiatives involving the risk of failure, and a tendency to be more uneasily anxious in competitive situations and more overwhelmingly mortified by the shame of failure. One can think of a number of good reasons why this sort of sense of honour is most likely to be found in a closed stratified society such as Japan before 1870 (or medieval Europe for that matter), a society in which a man's status and occupation was largely determined by birth and in which even in the cities men's lives were lived in small communities. Where there was little possibility of overt competition for position and occupational opportunities men rarely had the chance to experience – and get used to the experience of – being defeated or rejected. Again, failure in another sense, being accused of not living up to the expectations implicit in one's hereditarily assigned role, was the more totally damaging to a man's self-respect in that there was little possibility of moving on and starting afresh. Equally, where life was not segmented into different spheres of work and recreation and family life, the embarrassment of failure in one sphere could not be compensated for by retaining the regard and affection of members of quite separate spheres. One's small community contained all one's life activities; it judged one as a whole man, and there was small chance of escape. The more open, mobile society of modern Japan, where schools and employers recruit by selective competition and where leadership in politics and trade unions and women's institutes is decided by competition for votes, is likely to breed different personalities. The unusual aspect of Japan was that until 1945 the change in personality which one might expect to follow from the changing structure of society was slowed down by deliberate Government policy. Elements of the feudal code of personal relations – particularly the emphasis on duty and the punctilious fulfilment of obligations to superiors – were reformulated in the late 19th century into an officially sanctioned 'uniquely Japanese moral code' and instilled into every Japanese in the schools, in the army, through the press and through the radio – a feature the importance of which Ruth Benedict justly recognized.

Even in 1945, however, it was already doubtful whether it made any sense to talk of *the* typical Japanese personality. It is even more doubtful today after over twenty years of freedom from the incubus of state indoctrination in the 'Japanese spirit' and after a decade of the most rapid industrialization the world has ever seen. An industrial nation of nearly 100 million people is bound to be so differentiated by regional, class and individual variation that any generalization must admit of very large exceptions. The modern Japanese jazz musician probably has much more in common with an English jazz musician than he has with a Japanese civil servant. It still remains possible that the difference between the average Japanese and the average English jazz musician, and the differences between the average Japanese and the average English civil servant, lie in a consistent direction. Thus, to take a hypothetical example, a patient sociologist who invented a scale of 'politeness' might find that the following proportions of his samples were by his criterion 'polite people'.

	Japanese	*British*
Jazz musicians	40 per cent	30 per cent
Civil servants	80 per cent	70 per cent

It is only in this limited statistical and comparative sense that one can legitimately talk of national character. Thus, the assertion 'the Japanese are a polite people' has to be interpreted 'most Japanese are more polite than is usual among their counterparts in my (the asserter's) country'.

THE NATIONAL CHARACTER

This being said, what are the characteristics which, in this limited sense, might still be said to differentiate the Japanese from other people? It seems clear that some parts of the Western stereotype of Japan now have to go. The 'mere imitators lacking in originality' notion derives from the 19th century when Japan was quite clearly hell-bent on catching up with the West. Now that she has in large measure caught up, the Japanese are beginning to make their own fair share of original contributions to science and technology as they have always done in the field of art. Nevertheless such stereotypes are persistent, not least among the Japanese themselves. In 1958 a large national sample was asked to choose from a list of adjectives all those which they thought could justly be used to describe the Japanese people. The adjectives, and the proportion of the sample choosing each of them, were as follows: rational (12 per cent), diligent (55 per cent), freedom-loving (15 per cent), *tampaku* (something like 'unemotional', 'frank', 'indifferent') (19 per cent), persevering (48 per cent), kind-hearted (50 per cent), originally creative (8 per cent), polite (47 per cent), cheerful (23 per cent), idealistic (33 per cent).

Such stereotypes are unlikely to be an accurate mirror of reality. On the other hand, they probably have some foundation in reality even if it is the reality of a generation ago. My own list of the features which (in the limited statistical and necessarily comparative sense indicated above) differentiate the modern Japanese from the modern Englishman would be somewhat as follows. For each characteristic one may choose either the approving or the pejorative term according to taste as in the declension: 'I am a man of principle, you are obstinate, he is bigoted'. The Japanese, then,

are less self-confident and more neurotically preoccupied with retaining the good opinion of others.	have a keener sense of personal honour and are less complacently self-righteous.
are more imitative.	have a more realistic willingness to learn from others.
are more ambitious.	have a keener desire for self-improvement.
are more slavishly diligent.	are less afraid of hard work.
are more submissive to superiors.	have a more realistic appreciation of the need to co-operate in society.
are less willing to stand up for individual rights.	are less selfish.
are more dishonest and indirect in speech.	are more sensitive to, and less willing to offend, the feelings of others.
are less men of principle.	are more willing to forgo the pleasures of self-assertion in the interests of social harmony.
have less sense of social responsibility to remove abuses in their own society.	are less busybody, with a more tolerant willingness to live and let live.
are more childishly naïve.	have more good-humoured cheerfulness.
are more introverted.	are more shy about imposing their views and feelings on strangers.
are more sentimental.	show greater affectionate warmth and quicker emotional responses in intimate relations.

How many of these qualities – assuming that they really do characterize the modern Japanese – will be modified by further social change, and how far they will remain a permanent part of the Japanese variant of industrial man, it is difficult to predict. Equally problematical is their meaning for the future place of Japan in the world. In the short run, at least, the qualities of drive and willingness to learn seem to promise that Japan's rapid economic progress will continue. The limits placed on self-assertiveness might suggest that the cohesiveness of Japanese society will continue to be able to contain disruptive social conflict. (Though this is not necessarily the case; the same trait can help re-inforce the cohesiveness of sectional groups within the nation and so harden the lines of division which exist.) The continued sensitiveness to the good opinion of others suggests that, now that Japan is no longer able to force grudging admiration by the aggressive display of strength, her leaders will continue to follow a policy of international co-operation and punctilious observance of her obligations to her chosen allies – whoever, at the time, they happen to be.

BIBLIOGRAPHY

Frank Gibney. *Five Gentlemen of Japan. Portrait of a Nation's Character.* (Gollancz, 1953.)

I. Kawasaki. *The Japanese Are Like That.* (Tuttle, Tokyo, 1956.)

E. O. Reischauer. *The United States and Japan,* Part III. (Harvard University Press, Cambridge, Mass., 1957.)

THE IMPORTANCE OF
ASIA TO RUSSIA AND THE
WESTERN WORLD

K. M. Panikkar

ASIA covers a very large area of the land surface of the world. It contains over half of its population. In essential resources for industrial production it is richer than the other continents. Naturally, in an era when the world is organized into camps, the control of Asia, its space, its manpower and its natural resources, can tilt the balance of power.

Before the Second World War, all Asia outside Japan was divided into two almost equal parts, one forming part of the territories of the Soviet Union and the other under the authority or influence of the Western powers. A line from the Black Sea border of Turkey along Iran, Afghanistan, the Pamirs and China to the Pacific marked the boundary. The area to the north was a part of Soviet Russia, occupied, administered and developed as part of a federated union of states. The great Western powers shared the area to the south of this line which, before the war, contained no less than 1,250 million people.

Britain, basing her power on her Indian Empire, spread her authority into the Far East. Her outstretched arms spread into Tibet and into Sinkiang. France had, in the second half of the century, built herself an empire in the valley of the Mekong and the Meenam. From there she sought to extend her influence over south China. The Dutch ruled over the Indonesian archipelago and controlled its immense riches. Even America, after the occupation of the Philippines, became for a short time an Asian power. The areas of the Middle East were equally under European influence if not direct authority. Iran maintained a precarious independence as a buffer state between the British and the Russians, subject to the pressure of both. The oil-rich Arab kingdoms and principalities were areas of British and American influence. Palestine was ruled by the British under a mandate, while Syria and Lebanon were under French authority. Turkey had opted out of Asia and claimed to be a part of Europe.

The area under Russian control had a different history. In the 19th century the Tsarist Empire had, by slow but determined steps, moved on to the Pamirs, the frontier of Britain's Indian Empire. In the process she had annexed the Muslim Khanates and territories in the historic Central Asian region. Across the steppes of Siberia, she had planted colonies of Russians even in Tsarist times. In the period between the Revolution and the Second World War the Soviet Union followed in its Asian territories a vigorous programme of economic development as a defence against Nazi attack.

A basic difference between the Western and the Russian approach to the Asian countries needs to be emphasized. The importance of Asia to the Western powers lay mainly in trade, development and utilization of economic resources, political authority and use of manpower for purposes of warfare. They were not interested in colonization in the strict sense, in peopling the areas of Asia with men of Western stock. The case was different with Russia, as we shall see later. In none of the Asian countries under Western occupation was there a settled European population or even a considerable number of people of mixed blood.

Russia extended its influence very greatly when the Russian Revolution led to the establishment of Communist parties, open or secret, in many Asian countries. They were usually open to direction from Moscow. Through guidance of their activities, Russia greatly extended its range of influence throughout Asia.

The period following the Second World War witnessed the withdrawal of the Western nations from Asia. Within a period of ten years ending in 1957 practically every portion of Asia over which the Western nations exercised political authority was liberated.

But this withdrawal did not affect the Soviets except in Manchuria where, in agreement with the People's Republic of China, such rights as she possessed over the Manchurian railway and Port Arthur were surrendered shortly after the Communist revolution in China. Not only did the Soviet Union not have to withdraw from the vast areas of Asia into which she had overflowed but she affirmed in unequivocal terms her position as a great Asian state. In his famous speech at Srinagar in 1954 Mr Khrushchev claimed that China and India, along with the Soviet Union, constituted the three great powers of Asia.

ASIA AND THE WEST

The importance of Asia to the West, in spite of the elimination of political power, is very considerable. The West draws a good deal of its industrial raw material from the countries of Asia. A substantial portion of the oil supply of the West comes from the Arabian peninsula, Iraq, the trucial sheikhdoms and Indonesia. The investment of the

West in the half of Asia outside Communist control is considerable and, in fact, is greater than at the time of imperial authority. In India, for example, British investment at the time of independence amounted to only £155 million. In 1959 it was over £300 million, or had doubled itself. America was practically an unknown factor in South and South-East Asia outside the Philippines in the period before the Second World War. Today she has a major share in investment and trade.

But this is not a position which is stable, as the Asian countries are not content to remain the suppliers of raw material or markets for capital goods and manufactured products. Nor do they desire to be, for long, areas of profitable investment. India, the largest of the non-Communist countries, has already progressed a good way towards the creation of a self-sustained industrial economy; the other countries will also tread the same path. While non-Communist Asia of over 900 million (with Japan) will continue to be a major trading partner of the West, it is obvious that the future interest of the West in those regions will not continue in the field inherited from the days of colonialism. A return to political authority, economic dominance, restriction of production to raw materials or industry under the control of the West, as at one time in Shanghai and Calcutta, would be clearly impossible.

There is a sphere, however, where the importance of Asia to the West is a growing one. It is necessary to recognize that non-Communist Asia has to a large extent become integrated with the culture of the West. Education in all these countries is being developed largely in co-operation with Europe and the USA. The universities of the former British Empire in Asia are linked with their counterparts in countries of the Commonwealth. They also maintain close relations with America. In matters of scientific research there is a great deal of exchange between Europe and countries like India and Japan. The literature and artistic life of new Asia, outside the Communist world, is also closely connected to movements in the Western world.

ASIA AND RUSSIA

The importance of Asia to Russia lies in other factors. The original colonial position, especially in the Central Asian area, has been transformed already by a large-scale migration of people. The following figures of population in the two major areas of this region will show the magnitude of the transformation that has already taken place. The Republic of Kazakhstan is an immense territory lying between lower

Volga, Sinkiang and Mongolia. It has an area of 1,263,000 square miles, or nearly the same as India. Its population, however, is only 10 million, of which in 1956 over 35 per cent was of Russian stock. With the immense development schemes that the Soviets have in hand, it is obvious that in a few years the population of Kazakhstan will not only go up by leaps and bounds but that it will soon have a majority of people of Russian stock. Again Turkmenistan with an immense area has a population of only a million and a half, of which 20 per cent are already Russians. Siberia, which is much larger in size than the whole of Europe, is overwhelmingly Russian in the composition of its population. Thus over vast areas of Asia constituting more than half of the continent, Russia is fast ceasing to be a colonial power. It is becoming part of the Russian homeland. In the former colonial territories of Central Asia, the integration of the local proletariat with the fast-growing Russian population is itself a major factor. Besides, the economic and social developments of these areas have modernized their traditional economies and helped to create a society which has broken away from Muslim traditions. These areas in fact constitute Russia's New Frontier, the great challenge to the constructive ability of the Soviet Union.

But apart from the areas which form part of the USSR, there are two other sectors of Asia which are of importance to the Soviets. There is the Communist bloc of Asian countries – the People's Republic of China, Mongolia, North Korea and North Vietnam, which between them have 700 million people. What is the importance of this area to Russia? This would be best appreciated by imagining what the position would be if China, instead of going Communist, had reorganized herself effectively and been a member of the Western bloc. It is the change that has taken place in China and the Communist countries of Asia that has brought the Pacific areas within the Communist challenge. It is not necessary to emphasize that but for the growth of Communist Asian states Soviet power would have been effectively contained and limited as before the Second World War.

The problem of Asia's importance to Russia has another dimension and that is the position of the non-Communist half of the continent. To the south of the Soviet and Chinese territories lies a continental area which together with Japan, Indonesia, Ceylon and Taiwan has a population of over 900 million. It is difficult to over-estimate the importance of this area both to the West and to Russia. Apart from what may be called the long-term interest of converting every country to the gospel of Communism, the importance of this area to the Soviet

Union lies in the fact that the Western end from Turkey to Pakistan lies close to the sparsely populated Central Asia. Also from the eastern border of India to the South China Sea the territory is a battle ground where an expanding Communism faces the peoples of South-East Asia. The Soviet Union is for the time being content, so far as this area is concerned, to ensure that the states of South-East Asia should not be used as military bases by the Western bloc. She, therefore, supports a policy of non-involvement, such as is followed by India, Nepal, Burma and Indonesia, and extends to them technical and economic support.

Russia received a setback at the time of the Bandung Conference. It claimed that the Asian Republics of the USSR should attend. This claim was rejected, and Russia was held firmly to be a European power. The official claim by Russia that the constituent republics of the USSR were autonomous was questioned. This was before the days of the break with China, but Russia cannot have found it agreeable that China should have been the main Communist representative at the Conference.

At the end of the 1950s there broke out the quarrel with China. This caused a profound change in all Russia's policy in Asia. In claiming to be the proponent of Communism in Asia, it had to define its attitude towards Communist China, and it never succeeded in doing so convincingly to the intelligentsia of Asia.

As the quarrel developed, Russia was inclined to back up and to strengthen India economically, hoping that it would prove a counterweight to China. The encouragement which it gave India considerably annoyed China, which felt that, but for this, it might have fared better in its border dispute. A particular cause of offence was the considerable sums which Russia was advancing to India. According to Chinese calculations, this money might have made a great difference to the position of Communism if it had been invested in China.

The Russian backing of India did not, however, lead Russia on to commit itself more deeply to support India in its dispute over Kashmir. On the contrary, Russian policy veered considerably towards a more open-minded attitude between India and Pakistan. Khrushchev's enthusiastic support of India was replaced by a much more temporizing attitude by his successors. Russia avoided any direct participation in the Kashmir clash between India and Pakistan in 1965, and immediately afterwards it sought, by persuading both parties to the dispute to come to the conference at Tashkent, to extend Russia's moral influence in Asia. Russia's initiative made a great stir throughout all Asia; it has scarcely exploited this as it was expected to do. Pakistan has, however, made skilful use of the hostility between Russia and China, has played off one against the other, and has accepted surprisingly large arms deliveries from China.

The collision between Russia and China is reflected in the division in the Indian Communist party. One part of the party is pro-Russian; another part, especially in Bengal and in the far south, in Kerala, is avowedly pro-Chinese.

In 1965 a further Asian Conference, on the lines of Bandung, was to be convened at Algiers. Russia was bent on being admitted this time, the more persistently because of its disputes with China. Its claims were supported by India. China, however, persisted in its objections. Clearly the quarrel made the project of holding such a conference of doubtful value, and it was abandoned by all concerned when the overthrow of Benbella, the head of the host government, made a venue at Algiers suddenly unsuitable.

THE 'BATTLE FOR SOULS'

The importance of this area to the West has already been briefly discussed. Basically it is that the countries and peoples of non-Communist Asia, constituting over a third of the world's population, should not fall under Communist influence and be lost to the free world; for the West realizes full well that if South and South-East Asia fall within Communist orbit, the ultimate victory of Communism would be assured. To the West, therefore, it is the freedom of the non-Communist half of Asia that is important.

Thus a battle for souls is being waged in Asia with Russia entrenched in her Asian territories and China in her sphere of influence, and the West associated in economic development, technical and educational spheres. The West also shares with this area a common, though perhaps a weakening, liberal tradition, which has played a notable part in shaping its present life.

BIBLIOGRAPHY

G. F. Hudson. *Questions of East and West*. (Odhams, 1953.)

K. M. Panikkar. *Asia and Western Dominance*. (Allen & Unwin, revised edn, 1959.)

THE AUSTRALIAN
ATTITUDE TOWARDS ASIA

C. P. FitzGerald

EARLY in the 19th century a party of convicts, transported to Australia, escaped from custody and started to travel north in the belief that they would be able to reach China – overland. Apart from the probability that they would have been sadly disappointed by their reception if they had been able to accomplish such a journey, the story illustrates the general ignorance of uneducated persons of the true situation of Australia, and at the same time the realization that it was, indeed, a very great way from Europe. In the century and more that followed Australians had little desire to voyage to China or anywhere else in Asia: if they could afford to travel overseas they came 'home' to the United Kingdom, to visit relatives, to see for themselves the land from which their fathers, or grandfathers, had emigrated.

Asia remained a sealed book. It was largely under the safe rule of the European colonial powers, of which their own Britain was the greatest; and Britannia Ruled the Waves. There was no conceivable danger from Asia; Asians were backward; they were not Christians. They were therefore a suitable field for missionary endeavour, and many Australians took part in that enterprise. Some of them came back to retire in their homeland. They were much in demand to speak of their experiences, raise money for the missionary work, and in this way they exercised a real influence over the mind of the rising generation. It was necessarily a rather one-sided and even distorted picture of Asia which was received. A great continent of pagans – or 'heathen' – as yet barely touched by the light of the Gospel. A region which could not hope to progress until that light shone more widely; a land of toiling millions, benighted and poverty-stricken masses of humanity. Missionaries did not come into close contact with the educated and ruling classes of Asia, and when they did, they found these people unco-operative, obstructive and opposed to the work of the missions. They were therefore just as benighted as their uneducated countrymen, with less excuse.

These notions have not yet wholly faded from the consciousness (or perhaps the unconscious) of many of the older generation, not excluding

576

the eminent. They persisted in spite of the existence of a small but competent group of Australians who really did know Asia and followed its politics with close attention. Such men as George Morrison, correspondent of *The Times* in Peking for many years at the end of the 19th and in the early 20th century; W. Donald, who was the intimate adviser of General Chiang Kai-shek in the years before the war; and many of lesser fame in business, mining and industry could have been the leaders of an informed public opinion. In fact they exercised little or no influence upon opinion in their homeland. They only rarely returned to it; their contacts were increasingly with Europe or America. Effective policy towards Asia was not made in Australia; capital for enterprises in Asia was not raised in Australia.

BRITISH AND AMERICAN PROTECTION AGAINST JAPAN

Until a few years before the outbreak of the Second World War Australia had no independent diplomatic representation overseas, and no Ministry of External Affairs. Parliament and public left the conduct of foreign affairs to Whitehall. As far as Asia was concerned this did not matter, as there was only one Asian state which could have any significance for Australia either as a threat or as an ally: Japan. For a long period Japan was the ally of Britain, and therefore a friend. When this situation came to an end and Japan gradually became a threat, Australia responded very slowly to the change. Yet it is significant that among the very few diplomatic missions sent to a foreign power in the years shortly before the Second World War, Japan was one. Informed people were aware by 1938–9 that Japan was on the march, her ambitions far-reaching, and that Australia was in a very exposed position. The ease with which Japan had flouted foreign privileges in China, derided the protests of the powers, and employed force and violence without incurring any penalty opened the eyes of thinking men to the very real dangers ahead.

The general public remained unaware, confident and indifferent. If there was trouble, Britain would protect her kith and kin. British sea power was so strong a tradition that only close students of the changing world could assess its present limitations. Australians were generously ready to spring to arms to defend the 'home country'. The traditions of Flanders and Gallipoli lived vividly in the national memory, enshrined in the national day, Anzac Day, which for most still had (and has) a far greater significance than the commemoration of the first settlement of the Continent, or the foundation of the Commonwealth of Australia. But war to Australians had essentially this chivalric, detached, remote quality. Patriotic men enlisted to fight for the Empire in some far-off foreign land. They fought for principles, not for self-defence. No one really ever supposed that the Germans or the Turks could or would invade Australia. Few Germans were then found in Australia; it is very doubtful whether more than a very few individuals of the thousands who landed at Gallipoli had ever before set eyes on a Turk.

When invasion nearly came in the Second World War, when the Japanese had seized Malaya, landed in New Guinea, launched their naval power to take command of the Western Pacific, and only been checked at the last moment by the Battle of the Coral Sea, Australia experienced a traumatic shock. It became known that the military had had to base their plans on the 'Brisbane Line', which would have yielded the northern sparsely inhabited half of the continent to the invader without resistance. American sea power saved Australia. The historical fact is well known, but all its consequences have yet to sink into the general understanding of Australians.

The war left the Australian people with a sense of gratitude to America, but much more strongly with a sense of fear and horror of Japan. This is often attributed mainly to the sufferings of Australian prisoners of war, captives of a people whose military tradition did not admit clemency. But this was not all; underlying it was the realization that the Japanese had destroyed a dream, and violated a sacred shrine: the dream of Australia's perfect security behind the shield of Britain's Navy; the shrine of the Just War fought for pure patriotism and high principle, far away, in strange lands, against impersonal foes from remote nations.

The Japanese were not far away, they had come right down to New Guinea, an Australian territory. The war was not only for principles, but for survival; the penalty for defeat was not severe casualties and a heroic rear-guard action, but invasion, conquest, perhaps permanent subjugation. Such had indeed been the fate of many peoples for varying lengths of time. Those who have had the experience never forget it: conquest, partial or total, marks a watershed in the national history. If permanent, as with the Normans, it takes centuries to complete the fusion of the two peoples, to eradicate the last vestiges of privilege stemming from victory, of bondage stemming from defeat. It may be that the Japanese could never have conquered Australia, or held it if they had at first overrun the defence; but to the Australians this was certainly not apparent, and is in any case speculative. What was certain was that Asia could never be ignored in future. Japan might be defeated, occupied, disarmed; but who could guarantee that she would not rise again within a generation, just as Germany had risen.

The answer to this question was, and is, 'America'. The second lesson of the Second World War was that America was the only force in the world which could, if she would, save Australia, and protect Australia. But this lesson is learned much less easily, and is far less welcome. Attachment to Britain is strong, especially in the age group from which political leadership comes. It is not easy to recognize that Britain cannot now fulfil her traditional role. If the fact is recognized, it is not easy, nor politically wise, to over-emphasize it. To accept American preponderence in the Western world, and total domination of the Pacific Ocean, is comforting so long as it is certain that America won't forget her white cousins on the Western side. But from time to time it becomes uneasily apparent that American ideas on Asia and the aspirations of Asians are not always in harmony with Australian sentiment.

THE NEW ASIA

In the post-war world Australia was faced with an entirely new Asia. Japan, the one real terrible danger, was eliminated. But so, all too soon, were the old colonial empires, which had hitherto put the whole of South-East Asia into a kind of political cold storage. It was with London, The Hague or Paris that one used to deal if ever the affairs of Malaya, Indonesia or Indo-China impinged on Australian interests. Now it was with new men in new places, all unfamiliar. Everything was changed; China had been the ally in the war, distant, ineffective, vaguely romantic, but a friend. Very soon the Australians were being told, above all by the Americans, that the new Communist China was the enemy, far worse than Japan, ideological as well as military. It was more than hinted that Australian fears of Japan were outmoded and unreal; they should be taking heed of the new danger and assessing the new enemy. But the Australian people have been very slow to learn this lesson; in fact, very many of them repudiate the teaching.

Australia accepted, with reluctance, the lenient terms imposed on Japan at San Francisco. The re-arming of Japan, even on a limited scale, is viewed with deep suspicion. On the other hand the thesis that China is the new enemy is not widely accepted outside the right wing of both the Liberal (conservative) and Labour Parties. In the first group, the knowledge of servicemen of what war they are bound to prepare for influences opinion; in the second the strong proportion of

Roman Catholics in the Labour Party influences the view of China from an ideological rather than a practical or military standpoint. A majority of Australians are not under these special influences. The country, although not at present ruled by the Left, has always had a Left outlook. Communism as such may be unattractive, but there is a widespread knowledge that the Asian working class had been oppressed, ill-paid, and down-trodden; that the Chinese revolution was due to these facts and not to some 'Communist conspiracy'. The mass of the Australian people still hold their own colonial past in bitter memory; they are not unresponsive to others who feel the same.

There thus work in the Australian mind two rather contradictory impulses in respect of Asia: fear and sympathy. The old missionary village-hall lecturer has left his mark, sometimes in an unexpected way. The toiling millions may not yet be converted; but the modern Australian tends to remember their existence, both to fear their potential strength, and to feel concerned at their low standard of living. He is more alarmed by their poverty than distressed by their unbelief. If the poverty can be relieved, the pressure for revolutionary change can be eased, and thus the fear of violent upheavals, aggressive wars, and possible invasions reduced. Fear and sympathy dictate to many a similar approach; Australia's task in Asia is to assist development.

There is a considerable resistance to the approach which is dictated more by fear than sympathy. To contain Communism without trying to discover what makes Asians inclined to follow that doctrine; to form military alliances which bolster up very undemocratic regimes, but which seem none the less unable to win enthusiastic support from Asians; to many Australians, broadly, but not only, those of the Left, all this seems wrong-headed. There is thus a further dilemma facing Australians in their approach to the new Asia. The history of the last war has shown, beyond dispute, that Australia depends on America for her survival in a major war. But much of American policy in the East of Asia has seemed either unsound or positively contrary to Australian interests. Nor is this confined to matters concerning China and Communism.

WESTERN NEW GUINEA

Australia feared that Japan was being let off too lightly; although trade with Japan now flourishes, many still feel that American policy towards that country wholly ignored Australia's point of view. Indonesia has been an uneasy neighbour for Australia: her closest Asian neighbour, but unstable, with a large Communist Party, a rickety economy, and unsatisfied claims on Western New Guinea. Western New Guinea is divided from Eastern, Australian, New Guinea by a meridian of longitude, a line without reality in geographical terms, undemarcated, and unrelated to tribal boundaries or ethnic divisions. The Australians felt that if this territory was to become Indonesian just because it had been part of the Dutch Empire, then there was no reason in logic or geography why Indonesia would not claim Eastern New Guinea also. In any case they had little confidence in the ability of the Indonesian state to develop, govern and improve the trackless jungles of a most difficult region. Their own, not very clearly formulated plans for the future development of Eastern New Guinea, in which English would be the language of education and democracy the form of government, might be prejudiced by the creation of an artificial Indonesian nationalism in Western New Guinea. Therefore the Australian Government, with the support of the Opposition, and the undoubted backing of the electorate, upheld Dutch sovereignty and hoped it would continue.

President Sukarno was determined to gain Western New Guinea. When diplomacy failed he resorted to covert but increasing use of force, aided by the re-armament of his army and air force with Russian war material. It became obvious that the Dutch could not resist this pressure for long. New Guinea, and the ambitions of Indonesia in New Guinea, are questions very real to Australians. The campaign to keep the Japanese out of southern New Guinea was a heroic chapter in the war annals of Australia. Here was a matter where Australia conceived she had a vital interest at stake, where reliance on the American alliance should decide the issue, where that power was essential if Indonesian ambition was to be restrained.

But the United States of America had never taken up a defined attitude on the question of Western New Guinea. Australia had never obtained any promise from America in respect of this country, had not demanded – or had been refused – such a *quid pro quo* for accepting other American policies in the East of Asia. When early in 1962 it became clear that Indonesia and Holland would soon be at war, America stepped in to enforce mediation, under the chairmanship of an American diplomat. The result was an agreement which yields the territory to Indonesia, after a transitory and doubtless unreal condominium with the United Nations. By the middle of 1963 Indonesia was to be firmly in possession. Within a few months Indonesia opened her policy of confrontation directed against the new Federation of Malaysia, a policy intensified in 1964. The Australian Government has increasingly been compelled to manifest its complete disapproval of this aggressive policy.

POSSIBLE FUTURE POLICIES

Australia has three possible policies which could be pursued in respect of Asia. She could adopt a form of neutralism, sever her alliance with America by leaving the SEATO and ANZUS pacts, recognize Communist China, and thus endeavour to follow in the South-West Pacific the line which India has made her own. Such a transformation has had few advocates in Australia, and recent events in India are not likely to have made more Australians ready for such a policy.

Australia can also continue with the policy now followed by the present Liberal-Country Party coalition Government, but which the Labour Opposition would at least modify. This is to rely upon the American alliance and the British Commonwealth, with the emphasis on the American alliance. Communist China must not be recognized, although Britain does this. Australia does trade with China, travel and cultural exchange is free, but in deference to American opinion no move is made to regulate diplomatic relations, an Ambassador from Formosa remained in Canberra and in 1966 the Australian Government opened an embassy in Taipei. The Labour Party has declared that it would recognize China, and perhaps also withdraw from or modify Australian commitments to send troops to Asia under the SEATO pact. Probably the majority opinion in the country acknowledges that the American alliance is the only policy possible, even while increasingly recognizing that American aid is conditional on serving American interests, and that these are not always identical with Australian interests. With this recognition goes a determination to develop friendship with Asian countries in every non-political way possible. That this attitude betrays a secret doubt can hardly be concealed.

A third policy would, no doubt, be the most logical, a kind of Western Pacific counterpart of the European Community: an alliance between Australia, New Zealand and Japan, the three developed capitalist countries of the Western Pacific. The Philippines and the emergent Greater Malaysia could be also included. This combination could be strong enough to defend itself without exclusive reliance on America, and independent enough to follow its own policies where America was either not interested or not willing to take a stand in opposition to local nationalism (as in Western New Guinea).

The real obstacle to such a development is the abiding fear of and hostility to Japan still very much alive in the Australian electorate. Many Australians know that this would be a solution for their dilemma, a situation which would neither compromise their friendship with the parent countries of the West nor jeopardize their hope of making lasting friends with the countries of Asia. It is politically impossible at this time, but it may well be that the logic of events and the developing power structure of post-war Asia will push Australia gradually towards this possibility.

Australia has only had to take real account of Asia since the end of the Second World War. During this period many very great changes have occurred, with extreme rapidity. It is hardly surprising if public opinion is still floundering in the wake of events, and political parties are still uncertain of their footing. There is a marked cleavage between the views of the older and younger generations, many of the latter being ready to give an exaggerated importance to relations with Asia, without taking full account of the real ties which must bind Australia to America and the West. 'Australia is part of Asia' may be a geographical fact (although not one accepted by geographers) but Australians are certainly not Asians either by descent or by culture. No attitude which ignores either the geographical propinquity, or the racial and cultural affinity, can adequately serve as an Australian response to the problems which the new Asia presents to a community of some ten million people of European descent inhabiting a continent located in the South-West Pacific.

BIBLIOGRAPHY

W. Macmahon Ball. *Nationalism and Communism in East Asia.* (Melbourne University Press, Melbourne, 1952.)

John Burton. *The Alternative.* (Morgan's Publications, Sydney, 1954.)

G. Greenwood and N. Harper (Eds.). *Australia in World Affairs.* (F. W. Cheshire, Melbourne, 1957.)

Donald Horne. *The Lucky Country.* (Penguin Books, Sydney, 1964.)

R. N. Rosecrance. *Australian Diplomacy and Japan, 1945–1951.* (Melbourne University Press, Melbourne, 1961.)

Aspects of Society

PROBLEMS OF
DEVELOPMENT IN ASIA

Werner Klatt

DEVELOPMENT is as painful a process as the change from boyhood to manhood. There are now well over twenty countries in Asia that are undergoing this change, and nothing – short of war – will stop it. Leaders of countries emerging from the colonial past insist on a rapid change from what they see as social backwardness and economic stagnation to mobility and growth, even if aware that this might cause more distress than happiness. The clash between traditional forms of life and dynamic societies which occurred during colonial rule has left behind a ferment that cannot be stopped. As a result the end-products of Western society seem desirable even if the intellectual and technical processes that made them possible appear less worthy of acceptance or imitation.

It would be presumptuous to think that the representatives of developed countries are necessarily qualified to solve the problems of developing ones. The problems of the latter are unique in kind and unprecedented in scale. In fact, both developed and underdeveloped countries are facing a new phenomenon, and it may be that only few are qualified to provide answers – partial answers at best – to the many questions which are raised in the course of development. Because of the high degree of specialization of modern society, most experts have become technicians in a highly departmentalized world; yet what is needed is a universal approach to the problems of change. The econo-mist who refuses to concern himself with the significance of tabus is bound to fail, as is the engineer who disregards the role of a racial minority. The life of nations and individuals is undergoing many changes; if major errors of judgement are to be avoided, it has to be studied in all its aspects, and in its reaction to many forms of outside interference.

The literature on matters of development has grown as fast as the problem itself. It is no longer possible to do justice to it in brief. Leaving aside all matters of detail, one may distinguish between those authors who are guided by the desire for orderly processes of balanced development and those who emphasize the need for tensions in a process of growth which is bound to be erratic and disorderly in the best of circumstances. Within this framework of alternatives there is place for an almost unlimited amount of advice ranging from a concentration of effort on improving agriculture to a selection of targets in the steel, cement and engineering industries, or from a preference for a widely dispersed programme of basic education to the creation of a highly centralized planning apparatus.

In its most extreme forms the argument boils down to the age-old controversy between revolutionaries and revisionists. One must be prepared, however, for both evolution and revolution; where the former fails, the latter is bound to take its place. Stagnation is marked by a series of vicious circles; to break any one of them amounts to breaking with the *status quo*. This is bound to cause stresses and strains, be they political, social or economic. By no means all traditional institutions are incapable of adjustment to new circumstances, however. The more existing patterns are utilized in any process of change, the smoother it is likely to be. To be acquainted with such patterns is a prerequisite of success in any attempt to change them.

RURAL BASIS

Throughout Asia society is still based on farming as the chief occupation of the majority and on the village as the traditional form of society. This is true even of Japan and of Soviet Central Asia, where urbanization and industrialization have dislodged from their previous positions both agriculture and rural society. Its closely knit pattern is broken where plantations have been superimposed on the broad basis of subsistence farming, but the latter still prevails in more than a million villages of Asia. The pattern of farming, though by no means unalterable, is fixed by circumstances in most instances. The production of food grains for consumption on the farms and for sale in the markets forms the basis; all else tends to be of marginal significance except in the relatively rare cases where the production of a cash crop has led to specialization. Whilst the cultivators are not necessarily hostile to new ideas, most farm operations have not changed for centuries. The art of animal husbandry is largely unknown; nor does fruit and vegetable gardening take up more than an insignificant part of the land used. As a result the diet, like the farm pattern, tends to be monotonous.

The application of modern farm requisites is limited to the relatively few farms that specialize. In many villages four fifths of the farm produce is excluded from any cash transaction. Though local transport services are increasingly widening the horizon, the village community remains largely a world of its own. In Japan and Taiwan (Formosa) rural self-administration and social mobility resulted from fairly drastic agrarian reforms which were carried out in the wake of the last war. Elsewhere in Asia some of the excesses of landlordism and money-lending may have been eliminated, but the polarization of the village community has not yet been broken everywhere. Thus the way of life in the villages is often still circumscribed by a code of behaviour to which all but the very few conform, anchored to the expanded family and the village shrine. Traditional loyalties are rarely questioned.

If the picture which emerges is one of uniformity and conformity, this should not be taken to mean that there is no individuality and colour. There is plenty of both, particularly in areas where different races and religions exist side by side. Leaving on one side Confucianism, which is a philosophical concept and a way of life rather than a religion, Buddhism probably more than any other Asian belief is capable of accommodating itself to the requirements of a changing society. Against this, Islam, though closest to Christianity, seems to cling most tenaciously to an established code of conduct. Muslims do not allow pigs on their farms nor pork on their tables; they thus deprive themselves of the best scavenger of household refuse. Elsewhere in Asia the Hindu attitude towards cattle represents one of the most insurmountable barriers to advance in farming and food supplies.

It is to nobody's advantage to gloss over the damage that tabus towards livestock and towards women can cause to development in Asia. The exclusion of women from work in the fields and from public life is the most serious handicap to the rate of change, since the next generation is largely the product of maternal efforts in countries in which primary and secondary education is still the privilege of the few rather than the custom of the many. It would be wrong to conclude that religious beliefs are invariably 'enemies of the people'. Those who hold this view may ponder with profit the changes which Christianity has undergone since it was first conceived 2,000 years ago. At the same time it cannot be denied that development only begins where religious beliefs are brought into line with secular interests.

Without the rationalization of theological concepts and the secularization of political thought there is no prospect of social and economic advance nor of modern forms of government. Those who desire the end products of Western society may be reminded that Europe's communities accepted the changes brought about by renaissance, reformation, counter-reformation and enlightenment before they became what they are today, willing to abandon conformity and to take the risks that this entails. Racial, like religious, minorities are a factor of importance in Asian society and its change. Where race barriers are maintained, the prospects of general advance are limited, although the racial minority in its struggle for survival may do well for itself. Whilst religious minorities are often secluded from the world, racial minorities tend to be down-to-earth. The Chinese in South-East Asia have shown this more than any other minority. Where they have been allowed to integrate, they have brought advantages to themselves and to their host country. Many of the towns of Asia would not exist if it were not for the trading communities of migrants from other lands.

URBAN AMBITIONS

The towns in Asia are the centres of change. Some 90 million people now live in forty towns, each of which gives a home of sorts, if not work, to more than one million people. There are many more millions of urban dwellers who live in towns of less than one million inhabitants. The majority of them are labourers. The middle classes are still thinly spread in Asian societies. The towns are the refuge of those who choose to escape the villages where opportunities are limited. No wonder that towns in Asia often give the appearance of villages that have grown beyond their bamboo or cactus fences without having lost the characteristic features of rural communities. The process of urbanization progresses with frightening speed; in some towns the number of inhabitants has doubled within one decade. The towns attract those with the greatest initiative, but they also accept those who will be redundant in any society. Thus the towns are not only the centres of change but also the receptacles of the unwanted and the hotbeds of extremism. Among the intellectual leaders are many who are dissatisfied with the economic backwardness around them and impatient for social and political change. They find little in their country's past that they regard as worth keeping. It would be asking too much of them to expect them to recognize the assets of their colonial past, such as the infra-structure left behind, including a language that gives them access to the world of science and technology and to the United Nations. In their quest of the future they usually regard industrialization as the universal remedy for all social and economic ills and they see in planning the mechanism by which to fulfil their personal and national ambitions. They tend to associate private enterprise with imperial rule and farming with the monotony which they left behind when they chose the city as their home and their place of work.

As the life span of a generation is still short in Asia, its intellectual elite and its ruling groups are young by Western standards; they should not be misjudged on account of their age. They are usually earnest in their desire to lift their country in one great swoop from medieval backwardness into the twentieth century. They are passionately patriotic, at times chauvinistic and xenophobic. When things go wrong, they are readily accused of corruption; more often than not it is a case of nepotism rather than corruption, a relapse into the mentality of the villager who prefers a member of the family to the outsider. As skills are in short supply, they tend to take on more than they are qualified to carry out. As most of them have been educated in Western academic institutions, or institutions modelled on them, all too often they judge their own problems with eyes trained on Western targets. They are apt to travel too much in Europe and America, and too little in their own countries. As a result they sometimes overlook indigenous opportunities and rely too heavily on Western 'panaceas'.

DEGREES OF DEVELOPMENT

The problems of development that the political, administrative and managerial elite has to face vary considerably from country to country. Historical experience and national environment, natural resources and human skills are among the factors that account for considerable differences in the degree of development and the chances of further advance. International comparisons are handicapped by a lack of data; they are also invidious as they may be wrongly considered as value judgements rather than as mere tools to assess the degree of development achieved and the possibilities that lie ahead. As Chester Bowles has said: 'Economic progress measured in statistical terms of steel production, irrigation water, improving health standards and literacy is only one facet in the critical competition. An even more important measure for the long haul may be the sense of participation, of belonging, of community purpose that accompanies the material gains.'* Without certain indicators no comparison is possible, however; in using them one should leave no doubt that every indicator implies an asset and a liability at the same time. If it is taken as a criticism of the past, it should be read also as a challenge for the future.

* Philip W. Thayer (Ed.). *Nationalism and Progress in Free Asia*. (Baltimore, 1956.)

In most cases Japan figures as the country with the largest number of points. This is not surprising. Japan can legitimately be regarded as the most advanced country in Asia – socially, economically, and politically. This is not necessarily identical with being the happiest country. At the other end of the scale stands Pakistan; it might be displaced by Indonesia or one or another small Asian country if factual documentation were sufficient to permit of a comparison. This is not to say that Pakistan is a particularly unhappy community; development is not synonymous with happiness, but it is an aim of the leaders' policy. In any event, the differences are great enough to deserve recording; in some cases they are startlingly great.

Japan has a density of population of over 250 per square kilometre; Pakistan's density is slightly more than 100. Japan's population increases by less than 1 per cent a year; in Pakistan the rate of growth of the population is nearly 3 per cent. Almost two thirds of Japan's population live in towns as against one eighth in Pakistan. The gross national product, as calculated by the statistical office of the United Nations, is almost $600 per head (£250) in Japan as against $80 (£33) in Pakistan. Japan's gross national product has increased annually by over 10 per cent in recent years; in Pakistan the increase has been less than 3 per cent. In Japan a little over one half of the gross national product is accounted for by private consumption; in Pakistan it absorbs three quarters. In Japan, one third of the gross national product falls on fixed capital investment; in Pakistan it is less than half as much. In Japan the amount of energy available per head of population is equal to almost 1,800 kilos (or 1·8 tons) of coal; in Pakistan it is equal to 90 kilos. The corresponding figures for steel available per head of population are over 400 kilos (or 0·4 ton) and a little more than 10 kilos respectively. In Japan the yield of paddy (rice) per hectare is over 5 tons; in Pakistan it is 1·7 tons. The corresponding figures for the milk yield per cow are 4·3 tons and 0·4 tons respectively. In Japan 440 newspapers and 330 radio and television sets are available per 1,000 inhabitants; in Pakistan, five newspapers and four radio sets. In Japan over 90 per cent of all children between the ages of 5 and 19 years are enrolled in schools; in Pakistan, one quarter of all children in this age group. Finally, in Japan, on average, one medical doctor lokos after 900 inhabitants; in Pakistan he looks after 6,450.

DEVELOPMENT MEASURES

The difference between the levels of development demonstrated in the two cases of Pakistan and Japan are so wide as to justify a narrowing of the gap without one country necessarily imitating the other. In fact, all countries in Asia have development plans aiming at economic growth and designed to reduce the gap between themselves and other, more advanced countries. Only Russia and China, both of which have the most highly centralized forms of state planning in Asia, have been obliged in recent years to abandon their long-term plans and to replace them temporarily by annual plans.* Other countries have been more fortunate in that they have been able to uphold their plan targets, but no country has succeeded in fulfilling its plan in all its detail; nor is this essential. In most cases plans are no more than expressions of intent; nor should they be more. However, only in a few cases are they comprehensive – as they should be – that is to say, they cover all major aspects of development and anticipate as well the effects of the changes planned. There are, of course, not the same needs everywhere. A country such as Burma, that is richly endowed and not overpopulated by present standards, is clearly less exposed to tensions as a result of development than say West Bengal (India) or Java (Indonesia) where the pressure of the growing population on limited resources has reached explosive proportions. To be met effectively the so-called population explosion needs to be defined in quantitative and geographical terms.

Irrespective of regional peculiarities, certain measures may be singled out for the attention and consideration of planners in developing countries; but it must be understood that they should not be regarded as *panaceas*. Each case must be judged on its own merit; and each measure must be considered, in conjunction with other measures, as to its likely impact on existing social and economic patterns. As all Asian societies except Japan are agrarian in character, no single measure is likely to release social and economic forces as effectively as a reform of land ownership and tenure including the level of land rents and interest rates. This reform should not be interpreted as a measure designed to create an egalitarian society; but by eliminating justified grievances it would be likely to contribute to the development of intensive forms of farming, including animal husbandry, without which the growing urban population must go short of protein in its

* Recently India was forced by the failure of the monsoon in two consecutive years to defer the start of the fourth five-year plan.

diet. Any improvement in the average diet and thus in the condition of health is likely to require an annual growth of farm output of 3 per cent or more. Where plantation crops earn foreign exchange, the industry deserves to be kept competitive and not to be starved of capital investment.

In view of the current high rates of growth of population, most countries in Asia may find it a task beyond their means to employ more than the natural increase of population outside agriculture. At present prices it costs at least $2,000 (over £800) to absorb a man outside agriculture; it may cost ten times as much. As this outlay may prove too great an undertaking, most countries in Asia are likely to remain predominantly agrarian in character for many years to come. As productivity tends to be at least twice as high in industry as in agriculture, however, any human, physical and financial resources available beyond the needs of agriculture are best utilized outside it. In order to husband them, the non-agricultural sector must be so designed as to absorb a maximum of labour at a minimum of financial outlay. It will therefore be advisable to concentrate on investment in industries that are capital extensive rather than intensive; the industries that serve a large domestic market deserve special attention in this respect.

To generate growth a modern industrial sector is necessary. Here the choice is particularly difficult, and the temptation to select impressive targets for reasons of prestige may be irresistible. Expert advice is particularly wanted here, yet badly lacking at times. The demands on indigenous and foreign capital, on knowledge and initiative will be heavy; yet at this stage of development the shortage of entrepreneurs, technical and managerial skill and, last but not least, capital often presents almost insurmountable obstacles. Unless it is accepted that the capital required is provided, at least initially, by the taxpayers of other countries, domestic financial resources will have to be mobilized in large sums and handled with great care. Even so, the creation of a modern industry is bound to entail a period of reduced rather than improved standards of living. All development processes are painful and costly, but some are more painful and costly than others. To be successful the modern industrial sector of a developing society requires not only the contributions of engineers and economists, but also the co-operation of sociologists, demographers, anthropologists and the specialists of many other disciplines of current knowledge. There is no limit, in fact, to the help required by countries engaged in the process of development.

INDICATORS OF DEVELOPMENT IN ASIA

TABLE 1: GENERAL INDICATORS

Country	Population Density (persons per sq. km.)	Population Increase (per cent per year)	Urban Population (per cent of total)	Age Group under 14 and over 65 (per cent of total)	Illiteracy Rate (per cent of over 15 years)	School Enrolment (per cent of 5–19 years)
India	165	2·5	18·0	n.a.	77	31
Pakistan	111	2·8	13·0	48·0	72	26
Ceylon	175	2·8	15·5	44·5	24	74
Thailand	61	3·3	12·0	46·0	14	58
Malaya	67	2·9	42·5	47·0	29	62
Taiwan	356	2·7	n.a.	47·5	16	74
Philippines	112	2·1	35·5	48·5	24	70
Hong Kong	3,601	2·0	76·5	44·0	9	66
Singapore	3,293	2·4	63·0	44·5	31	77
Japan	267	0·7	63·5	36·0	negl.	91
Comparison						
USSR	10	1·1	53·0	38·0	negl.	78
UK	225	0·6	78·5	35·5	negl.	85
USA	21	0·9	70·0	41·0	negl.	100

n.a. – not available.

TABLE 2: SOCIAL INDICATORS

Country	Private Consumption (per cent of GNP)	Food and Drink (per cent of private consumption)	Calorie Intake (per day)	Protein Intake (grammes per day)	Urban Housing (persons per room)	Inhabitants per Physician (thousand)
India	n.a.	n.a.	1,980	49	2·6	5,800
Pakistan	73	n.a.	2,260	51	3·1	6,450
Ceylon	73	55	2,180	47	2·3	4,600
Thailand	74	47	2,120	45	n.a.	7,600
Malaya	63	50	2,400	54	3·0	6,500
Taiwan	65	52	2,340	58	n.a.	2,400
Philippines	71	50	1,980	48	n.a.	1,400
Hong Kong	n.a.	n.a.	n.a.	n.a.	n.a.	2,650
Singapore	n.a.	n.a.	n.a.	n.a.	n.a.	2,300
Japan	53	43	2,320	74	1·2	900
Comparison						
USSR	n.a.	n.a.	(3,000)	(85)	1·5	500*
UK	65	33	3,360	92	0·7	850
USA	63	23	3,140	92	0·6	700

n.a. – not available.   ( ) – estimate.   *including orderlies.

Sources: UN Statistical Yearbook 1966; UN National Accounts 1964; ILO Labour Statistics 1966; FAO Production Statistics 1966.

TABLE 3: AGRICULTURE AND EDUCATION

Country	Agricultural Working Population (per cent of total working population)	Rice (Paddy) Yield (tons per hectare)	Milk Yield (tons per cow)	Education Expenditure (per cent of GNP)	Newspapers (per thousand inhabitants)	Radio and TV Receivers (per thousand inhabitants)
India	73	1·31	0·19	2·4	12	7
Pakistan	75	1·68	0·42	1·2	5	4
Ceylon	51	1·77	n.a.	4·5	35	38
Thailand	82	1·51	0·50	2·5	12	12
Malaya	55	2·71	0·55	n.a.	57	41
Taiwan	50	3·78	2·90	3·3	64	72
Philippines	57	1·31	n.a.	3·2	17	30
Hong Kong	7	2·44	(2·80)	n.a.	239	60
Singapore	8	(2·50)	2·81	n.a.	248	109
Japan	27	4·95	4·34	6·5	439	330
Comparison						
USSR	36	0·95*	1·60	1·5	229	235
UK	5	3·75*	3·80	4·2	523	520
USA	7	3·05*	3·66	6·2	314	1,305

TABLE 4: DEVELOPMENT INDICATORS

Country	Gross Nat. Product ($ per head of population)	Recent Growth Rate (per cent p.a.)	Fixed Capital	Industry, Mining, Construction (per cent of GNP)	Energy† Consumption	Steel Consumption (kilos per head)
India	78	3·5	(15)	18	172	15
Pakistan	80	2·7	(15)	16	90	12
Ceylon	129	2·2	14	13	114	7
Thailand	102	5·4	20	19	110	19
Malaya	241	4·1	15	20	338	43
Taiwan	165	7·1	17	27	654	40
Philippines	191	4·1	13	24	209	22
Hong Kong	258	n.a.	n.a.	n.a.	603	155
Singapore	361	n.a.	n.a.	n.a.	578	n.a.
Japan	577	10·8	36	39	1,783	415
Comparison						
USSR	(1,300)	(5·0)	18	(63)	3,611	390
UK	1,910	3·4	17	44	5,151	500
USA	3,270	4·3	17	36	9,201	605

n.a. – not available   ( ) – estimate   * – all grains   † – coal equivalent
Sources: UN Statistical Yearbook 1966; UN National Accounts 1964; ILO Labour Statistics 1966; FAO Production Statistics 1966.

BIBLIOGRAPHY

P. T. Bauer. *Economic Analysis and Policy in Underdeveloped Countries*. (Routledge & Kegan Paul, 1965.)

Eugene R. Black. *The Diplomacy of Economic Development*. (Harvard University Press, Cambridge, Mass., 1960.)

N. S. Buchanan and H. S. Ellis. *Approaches to Economic Development*. (The Twentieth Century Fund, New York, 1955.)

A. K. Cairncross. *Factors in Economic Development*. (Allen & Unwin, 1962.)

Sally H. Frankel. *The Economic Impact on Under-developed Societies*. (Blackwell, Oxford, 1953.)

John Kenneth Galbraith. *Economic Development*. (Harvard University Press, Cambridge, Mass., 1964.)

Albert O. Hirschman. *The Strategy of Economic Development*. (Yale University Press, New Haven, 1958.)

Bert F. Hoselitz (Ed.). *The Progress of Underdeveloped Areas*. (University Press, Chicago, 1952.)

W. Klatt *et al.* *The Fertiliser Industry of the Asian and Far Eastern Region* (Mimeograph, Rome, 1960.)

Simon Kuznets. *Six Lectures on Economic Growth*. (Harvard University Press, Cambridge, Mass., 1964.)

William A. Lewis. *The Theory of Economic Growth*. (Allen & Unwin, 1955.)

H. Mint. *The Economics of Developing Countries*. (Hutchinson, 1954.)

Gunnar Myrdal. *Economic Theory and Under-developed Regions*. (Duckworth, 1957.)

Ragnar Nurkse. *Problems of Capital Formation in Underdeveloped Countries*. (Blackwell, Oxford, 1955.)

W. W. Rostow. *The Progress of Economic Growth*. (Clarendon Press, Oxford, 1960.)

Eugene Staley. *The Future of Underdeveloped Countries*. (Harper, New York, 1954.)

ASIA'S POPULATION PROBLEM

S. Chandrasekhar

TODAY the total world population has exceeded the 3,000 million mark. The world's population has been increasing at a faster rate during the last fifty years, especially during the last two decades, than ever before in human history. According to some 'guestimates' there were probably no more than 10 to 15 million people in the whole world at the end of the Stone Age. At the birth of Christ the population had probably increased to about 250 million. By 1650 A.D. it was about 500 million, and a century later, in 1750, about 695 million. In 1850 total population had passed the 1,000 million mark to become 1,091 million, and half a century later, that is at the beginning of the 20th century, it rose to 1,500 million. But during the last sixty years (1900–1960) the world population has doubled and become 3,000 million. Thus it took man many thousands of years to multiply to 1,000 or 1,500 million but it took only a little more than half a century to double that number – an incredible and unprecedented rate of increase.

Every year more than 120 million babies are born and 60 million people of all age groups die, leaving a net yearly addition of some 60 million to the existing population. And now the United Nations estimates that at the current rate of increase the world might have over 6,000 million by 2000 A.D.! Thus, 'viewed in the long-run perspective, the growth of the earth's population has been like a long thin powder fuse that burns slowly and haltingly until it finally reaches the charge and then explodes'.

GROWTH OF ASIA'S POPULATION* (IN MILLIONS)

Year	1650	1750	1800	1850	1900	1950†	1962
Asia's population	327	475	597	741	915	1,384	1,764‡
Total world population	545	728	906	1,171	1,608	2,509	3,135
Percentage of Asia's population to world total	60·0	65·2	65·9	63·3	56·9	55·1	56·3

*Source: the figures for 1650 to 1900 are A. M. Carr-Saunders's estimates.

† *Demographic Year Book* (United Nations, New York, 1963), pp. 32–5.

‡ Of this, some 1,670 million are the subject of this chapter; the remaining 94 million live in the Middle East (including Afghanistan). The population of Soviet Central Asia, Siberia and the Soviet Far East is excluded.

Of the world's 3,000 million people, Asia claims over one half, and this huge population is confined to about a fifth of the total world area. Asians are today increasing faster than Europeans (this was not true in the more distant past) and since Asia's population is a young one, the potential for rapid population growth is great. At the current rate of increase Asia may have to take care of 60 per cent of the total world population by 2000 A.D. – an increase she can hardly afford in the light of her present standard of living and at the current rate of her economic development.

Asia possesses the two most densely populated countries in the world: China with over 750 millions (if her published 1953 census figures and birth and death rates between 1954 and 1960 are assumed to be correct) and India with her 520 millions (based on the 1961 census). Between them, China and India account for more than one thousand million people. Only three other countries in Asia are of major importance from the point of view of population numbers – Japan, Pakistan and Indonesia. Although it is difficult to generalize about so large an area since in almost everything both extremes are possible, major trends and predominantly common features can be pointed out.

DENSITY

Asia as a whole is the second most densely populated continent in the world. Despite the fact that nearly 80 per cent of the Asian population is rural, the density per square mile in some Asian countries is higher than the density of some thickly populated European countries. While in the United States the density per square mile is 50 and in Europe 220, it is 820 in Taiwan and 670 in Japan. The density per square mile in India and Pakistan is 384 and 265 respectively. It is even higher in East Pakistan where the majority of the Pakistanis live. And certain areas within some of the Asian countries are even more densely populated. Kerala (1,125 per square mile), and West Bengal (1,031 per square mile) in India, Java (1,050 per square mile) in Indonesia are examples of extremely dense settlements.

AGRARIAN ECONOMY

Asia's population is predominantly rural and consequently agrarian. All Asian countries except Japan depend on agriculture for the meagre livelihood of a majority of their people. The man–land ratio in Asia is so adverse and the pressure of population on the soil so great that agriculture is, by and large, more a pathetic and sentimental way of life than a successful business or commercial proposition. In almost every Asian country between 70 and 80 per cent of the population is dependent on the soil for a livelihood. Hunger, particularly in India and Communist China, is almost endemic.

The problems of Asian agriculture are well known – too well known to need any pointed discussion. In some parts of the continent the outmoded, feudalistic land revenue system gives little right to the tiller of the soil. Variations of absentee landlordism and the share-cropping system with all their drawbacks still continue in many regions. The peasant is illiterate and ignorant of all that may be called modern scientific agriculture. The traditional methods he employs are quasi-primitive and yield no worthwhile results. He is in poor health, largely the result of his insanitary and unhygienic rural environment, poor diet and the want of rural medical aid. He is perennially in debt as he has little or no resources to improve himself or his livestock. He is usually in the grip of the usurious village money-lender unless the government can give him credit. And last, no matter what his resources, unwanted children keep arriving at regular intervals, depressing his already poor level of living.

As for his land, it is a fragmented and subdivided bit of a plot, too small to become a successful agricultural proposition. From year to year the cultivator is dependent upon the availability of good seed, natural manure or fertilizer, seasonal rainfall or government irrigation, factors often beyond his control. Then there are problems of pest control, soil erosion, storage and marketing. It is true that in recent years the governments in most Asian countries have been dedicated to improving the general welfare of the peasant, but the pace of reform has been slow, and where reforms have been revolutionary, as in Communist countries, the long-range outcome for both the peasants and production has been disastrous. The problem of food – adequate nutrition in quantity and quality for the people – continues to be a major problem in most Asian countries.

YOUNG POPULATION

An examination of the age structure of those Asian countries for which reliable age statistics are available reveals that Asia's population is predominantly young. On the whole, roughly two persons in every five are under 15 years; about 55 per cent are 15–59, and about one in twenty is 60 years or over. This has two undesirable consequences. One is that the number of dependants per adult is relatively large. For the economy as a whole the number of gainfully employed is disproportionately small in relation to the two unproductive groups who are dependent on them – children and old people. Secondly in view of Asia's current birth rate, the age structure is favourable for large additions in the future to the existing massive population.

PER CAPITA INCOME

Asia, with about 18 per cent of the world's land surface and 55 per cent of the world's population, receives only 12 per cent of the world's income. The *per capita* income of a vast majority of Asians is below the poverty line. It ranges between 50 and 120 US dollars and is in striking contrast to the *per capita* income of some $2,000 in the United States and Canada and about $1,000 in Europe excluding the Soviet Union. This low income is both the cause and consequence of the misery of the underdeveloped countries in Asia.

LITERACY AND EDUCATION

As for literacy and primary education, more than half the world lives in unlettered darkness. While Asia claims more than half the world's population, her share of illiterates is disproportionately high. The illiteracy rates range from 75 per cent in India to 4 in Japan. Leaving aside the adult illiterates, all the Asian countries find it impossible to provide educational resources to catch up with the birth rate. The governments are simply unable to provide trained teachers and textbooks, school buildings and equipment to take care of the children reaching school age every year.

HIGH BUT DECLINING DEATH RATES

The tremendous increase in the world's population and particularly the population of Asia in recent years is due to man's increasing control over disease and death. The effectiveness of death control is not uniform all over the world, for while the death rate in the Soviet Union and most countries of North-West Europe is about 10 per 1,000, the rates in Asia are relatively high – about 30 to 35 per 1,000 in Burma and Nepal, 20 in India and Indonesia; they are about 10 in Ceylon and Japan only.

However, during the last decade and more the death rates in many Asian countries have begun to decline thanks to the work of the World Health Organization, American technical aid, Colombo Plan assistance and the efforts of the various national governments in providing a modicum of modern sanitation and environmental hygiene, health education, wonder drugs and basic health services. In Ceylon, for instance, between 1945 and 1955 the death rate was cut by more than 40 per cent; in India within a few years by 33 per cent. What is more, once underground drainage, potable water supplies, modern conservancy measures and up-to-date preventive, diagnostic and curative medical services are made available, the death rates in even the most under-developed Asian countries will register even more dramatic declines.

The infant mortality rate, which is considered a sensitive index of a community's level of living and cultural milieu, is also declining in many Asian countries. While in North-Western Europe, Canada and the United States of America the infant mortality rate is between 20 and 25 per 1,000 live births, the rates in Asian countries, which were considerably above 100 before the Second World War, have dropped to 98 in India and Indonesia, 67 in Ceylon, 41 in Japan and 35 in Taiwan in recent years. The rates are still high in Burma and the Philippines, about 150 and 110 respectively. Even the lower rates are uncivilized and there is room for considerable further decline. However, it must be remembered that in some parts of Asia the rates were between 150 and 200 only twenty-five years ago.

HIGH BIRTH RATES

The average world birth rate during 1955–60 was estimated to be about 35 per 1,000 population. On a continental basis, Africa has the highest estimated birth rate of 45 per 1,000. Asia has the next highest birth rate of about 40 per 1,000.

Within Asia birth rates range from 50 per 1,000 in Burma to 40 per 1,000 in Malaya and India and about 35 per 1,000 in Ceylon and Thailand. Regionally during the last decade the birth rates have ranged between 42 per 1,000 in West Asia to 35 in East Asia.

Thus with a definitive decline in the death rate and a high and near stationary birth rate, the survival rate is high, yielding huge net annual additions to the existing population. For instance, the population of India alone increased by more than 77 millions during the decade 1951–61.

THE PROBLEM

The population problem of Asia is partly a legacy of European imperialism. The balance sheet of Western colonialism in Asia is a mixed one. Asia lost her political freedom and with it the chances of rapid economic development as her raw materials were taken off to feed hungry machines in Europe, while the manufactured products were dumped on Asian markets with the aid of preferential tariffs. But, on the other hand, Europe brought a measure of peace, democratic political institutions and above all a revolution in health and modern science and technology. The abolition of internecine struggles and wars and the control of epidemics and famines brought down the death rate. But at the same time the Europeans interfered little with the indigenous cultural mores conducive to a high birth rate. And so with a declining death rate, a high birth rate and a poor agrarian economy without any industrialization, Asia was reduced to poverty. The seeds of Asia's current population explosion were sown more than a century ago by well-meaning British, French and Dutch administrators.

Thus today the basic economic and social problem in Asia is really demographic, for here more people means more poverty, and vice versa. How can Asia raise the standard of living (which means more of food, clothing, housing, education and other goods and services for everybody) and cut down the still relatively high death rate (which means keeping alive more people and taking care of them), when it is so difficult to support the existing population even at a low standard of living, *if* the population continues to increase by about 30 millions every year?

Asia cannot lower her level of living any further. Nor can anyone suggest raising the death rate! From the Asian point of view, the way out appears to be rapid economic development with foreign aid and a drastic reduction in the birth rate. Planned internal migration whenever possible and the exploration of outlets for Asian emigration to thinly populated regions of the world may help some, but the major emphasis must be on rapid economic development and birth control.

POPULATION POLICIES

Four major countries in Asia – Japan, India, China and Indonesia – have attempted to formulate national population policies. These policies have been carried out with varying degrees of success.

Japan was faced with a desperately serious population problem at the end of the Second World War, with the loss of her empire and the repatriation of her overseas nationals. Actually population pressure was a serious problem for Japan before the last war and was one of the factors that turned her into a belligerent nation. With a war-shattered economy, Japan had to support some 78 million people on an area the size of the state of California. To meet this situation, Japan passed in 1948 the Eugenic Protection Law which 'authorizes voluntary and even compulsory sterilization in certain cases, the public sale of contraceptives which had hitherto been forbidden, and the performance of abortion in the event that continued pregnancy or parturition is likely to harm the mother's health on account of physical or economic reasons'. Japan thus reversed her pre-Second World War pro-natalist population policy. Today, officially a million (and unofficially about two million) abortions are performed in Japan every year. Japan's population increased from 78 million in 1947 to 93·3 million in 1957. But the annual number of births fell from 2·7 to 1·6 million during the same period. That is, Japan's birth rate dropped from 34 per 1,000 in 1947 to 17 in 1957. The country's birth rate was halved in ten years.

With her high literacy and education rates, disciplined national consciousness and adequate medical resources (more than 763 health centres in 1960) Japan has been able to reduce her birth rate through the drastic, costly and unhappy method of induced abortion.

India, where the problem is not as pressing as in Japan, embarked on an official policy of population control in 1951 when the Government Planning Commission was set up. The Government realized that a rapidly growing population in an under-developed agrarian country like India is more a hindrance than a help in raising the nation's standard of living, for with a high birth rate every increase in national effort was being used up to maintain the existing low standard of living.

But, unfortunately, non-Catholic, secular India lost nearly a decade foolishly experimenting with the safe period or rhythm method of birth control because of the Gandhian ideology of the then Minister of Health. (Mahatma Gandhi was opposed to scientific contraception.)

Today the Government of India has taken a progressive stand on this question and is in favour of all mechanical, chemical and surgical methods of family planning. It has been found, however, that under backward rural conditions conventional contraceptives are not successful as they require a clinical consultation, some knowledge of the physiology of reproduction and a relatively high level of living. Indian experience shows that sterilization or surgical methods of permanent conception control (vasectomy for fathers and salpingectomy for mothers) is really the answer to effective curbing of population growth. Therefore, today several states of the Indian Union have embarked on a programme of subsidized voluntary sterilization.

A rough calculation shows that India's birth rate can be halved if about five fathers or mothers out of every thousand of the total population undergo sterilization. India's vital statistics are none too reliable but the latest statistics show that the death rate is definitely declining while the birth rate is stationary at a high level, yielding a net annual addition of some thirteen million to the existing population. It is hoped that India can stabilize her population at no more than 650 million.

As for Communist China, her population today is over 750 million if her published statistics are accurate and reliable and not padded as her production figures are. Among all the under-developed countries China has been the *locus classicus* of the Malthusian dilemma. But when the Communists conducted the country's first census and discovered that the mainland's population in 1953 was around 583 million, they apparently found the figures an occasion for jubilation. Later, however, the plight of the economy, and particularly the food situation, was so bad that the country became a surprising convert to family planning. For nearly two years an intensive and unconventional campaign in favour of birth control was waged all over the country through all the available mass media. But at the end of 1958 the country reversed its stand on ideological grounds. Marx won, Malthus was overthrown, and the traditional Communist dogma that over-population is a vicious figment of the bourgeois imagination asserted itself.

Following the agricultural failures of 1960–62, rising population again became a major problem and the campaign for family planning was officially resumed. By 1964 the most popular method in urban areas was the intrauterine device (IUCD) – unperfected in China, in contrast to its success in Hong Kong, where cheap manufacture has been achieved. In 1965 the oral pill was under trial and in demand. The spread of education in all parts of China and the extensive control of the People's Communes would seem to make it possible for any technical achievements in birth control to become effective comparatively rapidly in Asia's most highly populated country.

Indonesia, with an area of 569,000 square miles, has to support more than 100 million people. Indonesia's population problem is in a sense regional and not national. The density on the main island of Java is very high, whereas many outer islands are relatively sparsely populated. Java contains about one eleventh of the area of Indonesia but about two thirds of the entire population. While the land in the outer islands is probably less fertile than that in Java, it is good enough to carry many millions. So even before Indonesia became free, emigration of peasant families to Sumatra and Borneo was organized, but the cost per settler was high and the Javanese farmer was not too willing to migrate to neighbouring under-developed islands. In recent years there has been some talk of pursuing settlement schemes in other Indonesian islands but nothing substantial has come of it. Apart from the theoretical schemes of redistributing the Indonesian population among the various islands, the Government has given no thought to any policy of population control, possibly on the assumption that there is plenty of land in the country as a whole.

More recently Indonesia has successfully demanded from the Dutch the return of the western half of New Guinea, now called West Irian. This region has an area of 180,000 square miles and an estimated population of some 750,000. From the demographic point of view, Indonesia needs this land, provided she can successfully colonize it with the Javanese.

As for other Asian countries, Pakistan, with a population of 100 million, has embarked under President Ayub Khan on a policy of population control. Birth control clinics have been opened in both wings of the country but the Muslim masses have not been attracted to them in substantial numbers as yet. Ceylon is also officially in favour of population control but determined Government efforts are not visible. Formosa, Hong Kong and Singapore have active voluntary family planning associations which are doing useful work with some Government encouragement.

On the other hand Burma and Thailand, for reasons best known to their Governments, consider themselves under-populated or at any rate free from population pressure. The levels of living in these countries are not particularly high in relation to other Asian countries, and there is no reason to suppose that their *per capita* incomes would increase if there were more people.

FAMILY PLANNING: THE 1968 POSITION

The latest (1966) surveys* estimate the population of the 42 countries which form the continent of Asia at a little over 1,750 million. To this

* United Nations Demographic Yearbook.

figure, Russia contributed two hundred million people (233,200,000), India nearly five hundred million (498,680,000) and China over seven hundred million (710,000,000). The size of the smaller countries varied between Sikkim, with a population of 180,000, and Indonesia with 107,000,000.

In the decade 1950–60, over the whole of Asia the death rates fell in the wake of improved hygiene and medicine, but the birth rates were controlled only by great efforts made notably in Hong Kong, Singapore, Taiwan and Korea. Throughout Asia, economic growth rates and per capita income increased only marginally but in the years between 1960 and 1966 the average annual birth rate – 38 per thousand – was more than double the average annual death rate of 18 per thousand.

During this period however several Asian governments* overcame initial doubts and were convinced that some form of control over the birth rate was essential to their countries' welfare. The main difficulties in making family planning programmes available in Asia are geographical and administrative and not religious. Several of its countries now manufacture IUCDs and orals and include these modern methods in the immense schemes of family planning which are sponsored as part of governmental medical and child health programmes.

CONCLUSION

The solution to Asia's population problem lies as much in population control as in economic and social development. While every Asian country is trying to modernize its agriculture and embark on planned large-scale industrialization, only a few have tried to curb their population growth.

However, the successful and widespread implementation of planned parenthood implies not only a reasonable standard of living but, more important, women's social emancipation. Once the women of Asia are liberated from ignorance and apathy, and education in the liberal sense of the word becomes widespread among the people of Asia, a new awareness of the dignity and worth of the individual is bound to dawn.

And last, no Asian country can develop its resources without substantial aid from the advanced Western nations. Such aid should

* Ceylon, India, Indonesia, Japan, Korea, Malaya, Nepal, Pakistan and Singapore have Government family planning programmes. Fifteen of the 42 countries of Asia are already among the 26 members of the International Planned Parenthood Federation.

not be confined to agricultural and industrial development alone but must extend to all the available 'know-how' on health and family planning. In the long run, Asia must be enabled to lower both her birth and death rates to civilized levels. When every Asian woman delivers two babies instead of the four or six she delivered before, and when every Asian farmer grows two ears of corn where one or none grew before, Asia's demographic and economic problems will be solved. A relatively rich Asia is bound to have beneficent repercussions even on the affluent West, for prosperity like peace is one and indivisible.

BIBLIOGRAPHY

George W. Barclay. *Colonial Development and Population in Taiwan.* (Princeton University Press, Princeton, N.J., 1954.)

Census of India, 1951. Part I-A. Report. (Govt of India, New Delhi, 1953.)

Census of India, Paper No. 1 of 1962. 1961 Census. (Govt of India, New Delhi, 1962.)

S. Chandrasekhar. *China's Population: Census and Vital Statistics.* (Oxford University Press, 2nd edn, 1959.) *Red China: An Asian View.* (Praeger, New York, 1962.) *Population and Planned Parenthood in India.* (Allen & Unwin, 2nd edn, 1961.) *Hungry People and Empty Lands.* (Allen & Unwin, 3rd edn, 1955.) *Asia's Population Problems.* (Allen & Unwin, 1967.)

Chu Chong-Lwan. 'Korean Economy and Population Problem'. (*Korea Journal,* Seoul, November, 1961, Vol. I, No. 3.)

Ansley J. Coale and Edgar M. Hoover. *Population Growth and Economic Development in Low-Income Countries.* (Princeton University Press, Princeton, N.J., 1958.)

Kingsley Davis. *The Population of India and Pakistan.* (Princeton University Press, Princeton, N.J., 1957.)

Demographic Year Book. (United Nations, New York.)

Dennis Kux. 'Growth and Characteristics of Pakistan's Population.' (*Population Review,* Madras, January 1962, Vol. 6, No. 1.)

John Robbins. *Too Many Asians.* (Doubleday, New York, 1959.)

Irene Täuber. *The Population of Japan.* (Princeton University Press, Princeton, N.J., 1958.)

Warren S. Thompson. *Population and Progress in the Far East.* (University of Chicago Press, Chicago, 1959.)

Justus M. van der Kroef. 'Cultural Aspects of Indonesia's Demographic Problem.' (*Population Review,* Madras, January 1960.)

Guy Wint. *Spotlight on Asia.* (Penguin Books, 1955.)

LABOUR IN ASIA

Werner Klatt

MOST of the working men and women in Asia are engaged in agricultural pursuits. Outside Japan – the only country that has progressed beyond the stage of agrarian backwardness – the rural population accounts for at least three out of four, sometimes even four out of five of the total population. As Louise Howard said in her book on farm labour: 'For millions of persons born in rural districts there is no escape from an agricultural career.'* The villages provide a home not only for those who till the land, but also for indigenous craftsmen and local traders. Much of the non-agricultural occupation is thus centred in hamlets and country towns rather than capital cities which accommodate primarily the administrative, academic, commercial and military sections of society, but little industry. In most parts of Asia the age of the congested areas holding the proletariat of modern industry is yet to come. This is not to say that Asia is a continent of bucolic peace and rural prosperity. On the contrary; even where it is not overcrowded by present, or indeed by any, standards of production and productivity, the countryside is at best a backwater of development; at worst it provides back-breaking toil and the hazards of intestinal disease.

PREDOMINANCE OF FARM LABOUR

The predominance of the villager in general and the agriculturist in particular is overwhelming. The share of cultivators, tenants and farm labourers in the total labour force accounts normally for two thirds, but in some of the least industrialized areas for as much as three quarters of the labour force. Any survey of its size, its forms of employment and of any changes in its composition would therefore be incomplete without an assessment of the agricultural sector. However much they despise life on the land, even administrators, intellectuals, traders and industrialists are closely tied in their mentality and in their relations to the villages from which they are often removed by not more than one generation.

Surveys of agricultural labour and of rural working conditions are

* Louise E. Howard, *Labour in Agriculture. An International Survey.* (Oxford University Press, 1935).

still relatively scarce in some parts of Asia, as indeed they are throughout the world; yet the planning of social and economic change is closely linked to an understanding of the rural communities and their role in society. Often even basic statistical data cannot be had easily. Certain salient features are, however, so pronounced as to provide an impression, at least in qualitative, if not in quantitative terms. Frequently one fifth to one quarter of the village population is engaged in non-agricultural activities. This section usually embraces the local rebels as well as the innovators. From here stems the beginning of social mobility; here can be found the ancestors of the foremen of factories, if not the entrepreneurs, exporters, officers and civil servants. The division between agricultural and non-agricultural pursuits is rarely rigid, except where the rules of caste prescribe men's status in life and death. Trading and handicraft are by necessity tied closely to the needs and the opportunities of the village community. Occupational choices are thus interwoven and interchangeable.

Even within agriculture the lines of division between cultivators, tenants and labourers are fairly fluid. Generalizations are more dangerous here than elsewhere, but in the rice economies of South and South-East Asia the farm labourers seem to account for between one third and two fifths of the total agricultural labour force. Its magnitude and composition is, of course, determined largely by the size of the holding. The smaller the farm, the more it depends on family labour. In some communities the owner-occupiers and tenants try to maintain a social status different from that of the labourers, but any such segregation tends to break down. Where the land available is limited and much sought after, cultivators and tenants may have to seek supplementary manual work to support themselves and their families. There are also agricultural workers who own some land and who thus stand somewhere between the landless labourer and the owner-occupier, tenant or share cropper. However, the labourer turned owner is as rare a specimen in Asia as is the lord of the manor.

During the depression of the late twenties many cultivators lost their land and became labourers. Where agrarian reforms have been carried out meanwhile, it has been one of their purposes to eliminate some of the worst features of landlordism and money-lending. Where these reforms have been successful, as in Japan, the village community has become more homogeneous than it was in the past in its social composition, in its economic interest, and in its political affiliation. In this situation tenants tend to gain by comparison with owners, and labourers sometimes gain by comparison with both.

HIDDEN UNEMPLOYMENT

Where modern Western society is plagued by urban unemployment, Eastern society's greatest blot is the under-employment in the rural communities. As the last of the various Indian famine reports pointed out, 'perhaps the most important, and in many ways the most intractable of all rural economic problems is that of under-employment'.* It is sometimes concluded that the withdrawal of farm labour and its transfer into industry is an easy process able to solve both rural underemployment and industrial growth. In fact, the position is too complex to lend itself to ready solutions. There is chronic as well as seasonal under-employment, and much of the disguised unemployment does not express itself in complete idleness but in work with insufficient or unsatisfactory tools that make for low productivity and excessive input of labour.

The extent of rural unemployment is clearly related to the amount of land available and the form of farming chosen. Where paddy (rice) is grown on wet ground and wheat, pulses and oilseeds are grown on dry land, some 200 working days are needed under present conditions on ten acres of land; to this have to be added the days taken up for repairing the house, the bunds, the implements; for collecting firewood and fodder and carrying farm products to the market. This adds up to almost uninterrupted employment from one end of the year to the other. There is not enough work, however, for the breadwinner and not enough food for his family, if the holding is substantially smaller than ten acres, and this applies in many, if not most, instances throughout Asia; often even five acres can be considered a gift of the gods.

In these circumstances underemployment and poverty can be averted only if the level of intensity of farming can be raised or supplementary or alternative employment can be found outside agriculture. Within farming, output and productivity cannot be raised substantially without the application of farm requisites additional to those available at present. Supplementary mechanical power and commercially produced plant nutrients are the most prominent among the many requisites for giving a new lease of life to the farming communities of Asia. Badly needed animal protein cannot be produced without additional supplies of fodder, the chief by-product of double cropping and mixed farming. Once animal husbandry plays its full part, it is bound to create new jobs on the farms, but this development has to await the growth of an

* Famine Enquiry Commission's Final Report (Madras, 1945).

urban consumer market that is yet to come in most of Asia. Thus farm and factory are two aspects of one and the same phenomenon.

As a result of improvements in transport facilities, villagers in Asia find it easier than in the past to secure supplementary employment and thus additional income, but these activities rarely contribute substantially to reducing seasonal unemployment, which is more marked in plantations than in subsistence farming; yet the plantations have brought a sense of labour discipline and an understanding of the money economy without which industrialization is unthinkable. Even allowing for supplementary earnings, total farm income is rarely large enough to provide more than a bare subsistence; sometimes it is less than that. In typical Asian farming communities some 75 to 80 per cent of the total net income is spent on food, the remainder being divided fairly evenly between clothing, shelter and other daily necessities. Two thirds to three quarters of the food bill is accounted for by cereals which provide the bulk of the daily calorie intake. Whilst the diet is overburdened with starchy foods, its content of animal protein is low. After weaning, the consumption of milk is insignificant. Its absence in the diet of the adult causes shortages of calcium and riboflavin. Where rice is highly milled, the diet lacks thiamin, as a result of which cases of beri beri can be found. Short stature, low body-weight and high frequency of stomatitis are the nutritional marks of societies in need of occupational change.

OCCUPATIONAL CHANGES

The workers employed in Asia's industry and commerce are the brothers and sisters, the sons and daughters of those remaining in the villages. Their problems are similar and they are interrelated. Some take temporary employment but return to their farm plots during harvest time. The industrial workers thus react to their new environment not unlike their rural relatives; yet their new conditions of work are far removed from their previous mode of life. The disruption caused by physical and mental dislocation is as violent in Asia as it has been in urban communities elsewhere in the world. Its by-products are reminiscent of Europe's industrial past. Some of the tenements of Asian industrial and urban centres bring to mind the worst features of early industrialization in Europe, but remarkably good housing and modern social services can be found in the most developed of the underdeveloped countries of Asia. If the political instability in many parts of Asia is taken as a sign of immaturity, this diagnosis is correct in so far as it describes the end of an old-fashioned rural society with its own built-in equilibrium and the beginning of the painful growth of new forms of living and working together in conditions where the monotonous, regular rhythm of the machine takes the place of the irregular, yet no less powerful rhythm determined by sun-rise and sun-set, by dry season and by wet.

The non-agricultural labour force of Asia may seem small if related to all those described in the official records as gainfully employed; yet in absolute numbers it represents a formidable force by any standards. Admittedly the statistical counts are neither complete nor accurate. The records of the International Labour Office, which was founded in 1919 and now advises on questions of labour on behalf of the United Nations, show almost 50 million workers employed in mining, construction and manufacturing industries in the countries of Asia outside the Communist bloc. There are many more outside these industries who have not been counted; they represent the potential on which entrepreneurs in all walks of urban life can draw. Urban labour includes not only factory hands, but also white-collar workers, as well as labourers in transport, trade and communications. The administrative grades often carry not only better remuneration, but also higher social status than the other groups. Whilst they provide a large portion of the elite of Asia, the members of the trading communities are often of alien origin and thus find it difficult to integrate in the indigenous labour force.

The flow of migrants from the rural areas to the urban centres of Asia has gained momentum since the end of the last war, when transport and communications began to provide the preconditions of mobility on an unprecedented scale. As a result the process of urbanization has been faster in Asia than it was at a similar stage of industrial development in Europe. Many towns of Asia have become the receptacles of the rural under-employed. Urban unemployment may thus be seen as the other side of over-population, at present levels of production, in the villages.

On the whole the new recruits to industry in Asia have shown a remarkable degree of adaptation to alien conditions. To be sure, there have been serious difficulties in some industries and there are still some to be overcome. Only the impatient or the rapacious, however, would have reason to be dissatisfied. Where indigenous skills were not dislodged as a result of the international division of labour, the training of industrial recruits has been easiest. At the middle layer of the industrial – as indeed of the administrative – hierarchy it seems most difficult to train large numbers fast enough. The programmes of international organs, such as the Technical Assistance Board of the United Nations or the Consultative Committee of the Colombo Plan, have provided some assistance in the training of suitable industrial staff, but the Western expert is not automatically the most suitable teacher of Asian managerial or engineering personnel. Much suitable human skill exists, as yet uncovered, in Asian villages and small towns that are rarely visited by government officials or their foreign advisers; it will pay handsome dividends to tap this.

THE STATUS OF LABOUR

As the supply of unskilled and semi-skilled labour usually surpasses the urban and industrial demand, workers are in a weak bargaining position. As a result, wages and working conditions tend to be unsatisfactory by Western standards. Even so, industrial workers of low skill usually earn twice as much and skilled workers may earn more than three times as much as agricultural labourers. This does not necessarily mean that urban living standards are correspondingly higher than those obtaining in villages where a large part of the income accrues as part of the subsistence economy and thus is cheap if not free of charge. As earnings are low, women have to earn in addition to men. Of this a great deal can be seen in Asia. The working women of Asia carry, as a rule, an even heavier burden than men. Except during the last stages of pregnancy, women of working-class origin, apart from running their households, are in fact invariably engaged in some form or other of paid employment. Child labour, though forbidden in several countries of the area, is not entirely unknown either. In these conditions absenteeism from work is frequent; it should not be seen as either a sign of income saturation or of laziness. On the whole Asian workers are industrious, though ill-paid. They have yet to reach the social and economic status that industrial workers have gained for themselves in Western society.

As private savings are small or non-existent, the opportunities for private large-scale capital investment are limited in Asia. In these circumstances the State steps in on many occasions which remained the preserve of the individual entrepreneur in the Western world for a century or more. The State is thus becoming rapidly the largest employer even where it is not the only one – as in the Soviet Union and in China. It is thus not surprising that labour relations and the struggle for the rights of the working man have taken forms in Asia that are distinct from those known in the older industrial countries of the world; for example, government legislation regulating conditions of work and labour relations has been introduced in several Asian countries at an early stage of industrial development. As a result civil servants have tended at times to regard labour matters – not unlike those concerning the co-operatives – as the prerogative of government departments rather than that of independent arbitration machinery. These tendencies have been encouraged in Asia by the weakness of organized industrial labour.

ASIAN TRADE UNIONS

The trade unions in Asia are numerically second to none, but they include, according to an estimate of the International Confederation of Free Trade Unions (ICFTU), 'not more than one quarter of the trade union potential in the non-Communist countries of Asia'.* Some 24 Asian trade union organizations from 12 territories in Asia and representing more than 7·6 million members are affiliated to the ICFTU which maintains, through its Asian Regional Organization (founded in 1951), close relations with the Asian trade unions and labour associations. It also maintains in Delhi a training college for labour organizers and trade union officials; it holds conferences and seminars throughout the region; and it has sent goodwill missions from time to time to territories where intractable difficulties within the trade union movement seemed to justify the dispatch of experienced officers of the international organization. A good many non-Communist labour unions have remained outside the international framework provided by the ICFTU, particularly in Japan. Whilst their total membership is uncertain, it is unlikely to add more than 2–3 million to the total non-Communist trade union membership. The numerical strength of the Communist and Communist-dominated organizations in Asia does not exceed 2 millions; they are affiliated to the World Federation of Trade Unions (WFTU) which has had to face certain internal difficulties lately due to the Sino-Soviet ideological dispute.

Japan, being the country with the largest industrial labour force in Asia, has almost 8 million workers who are organized in trade unions; this number falls little short of the membership of the Trades Union Congress of Great Britain. India has approximately 4 million trade union members, Pakistan claims half a million and Ceylon, Malaysia, South Korea and Taiwan (Formosa) have approximately one quarter

* ICFTU, Report to the Seventh World Congress (Berlin, 1962).

AGRICULTURAL AND NON-AGRICULTURAL LABOUR FORCE

Country	Economically Active Population (per cent of total population)	Population Engaged in Agricultural Pursuits (per cent of total employed population)	Industrial Workers in Mining, Manufacture, Construction (million)
South Asia			
India	43	73	20·0
Nepal	49	93	0·1
Pakistan	33	75	2·8
Ceylon	37	51	0·4
Central Asia			
Tibet	n.a.	n.a.	n.a.
Mongolia	n.a.	n.a.	n.a.
Russian Central Asia	n.a.	n.a.	n.a.
Far East			
China	n.a.	(70)	n.a.
Taiwan	30	50	0·4
Hong Kong	39	7	0·6
Japan	50	27	14·6
South Korea	32	54	1·0
North Korea	n.a.	n.a.	n.a.
Russia Siberia and Far East	n.a.	n.a.	n.a.
South-East Asia			
Burma	n.a.	n.a.	n.a.
Thailand	53	82	0·5
Cambodia	45	81	0·1
Laos	n.a.	n.a.	n.a.
South Vietnam	39	n.a.	n.a.
North Vietnam	n.a.	n.a.	n.a.
Malaya	34	55	0·3
Singapore	33	8	0·1
Sarawak	39	81	n.a.
Sabah	39	77	n.a.
Indonesia	36	72	2·6
Philippines	35	57	1·2

n.a. – not available   ( ) – estimate
Source: ILO, *Yearbook of Labour Statistics* (Geneva, 1966)

of a million each. Hong Kong has half as much as that. Whilst amalgamation progresses among trade unions in the Western world, Asian trade unions are marked by a tendency towards fragmentation, if not fratricide. In Japan as elsewhere, industrial workers are frequently organized according to place of work rather than occupation. Some 40,000 unions share the total membership and the average is thus a mere 200 members per union. Of the two main unions, the General Council of Trade Unions (Sohyo) and the Japanese Confederation of Labour (Domei), the latter is affiliated to the ICFTU. Together they absorb the bulk of Japan's organized industrial labour force. Sohyo draws its membership principally from workers in public enterprises, whilst Domei operates mainly among workers employed by private industry.

In India the average membership per union is 400. In many cases more than one union operates on the factory floor. The two largest unions are both affiliated to the ICFTU. The Indian National Trade Union Congress (INTUC) is exceeding the 2 million mark in membership, whilst Hind Mazdor Sabha (HMS) has less than half as many members. Elsewhere in Asia trade unions have a hard time, if they are not in fact restricted in their activities, as in Pakistan. In Ceylon, Malaysia, Hong Kong and Formosa they are fairly effective organs. Nowhere in the area do farm labourers represent more than a tiny section of organized labour. Most rural districts have not yet seen a trade union organizer.

The concept of political independence is not yet generally accepted by the unions in Asia. Some of them are associated with political parties, but on the whole work in the unions is not undertaken in the interest of political advance but rather with a view to genuine negotiation and arbitration. In spite of certain shortcomings, the trade unions in Asia represent an important factor in public life. The more effective of them are on the road to fulfilling functions not dissimilar to those undertaken by their counterparts in Europe and North America.

TRADE UNIONS IN NON-COMMUNIST COUNTRIES IN ASIA

Country	Name of Trade Union	Membership (in thousands)	ICFTU Affiliated	WFTU Affiliated
India	Indian National Trades Union Council (INTUC)	2,015	+	
	Hind Mazdoor Sabha (HMS)	760	+	
	All-India Trades Union Congress (AITUC)	500		+
Nepal	All Nepal Trade Union Organization	banned		

Country	Name of Trade Union	Membership (in thousands)	ICFTU Affiliated	WFTU Affiliated
Pakistan	All Pakistan Confederation of Labour (APCOL)	330	+	
	All Pakistan Federation of Labour (APFOL)	360	+	
	Pakistan National Federation of Trade Unions (PNFTU)	15		
Ceylon	Ceylon Workers' Congress (CWC)	135	+	
	Ceylon Trade Union Federation (CTUF) (pro-Chinese)	unknown		+
	Federation of Trade Unions of Ceylon (FTUC) (pro-Soviet)	unknown		+
Taiwan	Chinese Federation of Labour (CFL)	285	+	
Hong Kong	Hong Kong and Kowloon Trade Union Council	125	+	
	Hong Kong Federation of Trade Unions (Communist-supported)	unknown		
Japan	General Council of Trade Unions (SOHYO)	5,765		
	Japanese Federation of Industrial Unions (SANBETSU)			
	Japanese Confederation of Labour (DOMEI)	1,850	+	
	Japanese Postal Union (ZENTEI)*	200	+	
	Coalminers; Metal; Municipal; Broadcasting Workers Unions*	135	+	
South Korea	Federation of Korean Trade Unions (FKTU)	275	+	
Burma	Trade Union Congress, Burma (TUCB)	banned		
Thailand	Thai National Trade Union Congress	banned		
South Vietnam	Vietnam Labour Union (VLU)	50		
	Vietnamese Confederation of Labour (VCL)	unknown		

Country	Name of Trade Union	Membership (in thousands)	ICFTU WFTU Affiliated
Malaysia	Malayan Trade Union Congress (MTUC)	255	+
Singapore	Singapore Association of Trade Unions (SATU)	unknown	
	National Trade Union Congress, Singapore (SNTUC)	100	+
Indonesia	Gabungan Serikat Buruh Islam Indonesia (GASBIINDO)	250	+
	Kongress Buruh Islam Merdei (KBIM)	130	+
	Gerahau Organisasi Buruh Sjarikat Islam Indonesia (GOBSI)	50	+
Philippines	Philippine Trade Union Council (PTUC)	80	+
	Katipunang Manggagawong Philippino (KMP)	500	
	Philippine Labor Center	265	+
Okinawa	Okinawa Government Employees' Union (KANKORO)	5	+
	All Okinawa Military Employees' Trade Union (ZENGUNRO)	15	+

*These unions are affiliated to both the ICFTU and SOHYO.

Sources : ICFTU, Report of the Eighth World Congress. (Amsterdam, 1965.)
ICFTU, Supplementary Information. (Amsterdam, 1968.)

BIBLIOGRAPHY

Abdul Aziz and W. Klatt. 'The Development and Utilization of Labour Resources in South East Asia' in Philip W. Thayer (Ed.), *Nationalism and Progress in Free Asia.* (Johns Hopkins University Press, Baltimore, 1956.)

Tadashi Fukutake. *Man and Society in Japan.* (University of Tokyo Press, Tokyo, 1962.)

Louise E. Howard. *Labour in Agriculture. An International Survey.* (Oxford University Press, 1935.)

International Confederation of Free Trade Unions, Reports of the Seventh and Eighth World Congresses. (Berlin, 1962 and Amsterdam, 1965.)

International Labour Organization. *Agricultural Wages and Incomes of Primary Producers*. (Geneva, 1949.) *Basic Problems of Plantation Labour*. (Geneva, 1950.) *Yearbook of Labour Statistics*. (Geneva, 1966.)

W. Klatt. *Land and Labour in Burma*. (Mimeograph, Rangoon, 1956.)

Radhakamal Mukerjee. *The Indian Working Class*. (Hind Kitabs, Bombay, 1951.)

Surendra J. Patel. *Agricultural Labourers in Modern India and Pakistan*. (Current Book House, Bombay, 1952.)

B. Ramamarti. *Agricultural Labour. All-India Agricultural Labour Enquiry* and *Report on the Second Agricultural Labour Enquiry*. (Government of India, Delhi, 1954 and 1960.)

R. H. Tawney. *Land and Labour in China*. (Allen & Unwin, 1932.)

THE ASIAN INTELLECTUAL

Edward Shils

THE PROBLEMS OF THE ASIAN INTELLECTUALS

THE intellectuals of Asia, like their counterparts everywhere, are defined by the relative elaborateness of their intellectual activities, professional and vocational, such as those of university teachers, scientific research workers, literary men, theologians and journalists; or avocational, such as are sometimes found among businessmen, politicians, civil servants, physicians and engineers. The level of development of the intellectual classes, and their intellectual institutions, differ profoundly from country to country in Asia. At the one extreme is Japan with its many universities and research institutions, and with a vast output of science and scholarship, an impressive literary productivity, a tremendous and prosperous press and publishing industry and a dense and well-organized bookselling business; and India and Pakistan with great numbers, occasionally high quality and a profuse though disorganized system of intellectual institutions, through Burma, Indonesia and the Philippines, and the smaller countries like Laos and Cambodia with small bodies of intellectuals and very motley institutional systems.

The Asian intellectual classes of all countries, including even Japan, have in common the recent and exogenous origin of their modern culture. All the Asian countries, unlike most of Africa, have a rich tradition of religious–philosophical culture, well developed in written form and cared for by a class of professional custodians. In Asia, modern culture, introduced from the West, had, by the beginning of the 20th century, developed an elaborate set of institutions, universities, learned societies, periodicals, etc., through which modern culture was reproduced and applied to indigenous problems and traditions. Together with these there developed a considerable indigenous personnel, well schooled in the techniques and outlooks of modern culture. Japan and India were in the forefront. In Japan, of course, the initiative was Japanese, in India, Indian and British initiatives were intermixed. In China too, mixed initiatives were giving rise to a modern intelligentsia, academic, journalistic, and literary. In the other parts of South and South-East Asia under foreign rule, numbers were much smaller, but still some persons with a modern education – mainly lawyers and businessmen – existed to express an indigenous demand, to serve as a

621

pressure group for the establishment of advanced modern higher educational institutions, and as a public for modern intellectual works, preponderantly of metropolitan origin. All these intelligentsias, large and small, with well equipped and well functioning institutions or poorly equipped and poorly functioning, a century old in their rooting in Western culture or relatively recent, all faced, and still face, certain common problems and have certain common responses. Nationalism, populism, xenophilia and xenotropism generally, xenophobia and nativistic revivalism, inferiority feelings, curiosity and resentment in the face of the metropolitan culture are found throughout the continent. Countries like Japan, which retained their sovereignty throughout, as well as those which were ruled by Western powers, manifest these attitudes.

THE SCIENTIFIC-TECHNOLOGICAL VOID

In their occupational structure, the intellectual classes of the formerly colonial territories still bear the marks of their colonial inheritance as well as of the present economic backwardness of their countries. In the colonial period, except in India, the highest administrative posts were reserved for expatriates, but the middle ranks of administration afforded numerous opportunities for indigenous educated persons. High posts for scientists and technologists in industry and in government technical services were similarly reserved and few in number. There was little advanced scientific research and teaching, the poverty of the population meant a low effective demand for medical services. Outside the services of government, the main opportunity for the educated to deploy their skills with a prospect of substantial financial reward was in the legal profession. As a result, the educated classes in almost all the Asian countries, except Japan, are markedly skewed in the direction of the arts subjects – literature, languages, history – and the social sciences, while the scientific and technological categories are rather poorly represented. Japan and, latterly and incipiently, China are the only Asian countries which, possessing a modern industrial system and a more or less modern system of mass communications, have an intellectual class in which the technological component resembles that of the advanced Western countries.

The governments of most of the Asian countries have, in recent years, tried to establish or develop further technological education, medicine, and scientific research. Yet the fact remains that indigenously established industry, except in Japan and, to a much smaller extent, China, is both rudimentary and reluctant to give a prominent place to technologists, scientists, and engineers. (In India, for example, which is one of the more advanced countries of Asia, one third of all engineers are employed in industry and two thirds in government departments where, in some Western countries, the proportions are four fifths in industry and one fifth in government departments.)

Since government departments are still the major employers of highly educated persons, the old tradition persists. It is indeed reinforced by the simple fact that the powerful drive to education, so characteristic of the new states of Asia, encounters no resistance from the arts faculties – more students can always be crowded into the lecture halls and standards are less exacting – whereas the scientific, medical and technological departments limit admissions more or less proportionately to the space available in laboratories. (Furthermore, since the latter are much more expensive to construct and equip than lecture halls, the expansion proceeds more slowly.)

DISCOURAGING CONDITIONS

In income and wealth the Asian intellectual is generally a very poor man. Recruitment into the intellectual professions in Asia, although markedly biased in favour of persons of middle-class origin, is really too wide to remain a monopoly of the offspring of the wealthy classes. Intellectuals are therefore dependent on their earned income – often gained in several occupations concurrently practised – and supported by kinsmen in accordance with the traditions of the extended family system. Civil servants at the level of permanent secretaries and other members of the highest categories, some very successful physicians and lawyers, a handful of journalists and university professors, a small number in business, similarly small numbers of literary men, especially those who write for films, have incomes which permit them to live in what could be called, according to Western criteria, a middle-class manner. The mass of journalists, secondary school and college teachers, literary men who write in the vernacular, most lawyers and doctors, although much better off than the masses of their countrymen, live in relative poverty. In their housing they are crowded far past the point where privacy of any sort is possible; they are unable to purchase books. Those with regular employment and income in the profession of their choice are the fortunate ones. At the bottom are the educated who have never been able to find a position corresponding even to very modest aspirations. About a tenth find no employment at all on the completion of their university studies, and this period of unemployment may persist for several years. Great numbers of the educated unemployed ultimately do find posts which, even though they are not what was sought, are sufficient for a scant livelihood. This is common to all the underdeveloped countries of Asia and even Japan, as a result of the tremendous expansion of university studies, has a moderate amount of intellectual unemployment.

This situation is most pronounced in India which had numerous universities before independence and a corresponding surplus of graduates. It has also become true of countries whose higher educational system has taken definite shape only since independence. Few governments have taken any steps to cope with the unemployment of the educated.

In all these countries, intellectual unemployment is an urban phenomenon. Unwillingness to accept posts as village teachers and community development workers, because of the lack of amenities and low salary, is fostered by the extended family system.

The traditional intellectuals – monks, priests – live in their traditional mendicant poverty, perhaps even less well than they lived under the colonial regime because of the diminution of patronage and charity resultant on reforms in land ownership and the contraction of the princely orders. Despite the political concessions made to them by governments in Pakistan, Ceylon and Burma and the flattery which, almost everywhere except Japan and the Communist states, is directed towards the traditional culture and its custodians, Asian governments have done very little to improve the economic lot or even the institutional provision for traditional intellectuals.

INTELLECTUAL INSTITUTIONS

The three major Asian countries, Japan, India and China, are the only ones which have a relatively highly developed system of intellectual institutions. The Japanese system is the only one which has a full range of well-working universities, technical colleges, secondary schools, teacher training institutions, scientific and technological laboratories, libraries, museums, bookshops, broadcasting and television services, daily and periodical press, scientific press and book reviewing system.

The Indian system of intellectual institutions is, by virtue of its differentiatedness and amplitude, the most advanced of any underdeveloped country. It is less self-sustaining than the Japanese; it depends, like that of practically all underdeveloped countries, on government subvention and sponsorship. This is a consequence of the small size of the public willing and able to pay for intellectual goods and services. The literary market is very much smaller in India than it is in Japan. The supportive capacity of this small market is further diminished by the fragmentation of the country into a multitude of heterogeneous non-communicating cultures. The situation is no better in many of the other countries, in contrast with Japan where the public is linguistically homogeneous. For these reasons, journalism and literary institutions, which suffer in any case from inadequate professional, commercial and technical traditions, are further impeded by poverty.

The universities of most Asian countries are usually overcrowded and understaffed (often by part-time teachers), their libraries are small and random. The scientific research carried on in universities almost everywhere except Japan is scant in quantity and seldom important in quality. The publication of books and periodicals is ill-organized and often unscrupulous; the system of book distribution is haphazard. Scientific research outside Japan, China and India is very poorly provided for. Relatively little was inherited from the colonial regimes and although the new governments have created many research institutions, their performance has generally been meagre – as could have been expected in situations where the tradition of modern scientific research has not been well implanted and where highly qualified personnel have been in short supply.

MODERNITY AND TRADITION

The culture of the intellectual classes of most of the Asian countries is of a threefold composition. There is, first, the modern culture which involves an appreciation of the validity of science and of a rational, non-magical approach to the problems of individual life and social organization; it involves knowledge of some of the main works of modern culture in science, literature, history, and a continuous contact with some stream of modern culture. The second culture is a mixture of the traditional and indigenous with the modern. It is a culture which entails familiarity with the lately metropolitan language, and an acquaintance with some of the main works in it; much of this second culture is in the indigenous language. The products of this culture are an unstylized, matter-of-fact intermingling of indigenous traditional and exogenous modern. The third culture is the traditional religious-philosophical culture.

Higher civil servants, the more important university teachers, scientists, engineers, outstanding lawyers, physicians, editors of leading newspapers and their more prominent correspondents, some politicians, are the major participants in the modern culture. The second, mixed culture, is shared largely by elementary and some secondary school teachers, particularly in rural areas and small towns, journalists in vernacular newspapers or in the provincial press, middle and lower rank civil servants, and most politicians, particularly those outside the central political elite. The traditional culture is carried by priests and monks, practitioners of indigenous or folk medicine, and religious teachers; although increasingly the bearers of the first and second cultures are taking their share in certain selected aspects of the third culture.

Since the acquisition of independence by the newly sovereign states, the balance has shifted somewhat more in the direction of the second class, from the first class which for so long had, jointly with the foreign ruler, played so vital a part in the implantation of the seeds of modernity in their societies. Even now the first class still occupies the central position of influence in their respective societies, in the higher civil service, in the law courts, in the leadership of the political parties, in the army, in journalism and in the universities. Since, however, the new regimes of Asia are either democracies, or populistic oligarchies, the second class and the third too have come forward to greater prominence and influence. In Japan, even the extremes of nationalism and hostility towards the West among the intellectuals have however in recent years not resulted in any marked upsurge of cultural revivalism.

Of course, in no Asian country is even the first class, the modern or 'Westernized' intellectuals, so modern or 'Westernized' that they preserve no traces of the indigenous traditional culture in their outlook, in their tastes and social relationships, in their self-identification, or in their loyalties. At the other end of the continuum, there must be very few in the third class who are entirely untouched by modern Western ideas and practices, and who do not respond in some way to their challenge.

The first class is often referred to as a class of 'Brown Englishmen' or 'Brown Frenchmen' or 'Brown Sahibs', as 'uprooted intellectuals, suffering from schizophrenia', as men 'suspended between two worlds, belonging to neither'. They are alleged by their critics, often less educated politicians or littérateurs from their own circles, as being 'out of touch with the people'.

These criticisms notwithstanding, most of the Westernized intellectuals in the Asian countries retain in their outlook, in their family relationships and in their tastes, a great deal of their indigenous culture. Many of them know a great deal about their indigenous culture too, often more than the less well educated politician, whose education, such as it is, was also a modern Western education and whose indigenous culture is more a matter of espousal than of knowledge. The 'Westernized intellectuals' of Asia usually know more about the higher content of the traditional culture than their peasant fellow-countrymen with whom they are so often and so unfavourably compared. They are also more attached to the national idea than most of the rest of their fellow nationals in their country, they are likely to be less sectional, less regional, less communal, less caste-bound. Not that the 'Westernized intellectuals' are entirely free from these sectional attachments, they are just more free than most of their fellow countrymen.

AMBIVALENCE AND ITS CONSEQUENCES

Their attachment to their country and their appreciation of its past and its traditions generally coexist with some disbelief in the traditional, indigenous view of the world and of man's place on earth. They are, generally, more secular in their understanding of the world, more hedonist in their conception of a good life, more egalitarian in principle, more accepting of science, technology, progress and the potentialities of human initiative in changing society. This complex of beliefs has proved to be fairly compatible with a considerable degree of embeddedness in traditional familial institutions and the retention of indigenous elements in their style of life. Internal strain and conflict, at least on the level of consciousness, do not always result, nor need they do so. Yet, so deeply had this self-image of a 'split personality', alienated from its society, penetrated into the consciousness of the modern Asian intellectual that it has become a secondary *malaise*. Their feeling of being *à l'écart* with respect to populistic and demagogic politics since independence had led many to accept as true the charge of 'being out of touch with the people'.

The intellectuals of the second class are much less afflicted by this problem. They do not possess so much modern culture that they feel themselves under attack when 'uprooted intellectuals' are being criticized. Most of their cultural life is lived in the medium of their mother tongue and its literature. So much of their professional activity as school teachers, local officials, journalists and authors is carried on in it and so unintense is their concern with the modern culture conducted in English or French that they feel no conflict or remorse. It does not occur to them to look on themselves as alienated. They are too concerned with local problems which always have an indigenous accent.

The traditional intellectuals, at least the more sensitive and more alert among them, feel themselves on the defensive, under pressure from the secularizing tendency of the 'Westernizing' intellectuals and higher civil servants of the big cities. Even where Buddhism or Islam is established as the state religion or where the state is designated as a Buddhist or Islamic state, the traditional intellectuals know that this has been achieved against the resistance of the political, administrative, and intellectual elite of the country. The conflict in which they are engaged is an external conflict, not an internal one within their own minds.

CREATIVITY AND INTELLECTUAL INDEPENDENCE

In its modern culture, much of Asia is still uncreative. In Japan the novel flourishes; in India there are some literary men of genuinely high quality. There are some interesting painters. On the whole, the tendency is towards reproduction rather than creation. In mathematics and the natural sciences, Japan has become a fully modern culture. In India there has been some work of high quality in physics and Indians abroad have done distinguished work in this and in related fields. In India, research in the natural sciences is carried on on a large scale but the quality of the scientific output in India, throughout practically all the fields of science, is not generally thought to be up to a very high international standard. The situation in Pakistan seems even poorer, both quantitatively and qualitatively. In both of these countries, which, with Japan and China, are the most advanced in modern culture in Asia, there is a very marked tendency for some of the ablest young scientists to emigrate from their countries, temporarily, if not permanently, to Western Europe or North America. Throughout South-East Asia, scientific research scarcely exists. In the social sciences creative, and even routine, work at a high standard of proficiency is still scant. Valuable work is being done in the historiography of the region, and in the study of the indigenous traditional cultures. In these fields, the leading Asian scholars are now beginning to enter into collegial equality with some of the best metropolitan scholars.

The modern intellectuals of most Asian countries depend for their intellectual sustenance on the output from Western Europe and North America, and the level of intimate knowledge of this output is often very high. It is perhaps even too high for its own dignity, being impelled sometimes by a preoccupation with the culture of the old imperial metropolis almost as much as by a love of its intrinsic substance. Even in Japan, which in many fields of work is a full-fledged member of the world intellectual community, there is a strong xenotropic tendency. This preoccupation with the West as an intellectual metropolis is intimately connected with the continuation of substantial intellectual dependence on the West. Except for Japan, which has a very productive modern culture, nearly as self-sustaining as any modern culture in the world, Asian intellectual life continues to suffer from a many-faceted intellectual dependence on the old metropolitan centres.

The problem becomes acute in connexion with the medium of instruction in the universities and the availability of textbooks. Practically all the other countries must still use textbooks in English or French, or textbooks which are translations and adaptations of European or American textbooks. Since, except in Japan, China and Indonesia, the medium of instruction has in the main been the metropolitan language, the situation could scarcely be otherwise. The introduction of a local medium of instruction, for which there is powerful motivation, is moving ahead. National self-regard, persistent preoccupation with colonialism, considerations of populistic politics and a conviction of the anomaly of the high culture of the country being conducted in a language foreign to the mass of the population, all give impetus to the drive, and only strong determination by educators and high administrators is able to hold it in check, while slowly yielding to the inevitable pressure.

The present and the oncoming generations of students face a situation in which they must either conduct their higher education in a language which they have very imperfectly mastered – owing to unsatisfactory language instruction – or, if they are instructed at a university in their mother tongue, they still have to depend for their reading on literature in a foreign language or on a very inferior kind of literature produced in their mother tongue. The consequences of this linguistic interregnum for the quality of culture of the Asian intellectuals are apparent. Their contacts with the more creative metropolitan culture will be attenuated before their own cultures have become creative. The high points of intellectual cultivation and urbanity attained in the Asian societies by a small proportion of the intellectual class will undoubtedly be maintained, but the proportion of those at the heights will be reduced while the proportion of the second class of intellectuals will increase very markedly, and many of the latter will therefore have to be drawn on to occupy roles such as university teaching, journalism and higher civil service.

The linguistic interregnum must, for a time, hamper the creativity of the indigenous modern culture, and thus will prolong the period of dependence. At the same time the metropolitan culture which comes to the Asian countries is dilapidated by the promotion of indigenous culture and the ramshackle quality of schools and universities, bookshops and libraries, periodicals and newspapers.

This cultural dependence has always carried with it overtones of inferiority. The response to this inferiority almost everywhere among Asian intellectuals has a propensity towards revivalism. This has entailed, in the new states, an effort to rehabilitate the indigenous culture, to make it more prominent and more appreciated. Among the most Westenized intellectuals, there has been a quickening of interest in the traditional artistic, architectural and religious inheritance. Here and there are efforts to modernize by reformulation in the modern idiom and to discover points of continuity between the cultural inheritance and the aspirations towards modernity.

INTELLECTUALS IN POLITICS

The political life of the Asian states, except Japan, is in many important respects the creation and the affair of the modern educated class. The political elites of the new states of Asia were constituted almost exclusively from the parties and groups which had been in opposition under the colonial regime. The longer history of the Indian political movement and the relatively early and large supply of educated and cultivated lawyers, businessmen, publicists and social workers permitted the formation of a political elite of mature men. Similarly, the longer experience of the Indian movement for a larger share in government – and ultimately for self-government and its much larger scale – permitted the emergence of a differentiated body of specialized politicians, party organizers and 'bosses'. In the other countries of Asia, the movement was of more recent growth and tended to draw on a younger generation, particularly from the student population.

The political leaders in Asia – except for Japan, where an older aristocracy and plutocracy could provide personnel for politics – were drawn from the modern intellectual class. There were indeed few other groups from which a political elite could be drawn. Landowners and merchants lacked civic spirit and national concern; the latter were often alien in race and culture, and they and the landowners prudently sought to avoid incurring the displeasure of the colonial rulers. Teachers in government schools and colleges and civil servants were barred from public political agitation, unless they were ready to give up their coveted stability of employment. Hence misemployed educated young persons, some of the prosperous lawyers and physicians, and more of the less successful lawyers with time on their hands supplied the personnel of political agitation. The tradition, endemic in the oriental religions, which authorizes the religiously learned and devoted to eschew the daily comforts and routine responsibilities of this world and to live from the charity of others, both impelled many of the intellectuals to turn towards the higher cause of politics and enabled them to live in a calling which offered no significant income.

The political intellectuals of Asia, particularly those who came into politics after the First World War, were to a man nationalist and anti-imperialist. Anti-imperialism tended almost automatically to be anti-capitalist and therefore, by implication, socialist. Asian intellectual politics have also become increasingly populist; the more insistent on complete independence, and the less they were inclined towards the piecemeal enlargement of the sphere of self-government, the more populist they tended to be. For the most part they were culturally modernist and anti-traditional as well, although the need to provide a cultural legitimation for nationalist political aspirations led to a more affirmative attitude towards selected elements of the traditional indigenous culture. Finally, the politics of the intellectuals in Asia before independence were oppositional and agitational, and often merely obstructive since, with the exception of a short period in India in the second half of the 1930s, there was no constitutional possibility for a nationalist political movement to assume power as long as the foreign ruler remained.

With the attainment of independence, the political outlook of the intellectuals retained much of its earlier content. Those who took over the responsibilities of government became professional politicians to a greater extent than before. As members of the government, they had regular incomes. They also had to pay more attention to their party machinery; this entailed for the major parties, to a greater extent than before independence, the creation of a party apparatus, which required full-time, regularly paid political employment.

This led to a fissure in the ranks of the intellectuals between those who now had a stake in the new government and its supporting institutions and those who remained outside. The former soon lost their oppositional disposition; the latter retained it and even deepened it.

The routines and the pitfalls of governing have produced a type of man and a type of rhetoric which fits poorly with the Asian intellectual's reverence for selflessness and for a pattern of life in accordance with a high, quasi-religious, ideal. The result has been disillusion with politics. In some cases the disillusionment is accompanied by a greater realism and a resigned reconciliation with the breed of politician available and with the rigours of the politician's task; in others disillusionment has led to alienation from politics, not only in action but in sentiment and belief. De-politicization is the end-product.

What is striking about the Asian intellectuals, given the importance of the political culture of the European thirties which is so important in their political tradition, their anti-imperialism, their collectivistic outlook in economic matters and their fluctuating anti-Western impulses, is that so few of them have become active Communists or even sympathizers with the Communist Parties in their countries. 'Fellow-travelling' is certainly common among Asian intellectuals – it is in a sense the 'natural' political outlook of the Asian intellectual – but membership and active support of Communist parties, legal and illegal, has, with the possible exception of Indonesia, certainly not been widespread.

No discussion of the politics of the Asian intellectual can overlook the importance of the university student and even of the high-school student. In the independence movements, they supplied many of the lower-rank agitators. Demonstrations, which are an essential part of Asian politics, almost always draw heavily on student support.

To cite a few instances: the Japanese students are of an extreme and passionate turbulence, of which the wild demonstrations prior to the projected visit of former President Eisenhower to Japan gave only one instance. In Burma, the government of General Ne Win recently felt called upon to destroy physically the Student Union because it was a nest of student agitation. The restless demonstrativeness of the Indian students has often been noted in political as well as non-political events. In Pakistan the students, even in the more repressive phase of General Ayub's military government, reconciled themselves to the regime less passively than any other section of Pakistani society. In South Korea student demonstrations played an important part in bringing down the government of Dr Syngman Rhee. In Indonesia, they played a part in unseating President Sukarno.

The tradition is an old one, as old as the independence movements and modern higher education in Asia. Adolescent rebelliousness, the decline of traditional authority, the impoverished conditions of student life, the lack of prospects, economically, of the students on graduation, youthful idealism, have all been significant factors. The deliberate machinations of party politicians, especially amongst the opposition within and outside the ruling parties, aggravate the situation.

THE PROSPECT

In the coming decades, the intellectuals of the Asian countries are bound to increase in number. The rapid expansion of the university population throughout Asia guarantees that there will be more university teachers, and that from among the growing number of graduates there will be an indeterminate number who will follow intellectual occupations or who will develop and pursue intellectual interests avocationally. It is also likely that the governmental cultural bureaucracy – in communications, in the administration of academies, etc. – will increase. The belief in the need for technologists and applied scientists will also increase facilities, create posts and undoubtedly attract many persons.

The vocational opportunities will undoubtedly be outnumbered by the aspirants with the formal qualifications of university degrees and diplomas. The rate of economic development of the Asian countries is not likely to be great enough to absorb all who aspire to follow an intellectual occupation. There is bound to be an increase in those in lesser administrative and clerical posts and a large number who feel themselves misemployed.

The large numbers who enter into government service in one form or another will not greatly enhance the status of the intellectual in Asia. Government service, aside from the security it confers, is not such a claim to deference now as it was before independence. There are too many persons in it with a marginal economic existence; it is no longer believed to be the only proper place for young men of the highest intelligence, and the low esteem in which politicians are held will not enhance the reputation of those who staff their governments.

Teaching in colleges and universities is likewise not likely to increase in prestige, in so far as income and dignity of employment are sources of such prestige. The large numbers of students, the indifferent quality of the instruction which they seem destined to receive in the near future, and the undistinguished intellectual output of university staff will also not enhance their position in their respective societies.

What then are the chances for greater creativity where there has been little recently, or for the development of a higher standard of performance, which, even though not creative in a deep sense, would markedly raise the average level of intellectual attainment? Regarding the former: in literature, in painting or in the arts generally, such a development is not inconceivable. The improvement of performance in the non-artistic spheres of cultural life, of scientific and scholarly research, of university teaching, of journalism, of the learned professions, is more subject to policy, and therefore to wise policy, than in the artistic sphere. Much depends on the leadership of the universities. The difficulties which the near future will inherit from the present will be very great. Throughout India, Pakistan, Burma, the Philippines, and Indonesia, the universities are in a poor way. In China, they have no opportunity to exercise leadership. Only in Japan have some universities managed to distinguish themselves from the motley of mediocrity, and therewith maintained, at least in certain fields of science and scholarship, a standard which reminds the deficient of their deficiencies. Yet, in the rest of non-Communist Asia, the situation is not hopeless. The human material is there. Many outstandingly intelligent young Asians manage, despite their university systems, to come through to qualify themselves, and to do excellent post-graduate work overseas. (Many, of course, are so poorly trained that, when sent overseas, they are incapable of doing competent work.) Many of them who do good work overseas are wasted in all sorts of ways when they return home. Sheer difficulty in finding fitting employment is one source of waste; another is life in an unstimulating intellectual environment in isolation from other talented men and women of their own generation and interests. There are no reasons, other than political hesitation, bureaucratic indifference and the jealousy of older mediocrities in prominent positions, why this waste of talent should be allowed to go on. A little more courage by politicians, a little more alertness on the part of bureaucrats, a little more generosity on the part of the elders, would make it possible for one or a few high-grade universities in the more populous countries, one high-grade regional university in the French-speaking countries of South-East Asia, to emerge. It would not be necessary, to attain this end, to change the open admissions policy which is now followed and which is one of the factors in the dilapidated condition of intellectual life of this area. All it would require is a little determination to concentrate resources more circumspectly than is done at present. Such a concentration helps to explain the superiority of Japanese intellectual life. If this were done, there would be grounds for hope that the intellectual life of the Asian societies would find a new centre of gravity. The civil service which depends on the universities would be immensely benefited, economic policies would be improved, public criticism would be better informed and more realistic. The formation of a highly qualified specialized corps of scientifically trained technologists would be furthered. Science and scholarship would become sufficiently productive and small but effective intellectual communities would grow up. Intellectual dependence and provinciality would begin to fade. The Asian intellectuals would begin to become equal members in the world-wide intellectual community.

SCIENCE IN ASIA

Alan Mackay

WHEN examining a particular society or civilization it is now obligatory
to ask about the level of science and its place in that society. The
relationship of technology to society is clear (and serves to characterize
primitive societies – as 'stone age', 'iron age', etc.). Technology
produces wealth and contributes to the gross national product (GNP).
However, the connexion between science and technology is not so
clear and is a subject for active research. Questions such as 'how does
innovation occur?' and 'how can innovation, both social and material,
be planned and promoted?' must be asked. We can roughly distinguish
two main facets of science: science as a part of culture, forming a view
of the world, man's place in it and his relationship to other men and
organisms; and science as the basis of technology – controlling and
changing the world and man too. Technology is not just applied science
and today, while it is generally believed that money laid out on science
will eventually return a hundredfold, the relationship between pure
research and national productivity is an indirect and subtle one.

Nowadays science is ecumenical – in Needham's metaphor the
individual streams of national or locally coloured science have now
merged into the sea of science to which all peoples, in principle, have
access. 'There is no national science, just as there is no national
multiplication table; what is national is no longer science' (Anton
Chekhov). Technological know-how, on the other hand, is not so widely
published but diffuses as a marketable commodity.

Science has the strange characteristics, consequent on the communication system of civilization, that it is cumulative and self-
correcting, while technology needs rebuilding each generation or so.
Euclid had been unchanged for 1600 years; his work has been supplemented but not superseded by modern non-Euclidean geometry.
Progress has thus been fairly continuous since the times when the
urges of early man to feel at home in his environment were temporarily
satisfied by mythologies and magic (applied mythology) in which
familiar phenomena had names but remained capricious and uncontrolled. Steadily myth has retreated from physics, chemistry,
meteorology, astronomy, and in our own times, from biology.
We may expect that in the future it will desert religion, sociology and

other branches of psychology which relate to the individual and collective behaviour of man. It is characteristic of the present stage of world science that advances are being made into the fields of the less exact sciences ('soft sciences') with the full panoply of experiment, mathematics and logic ('hard science'). Subjects at present investigated include economics, linguistics, animal behaviour, memory and other regions considered to be the preserve of the humanist.

Scientists are, often without willing it themselves, agents of change. They therefore bring problems as well as solutions for societies and governments. They destroy state myths; they communicate with colleagues abroad; they emigrate; they owe allegiance to other gods than the nation provides; they ask questions and interfere; they cause economic trouble by inventing things (for example, the appearance about 1900 of synthetic indigo in quantity led rapidly to the decline of the Indian indigo industry). Translated by technology into everyday experience, these inventions mean that a man's life is less and less like that of his father, so that problems can less and less often be solved by appeal to precedent. This has sapped the strength of traditional societies.

Scientists can bring national prestige, either by winning personal honours such as Nobel prizes or by generating military power in the shape of bombs or earth satellites; but to be an isolated scientist in a backward country is to be cut off from colleagues and facilities in the rest of the world by uncomprehending countrymen. To produce good work in such circumstances is extremely difficult as scientific success goes by the Matthew principle 'To him that hath shall be given'.

There has always been considerable indigenous scientific activity in Asia, particularly in the settled cultures of China, India and the Middle East. There has always been a reservoir of technology waiting to be applied and, behind it, a corpus of scientific results waiting to be developed. This development has usually been limited by lack of social rather than technological inventiveness, so that the vast variety of Asia now comprehends societies at all stages of evolution, from those which have still hardly produced a settled agriculture, to those which are at work applying automation to industry and television to conscious social engineering. The full story of this evolution has not yet been told. The history of science in China has been recounted in Joseph Needham's masterpiece, and in the Islamic world by George Sarton. Tsuge has produced an introduction to science in Japan, most of which was derived from China before 1600 and after that date from Europe. The definitive histories are still being written by the History of Science Society of Japan.

(Details of these works are given in the bibliography.) The history of science in India is still fragmentary.

We know, however, that India was most probably the home of the first university in Asia, the University of Nalanda near Patna (*floruit* 630 A.D.), which was a definite invention for social purposes and was financed by the taxes exacted by the state from hundreds of villages. The first research institute with full-time research workers working on state problems (among them the production of temple miracles) was probably the Museum of Alexandria. Examinations for selecting talent were invented in China about the second century B.C. and, in short-lived reforms of the 11th century, scientific subjects were introduced there. Physics and mathematics were finally introduced into the Chinese Civil Service examinations in 1877, some years before this happened in Britain. It is in Asia too that we see the first of a new kind of institution, the science city; the first, in the USSR at Novosibirsk, is trying out many new forms of scientific work and another, the Mount Tsukuba Research Park near Tokyo, is just beginning to be constructed. Institutions which are in fact science cities had, however, evolved earlier in the USA.

Today Japan, China and India are the chief among those nations of Asia which have developed appreciable scientific activity for their own purposes. Their societies are very different but they are all seeking to use the same tool for raising their material and cultural standards. Each will be considered in turn.

JAPAN

Japan was the first nation in Asia wholeheartedly to adopt modern science and technology and, after the Meiji Restoration of 1868 and the Imperial rescript on education (1872), a policy of modernization was pursued to the point where Japan has become a coherent mass society of 100 million people, which in 1966 produced nearly as much shipping as the whole of the rest of the world put together and exceeded all but the USA in the production of motor cars.

Japanese life gives a great impression of coherence, in spite of continuing class struggles. Japan is almost unique in having changed from a closed feudal society, through industrialization, extreme militarization and imperialism, defeat in war and loss of empire, to a modern capitalist society, without revolution or civil war. There was little ideological objection to the introduction of science and technology, which were adopted deliberately as aids in the modernization necessary for military and commercial conquest. Now technology is the foundation of business, which attracts more popular support than war. Since 1945 the class bases of power have not seriously changed except for the decline of the military, but now the leaders of industry have the policy of encouraging a booming consumer market at home (formerly the home market was kept down to the barest subsistence level) and the population responds by re-investing its savings in industry. This has been accompanied by increasingly democratic government and a spreading of industrial and political power so that the Japanese people are now able to express more of their thoughts and feelings than ever before.

In the period 1945–65 Japanese industry was completely rebuilt using know-how from abroad, foreign (US) companies being given interests in exchange (limited in the case of strategic industries). While education also boomed, the expenditure on research and development was relatively limited (about one per cent of the GNP). Now that Japan has reached a position where its products are as good as those of its competitors, it is found that know-how for further advance cannot be bought, but that the research and development must be done at home. The development side has thus drawn people from universities into industry so that it is now realized that more university research is required to back up the development work. In spite of the expansion of education (the products of the post-war baby boom now leaving the universities) the status of university staffs remains poor by world standards. Nevertheless emigration is not yet a serious problem.

The single most important change in emphasis in the Japanese domestic research policy of the past decade is the effort to promote that quality which underlies the very process of research and innovation: scientific creativity. (OECD Report, 1967.)

Considerable developments on the science side are thus taking place and more than half of the modest ($7 million in 1964) expenditure on space research is going into universities. Space research is angled towards communication satellites.

The nuclear energy expenditure is similarly modest ($29·5 million in 1964), the bulk going to the Atomic Energy Research Institute, but there is no doubt that Japan could build whatever nuclear weapons were necessary. The low expenditure on defence (only 1·1 per cent of the GNP as compared with 8·9 per cent in the USA and 6·7 per cent in Britain) has been of great benefit in permitting the Japanese to concentrate on goods for export.

A salient feature of university life is the difficulty of getting research students at the current rates of stipend. There were only about 2,000 Ph.D. students in 1963 and only 800 applicants for 1,269 places. The hard core of Japanese research scientists is surprisingly small and, in contrast to India, the great industrial strength depends on the highly skilled and hard-working middle and lower personnel, who have been literate for several generations.

There are two key bodies concerned with science. The first is governmental, the Council for Science and Technology, which determines state policy, includes the Prime Minister, the Ministers of Finance and Education, the Directors of the Economic Planning Agency, of the Science and Technology Agency of the Science Council of Japan.

The Science Council of Japan, formed in 1949, consists of 210 members (thirty in each of seven subject divisions) elected democratically by the whole scientific population and is an organization in which science policy in its social, political, ethical, organizational and planning aspects can be discussed, and through which scientists in general can have a voice in public affairs.

The Science and Technology Agency (formed in 1956) is the chief executive organ responsible for the administration of national institutes, the Atomic Energy Bureau, for planning and for resources, etc.

In Japan it is possible to see a group of fifty fishermen carry out a complex operation like hauling in a system of nets, without evident leaders and without commands, the group working collectively, just doing what has to be done. Decision-making in Japan has a uniquely Japanese character and this is evident also in the scientific world.

M. Piganiol (concluding the OECD review of science policy in Japan) expressed a similar view of the Japanese ways of doing things:

Japan appears to be a past master in the art of reconciling contradictory approaches. . . . She seems to have reconciled a high level of academic freedom with a real effort at coordination. She has reconciled freedom of enterprise in industry with governmental action which is extensive but efficacious. In research itself she has reconciled an approach by discipline taking into account the structure of science. Everything happens as if, beneath the structure and the organization charts, the power of persuasion was accompanied by a very powerful expression of the national will.

CHINA

China has at last undergone a thorough revolution which has entirely changed the basis of its society. The present convulsions of the 'Great

Leap Forward' (1958) and the Cultural Revolution (1966) can be understood perhaps better in terms of general systems analysis than in European political terminology. The Chinese have attacked a number of basic stabilizing factors in their civilization. Mao Tse-tung said, 'Correct ideas can only come from social practice, from the three kinds of social practice, namely, production struggle, class struggle, and scientific experiment.' This means innovation in industrial and agricultural production, in social engineering and deliberate experiment in all fields of life. The Confucian respect for dogmatic authority has been undermined. The idea that manual labour was degrading has been reversed. The bases of land ownership have been changed. The family has been changed. In fact the whole traditional system of checks and balances, of positive and negative feedbacks, has been affected. Pressures of people on each other have been generated so that the great mass of the population is affected by changes, mentally, physically, and economically. Quite tremendous forces have been unleashed and are clearly not entirely under control.

Because of the cultural revolution, education, which was expanding rapidly in a well planned way, has been in abeyance for a year, so that scientific work will have received a set-back. It appears that the ambitious twelve-year plan for science formulated in 1956, in which China aimed to catch up the rest of the world by 1968, has been abandoned, although, with the tremendous achievement of the synthesis of physiologically active insulin, and the skill in nuclear technology manifested by seven explosions, it is clear that in some fields China has reached the front lines of research. In spite of recent disturbances the production of nuclear weapons, planned since the early 1950s and culminating in explosions of U235 bombs in 1964 and 1965 and a lithium deuteride fusion bomb in 1967, has apparently continued steadily.

Some of the early observers of China, noting that an ivory carver could begin work on a complicated object, which his son would continue and his grandson would finish, asked: 'What kind of people is this that have such confidence in the continuity of their civilization?' Although the 'Great Leap Forward' and the cultural revolution have appeared as recessions in the rising curves of production, it is the very long-term effects which will be the important ones, and these are still unclear. Similarly in the scientific field the significance of present Chinese work lies in what it may portend.

Science and its methods of experimentation have been chosen as the agents of progress towards the goal of making a modern industrial nation of 1,000 million by the end of the century.

Towards this objective, although perhaps interrupted, the educational measures necessary at the primary, secondary and tertiary levels are being carried through. Starting from a thousand or so workers with higher degrees in science, and some 10,000 graduates, the numbers of qualified technical personnel now amount to about a million. Their allocation to work is directed. The Chinese Academy of Sciences is responsible for basic science to back up technology and much pure science is carried out. Proper arrangements for preserving the long-term balance between pure and applied science appear to have been made. For example, although the training of doctors has to be as rapid and as standardized as possible, special facilities are made for the training of selected students for future medical research; these are given an eight-year medical course with special emphasis on fundamental chemistry and biology. The Academy operates over a hundred research institutes and various ministries are responsible for research in their own fields.

Following the withdrawal of Russian aid in about 1962 the Chinese have had to develop science almost entirely on their own, using only the international literature. We can only wait to see what progress has been achieved when the political convulsions die down.

INDIA

India has been unfortunate in the way in which modern science has replaced the traditional systems. The volume of indigenous science and technology was quite considerable, particularly in mathematics, medicine, astronomy and linguistics. Two circumstances have had lasting effects on science. First, the native Indian materialist schools of philosophy, associated with non-conformist social and religious views, but also with alchemy, were suppressed by the official idealist schools. There were few experimentalists after the 8th century A.D. Secondly, on both occasions when new science arrived it came in the train of foreign invaders; in the medieval period the Muslim invasion preceded the flourishing science of the Mogul courts; in the modern period international science was brought in by the British Raj. Thus, active nationalists tended to view science as un-Indian and collaborationist. Even in the most recent times the anti-cow-slaughter movement and the Hindi-language riots unite xenophobic and anti-scientific elements. India is still not a mass society; the stone age and the atomic age coexist; and the rational temper is not so common even among scientists. The rise of mass education is just beginning to disturb the social structure, so cleverly and (judging by the Arthashastra which describes the government of the Mauryan empire, when in 300 B.C. Patna was one of the finest cities in the world) so deliberately engineered for hyperstability. Traditional society is beginning to be disturbed and it appears that there may be a long stage of disorganization while new social forms develop. This, of course, reacts on science. For example traditional habits such as hoarding savings as gold instead of reinvesting them as the Japanese do voluntarily and the Chinese compulsorily, greatly hinder economic growth.

India is so large that (as with China) it is only by its own efforts that it can become a modern mass society in place of the present group of communities with conflicting interests.

Modern attempts at limiting the population (now about 500 million), the increase in which fundamentally threatens Indian civilization and which has brought a series of five-year-plans to nought, have been made with a Mauryan ruthlessness (the compulsory sterilization of all males who have fathered three children is intended) but, as it is unimaginable that they should be carried out, such attempts can only lead to discredit.

In looking at India as the poorest of the rich and powerful countries it is easy to forget that she is also (scientifically as well as economically) the richest of the poor. It is clear that India, with a number of nuclear power stations coming into commission, could, unassisted by foreigners, make a nuclear bomb; fourteen Indians are, or have been, Fellows of the Royal Society; there are about fifty universities; there is considerable heavy industry and production of electrical power. It is just that, on a *per capita* basis, there is not much to go round for a population of nearly 500 million.

Science is relatively well supported by the government (but less well by the private sectors of industry) and the Council for Scientific and Industrial Research operates the principal technological laboratories on the British model. Fundamental science is also done in universities, and in the establishments of the Department of Atomic Energy, which is of very high standard. The level of scientific work in India is very variable and it has recently been the policy to concentrate the best into a number of centres of excellence so that it may have the maximum effect. Scientific manpower is not directed but unemployment among university graduates has a depressing effect on the market for scientists and emigration is not restricted (except financially). With the appearance of a free world market in manpower this has meant a tremendous loss of the better qualified and most enterprising people such as to nullify most of the technical aid supplied by the richer countries.

India's exports of tea, jute, leather, cotton (56 per cent of all her exports) are extremely vulnerable to scientific developments (such as the synthesis of indigo already mentioned) but it seems that an inadequate part of the scientific effort is employed in keeping them competitive and in developing new exports.

THE USSR IN ASIA

The larger part of the USSR lies in Asia and, although contacts with other countries of Asia are not great, the influence of the USSR, scientifically as well as politically, is enormous, since it represents one of the great alternative models which the developing countries might follow. From the beginning the USSR officially espoused science and used the slogan 'Communism is Soviet power plus the electrification of the whole country' to indicate the importance of new social forms and new technology. The USSR provides modest amounts of scientific aid, particularly to India, and of course much help was given to China before the Sino-Soviet rift.

The two huge Asian regions, Siberia and Central Asia, are not densely populated, although there is a large indigenous population in Central Asia, and every encouragement is being given for their settlement by people from the west of the USSR. Parallel with industry and population, scientific activity in these regions is growing too, the distance from Moscow being in some respects an advantage. Hitherto above half of the science of the USSR has been concentrated in Moscow and Leningrad but now efforts to construct viable concentrations of science elsewhere are being made. These counteract the internal brain drain. The principal new centre, where experiments in new forms of scientific work and education are being made, is the Academic Township of Novosibirsk. This is a complete town of some 35,000 people dedicated to the support of a range of scientific institutes of the Siberian Section of the Academy of Sciences of the USSR and to the development from them of experimental factories pioneering new products and processes. Irkutsk also is due to develop such a centre.

There are Academies of Science in the Republics of Uzbekistan (with Tashkent as a major centre), Kirgizia, Tadzhikistan and Turkmenistan, although these are largely subordinate to the Academy in Moscow. All together they run over a hundred institutes where about 1,200 scientists with higher degrees pursue their research. The general standards of science, education and public welfare are almost on the same level as in the European parts of the USSR and are far higher than in neighbouring countries. The Asiatic part of the USSR cannot be considered separately from the rest but, although the Asian societies are being integrated into a modern super-state, they have preserved their national characteristics and languages.

It is probable that many of the nuclear and space establishments of the USSR are located in Siberia and Central Asia but these form a separate network so that the 'technological fall-out' of skills and products does not influence civilian science nearly as much as it does in the USA.

Science in the USSR is planned through the State Committee for the Co-ordination of Scientific Research, descriptions of which can be found elsewhere.

BIBLIOGRAPHY

General

J. D. Bernal. *World Without War*. (Routledge & Kegan Paul, 1958.)

Ruth Gruner (Ed.). *Science and the New Nations*. (Basic Books, New York, 1961.)

D. J. de S. Price. *Science since Babylon*. (Yale University Press, New Haven, 1962.)

G. Sarton. *History of Science*. (Oxford University Press, 1953–9.)

World Federation of Scientific Workers. *Scientific World*. (London, 1957 and onwards.)

China

American Association for the Advancement of Science (AAAS). *Sciences in Communist China*. (Washington, 1961.)

China Quarterly. No. 6, pp. 19–169. (1961.)

J. Needham. *Science and Civilisation in China*. (Cambridge University Press, 1954–62.)

D. Wilgress. 'China's Leap Forward in Science'. (*Discovery*, November, 1960.)

Japan

Hideomi Tsuge. *Historical Development of Science and Technology in Japan*. (Tokyo, 1961.)

A. L. Mackay. 'Science in Japan'. (*Impact* (UNESCO), No. 12, 1962.)

Science and Technics Agency, Tokyo, Reports.

India

Information Service of India, London, Annual Reports.

Council of Scientific and Industrial Research, New Delhi. Reports.

USSR

N. de Witt. *Education and Professional Employment in the USSR*. (NSF, Washington, 1961.)

THE ASIAN PRESS

E. J. B. Rose

MANY people of Asia outside China are not yet reached by any of the modern media of mass communication. In a population of approximately 1,000 million the total circulation of all daily newspapers is 55 million, of which 43 million are sold in Japan. Whereas in Japan every two persons have one newspaper between them, in India and Indonesia a hundred people may have one newspaper between them.

In some countries the figures fall startlingly below even the overall low average. Thus in Pakistan which has a population of 110 million total newspaper circulation is not more than 600,000. or little more than the circulation of newspapers in the Philippines with a population of one quarter of its size.

Burma and Thailand are fairly representative countries with 250,000 and 300,000 daily newspapers sold in populations of 23 and 28 millions; but even in a relatively developed country like Ceylon, with a circulation of over 350,000 newspapers, a great part of the 11 million citizens never see a daily newspaper.

FACTORS LIMITING CIRCULATION

There are various economic factors which at the moment set a limit to the circulation of the press. Chief among these is of course the poverty of the people and the price of the newspaper. In India a month's subscription to a newspaper is the equivalent of one day's pay of an average worker. The cost of a cheaper newspaper in India is the equivalent of twenty minutes of labour. In Thailand, a morning paper costs 1 tekel. For 1·50 tekels a man can buy a bowl of noodles which is sufficient for his midday meal.

The result is that newspapers are passed from hand to hand and the average newspaper may be read by at least seven people. In Hong Kong and Singapore readership may be as high as 30 a paper as the teashops rent out newspapers to their customers. In the shops, where there is little work to do, the paper is passed from the owner down through the employees and, when it has been read fully by the apprentice, it is exchanged for another newspaper with the neighbouring shop.

In India and elsewhere newspapers are read aloud to groups of illiterates in the villages.

A second limiting factor is the low level of literacy, but poverty and illiteracy cannot fully account for the position in a country like India. The latest UNESCO survey estimates literacy at 25 per cent, which would give a figure of over 100 million literates, but the total circulation of all daily newspapers in all languages is barely more than 6 million. Supposing that half the literate population could not afford to buy a newspaper this would still leave more than 10 million families able to read and able to pay who at present do not buy a daily newspaper.

All governments in Asia are giving high priority to education and it is estimated that literacy rates in many countries are rising by 8 per cent a year. There is therefore going to be an ever-widening reading public which at present is not being reached by the press. It is not being reached chiefly because publishers are not producing the kind of newspaper which appeals to the new literate and to the rural worker. This is largely a matter of skills, but there are also other causes which lie in the recent colonial past.

THE VERNACULAR PRESS

The future rests with the vernacular press in Asia. English is a fading language and the standard of English is in many places declining. In Burma 99 per cent of those who fail to matriculate fail in English. In many countries English is no longer used as a medium of instruction and children now only begin to learn English at ten whereas formerly it was taught in the first grade.

However in most countries which were formerly under British rule the local language press is at present the poor relation of the English press. This is particularly true in India, Malaysia, and Pakistan. Even in Rangoon where the bulk of the newspaper circulation is in Burmese two of the three leading newspapers are produced in English. In Malaysia where half the population is Malay hardly one third of the newspaper circulation was, until very recently, in the Malay language.

In almost none of these ex-British countries has the language press got a strong economic base. Nor has it yet developed a character of its own. The English language press, very often modelled on the old British 19th-century pattern, is too political and is addressed to a small elite of businessmen, civil servants, and intellectuals. It lacks vitality. The language press mistakenly follows this pattern. Too much emphasis is placed on the leading article. Many language papers are in fact the direct descendants of the English 18th-century pamphlet. They can be disguised as newspapers because of the existence of news agencies which enable them to put news on their front and back pages, but the quality of this news, its interest for their readers and the criteria for its selection are doubtful.

Nevertheless this position is bound to change with the national awakening, the growth of literacy and as new skills are acquired. Mass circulations, when they come, will only be attained in the vernacular press.

It must not be forgotten that in some countries the press, as we know it, is not yet twenty years old. This is the case in Indonesia and Pakistan. Before 1947 there were very few Muslim journalists in India and the press of Pakistan has suffered from lack of traditions as much as from shortage of skilled workers. In India under British rule the native press was largely agitational in character; the papers were run at a loss, the editor was supported by his family and was an honoured member of the community whether in or out of gaol. After liberation all this was to change. Newspapers had to become commercial propositions and very often passed into the hands of businessmen who found them a useful adjunct to their other activities. These men have not been primarily concerned with the profession of journalism and have not promoted it adequately. Not only in India but in most of Asia the pay and conditions of employment in journalism are wretched; the journalists' morale is often very low, the standing of the profession suffers and it is hard to maintain good ethical standards.

Some of the problems of the language press in Asia spring from the nature of the languages themselves and these are mainly production problems. All news agency copy is supplied in English and has to be translated in the newspaper. This imposes an added burden on the budget as most newspapers have to employ several translators.

As the body type of most of the scripts is a minimum of nine point – in most cases it is twelve point or nearly twice the size of the body type in an English language paper – and as the languages are wordier than English and in translation run as much as 50 per cent longer than the corresponding English text, it will be seen that the amount of space available for agency news in a six- or eight-page paper is severely restricted.

In the process of translating and condensing almost all background information gets cut out and the resulting text may easily be distorted.

TECHNICAL PROBLEMS AND PRESENTATION

There are very great contrasts within the continent of Asia – ranging from the most modern methods of production in Japan, where the *Asahi Shimbun* of Tokyo produces an edition by facsimile 900 miles away in Hokkaido through a television process, to the Urdu newspapers in West Pakistan and north India which are still in the pre-Caxton age. On most Urdu papers there is not even hand-setting of type; the newspapers are written by calligraphers and then produced by lithography. The Hokkaido edition of the *Asahi* is printed within seconds of transmission of the signals from Tokyo; the first two pages of an eight-page Urdu paper have to be 'composed' nearly 24 hours before press time.

Between these extremes there are many successful newspapers and many interesting experiments. Some of the largest circulations in South and South-East Asia are in the language press. In almost all cases, except for the Chinese papers in Singapore and Hong Kong, these successful papers are written in simple direct language and carry a certain amount of entertainment features. They are not heavily political. One Tamil paper published in Madras has raised its circulation from 8,000 to 150,000 in ten years through adapting the techniques of the popular tabloid press in the West; all stories in the paper are short and tightly written; the content is on the whole sensational and is sensationally presented. In the same state of Madras there are two weekly family magazines, again in Tamil; each sells more than 100,000 copies and each must have more than half a million readers. Out of 100 pages only eight are given to politics; the rest contain short stories, serials, much of Tamil traditional culture and features for the home.

Much research and development is needed in evolving typewriters, teleprinter keyboards, and mechanical methods of setting type in the various scripts. Much is already being done. However, the future for many papers may perhaps lie with cold-type and some form of photo composition. The many difficult scripts are an obstacle to literacy and to modern production methods; the real expansion of the vernacular press may come when newspapers go over to romanized script as was done in Indonesia after the war and is now being successfully pioneered by one newspaper in Malaysia. Such a reform, though badly needed, would be a most radical step in many countries and should first be taken in the schools. The Chinese are simplifying the characters of their script, of which some three or four thousand are still needed, however, for full understanding; this could mean a great leap forward to literacy. For other languages to convert to romanized script would be a far simpler operation.

JAPAN

Japan is the shining exception in Asia. With one newspaper for every two persons in the population Japan has the highest density of newspaper readership of any country in the world except Britain. Two newspapers in Tokyo, each selling six million copies a day, have the largest daily circulations in the world. These circulations are achieved through intensive methods of distribution and because there is a *cachet* attached to reading a Tokyo newspaper. But the provincial newspapers do not allow themselves to be dominated by Tokyo and there are several papers published in the provinces with circulations of over one million.

The editorial standard of the multi-millionaire papers is remarkably high as is the overall standard of literacy throughout the country. But for the problem of language the Japanese press might well offer technical assistance to the rest of the press of Asia. It is certain that new and cheaper methods of production will be evolved in Japan for the benefit of a future Asian press.

CHINA

If Japan is a special case Communist China is a world of its own. The whole business of communication is strictly controlled in the interest of the Party and the Government and follows the Leninist pattern perfected in the Soviet Union, with some variations which are peculiar to China.

The total circulation of newspapers is estimated to be 12 million daily. This may seem to be a low figure in a population of 700 million but it must be related to the highly developed system of public reading groups which the Communists have organized and which they strictly supervise. The schools have adopted newspaper reading as part of their official curricula; and Government agencies, mass organizations, military units, commercial firms, industrial enterprises, and collective farms have organized newspaper reading groups in which literate persons read the papers to those who are illiterate. The Government carries out periodic tests to make sure that in fact the newspapers are being effectively read.

In Communist China the Government decides when, where and how many newspapers should be founded. The Government also decides who or what organizations are to be responsible for editing them. It also decides among what groups of people the various newspapers should respectively seek circulation.

Thus in recent years the Government has been concentrating on founding a regional press directed to the rural population; for example a directive issued by the Central Committee of the Party in 1956 called for the establishment of 360 new regional newspapers as a means of strengthening the Party's ideological leadership at a time when agricultural collectivization was being vigorously promoted. Up till then there had been, as in most other countries in Asia, far too much concentration of newspapers in the large cities.

In addition to the newspapers with 12 million circulation there are countless handwritten wall-newspapers in villages, factories, and in all units of the armed forces.

A most interesting feature of publishing in China is that newspapers have to try to pay their way. Subscription rates are set to cover the cost of the newsprint. The press can even take advertisements for publishing houses and certain commercial enterprises. There is very tight managerial control and a good revenue from job printing. The national dailies do in fact pay their way. In this respect the Chinese system differs almost completely from that in most other Communist countries.

Distribution over great distances is one of the greatest problems facing the press in all developing countries. In China the newspapers are distributed through the post offices. Postmen deliver and also renew and open new subscriptions. They exercise considerable pressure on the public. They also help to organize reading groups.

There is the most rigid control over the contents of the press in China. This control is exercised through selection and indoctrination of the staffs who are appointed by the Party (far more effective than censorship); through ground rules, directives and scrutiny of the press. Most news comes from the central New China News Agency. The control is in fact as nearly perfect as it can be working through human material. But it has its disadvantages. The papers are far too full of propaganda; they tend to neglect items of human interest. They are therefore dull and monotonous and to that extent not as effective an instrument of government as they might otherwise be.

GOVERNMENT CONTROL AND FREEDOM

In the rest of Asia, while there is nothing to compare with the systematic thought control practised in China, there are now only four countries where the press is free. These countries are India, Japan, Malaysia and the Philippines. In Malaysia, however, the Government is sensitive to criticism and the press finds it prudent not to be too critical; it operates a form of self-censorship; and in India few papers are financially strong enough to be indifferent to the revenue from Government advertising. Government influence particularly at the state level is often exercised through this form of patronage. However in spite of this and other kinds of pressure the Indian press does operate in a climate of freedom. Elsewhere in Asia the situation of the press has fluctuated in the last ten years. The scene is familiar and repetitive. Military dictatorships, police states, 'guided democracy' have crippled or crushed the independent press. There have been some victories by the press, notably in Japan, India and most recently in South Korea, but a press that was relatively free had been subjected in Burma, Thailand, Pakistan and, until recently, in Indonesia. In Formosa there is virtually no native press and the Chinese publications have never known freedom. In other countries what press there is is completely subservient.

As elsewhere in the world, the strongest supporter and competitor of the press in Asia is broadcasting; but as the number of intellectuals grows and the politically conscious gain influence, the press is bound to increase in volume and to improve in content. It may never become as important, however, as it is in Europe and America.

BIBLIOGRAPHY

World Press, Newspapers and News Agencies. (UNESCO, Paris, 1964.)

Economic Affairs

THE ECONOMY OF INDIA

Taya Zinkin

A RURAL ECONOMY

INDIA is a country of poor peasants. Five sixths of the population live in the countryside. Three out of four depend on agriculture. Four in five of those who live off the land own something; but a half of all the farmers own an acre or less, and large estates are so few that if everything over 30 acres were confiscated, only about 10 per cent of the land would become available.

The average size of a farm varies with the part of the country and the quality of the land. Three acres is quite a good holding of coconuts and areca nuts and rice in Kerala; fifteen is only just enough in the dry millet lands of the Deccan. Taking the country as a whole, five acres is about the mean.

With holdings of this size, poverty, by European standards, is inevitable. Moreover, yields are low; eight cwts. of wheat per acre, ten cwts. of paddy, are in India very reasonable yields. In England, the farmer expects to get three times as much wheat from his acre, and the Japanese farmer gets three times as much paddy from his.

Most of what is grown is used for the subsistence of farmer and family. Only one third of the foodgrains grown is sold, the rest is eaten by the farmer and his family. This does not always make for the most efficient use of land; a man will grow millet when it would be much more profitable to grow cotton or groundnuts because he wants to be sure of his food.

Five acres at 800 lbs. of wheat to an acre must mean poverty. Naturally the Indian income per head is only 10s. per week. In the countryside indeed, it is lower than 10s., for people are slightly better off in the small towns, and very much better off in the big ones, especially in the great cities of Bombay, Madras, Calcutta and Delhi – each of them bigger than any English town except London – where incomes are at least twice the national average.

Although the farmer grows mainly foodgrains, these are not his only crops. He gets his protein mainly from pulses, though he does also eat some animal protein, mainly goat or chicken and, in the coastal or riverain areas, fish; he does not eat beef, and India has very little mutton or lamb. India also grows some 5 million bales of cotton a

655

year and over 5 million bales of jute, enough to keep going the world's largest jute industry and its second largest cotton textile industry.

The small size of Indian farms is the result of a combination of two circumstances, the pressure of population on the land and very labour-intensive agricultural techniques. Until 1920 or so, the population grew slowly. It may have been little larger in 1900 than in 1800, and between 1890 and 1920 it hardly grew at all. But since 1920 it has been growing at an increasing pace, which is now probably more than $2\frac{1}{2}$ per cent per year and, up to now, most of this increase has had to find its place on the land. The percentage of the population living in towns may well be no higher now than 150 years ago.

This concentration on the land is made worse by the Hindu and Muslim laws of inheritance. Every son is entitled to a share of the family estate. If there are four acres and four sons, each son gets one acre; and once a man has some land, he tends to be tied to his village. Land gives so much prestige that nobody will cut himself off from his village if he can help it. Every factory, even today, has to face a large demand for leave from its employees as soon as the harvest season comes round.

This fragmentation of ownership, however, only exacerbates a tendency already inherent in Indian techniques of cultivation. The plough animal over most of India is the bullock – in paddy land it is sometimes the buffalo. Even on light dry land a pair of bullocks cannot manage more than fifteen acres or so; in heavy or wet land they can manage less still; and in areas like Orissa or Tanjore, where the cattle are poor, one may need more than one pair to plough the same field; one can sometimes see as many as eight pairs operating in tandem. And each pair of bullocks requires a ploughman. Methods of transplantation and of harvesting are similarly extravagant of labour. At transplanting each paddy plant has to be put in separately; this requires whole teams of women for every field. At harvest each stalk is either pulled out or cut with a little sickle, individually. This too requires whole teams of men and women for every field.

The Indian peasant is skilled in his own tradition; and he is much quicker than is generally believed to accept profitable innovations. But many of his methods are basically inefficient. He treats the cow as sacred; so there are two cattle for every three people, many cattle give neither milk nor labour, and the Indian rice areas swarm with the world's poorest animals. He is only beginning to learn how to select his seed; proper seed-farms did not exist until recently. He uses most of his cowdung for fuel; he has no option, he cannot get coal and most villages are lacking in wood. Chemical fertilizers are a new idea, and, though demand now exceeds supply, this is because the supply is still so pathetically small, a million or so tons in terms of nitrogen per year. Erosion is, in all the unirrigated areas, an ever present threat. Cereals are grown on the same land year after year; the farmer very often ploughs downhill instead of along the contours; the rains come in torrents and cut great gullies out of the bare slopes. Not nearly enough legumes are grown for a proper rotation. Most animal breeding is casual, without any deliberate selection of the sire.

The poverty that comes from too small holdings and too little application of modern methods is compounded by the high charges the peasant has to pay when he borrows or rents or sells. Tenancy has been greatly reduced of late years by legislation enabling the tenant to buy his landlord out; but a good deal – just how much nobody knows – still remains, and despite laws prescribing lower levels, the tenant still usually pays half his crop as rent. Moneylenders now have to be licensed, and interest is limited by law; but most borrowing is still from patrons or relations or shopkeepers or merchants, and at rates well above the legal maximum: 18 per cent to 25 per cent is frequent, anything under 12 per cent exceptional. There are co-operative societies for the giving of credit, and the Government has been pouring funds into them, but they still do only a small part of all rural lending. This is partly because so many of the rural population are not creditworthy by any reasonable business standards, partly because so much of the borrowing is for unproductive purposes. A man will hesitate to put himself deeply in debt for fertilizer or to build a well. He cannot hesitate if he has a daughter to marry, a son's thread ceremony to perform, or a mother's funeral to conduct. These social obligations are expensive. A wedding can easily cost a year's income.

The peasant also loses when he comes to sell. He needs money quickly when his harvest comes in. He has the land revenue to pay, his creditors may be pressing, he has things he wants to buy. So prices dip at harvest time, and the frequent unscrupulousness of the merchant means that the simpler farmers do not even get the whole of the lower price. Even if the merchant is totally honest, the price in the village is bound to be low. The collection of many small parcels and their storage over several months is an expensive business, especially when, as happens very often, the peasant does not take his crop to market but expects the merchant to come and fetch it in the village. This is particularly expensive because communications are bad. Most villages are not on a road of any sort. When the rains come, they are cut off;

and even when there is no rain, there are usually two or three unbridged streams between them and the main road; the strain of pulling a load up the banks of these streams is severe, so the bullock carts carry less than they would if the roads were good.

Nature, too, is against the villager. Many soils are light, and exhausted by hundreds of years of cereal growing. When there is water, there is often too much; the rain pours down, inches in a day, and there are floods. But most of the time, over most of the countryside, there is not enough water. Crops fail, or are not as good as they might have been because the rain was inadequate, or did not come at the right time, or was too heavy when it did come. Some 80 million acres are now irrigated, and along the coasts, especially, there are areas whose rain is reasonably certain. But even in the irrigated areas, the water can fail if there is no rain in the catchment areas away in the hills; and the unirrigated areas of uncertain rainfall are still perhaps three quarters of the total.

Traditionally, the Indian peasant provided for extra sons by reclaiming new land. In some areas this process was still in full swing in the 1930s. But now it is virtually finished. Over half of India's land surface is now arable; in most States the forest has been reduced well below what is desirable, and many villages have no pasture-land left at all. There is still some room for reclamation, but it is no longer of the old sort. Now it involves tractors and a major effort by the State to make ravines cultivable, or to get rid of Kans grass. For more people to be able to get a living from the land in future, agriculture will have to become more intensive. There will have to be more fertilizer, better seed, more water, more artificial insemination in the flocks and herds, more changing over from farming for subsistence to farming for cash.

For this to happen more knowledge and more capital must be applied to the land. Better seed means seed-farms and money to buy it with. More fertilizers means fertilizer factories, and again money to buy them with. More artificial insemination means more veterinary surgeons, more good sires, more veterinary clinics, and, in due course, money to pay a fee with. More water means more wells, more dams, more canals, and money to pay the water rate with. All of it means more activity by the Government. There has to be more extension work. There has to be more credit, without which the farmer will not be able to pay for the fertilizer, the seed, the wells, or any of the other hundred and one improvements, from gully-stopping to orchards, which his land may need. More credit means more co-operative societies, and more

Government money for them so that they will have enough to lend. There was virtually no Government money in the co-operative movement in 1947; there is now several hundred million pounds.

Poorest of all in the countryside are the agricultural labourers. Just how many of them there are is hard to say. Most small owners, and nearly every tenant, also do some agricultural labour. When a man has no work to do on his own land, he ekes out his living by working on somebody else's land; when there are two brothers sharing a farm hardly big enough for one, one or other will spend much of his time working for other people. On the other hand, many of those who return themselves in a census as labourers probably have at least a cottage-garden; a considerable proportion will have half an acre or so of their own or perhaps on lease. But the number of those who are predominantly labourers must be approaching twenty million; those who do some agricultural labour may be three times that or more.

The lot of the agricultural labourer, like everything else, varies a good deal from one part of the country to another. In parts of the Punjab, where irrigation has just been provided and labour is still scarce, a man may earn 4s. a day and have work for virtually as many days as he wishes. In parts of Madras or Kerala where population has been rising rapidly and no new land has come under cultivation he may earn 1s. 6d. a day and count himself fortunate if he works 180 days a year, though this will be supplemented by work at lower rates for the wife and children at such peak times as harvest.

The peasant spends two thirds of his income on food alone though much of this of course is not expenditure in the market sense of the word but home-grown produce consumed in the home. After that, and after ceremonies and taxes, he does not have much left over for anything else. He buys salt from the town, perhaps sugar, almost certainly kerosene and matches, probably soap; sometimes he will have a cup of tea or coffee; occasionally he may buy a newspaper or visit a cinema or go on a pilgrimage by train or to town by bus, or get a rim for his cart-wheel or a sari for his wife. That is virtually all. His demands on the rest of the economy are limited in the extreme; which is why the rest of the economy is so small.

India has, it is true, a very considerable railway system, over 40,000 miles of line connecting up every major centre; and this railway system is so heavily loaded that it is one of the few left in the world which still makes a profit. India has a cotton textile industry which produces more than 7 billion yards of cloth a year (including handloom production), a jute industry which produces a little over a million tons of jute cloth a year, a steel industry which will soon produce 6 million tons of steel a year, and growing chemical and engineering industries. But that is the whole of India's modern industry. In relation to the country as a whole it is tiny. All factory employment put together is less than one fiftieth of total employment. Industry is still a few small islands in a very large ocean, important in perhaps a dozen cities, and that is all.

INADEQUATE INFRASTRUCTURE

India does not even have yet an adequate infrastructure. The railways are overloaded; low priority traffic sometimes has great difficulty in moving at all, while a third-class passenger coach is the nearest human equivalent to a sardine tin known. Electric power, although it doubles every five years or so, is still only a fraction of that available per head in Western countries, and is quite inadequate; there is hardly any part of the country which has not suffered severely from power cuts over the last few years, and which does not anticipate more power cuts to come. The road system is improving, but it is still equally inadequate. Many major rivers are still unbridged; the asphalted parts of roads are often wide enough only for one vehicle; only the major roads are asphalted at all. Buses and lorries manage somehow to get their passengers and goods even over dirt tracks without culverts; but wear and tear is enormous, and makes worse the already high costs resulting from punishing high taxation.

Motor vehicles are not alone in paying high taxes. Although the percentage of the national income which goes in tax is relatively low, this is because the people are poor, not because the taxes are low. India has a combination of taxes on the rich – income-tax, super-tax, capital-gains-tax, wealth-tax, gifts-tax, estate-duty – equalled elsewhere only by Ceylon. A rich Indian cannot pay all his taxes and be left with anything to spend unless he is very good at making capital gains. Nor are indirect taxes light. Everything is taxed (except salt because of the memory of Gandhi's salt march), everything, from kerosene to soap, from steel to cooking fat; and taxes are high; between municipal octrois and State sales taxes and Central excises 25 per cent is a frequent level, and on such necessities as cloth and sugar it is usually higher still. Not much except foodgrains and certain handicraft articles is exempt from tax, and even that is not universal.

Although taxes are high, revenues are low. The State is poor; or perhaps one should say the States, for India is a federation, where the centre has the main taxes and controls the economy as a whole but where the States are entitled to such important taxes as the sales tax and the land revenue, together with a share of certain central taxes, and look after such vital subjects as education, health, agriculture and law and order.

The poverty of the State reflects itself in many ways. The armed forces are small for a country of 500 million people, and the part with modern equipment is smaller still. The need to increase them to meet the Chinese threat is placing a crushing burden on the economy. It will be the end of the sixties before all children even in the age group 6–11 are at school; at present more than half the girls get no education at all; and it is a rare villager who gets to secondary school, let alone to university, though a large percentage of townsmen do both. Most villagers see a doctor only in an epidemic or when seriously ill; there is rarely a doctor in the village, and the nearest dispensary is normally some miles away. They see a nurse more seldom still; there is only one trained nurse for every 11,000 people. Social services are virtually confined to clerical staff and factory labour. They get a health service and provident funds, though not unemployment pay. The rest of the population gets nothing, except for a very modest beginning with old-age pensions in Andhra; though the hospitals are free, when there is a hospital.

DEVELOPMENT

The most serious effect of the poverty of the State and the community, however, is upon development. It is difficult for a poor country to make the savings which are necessary for development. It is almost equally difficult for it to find the money to develop the many specialized skills development needs.

In 1947 in India probably about 5 per cent of the national income was saved. This was just about enough to ensure that the increase in population – already then over one per cent per annum – did not lead to a positive drop in standards; it was not enough to provide for any improvement. Income per head in India in 1950 may well have been no higher than in 1880. There has been a steady effort to increase savings, but even now they are not more than 10 per cent of the national income. Moreover, three quarters of the savings are invested directly by the people who make them. Most Indians, perhaps as many as 80 per cent, are self-employed, as peasants, as shopkeepers, or as craftsmen; when they save, they put the money straight back into their own enterprises. The shopkeeper buys more stock or gets a bigger shop; the craftsman may take in an assistant or two; the peasant digs a well, or makes some contour bunds, or buys a new pair of bullocks. All of them build themselves houses, even if only of mud and wattle, or timber and bamboo; the really successful villager may build in brick or stone. This habit of self-finance extends into industry. About half of the profits of companies after tax are ploughed back, and this is the major source of company finance, though it is possible for a company with a progressive profit record or a well-known foreign collaborator to raise money in the market.

The Government gets about one fifth of total savings; some of this comes from savings certificates, but much of it is the result of the legal requirement that provident funds must be invested in Government securities and of the Government's ownership of the Life Insurance Corporation, the Reserve Bank (the Central bank) and the biggest commercial bank. The Government also makes a profit on certain of its enterprises, notably banks and railways.

Modern skills are nearly as difficult as savings. What managers India has got are, on the whole, good, but in an economy which is now really beginning to expand, they are inevitably scarce. In chemicals and engineering and steel, where in the past the Indian industry was very small, there are very few people with the necessary training and experience, and each new factory means a new training programme. Moreover, the Indian universities before the war produced overwhelmingly arts graduates. Only since the war has it become the fashionable thing for the bright young man to do physics or engineering. Engineering colleges, science faculties, polytechnics and medical colleges are now being built as fast as the staff can be found for them, but management is still a bottleneck.

Nor is management the only bottleneck. There are equally serious difficulties lower down, at the level of the foreman, the fitter, and the overseer of public works; and this bottleneck is even harder to cure, for so much of the training has to be practical and on the job. It takes longer to make a good overseer than a good engineer.

The most backward area of all in the Indian economy is small industry, under which name one may include both the handicrafts and such artisan professions as motor repairing or very small-scale engineering. This is traditional in its methods, badly lacking in modern equipment, and very short of capital. There is very considerable Government assistance, for the small industrialist through such measures as industrial estates, special advisory services, and special financing arrangements, for the handicraftsman through training schemes, tax preferences and sometimes limitations on the big business right to expand. This special assistance has had some success. Handloom weaving, for instance, which had been declining for a century, is now beginning to expand again.

THE FIVE-YEAR PLANS

This burgeoning, like the extension service in agriculture or the new colleges, is one of the results of India's new five-year plans. The first plan began in 1951. Three have been completed so far, and the fourth is due to start. Achievement already is very considerable. The national income increased by two thirds over the fifteen years of the first three plans, and this included an increase in agricultural production of very nearly as much. There are now one and three quarter million students at university, seven times as many as pre-war, and roughly as many in proportion to the population as in Great Britain, though standards are of course lower; most students do pass degrees. The death rate has been nearly halved, and malaria brought under control by a nation-wide campaign of DDT spraying. Improved varieties of wheat and rice promise revolutionary improvements in yields wherever water and fertilizer are available; and there is hope that similar improvements may soon be achieved with millet. Millions of acres have been contour-bunded, hundreds of thousands of holdings have been consolidated, there is a bigger demand for fertilizer than the Government can satisfy, absentee landlords have been got rid of, a stable industrial labour force has been created, industrial peace has been largely preserved by an elaborate structure of compulsory arbitration. The figure for steel production increased from one to nearly seven million tons by 1967. There have been some promising discoveries of oil, four refineries have been built, and two more are building. A machine industry has been established. India now makes most of its own textile and sugar machinery, and nearly all its own diesel engines, for instance. Production of chemicals has grown threefold and India now produces most of the standard chemicals like sulphuric acid or chlorine or caustic soda for itself. Banking has been pushed into the smallest towns, life insurance is being sold throughout the middle classes, the co-operative movement has been reorganized, the range of taxation has been greatly widened. In short, an economy which had been stagnant for centuries is, at last, getting off the ground in a way that is obvious not only in the figures, but to the naked eye. Wherever one goes around India, one can see new power stations, new roads, new bridges, new schools, new dams, new electrified railways, new dispensaries, new factories, new contour bunds, new canals, taller crops and better cattle.

Development of this sort very rapidly acquires its own momentum. Every year the national income increases, savings increase, the number of the specially skilled increases, the taxable capacity increases, the effect of the extension services increases. There is a benevolent as well as a vicious circle in economics, and until 1965 India was turning on this bright circle, despite the diversion of resources to defence which followed the Chinese attack of 1962. But then came the monsoon failures of 1965 and 1966, and the war with Pakistan of 1965. Now everything has been plunged back into doubt, as the economy labours and the Fourth Five-Year Plan is postponed. A couple of good monsoons will start the economy up again, but certain requirements will remain. Above all, there is the need for foreign exchange for the import of machinery and raw materials. The need for these goes up and up; India's capacity to pay for them does not. India's main exports are tea, cotton textiles, and jute textiles, and for all of these world demand is sluggish. Nor is it easy to find new exports. India's new industries can rarely export; their costs are too high or their quality is too low or their products are too urgently needed at home. Agriculture no sooner increases its production than the cotton or rice or groundnuts or whatever it may be is absorbed by the insatiable demand at home. The foreign exchange deficit is at least £500 million per year. If this foreign exchange is not found, India's rate of progress will slow down until it is barely able to provide for the growth of population; or, alternatively, India will have to become more totalitarian in order to squeeze the necessary sacrifices of consumption out of its population. But if the foreign exchange is found there is no reason why this century should not see the end of India's age-old problem of poverty. India will still not be rich, in the Western way; but it may at least be moderately comfortable.

THE THIRD PLAN

	1960–1	1965–6 Targets	1965–6 Achievements
Foodgrains production (in million tons)	76·0	100·0	77·0
Nitrogenous fertilizer consumed (thousand tons of N)	230·0	1,000·0	600·0
Area irrigated (in million acres)	70·0	90·0	77·0
Co-operative advances to farmers (in million £)	150·0	397·0	285·0

	1960–1	1965–6 Targets	1965–6 Achievements
Steel ingots (in million tons)	3·5	9·2	6·2
Aluminium (in thousand tons)	18·5	80·0	74·0
Machine tools (value in million £)	4·2	22·5	16·5
Sulphuric acid (in thousand tons)	363·0	1,500·0	675·0
Petroleum products (in million tons)	5·7	9·9	9·9
Mill made cloth (in million yards)	5,127·0	5,800·0	5,100·0
Other than mill made (in million yards)	2,349·0	3,500·0	3,450·0
Iron ore (in million tons)	10·7	30·0	22·0
Coal (in million tons)	54·6	97·0	67·0
Exports (in million £)	480·0	640·0	–
Power (in million kilowatts)	5·7	12·7	10·2
Railway freight carried (in million tons)	154·0	245·0	205·0
Vehicles on the road (in thousands)	210·0	365·0	328·0
Students in school (in millions)	43·5	63·9	60·0 (1963–4)
Hospital beds (in thousands)	186·0	240·0	240·0
Practising doctors (in thousands)	70·0	81·0	86·0
Food (in calories per capita per day)	2,100·0	2,300·0	–
Cloth (in yards per capita per year)	15·5	17·2	–
Cement (in million tons)	8·5	13·0	10·5 (1965)

Production of Major Crops

	1960–1	1965–6 Targets	1965–6 Achievements
Foodgrains (in million tons)	76·0	100·0	76·0
Oilseeds (in million tons)	7·1	9·8	7·5
Sugarcane (in million tons)	8·0	10·0	12·3
Cotton (in million bales)	5·1	7·0	5·4
Jute (in million bales)	4·0	6·2	4·5
Tea (in million lbs.)	725·0	900·0	827·0

Transport and Communication

	1960–1	1965–6 Targets	1965–6 Achievements
Railway new lines (in miles)	800·0	1,200·0	–
Railway new double lines (in miles)	1,300·0	1,600·0	–
Railway freight carried (in million tons)	154·0	245·0	205·0
Post offices (in thousands)	77·0	94·0	98·0
Telegraph offices (in thousands)	6·5	8·5	8·6
Telephone connexions (in thousands)	460·0	660·0	873·0

BIBLIOGRAPHY

F. G. Bailey. *Caste and the Economic Frontier*. (Humanities Press, New York, 1958.)

C. Bettelheim. *L'Inde indépendante*. (Armand Colin, Paris, 1962.)

T. S. Epstein. *Economic Development and Social Change in South India*. (Manchester University Press, Manchester, 1962.)

W. Malenbaum. *Prospects of Indian Development*. (Allen & Unwin, 1962.)

W. B. Reddaway. *The Development of the Indian Economy*. (Allen & Unwin, 1962.)

G. Rosen. *Democracy and Economic Change in India*. (University of California Press, Berkeley, 1966.)

The Third Five Year Plan. (Planning Commission, Government of India, New Delhi, 1961.)

M. Zinkin. *Development for Free Asia*. (Chatto & Windus, 1961.) *India*.

T. Zinkin. *India*. (Thames & Hudson, 1965.) *Challenges in India*. (Chatto & Windus, 1966.)

THE ECONOMY OF CHINA

Werner Klatt

CHINA is undergoing a process of change the like of which has probably never been experienced in modern history. The degree of success or failure of the experiment, carried out under the strict control of the Communist Party which has ruled the country since 1949, will affect directly more than a quarter of the human race. It is bound to have an impact also beyond the borders of China in countries recently freed from Western colonial rule and bent on solving their political, social and economic problems without giving the appearance of Western tutelage. The Chinese model, being Asian in its practical application even if European in its doctrinal origin, tends to have its attraction where the Soviet variant of Communism is suspected of being only another form of domination by whites over non-whites.

The Chinese pattern is watched with all the more interest as it represents an attempt to turn an overpopulated, underdeveloped agrarian society, in the shortest possible space of time and with the minimum of foreign assistance, into the third most highly industrialized nation on earth. Unlike Russia which had experienced some of the birth pains of industrialization when it entered the phase of Communist revolution, China showed all the marks of economic backwardness and social stagnation of an underdeveloped country when the Communists dislodged the Kuomintang from its seat of power.

OVERRIDING POLITICAL CONSIDERATIONS

Born a child of the revolution, China's economy cannot deny its political parentage. It would thus be futile to describe development during the last decade as if it was an economic phenomenon free of political overtones. Some observers believed for a good many years that Chairman Mao, the founder of the new China, was a mere agrarian reformer. By now there can be no doubt about the solid Marxist training of all the leading Chinese Communists. This is not to say that they applied uncritically the formulae of the Soviet textbooks in their own revolutionary situation. On the contrary, they displayed a large measure of originality when faced with problems which none of the European Communist leaders could have anticipated.

This is not the place to argue whether and to what extent the Chinese model is a mere variant of the Soviet one. The Chinese leaders originally consulted the Soviet precedent whenever they were faced with a new problem. At the same time they have shown much ingenuity on more than one occasion when instigating institutional changes of their own in a specifically Chinese situation. The 'Great Leap' and the 'Cultural Revolution' are only the most eminent and the most recent cases in point. The short history of Communist China's development provides other instances.

WARTIME DESTRUCTION

When the Chinese Communists came to power in 1949, they inherited a country which had been disrupted by many years of war and civil war. Moreover, Manchuria, the only industrial base of the country, where investment had been increased fivefold during the ten years of Japanese occupation, was largely depleted of its industry. Industrial equipment was dismantled and removed when the Soviet Army entered the country. In the rural areas China had suffered more from lawlessness and lack of security than from the destruction of transport and communications; the most important part of an infrastructure was still in its infancy at the time of the Communist seizure of power. The majority of the population was able to live and work in the villages provided rivalling warlords allowed it to do so.

At least four fifths of the population were villagers and the bulk of them worked on the land, the non-farm population being engaged in local handicraft and trade rather than industry and commerce which was limited to a few urban areas along the seashore. After years of war and internal strife farming operations were not at their best. In particular irrigation canals had been neglected all too long. Even so output per acre was higher than in most other parts of Asia outside Japan. Against this, productivity of labour was as low as elsewhere in Asia. Farming provided little beyond the meagre subsistence level maintained by the producer. Inequalities in rural areas were great as the polarization of the village community had reached extreme forms. Landlords and tenants were worlds apart.

The true picture of the level of production in 1949 will probably never be known, but even if it had not declined as much as Communist statements maintained later on, there can be no doubt that it was low by previous standards. Its recovery was dependent upon the restoration of law and order so long absent from rural areas and urban centres of production. The Communist leadership made this its first task. It was of course a Communist type of law and order that was created. Side by side with the establishment of political and administrative control, the stabilization of prices, the introduction of a unified tax system, the repair of industrial plant and transport equipment, and the redistribution of land, violent campaigns were directed against landlords, industrialists, and traders, many of whom were treated as counter-revolutionaries. The 'anti-campaigns' against the enemies of the revolution and their excesses were intensified after the outbreak of the Korean war in 1950.

PERIOD OF RESTORATION

During the period of restoration, from 1949 to 1952, China's economic policy was governed by the Common Programme which had been adopted by the Chinese People's Political Consultative Conference in September 1949. Five years later it was superseded by the Constitution of the Chinese People's Republic which was adopted by the National People's Congress in September 1954. During the period of transition certain concessions were made to existing institutional conditions, but the ultimate aim was the 'socialist' transformation of agriculture, handicraft, industry and commerce and in particular the creation of the 'socialist' industrialization of the country. This meant that expropriation of foreign and indigenous capital, industrialization of the heavy type and collectivization of agriculture represented the overriding political targets of Communism in China. Whereas in the first stages of the revolution a policy of a united front was pursued and collectivization was rejected as an immediate aim, the ultimate pattern of the economic policy was never in doubt.

By the end of the period of restoration institutional changes were well under way; they had followed familiar Communist patterns. As to economic performance, the Chinese Communists claimed that pre-war peak levels of output had been surpassed by 16 per cent in the case of producer goods and by 32 per cent in consumer goods. Whilst these were exaggerated claims, by the end of 1952 the pre-war level of output had on balance been restored. China was thus ready to embark on a programme of 'transition to socialism' which was expected to take three five-year plan periods, i.e. from 1953 to 1967. The plan was to be worked out by the State Planning Committee (later named State Planning Commission). Later a National Economic Commission was created to supervise the drafting and implementation of the annual portions of the Plan.

THE FIRST FIVE-YEAR PLAN

Although work on the first five-year plan had begun in 1951, it was not ready for adoption by the State Council until the middle of 1955, two and a half years after the plan era had been officially inaugurated. Statistical services were far from perfect and statistical data were subject to extensive revisions until the end of 1954. The plan when eventually published showed the marks of the Soviet pattern. In fact the Soviet Union was mentioned explicitly as the model for China. Nearly 60 per cent of all investment was earmarked for industry, and nearly nine tenths of this amount was allocated to heavy industry, little over one tenth being available for the development of consumer industries. Less than 8 per cent of total investment was set aside for agriculture, forestry, and water conservation.

Shortly after the publication of the first five-year plan Mao Tse-tung asked for the rapid collectivization of agriculture which had hardly recovered from the effects of a drastic land reform. The planners had not allowed for a major institutional change of this kind to be carried out before the end of the first plan. It led almost immediately to difficulties in food supplies which necessitated strict rationing in cities as well as villages. This was only the first major unplanned dislocation of production in the countryside.

RELIABILITY OF STATISTICS

So as not to create a misunderstanding about the significance of data quoted in this essay, something will have to be said about the nature of Chinese statistics. As in Russia, they are regarded as a political instrument of the Communist regime rather than a technical device with which to record and assess economic and social processes. As statistics are considered of vital importance to the state, their disclosure has been made a capital offence. In trying to penetrate the partial blackout of information on economic development, Western observers have thus to rely on the very limited amount of factual information released by the Chinese authorities. This was regarded on the whole as free from deliberate falsification until the end of 1957, but even then data on industrial production or foreign trade in physical units could be trusted more than farm statistics, aggregate value data, or indices of gross production, labour productivity and national income.

China does not publish statistical yearbooks or reports of the kind now generally available in countries of the Soviet bloc. As statistical services are extended, there is a tendency towards increased secrecy in reporting. Discrepancies are generally regarded as due to obscurity in methodological concepts and statistical definitions rather than deliberate distortions, but a caveat has to be entered here with regard to the year 1958 when the attempt was made to establish a network of primary statistical units throughout the rural districts of China. This move coincided with the 'Great Leap Forward' and led to 'mass participation' in statistical work under Party leadership. Statistics handled became a tool in the hands of local political cadres instead of being handled by trained men of professional integrity. All statistical progress reports suffered from a strong upward bias, if they were not outright fabrications.

The revised agricultural targets for 1958, the first year of the second five-year plan, called for doubling the grain output within one year; the plan results not surprisingly recorded an all-time record harvest of 375 million tons compared with 175 million tons in 1957. The disaster that was to follow this gross exaggeration, though dismissed as improbable by some observers at the time, could be foreseen. After half the crop had been consumed, statistical recounts were ordered which yielded a revised grain estimate of 250 million tons, a figure which was probably still overstated by at least 12 per cent. Similar exaggerations occurred in other sectors of the mass production drive, such as in small-scale iron and steel production. Since 1958 Chinese statistical reports have become less and less frequent. The volume of data flowing from Peking can be regarded as a measure of success or failure not only of the statistical services, but of the whole system of economic planning.

THE SECOND FIVE-YEAR PLAN

Draft proposals for the second Five-Year Plan due to start in 1958 were made known in 1956. The new plan was even more ambitious than its predecessor. Material production of industry, handicraft and agriculture was to increase in five years by as much as 75 per cent compared with the plan figure of 51 per cent in the previous plan. The emphasis was even more than before on the increased output of producer goods whose share in total industrial production was expected to rise from 38 per cent as planned for 1957 to 50 per cent in 1962. Consumer goods were to decline correspondingly from 62 per cent previously to 50 per cent at the end of the second plan. These were ambitious targets which were said to require twice the amount of capital investment set aside during the first plan when it absorbed between one fifth and one quarter of the nation's total efforts.

When the plan was due to start in 1958, no detailed targets were known. Like its forerunner it represented little more than an expression of intent. The political leadership saw it within the wider framework of its economic policy which was to aim, within fifteen years, at over-taking Britain in the output of iron, steel and other important industrial products. During the last year of the first plan the economy had been so seriously overtaxed that the pace of economic development had to be slowed down and intellectuals and professionals had to be given a period of grace. As Mao's advice to 'let a hundred flowers bloom' had led to outspoken criticism on a large scale, new ways had to be found to mobilize the bourgeoisie as well as the masses in the interest of the second plan.

The Soviet leaders had shown the way when they replaced bureau-cratic centralism by decentralized forms of control. The sweeping institutional changes that were introduced in China during the first year of the second plan were an adaptation rather than an imitation of the Soviet model. They were nevertheless ill-conceived since the economic planners had in no way provided for them. The new course was introduced by Liu Shao-chi, the Party's theoretician, at the second session of the eighth Party Congress held in 1958. Representing the wing of the Party which wished to forge ahead without making con-cessions to public sentiments, Liu asked for a great leap forward in economic development through mass participation on a nation-wide scale. This led to feverish activities which were directed by local Party cadres and which were aimed at achieving the production targets of the second plan in the course of one year instead of five. By the autumn of 1958, some 600,000 small-scale furnaces were reported to have been set up, employing over a million people with no previous experience in industrial processes. The steel target of the year was raised from 6·2 million tons early in 1958 to 8 million tons in the summer and nearly 11 million tons, or twice the output of 1957, in the autumn of 1958. At the end of the year it was claimed that gross industrial output had increased by 65 per cent within the preceding twelve months.

THE 'GREAT LEAP FORWARD'

The targets set for agriculture were no less fantastic. Some 100 million cultivators were apparently organized for the purpose of building irrigation canals which were to raise the acreage under wet crops by 30 per cent within one year. At the same time home-produced fertilizers were to be manufactured, deep ploughing, close planting and other new farm techniques were to be introduced on a massive scale. The direction and control of labour in a campaign of such vast dimensions required forms of organization for which there was no precedent in the history of Communism. In the autumn of 1958, the so-called People's Communes were created and by the end of the year over 700,000 agricultural producer co-operatives (set up as recently as 1957) were reported to have merged into some 26,000 communes with an average of almost 5,000 rural families and 10,000 acres of land. Urban communes were to be set up on a similar pattern.

Much has been written in the last few years about the principal features of the communes, their multi-character within the setting of the second Five-Year Plan and the 'Great Leap Forward'. Apart from mobilizing surplus labour for the dual purpose of raising the output of industry without impeding farm production, the communes were designed to effect drastic changes in the structure of Chinese society, in family relations, and in the values and loyalties of the individual. Whereas it is still too early to draw the final balance sheet of this mass experiment in social engineering, there can be no doubt that the price paid, in human terms, has been heavy indeed. The dislocation of work in the fields at the height of the paddy harvest set in motion a downward trend in agriculture which has only recently been brought to a standstill. The resentment caused was such that a halt had to be called in 1959 which led to a period of economic and organizational retrenchment. Since 1960 the communes have ceased to control agriculture. Administrative authority is now vested in the production brigades which supervise, much like the former agricultural producer co-operatives, on average some 250 households. Work in the fields is done under contract by production teams, consisting as a rule of some 40 households. Private plots and rural markets which were eliminated in 1958 are allowed again so as to provide incentives to the cultivators. However, in three successive years of poor yields caused by bad weather and political mismanagement farm production fell well below the level reached in 1957. This level was surpassed for the first time in 1964 and it was maintained during the following three years.

At first the Chinese Communist leaders were so certain of success that they claimed a major shortcut on the way towards Communism to be possible owing to the creation of the communes. This led to an ideological clash with the Soviet Union with whom relations had not been any too cordial since the time of the uprising in Eastern Europe. China, preoccupied with the completion of her first plan and the drafting of the second, was pained to see $1,000 million worth of

Soviet aid go to unreliable European members of the bloc; all the more so as, though badly in need of foreign aid herself, she was in fact repaying short-term Soviet trade credits. The second plan was thus designed on the assumption that China had to rely on her own resources and could not expect foreign aid for her economic development.

SINO-SOVIET ECONOMIC RELATIONS

Only the two Soviet loans of February 1950 and October 1954, providing the equivalent of $430 million, are known for certain. Military aid during and after the Korean war was given, but the amount granted remains a closely guarded secret. In addition China accumulated between 1950 and 1955 almost $1,000 million in short-term trade balances. In 1956 she began to repay these and her trading deficit with the Soviet Union turned into a surplus by 1962 of approximately $125 million. In 1964 only a small amount was outstanding on the repayment of the Soviet long-term loans. China's balance of payments position is not known, but the surplus was sufficient to meet the commitments which fell due in 1961 to 1964, when after some poor harvests over $250 million had to be made available each year for the purchase of 5 million tons of Canadian, Australian, and West European grains. Foreign exchange commitments of this kind have to be met from savings in imports and from earnings through exports of commodities and bullion as well as overseas Chinese remittances. China's trade has been adjusted drastically to the policy of economic retrenchment. Imports of plant equipment have been cut severely so as to make room for foodstuffs. At the same time exports have been kept up fairly well, though their volume is also reduced. Sino-Soviet trade turnover in 1963 amounted to less than one half of the average of the previous five years. China's exports to the Soviet Union were halved within three years and her imports from the Soviet Union were reduced at the same time to one fifth. Even so, Soviet Russia's contribution to China's industrial development must not be underrated. Before China was obliged to settle on a policy of economic retrenchment, she had received Soviet plant and factory equipment worth over $2,000 million. Without this, her rapid industrialization would have been impossible.

Apart from machinery, Soviet technicians and know-how were of vital importance since they became available to China at a crucial period of her economic development. All in all, over 10,000 Soviet specialists worked in China at one time or another. The withdrawal of 1,000 to 1,500 technicians at the height of the Sino-Soviet discord aggravated a situation which was precarious in itself. Following the temporary settlement of the dispute the Soviet Union granted China in 1961 a moratorium on her loan services and on the payment for 50,000 tons of sugar; it also returned some industrial specialists to China. There is no evidence, however, of a revival of large-scale Soviet shipments of industrial plant. In their absence China's industrialization programme has to rely on strictly limited domestic resources, and this means that China has to mark time.

OUTCOME OF THE SECOND PLAN

As no production data have been published since 1960 and no plan or budget data were made known at the sessions of the National People's Congress held in the spring of 1962, the autumn of 1963 and the winter of 1964, it is difficult to estimate the effects of the current policy on the likely results of the long-term plan. Allowing for yet further mediocre harvests which must be expected by the Chinese authorities, there are bound to be shortfalls in those sectors of the economy which are dependent on the performance of the farming industry. However, as the output of at least some of the basic raw materials and semi-manufactured goods was above the original target set for 1962, there is bound to have been a certain increase in the overall gross industrial output. Against this, farm production has been lagging badly behind the plan. Even an exceptionally good harvest in 1963 would have failed to raise agricultural output substantially above the level attained in 1957, the last year of the previous plan. In fact, the crop of 1963 was only marginally better than the crops which preceded it. This means that the goal set for the total national product is unlikely to have been reached by the end of the second Five-Year Plan period.

The Ten-Point Programme, outlined by Chou En-lai, the Chinese Prime Minister, at the National People's Congress in 1962, reflected the temporary victory of caution over enthusiasm in economic policy. Agriculture was given priority over industry, and in the industrial sector the emphasis was on consumer goods which were to provide rewards to those at home and abroad who helped China out of her economic predicament. In this context the emphasis on consumer industries should be seen as interrelated with the aim of expanding foreign trade. Although improved supplies of consumer goods were promised to domestic producers in factories and farms, they take second place to those of her customers able to supply the foreign exchange badly needed for the purchase of capital equipment and spare parts.

RECOVERY FROM RETRENCHMENT

In his report to the National People's Congress held at the end of 1964, Chou En-lai was able to speak of a turn for the better and of a new period of development lying ahead. The period of retrenchment was over, and the years of consolidation had borne fruit. Steel output was close to 10 million tons against 5 million tons in 1957 and 13 million tons in 1959. Though a marked recovery had taken place, the claim of an industrial growth rate of 15 per cent in one year could be regarded as an exaggeration. In agriculture 50,000 tractors were available compared with ten times as many in Britain on an acreage that is approximately one fifteenth of China's. Some 3 million tons of fertilizers were available equal to 3 kilos (7 lbs) of nutrients per acre or one twentieth of the amount used on farms in Britain. The grain harvest, though well below that of 1958, was probably somewhat above that of 1957, i.e. perhaps 190 million tons.

The priorities laid down early in 1962 were to determine economic policy in the years ahead. As before agriculture was described as the foundation and industry as the leading sector of the economy. Self-reliance remained the yardstick where foreign economic relations were concerned, but grain imports of the order of 5 million tons, costing about US$400 million, continued to be needed every year. Just the same, the road of development was once again charted.

At the end of 1965 the National People's Congress failed to meet, and a leading article in the Communist Party's official organ had to suffice to fill the gap in factual information. The article gave the first official account of what had happened in the years since the 'Great Leap forward'. The second Five-Year Plan, launched in 1958, was said to have been fulfilled in 1960, two years ahead of schedule. During the next three years, the national economy had been readjusted in a general way, and in the last two years of the transition period a new upsurge of the national economy had been organized and was said to have created sound and adequate foundations for implementing the third Five-Year Plan. Certain shortcomings and mistakes were admitted for the years 1959 to 1961, the years following the 'Great Leap Forward', when the economy was seriously dislocated and the population suffered great hardships. No data were made known, however, on China's economic performance prior to 1966; nor were any forecasts or plan targets published for the period of the third Five-Year Plan, ranging from 1966 to 1970.

China's industrial base was still that of a pre-industrial society. Energy available per head of population equalled less than 300 kilos of coal or 6 per cent of the energy available *per capita* in the United Kingdom. Worse still, in China some fifty persons have to make do with the electricity supply that one person has at his disposal in the United Kingdom. At seventeen kilos per head China's steel consumption equals one thirtieth and one fortieth respectively of the levels attained in the United Kingdom and the United States. According to current Chinese thinking, it will take twenty to thirty years before China will be able to catch up with Western industrial nations. Thanks to the highly selective nature of the industrial programme, remarkable achievements in some spheres have gone side by side with stagnation in others.

China's nuclear programme, which was given priority in the allocation of human, material and financial resources, progressed much faster than was generally expected. The first nuclear test explosion took place in October 1964. Others followed in May 1965 and in May, October, and December 1966. These tests revealed a high degree of sophistication in China's scientific and technological advance. There is reason to think that the pace at which this programme has been developed cannot be maintained.

IMPACT OF THE CULTURAL REVOLUTION

Had it not been for the cultural revolution, progress on a broad front might have been possible during the third Five-Year Plan. As it is, China is – once again – in the throes of an upheaval, in the course of which – in the Chinese phrase – politics have taken command of economics. The outcome of this latest turn of the revolution cannot be foreseen with any degree of certainty. If the *status quo ante* as it existed prior to the cultural revolution could be restored speedily, an increase of gross industrial production by 50 per cent during the current Five-Year Plan might still be possible; but with every day that passes without a settlement of major political issues this achievement seems less likely. As some of China's industrial capital is in need of repair, if not replacement, an annual industrial growth rate of $8\frac{1}{2}$ per cent might well be unattainable even under conditions of internal stability. Much would, of course, depend on the performance of the farming industry which has to supply not only food and agricultural raw materials for the rural and urban population, but also the financial means of 'primitive accumulation' – to use a Marxist term – without which industrialization cannot proceed. For the time being nature rather than man determines the level of farm production. Few farm requisites capable of levelling out the effects of natural hazards and of levelling up the yields of the main crops are likely to become available before 1970, the terminal year of the current plan. Thus the growth rate of the farming industry may not exceed that of the population; it may even lag behind it. In these circumstances gross domestic product and expenditure are unlikely to rise by more than one third during the period of the current plan, or by an average of $5\frac{1}{2}$ to 6 per cent per year. This would correspond to the rate of performance during the first plan.

Progress at this rate presupposes a speedy return to stability in domestic and foreign relations. At present China seems to be far removed from such a state of affairs. If the conditions of life and work remain disrupted for a further year or more – as they were after the 'Great Leap Forward' – the consequences might even be more serious than they were then. In that case, not only might China's industry lose the momentum regained not so long ago; but the population might suffer even more serious hardships than in the years following the 'Great Leap Forward'. Periods of stagnation and retreat under conditions of internal and external warfare have not been unknown in the fifty years of Communist history. If it were to be China's fate to experience what Russia had to endure in the years from 1928 to 1944, the increase of the population might provide the only growth rate of the nation, and even that might disappear.

THE ECONOMY OF CHINA

RATES OF ECONOMIC GROWTH

Output	First-Five Year Plan 1953–7 Five-Year Plan target 1952 = 100	actual estimated	Interim Period 1958–65 Five-Year Plan target 1957 = 100	actual estimated	Third Five-Year Plan 1966–70 forecast estimated 1965 = 100
Gross agricultural output	123	115	135	100	110
Gross industrial output	190	200	200	160	150
Gross material output	151	150	175	135	130
National income	143	135	150	130	130
National income, per head of population	131	124	141	116	119

RATES OF INDUSTRIAL GROWTH

Industrial output	First Five-Year Plan 1953–7		Interim Period 1958–60		Third Five-Year Plan 1966–70
	Total Industry	Modern Industry	Total Industry	Modern Industry	Total Industry
Industrial output	*1952 = 100*		*1957 = 100*		*1965 = 100*
Gross national output					
(Official)	228	252	n.a.	145	n.a.
Net industrial output					
(Official)	n.a.	n.a.	277	n.a.	n.a.
(K. Chao)	186	196	n.a.	190	n.a.
(Y. L. Wu)	189	223	183	172	n.a.
(Liu-Yeh)	194	240	n.a.	160	n.a.

NATIONAL INCOME, FIRST FIVE-YEAR PLAN
(in 000 million Yuan, 1952 value)

Year	Net Material Product (Official)	Gross National Product (Hollister)	Net National Product (C. M. Li)	Net National Product (Liu-Yeh)	Net National Product (Y. L. Wu)
1952	61·1	67·9	72·9	71·4	72·4
1953	70·0	77·1	80·2	75·3	75·4
1954	73·9	81·9	86·6	79·3	78·3
1955	78·8	85·4	93·8	82·3	82·0
1956	88·7	97·2	107·3	92·1	91·7
1957	93·5	102·4	111·8	95·3	94·8
Av. growth rate (per cent per year)	9·0	8·6	8·8	6·0	5·6

INDUSTRIAL PRODUCTION
(in million physical units)

Industrial production	1952 actual	1957 actual	1959 claim	1964 estimated	1966 estimated
Electricity (000 kwh)	7·3	19·3	41·5	33·0	50·0
Coal (tons)	66·5	130·7	347·8	220·0	250·0
Crude oil (tons)	0·4	1·5	3·7	6·0	9·0
Crude steel (tons)	1·3	5·3	13·3	10·0	12·0
Cement (tons)	2·9	6·9	12·3	8·0	10·0

AGRICULTURAL PRODUCTION AND LIVESTOCK

Crops and livestock	1952 actual	1957 actual	1959 claim	1964 estimated	1966 estimated
Acreage (million hectares)					
Rice	28·4	32·2	n.a.	29·5	30·0
Wheat	24·8	27·5	n.a.	25·5	25·0
Other grains and pulses	50·4	50·6	n.a.	52·5	53·5
Potatoes	8·7	10·5	n.a.	12·5	11·5
Total grains	112·3	120·9	121·0	120·0	120·0
Soya beans	11·5	12·6	12·8	8·5	10·0
Cotton	5·5	5·8	6·0	4·5	5·0
Production (million tons)					
Rice	68·5	86·8	n.a.	87·5	85·0
Wheat	18·1	23·7	n.a.	24·5	21·5
Other grains and pulses	51·5	52·6	n.a.	55·0	53·5
Potatoes (grain equivalent)	16·4	21·9	n.a.	23·0	20·0
Total grains (grain equivalent)	154·5	185·0	270·5	190·0	180·0
Soya beans	9·5	10·0	11·5	7·5	10·0
Cotton	1·3	1·6	2·4	1·5	1·7
Yield (tons per hectare)					
Rice	2·41	2·70	n.a.	2·96	2·83
Wheat	0·73	0·86	n.a.	0·96	0·86
Other grains and pulses	1·02	1·04	n.a.	1·05	1·00
Potatoes (grain equivalent)	1·86	2·08	n.a.	1·84	1·74
Total grains (grain equivalent)	1·38	1·53	2·32	1·58	1·50
Soya beans	0·83	0·80	0·90	0·90	1·00
Cotton	0·24	0·28	0·38	0·33	0·35
Livestock (millions)					
Horses, donkeys, mules	19·6	19·8	20·0	n.a.	n.a.
Cattle and buffaloes	56·6	65·8	65·4	65·0	65·0
Pigs	89·8	145·9	180·0	180·0	180·0
Sheep and goats	61·8	98·6	112·5	n.a.	100·0

FOREIGN TRADE ESTIMATES

(in 000 million US $)					
Trading Area	*1952*	*1957*	*1959*	*1966*	*1967*
Imports					
Soviet Union	0·5	0·5	0·9	0·2	0·1
Other Bloc countries	0·2	0·4	0·5	0·2	0·2
Total Soviet Bloc	0·7	0·9	1·4	0·4	0·3
Developing countries	0·2	0·2	0·2	0·4	0·4
Other non-Bloc countries*	0·1	0·3	0·5	1·1	1·2
Total non-Bloc countries	0·3	0·5	0·7	1·5	1·6
Total world	1·0	1·4	2·1	1·9	1·9
Exports					
Soviet Union	0·4	0·7	1·1	0·1	0·1
Other Bloc countries	0·2	0·4	0·5	0·3	0·3
Total Soviet Bloc	0·6	1·1	1·6	0·4	0·4
Developing countries	0·2	0·2	0·2	0·5	0·6
Other non-Bloc countries*	0·1	0·3	0·4	1·2	1·1
Total non-Bloc countries	0·3	0·5	0·6	1·7	1·7
Total world	0·9	1·6	2·2	2·1	2·1
Turnover					
Soviet Union	0·9	1·2	2·0	0·3	0·2
Other Bloc countries	0·4	0·8	1·0	0·5	0·5
Total Soviet Bloc	1·3	2·0	3·0	0·8	0·7
Developing countries	0·4	0·4	0·4	0·9	1·0
Other non-Bloc countries*	0·2	0·6	0·9	2·3	2·3
Total non-Bloc countries	0·6	1·0	1·3	3·2	3·3
Total world	1·9	3·0	4·3	4·0	4·0
Balance					
Soviet Union	−0·1	+0·2	+0·2	−0·1	+0·0
Other Bloc countries	+0·0	+0·0	+0·0	+0·1	+0·1
Total Soviet Bloc	−0·1	+0·2	+0·2	+0·0	+0·1
Developing countries	+0·0	+0·0	+0·0	+0·1	+0·2
Other non-Bloc countries*	+0·0	+0·0	−0·1	+0·1	−0·1
Total non-Bloc countries	+0·0	+0·0	−0·1	+0·2	+0·1
Total world	−0·1	+0·2	+0·1	+0·2	+0·2

*Including Hong Kong.

BIBLIOGRAPHY

A. D. Barnett. *Communist Economic Strategy: The Rise of Mainland China*. (National Planning Association, New York, 1959.)

J. L. Buck. *Land Utilization in China*. 3 vols. (Nanking University, Shanghai, 1937.)

J. L. Buck, O. L. Dawson and Y. L. Wu. *Food and Agriculture in Communist China*. (Pall Mall Press, 1966.)

S. Chandrasekhar. *China's Population*. (Hong Kong University Press, Hong Kong, 1959.)

K. C. Chao. *Agrarian Policy of the Chinese Communist Party*. (Asia Publishing House, London, 1960.)

A. Eckstein. *The National Income of Communist China*. (The Free Press, Glencoe, Illinois, 1961.)

W. W. Hollister. *China's Gross National Product and Social Accounts 1950–1957*. (The Free Press, Glencoe, Illinois, 1958.)

R. Hsia. *Economic Planning in Communist China*. (Institute of Pacific Relations, New York, 1955.)

T. J. Hughes and D. E. T. Luard. *The Economic Development of Communist China 1949–1960*. (2nd edn, Oxford University Press, 1961.)

E. S. Kirby *et al. Contemporary China*. Vols I–V. (Hong Kong University Press, Hong Kong, 1955 ff.)

C. M. Li. *Economic Development of Communist China*. (University of California Press, Berkeley and Los Angeles, 1959). *The Statistical System of Communist China*. (University of California Press, Berkeley and Los Angeles, 1962). Ed. *Industrial Development in Communist China*. (Praeger, New York, 1964.)

T. C. Liu and K. C. Yeh. *The Economy of the Chinese Mainland: National Income and Economic Development, 1933–1959*. (Princeton University Press, Princeton, N.J., 1965.)

C. F. Remer *et al. International Economics of Communist China*. (University of Michigan Press, Ann Arbor, 1959.)

W. W. Rostow *et al. The Prospects of Communist China*. (John Wiley, New York, 1954.)

T. Shabad. *China's Changing Map*. (Praeger, New York, 1956.)

T. H. Shen. *Agricultural Resources of China*. (Cornell University Press, Ithaca, N.Y., 1951.)

R. H. Tawney. *Land and Labour in China*. (Allen & Unwin, 1932.)

Y. L. Wu. *An Economic Survey of Communist China*. (Bookmen Associates, New York, 1956.)

Y. L. Wu. *Economy of Communist China*. (Pall Mall Press, 1965.)

H. Yin and Y. C. Yin. *Economic Statistics of Mainland China*. (Harvard University Press, Cambridge, Mass., 1960.)

THE ECONOMY OF CHINA

JOURNALS

Economic Survey of Asia and the Far East. (Bangkok.)
Economic Bulletin for Asia and the Far East. (Bangkok.)
Far Eastern Economic Review. (Hong Kong.)
Problems of Communism. (Washington.)
The China Quarterly. (London.)

THE ECONOMY OF JAPAN

R. N. Wood; revised by S. A. Broadbridge

THE chaotic conditions which accompanied the end of the war make it difficult to assess with any accuracy what defeat meant for Japan in material terms. It is probable, however, that the real national income in 1945–6 had fallen back to the level achieved fifteen or twenty years before. The reduction of individual incomes was even more serious, since the 1945 population was much higher than it had been in the mid twenties. Many people lived on the verge of starvation and, with a major part of the country's economic assets destroyed, it looked as if it would be a long time before recovery.

POST-WAR RECOVERY

The post-war recovery – as in West Germany and Italy – was however remarkably rapid. A great deal of the credit for this must go to the United States, the principal influence in the formation of the policy of the occupation forces (SCAP). Very generous financial assistance was given to the stricken country, and SCAP made every effort to encourage the improvement of living standards. This enlightened policy together with the industry and enterprise shown by the Japanese produced most gratifying results.

Between 1946 and 1953 – the year after independence was regained and which is taken here as the end of the post-war recovery period – the national income more than doubled in real terms, bringing an increase of nearly 90 per cent in income per head. In the immediate post-war years there was, it is true, rapid inflation, but increases in production were rapid too and by the end of 1950 inflationary pressures had been reduced to modest proportions.

One of the most significant and successful measures introduced by SCAP was the land reform. Although the reform was carried out on strictly orthodox lines, with provisions for compensation for the old landowners, the burden of debt on the peasants was appreciably reduced by inflation. Since most of the land had been in the hands of small landowners, and had been let out in small units, the transfer of title to the tenants did not disrupt what had been, for many decades, a successful system of agriculture. On the contrary, there is no doubt that the reform contributed greatly to the ever increasing yields of Japanese agriculture. Between 1945 and 1953 total agricultural production increased by two thirds, despite the fact that 1953 was an unusually bad year. Rice is the main crop, and the growth of its output was the main factor contributing to the overall increase. The most rapid advance, however, was in the production of livestock, which rose nearly six times during this period.

Japan's mineral output is dominated by coal, though there are small quantities of many other minerals. Total mining production rose by 83 per cent between 1945 and 1953. Coal production declined sharply in 1946, however, and over the period production rose by only 53 per cent.

The major growth sector both in the early post-war period and more especially after 1953 was manufacturing industry. It was here that the effects of defeat in war were felt most acutely. In 1946 the index of manufacturing production was two thirds lower than it had been in 1945. By 1953, however, it had reached a level of 96 per cent above that for the year of Japan's surrender. Progress in basic items such as iron and steel, rolling stock, textiles, and foodstuffs was much more rapid than average – though the machinery industry, to be one of the front runners in the later period, was rather slow to recover.

The post-war progress of manufacturing was closely linked to the success of Japan's exports. Here, too, the enlightened policy of the United States was important, for, in contrast to West European countries, it maintained a liberal attitude to imports from Japan. South-East Asian markets also proved fruitful, with reparations agreements smoothing the path of exports. The total value of exports rose fourteen times between 1945 and 1953.

CHANGES IN ECONOMIC STRUCTURE

While Japan's recovery after the war was remarkable, it is to a large extent overshadowed by the speed of advance since the end of the reconstruction period. Between 1953 and 1966 the gross national product more than trebled in real terms, giving an annual average rate of growth of nearly 10 per cent. No other country in the free world (and probably not in the Communist world either) can boast of such a dynamic achievement. Intensive Government campaigns greatly reduced the birth rate in comparison with the pre-war period, so that the increase in total output was not greatly eroded as a result of population growth; the real annual rise in GNP per head over the period 1953–66 was also nearly 10 per cent. The rapid rise in production was accompanied and promoted by an upsurge in investment. Gross fixed capital formation in 1965 was $4\frac{1}{3}$ times higher in real terms than in 1953 and amounted to as much as 34 per cent of GNP. Foreign trade, too, expanded very rapidly during this period. Between 1953 and 1966 the quantum of exports rose 8 times and imports more than quadrupled.

The swift progress of these years had been accompanied by great changes in economic structure. While in 1953 agriculture, forestry, and fisheries contributed 22 per cent of the domestic output, by 1965 their share had dropped to a mere 11 per cent. Manufacturing, on the other hand, increased its share of the total from 24 per cent in 1953 to 28 per cent in 1965. These changes are reflected, though to a lesser extent, in the employment figures. In 1953 45 per cent of the total labour force was engaged in agriculture, forestry, and fisheries; by 1966 the proportion had shrunk to less than one quarter. Over the same period the proportion of the labour force in manufacturing rose from 17 per cent to 25 per cent. There is no doubt that this flow of workers from the countryside into more productive employment in the towns has been one of the major factors in Japan's economic success.

This is not to say that agriculture stagnated. Between 1954 (1953 was an exceptionally bad year) and 1965 the overall index of agricultural production rose by well over half. Domestic production of rice rose from 9 million tons in 1954 to 13 million tons in 1962, but has since declined slightly to $12\frac{1}{2}$ millions. This decline has been accompanied by a sharp recovery of imports, which had become insignificant in the early 1960s. Imports of other cereals have also increased rapidly, particularly those of maize and wheat. These are a result of the swift advance in livestock, milk, and egg production. The Japanese now enjoy a better, and more varied, diet. The land reform made a major contribution to this rise in agricultural production by giving the peasants a stake in the soil. Many of the individual holdings are small, however, and prevent the fullest and most economic use of new machinery and techniques. In recent years, therefore, the land reform measures have been amended, and a programme for larger holdings and increased mechanization has been started in a number of communities with the emphasis on commercial crops and dairy products. Larger-scale operations are essential not only to boost agricultural output further, but also to enable a sufficent number of workers to move to employment in the towns and so prevent industrial labour costs from rising unduly.

Since 1953 mining has been, perhaps, the least successful of the major industrial sectors. To a large extent this reflects the problems of the coal industry, the main traditional centre of which is the southern island of Kyushu. Much of the coal is of poor quality, while the seams are narrow and have become increasingly difficult to work. Total mineral production rose by only one third between 1953 and 1963; coal production increased by a mere 11 per cent and has actually declined since 1963. The index of iron ore production has also fallen since 1960, yet Japan is importing vast quantities of both coking-coal and iron ore for its steel industry.

The Government has been prepared to protect mining, partly to conserve foreign exchange and partly for social and political reasons. In future, however, it is intended to rely increasingly on imports of better quality minerals, including petroleum.

MANUFACTURING INDUSTRY

It is manufacturing industry, of course, which has been the star turn of the Japanese economy. Between 1953 and 1966 manufacturing production increased more than fivefold. There have naturally been big differences in the performance of the various sectors. Traditional light manufactures, such as cotton textiles, ceramics, food production, etc., have lost ground to technically advanced heavy industries. Production of cotton fabrics, for example, rose by about 40 per cent between 1953 and 1961 but has since declined.

The rather mediocre performance in these areas was offset by some quite outstanding results in others. Machinery production in 1966 was nine times above that for 1953. A major growth sector was the electrical machinery industry. Production of television sets rose from 14,000 in 1953 to $5\frac{1}{2}$ million in 1966. But even more impressive has been the record in shipbuilding, motor-cycles, automobiles, and steel: Japan's world position in these commodities is first, first, second, and third respectively.

The chemical industry has also gone ahead very fast, particularly on the organic side. Japan's progress with synthetic resins and non-cellulose based plastic materials has been astounding, and it now produces as wide a range of these products as any other country in the world. Synthetic textiles have been the only really buoyant part of the textile industry, and have greatly enhanced overall results there.

GOVERNMENT POLICY

Government expenditure lagged behind advances in trade and industry in the fifties, but has accelerated in recent years. Since 1953 Central

Government outlays – including those of public corporations and special institutions – have probably quadrupled. Even so, many basic facilities relying on Government support, such as roads, ports, sewerage and housing, have become increasingly inadequate to cope with the rapidly expanding economic and social needs.

The Government's impact on the economy has been more in the direct influence it has exerted on private industry. There are indications, however, that the opportunities for this sort of Government interference may be reduced. Its most powerful weapons in controlling the private sector have derived from its power to regulate foreign trade and exchange. Since Japan possesses hardly any of the raw materials necessary to support its industry, it is argued that its balance of payments – already unstable – is likely to be subject to greater strains than elsewhere. This is usually put forward as justification for the structure of trade and exchange controls. Other factors have been the Government's wish to regulate competition and to control the domestic economy, and its fear lest too large a part of Japan's assets should fall under foreign control. Under pressure from other industrial countries the authorities are liberalizing the external restrictions. This process has now gone some distance since 1964, when Japan was admitted to full membership of the IMF and OECD, though a significant number of items is still subject to restrictions. Further liberalization is planned, however, and as these defences disappear, the Government's power over private industry will diminish, unless it is successful in its attempt to substitute less visible controls, such as 'administrative guidance'.

THE FUTURE

Japan's progress has been remarkable. What of its future? In 1961 the Government published its Long-Range Economic Plan, setting out the targets for the sixties. The plan called for the following objectives to be reached by 1970 (increase over 1956–8 given in brackets): national income per head £207 (2·4 times), gross domestic capital formation £2,958 million (2·8 times), exports £3,329 million (3·5 times), and imports £3,534 million (3·2 times). These targets may have looked ambitious in relation to economic performance elsewhere, but viewed against the background of Japan's own progress they were by no means unreasonable. Indeed, owing to the extraordinary rate of growth achieved in the years 1959–61, Japan began the plan far ahead of the start-line envisaged by the planners.

Gross national product in 1960 was £16 billions. By March 1967 it had risen to £27½ billions, calculated in 1960 prices. That the growth potential of the Japanese economy remains unexpectedly high, is shown by the forecast that during the fiscal year 1967-8 it would rise by 12 per cent to £30½ billions. This means that by the spring of 1968 Japan's GNP would be 91 per cent greater, in real terms, than it was in 1960, and, short of catastrophe, it is certain that the Income Doubling Plan will be achieved by mid 1969, well ahead of schedule.

The huge expansion in sectors such as steel, shipbuilding and the motor industry has proved unfounded the fears expressed in the early 1960s that Japan's growth rate would drop sharply during the decade. The diminished supply of labour from the countryside, the narrowing of the technological gap, the comparative lack of original research and development, the growing need to expand social capital, and the restrictions imposed by an unstable balance of payments, have been and still are advanced as reasons why growth will be less rapid. The potential difficulty of these aspects is undeniable, but Japan has shown herself able to grasp every conceivable opportunity to expand and, providing that the United States, on which she is very dependent, continues to be buoyant there seems to be no reason why she should not still be expanding by some 10 per cent per annum at the end of the 1960s. She is already the world's fourth largest economy and has the world's third largest industrial sector. In fact, it could be that the biggest question mark hanging over her future is the antagonism that might be aroused by her headlong progress.

BIBLIOGRAPHY

G. C. Allen. *Japan's Economic Expansion*. (Oxford University Press, 1965.)

J. B. Cohen. *Japan's Postwar Economy*. (Indiana University Press, Bloomington, 1958.)

L. Hollerman. *Japan's Dependence on the World Economy*. (Oxford University Press, 1967.)

S. S. Kuznets (Ed.). *Economic Growth: Brazil, India, Japan*. (Duke University Press, Durham, North Carolina, 1955.)

S. Okita. *The Rehabilitation of Japan's Economy and Asia*. (Ministry of Foreign Affairs, London, 1956.)

S. Takahata. *Quo Vadis, Japan?* (Institute of Pacific Relations, Kyoto, 1954.)

The Japanese Economy. (Economist Intelligence Unit for Federation of British Industries, London, 1962.)

BUDDHIST ECONOMICS

E. F. Schumacher

'RIGHT LIVELIHOOD' is one of the requirements of the Buddha's Noble Eightfold Path. It is clear, therefore, that there must be such a thing as Buddhist Economics.

Buddhist countries, at the same time, have often stated that they wish to remain faithful to their heritage. So Burma: 'The New Burma sees no conflict between religious values and economic progress. Spiritual health and material well-being are not enemies: they are natural allies.'[1]* Or: 'We can blend successfully the religious and spiritual values of our heritage with the benefits of modern technology.'[2] Or: 'We Burmans have a sacred duty to conform both our dreams and our acts to our faith. This we shall ever do.'[3]

All the same, such countries invariably assume that they can model their economic development plans in accordance with modern economics, and they call upon modern economists from so-called advanced countries to advise them, to formulate the policies to be pursued, and to construct the grand design for development, the Five-Year Plan or whatever it may be called. No one seems to think that a Buddhist way of life would call for Buddhist economics, just as the modern materialist way of life has brought forth modern economics.

Economists themselves, like most specialists, normally suffer from a kind of metaphysical blindness, assuming that theirs is a science of absolute and invariable truths, without any pre-suppositions. Some go as far as to claim that economic laws are as free from 'metaphysics' or 'values' as the law of gravitation. We need not, however, get involved in arguments of methodology. Instead, let us take some fundamentals and see what they look like when viewed by a modern economist and a Buddhist economist.

There is universal agreement that the fundamental source of wealth is human labour. Now, the modern economist has been brought up to consider 'labour' or work as little more than a necessary evil. From the point of view of the employer, it is in any case simply an item of cost, to be reduced to a minimum if it cannot be eliminated altogether, say, by automation. From the point of view of the workman, it is a 'dis-utility'; to work is to make a sacrifice of one's leisure and comfort,

* References are listed on page 697.

and wages are a kind of compensation for the sacrifice. Hence the ideal from the point of view of the employers is to have output without employees, and the ideal from the point of view of the employee is to have income without employment.

The consequences of these attitudes both in theory and in practice are, of course, extremely far-reaching. If the ideal with regard to work is to get rid of it, every method that 'reduces the work load' is a good thing. The most potent method, short of automation, is the so-called 'division of labour' and the classical example is the pin factory eulogized in Adam Smith's *Wealth of Nations*. Here it is not a matter of ordinary specialization, which mankind has practised from time immemorial, but of dividing up every complete process of production into minute parts, so that the final product can be produced at great speed without anyone having had to contribute more than a totally insignificant and, in most cases, unskilled movement of his limbs.

WORK

The Buddhist point of view takes the function of work to be at least threefold: to give a man a chance to utilize and develop his faculties; to enable him to overcome his ego-centredness by joining with other people in a common task; and to bring forth the goods and services needed for a becoming existence. Again, the consequences that flow from this view are endless. To organize work in such a manner that it becomes meaningless, boring, stultifying, or nerve-racking for the worker would be little short of criminal; it would indicate a greater concern with goods than with people, an evil lack of compassion and a soul-destroying degree of attachment to the most primitive side of this worldly existence. Equally, to strive for leisure as an alternative to work would be considered a complete misunderstanding of one of the basic truths of human existence, namely, that work and leisure are complementary parts of the same living process and cannot be separated without destroying the joy of work and the bliss of leisure.

From the Buddhist point of view, there are therefore two types of mechanization which must be clearly distinguished: one that enhances a man's skill and power and one that turns the work of man over to a mechanical slave, leaving man in a position of having to serve the slave. How to tell the one from the other? 'The craftsman himself,' says Ananda Coomaraswamy, a man equally competent to talk about the Modern West as the Ancient East, 'the craftsman himself can always, if allowed to, draw the delicate distinction between the machine and the tool. The carpet loom is a tool, a contrivance for holding warp threads at a stretch for the pile to be woven round them by the craftsmen's fingers; but the power loom is a machine, and its significance as a destroyer of culture lies in the fact that it does the essentially human part of the work.'[4] It is clear, therefore, that Buddhist economics must be very different from the economics of modern materialism, since the Buddhist sees the essence of civilization not in a multiplication of wants but in the purification of human character. Character, at the same time, is formed primarily by a man's work. And work, properly conducted in conditions of human dignity and freedom, blesses those who do it and equally their products. The Indian philosopher and economist J. C. Kumarappa sums the matter up as follows:

If the nature of the work is properly appreciated and applied, it will stand in the same relation to the higher faculties as food is to the physical body. It nourishes and enlivens the higher man and urges him to produce the best he is capable of. It directs his freewill along the proper course and disciplines the animal in him into progressive channels. It furnishes an excellent background for man to display his scale of values and develop his personality.[5]

If a man has no chance of obtaining work he is in a desperate position, not simply because he lacks an income but because he lacks this nourishing and enlivening factor of disciplined work which nothing can replace. A modern economist may engage in highly sophisticated calculations on whether full employment 'pays' or whether it might be more 'economic' to run an economy at less than full employment so as to ensure a greater mobility of labour, a better stability of wages, and so forth. His fundamental criterion of success is simply the total quantity of goods produced during a given period of time. 'If the marginal urgency of goods is low,' says Professor Galbraith in *The Affluent Society*, 'then so is the urgency of employing the last man or the last million men in the labour force.' And again: 'If . . . we can afford some unemployment in the interest of stability – a proposition, incidentally, of impeccably conservative antecedents – then we can afford to give those who are unemployed the goods that enable them to sustain their accustomed standard of living.'[6]

From a Buddhist point of view, this is standing the truth on its head by considering goods as more important than people and consumption as more important than creative activity. It means shifting the emphasis from the worker to the product of work, that is, from the human to the sub-human, a surrender to the forces of evil. The very start of Buddhist economic planning would be a planning for full employment, and the primary purpose of this would in fact be employment for everyone who needs an 'outside' job; it would not be the maximization of employment nor the maximization of production. Women, on the whole, do not need an 'outside' job, and the large-scale employment of women in offices or factories would be considered a sign of serious economic failure. In particular, to let mothers of young children work in factories while the children run wild would be as uneconomic in the eyes of a Buddhist economist as the employment of a skilled worker as a soldier in the eyes of a modern economist.

While the materialist is mainly interested in goods, the Buddhist is mainly interested in liberation. But Buddhism is 'The Middle Way' and therefore in no way antagonistic to physical well-being. It is not wealth that stands in the way of liberation but the attachment to wealth; not the enjoyment of pleasurable things but the craving for them. The keynote to Buddhist economics, therefore, is simplicity and non-violence. From an economist's point of view, the marvel of the Buddhist way of life is the utter rationality of its pattern – amazingly small means leading to extraordinarily satisfactory results.

STANDARD OF LIVING

For the modern economist this is very difficult to understand. He is used to measuring the 'standard of living' by the amount of annual consumption, assuming all the time that a man who consumes more is 'better off' than a man who consumes less. A Buddhist economist would consider this approach excessively irrational: since consumption is merely a means of human well-being, the aim should be to obtain the maximum of well-being with the minimum of consumption. Thus, if the purpose of clothing is a certain amount of temperature comfort and an attractive appearance, the task is to attain this purpose with the smallest possible effort, that is, with the smallest annual destruction of cloth and with the help of designs that involve the smallest possible input of toil. The less toil there is, the more time and strength is left for artistic creativity. It would be highly uneconomic, for instance, to go in for complicated tailoring, like the modern West, when a much more beautiful effect can be achieved by the skilful draping of uncut material. It would be the height of folly to make material so that it should wear out quickly and the height of barbarity to make anything ugly, shabby or mean. What has just been said about clothing applies equally to all other human requirements. The ownership and the consumption of goods is a means to an end, and Buddhist economics is the systematic study of how to attain given ends with the minimum means.

Modern economics, on the other hand, considers consumption to be 'the sole end and purpose of all economic activity', taking the factors of production – land, labour, and capital – as the means. The former, in short, tries to maximize human satisfactions by the optimal pattern of consumption, while the latter tries to maximize consumption by the optimal pattern of productive effort. It is easy to see that the effort needed to sustain a way of life which seeks to attain the optimal pattern of consumption is likely to be much smaller than the effort needed to sustain a drive for maximum consumption. We need not be surprised, therefore, that the pressure and strain of living is very much less in, say, Burma than it is in the United States, in spite of the fact that the amount of labour-saving machinery used in the former country is only a minute fraction of the amount used in the latter.

PATTERN OF CONSUMPTION

Simplicity and non-violence are obviously closely related. The optimal pattern of consumption, producing a high degree of human satisfaction by means of a relatively low rate of consumption, allows people to live without great pressure and strain and to fulfil the primary injunction of Buddhist teaching: 'Cease to do evil, try to do good.' As physical resources are everywhere limited, people satisfying their needs by means of a modest use of resources are obviously less likely to be at each other's throats than people depending upon a high rate of use. Equally, people who live in highly self-sufficient local communities are less likely to get involved in large-scale violence than people whose existence depends on world-wide systems of trade.

From the point of view of Buddhist economics, therefore, production from local resources for local needs is the most rational way of economic life, while dependence on imports from afar and the consequent need to produce for export to unknown and distant peoples is highly uneconomic and justifiable only in exceptional cases and on a small scale. Just as the modern economist would admit that a high rate of consumption of transport services between a man's home and his place of work signifies a misfortune and not a high standard of life, so the Buddhist economist would hold that to satisfy human wants from far-away sources rather than from sources near by signifies failure rather than success. The former might take statistics showing an increase in the number of ton/miles per head of the population carried by a country's transport system as proof of economic progress, while to the latter – the Buddhist economist – the same statistics would indicate a highly undesirable deterioration in the *pattern* of consumption.

NATURAL RESOURCES

Another striking difference between modern economics and Buddhist economics arises over the use of natural resources. Bertrand de Juvenal, the eminent French political philosopher, has characterized 'Western man' in words which may be taken as a fair description of the modern economist:

> He tends to count nothing as an expenditure, other than human effort; he does not seem to mind how much mineral matter he wastes and, far worse, how much living matter he destroys. He does not seem to realize at all that human life is a dependent part of an ecosystem of many different forms of life. As the world is ruled from towns where men are cut off from any form of life other than human, the feeling of belonging to an ecosystem is not revived. This results in a harsh and improvident treatment of things upon which we ultimately depend, such as water and trees.[7]

The teaching of the Buddha, on the other hand, enjoins a reverent and non-violent attitude not only to all sentient beings but also, with great emphasis, to trees. Every follower of the Buddha ought to plant a tree every few years and look after it until it is safely established, and the Buddhist economist can demonstrate without difficulty that the universal observance of this rule would result in a high rate of genuine economic development independent of any foreign aid. Much of the economic decay of South-East Asia (as of many other parts of the world) is undoubtedly due to a heedless and shameful neglect of trees.

Modern economics does not distinguish between renewable and non-renewable materials, as its very method is to equalize and quantify everything by means of a money price. Thus, taking various alternative fuels, like coal, oil, wood or water power: the only difference between them recognized by modern economics is relative cost per equivalent unit. The cheapest is automatically the one to be preferred, as to do otherwise would be irrational and 'uneconomic'. From a Buddhist point of view, of course, this will not do; the essential difference between non-renewable fuels like coal and oil on the one hand and renewable fuels like wood and water-power on the other cannot be simply overlooked. Non-renewable goods must be used only if they are indispensable, and then only with the greatest care and the most meticulous concern for conservation. To use them heedlessly or extravagantly is an act of violence, and while complete non-violence may not be attainable on this earth, there is none the less an ineluctable duty for man to aim at the ideal of non-violence in all he does.

Just as a modern European economist would not consider it a great economic achievement if all European art treasures were sold to America at attractive prices, so the Buddhist economist would insist that a population basing its economic life on non-renewable fuels is living parasitically, on capital instead of income. Such a way of life could have no permanence and could therefore be justified only as a purely temporary expedient. As the world's resources of non-renewable fuels – coal, oil and natural gas – are exceedingly unevenly distributed over the globe and undoubtedly limited in quantity, it is clear that their exploitation at an ever increasing rate is an act of violence against nature which must almost inevitably lead to violence between men.

THE MIDDLE WAY

This fact alone might give food for thought even to those people in Buddhist countries who care nothing for the religious and spiritual values of their heritage and ardently desire to embrace the materialism of modern economics at the fastest possible speed. Before they dismiss Buddhist economics as nothing better than a nostalgic dream, they might wish to consider whether the path of economic development outlined by modern economics is likely to lead them to places where they really want to be. Towards the end of his courageous book *The Challenge of Man's Future*, Professor Harrison Brown of the California Institute of Technology gives the following appraisal:

Thus we see that, just as industrial society is fundamentally unstable and subject to reversion to agrarian existence, so within it the conditions which offer individual freedom are unstable in their ability to avoid the conditions which impose rigid organization and totalitarian control. Indeed, when we examine all of the foreseeable difficulties which threaten the survival of industrial civilization, it is difficult to see how the achievement of stability and the maintenance of individual liberty can be made compatible.[8]

Even if this were dismissed as a long-term view – and in the long term, as Keynes said, we are all dead – there is the immediate question of whether 'modernization', as currently practised without regard to religious and spiritual values, is actually producing agreeable results. As far as the masses are concerned, the results appear to be disastrous –

a collapse of the rural economy, a rising tide of unemployment in town and country, and the growth of a city proletariat without nourishment for either body or soul.

It is in the light of both immediate experience and long-term prospects that the study of Buddhist economics could be recommended even to those who believe that economic growth is more important than any spiritual or religious values. For it is not a question of choosing between 'modern growth' and 'traditional stagnation'. It is a question of finding the right path of development, the Middle Way between materialist heedlessness and traditionalist immobility, in short, of finding 'Right Livelihood'.

That this can be done is not in doubt. But it requires much more than blind imitation of the materialist way of life of the so-called advanced countries. It requires, above all, the conscious and systematic development of a Middle Way in technology, of an 'intermediate technology', as I have called it,[9, 10] a technology more productive and powerful than the decayed technology of the ancient East, but at the same time non-violent and immensely cheaper and simpler than the labour-saving technology of the modern West.

REFERENCES

1. *Pyidawtha, The New Burma.* (Economic and Social Board, Government of the Union of Burma, 1954, p. 10.)
2. ibid., p. 8.
3. ibid., p. 128.
4. Ananda K. Coomaraswamy. *Art and Swadeshi.* (Ganesh & Co., Madras, p. 30.)
5. J. C. Kumarappa. *Economy of Permanence.* (Sarva-Seva-Sangh Publication, Rajghat, Kashi, 4th edn, 1958, p. 117.)
6. J. K. Galbraith. *The Affluent Society.* (Penguin Books, 1962, pp. 272–3.)
7. Richard B. Gregg. *A Philosophy of Indian Economic Development.* (Navajivan Publishing House, Ahmedabad, 1958, pp. 140–41.)
8. Harrison Brown. *The Challenge of Man's Future.* (Viking Press, New York, 1954, p. 255.)
9. E. F. Schumacher. 'Rural Industries' in *India at Midpassage.* (Overseas Development Institute, London, 1964.)
10. E. F. Schumacher. 'Industrialisation through Intermediate Technology' in *Minerals and Industries,* Vol. 1, no. 4. (Calcutta, 1964.)

OIL IN ASIA

W. J. Harris

ONE of the most interesting features of Asia's oil industry is its antiquity. It is indeed believed that the Chinese recovered oil over two thousand years ago, when sinking wells for brine in the province of Szechuan.

Although recorded history does not extend as far back in the case of other Asian countries, Burmese oil is mentioned in Chinese documents of the 13th century. This oil was being exported to Britain and to other countries by the middle of the last century, and before the end of that century, large-scale production had begun in a number of Asian areas. In consequence, Asia then became one of the main sources of world oil supplies. As recently as 1938, Indonesia (then known as the Dutch East Indies) ranked as the fifth largest producer in the world. Burma and British Borneo were also important oil exporters at that time.

Although Asian oil output is currently running at several times its pre-war level of just over 10 million tons annually, the area possesses only relatively small petroleum resources compared with those of the USA, the Middle East, Latin America, the USSR, and Africa. Asian annual production is falling short of the region's rising oil requirements, so that substantial imports are needed to balance demand against supplies. Details of the individual oil-producing countries are as follows:

INDONESIA

Production

Indonesia is by far the largest crude oil producer and exporter in Asia. Production in 1967 amounted to approximately 25¼ million tons, of which about half was available for export. However, despite numerous discoveries made in that country, the output of individual fields remains small. Production comes from Sumatra, Kalimantan (formerly Dutch Borneo), Java and West Irian.

War damage sustained by the oil industry during the Japanese invasion was extensive and immediate post-war political complications hindered the international oil companies in their efforts to resume

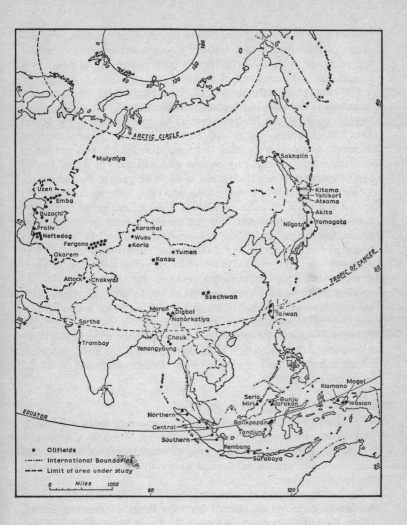

ARCTIC CIRCLE

Mulymya

Sakhalin

Uzen
Emba
Buzachi
Proliv
Neftedag
Okarem

Karamai
Wusu
Korla

Kitamo
Yshikori
Atsama
Akita
Niigata
Yamagata

Fergana

Yumen

Kansu

Attock
Chakwal

Szechwan

TROPIC OF CANCER

Moran
Digbol
Nahorkatiya

Taiwan

Sartha

Chauk

Trombay
Yenangyaung

Klamono
Mogoi

Seria
Miri

Bunju
Tarakan

Wasian

Northern

Central

Balikpapan

Tandjung

Southern

Rembang

EQUATOR

Surabaya

● Oilfields
—·—·— International Boundaries
— — — Limit of area under study

0   Miles   1000

operations in Indonesia. Nevertheless, despite these obstacles, rehabilitation of the industry went ahead vigorously and successfully until a few years ago, when this progress was again interrupted by new moves to nationalize the country's oil interests.

Following the introduction of fresh legislation in 1960, the Indonesian Government began negotiating with the three major international oil companies operating in the country – the Royal Dutch/Shell Group, Caltex and Stanvac. In 1963, these companies accepted terms whereby their refining, distribution and marketing facilities would subsequently become nationalized. The Royal Dutch/Shell Group completed the transfer of all its interests to the Indonesian Government as from 1 January 1966, and since then has taken no part in the country's oil industry. Caltex, Stanvac and other foreign oil companies have remained, but are currently functioning solely as contractors working for the State-owned concern, Permina. This company has been set up by the Indonesian Government to administer all exploration and production activities. However, latest developments in the country's political authority have brought a halt to this nationalization trend. Although no steps taken by the previous regime have yet been reversed, one indication of a new attitude has been a suggestion by the Indonesian Foreign Minister that some way might be found to induce Royal Dutch/Shell to re-enter the country. Certainly it looks as if there is to be a more broadly based industrial system, in which there will be a place for direct foreign participation in the country's oil industry.

Sumatra

The oldest of Indonesia's individual oil-producing areas is Sumatra, still the country's most important single source of supply. Commercial operations began as early as 1893, although many of the oilfields contributing to current production have only been discovered within the last thirty years.

Oil has been found in three separate parts of the island. In North Sumatra, operations are centred upon the Pangkalanbrandan district, where the initial discovery was made. In South Sumatra, oil was also found before the end of the last century. The third area is Central Sumatra, where some fields were found shortly before the Second World War and where further promising discoveries have been made in recent years. All these fields lie to the east of a high mountain range, nearly 1,000 miles in length, which forms the backbone of Sumatra. It is not expected that commercial discoveries will be made to the west of these mountains. Sumatra's production exceeded its pre-war level as early as 1949 – a tribute to the energy put into the reconstruction programme.

More recently, owing to political developments, the Indonesian Government and Japanese oil interests have concluded an agreement whereby the Japanese are operating oilfields formerly worked by British and Dutch interests – an agreement which now extends to offshore exploration along the coast of North Sumatra.

Kalimantan

Oil has been found in three different areas in this part of Indonesia, the first locality being at Takaran Island, off the north-east coast. The second area lies on the east coast, to the north of Balik Papan. The third discovery was made in 1938 at Tandjung, 120 miles south-west of Balik Papan. Owing to the intervention of the war, regular production at Tandjung did not start until 1961, when a 150-mile pipeline came into operation linking the field with a refinery near Balik Papan.

Java and Ceram

As in the case of Sumatra and Kalimantan, Java's oil industry dates back to the latter part of the 19th century. There are two main producing zones – at Rembang, in the centre of the island, and at Surabaya, on the east coast. In 1938, the combined output of these fields amounted to almost 900,000 tons. There was also a small pre-war production obtained from the island of Ceram.

Post-war political complications severely hampered the resumption of oil products in this part of Indonesia and even as recently as 1966, Java's output amounted to only some 200,000 tons. Nor has any progress so far been possible in Ceram.

West Irian

Seepage oil was noted in West Irian (formerly Netherlands New Guinea) early in this century. An extensive search began in 1936, when a mixed British, Dutch and American company started prospecting in the Vogelkop, the peninsula forming the extreme north-west section of the island. This search met with swift initial success, indeed in the same year that the venture started, the Klamono field was discovered and in 1940 two other fields were found at Wasian and Mogoi.

Commercial development of these discoveries had to await the end of the war, operations at Klamono beginning in 1948. Production from the other two fields started in 1954, but their yield soon declined until, by 1964, their output was only negligible.

West Irian provides an outstanding example of the difficulties that can sometimes complicate oil operations. The climate is atrocious: as much as 120 inches of rain have been recorded in a single month. By comparison, an unusually bad month in England and Wales will only register a rainfall of about 5 inches. The terrain varies from high mountains to swamp, and it is in the latter that the oil discoveries have been made. In such country, it is almost impossible to transport heavy equipment by conventional methods, although in recent years helicopters have proved invaluable substitutes for land vehicles. Many of the early wells in the Vogelkop were drilled by light, manually operated rigs, carried section by section to the sites by bearers. In order to convey the oil to the coast for shipment, a pipeline had to be built to a harbour at Sorong. This was a distance of only thirty miles, but it took two years to build a road and then lay the pipeline.

After the tremendous effort which has gone into developing the West Irian oilfields, it is disappointing to record the subsequent decline in production and the decision, in 1960, to abandon further exploration as no longer justified.

Refining

Indonesia has a current annual refining capacity of about 14 million tons. The principal plants are at Pladju and Sunei Gerong in South Sumatra, Balik Papan in Kalimantan, and Wonokromo and Tjepu in Java. Between them, these installations can process more than enough crude oil to meet Indonesia's own requirements, leaving a substantial surplus of finished products for export.

FEDERATION OF MALAYSIA

Production

Formed in the autumn of 1963, Malaysia was originally a Federation incorporating Malaya, Sabah (the colony of North Borneo), Sarawak, and Singapore. The last-named country, however, withdrew from the Federation in 1965. Nor does Malaysia include the independent State of Brunei, even though this territory lies between the federated countries of Sarawak and North Borneo.

Sarawak

This is the sole oil-producing country in the Federation. Its only oilfield, Miri, was found in 1910. Peak production was reached in

1926–30, when annual outputs were averaging around 700,000 tons. Output then declined to about 200,000 tons annually by the outbreak of the war. Despite extensive post-war exploration, no further oilfields have been found and current production is running at no more than about 50,000 tons a year.

Refining

The Federation has an annual refining capacity of slightly more than 5 million tons. There is one refinery at Lutong, Sarawak, which has an annual capacity of about 2½ million tons, and two somewhat smaller plants at Port Dickson, Malaya, with a combined annual capacity of just over 2½ million tons.

BRUNEI

Production

Until the inauguration of the Federation of Malaysia, Brunei was associated with the territory of British North Borneo and Sarawak in British Borneo. Since then, it has remained outside the Federation as a separate State.

Brunei is among the more important Asian producers. Its one inland field, Seria, was discovered in 1929 and by 1939 annual production was running at around 700,000 tons. Although virtually destroyed during the war, its post-war rehabilitation was astonishingly swift. By 1956 it was producing at a record rate of about 5½ million tons a year. At that point, its output began to dwindle, but at the same time offshore exploration gave Brunei new production prospects. Thanks to the subsequent development of her underwater resources, she is still producing just over 5 million tons of oil a year. Most of this output is shipped for refining at the Lutong refinery in Sarawak. The remainder goes mainly to Australia and Japan.

SINGAPORE

Refining

Although lacking any crude oil production, Singapore now possesses three refineries having a combined annual throughput capacity of some 3½ million tons. The first plant to come on stream was at Pulau Bukom in 1961. This has a current annual capacity of 1¾ million tons. The other two plants are at Pasir Panjang (annual capacity: 750,000 tons) and Jurong (annual capacity: 1 million tons).

BURMA

Production

Mention has already been made of the antiquity of Burma's oil industry, though for many centuries production was limited to hand-dug wells lined with timber. Modern drilling techniques were introduced into Burma in 1899.

The oilfields lie along the Irrawaddy River, the two most important fields being Chauk and Yenangyaung. Development was difficult owing to the general lack of communications and other facilities in this isolated area, but although operating costs were correspondingly heavy, the crude oil was of exceptionally high quality. By 1938, annual output was running at over one million tons.

Following almost total destruction during the war, the rehabilitation of the fields proved a protracted task, output reaching no more than half its pre-war level by 1959. In 1963, the industry was taken over by the State, but with no significant improvement in production. This amounted to only some 600,000 tons in 1967, but exploratory drilling is continuing and more rewarding results may follow.

Refining

Burma's single oil refinery – at Rangoon – was rebuilt in 1957. This plant has an annual throughput capacity of one million tons and is fed by river barge.

INDIA

Production

The main oilfields of India are those at Nahorkatiya and Moran, in Upper Assam, and at Ankleshwar, in Western India – the latter field being the present largest producer. Combined output of these fields in 1967 was about 5 million tons. As well as further inland exploration, future plans include test drilling in the Gulf of Cambay.

Refining

India has long possessed a substantial oil refining industry, whose current annual capacity is now in the region of 16 million tons. At Trombay Island, near Bombay, two important refineries have been built with an aggregate capacity of nearly 6½ million tons annually. Other plants are at Vishakhapatnam, on the east coast, and a smaller plant at Digboi, Assam. Four major new refineries to come on stream since 1962 are at Koyali ($3\frac{1}{2}$ million tons a year), Cochin-Kerala ($2\frac{1}{2}$ million tons), Barauni (2 million tons) and Gauhati (just under one million tons). The latter two plants were built in consequence of the development of the Nahorkatiya and Moran oilfields, these fields being linked to the refineries by pipeline.

PAKISTAN

Production

This country's oil production comes mainly from the Punjab fields, which have been in operation for many years. Output is small, however, and in 1967 amounted to only 500,000 tons. A most useful contribution to the country's national fuel economy is now being made by natural gas. The chief gas fields are at Sui and Sylhet – in West and East Pakistan respectively. Both fields have been linked by pipeline to centres where the gas is used for industrial purposes as well as for domestic consumption. Another major gas field has been found at Mari, to the south of Sui, but this field is not yet in commercial production. In East Pakistan, another new field – discovered at Titas and rated as large as Sui – is now supplying natural gas to Dacca via a 50-mile pipeline.

Refining

The country's refining interests have so far been confined to West Pakistan, where an old-established plant at Rawalpindi is handling about 450,000 tons of crude oil annually. In 1962, a much larger refinery was opened near Karachi, with an annual capacity of some $2\frac{1}{2}$ million tons. A smaller plant in the same area came on stream in 1966 with an annual throughput capacity of 650,000 tons. These plants are now able to meet nearly all of West Pakistan's oil requirements. In East Pakistan, another refinery, with an annual capacity of one million tons, has just come on stream at Chittagong.

JAPAN

Production

As might be expected in view of her intensive industrial development, Japan is now using very substantial quantities of petroleum products. Indeed her oil consumption in 1966 amounted to about 90 million tons – nearly 20 million tons more than the United Kingdom's inland consumption during that same year.

Japan's indigenous oil production, however, is relatively insignificant, totalling just under 800,000 tons in 1967. This output comes from a large number of small fields that have been discovered during the past ninety years. The most important of these are on the main island of Honshu.

At one time, Japan held an oil concession from the USSR in the northern part of Sakahlin Island, but this was cancelled in 1944. She has also forfeited some shale oil deposits which she formerly worked in Manchuria and some natural gas fields in Taiwan (Formosa).

In recent years, Japanese companies have been active in seeking concessions overseas. A first step was taken in 1958 with the formation of a company to operate the Persian Gulf offshore field at Khafji, in the Kuwait/Saudi Arabia Neutral Zone. Crude oil shipments from this field have been reaching Japan since 1961. And, as mentioned earlier, Japanese interests are now participating in oil operations in North Sumatra under contractual agreement with the Indonesian Government.

Refining

Japan now has nearly forty refineries whose combined annual throughput is a little over 100 million tons. In consequence of this tremendous post-war construction programme, she now possesses a greater annual throughput than any other country in the world except the USA and the USSR. Closely associated with this refining industry is a major petroleum-chemical industry, and both these interests are to be extensively expanded in the near future.

CHINA

Production

Despite her long-standing interests in petroleum, China has never ranked as a major producer. She has, however, made strenuous efforts to develop her indigenous resources, with the result that in 1967 her output amounted to about 10 million tons (inclusive of synthetic supplies obtained from coal and shale).

Most of her crude oil production comes from the province of Kansu, in north-west China, though small quantities of oil and natural gas have been obtained in other parts of the country.

In its efforts to implement an ambitious industrialization programme, the Chinese Government is making self-sufficiency in oil supplies a main objective. Exploration in the northern part of the country has led to reports of further substantial discoveries but no detailed assessment of these discoveries has yet been published. There is no doubt that China faces formidable problems in her efforts to increase indigenous production, the chief obstacles being an acute shortage of technicians and equipment. Under China's present political constitution, it is difficult to see how these problems are to be overcome.

Refining

The country has only a relatively small refining industry whose aggregate annual capacity now approximates to 8 million tons. The two principal plants are at Lanchow and Shanghai, with capacities of 3 million tons and $1\frac{1}{4}$ million tons respectively.

OTHER COUNTRIES

Exploration

There are a number of other Asian countries where intensive exploration has so far failed to lead to discovery of petroleum. In particular, exhaustive search has been made for many years in Papua, New Guinea, where surveys have extended over 35,000 square miles at a cost of nearly £40 million. Lack of encouragement led to a curtailment of activity here in 1961, but the venture has not been completely abandoned.

Refining

Several countries without indigenous oil resources now have limited refining capacities apart from those already listed. They include Thailand, Korea, the Philippine Islands and Taiwan.

FUTURE PROSPECTS

Although Asia's oil production cannot claim an importance comparable with that of the main oil-producing areas, this does not mean that there are no grounds for future optimism. On the contrary, there are still extensive onshore and offshore areas awaiting exploration, and but for post-war complications in the political sphere, much of this exploration might by now have been in full swing.

However, recent governmental decisions in some Asian countries have made it difficult or impossible for independent overseas oil companies to continue operations. This is a particularly serious development when a country lacks the technical or financial resources to carry out oil exploration itself. In such a case, the only alternative to accepting the presence of independently owned overseas oil companies is that of seeking State aid from foreign governments.

No matter how these political issues are solved, increased oil supplies are vital to the continued economic growth of the Asian countries. This growth cannot be maintained unless such supplies are forthcoming, and if they are not obtainable from indigenous sources they will have to be imported – if necessary as finished products. Obviously, however, from the point of view of Asia's economy, it is highly desirable that all the countries there should be as self-sufficient as possible in the matter of fuel supplies. Therefore it would seem in Asia's own best interests to make overseas participation in oil production as attractive as could reasonably be expected.

DEVELOPMENT AID TO ASIA

Werner Klatt

WITHOUT aid there would be no development worth its name in Asia. Outside Japan, Asia consists of countries that are marked by their lack of economic development, industry, and social services. They are described as backward, underdeveloped or pre-industrial. Whilst none of these terms is entirely fitting, and some have an unfortunate ring of paternalism, most of the countries of Asia have certain features in common which are absent in the case of fully developed industrial societies. One of the most important characteristics is the role played by farming as the most frequent form of economic activity, and by village life as the most prominent form of society.

Economic and social change is associated with urbanization and industrialization. These are costly processes which are enforced by dictatorial regimes where they are carried out with great speed and paid for out of the forced savings of the cultivators. This is the form of development which has been chosen by the Communist regimes of China, North Korea, North Vietnam, Mongolia and Tibet. Elsewhere in Asia, economic development, though instigated as a matter of urgency, has been carried out at a less rapid pace and it has been financed to a large extent through contributions from abroad.

MULTILATERAL AID

The forms of development aid are so manifold that it is impossible to give a complete picture within the compass of a brief review. The two principal types to be distinguished are multilateral and bilateral aid, the former being channelled through international organs, such as the agencies of the United Nations and the Colombo Plan, whilst the latter is usually given on the basis of agreements between the governments of the donor and the recipient country. To this has to be added the not insignificant contribution which is made to development by private capital investment.

Foreign trade is, of course, the oldest form of economic assistance. Development aid ought to be considered, therefore, in relation to foreign trade transactions which are often the outward sign of aid programmes being implemented. This is particularly so in the case of bilateral aid offers made by countries of the Sino-Soviet bloc which implement their development programmes as a rule through barter trade transactions.

The largest foreign contributor to the economic progress of Asian countries is the United States, which ranks ahead of all other countries in both multilateral and bilateral development programmes. The next largest contributor is Britain. In recent years Germany has entered the sphere of economic development aid on a rapidly increasing scale, but her aid is directed primarily to countries in Africa. Japan deserves also to be mentioned among the donors of foreign aid.

THE WORLD BANK

Of the international organs that have contributed towards economic progress in developing countries of Asia, the World Bank deserves to be singled out because of the size and nature of its development programme. The principal objectives of the World Bank, founded in 1944 as a specialized agency associated with the United Nations, are implicit in its official title – International Bank for Reconstruction and Development. When the most immediate post-war tasks of reconstruction had been fulfilled, the World Bank turned its attention towards aiding the economic growth of developing countries.

The World Bank has made over three hundred loans to some sixty countries, totalling well over US$7,000 million. It obtains funds for these loans from capital subscribed by its seventy-five member countries, from sales of Bank bonds in the various capital markets of the world, and from net earnings on its operations. In addition, sales of portions of Bank loans to other investors and repayments of loans permit the Bank to recover its funds and thereby serve to reduce the amount which the Bank must obtain from other sources for its lending operations.

From its very beginning, the World Bank's emphasis has been on serving as a bridge for the movement of private capital into international investment. This explains why many of its financial resources and more than half its loans have come from private investors. The larger part of this investment has come from outside the United States.

From its inception the World Bank has operated a lending policy patterned on the practices of private investment banks. Thus, in making loans it must give due consideration to the possibilities of repayment. The loans must be for productive purposes and, whether given to government agencies or private enterprises, must carry the guarantee of the government of the country in which they are placed. Before considering a loan the Bank must satisfy itself that the proposed project is economically justified, that the plans for carrying it out are sound and that the borrower will be able to meet payments of interest and principal on the loan when they fall due. The Bank must also determine that the borrower cannot obtain the loan from private sources on reasonable terms, within the prevailing market conditions. The rate of interest charged on Bank loans is based on the rate which it would itself have to pay to borrow money at the time the loan is made, plus a commission charge which is allocated to a Special Reserve, and a small charge to meet administrative costs. In practice, the long-term lending rate of the Bank varies between five and six per cent.

Normally World Bank loans cover only the foreign exchange costs of a project. The Bank feels that it can best serve the interests of its developing member countries by concentrating its loans on basic services, such as electric energy and transportation, without which economic progress is almost impossible. These projects, because of their high costs and low returns, tend to attract little private investment.

At the same time, the Bank has sought to promote the development of private industry. In some cases it has made loans directly to private industries, by contributing to projects such as the production of steel in India and by helping national development banks which use the World Bank's funds for their own lending operations. However, the requirement of a governmental guarantee for all its loans has limited the Bank's action in the field of private investment.

INTERNATIONAL FINANCE CORPORATION

Governments are reluctant at times to guarantee loans to particular private enterprises which, on their part, sometimes fear official interference as a result. To overcome these difficulties, the International Finance Corporation was established in July 1956. Over sixty nations became members of IFC which has funds close on US$100 million and shares its President and Executive Director with the World Bank.

IFC performs a particularly useful function in the field of underwriting stock issues, since in many of its member countries capital markets, where they exist at all, are not yet fully developed. In Asia it has made investments in India and in Pakistan in companies producing cement, steel, pumps, refractory bricks and textiles.

INTERNATIONAL DEVELOPMENT ASSOCIATION

The need for outside capital has been increasing faster than the ability to service conventional loans. Some countries have already begun to draw close to the limit of the debt they can prudently assume on conventional terms. It was awareness of this problem which led to the founding of the International Development Association as an affiliate of the World Bank. The establishment of IDA came after many years of discussions of the desirability of accelerating economic growth in the less developed areas by adding international funds, repayable on other than conventional terms, to the flow of development capital. By 1962, over sixty countries had joined IDA and had subscribed a total of over US$900 million. More than 80 per cent of IDA's subscribed funds is in convertible form. Ten Asian countries have joined IDA.

IDA is closely linked with the World Bank. The President of the World Bank is *ex officio* President of IDA, and the officers and staff of the Bank serve as officers and staff for IDA. A project submitted for IDA financing is expected to meet the same technical, economic, financial, and administrative standards as the World Bank itself would look for if the Bank were making a loan for the project on conventional terms.

It is IDA's primary purpose to provide development capital for countries whose balance of payments prospects would not allow them to incur external debts on conventional terms. Thus most of the IDA credits have been extended for projects which are of a type traditionally financed by the World Bank, but IDA is allowed to finance projects in the field of social investment which the Bank has hitherto not undertaken. In the past IDA has assisted municipal water supply projects in Taiwan and it is investigating the possibility of assisting school construction programmes in some countries. Development credits have been extended for fifty years without interest, amortization to begin after a ten-year period of grace, thereafter, in most cases, one per cent of the principal being repayable annually for ten years and three per cent during the final thirty years.

UNITED NATIONS CREDITS TO ASIA

Throughout Asia and the Far East* some fourteen countries (Afghanistan, Burma, Ceylon, Taiwan, India, Japan, Korea, Laos, Malaysia,

*This term, which includes Afghanistan, is used here as it appears in some of the sources upon which this chapter is based, and in certain cases it is impossible to separate figures for Afghanistan from those for other countries of the area.

712

Nepal, Pakistan, Philippines, Thailand, and Vietnam) are members of the World Bank; most of them (all except Cambodia and Indonesia) are members also of the Bank's affiliate, the International Development Association. Total lending in the area by the two institutions amounts to almost US$4,000 million. Up to 1966 nine had received loans, amounting to well over a quarter of all the World Bank's loans and three quarters of all development credits extended by the International Development Association. The emphasis has been on the development of basic services. Loans for transportation by road, rail, sea, and air amounted to about two fifths of the total. Electric power and industrial development each accounted for approximately a quarter, and most of the remainder had been devoted to agriculture, which also benefited from increased transport and electricity supplies.

The World Bank and IDA have granted loans for railways in Burma, India, Japan, Pakistan, and Thailand; for ports in all these countries except in Japan, and in addition in Taiwan and the Philippines; for roads in India and Japan; and for a natural gas pipe-line in Pakistan.

Seven countries have borrowed from the Bank or IDA so as to finance electric power projects. The loans have helped to finance fifteen major dams and hydro-electric stations, eleven thermo-electric stations, many thousands of miles of transmission lines, and extensive distribution facilities. When all the projects are complete, they will add over 3 million kilowatts to the total generating capacity of countries in Asia and the Far East.

Bank loans for agriculture have helped to increase food production in India through the reclamation of lands, while IDA credits have financed irrigation and drainage schemes. In Pakistan, a Bank loan financed heavy machinery used to prepare land for settlement in the Thal irrigation areas, and IDA credits are helping to pay for a pilot irrigation project and a major scheme to restore waterlogged and salty land to full production. In Japan, the Bank made a loan for equipment to clear and stock new farms established in remote areas, and for imported cattle. A Bank loan to Thailand helped to increase rice production in the Central Plain.

Most of the Bank's lending for industry in Asia and the Far East has been used to finance the expansion of the iron and steel industries of India and Japan. Between them, the two countries have borrowed well over US$300 million for this purpose, installing *inter alia* six blast furnaces, five strip or plate mills, seven converters and two open-hearth furnaces. Coal production in India will be expanded with the help of a Bank loan and IDA credit. In Pakistan, a Bank loan helped to pay for construction of a paper mill. In addition, the Bank and IDA have extended loans and credits amounting to near US$100 million to development banks interested in small industrial companies in India, Pakistan, and Taiwan.

A Bank loan of US$90 million was made to Pakistan towards the cost of works to be carried out under the terms of the settlement of the dispute between Pakistan and India over the use of the waters of the Indus River and its tributaries.

In addition to its lending, the Bank has provided survey missions, whose reports on Ceylon, Malaya and Thailand provide valuable information and advice. Bank missions have kept in particularly close touch with the economic problems of India and Pakistan and have given advice to their governments on various aspects of their development plans and on setting up development banks. Last, but not least, the Bank has concerted the efforts of developed countries to provide aid to the two countries under the auspices of the 'Aid to India' and 'Aid to Pakistan' consortia.

UNITED NATIONS TECHNICAL ASSISTANCE

The deployment of credits and loans on development projects has disclosed a gap at the pre-investment stage that needed closing. The United Nations Special Fund which started its work in 1959 with an initial fund of some US$26 million was charged with creating conditions which make capital investment either feasible or effective. Its assistance consists mainly of surveys, research and demonstration, and its emphasis is on water, irrigation, power and soil surveys. Approximately one third of the Special Fund's contributions have been earmarked for Asia and the Far East. In Thailand an investigation was financed into the silting conditions in Bangkok harbour which was to provide the data necessary for investment in remedial works to be undertaken by the port authority. Other pre-investment schemes include survey work on hydraulic projects in Taiwan, soil surveys in East Pakistan and mineral surveys in West Pakistan.

Whereas the normal minimum sum involved in schemes of the Special Fund amounts to US$250,000, the projects of the Technical Assistance Programme of the United Nations and eight of its specialized agencies rarely surpass one fifth of that sum. The programme has been in operation since 1948 and its main functions are to arrange for experts to visit countries in need of advice; to provide for fellowships for training of experts from developing countries; and to provide equipment required in the course of these activities. A Technical Assistance Board is responsible for the co-ordination and supervision of the programme.

Since its inception, over US$300 million have been expended, some 10,000 experts have been provided and 20,000 fellowships have been awarded. The Food and Agriculture Organization and the World Health Organization usually have the heaviest call on the funds of the technical assistance programme. Much of the work of the experts is concentrated on what is nowadays called 'impact' projects, assistance which – like that financed by the Special Fund – will pave the way for later development. Emphasis is placed on eliminating illiteracy and promoting vocational education; on improved human and animal health; on improved strains of plants and increased use of farm requisites; on surveys of natural resources; on feasibility studies in industry; and on training of technicians, foremen, managers and administrators. In recent years some US$10 million have been expended under this programme in countries of Asia and the Far East, involving 1,000 each of foreign experts and national trainees.

A special form of assistance provided by the World Bank is the training it provides to officials of its member countries. In all, almost a hundred officials from twelve Asian countries have attended the six-month courses of the Economic Development Institute in Washington, D.C., which was established in 1955 with the object of improving the quality of economic management in government in developing countries. Other officials have undergone training at the Bank itself.

The Economic Commission for Asia and the Far East (ECAFE) has played an increasingly active part in matters of technical assistance and the aid programmes of the United Nations. Its annual economic surveys, the reviews of specific aspects of economic development in its quarterly economic bulletins and the reports of its committees are among the indispensable sources of factual information on Asia. They also provide food for thought on a wide range of problems, of which development aid, though not the least important topic, is only the most recent subject for discussion among Asian planners, managers, economists and their foreign experts.

THE COLOMBO PLAN

The survey of multilateral aid would be incomplete without mention being made of the Colombo Plan, the only multilateral programme which applies to Asian countries only. It was created early in 1950 for the furtherance of economic development in South and South-East Asia, and a consultative committee was set up to consider the needs and to assess the resources available and required in the area. Development programmes of the original South and South-East Asian members (India, Pakistan, Ceylon, Malaya, and British Borneo) were drawn up and compared for the six years starting from July 1951, and technical co-operation was instigated from that date. In the meantime, the Colombo Plan has been extended several times, and it has been joined from within the region by Afghanistan, Bhutan, Burma, Cambodia, the Maldive Islands, Nepal, Indonesia, Laos, the Philippines, Sarawak, Singapore (observer), South Korea, South Vietnam, and Thailand. The members from outside the region, i.e. the United Kingdom, Canada, Australia and New Zealand have been joined by the United States and Japan.

The original plans of the South-East Asian member countries were marked by their emphasis on the development of agriculture and transport, each of which were to take a share of one third of the total estimated cost of their plans, the remainder being shared almost equally between the cost of social services (housing, health, education) and industrialization (industry, mining, fuel and power). It was assumed that by far the largest portion of the cost of each plan would have to be met by each country itself. The contributions of the developed member states of the Commonwealth rested in (a) their willingness to provide experts and training facilities; (b) Britain's willingness to release close on £250 million from the sterling balances of the member countries in South-East Asia. During the first ten years of the plan approximately £250 million were spent on experts, trainees and equipment and more than 1,700 experts and over 15,000 training places were supplied. During the same period some £2,850 million from indigenous and foreign sources were committed in the area of South and South-East Asia on economic development projects, and marked progress was achieved in most countries of the area. At the same time sterling reserves were withdrawn at an unexpectedly fast rate and requirements of foreign aid proved to be much larger than anticipated originally.

AID PROGRAMMES OF THE UNITED STATES

Without massive bilateral aid Asia would be in a bad way. As it is, the bulk of credits and grants is of the bilateral kind, and the overwhelming portion of these is American in origin. The American aid programme can be traced to the outbreak of hostilities in Korea, although this gave only a new urgency to problems which had been recognized before that event. In 1950 the activities of the Economic Cooperation Administration, the United States aid organization which had previously operated in Europe, were expanded to Asia and other continents. The importance of technical and economic assistance was underlined in Point IV of President Truman's inaugural address of January 1949 which was to give its name to American aid throughout the world. The need for an expansion of this feature of American foreign policy was underlined in Gordon Gray's report to the President on 'Foreign Economic Policies' and that of the International Development Advisory Board which, under the chairmanship of Nelson Rockefeller, issued 'Partners in Progress'.

An important part of the foreign policy of the United States in this sphere has been the emphasis on creating conditions that will stimulate the investment of private capital in the areas earmarked for economic and technical assistance. In Asia it has been operated under different names, for the purpose of relief, reconstruction and development, including a wide variety of goods and services ranging from surplus farm produce to most modern capital equipment, and from teachers in primary education to specialists in computers and physicists familiar with the application of atomic energy for civilian uses. In strategically vulnerable areas, such as South Korea, South Vietnam, and Taiwan, a large part of the assistance was given under the Mutual Defence Assistance Act. Even where these projects have satisfied American security requirements in the first instance, they have benefited at the same time the recipient countries, in that they aimed at creating stability, provided scarce raw materials and equipment, saved foreign exchange and thus improved living standards. Even so, the result seemed not always to justify the expenditure, and therefore American, like other Western, aid has sometimes come under fire both at home and abroad.

The history of American aid to Asia is too long and varied to be recounted here in any detail except to recall that in March 1961 President Kennedy in a message to Congress redefined it under the following headings: (a) all forms of economic aid to be administered by a single agency; (b) military assistance to be separated from economic aid; (c) aid to be allocated for a period of five years instead of a year-to-year basis; (d) co-operation to be established with other donor nations; (e) aid to be given to nations willing to help themselves by their own economic and social efforts. A new Agency for International Development (AID) took the place of the former International Co-operation Administration (ICA) and it absorbed the Development Loan Fund.

The President was authorized to enter into long-term commitments and to spend US$7,200 million on development loans over a period of five years, subject to annual appropriations.

In the meantime, Congress has had second thoughts and the appropriation for 1968 at US$2,160 million was considerably less than had been requested and also less than had been appropriated in the previous fiscal year. As to the future, reports on United States aid failures are likely to keep Congress in a critical mood; they may lead to further economies. Even so, the American aid programme is of extraordinarily large proportions and surpasses anything ever done before in this sphere. Since the end of the Second World War close on US$40,000 million have been appropriated to Asia and the Far East (excluding the Middle East), of which 70 per cent were for economic projects and 30 per cent of a military nature. Of the economic aid, two thirds were grants and one third loans. The chief recipients were India, South Korea, Taiwan, South Vietnam, Japan, and Pakistan – in that order. The programme reveals the priorities which have prevailed in the past and which are now being exposed to criticism.

BRITISH AND EUROPEAN AID

Compared with American orders of magnitude Britain's foreign aid programme may seem modest. Just the same, since the end of the Second World War some £517 million have been allocated by the Exchequer to countries of Asia and the Far East. Of this sum over two thirds were offered as loans and the remainder were grants-in-aid. About half of the total was earmarked for India and about one fifth for Burma and Malaya together, Pakistan and other countries of the area sharing the remainder. Public and private projects range from government cover for a steel mill built by an industrial consortium in India to the provision of research staff for Burma and of arms during the emergency in Malaya.

In recognition of the importance of technical assistance to donor and recipient alike, all forms of aid of this kind were brought in 1961 under a single government agency, the Department of Technical Co-operation.

In 1964 the Government created a Ministry of Overseas Development under a Cabinet Minister who was given overall control of all aid operations.

Of other countries in Europe, France and West Germany are the principal donors, but both specialize mainly in areas other than Asia and the Far East, although a German industrial consortium has set up a steel mill in India. The European community has made some contributions of a general nature which are of significance also to the area under review. Under the auspices of the Organization for Economic Co-operation and Development (OECD – formerly OEEC) surveys have been undertaken of the flow of international capital from public and private sources which suggest that earlier estimates, published under the auspices of the United Nations, have underestimated the flow of resources from developed to developing countries.

The world total now runs at an annual rate equivalent to over US $8,000 million. Of this total, the share of Asia and the Far East may be estimated to be nearly 50 per cent. It used to be higher, but the recent emergence of independent countries in Africa has shifted the priority of aid programmes in favour of the latest claimants. Even at the high rates of financial assistance quoted it is estimated that only two thirds of the minimum requirements of the developing countries in foreign capital are being met at present. Unfavourable terms of trade and increasing debt services absorb a substantial and growing portion of the financial assistance of developing countries, and high rates of growth of population swallow much of the economic progress that is made.

In recognition of past shortcomings of Western aid programmes, the Development Assistance Committee of the Organization for Economic Co-operation and Development, in its first annual review of 1962, made some timely recommendations, e.g. the need for (a) securing public support for expanding aid programmes; (b) co-ordinating aid efforts to ensure their fullest effect; (c) linking aid to long-term development objectives; (d) increasing the earnings of foreign exchange of the developing countries by providing expanding markets for their products, including manufactured goods, in developed countries. Thus the awareness is growing that attention must be devoted, more than in the past, to the effectiveness of aid as against its mere size. This recognition has been brought about in part by a critical analysis in recent years of the methods practised in developing countries by members of the Communist bloc.

COMMUNIST BLOC AID

Soviet interest in developing countries is of fairly recent date. Even today, aid – like trade – is a residual rather than an essential part of Soviet foreign policy. However, since Stalin's death and more specifically since 1956 when the Soviet Union experienced its 'Indian mutiny' within its realm, the awareness of the problems of development has grown to the extent that the concept of 'peaceful coexistence' has replaced that of 'socialism in one country'.

Soviet publications claim that not only has Russia grown, within less than five decades following the revolution, from a backward country to a great power, but in particular it has developed tribal areas, kept by the Tsarist regime under conditions of feudal servitude, ranging from the areas of the small peoples of the extreme north to the territories of the aborigines in the Caucasian mountains. Although much of this is part of the national folklore rather than the historical record, it meets with a certain response in some of the newly emergent countries. Where Russia is regarded as too remote or too European, China's more recent experiment in development sometimes has a special appeal. This was at least so prior to the Sino-Indian border incidents and the failures of China's 'Great Leap Forward' and 'Cultural Revolution' (see chapter entitled 'The Economy of China', p. 667). In time, China may yet recover its appeal in Asia.

There is a certain affinity between the developing countries and the Communist bloc which has its origin in their predominantly rural character; their preoccupation with farming pursuits; their urbanization and industrialization through planning as conscious attempts to break with the medieval past; and, last but not least, their hostility to certain undesirable features of Western capitalism and colonial rule, if not to these phenomena as such. In these circumstances the attraction which the Communist bloc and its aid have is hardly surprising. Its contribution to development in Asia and the Far East has been smaller than the publicity given to it seems to imply.

Since Communist bloc aid was started in 1954, offers to developing countries equivalent to almost US $9,000 million have been made by members of the bloc. Of this total, Asia's share accounts for approximately half, the principal recipients being India (US $1,950 million), Indonesia (US $750 million) and Afghanistan (US $600 million). Indonesia also received a substantial part of the military aid offered to Asia.

Projects, like countries, are highly selected, more than half of the economic aid offered being earmarked to go to industrial projects where the emphasis lies with plants processing indigenous raw materials and manufacturing producer and capital goods. The largest project of this kind is the much publicized Bilai steel mill in India. Prestige projects, such as a sports stadium, a tourist hotel, or a technological institute have also received a good deal of public attention, but there are also less conspicuous, though no less useful projects, such as cement factories and sugar mills.

The actual financial outlay for Communist economic aid has been relatively small. Although official figures are not published, it can be estimated at little more than US $1,300 million, or one third of the offers made between the beginning of 1954 and the end of 1966. Military offers have been met from Soviet armament depots at a faster rate than non-military commitments, but here data are even less readily available and less reliable than in the sphere of economic aid.

As is usual, plant equipment is accompanied by technicians of whom there are at present some 5,000 from Soviet bloc countries operating in Asian countries. Simultaneously Asian students have been trained at universities and technical colleges throughout the Soviet bloc. Their present numbers are unlikely to total more than 2,500. Linguistic difficulties form a barrier for technicians and trainees even where other obstacles are ignored.

As Soviet bloc aid consists mostly of credits and is thus repayable in full, there is a close correlation between the trends of trade and aid. At present Communist bloc trade with developing countries in Asia and the Far East runs at an annual rate of about US $800 million in either direction, consisting of an exchange of industrial capital goods against agricultural and mineral raw materials. These are small transactions when compared with those of the traditional commercial partners of Asia. In fact, Communist trade transactions, like aid disbursements, amount to well under 10 per cent of the corresponding operations of non-Communist countries.

Even so, the Soviet – like the American – aid programme seems to have been the subject of a careful political reappraisal leading to a temporary decline in offers in 1962 due to certain strains in Russia's economy. In 1966 approximately US $800 million were offered to Asian countries from the Communist bloc. China, with limited resources, made hardly any offers of aid in 1966. Its foreign policy seems to favour revolutionary developments in preference to regimes composed of members of the 'national bourgeoisie' of developing countries.

CONCLUSION

Aid to developing countries is part and parcel of the conflict of a divided world. Seen from the developing countries, there is a *prima facie* case for taking economic aid irrespective of any political aspects of importance to the donor. The inclination in favour of non-alignment, though strong, has however been weakened in South and South-East Asia since the fallacy of this concept has become manifest in the recent past. As a result the rivalry between the industrial West and the Soviet bloc is recognized increasingly as a fact of life, of which economic aid has become an indispensable part.

TABLE 1

WORLD BANK AND INTERNATIONAL DEVELOPMENT
ASSOCIATION. LOANS AND CREDITS TO ASIA. 1944–66

(US$ million)

	South Asia	SE Asia and Far East	Total
Economic Aid:			
Bank Loans	1,400	1,325	2,725
IDA Credits	1,000	25	1,025
Total	2,400	1,350	3,750
thereof:			
India	1,650	–	1,650
Japan	–	750	750
Pakistan	700	–	700
Thailand	–	225	225
Malaysia	–	150	150
Philippines	–	100	100
Others	50	125	175
Tota	2,400	1,350	3,750
thereof:			
Transport	(950)	(550)	(1,500)
Industry	(600)	(250)	(850)
Power	(500)	(450)	(950)
Others	(350)	(100)	(450)
Total	(2,400)	(1,350)	(3,750)

( ) – estimate.　　　*Sources:* US Foreign Affairs Committee Report, 1967.

DEVELOPMENT AID TO ASIA

TABLE 2

UNITED STATES ECONOMIC AND MILITARY AID
TO ASIA. 1946-66
(US$ million)

	South Asia	SE Asia and Far East	Total
Economic Aid:			
Loans	6,925	2,975	9,900
Grants	3,460	14,390	17,850
Total	10,385	17,365	27,750
Military Aid (only partly declared)	–	10,235	10,235
Grand Total	10,385	27,600	37,985
thereof:			
India	6,770	–	6,770
Korea	–	6,675	6,675
Taiwan	–	4,900	4,900
Vietnam	–	4,590	4,590
Japan	–	3,970	3,970
Pakistan	3,070	–	3,070
Philippines	–	1,925	1,925
Thailand	–	1,090	1,090
Indonesia	–	830	830
Laos	–	475	475
Cambodia	–	345	345
Afghanistan	345	–	345
Others	200	2,800	3,000
Grand Total	10,385	27,600	37,985

Sources: International Co-operation Administration, U.S. Foreign Assistance 1945–61. Agency for International Development, US Foreign Assistance 1945–63. Washington 1963. Foreign Affairs Committee, US Overseas Loans and Grants, 1945–66. Washington 1967.

TABLE 3

UNITED KINGDOM. ECONOMIC AND TECHNICAL ASSISTANCE TO ASIA. 1945/46–1966/67

(£ million)

	Loans	Grants	Total
Economic and Technical Aid			
South Asia	314	12	326
SE Asia and Far East	20	87	107
Unspecified	22	62	84
Total	356	161	517
thereof:			
India	251	6	257
Malaysia	16	54	70
Burma	4	33	37
Pakistan	63	6	69
Unspecified	22	62	84
Total	356	161	517

Sources: Central Statistical Office, Annual Abstracts of Statistics, 1961 to 1967. London 1961 to 1967.

TABLE 4

COMMUNIST BLOC ECONOMIC AND TECHNICAL AID
TO ASIA. 1954–66

(US$ million)

	South Asia	SE Asia and Far East	Total
Economic Aid Offers			
Loans	2,750	850	3,600
Grants	300	100	400
Total	3,050	950	4,000
thereof:			
Soviet Aid	2,400	400	2,800
East European Aid	450	300	750
Chinese Aid	200	250	450
Total	3,050	950	4,000
thereof:			
India	1,950	–	1,950
Indonesia	–	750	750
Afghanistan	600	–	600
Others	500	200	700
Total	3,050	950	4,000
Economic Aid Drawings			
Loans	950	300	1,250
Grants	50	50	100
Total	1,000	350	1,350

	1962	1964	1966
Economic Experts	4,000	4,500	5,000
Students Trained	3,500	2,500	2,500
Foreign Trade Agreements	45	45	45
Foreign Trade Turnover (US$ million)	1,000	1,200	1,600

Sources: National Statistics. Estimates as of December 1967.

BIBLIOGRAPHY

BOOKS

R. L. Allen. *Soviet Economic Warfare*. (Public Affairs Press, Washington, 1960.)

H. J. P. Arnold. *Aid for Developing Countries*. (Bodley Head, 1962.)

F. C. Benham. *The Colombo Plan and Other Essays*. (Royal Institute of International Affairs, London, 1961.) *Economic Aid to Underdeveloped Countries*. (Oxford University Press, 1961.)

J. S. Berliner. *Soviet Economic Aid*. (Praeger, New York, 1958.)

A. A. Jordan. *Foreign Aid and the Defence of South East Asia*. (Praeger, New York, 1962.)

M. Kovner. *The Challenge of Coexistence*. (Public Affairs Press, Washington, 1961.)

R. F. Mikesell and J. N. Behrman. *Financing World Trade and the Sino-Soviet Bloc*. (Princeton University Press, Princeton, N.J., 1958.)

A. Nove and D. Donnelly. *Trade with Communist Countries*. (Hutchinson, 1960.)

OFFICIAL PAPERS

Commonwealth Consultative Committee. *The Colombo Plan for Co-operative Economic Development in South and South East Asia*. Cmd. 8080. (London, 1950.) *The Colombo Plan, The Tenth Report*. Cmd. 1600. (London, 1961.) *The Colombo Plan*. Cmd. 3189. (London, 1966.)

ECAFE. *Economic Surveys of Asia and the Far East*. (Bangkok, 1948–1967.) *Economic Bulletins for Asia and the Far East*. (Bangkok, 1950–1967.)

HM Government. *Technical Cooperation*. Cmd. 1698. (London, 1962.) *Technical Assistance from the United Kingdom for Overseas Development*. Cmd. 1308. (London, 1961.) *Annual Abstract of Statistics*. (London, 1967.)

OECD. *The Flow of Financial Resources to Less Developed Countries, 1961–1965*. (Paris, 1967.)

US Congress. *Economic Policies Towards Less Developed Countries*. (Washington, 1961.) *United States Foreign Policy: Asia*. (Washington, 1959.) *US Grants and Loans*. (Washington, 1967.)

US Department of State. *The Sino-Soviet Economic Offensive in the Less Developed Countries*. (Washington, 1958.) *Communist Economic Policy in the Less Developed Areas*. (Washington, 1960.) *Communist Governments and Developing Nations*. (Washington, 1967.)

US Government. *ICA, U.S. Foreign Assistance*. (Washington, 1962.) *AID, US Foreign Assistance*. (Washington, 1962.) *Mutual Defence Assistance Control Act of 1951*. (Washington, 1951–1965.)

United Nations. *ECOSOC, International Flow of Long-Term Capital and Official Donations 1960–1962*. (New York, 1965.)

United Nations. *Yearbook of the United Nations, 1965*. (New York, 1966.)

BIOGRAPHICAL NOTES
ON CONTRIBUTORS

W. A. C. ADIE, M.A., Senior Research Fellow, St Antony's College, Oxford. Formerly worked on Far Eastern and South-East Asian affairs at the Foreign Office and at posts in the area. Now engaged in research on recent and contemporary history of China. Author of articles in *China Quarterly*, *International Affairs* and other specialized journals, co-author of several books on Eastern affairs and member of the Royal Institute of International Affairs Working Group on China and the World.

MARTIN BERNAL read Chinese at Cambridge, spent eight months at Peking University 1959-60 and two years in the USA working towards a thesis on *Chinese Socialism Before 1913*. At present he is Fellow and Assistant Tutor at King's College, Cambridge and a contributor to the *New Statesman* and the *New York Review of Books*.

CARMEN BLACKER read Modern Greats at Somerville College, Oxford and studied Japanese at the school of Oriental and African Studies, University of London and at Keio University, Tokyo. Lecturer in Japanese at the University of Cambridge from 1958. A practising Buddhist.

S. A. BROADBRIDGE studied Economics and Economic History at Southampton University College and the London School of Economics. He has taught at Ibadan, Aberdeen and London Universities. Visiting Scholar of Institute of Social Science, Tokyo University, 1963-4. Now Senior Lecturer in Economic History, Sheffield University. He is the author of *Industrial Dualism in Japan* (Cass, 1966).

PROFESSOR SRIPATI CHANDRASEKHAR received his training from the Madras Presidency College, the University of Madras, and Columbia and New York Universities. After lecturing for two years in American universities he became Professor and Head of the Department of Economics, Annamalai University, South India, 1947-51. Director of Demographic Research, UNESCO, Paris, 1948-9. Professor and Head of the Department of Economics, Baroda University, Baroda. Nuffield Fellow, London School of Economics, 1953-5. Director, Indian Institute for Population Studies, 1956 onwards. Visiting Professor of Demography, University of Missouri, 1957, University of Pittsburgh, 1961. Has lectured before numerous universities in the USA, Canada, UK, Scandinavia, Middle East, Africa and South-East Asia. Has been a delegate to numerous international conferences. Is a member of several national and international learned bodies. Is a member of the Demographic Advisory Committee of the Government of India and the

International Union for the Scientific Study of Population. Elected a Member of Parliament (Upper House) at New Delhi, 1964. Appointed Professor of Demography, University of California, Riverside, 1965. Appointed a member of the Cabinet of the Government of India in charge of Health and Family Planning on 13 March 1967.

WALTER FRANK CHOINSKI. Educated in letters and law at the University of Wisconsin. On active duty in United States Army 1939–58: retired with rank of Colonel. Since 1958 associated with the American Institutes for Research in the Behavioral Sciences, Pittsburgh, Pennsylvania, where now Director of Research for the Military Assistance Institute of Washington, DC and Arlington, Virginia. Has lived and travelled extensively in Poland, Germany, Italy, France, North and South Korea, Laos, Cambodia, Vietnam, Thailand, Kashmir and Mexico. Has written books on fourteen countries which are now in use at the Military Assistance Institute by student officers assigned to duty in overseas areas.

EDWARD CONZE. b. 1904, London. Educated in Germany; studied philosophy at various German universities, and obtained the degree of Ph.D. at Cologne in 1928. In 1933 he returned to England, where he has conducted extra-mural classes for twenty-five years and written a number of books on Buddhism. In 1963–4 he went to the University of Wisconsin as a Distinguished Visiting Professor of Buddhist Studies, in 1964–5 he was a Research Fellow at Manchester College, Oxford, and in 1966–8 a Professor of Indic Studies at the University of Washington, Seattle. At present he is a Visiting Professor at the University of Lancaster. He is a Vice-President of the Buddhist Society, London.

R. P. DORE. Professor of Sociology with special reference to the Far East at the London School of Economics and Political Science and the School of Oriental and African Studies. Formerly taught at the University of British Columbia. Author of *City Life in Japan* (University of California Press, Berkeley and Los Angeles) and *Land Reform in Japan* (Oxford University Press, 1959). B.A. in Modern Japanese at London University.

BERTRAM H. FARMER. b. 1916. President of St John's College, Cambridge; Reader in South Asian Geography and Director of the Centre of South Asian Studies, University of Cambridge. Publications include: 'Ceylon' in O. H. K. Spate and A. T. A. Learmonth, *India and Pakistan* (Methuen, 3rd ed., 1967); 'Rainfall and Water Supply in the Dry Zone of Ceylon' in R. W. Steel and C. A. Fisher (Eds.) *Geographical Essays on British Tropical Lands* (George Philip, 1956); *Pioneer Peasant Colonization in Ceylon* (Oxford University Press for Royal Institute of International Affairs, 1957); *Ceylon: a Divided Nation* (Oxford University Press for Institute of Race Relations, 1963).

C. P. FITZ GERALD. b. 1902, London; educated at Clifton College, Bristol. Lived in China 1923–39, with brief breaks, and for four years after the war,

1946–50. Has subsequently paid two visits to China (1956 and 1958). Lever-hulme Fellowship for anthropological research in China, 1936–9. Worked at Tali, Yunnan province. Representative of the British Council in North China, 1946–50. Author of many books on China, including *The Birth of Communist China* (Penguin Books, 1955), *China: A Short Cultural History* (Cresset Press, revised edn, 1961) and *The Chinese View of their Place in the 1965 World* (The Royal Institute of International Affairs, 1964), and of the *Concise History of East Asia* (Heinemann, 1966).

RICHARD HARRIS. b. 1914 in China and lived there until 1928. Returned to China on war service, 1945; with British Embassy in China, 1947–50; joined *The Times* as correspondent in Hong Kong, 1951–3, and Singapore 1953–5. Since 1955 specialist on Asian Affairs for *The Times,* and now Deputy Foreign Editor. Author of *Independence and After* (Oxford University Press, 1962) and *America and East Asia* (Times Publishing Co., 1968). Has also taken part in broadcasting and television on Asian subjects.

W. J. HARRIS, of the Petroleum Information Bureau, is a member of the Petroleum Institution.

P. J. HONEY is Reader in Vietnamese at the School of Oriental and African Studies, University of London. Most of his published work is in the form of articles, but he has written three books, *North Vietnam Today* (Praeger, New York, 1962), *Communism in North Vietnam* (Allen & Unwin, 1965) and *Genesis of a Tragedy* (Benn, 1968). He has also lectured and broadcast extensively.

GEOFFREY HUDSON. Fellow of All Souls College, Oxford, 1926–54. Served in the Research Department of the Foreign Office, 1939–46. Worked part-time on the editorial staff of *The Economist*, 1946–54. Fellow and Director of Far Eastern Studies at St Antony's College, Oxford, since 1954. Advisory Editor of *The China Quarterly* since 1960. Author of *Europe and China: a Survey of their Relations in History to 1800* (Edward Arnold, 1931); *The Far East in World Politics* (Oxford University Press, 2nd edn, 1939).

D. INSOR has lived a number of years in Thailand and has written the only comprehensive account so far of present conditions (see page 297 above). He has contributed articles to the *Guardian* on South-East Asian affairs.

RAGHAVAN IYER. Educated in Bombay and Oxford (First Class Honours in Modern Greats, President of the Oxford Union). Spent a year with the Indian Planning Commission. Formerly Fellow and Lecturer in Politics, St Antony's College, Oxford. Visiting Professor at the Universities of Oslo, Chicago and Ghana. Edited *South Asian Affairs* (Chatto & Windus, 1960) and *The Glass Curtain Between Asia and Europe* (Oxford University Press, 1965). Now teaches at the University of California and is also associated with the Centre for the Study of Democratic Institutions, Santa Barbara.

NOTES ON CONTRIBUTORS

DR WERNER KLATT, O.B.E. is a Fellow of St Antony's College, Oxford. He was for many years economic adviser at the Foreign Office. As a consultant to United Nations agencies he has undertaken a number of surveys in various Asian countries. He has written for journals in England, America and the Continent and he edited and contributed to *The Chinese Model. A Political, Economic and Social Survey* (Hong Kong and Oxford University Press, 1965). He is now engaged in a research project on land and labour in Asia.

OWEN LATTIMORE (b. 1900) spent his early life in China engaged in business, journalism and research. Research Student at Harvard University, 1929. Fellow of Harvard-Yenching Institute in Peiping, 1930–1. Research Fellow, Guggenheim Foundation, Peking, 1931–3. Editor, *Pacific Affairs*, 1934–41. Lecturer, Johns Hopkins University, 1938–63. Director, School of International Relations, Johns Hopkins University, 1939–53. Political Adviser to Generalissimo Chiang Kai-shek, 1941–2. Director, Pacific Operations, Office of War Information, San Francisco, 1943. Economic Consultant, American Reparations Commission in Japan, 1945. Visiting lecturer at École Pratique des Hautes Études, Sorbonne, 1958–9, and University of Copenhagen, 1961. Foreign Member, Academy of Science, Mongolian People's Republic. Professor and Head of Department of Chinese Studies and Centre for Research on China, University of Leeds. Author of many books on Asia.

EDMUND RONALD LEACH. Provost of King's College, Cambridge, and Reader in Social Anthropology in the University of Cambridge. Author of *Social and Economic Organisation of the Rowanduz Kurds* (1940), *Social Science Research in Sarawak* (1948), *Political Systems of Highland Burma* (1954), *Pul Eliya: A Village in Ceylon* (1961), *Rethinking Anthropology* (1961), and numerous papers in anthropological journals. Graduated from Cambridge (Clare College) with a first class degree in Engineering (Mechanical Sciences) in 1932. During the period 1937–9 studied social anthropology at the London School of Economics under Professors B. Malinowski and Raymond Firth. Spent a brief period in Iraq in 1938. In 1939 was engaged in fieldwork among the Kachins of Northern Burma. Much of the war spent on 'irregular' activities in Northern Burma. In 1946 returned to LSE and completed a Ph.D. In 1947 spent six months in Borneo carrying out research on behalf of the Colonial Office. Was engaged in fieldwork in Ceylon in 1954 and again in 1956. Reith Lecturer 1967.

CHONG-SIK LEE is a native of Korea and an associate professor of political science at the University of Pennsylvania. He is the author of *The Politics of Korean Nationalism* and has contributed a number of articles on the Korean Communist movement and the North Korean regime to scholarly journals.

ALAN MACKAY is a Senior Lecturer in Crystallography at Birkbeck College (University of London). After taking his first degree at Cambridge in 1947 he worked in industry and then did crystallographic research at London

University. He has worked in the USSR and in Yugoslavia on exchange schemes; in 1961 he visited scientific institutions in Japan for three months and in 1963 visited India for the same period.

The past, present and future relations of science and society have been a major spare-time concern. Dr Mackay is co-founder of the Science of Science Foundation which organizes study in this field. He has written on symmetry, documentation and translation problems besides crystallographic and science study topics.

LOIS MITCHISON first went to Asia as a university teacher in Pakistan and travelled widely in India and Ceylon. She worked as a foreign correspondent for the *Guardian* in Asia, and later as a free-lance writer, visiting China and most countries in South-East Asia. Her articles and photographs have been published in the *Guardian, Neue Zürcher, Zeitung, New Statesman* and *Glasgow Herald,* and she has broadcast on the Asian, African and Home Services of the BBC. After a working visit to West Africa she wrote *Nigeria: Newest Nation* in 1960 (Pall Mall Press), *The Overseas Chinese* in 1961 (Bodley Head), *Gillian Lo* (Faber) in 1963 and *China* (Thames & Hudson) in 1966.

HUGH MORLEY. b. 1917, M.A., D.PHIL: educated at Queens' College, Cambridge and recently spent a period as a Research Fellow in Oxford. Has written on the affairs of South and South-East Asia where he has resided and travelled extensively.

LESLIE PALMIER made the first of several visits to Indonesia in 1951 as part of his graduate studies at the London School of Economics. He took his Ph.D. in 1956, and spent the next academic year as Research Fellow in Southeast Asia Studies at Yale University. From 1957 to 1962 he was head of the Department of Asian Studies at Victoria University of Wellington, New Zealand. He then served with the Unesco Research Centre on Social and Economic Development in Southern Asia, Delhi, and the United Nations Research Institute for Social Development, Geneva, before joining Bath University of Technology in 1967. He is an Associate Fellow of St Antony's College, Oxford. He has published *Social Status and Power in Java* (Athlone Press, 1960), *Indonesia and the Dutch* (Oxford University Press, 1962), and *Indonesia* (Thames & Hudson, 1965).

KAVALAM MADHAVA PANIKKAR (b. 1895; d. 1963). Vice-Chancellor, Jammu and Kashmir University; ex-MP (Rajya Sabha); D.Litt. (Delhi), LL.D. Member of the National Academy of Letters, India. Educated at Madras, Oxford; Scholar of Christ Church, Barrister-at-Law (Middle Temple). Career: Editor, *Hindustan Times*, New Delhi; Minister, Patiala State; Prime Minister, Bikaner State; Member, Constituent Assembly of India; Vice-President, Royal India Society, London; Vice-President, Indian Council for Cultural Relations; Member, Indian Academy of Letters; Ambassador in China (1948–52); Ambassador in Egypt (1952–3); Member,

States Reorganization Commission (1954–6); Ambassador in France (1956–9); Member, Rajya Sabha (Upper House of Parliament) (1959–61). Invited to deliver lectures at the Universities of Paris, Oxford, St Gallen (Switzerland), and at Indian universities. Author of numerous books on Asia; also published novels, plays and poems in Malayalam.

PETER PARTNER (b. 1924) is the author of *A Short Political Guide to the Arab World* (Pall Mall Press, 1960), and of various works on European medieval history. Teaches history at Winchester College.

CANON DAVID M. PATON was an Anglican missionary in China. Author of *Christian Missions and the Judgment of God* (S.C.M. Press, 1953) and *Anglicans and Unity* (Mowbrays, 1962), and editor of *Essays in Anglican Self-Criticism* (S.C.M. Press, 1958), *Church and Race in South Africa*, (S.C.M. Press, 1958), and of two collections of the writings of Roland Allen.

GEORGE N. PATTERSON went to China as a missionary in 1946 and from 1947 to 1950 worked among the Khambas of East Tibet. When China invaded Tibet he remained on the Indo-Tibetan border studying and writing on the political affairs of the Himalayan countries and tribes. He has been a freelance journalist, correspondent for the *Daily Telegraph* and the *Observer* and contributor to leading international journals. He has also lectured and broadcast on Asian affairs. His publications include *Tibetan Journey* (1954), *God's Fool* (1956), *Up and Down Asia* (1958), *Tragic Destiny* (1959), *Tibet in Revolt* (1960), and *Peking versus Delhi* (1963) (all by Faber & Faber). Other books include *The Unquiet Frontier* (Dragonfly Books, 1967), and *Christianity in Communist China* (World Books, Waco, Texas, 1968). He also contributed to *The Chinese Model*, a symposium by twelve international authorities on China, edited by Dr Werner Klatt (Oxford and Hong Kong University Press, 1964).

E. J. B. ROSE. Educated Rugby and New College, Oxford. Literary Editor of the *Observer*, 1948–51. First Director of the International Press Institute, Zurich, from 1951 to 1962. Under his direction the IPI launched a programme of Technical Assistance to the Asian Press in 1960 following a survey of the needs which he conducted in 1958.

SAUL ROSE, M.A., D.PHIL. Fellow of New College, Oxford. Lecturer in International Relations at Aberdeen University, 1949–52. International Secretary of the Labour Party, 1952–5. Fellow of St Antony's College, Oxford, 1955–63. Publications: *Socialism in Southern Asia* (Oxford University Press, 1959); *Britain and South-East Asia* (Chatto & Windus, 1963). Editor of *Politics in Southern Asia* (Macmillan, 1963.)

E. F. SCHUMACHER. b. 1911, Bonn; emigrated to England in 1937. Educated at the universities of Bonn and Berlin, Oxford (Rhodes Scholar), and Columbia, New York. After several years in business, farming and journalism joined the British Control Commission for Germany in 1946 as Economic Adviser. Economic Adviser of the National Coal Board, London, since 1950 and Director of Statistics since 1963. In 1955 seconded to United Nations as Economic Adviser to the Government of the Union of Burma; in 1962 invited by the Indian Government to advise the Indian Planning Commission on problems of Indian development policy. Has travelled widely in Europe, America and Asia and published many articles and several books on economic and philosophical subjects. In November 1963 received an honorary doctor's degree from the Technical University of Clausthal, West Germany. In 1966, became Founder/Director of Intermediate Technology Development Group Limited, at 9 King Street, Covent Garden, London WC2.

EDWARD SHILS. b. 1911; Professor of Sociology and Social Thought at the University of Chicago, and Fellow of King's College, Cambridge. His publications include *The Intellectual between Tradition and Modernity: The Indian Situation* (Mouton, The Hague, 1961) and *Political Development in the New States* (Mouton, 1963); joint author and editor (with Talcott Parsons) of *Toward a General Theory of Action* (Harper & Row, New York, 1962). Author of *Theories of Society: Foundations of Modern Sociological Theory* (Free Press, New York 1961). He is editor of *Minerva: A Review of Science Learning and Policy*.

ASLAM SIDDIQI. Author of *Pakistan Seeks Security* (Longmans, Branch, Lahore, 1960) and *A Path for Pakistan* (Pakistan Publishing House, Karachi, 1964), etc. Regular contributor to specialized journals. Active member of Pakistan Institute of International Affairs. Deputy Director, Central Institute of Islamic Research, Pakistan.

KHUSHWANT SINGH. Educated in England; practised law at Lahore till Partition. Thereafter with the Indian Ministry of External Affairs, All India Radio and the Planning Commission (edited *Yojana*). Long-term grant from Rockefeller Foundation to carry out research in Sikh history (1958) which resulted in a two-volume *History of the Sikhs* (Princeton University Press, Princeton, N.J., 1963–6). Other works include *Ranjit Singh – Maharaja of the Punjab* (Allen & Unwin, 1963) and two novels and three collections of short stories. Is visiting Professor at Princeton University.

DERRICK SINGTON. b. 1908; educated Wellington College and Trinity College, Oxford; free-lance journalist; commanded propaganda unit in North-West Europe campaign in Second World War; Deputy-Controller of *Die Welt*, the British-launched West German newspaper (1946–50); *Manchester Guardian* correspondent in South-East Asia, covering the war in Indo-China and the Malayan Communist insurrection (1950–2); staff leader-writer of *Manchester Guardian* (1952–4). Publications: *The Goebbels Experiment* (with Arthur Weidenfeld) (1942); *Belsen Uncovered* (1947); *The Offenders*, a book against capital punishment (with Giles Playfair) (1957); and *Malayan Perspective* (1952), a Fabian brochure.

PERCIVAL SPEAR took a B.A. in History from St Catherine's College Cambridge, and then proceeded to India, where he was a Lecturer in History at St Stephen's College, Delhi and an honorary Reader in the University of Delhi between the years 1924 and 1940. In 1937 he received a Leverhulme Research Fellowship for work on Indian history. In 1940 he joined the Government of India and became Deputy Secretary in the Department of Information and Broadcasting. After the war he became Fellow and Bursar of Selwyn College, Cambridge, and divided his time between administrative duties and Indian historical studies. In 1957-8 he was a visiting Professor in Indian History at the University of California (Berkeley). He is now a University Lecturer in History. Dr Spear's published works are as follows: *The Nabobs: English Social Life in India in the 18th century* (Oxford University Press, 1932; Oxford paperback edn, 1962); *Dehli: A Historical Sketch* (Oxford University Press, 1937); *India, Pakistan and the West* (Oxford University Press, 4th Oris edn, 1967); *The Twilight of the Mughals* (Cambridge University Press, 1951); *The Oxford History of Modern India* (Oxford University Press, 3rd edn, 1965); *India: A Modern History* (University of Michigan Press, Ann ⁺961); *History of India*, Vol. 2, (Penguin Books, 1965).

⸱. b. 1913 at Doncaster, Yorkshire. Educated at Repton ⸱⸱⸱ton College, Oxford. Lecturer at Otaru College of Commerce, Hokkaido, Japan, 1937–40. Army Officer in Egypt, Singapore, India, Burma and London, 1941–6. Research Scholar of the Australian National University, 1948–52. Research Fellow of the Australian National University, 1952–5. Roger Heyworth Memorial Research Fellow of St Antony's College, Oxford, 1955–60. Official Fellow of St Antony's College since 1960. Lecturer in Far Eastern Studies, University of Oxford since 1962. Visited post-war Japan in 1949, 1953–4, 1959–60, 1961. Publications: *The Double Patriots: A Study of Japanese Nationalism* (Chatto & Windus, 1957), *A History of Modern Japan* (Penguin Books, 1960), *Japan* (Oxford University Press, 1965), and (with F. W. Deakin) *The Case of Richard Sorge* (Chatto & Windus, 1966).

HUGH TINKER served on the Assam-Burma border in 1942. Professor of History, University of Rangoon, 1954–5. Now Professor of Government and Politics in the University of London.

S. V. UTECHIN. b. 1921 in Russia; educated at Moscow University (Faculty of History), Kiel University and Oxford (B.Litt.). Senior Research Officer in Soviet Studies at the London School of Economics and Political Science, 1958–62; Research Fellow at St Antony's College, Oxford since 1962. Publications: *Everyman's Concise Encyclopaedia of Russia* (Dent, 1961), *Russian Political Thought: A Concise History* (Dent, 1964), and many articles on modern Russian history and Soviet affairs.

GEOFFREY WHEELER was Director of the Central Asian Research Centre, London, from 1953 to 1968. He served for thirty-three years in the Army and Indian Political Service and was Counsellor in the British Embassy in Tehran from 1946 to 1950. Author of *Racial Problems in Soviet Muslim Asia* and *The Modern History of Soviet Central Asia*, and Joint Editor of *Central Asian Review*, London.

GUY WINT. b. London, 1910. Educated at Dulwich College, Oriel College, Oxford, and Berlin University. Member of St Antony's College, Oxford since 1957. Was a leader-writer for the *Manchester Guardian* and wrote for the *Observer* on Asian affairs. His publications include *Spotlight on Asia* (Penguin Books, 1955); (with Peter Calvocoressi) *Middle East Crisis* (Penguin Books, 1957); *Common Sense About China* (Gollancz, 1960) and *China's Communist Crusade* (Praeger, New York, 1965).

DAVID WOOD. b. 1934. Graduated in Economics from Magdalene College, Cambridge, 1957. University of Paris, 1957–8. Joined Institute for Strategic Studies, 1964. Author of *The Middle East and the Arab World: the Military Context*, July 1965; *The Armed Forces of African States*, April 1966; *Armed Forces in Central and South America*, April 1967; all for the Institute for Strategic Studies. Has been associated with the Institute's annual publication *The Military Balance*.

R. N. WOOD. Graduated from Oxford in Politics, Philosophy and Economics, 1958. Rockefeller Studentship in International Studies, London School of Economics and Political Science, 1958–9. Now Manager of Asian and Middle Eastern Department, Economist Intelligence Unit, London.

TAYA ZINKIN. b. 1918; studied medicine in Paris; research in bio-chemistry at the University of Wisconsin; married Maurice Zinkin of the Indian Civil Service in 1945; lived in India from 1945 to 1960. From 1950 to 1960 correspondent from India for the *Economist* and the *Guardian*, and from 1955 to 1960 for *Le Monde*. Author of: *India Changes!* (Chatto & Windus, 1958); *Rishi* (Methuen, 1960); *Rishi Returns* (Methuen, 1961); *Caste Today* (Oxford University Press, 1962); *Reporting India* (Chatto & Windus, 1962); *India* (Oxford University Press, 1963); *India* (Thames & Hudson, 1965); *Challenges in India* (Chatto & Windus, 1966); and in collaboration with Maurice Zinkin *Britain and India: Requiem for Empire* (Chatto & Windus, 1964).

M. ZUBERI. b. 1930. Studied at the Muslim University, Aligarh, India (B.A., 1949; M.A. in Political Science, 1951). Thereafter Lecturer in Politics at Aligarh University. Scholarship to Balliol College, Oxford; Senior Scholarship at St Antony's College, Oxford. Now writing a study of British policy in Asia during the late 19th and early 20th centuries with special reference to the defence of the Indian Empire.

A COMPANION VOLUME ON AFRICA

AFRICA HANDBOOK

Colin Legum

A modern and all-inclusive survey of the whole continent of
Africa, in which experts have assembled a mass of reliable
background information for the intelligent but non-expert
reader. The bulk of the handbook is devoted to individual
articles (with bibliographies) on each of the sixty or more
independent (and often newly named) territories, colonies,
and islands which make up the 'crisis continent': for each
country the political development and the economic situation
are outlined and the basic geographical and racial facts given.
In addition there are special essays on cultural and religious
subjects.

The contributors include Basil Davidson, James Duffy,
Ernest Gellner, Tom Hopkinson, A. J. Hughes, Harry Land,
E. G. Parrinder, Hella Pick, Tom Stacey, Clyde Sanger, and
other specialists on African affairs.